JESUS, RHETORIC
AND LAW

BIBLICAL INTERPRETATION SERIES

VOLUME 20

JESUS, RHETORIC AND LAW

BY

IAN H. HENDERSON

E.J. BRILL
LEIDEN · NEW YORK · KÖLN
1996

The paper in this book meets the guidelines for permanence and durability of the Committee on Production Guidelines for Book Longevity of the Council on Library Resources.

Die Deutsche Bibliothek – CIP-Einheitsaufnahme

Henderson, Ian H.:
Jesus, rhetoric and law / by Ian H. Henderson. - Leiden ; New York ; Köln : Brill, 1996
   (Biblical interpretation series ; Vol. 20)
   ISBN 90-04-10377-5
NE: GT

ISSN   0928-0731
ISBN   90 04 10377 5

CONTENTS

Preface vii

Introduction 1

Chapter I 73
    Defining Gnome

Chapter II 156
    Gnome and Wisdom Saying

Chapter III 196
    Logia, Aphorisms and Authenticity

Chapter IV 236
    Gnomai in Tradition and Redaction: Distribution
    and Distinctness

Chapter V 292
    Discipleship, Eschatology and The Projection
    of Character in Synoptic Gnomai

Chapter VI 353
    Gnomic Normativity and Law in Synoptic and in
    Pauline Reception

Epilogue 407
    What Did Jesus Sound Like?

Appendix A 410

Bibliography 414

Indexes 430

PREFACE

Jesus, Rhetoric and Law is the now quite distant descendant of my 1988 Oxford D. Phil. dissertation, *Sententiae Jesu: Gnomic Sayings in the Tradition of Jesus*, prepared under the generous yet permissive supervision of Professor E.P. Sanders. I have let this work simmer as long and as gently as I dared. In the result, the thesis remains, but I trust the dissertation has almost vanished.

I have allowed myself to employ freely and without further comment the abbreviations recommended by the *Journal of Biblical Literature* (*Society of Biblical Literature: Membership Directory and Handbook* [Decatur, GA, 1994] 226-240). I have supplemented these with abbreviations drawn from N.G.L. Hammond and H.H. Scullard, eds., *The Oxford Classical Dictionary* (2d ed., Oxford, 1970) ix-xxii. In addition, I have used throughout the abbreviation 'par' (e.g., "Mark 9:50 par" means, "Mark 9:50 and its parallels").

Translations into English are my own, unless otherwise indicated, though especially in relation to biblical and classical texts I have taken no steps to avoid accidental similarity to the myriad previous translations. If I have understood anything about gnomai, it is that they have long offered special temptations and opportunities to translators, but that they do not easily suffer copyright.

INTRODUCTION

The book which follows has two objectives. In general, I wish to argue for the relevance of Greek and Roman rhetoric as a whole to New Testament study. This might appear incontestable, judging from the increasing currency of rhetorical terms in books and articles on early Christianity. It is still the case, however, that use of rhetoric as a background for early Christian language is often fragmentary, superficial and indiscriminate. The relationship between modern and Hellenistic rhetorics remains confused and ambiguous, as do relations between rhetoric, however defined, and other current academic approaches (e.g., literary criticism or sociology). In addition, our cultural suspicion of rhetoric combines with declining competence in classical languages and the daunting technicality of the rhetorical tradition to ensure that few students of Christian origins have broad, independent knowledge of ancient rhetoric. In this way, for example, the *Progymnasmata*, the basic school–books of antiquity, are known and even read by scholars, but mainly for their chapters on chreia; Demetrius *On Expression* is cited, but as though its few paragraphs on letter–writing were the climax and centrepiece of its argument. The present book is meant to embody my aspiration and invitation to a wider rhetorical horizon; if this prescriptive, even polemical aim is most often left implicit, it is still central to what I hope to say.

My second objective, however, is to address a particular tangle of problems in the critical use of ancient rhetoric, and I wish to do so in relation to the concrete historical problem of relating early Christian rhetoric to the speech tradition of Jesus of Nazareth. On the part of rhetorical method, I want to explore continuities and discontinuities among modern rhetoric, ancient rhetorical theory, ancient rhetorical education, performance and literary composition. My chosen vector through this tangle is that of gnomic rhetoric, the systematic use of gnomic sayings to structure rhetorical composition, performance and memory. Gnomic sayings (Greek: *gnome*; Latin: *sententia*) are usually compact, but always syntactically separable from their contexts; they are ethically urgent (normative) and analogical in structure. Typical examples from the rhetoricians might be:

No one is a lover who does not love always.

Not death, but dying is bitter.

One gnome which certainly stems from Jesus is:

Let the dead bury the dead.

The uses of such gnomic language in differing rhetorics is a matchless starting-place for the exploration I have in mind: no aspect of rhetoric is more universally attested in both practice and theory than gnome-use. More specifically, though, there is a strongly shared predilection for gnomic rhetoric in Jesus' own speech tradition, in the earliest Christian epistolary literature and in the gospels' literary tradition. This makes a unique opportunity for tracing continuities and discontinuities of Jesus' influence as a public speaker.

Historically, an approach to Jesus' tradition as rhetoric and as specifically gnomic rhetoric can clarify the basic problem of early Christianity: the equivocal relationship between Jesus' expressed aims and the need for early Christian writers to translate his overcharged (e.g., provocatively legal) symbolism into functionally normative texts for young churches. It would, indeed, be astonishing if the personal, confrontational and allusive intensity of Jesus' rhetorical manner were not qualified and stretched, carefully forgotten as well as carefully remembered. In fact, the written evidence attests at least four phases in this stretching: first by the post-Easter, post-Biblical rhetoric of the gospel; then by the epistolary rhetoric and wisdom poetry of the earliest Christian literatures; and then again by traditional and redactional reconstructions as narrative and dialogue in the Gospels.

A rhetorical description of the interface between oral and literary aspects of early Christian tradition also has the potential to co–ordinate persuasively the insights of literary and historical criticisms. Historical critics of early Christian literature have increasingly assimilated the influences of, on the one hand, social scientific studies of culture and, on the other, literary–critical studies of literature. The latter process, however, of rapprochement between historical and literary study, has not easily achieved a theoretical basis, especially because literary criticism of the Bible has often been conceived of as a rebellion against positivist historicism. Rhetoric is the study of texts through time and social space, their production, reception and influence. Because this is so, rhetorical criticism is sincerely interested both in texts as uniquely expressive artifacts and in text-production as a process in social history. Rhetorical criticism seeks to advance arguments, topics and problems from both literary and historical perspectives with equal integrity.

It will often be easy to lose sight of these differing objectives amid the technicalities of literary criticism, rhetoric, New Testament studies and their several related disciplines. Technical jargon inevitably builds obstacles; I can only plead that attention to such obstacles may help me avoid some of the pitfalls of interpreting early Christian and classical texts just at a moment of crisis in modern academic culture. At the same time, my own increasingly restless reading habits warn me against supposing that many readers will read with equal interest all of the chapters which follow. I therefore turn now, for my own sake as well as the reader's, to map out with a minimum of scholarly apparatus my leading goals and the main lines of argument to be developed later.

I

THE RHETORIC OF JESUS

For most of a century, the words of Jesus, their influence, preservation and adaptation have been interpreted along an axis from eschatology to wisdom, with wisdom and Cynic anti-wisdom gradually gaining ground as critical models. Both wisdom and eschatology are important influences in early Christianity, but neither has provided—indeed both together have not provided—a comprehensive explanation of Jesus' aims in speaking, of his manner of speaking and of his impact as a speaker. Jesus probably used eschatological and sapiential motifs, but he did so in spoken performance, when motifs and mannerisms either fail and are forgotten or become meaningful and memorable as rhetorical first impressions. In Jesus' day as now there were few second chances in public speech and very few audiences willing to hear a speaker with only wisdom and eschatology to offer.

I believe it is a mistake, then, (it is certainly a persistent habit) to portray Jesus as a teacher of wisdom and his tradition (apart from its miracle-stories) as wisdom sayings. I don't mean by this that Jesus did not encourage people to become wise. I do intend to deny the historical usefulness of identifying Jesus, his goals, his language or his following, with any model of sagehood: biblical, scholarly, folkloric or even philosophical. Describing Jesus' language in terms of wisdom sayings, proverbs or aphorisms fails to explain either its unique influence or its curious limits.

Expecting Jesus to have been a wisdom teacher confuses his influence with that of wisdom books. There are certainly formative influences on early Christian writing from wisdom literatures, but these are often specifically literary influences, invoked to guide the transformation of speech into books; sayings produced or preserved by such wisdom are quite ambiguously related to any actual way of talking or listening in public.

There is a better way to describe Jesus' speech habits, their influence on the composition of the gospels and their surprising lack of influence elsewhere. This better way presents itself because Jesus' world supremely valued and carefully cultivated public speech, even to the point of writing books about speaking effectively. We can therefore know the basic rules of verbal communication in the world of Christian origins with a precision hardly imaginable among the complicated and fluid media of our own day.

In Jesus' world the cultural role of literacy was to inculcate, criticize, publicize, preserve and imitate good speech. In this way the simplest canons for oral performance and aural appreciation also closely conditioned the writing of letters and books. Such rhetoric could be heard and read without presuming either ancient metaphysical ideals of wisdom or modern sociological ideals of folklore, ethnicity or class. Greco-Roman rhetoric was, no doubt, sagely, idealized and ideological, in its full range the preserve and tool of very few. Still, in its most basic elements it successfully captured, formalized and inculcated the shared public speaking culture of Mediterranean antiquity. And it did so not least because it could plausibly feign a cultural and social universality more powerful than that of older wisdoms.

This achievement was intimately related to the balance of orality and literacy in Hellenistic rhetoric, a balance which it is difficult but essential for us to appreciate better. When I was first introduced in a

North American school to a discipline called rhetoric, it was defined and practised as the art of writing effectively, with speech-making a poor second; it was in sectarian Christianity that I encountered a living rhetorical culture, in which public speech remained a central medium of social life. In the ancient world, by contrast, composing, delivering, hearing and analyzing speeches were activities of fundamental social importance, far beyond the production and use of books. Respect for rhetorical practice was, moreover, common ground between the dominant, Hellenizing culture of Greco-Roman antiquity and the resistant, often older cultures of the ancient Near East.

The influence of rhetoric in the ancient world and its relevance for exegesis today therefore do not depend on its literary products as such: theoretical treatises, educational texts and written model orations. Instead, this vast and varied literature documents the essential, oral business of talking aloud in public and of listening discerningly to such public speech. Ancient rhetoric, even at its most literate and literary, retained this intentional, programmatic oral character, even while the literacy and politics of Hellenism became the means for globalizing Athenian and Roman patterns of eloquence into a quasi-universal theory and educational movement.

Rhetoric did not inherit such global pretensions without risking political and social trivialization and, more seriously, transformation into delusive, repressive ritual. One of the boldest, earliest and most essential steps toward the foundation of Christianity was the movement's appropriation and invigoration of the rhetoric of empires for the propaganda of an exotic gospel. Even the choice of Greek cannot have been obvious for the followers of a Galilean healer and sectarian rabbi. Yet the decision seems to have been made well before the decision to write books and perhaps before the decision to court non-Jews. With its adoption of Greek, early Christian oral tradition, for all its inner diversity, committed itself to an extraordinary rhetorical project. Early Christian literature is thus unusual for its presentation of a complex rhetorical tradition which consciously offered itself as an alternative to the established rhetorics of Jewish and Hellenistic elites: early Christianity, from its ethnic, sectarian and socially marginal origins, insinuated a new topicality and a new orality into rhetorical culture. Hellenistic rhetoric and its early Christian subculture both urgently raise the issue of persistent oral influences at the heart of sophisticated and self-conscious literacy.

The common denominator of rhetoric

Within ancient rhetoric it is, moreover, possible to specify narrowly "the minimum formal rhetorical equipment of any literate person from the Hellenistic period on," an equipment certainly shared by anyone capable of writing or of reading any of our gospels or their sources.[1]

The same equipment was, moreover, the stock in trade of public speakers and their audiences, literate or not, in Greek or not, at every educational level in a commonwealth of societies rich in literature, but powered by the well-spoken word. Especially in its lowest registers, Hellenistic rhetoric straddles the divide between oral and literate expression. The New Testament itself is evidence that this lowest common denominator of Hellenism exercised particular influence toward the social, cultural and geographical margins of the Greco-Roman world. This level of rhetorical practice and theory is also the most readily understood by moderns, among whom Greco-Roman rhetoric has a bad name for pedantry and sophistry.

Collectively, the elemental conventions of primary education, literary composition and oral performance were known and taught throughout the ancient world as *progymnasmata*, pre-rhetorical exercises. The four most basic of these progymnasmata were even more generally known, so that the Roman, Quintilian, calls them the *primordia dicendi* (*Inst.* I 9.1), the ABCs of speech. And so they were, not least in the culturally complex environment of lower Galilee.

These four most widely prescribed, used and appreciated techniques will be immediately familiar—if not by name—to the reader of the gospels: chreia (anecdote about a named personality); gnome (sententious analogy); *mythos* (fable or parable; fictional story); *diegema* (narrative; historical-mythical episode).

The claim of these categories to precedence in describing the gospels and their prehistory is clear: the gospels, like their sources and the traditions which inform them, were composed, revised and performed almost entirely in Greek and in a world where even the non-Greek-speaker and non-literate were inescapably exposed to the media of Hellenistic rhetoric. Chreia, gnome, *mythos* and *diegema* had some of

---

[1] F.W. Cairns, *Generic Composition in Greek and Roman Poetry* (Edinburgh, 1972) 75.

the ubiquity and socially broad, even cross-cultural appeal of modern mass publicity.

Consequently, there is no need to revive a false and prejudicial polarity between Hellenism and Judaism in order to apply Hellenistic rhetoric to gospel rhetoric. On the contrary, it is impossible to take seriously their mutual assimilation without focusing on the precise register of rhetorical culture which is historically most relevant to Jesus' Palestine and to Christian origins. At the crossroads of the Eastern Mediterranean, if anywhere, we should find intelligible patterns of interaction among the many levels of Hellenism—from Galilean tradesmen to apostolic letter-writers—among various styles of Jewishness—priestly, Pharisaic, folk, sectarian—and among differing modes of expression—from parlour gossip and itinerant preaching to epistolary and biographical rhetoric. The rhetoric of Jesus and his earliest tradition is important for the history of Greco-Roman rhetoric not least because, though richly documented, it remains noticeably provincial, sub-literary, un-Greek, unprivileged and sectarian.

This book is therefore not intended as a general introduction to the progymnasmata, not even to the four most basic of these exercises and not even as they illuminate New Testament rhetoric in general. Instead the goal will be to throw light on the particular question of historical and rhetorical continuity from Jesus' words, through oral tradition, to the Gospels. Along the way, I hope to ask and nuance questions about differing registers of rhetorical culture in antiquity and about the complex relationships among oral rhetoric, literary composition and social history.

The gnomic manner of speaking

I shall concentrate particularly on one of the progymnasmata, the gnomic saying (*gnome*). There are tactical reasons for this focus: *chreia* has recently attracted extensive, even excessive, attention among New Testament scholars. Similarly, gospel parables have been smothered with aesthetic and philosophical analyses. A rhetorical approach to *parable* can hope only to remind readers that neither Hellenistic *mythos* nor Hebrew/Aramaic *mashal/matla* presented Jesus' audiences with the world-ending mystery beloved of twentieth-century exegesis. Parable and its uses were alien to neither Jew nor Greek in Jesus' environment.

Finally, the flash of uniqueness in Jesus' parables is no less evident in the mini-parable of gnome.

There are also more positive reasons to examine especially the role of gnome in the formation of Jesus' tradition and in the composition of the gospels. Above all, gnome connects apparently divergent tendencies; this is a frequently attested function of gnome in rhetoric and should become its function in criticism.

> There is one major exception to the general rule that Greek popular culture tends to be neglected in the written record.... Traditional sayings, whether proverbs or fables, were widely used...as powerful devices of rhetoric to add persuasiveness, dignity or interest.... Proverbs and (more important) reflective sayings (*gnomai*) cast in the memorable style of proverbs are to be found everywhere in Greek literature.[2]

Thus gnome provides a bridge between chreia and more elaborate sister techniques of argumentation and narration. A chreia very often contains a gnomic saying and gnomai are often used to flesh out a chreia into a longer dialogue or argument form. But gnomai are also very commonly used to round off a fable/parable or to dramatize a narrative episode. On a larger scale, gnomai are among the very few rhetorical features common in both the main genres of early Christian literature (gospel and epistle). This aptness of gnome to link discursive, argumentative and narrative forms is important, if we wish to relate the discourses of Jesus to his successors' narratives and discourses about him.

Approaching early Christian language through Hellenistic, specifically gnomic, rhetoric also invites a more nuanced appreciation of the transformation in early Christian rhetoric of its biblical and folkloric heritage in wisdom poetry. Gnomic language and parabolic story-telling are the points of busiest contact and freest exchange between rhetoric and wisdom. Within this exchange, rhetoric seeks to sound wise. For its part, wisdom seems to have become rhetoric not only in the Hellenistic world's saturation with the techniques of speech, but also in the nature of Jesus' own and his successors' chosen task of public communication.

One goal of rhetoric is to bring wisdom into public speech. In Jesus' environment and in the early Church this conversion seems to have

---

[2] P.E. Easterling, "The Fable," *CHCL* I,4 (1989) 139–143, 140.

entailed not only the early adoption of the Greek language. It also included an even earlier commitment in Jesus' own public style to patterns of communication rooted in Israel's prophetic wisdom, yet also readily intelligible in the global vernacular of Hellenistic style. On the evidence of early Christian literature, gnome-use was one of the most durable and effective means, first, of facilitating Jesus' self-expression and, then, of translating it into Christian proclamation.

The point is not just the broad one that Hellenism was powerful even in the presumably un-Greek rhetoric of Jesus (as it certainly is in the Rabbis' scholastic rhetoric). The argument here is rather that specifically gnomic language provided a crucial vehicle both for communicating the Kingdom in Galilee and later for spreading the Gospel cross-culturally.

Its cross-cultural and durable persuasiveness is not the only reason for preferring gnomic rhetoric over wisdom tradition to describe public speech in Jesus' movement. Wisdom-traditional explanations are attractive for New Testament studies largely because no one knows quite what wisdom is: among other things, the notion of wisdom begs necessary questions about the functions and social settings of speech and of written text-production. In Jesus and in the earliest Church have we to do with the local folklore of Galilean peasantry? If so, does its co-option by the aggressively international, sectarian literature in and around the New Testament constitute an impassable break with Jesus' intended influence? Or, are the wisdom elements in early Christian literature results of the literary influence of biblical, aristocratic and professional wisdom on Christian writers? If heavy use of gnomic language is a trace of literary influence on church writers, must we not again discount any serious degree of verbal influence from Jesus? A rhetorical approach breaks through these quandaries by investigating the one culturally recognized social function, the one life-setting (*Sitz im Leben*) which really is attested for Jesus, for pre-gospel traditions, both oral and writing, and for the epistolary tradition: public rhetoric.

In this context of publicly performed rhetoric, the whole range of proverbial folklore, wisdom sayings, oracles, party slogans and critical aphorisms can be interpreted together as opportunities for gnome-use. Likewise, the largely unknown processes of oral tradition and the scarcely less inscrutable permutations of literary influence and reception are held together by an exceptional continuity of rhetorical aims and means in gnome. Gnome-use is neither simply the mark of literary influence nor the necessary residue of some pre-literary orality; it is both the cutting-edge of smart Hellenistic rhetoric and the carrier of conservative 'oriental' wisdom.

Early Christian writers did exploit gnomic rhetoric. So did Jesus: there are nearly one hundred gnomai attributed to Jesus in the Synoptic Gospels (Matthew, Mark and Luke). Most are attested from more than one pre-gospel source, and/or in more than one kind of context, and/or in several variants. No doubt some are falsely attributed to Jesus, but not all.

Moreover, Synoptic gnomai cohere as such within a single rhetorical category with well-attested sub-categories; there is no rhetorical criterion (e.g., no tendency to allegorize) for declaring some gnomai less authentic than others in ascription to Jesus. In consequence, gnome-use in the first three gospels is exceptionally likely to represent authentically Jesus' own speech style, even where many inauthentic examples are included indistinguishably among the authentic. Gnomic language is heavily enough attributed to Jesus and can be understood well enough from the standpoint of Hellenistic rhetorical theory to permit the conclusion that the evangelists and Paul and their informants were in this one respect in a position responsibly to retain the flavour and gist of Jesus' speech.

The net gain from identifying many New Testament proverbs, wisdom sayings, slogans and aphorisms as gnomai is that in this way they are brought into a context which is exegetically more powerful than wisdom or folklore and historically more relevant to questions of connection from Jesus and his immediate interpreters to the New Testament. This context is powerfully interpretive, however, not only because both gospel tradition and general educational and public speaking practice were irreducibly rhetorical, irreducibly oral and irreducibly gnomic. Further to help us interpret early Christian gnome-use we also have a rich secondary literature of philosophical and theoretical reflection contemporaneous with the birth of Christian rhetoric. Gnome-use is illustrated throughout Greek literature and not only in gnomological collections. It is defined, exemplified and pre-scribed in progymnasmatic textbooks, but it is also given more detailed and sustained philosophical analysis than any of the other progymnasmata.

Rhetorical theory and early Christian discourse

The centrality of gnome-use to Greco-Roman rhetoric is important for understanding early Christianity, *not* because Aristotle or the first-century Latin, Quintilian, might have influenced early Christian rhetoric directly—Aristotle's influence was incalculably remote to Palestine and Christian experience, while Quintilian was describing and criticizing rhetorical practice from the Roman and aristocratic, not the Jewish and provincial, margin of Hellenism. Instead, Aristotle and Quintilian epitomize Hellenistic technical and theoretical achievement in a discipline in which modern thought has not surpassed its ancient roots. The Greek and Roman rhetoricians are arguably still the finest theorists of public speaking. At any rate, they offer a body of theory and criticism designed, to be sure, for the higher registers of classical rhetoric, but more directly applicable than any modern (e.g., speech-act or literary-critical) theory to the beginnings of Christianity in speech. Hellenism itself provides a critical instrument of unsurpassed refinement, detachment and relevance for gospel rhetoric; the instrument provided in this way is one which emphasizes the theoretical as well as practical importance of gnomic language.[3]

The rhetoricians give particular attention to gnome for reasons which bear directly on the analysis of Synoptic gnomai. First, gnomai are among the most connotative, affective and elliptical patterns in ancient rhetoric. This means that attention must be given to their poetic qualities as a basis for their rhetorical effectiveness. The connotative power of gnomai helps to explain their flexibility and usefulness in every genre of rhetoric. It may also help to explain their interpretive difficulty and relative neglect in historical criticism of the New Testament. As exemplified by the progymnasmatists, by early Christian writers and by the rhetoricians, and as analysed by the latter, gnome is not so much metaphorical as analogical in its connotations. Metaphor is often used, but the essence of gnomic poetry is analogy, the comparison of

---

[3] For good summaries of Greco-Roman Rhetoric, see B. Vickers, *In Defence of Rhetoric* (Oxford, 1988) 1–82; R. Barthes, "L'ancienne rhetorique: aide mémoire," *Communications* 16 (1970) 172–229; R.A. Lanham, *A Handlist of Rhetorical Terms* (2d ed., Berkeley and Los Angeles, 1991) 163–180; and, at greater length, J.J. Murphy, ed., *A Synoptic History of Classical Rhetoric* (Berkeley, 1972; 2d ed. Davis, CA, 1983); M. Heath, transl., *"Hermogenes" On Issues* (Oxford, 1995) 3–18.

relationships, not their metaphorical creation. Thus Aristotle and, even more, later rhetoricians emphasize the confrontational tone of gnomic language, often contrastive and intensely specific, never abstract.

Gnomic rhetoric is therefore also much more personal in its origins, content and address than meets the untrained ear, especially where expectations of timeless, anonymous, proverbial wisdom interfere. The rhetoricians' careful distinction between gnome and proverb is a valuable and deliberate corrective to folkloric images of proverbial rhetoric as impersonal, uncontroversial and traditionalist. Hellenistic theory makes it clear that, while some gnomai are or become proverbs, many are sophisticated adaptations or bold contradictions of traditional proverb-use. Many go beyond the anti-proverbiality also audible in some modern advertising to deliver the challenge of graffiti, political slogans, oracles or even personal insults.

Ancient writers about rhetoric laboriously explain the art and dangers of making up and deploying gnomic language; clearly they do not think of gnomic speech as traditional wisdom. Many of the rhetoricians' gnomai and even more gnomai in Jesus' tradition are acute evocations of actual personalities, feelings and issues and not only of generalized or proverbial values. As one of the fundamental means of persuasion (*pisteis*), gnome belongs not only to argumentative content (*logos*), but also to the more personal, emotional and passionate (*ethos*; *pathos*) levels of rhetorical experience.

The rhetoricians are clear about the social and psychological complexity of using even the most innocuous-sounding gnomai. In this their judgement is confirmed by modern anthropologists. Their research tends to emphasize the variety and complexity of proverb-use, against simplistic expectations about folk-wisdom. Thus a surprising number of 'old proverbs' turn out in practice to be extempore adaptations or inventions. In fact, modern models for cross-cultural comparison of proverb-uses can help us go beyond the rhetoricians' scholasticism and cultural imperialism to appreciate the normative slant and inter-cultural influence of gnomic rhetoric.

In many traditional societies, as in Hellenistic rhetoric, gnomai figure prominently in social, political and judicial controversy. Didactic or speculative contextualization of gnomai in moral instruction (parenesis) or in literary wisdom collections, Greek or non-Greek, despite its allure for scholars of every age, is not typical of gnome-use in other literary genres or in speech outside the nursery and the classroom.

More often, certainly in the Hellenistic world, the speaker who chooses a strongly gnomic style is asserting personal authority in a rhetorical context where it need not be accepted; the speaker stakes credibility on a gnomic *tour de force*, wedding selected audience concerns to the speaker's own, significantly different, rhetorical *ethos* and argumentative goal. The typical function of gnome is to create a moment of complicity between speaker and audience, not in the vacuum of idealized wisdom, but amid the real risks of speech on real issues. If the speaker wins that complicity, however fleetingly, tentatively or subliminally, what I mean by rhetorical normativity is created, upon which the skilful orator may elaborate in less connotative rhetoric to influence norms of attitude and behaviour after speech.

Normativity before, after and during rhetoric

A vital distinction is implied here between rhetorical normativity and social normativity. Both are formally social, since the rhetorical act is intrinsically gregarious: Rhetoric always requires an audience (and a larger public) as well as a speaker. Consequently, rhetorical normativity always reflects and seeks to influence the practical norms of that audience and its wider public. Still, audience expectations and the intent of speakers seldom correspond simply to the actual communicative impact of speech on behaviour. Moreover, except in the smallest-scale societies, even the most representative audience does not perfectly embody its larger public.

Rhetorical normativity differs from social normativity in two ways then: Rhetoric is, first of all, wishfully normative speech. The normative slant of speech becomes actual only in the one social setting of public communication. At the same time, rhetoric, though pretending to general social appeal, is selective and partial in its choice of real audience and in its invention of an imaginative yet plausible rhetorical scenario. Rhetorical normativity, as it occurs, for example, in modern advertising, is more demagogic than democratic. Such normativity may be said to be implicit in texts, but only in so far as their meaning can be publicly grasped by some definite audience. Rhetorical normativity is the presumption of assent or at least of informed attention.

Speeches and texts, especially those which explicitly address social norms, are not primarily or directly about social normativity. Instead they are efforts to influence social history by creating an intermediate, rhetorical normativity in which the speaker dares to confuse his own values with those of an imagined audience in an imagined setting. Rhetorical normativity—especially in gnomai—expresses this risk-taking in all serious public speech. Even when the rhetorically normative moment is successfully created, it may ultimately fail to connect with social influence—a speaker may confirm, who intended rather to convert. Or again, the socially normative use of texts (e.g., as canon) takes on a life of its own, not wholly foreseeable from the rhetorical norms of the texts themselves in the setting of their implied audience. All rhetoric is tendentious; not all rhetoric, however, is equally, or predictably, or consistently effective.

In itself, the attempt to translate real and imagined norms into words and words into social influence tells us more about its speaker than about its actual audiences, settings or eventual receptions in social history. It allows us to hear what sort of gambler our speaker is and for what stakes, but not to know the outcome of the venture or the other players in the game. All public rhetoric has this myth-making, constructive and critical, even fictional or prophetic aspect, but gnome in particular is its oracular voice.

This is in part why I prefer to describe a speaker's implicit frame of reference or working hypothesis for winning an audience as 'rhetorical normativity' rather than as a "rhetorical or argumentative situation," despite the latter's currency in rhetorical theory since Lloyd Bitzer. "Situation" is a misleadingly static, deterministic and objective metaphor for a speaker's personally selective and heuristic construction of the terms for rhetorical engagement with audience or opponents. Rhetorical normativity cannot succeed if it fails to catch its audience's imagination; it can, however, succeed by dramatically distorting, even flouting actual social norms and situations.

Modern philosophical theories of argumentation are, in principle, aware that "rhetorical situation" is never simply identical with social reality either before or after speech and that argumentation is not the whole of rhetorical persuasion. Usually in argumentation theories, "rhetorical situation" means above all the motivating complex imagined by would-be speakers before speech. It doesn't usually mean the unmediated social setting, nor the broad range of topics and images which are "in the air," nor even the situation imagined in actual speech.

Yet only the last of these is more or less fully implicit in a rhetorical text.

The clear tendency in modern rhetorical theory and in its application to the New Testament is to confound these multiple situations into one. The result is a double fallacy of rhetorical determinism. First, we are tempted to read as though specific social, historical setting were so determinative of rhetorical artifice that "the actual rhetorical historical situation" could normally be salvaged, even from a difficult text, and then be used to clarify the text's very difficulty. Even beyond that excess of social-rhetorical optimism, however, is a second influential assumption, that rhetorical effect is so determined by patterns of argumentation that "calculating the persuasive force of an argumentation" will suffice to solve "the rhetorical equation."[4]

Such assumptions may well prove fruitful for criticizing contemporary rhetoric in a social setting well known to the critic; extended into the criticism of ancient texts and oral traditions, they quickly become fallacious and reductionist. Thus a rhetorical analysis of the language of the 1992 United States presidential campaign might well show that Bush and Clinton, even perhaps Perot, were using substantially the same persuasive strategies on the same topics to address the same audience, a surprisingly small minority of privately contented, though publicly more or less nervous voters. That is, all three may presuppose the same "rhetorical situation," though each within a different rhetorical character (*ethos*) as incumbent, opponent or outsider.

One theoretical problem relating rhetorical situation to social situations is that the speakers themselves may err in their analysis of social conditions: Bush, Clinton and Perot might all have misconstrued

---

[4] E. Schüssler Fiorenza, "Rhetorical Situation and Historical Reconstruction in 1 Corinthians," *NTS* 33 (1987) 386–403, 387; B.L. Mack, *Rhetoric and the New Testament* (Guides to Biblical Studies; Minneapolis, 1990) 15, 19–21; see A. Brinton, "Situation in the Theory of Rhetoric," *Philosophy and Rhetoric* 14 (1981) 234–48; S. Consigny, "Rhetoric and Its Situations," *Philosophy and Rhetoric* 7 (1974) 175–186; L. Bitzer, "The Rhetorical Situation," *Philosophy and Rhetoric* 1 (1968); R.E. Vatz, "The Myth of the Rhetorical Situation," *Philosophy and Rhetoric* 6 (1973); W. Wuellner, "Toposforschung und Torahinterpretation bei Paulus und Jesus," *NTS* (1978) 463–483; for a gentle critique see D.L. Stamps, "Rethinking the Rhetorical Situation: the Entextualization of the Situation in New Testament Epistles," in *Rhetoric and the New Testament: the 1992 Heidelberg Conference*, ed. S.E. Porter and T.H. Olbricht (Sheffield, 1993).

the audience. Much more probably, the topics and arguments selected by candidates may gravely misrepresent key issues, options and powers of public office, in this case of the U.S. presidency, in ways which it would not be possible to notice by rhetorical analysis alone.

But New Testament studies face an additional, more practical problem. Contemporary rhetorical critics and their audiences can know enough about their own historical, political and social situation to be able to make informed, detailed judgements about current rhetoric and to test them from a partly independent, non-rhetorical standpoint. It is possible for contemporaries to locate both electioneering rhetoric and rhetorical criticisms of such rhetoric—and to locate them accurately—within specific political, commercial and cultural processes. By contrast, my readers and I have little access to the social-historical context of early Christian speech-production and oral reception of Jesus' influence, apart from the early Christians' surviving texts.

Any rhetorical criticism which methodically moves from "rhetorical situation" to sociological reconstruction of the forces in and around early Christianity must claim the ability to construct the rhetorical situation and to reconstruct the 'social situation of the rhetorical situation' from the same texts. While this may occasionally be possible with the help of a historically controlled rhetorical theory, the project would seem to require a methodical humility not typical of contemporary rhetorical theory. Moreover, if this is a daunting challenge for rhetorical criticism of New Testament texts as literary products, it is an even more major obstacle to taking seriously the wider and never more than partially documented oral rhetorics of Jesus' movement and early Christianity.

This is not to disown the important modern question of the relation between production and reception of rhetoric and its social-historical setting. The notion of 'normativity' and the distinction between its rhetorical and social achievement are my attempt to pose this modern question with the critical diffidence demanded by the products of a bygone—in modernity often repudiated or distorted—rhetorical economy. Modern analyses of the purposeful and social dimensions of language use have been transformed, for richer and for poorer, by the influence of post-Freudian psychology and by the social sciences as well as by experiences of literacy, production and publicity alien to antiquity. There is wide scope for critical discernment as to how far ancient rhetoric is antithetical to or compatible with these revolutionary experiences of modernity. But such discernment cannot responsibly happen where ancient rhetoric is not understood and appreciated in its distinctiveness.

The modern construct of "rhetorical situation" as textual analogue to social situation is profoundly different from ancient expectations of the projection of intentionality and normativity in rhetorical performance. Rhetorical criticism in modern and especially New Testament study is regularly constructed from symbolic and formal-structural analysis "between the lines" and "across the grain" of ancient texts; it is to that extent more like ancient allegorical interpretation than it is like the normal, conventional text-processing which most early Christian texts invited in their pre-canonical contexts.

A criticism informed by traditional rhetoric must begin by recognizing the conscious and cultivated rhetoricity of early Christian and other Greek texts. This also means facing the deliberate representation in such texts of rhetorical normativity with conventionally explicit and conventionally limited claims to interpret and influence social normativity. Possibly the foundational myth of ancient and traditional rhetoric is the fiction that there are two sides to every question, two normatively opposite accounts (*logoi*) to be given about anything important (attributed to Protagoras [Diog. Laer. IX, 51]). This is, it must be admitted, a fiction: real experience and discourse are seldom matters of tidy binary oppositions (rhetorical *stasis*). Much post-modern thought is groping toward an authentic pluralism to escape the rhetorical dilemma as it lurks, often unacknowledged, behind modern dialectics. Traditional rhetoric, by contrast, thrives in the candid intention to co-opt the approval of its chosen audience. It therefore approaches social situations and social normativity with the reductive and tendentious aim of producing a rhetorical normativity within which an audience's perceived options will be two, one good and one bad.

Social description is not the purpose of rhetoric; the social function of rhetoric is rather to facilitate and guide public decisions and moods in social settings where community consensus can no longer be taken for granted. Two points, then, need to be emphasized: first, rhetorical normativity is consciously selective, reductive and prescriptive over against social normativity; second, the basic conventions of selection, reduction and prescription in ancient and traditional rhetoric are under experimental revision in much modern criticism. The modern critic must consequently work all the harder to recognize the rhetorical normativity of ancient texts before dissolving it in the alchemy of pluralizing social analysis.

Rhetorical texts and social determinacy

It was a major postulate of form and redaction criticism in New Testament studies that stylistic, generic and argumentative differences within and among early Christian texts mirror ideologically distinct groups and moments in Jesus' tradition. In form criticism this postulate depended on the perception of the gospels as *Kleinliteratur*: the texts about Jesus were sub-literary and folkloric, written by almost passive collectors. Curiously, redaction criticism, while rediscovering the gospel writers' creative authorship, maintained the postulate from a specifically theological point of view. Each redactional product was presumed to express a controlling theological position, which though authorial in expression was assumed to be programmatically related to a pre-existent, confessionally distinct social group. But can the edifying theological postulate of normative analogy between text-linguistic patterns and social worlds survive without reductively folkloric or theological definitions of 'community' and 'ideology'?

In so far as rhetoric is the study and practice of public speech, it postulates, like form and redaction criticisms, a normative relationship between discourse and some larger social collective. Rhetoric—and, I suspect, any mature socio-linguistic theory—emphasizes and in application exploits the gaps between social and rhetorical normativity, between actual community and textually projected public. As I understand the distinction between 'public' and 'community', the former points toward social organization in relation to the loyalty demands of a state or virtual state (e.g., Israel or the Church). A public dimension is a specialized and by no means universal aspect of community life. Public ideology demands politically sanctioned or canonized media. That is, a public is not only a social but also a political and rhetorical construct, based in exclusive conventions for talking out loud in a complex, mixed community.

In this role liberal rhetoric, ceremony, theatre and epigraphy were more important to the Greco-Roman world than literacy per se; it is no accident that throughout Greco-Roman antiquity public support for higher rhetorical education and accomplishment is far more common than public support for primary literacy. Nor is it an accident that early Christian writers, though engaged in an extensive literary outpouring, neither attest nor urge special Christian interest in primary literacy.[5] In itself basic literacy was widely useful in ordinary community life, but it is cultivated, articulate speech—liberal, bookish rhetoric—which is publicly valued, useful to Caesar and God. Such public order is in a self-consciously hierarchical and taxing relation to community and class loyalties and their institutions.

In the ancient Near East the Hellenistic and Imperial centuries are marked by the massive, progressive projection of public onto community and class interests through rhetorical/linguistic, architectural and military/fiscal intervention. Within that intervention, early Christianity, like Judaism, is a strikingly successful projection of alternate liberal rhetorics. Hellenism, Judaism and early Christianity are notable for their use of literature to project a public identity beyond any material possibility of actual community. Each of these *ekklesiai*, of free Greeks and Romans, of Jews and of Christians is characterized by the tension between the catholicity of their liberal rhetorical fraternity and the actual impossibility of face-to-face, day-to-day community: the whole public must be normatively modelled in a multitude of fragmentary communities, groups whose identities were co-determined by participation in less public dimensions of social organization.

Liberal rhetoric was an essential, imaginative link between actual communities—local, regional, ethnic and cultic—and the commonwealth of communities called for by public ideologies. Yet literacy, and through it Greco-Roman rhetoric, could not function in this way without the prior and continuing support of trans-community class consciousness in each potential public—despite egalitarian aspirations in each. Class solidarity stands over against both community and public identities and mediates critically between them. In the Greco-Roman Near East the persistent importance of regional networks of village communities is a major cultural and economic factor, easily underestimated by the reader

---

[5] P.E. Easterling, "Books and Readers in the Greek World: the Hellenistic and Imperial Periods," *CHCL* I,4 (1989) 169–97, 180, 193–5; W.V. Harris, *Ancient Literacy* (Cambridge, MA, 1989) 129–146, 244–5; E.A. Judge, "A state school teacher makes a salary bid," in G.H.R. Horsley, *New Documents Illustrating Early Christianity* 1 (1981) 72–8 (#26); A.H.M. Jones, *The Greek City from Alexander to Justinian* (Oxford, 1940) 220–26.

of textual sources. Recent research into the genesis and gradual development of the sayings-gospel Q seizes on this level of social organization, not least because the Galilee of Q, of the narrative gospels and of Josephus is easily the best documented example of such a regional society before AD 70.

Against precisely that background, however, the production of extended texts, full of local colour but clearly Greco-Roman in rhetoric as well as language, appears as a baffling anomaly. The hypothesis of ideologically distinct communities at the village network level scarcely clarifies the ambiguous, semi-public quality of the gospel rhetorics. These experimentally combine dramatic and well-informed reference to Jesus' Galilee and Jerusalem, and intense Greco-Jewish and Synoptic intertextualities, all within an irreducibly Greco-Roman rhetorical and literary culture. It is remarkable enough that the Jesus of Nazareth crucified in Jerusalem should become the focus of a rhetorical tradition in Greek; that this tradition of public speech came to include a complex literary project in multiple, closely related recensions and revisions requires something more and something other than local remembrance at the social base of Jesus' onetime activity.

As rhetorical and written artifacts the gospels seem rather to index an ideologically radicalized but still distinctly liberal and (in the Greco-Roman sense) urban class. Galilean "peasant social unrest" may, in J.D. Crossan's words, be "the most proximate background for Jesus." For the production of gospels, however, and for their initially rather private circulation and revision in Greek, unrest of a different social order seems required. Moreover, social analysis of the Greco-Roman Near East emphasizes clearly the importance of class identities as mediating between community and public spheres and as central to the production and dissemination of texts which are not only written but publicly articulate. In particular, the career and liberal rhetorical production of Josephus illustrate the tense interplay of class identity with public Jewish and public Greco-Roman loyalties—and specifically their ambiguous relation to local agrarian communities.[6]

---

[6] F. Millar, *The Roman Near East 31 BC—AD 337* (Cambridge, MA and London, 1993) 337–66, esp. 342–3; J.D. Crossan, *The Historical Jesus: The Life of a Mediterranean Jewish Peasant* (San Francisco, 1991) quoting 100; G. Theißen, *Lokalkolorit und Zeitgeschichte in den Evangelien: Ein Beitrag zur Geschichte der synoptischen Tradition* (NTOA 8; Göttingen and Freiburg, 1989)= L.M. Maloney, transl., *The*

W.V. Harris' study of literacy in antiquity has made it clearer that Greek literacy—without which Greco-Roman rhetoric could not have been sustained—was confined to a very small proportion of the populace of any eastern Mediterranean region. The same could probably be said of Hebrew and Aramaic literacies. One implication of this is that there was no popular literature written in the ancient Mediterranean world. Among Palestinian Jews, popular receptions of the rhetorics of public liberal traditions did on occasion mobilize genuinely mass protests. But such receptions were inevitably mediated through public performances by elites and their retainers, loyal or disaffected, Jewish or imperialist Gentile, and keyed to public institutions of Torah and Temple. Liberal rhetorics were public, but not therefore popular in origin or reception.

Production of long texts was directly conditioned by the interests of very small minorities of active writers and readers. Such minorities were socially diverse and geographically dispersed: some magnates were nearly illiterate and others affected illegible handwriting, while some of their slaves and freedmen could indeed write and circulate complex documents—and exert telling social influence. Class is not simply social status, but has to do with how social status is produced. Again, in the Greco-Roman world it is not literacy itself which marks an exclusive class threshold, but liberal rhetoric, the graded ability to produce publicly influential discourse.[7]

The gospel writers were far more than literate in Greek. They had mastered at least the basic progymnasmata ("the only thing approaching a common [educational] experience for the elite") with a confidence which permits their revolutionary hybridization with biblical narrative and wisdom. The gospel writers' achievements and their influence on one another are a far cry from the form letters, stereotyped certificates

---

Gospels in Context: Social and Political History in the Synoptic Tradition (Minneapolis, 1991); M.D. Goodman, *The Ruling Class of Judaea: The Origins of the Jewish Revolt against Rome AD 65–70* (Cambridge, 1987); J.S. Kloppenborg, "The Sayings Gospel Q: Recent Opinion on the People Behind the Document," *Currents in Research: Biblical Studies* 1 (1993) 9–34; J.S. Kloppenborg, "Literary Criticism, Self-Evidence and the Social History of the Q People," in *Early Christianity, Q and Jesus*, ed. J.S. Kloppenborg and L.E. Vaage=*Semeia* 55 (1991) 77–102.

[7] Harris, *Ancient Literacy*, 248–84.

and halting signatures of the few village scribes we know about.[8] Instead gospel literature shows its authors to be members of an exclusive though variegated class by virtue of their access to the widely but thinly spread technology of Greco-Roman liberal rhetoric. Thus even those few texts which, like Josephus and the gospels, refer to the communities of the tributary majority do not do so from within. The gospels are unique in their sympathetic and informed perspective on Galilean village life pre-30, but the genesis of such texts is the very opposite of evidence for identifying their authors socially with later, otherwise undocumented phases of minority development in those same communities.

> Any assumption that the intellectually less demanding genres of Hellenistic literature aimed at, or reached, a truly popular audience of readers should be resisted. The papyri show conclusively that popular literature did not exist in any ordinary sense of that expression: the literary texts which were most copied were the classics....And if we look at genres of writing which might strike scholars as being undemanding, we do not find works which were intended for mass consumption....Popular culture had little to do with reading.[9]

Early Christian communities were consequently not demonstrably or even probably 'gospel' communities in anything like the way routinely posited by both redaction criticism and rhetorical criticism of the gospels. When Christian epistles address local, cultic groups of Christians living with their neighbours in actual communities, the communities addressed scarcely represent direct socializations of specific pre-gospel rhetorics. It is hard enough to reconstruct Corinthian or Galatian communities from documents which at least ostensibly assert the existence of groups in Corinth and (somewhere) in Galatia; by contrast, no texts anywhere prove the existence of actual communities (e.g., in Galilee) which correspond distinctively to the ideology of

---

[8] Harris, *Ancient Literacy*, 276–82; R.A. Kaster, *Guardians of Language: The Grammarian and Society in Late Antiquity* (Berkeley and Los Angeles, 1988) 24–7, quoting 26.

[9] Harris, *Ancient Literacy*, 3–24, quoting 126; H.Y. Gamble, *Books and Readers in the Early Church: A History of Early Christian Texts* (New Haven and London, 1995) 32–40.

the implied public of any gospel. It is an important trait of gospel rhetorics that their community references look explicitly to an idealized past or to an eschatological future. Even Q shares this essentially retrospective attitude.[10]

The Christian public implicitly addressed by the gospels did not yet exist except as a possibility of hybridizing the universal ideal of Hellenistic literacy and liberal rhetoric and the actual alternative community experiences of early Christians. But this possibility of creating a new public within both Greco-Roman and Jewish public literatures existed materially only in the tutored imaginations of a very small minority of Christians. This few are not demonstrably linked in any local, cultic community, but rather by the convergence of apparently clashing social identities: the technical literacy of trans-cultural Hellenism and the marginal, liminal definition of community by adherents of Jesus.

This may be pointedly illustrated with reference to the enormous scholarly energy now being expended on socially locating the "Q community" and on coordinating its history with the three-phase redactional history of the Q sayings gospel. J.S. Kloppenborg has summarized and defended this direction in Q research—and has, I think, nuanced it almost to the brink of replacing local community with a cadre defined instead by Greco-Roman and biblical class literacy and social alienation. Kloppenborg certainly intends to defend the tendency to identify public and community behind Q and, further, to assume changes in a continuing "Q community" analogous to changes in rhetoric and genre in succeeding textual redactions. He does so, however, without concealing the tension between the productive milieu of potential gospel writers and any communities their works might encode.

Thus Kloppenborg knows that the development of Q through repeated, mostly cumulative redactions and the sapiential genres basic to the composition of Q are not enough to posit a "Q community"; these features are characteristic of "other social locales—most notably the scribal school—that would scarcely qualify as 'communities' in the sense in which we are here speaking." Although Kloppenborg does not

---

[10] L.M. White, "Sociological Analysis of Early Christian Groups: A Social Historian's Response," *Sociological Analysis* 47 (1986) 249–66, 256; cited by Kloppenborg, "Q: Recent Opinion," 17.

yet dispense with the postulate of a local (Galilean) community, structurally and functionally analogous to a detailed, social-scientific reading of the text, he can take seriously the role of a "scribal class" and the "'public' character of the scribal pursuit."

> [T]he scribe's responsibility is ultimately to the public and public approbation in the form of honor and fame crowns the sage's achievement.[11]

Kloppenborg's scribal sage, rewarded with fame, seems an unnecessarily biblical and professional description for the anonymous redactors of a Greek sayings-gospel, however steeped in some aspects of translated Israelite literature. Yet it is his Greek-reading public which is least likely to be a local, cultic, Galilean "Q community." The material evidence of the sayings-gospel Q points to different trustees of public identity, who are members of the writers' own ideologically mobile class, albeit also devotees of Jesus of Nazareth. No doubt the gospel writers were somehow related to Christian groups, but that these actual groups were the direct referents of remarks in the texts which model community life is an unverifiable guess.

What is materially certain is that gospel writers wrote well enough to locate themselves and their friends in a trans-local, Greco-Roman minority interested in the production and largely private consumption of ideologically universalizing literature. It is also materially certain that the authors of Q^1, Q^2, Q^3, Mark, Matthew and Luke specifically read and appreciated each other's works well in advance of any sign of the gospels' wider circulation or local canonization. The obvious social matrix for gospel literature is, to this extent, a small, dispersed cadre of Christians, very respectably articulate in public Greek, though also biblically well-read; the public which they address is an alternative construction of that universal public imagined by Greco-Roman literature and only partially, unevenly and gradually actualized in regional and local communities. The communities described in gospel literature belong in its past and are socially quite unlike the social class able to compose, read and copy such rhetorical texts; even less do the ideologically pure and distinct communities reconstructed by modern

---

[11] Kloppenborg, "Q People," 79, 100, 83; and "Q: Recent Opinion," 25.

critics, notably the "Q people," resemble the few local groups specifically known for early Christianity.

Normativity and legality

The goal of gospel rhetorics, then, was to envision a new public, not to regulate old communities. Some distinction like that between rhetorical normativity—creating an audience or even a public—and social normativity—governing a group—seems to be anticipated in the rhetoricians' perception that gnomai are *like* laws and civil decrees, but are not the same. Every community enforces social norms some of which are expressed as laws. Gnomic rhetoric often mimics such lawmaking, but its normativity is specifically limited to speech; a gnome is, if you like, a law unsanctioned except in speech performance.

The difference between rhetorical and social normativities is also implicit in the difference between Aristotle's characterization of gnome as part of rhetorical (not usually logical) "proof" (*pistis*) and the inclusion of gnome instead under "ornament" by Quintilian. Aristotle and Quintilian do not disagree that the rhetorical function of gnome is to crystallize normative influence in the experience and memory of an audience. By embracing the (rhetorical) normativity of ornament, Quintilian goes further than Aristotle toward recognizing that socially normative influence is not a matter of rational proof, even rhetorically simulated, so much as of a complex interaction of personal authority and rapport, aesthetic effect, audience susceptibilities and social setting. In its normative tendency, especially as captured in gnomai, rhetoric models what social norms might be and might become; even subliminally, it is not their uncritical mirror, as historians so often suppose.

This has its most urgent implications where New Testament gnome-use impinges on the sacred normativity of the Law. Here is a problem central to the rhetoric and to the social history of both Judaism and early Christianity: God-given Law is a major focus of social conflict and loyalty in both Judaism and its offshoot. At the same time, the rhetorical character of the Law's normative influence is inescapable; whether as a book or as a tradition, Torah cannot be communally obeyed until it is publicly talked about. Its impact on social normativity is to that extent always debatable and debated.

In Jewish and early Christian rhetoric there are notable correlations between gnome-use and topics or imagery which invoke the normativity of Law. Particularly in rhetoric ascribed to Jesus, however, legally symbolic topics and potentially legal topics (e.g., Sabbath, burial, food, fasting, marriage, taxes) are almost always associated with gnomic sayings. Nearly a quarter of all Synoptic gnomai refer to such topics or use such imagery. In fact, these topically legal gnomai are so numerous, so well attested across source- and form-critical boundaries and so rare outside the gospels as to sustain a presumption that they authentically represent one major type of gnome-use in pre-gospel tradition, stemming ultimately from Jesus.

Shared topics and collective authenticity in gnomai

The argument that legally topical gnomai attributed to Jesus are collectively, if not individually, authentic and representative of his public speech is thus essentially the same as that offered for Jesus' gnome-use in general. Representative authenticity is even more important in the topically legal examples, however, because the frequency of legal-sounding gnomai is the most distinctive aspect of gnome-use in the Synoptic Gospels and because the issue of the Law is one of the most troubled in historical study of Christian origins.

The very form of this argument for the authenticity and importance of gnomic language and specifically of legal gnomai adds to understanding Jesus historically as a speaker and as an influence on the gospels. I am not arguing that every gnome or every legally topical gnome was actually used by Jesus of Nazareth; instead I am saying that Jesus certainly used gnomic rhetoric heavily, even by the standards of his day and setting, and that at least some of those preserved in his name are characteristic of his actual usage.

Historical reconstructions of Jesus' public speaking are still usually based on the assumption that when he talked, he intended, on balance, to teach committed disciples rather than to create, persuade or dissuade uncommitted audiences. Even more prejudicially, historical reconstructions have for years attempted to authenticate Jesus' alleged sayings one by one and to authenticate them by contrast with their rhetorical environment; Jesus is most often assumed to have said those things which are least typical of either Palestinian Judaism or emergent

Christianity. The expectation is that early Christian tradition preserved and interpreted Jesus' speech patterns at best haphazardly or even against its own vested interest in a post-Easter Lord, speaking through the Spirit in the Church. This approach exposes a few relative singularities in Jesus-tradition, e.g., the topic of divine kingship and heavy parable-use, but it is unlikely to identify any database of sayings, each one of which will be demonstrably authentic and yet all of which will make sense as representative parts of a coherent rhetorical programme on Jesus' part.

Indeed, by aligning authenticity with originality, idiosyncrasy, even unorthodoxy, this procedure precludes discovery of an authentic whole among authentic fragments. It also kills any hope for interpretative consensus on individual sayings: any interesting saying attributed to Jesus attracts both pro- and anti-authenticity readings. The very notion, 'saying', is perplexing. Unless it is credibly placed in a specific context of social interaction—folklore or wisdom school or rhetoric—a 'saying' remains an arbitrary, historically inscrutable extract from a book. Such fragments, more or less plausibly authenticated, cannot reliably yield a representative sample of anyone's discourse. The overused criteria of 'dissimilarity' have demanded from 'authentic' words of Jesus not only an unlikely distinctness from Jewish, Hellenistic and Christian norms, but also the intelligibility of 'sayings' apart from and prior to placement in a possible rhetorical context, that is, in speech. More recently, a return to emphasizing early or multiple documentary attestation is still unable to escape an inevitably fragmentary result, in order to pull together a rhetorically competent Jesus, capable of more than a sentence or two at a time. The Jesus of twentieth-century historiography can generate haunting imagery, but hardly a coherent discourse; his influence remains a paradox.[12]

---

[12] E.P. Sanders, *Jesus and Judaism* (London, 1985) 13–16 for the challenge; R.W. Funk, "Unravelling the Jesus Tradition: Criteria and Criticism," *Forum* 5 (1989) 31–62, esp. 33; R.W. Funk, R.W. Hoover and the Jesus Seminar, *The Five Gospels: The Search for the Authentic Words of Jesus* (New York, 1993) 1–38; Crossan, *Historical Jesus*, xxx–xxxiv for nuanced, but in my view still rhetorically incoherent responses. For a recent list and bibliography of "criteria of authenticity" see J.P. Meier, *A Marginal Jew: Rethinking the Historical Jesus*, vol I: *The Roots of the Problem and the Person* (AB Reference Library; New York, 1991) 167–195.

An approach to Jesus' public speaking as rhetoric, stressing his gnome-use, alleviates many of these difficulties. In the first place, it portrays Jesus as a grassroots Jewish-Hellenistic rhetor with a real audience and not only as the teacher-poet of a select few. On this basis, no very strenuous critical or apologetic gymnastics are required to identify significant stylistic and thematic continuities between Jesus' public speech and that of the early Church, notwithstanding the revolution of the Easter message. Account must still be given of the transformations of tradition between Jesus' rhetoric and the rhetorics of gospels and epistles, but such change can now be evaluated along a well-understood rhetorical continuum: the Hellenistic rhetorical habits of gnome- and parable-use.

Indeed the continuity of gnome-use can help us to model and understand the more perplexing continuum between orality and literacy in both Hellenistic and early Christian rhetorics. Jesus did not speak only in gnomai and parables/*mythoi*, but his preference for them was sufficiently marked and sufficiently attractive to audiences and bearers of tradition to influence noticeably each strand of tradition and each author claiming Jesus' authority. Above all, the thorough contextualization of gnome-use in Greco-Roman rhetorical theory and practice can partly make up for the impossibility of contextualizing Jesus' 'sayings' within the texts of full-length speeches to definite audiences on definite occasions.

Synoptic gnomai are authentically representative of Jesus' rhetoric because they are a rhetorically definite, tradition-historically ubiquitous class; no reconstruction of Jesus' speech patterns is possible which does not prominently include gnomai. This is true even when the criteria of reconstruction ignore the rhetorical culture of Jesus' world and the rhetorical character of his ministry and tradition. Indeed, Jesus seems to have cultivated the gnomic manner to a degree which Roman rhetoricians like Cicero and Quintilian condemned as typically 'Asiatic' and newfangled.[13]

This kind of general authenticity does not depend on the demonstrable authenticity of any one gnome. Strong cases can be made even on the old, atomistic logic for the authenticity of several key gnomai.

---

[13] Cic. *Brut.* 95, 325; *Orat.* 49, 165 and Quint. *Inst.* VIII 4, 29; 5, 15–34; XII 10,48.

But to know that Jesus and his hearers liked gnomai and liked to sharpen them with legal topicality is far more important than to know which individual examples are most probably Jesus' own inventions. This is especially so when the criteria for authenticating individual items actively select *against* representativeness. My essential point in this study is that, even though early Christian tradition was not interested in preserving texts of Jesus' speeches, Jesus and the rhetorical culture of his day created in gnome the conditions for specific and, within discernible limits, successful re-creation of his style and thought in one of its most characteristic aspects.

Gnome and parable in Jesus' rhetoric

The logic for the authenticity of gnome is very like that widely accepted for the authenticity of parable. Thus Jesus' unusually intense use of parables is an authentic and essential fact about him, whether or not I can reconstruct or authenticate or even understand any particular example.

Gnomai differ from parables, however, in ways which identify the former as more broadly representative of Jesus' rhetoric and as more promising objects for rhetorical insight than the less flexible parable (*mythos/paradeigma*). Unlike gnomai, parables (or fables: *mythoi*) are formally narrative and fictional. These qualities expose parables more than most gnomai to serious modification in successive re-membering, re-telling and re-writing. Thus, although the popularity of *mythoi* is as ancient among the Greeks as their taste for gnomai, surviving examples of the former

> are almost entirely the product of late antiquity. Being normally rather longer and more circumstantial..., the fable offered more scope as a potential literary form in its own right.[14]

The story-teller's art is to make the old tale seem novel. The gnome-speaker wishes rather to make a new argument and a unique rhetorical

---

[14] Easterling, "Fable," 140. See also Mary Ann Beavis, "Parable and Fable," *CBQ* 52 (1990) 473–98.

context seem charmingly or menacingly familiar. Certainly, parables in different gospels, say Matthew and Luke, differ significantly more than the same authors' gnomai.

Moreover, the same qualities which make the gist of a gnome more resistant to modification than are the plot and characters of a parable also allow gnomai to be used in a wider variety of rhetorical contexts. This mercurial effectiveness of gnomic language in almost any speech setting might seem a liability against interpretation of Jesus' style as gnomic. It does, however, imply two advantages.

First, it forces us to respect the limits of historical exegesis of Jesus' language. Since we cannot in any case fully reconstruct even the rhetorical context, let alone the social and historical settings of Jesus' words, we had better begin historical interpretation with the category of speech which rhetorical convention expected to be most separable from its possible contexts. The fact that gnomai found in the Synoptic Gospels are legitimately understandable in the broad but well-documented context of rhetorical conventions, should in part obviate speculation about the social settings and original forms of Jesus' speeches.

Second, the resistance of gnomai to specialized contextualization in any particular kind of rhetoric paradoxically holds out the promise of a more universally and integrally representative sample of Jesus' speaking tradition. Synoptic association of parable with 'Kingdom' and the dissociation of 'Kingdom' from 'Son of Man' language are sharp enough to suggest that these turns of language, though undoubtedly authentic mannerisms of Jesus, may have been confined by him to special rhetorical and perhaps social contexts. By contrast, rhetorical convention allows that Jesus may have used gnomic language in any context chosen by him for public speech. The distribution of gnomai in the gospels and the distribution of imagery and topics among Synoptic gnomai confirm this expectation. Gnomai are the only sayings-type which was not only authentically used by Jesus, but also was likely to have been used by Jesus in the whole of whatever range of rhetorical situations he addressed.

The rhetorical function of gnomic language

This brings us back, however, to the problem of normative function in gnomai. The conventional rhetorical function of gnomai is to create rhetorical normativity, to confirm or redefine the relationship between speaker and audience. It does not do so in a rhetorical vacuum, however. Rhetorical complicity of this kind is created with a view to influencing some post-rhetorical world, to influencing social normativity after the present speeches are done. Gnome is well-suited to this ulterior motive as it creates rhetorical normativity by seeming, in its form and imagery, to crystallize or challenge social norms. Still, gnomic allusion to social normativity is quite ambiguously related to actual social setting and eventual influence. The aspect of social normativity which is most evident in the rhetorical text may not be the actual social setting or intended field of influence: a "stitch in time" seldom encourages real sewing. It is even harder to tell how far Jesus' gnomic normativity was fictional and utopian, programmatic and prophetic, or ostensibly descriptive in its allusion to social norms.

Negatively, this means that I do not know how far Jesus' rhetoric proved concretely, socially relevant to his intended audience. Some disciples were certainly called and an oral tradition began, but no school or party was instituted and few visible traces left on Palestinian society. Nor do I know how widely the memory of Jesus' own rhetoric influenced the remarkable post-Easter christological and ecclesial development of his movement. Pre-gospel tradition was apparently useful in these directions to the few who wrote gospels, but apparently not to the writers of Christian letters.

Sayings in general and gnomai in particular support direct reconstruction only of the rhetoric of Jesus and those influenced by his tradition; inferences about socially normative impact must be indirect, occasional and partial. Inferences from rhetoric to underlying, implicit, abstract and possibly subconscious attitudes (notably toward the Law) are even more speculative.

This is especially true of topically legal gnomai, despite their appearance of immediate social and ideological relevance. A speaker (or nowadays a broadcaster) can topically exploit an issue of the day (say, Law) to great effect without holding any coherent philosophical, political or theological position on the Law. Such controversial topicality can be of special use for establishing a speaker's stature, credibility and rapport with the particular audience for which a topic is most resonant. It is one thing, therefore, to know that Jesus could speak out aggressively on legal topics and another thing to know what the ideological, programmatic tenor of such speech may have been. A loyal Jew speaking among trusted friends might innocently say things about Law which on less loyal lips or on a more public occasion might become deeply antinomian or even offensively anti-Jewish.

What Jesus and his imitators say about key social and religious issues and values of his day is deliberately couched in an idiom which assumes more social or religious information than it yields. As often with personal and occasional wit, only contemporary insiders could reliably apply Jesus' gnome-use to specific social settings or attitudes. This is because the essential rhetorical function of gnome was less informative and argumentative (*logos*) than relational (*ethos*; *pathos*). Over time Jesus' definition of a particular rhetorical *ethos* and his invitation to rhetorical *pathos* became integral to the gospel's social function within the canonized, christological discourse (*logos*) of a gospel-reading sub-culture which was significantly unlike Jesus' own actual audiences. But the pervasive concern of Jesus' and the gospels' rhetoric with the task of communicative self-definition is in itself eloquent of Jesus' historical aims and historic influence.

Analysis of gnomai from the Synoptic Gospels does therefore allow significant social-historical carry-over to a more rhetorical model of oral tradition and gospel composition, and to Jesus' understanding of himself as a speaker. In keeping with the rhetorical function of gnome, to 'normalize' the relationship between audience and speaker, the rhetoricians are very clear that gnome-use has an exceptionally clear bearing on the speaker's communication of his chosen *ethos*. This seems, if anything, unusually true of Jesus' self-presentation; in a rhetorical world where everyone used gnomai and many to excess, Jesus' speech impressed his most sympathetic audience as distinctly gnomic and personal.

We should not try to determine too closely the social grounds for Jesus' adoption of a strikingly gnomic as well as parabolic style: perhaps intensive gnome-use helped Jesus to plan and organize speeches without writing or verbatim memorization; perhaps gnomai served him, as they seem to have served his Cynic contemporaries, in the unusually close speaker-audience interaction of soapbox improvisation; gnomic and parabolic style may mark the extent of Jesus' and/or his audiences' assimilation of Hellenistic 'pop' rhetoric; it may be that the instant rhetorical self-definition of gnome was necessary to turn a healer's clientele and spectators into a speaker's audience. Again, it would be naive to expect gnomai—even authentic gnomai—to tell us Jesus' social or political agenda or to expose his inner experience.

Gnomai do, however, cumulatively represent Jesus' chosen public voice better than any other sample of sayings tradition. Reasonable assurance is thus possible on four important points: Jesus noticeably affected a gnomic style; he did so deliberately; he intended thereby particularly to define his chosen rhetorical *ethos*; and he expected his hearers to understand this and hence to see themselves as an audience constituted by his speech. In this way gnomic rhetoric is an important antecedent for the gospels' christological reception of Jesus' speech.

Jesus, Paul and gnomic topicality

At the same time, a rhetorical approach to Synoptic gnomai suggests why there is so little evidence for widespread normative appeal to Jesus' words within the early Church. For a reader of the gospels, the lack of appeals to Jesus' sayings elsewhere in early Christian literature should be puzzling. Paul in particular seems actively to avoid citing Jesus' words even when he professes to know them. Rhetorical theory reminds us, however, that Jesus' gnomai would have been in their day recognizably neither didactic wisdom nor enforceable law. Instead, they express the speaker's adoption of a quite particular rhetorical *ethos*, neither didactic nor legal, toward his projected audience.

It is understandable that such rhetoric was therefore not directly usable by apostolic and pseudepigraphic letter-writers, for whom Jesus' rhetorical *ethos* had become a christological *persona*. A. Loisy's (gnomic!) paradox of Christian origins, that Jesus proclaimed the Kingdom, and the Church came, is tempered by the realization that Jesus' proclamation, whatever its conceptual or symbolic content, was concerned rhetorically to win and to move a selected audience; this audience, more than the sayings of the Kingdom, is the matrix of the Church. After the Cross and the Resurrection, this Church, spiritually empowered to listen to and speak for the Risen Lord, could practically ignore the historic sayings of Jesus, at least until these entered a more public domain as written documents with implications no longer under the control of charismatic leaders and congregations. Put simply, the kinds of normative language (wisdom and law) needed by early Christian writers and by their audiences could actually be undermined by the highly personal and emotive normative language in fact provided by gnomic sayings tradition.

The historical identification of gnomai as expressions of Jesus' conscious rhetorical stance is especially basic to the interpretation of topically legal gnomai. Here again, the gap between rhetoric's normative tendency and actual social norms imposes initially negative expectations; legal topics and imagery do not turn gnomai into laws. Topically legal gnomai in the gospels do not make a coherent or applicable body of rules (*halakah*) nor do they add up to a theory or theology of the Law, even assuming Jesus had one. On the other hand, they do positively model a Jesus whose rhetorical stance is not one of silence regarding the Law and its most symbolic topics. Instead, the gnomic Jesus defines himself and his audience by referring often to topics where the rhetorical normativity of the Law meets actual social sensitivities about day-to-day norms.

In the gospel gnomai, Jesus is not only keeping a guarded silence about the Law, nor is he simply abstaining from formulating rules on urgent practical questions about the Law's social use. He does both of these while aggressively defining his rapport with his audience in terms of just those topics over which lawyers, scholars, scribes, priests, prophets, judges and rulers might be expected to dispute his right to speak. He is able to do so by evoking legal issues non-legally in gnomic sayings.

Here Jesus' rhetorical interest in the Law contrasts with the more equivocal, often genuinely legal and theological attitudes of, e.g., Matthew and Paul to the Law and to the Church's need for laws. Jesus' tradition was always interested in the Law as a source of urgent rhetorical normativity and topicality; Paul and Matthew are interested in the Law as a topic *per se*. I shall argue later that Jesus' rhetorical stance is not taken in relation to the issue of the Law as a whole, though in "Galilee of the Gentiles" he could have done so. Instead Jesus seems to focus on the normative and topical quality of a few centrally representative laws. And he does so within the overarching topic of God's Kingship, a strategy which makes sense in addressing essentially Jewish, more or less Law-observant audiences.

As well, Paul's extraordinary reticence about Jesus as speaker makes sense as a response to the general difference of rhetorical *ethos* and audience between Jesus and the apostle. Specifically, it makes sense as a response to the barely repeatable, potentially misleading nuances of legal topicality in many of Jesus' gnomai. Paul may have had the defensible intuition that Jesus' rhetoric, simply repeated in Paul's context, would belie Jesus' original rhetorical aims; conversely, it may well be that Paul's rhetoric and Jesus' rhetoric, though quite different in their selection and use of key topics, may have sought much the same normative transformations in their different audiences. In both cases, however, it is important to remember that we are talking about a rhetorical, not a theoretical or theological attitude to Law—Law as source of topics, not Law as religious idea.

Paul's occasional, diffident allusions to Jesus as an authoritative speaker almost all refer to subjects about which the Synoptic Gospels attest topically legal gnomai. In view of general cultural sensitivity to gnomic rhetoric and the prevalence of gnomai in Synoptic tradition, this selective allusiveness cannot be coincidental, especially since Paul otherwise freely uses gnomai in controversy, legal epitome and ethical instruction (parenesis). Instead it implicitly recognizes that Jesus' gnomic rhetoric was non-didactic and non-legal, even when touching legal topics. Whether consciously or instinctively, Paul discerns that the personal and affective intensity (*ethos* and *pathos*) of Jesus' legal gnomai makes their conceptual aspect (*logos*) difficult to apply in a new setting. Jesus relates through gnomai and through daringly legal topics to an audience and with an authority not like Paul's. To that extent the apostle is rhetorically as well as christologically prudent to exclude Jesus' words as far as possible from his own moral instruction, from his discussions of legal topics and from the apologetic and polemic definition of his own *ethos*, rhetorical settings in which he freely uses his own gnomic coin.

Jesus' gnomai cannot embody an integral attitude to the Law. Yet they do enshrine a communicative attitude to himself and to his audience which led him markedly to risk and enhance the personalism and value-laden urgency of gnomic language. On the other hand, this central, pre-christological, pre-canonical concern is tempered in the direction of an unspecifiable but undeniable social normativity by the frequency and boldness of gnomic allusion to social roles and to legal topics; Christian establishment and transformation of authoritative social institutions was not an arbitrary response to Jesus' rhetorical *ethos*, though it necessarily went well beyond the possible implications of his speech as *logos*.

The sensitivity of the ancient world to deliberately projected rhetorical *ethos* and perhaps a hint of the special volatility of gnomic allusion to legal topics may be conveyed by an extract from Peter Brown's discussion of "*Paideia* and Power":

> So much alert attention to deportment betrays a fact almost too big to be seen. We are in a world characterized by a chilling absence of legal restraints on violence in the exercise of power.... For centuries philosophers and teachers...grappled with the intensely personal nature of power in ancient society. Ethical writers of the early empire were obsessed by scenarios of acute dependence. From wives and slaves in the household to the abject courtiers of tyrannical rulers, the lives of so many persons in so many situations appeared to depend on the whim of their superiors. A lurking fear of arbitrary violence, untrammeled by legal and political constraints, insensibly shifted the weight of philosophical discussion towards ethical issues, involving self-formation and control of the passions. The emphasis on the "care of the self" that flourished in the first two centuries A.D. was in many ways the reaction of thinking persons to their own bleak perceptions of Roman society as one in which heightened self-control was the only, frail guarantee of humanity to others.[15]

To appreciate the risk, the sovereign or else churlish carelessness of self, in Jesus' gnomic rhetoric and use of legal topics, we need add only the heightened stakes arising from the resistant prestige of Torah-Law within the Roman commonwealth and certainly in pre-70 Galilee and Jerusalem. Unlike Jesus' parables, the frequent insolence and/or legal topicality of Jesus' gnomai ("Let the dead bury their own dead." Matt 8:22 par), if public, could contribute to public and arbitrary judgements. At the same time we may appreciate the nervousness of Paul, whose own rhetorically-projected apostolic *ethos* was vulnerable to Roman, Christian and Jewish opposition, as shamelessly lacking in self-restraint; the folly of Paul's own gospel was provocation enough, without directly

---

[15] Peter Brown, *Power and Persuasion in Late Antiquity: Towards a Christian Empire* (Madison, WI, 1992) 50.

borrowing the heritage of Jesus' aggressive gnomic self-definition and its frequent caricature of legal authority.

It is in the nature of gnomic rhetoric, then, that Jesus' gnomai and the rhetorical *ethos* they document did not exert an unambiguous influence, even on Jesus' most passionate devotees. Nor, rhetorically or theologically, should they have—in the gospels gnomic language and characterization are indispensable to constructing a new, biographical rhetoric for the literary character Jesus. Yet they are also subordinate to other motives (e.g., the story of Easter and the revelation of divine Wisdom). Outside the gospels it is even clearer that, if Jesus' gnomic habit should have inspired christology, it seldom did so directly. Even the exceptions reflect the evangelists' and Paul's need to find or to avoid a consistent attitude to Law and legal normativity, more than a direct interest in the pre-christological implications of gnomic rhetoric as such. In gospel and epistle, Law and laws are topics in their own right; in Jesus' recoverable (gnomic and parabolic) rhetoric, Law and legality are not topics but symbols borrowed to illustrate and intensify Jesus' rapport with his audience. In gospel and in epistle, Jesus is not the speaker; he is the subject of quotation, allusion and christological reflection. In Jesus' own rhetoric, the audience is not yet the Church and its World, and the identity of the speaker is not yet fully disclosed even to himself.

For rhetoric and hence, I think, for theology these nuances of difference are best heard in the ways dominical, epistolary and gospel rhetorics link Jesus and Law to gnome-use. For rhetoric they are, moreover, legitimate, even predictable adjustments to post-Easter rhetorical settings; acquaintance with the most basic categories of Hellenistic rhetorical theory and practice thus strongly suggests that rhetorical legitimacy is the nursery of theological insight in the historic re-integration of Jesus' rhetoric as Christian gospel.

II

A DEFENCE OF RHETORIC AGAINST ITS ADMIRERS

Thus far, a reader might be forgiven for expecting a book on gnomic rhetoric in Jesus' tradition to contribute to some branch of New Testament scholarship generally recognized as 'rhetorical criticism'.

This must, however, be doubly qualified by noting ambiguities in current references to rhetoric and fragmentation within the discipline of New Testament studies itself. In fact, ambiguities conceal real contradictions within the widening range of fashionable rhetorical contextualisms, a centrifugal movement of growing eclecticism, pluralism and uncertainty about methods for New Testament interpretation. Those who accept the label 'rhetorical criticism' for their own work do not by any means agree on its basic implications, while those who see rhetorical criticism in the work of others are not yet under much disciplinary pressure to go beyond labelling to real understanding of this scholarly phenomenon.

Certainly, there are important unresolved tensions between literary-poetic and social-historical uses of rhetoric. Within the latter there is, or should be, further tension. Exegesis may welcome rhetorical criticism technically as a source of greater realism for a more or less objective picture of the past. This is not easily wedded with a more hermeneutically-oriented exegesis, seeking to re-tell the past rhetorically not as impartial knowledge, but as an argument against a particular present and an apprehended future. In a still rare attempt to evaluate rhetorical criticism as a trend, Dennis Stamps has concluded:

> In terms of interpretive goals and methods, the poles could not be further apart. From one there is the rhetoric of the hegemony of the status quo, the maintaining of the sacred guild which determines the criteria by which a new critical method is allowed in the picture. From the other, there is the radical rhetoric of revolution and reconfiguration, the eclectic grasp for a new constellation.[16]

In fact, the situation is even more complicated than this might suggest. Despite his pluralist call for "a new constellation," Stamps is invoking the old Protagoran quest for two rhetorically and politically, if not logically, opposable sides as the first step toward victory over chaos. He is certainly right that there ought to be a vigorous debate about the use of rhetoric in future study of early Christian literature. It is dangerously misleading, however, to suppose there can be two cleanly opposed poles

---

[16] D.L. Stamps, "Rhetorical Criticism and the Rhetoric of New Testament Criticism," *Journal of Literature and Theology* 6 (1992) 268–79, 273–4; compare Bible and Culture Collective, *The Postmodern Bible* (New Haven and London, 1995) 149–186.

in such a debate. Both the "status quo" and allegedly radical rhetorics of "revolution and reconfiguration" are riven by internal dissensions as basic as any opposition between them, and as carefully repressed by common scholarly interest. Stamps is right that New Testament studies are still basically defined by positivist historicism (revolutionary enough in its suspicion of theological criticism). It remains unclear, however, that "the [*sic*] alternative understanding of texts" has a better title to the name of rhetoric—or even that an alternative really exists in the plurality of scholarly motives and interests.

Most academic writers on Christian origins are no longer addressing a theologically defined audience, but few of us can or will ignore the gospel's rhetorically avowed intention to transform a world. Nor are we likely to renounce meekly the old pretensions of biblical rhetoric and its professional exegetes to universal relevance, even where we are deeply divided and unsure what that relevance should be and to whom it should be responsible. The danger in this context of constructing and proclaiming a new, eclectic rhetorical criticism is that it may promote a false naivety about the motives of the revisionist academic rhetorics to which such criticism often belongs. Thus, for example, if we are drawn to the gospel as a model for socially redemptive, emancipatory rhetoric we should not expect easily to cut or re-tie historical and christological strings attaching it to a potentially intractable Jesus.

Stamps characterizes rhetorical criticism (and New Testament studies generally) as an undeclared war between historicist, theological and transcendent hermeneutics on one side and "a larger and ubiquitous critical practice which takes the critic...beyond rhetoric restrained to rhetoric reinvented."[17] This is a useful indication of the intensity of the conflict over rhetoric and of its location—among modern interpreters even more than among the old texts of ancient rhetoric and early Christianity. But Stamps' dialectic of radical reinvention expresses a falsely tidy consciousness of the struggle to legitimate Bible-reading within a North American academy which itself awaits social and ideological reinvention. The relationship between rhetorical criticism of the past and critical rhetoric for the future is as important and as unstable as the older relationship between historical criticism and

---

[17] Stamps, "Rhetorical Criticism," 277.

theological confession: neither relationship is mediated by a clean binary opposition of scholarly loyalties.

If even a potential or heuristic unity of New Testament exegesis is to be maintained, and with it the vestiges of former religious and social influence, some unifying yet flexible hermeneutic is needed, to which I believe the ethos of Hellenistic rhetoric is indispensable.[18] On the other hand, if putative cohesion is dropped in favour of radical exegetical pluralism, greater candour is needed to identify the intended audiences of our several distinct 'rhetorical criticisms'. My preference is for the former option, and I will return to it. But either way, I think it crucial to clarify the intended place of the present work and of Hellenistic rhetoric within the wider motives and debates of Early Christian studies and among competing critical appropriations of rhetoric.

---

[18]   I have in mind the *"wirkungsgeschichtliche Hermeneutik"* of K. Berger, "Rhetorical Criticism, New Form Criticism, and New Testament Hermeneutics," in *Rhetoric and the New Testament: Essays from the 1992 Heidelberg Conference*, ed. S.E. Porter and T.H. Olbricht (Sheffield, 1993) 390–396; K. Berger, *Exegese des Neuen Testaments* (UTB 650; Heidelberg, 1984) 242–69, on Rhetoric and *Wirkung*; *Einführung in die Formgeschichte* (UTB 1444; Tübingen, 1987) 164–7, 257–8; cf. E. Schüssler Fiorenza, "Rhetorical Situation," *NTS* 33 (1987) 386–403, 386; for a challenging, but sometimes unclear proposal relating rhetorics and hermeneutics, see W. Wuellner, "Hermeneutics and Rhetorics: From 'Truth and Method' to 'Truth and Power'," *Scriptura S* 3 (1989) 1–54 and "Rhetorical Criticism and its Theory in Culture-Critical Perspective: The Narrative Rhetoric of John 11," in *Text and Interpretation: New Approaches in the Criticism of the New Testament*, ed. P.J. Martin and J.H. Petzer (Leiden, 1991) 171–85. Wuellner is also part of the Bible and Culture Collective, see *Postmodern Bible* 157, 160. See also M.J. Hyde and C.R. Smith, "Hermeneutics and Rhetoric: A Seen But Unobserved Relationship," *The Quarterly Journal of Speech* 65 (1979) 347–63; H.P. Rickman, "Rhetoric and Hermeneutics," *Philosophy and Rhetoric* 14 (1981) 100–11; S. Mailloux, "Rhetorical Hermeneutics," *Critical Inquiry* 11 (1985) 620–41; J.P. Martin, "Towards a Post-Critical Paradigm," *NTS* 33 (1987) 370–385; S.M. Pogoloff, "Isocrates and Contemporary Hermeneutics, in *Persuasive Artistry: Studies in New Testament Rhetoric in Honor of George A. Kennedy*, ed. D.F. Watson (JSNTSup 50; Sheffield, 1991); and Evelyn R. Thibeaux, "Rhetorical Criticism as an Integrative Paradigm for New Testament Studies," presented to the SBL, Mid-Atlantic Region, 27 February, 1992, unpublished.

Rhetorical genre criticism (H.-D. Betz)

One deservedly influential model for rhetorical criticism of New Testament texts is the genre-critical rhetoric of H.-D. Betz, especially his commentaries on Paul's epistolary rhetoric.[19] Betz' interpretation of the Sermon on the Mount as Hellenistic *epitome* is less persuasive, but highlights the rhetorical status of a question which has become central to gospel criticism: What genre(s) and sub-genres should determine rhetorical conventions for reading the gospels and Q?[20] Such approaches are to be encouraged, but their focus is primarily on literary genres, in understandable overreaction against classical form criticism; it is hard to connect such criticism with legitimate questions about how, why and to whom early Christians and Jesus spoke in public.

Special pleading for continuity between conversation and literary form and for social-historical representativeness is possible for a few specific rhetorical categories. Thus, diatribic and epistolary texts do have a special, though still tricky, generic connection with actual conversation; the ancients did think that diatribe and letter should sound like one and a half sides of a telephone conversation. Nevertheless, it is significant that the best integration yet of literary insight from epistolary rhetoric with broader social-historical reconstruction rests on the letter to Philemon, surely an exceptional case for both epistolary and sociological approaches to Pauline writing.[21]

---

[19] H.-D. Betz, *Galatians* (Hermeneia; Philadelphia, 1979); *2 Corinthians 8 and 9: A Commentary on Two Administrative Letters of the Apostle Paul* (Hermeneia; Philadelphia, 1985); for an important critique of Betz' rhetoric see C.J. Classen, "Paulus und die antike Rhetorik," *ZNW* 82 (1991) 1–33, translated and updated as "St. Paul's Epistles and Ancient Greek and Roman Rhetoric," *Rhetorica* 10 (1992) 319–344 and in Porter and Olbricht, *Heidelberg Conference*, 265–291.

[20] H.-D. Betz, *Essays on the Sermon on the Mount* (Philadelphia, 1979); on gospel genres see E.P. Sanders and M. Davies, *Studying the Synoptic Gospels* (London and Philadelphia, 1989) chaps, 2, 17, 18, 19 and bibliography there; for Q see J.S. Kloppenborg, *The Formation of Q: Trajectories in Ancient Wisdom Collections* (Studies in Antiquity and Christianity; Philadelphia, 1987); R.A. Piper, *Wisdom in the Q-Tradition: The Aphoristic Teaching of Jesus* (SNTSMS 61; Cambridge, 1989).

[21] On the special problems and opportunities of epistolary rhetoric see Classen, "Paul's Epistles and Ancient Rhetoric"; on conversational typicality in letters see N.R. Petersen, *Rediscovering Paul: Philemon and the Sociology of Paul's Narrative World* (Philadelphia, 1985) esp. 53–65; W.G. Doty, *Letters in Primitive Christianity* (Guides

The present book is itself an instance of such special pleading for the exceptional importance of a single rhetorical category. I argue that gnome-use is the rhetorical habit which Jesus, early Christian speakers and early Christian writers were most likely to have in common. Gnome is exceptional, however, precisely because of its presence in every genre of literary and performance rhetoric. Among the progymnasmata, the overstudied chreia is most typical of the gospels as literature and most pivotal to their redactional development.[22] Chreia and its argumentative and narrative elaborations are a good model for the formation of the gospels' literary rhetoric. By the same token, however, they are inadequate for assessing Jesus' rhetorical influence, since Jesus' own style was gnomic and parabolic not, on the whole, chriic—this is true, too, of actual public speaking in Christian milieux, so far as we know anything about it at all.[23]

---

to Biblical Scholarship; Philadelphia, 1973) 11–17; R.W. Funk, *Language, Hermeneutic, and Word of God* (New York, 1966) 248ff; H. Koskenniemi, *Studien zur Idee und Phraselogie des griechischen Briefes bis 400 n.Chr.* (Helsinki, 1956); on dialogue style in *diatribe* see S.K. Stowers, *The Diatribe and Paul's Letter to the Romans* (SBLDS 57; Ann Arbor, MI, 1981) 45–8, 75–8; T. Schmeller, *Paulus und die "Diatribe"* (NTAbh 19; Münster, 1987); H. Thyen, *Der Stil der Jüdisch-Hellenistische Homilie* (Göttingen, 1955); R. Bultmann, *Der Stil der paulinischen Predigt und die kynische-stoische Diatribe* (Göttingen, 1910).

[22] V.K. Robbins, ed., *The Rhetoric of Pronouncement=Semeia* 64 (1993) esp. vii–xvii, V.K. Robbins, "Introduction: Using Rhetorical Discussions of the Chreia to Interpret Pronouncement Stories"; B.L. Mack and V.K. Robbins, *Patterns of Persuasion in the Gospels* (Sonoma, 1989); B.L. Mack, *A Myth of Innocence: Mark and Christian Origins* (Philadelphia, 1988) esp. Appendix I; V.K. Robbins, "The Chreia," in *Greco-Roman Literature and the New Testament: Selected Forms and Genres*, ed. E. Aune (Sources for Biblical Study 21; Atlanta, 1988) 1–23; H.A. Fischel, "Studies in Cynicism and the Ancient Near East: The Transformation of a Chria," in *Religion in Antiquity: Essays in Memory of E.R. Goodenough*, ed. J. Neusner (Leiden, 1988) 372–411; R.F. Hock and E.N. O'Neil, *The Chreia in Ancient Rhetoric*, vol I: *The Progymnasmata*, (Texts and Translations 27; Greco-Roman Religion 9; Atlanta, 1986); J.R. Butts, "The Chreia in the Synoptic Gospels," *BTB* 16 (1986) 132–8; D. Patte, ed., *Kingdom and Children: Aphorism, Chreia, Structure=Semeia* 29 (1983); G.W. Buchanan, "Chreias in the New Testament," in *Logia—les Paroles de Jésus—the Sayings of Jesus: Mémorial Joseph Coppens*, ed. J. Delobel (BETL 59; Leuven, 1982) 501–5; R.O.P. Taylor, *The Groundwork of the Gospels* (Oxford, 1946).

[23] Early Christian rhetorical performance seems to have abounded in strong assertions of personal and normative authority; its uses of scripture seem paradigmatic and enthymematic and, in parenesis, gnomic, but not often chriic in form or spirit. Cf.

Rhetorical "Poetics of Faith" (J. Muilenburg; A.N. Wilder)

Two voices have particularly inspired movement toward a self-consciously literary rhetorical criticism, more sensitive to the expressive unity and power of texts than classical form criticism could dare to be. Both James Muilenburg (in Old Testament studies) and Amos Wilder (in New Testament criticism) remained loyal to the heritage of form criticism, while seeking a more equal balance between reconstructing the oral prehistory of biblical texts and appreciating their actual composition as texts. A more specifically, perhaps exclusively, literary horizon defines the rhetorical criticism inaugurated by Muilenburg, perhaps because of its origin in the study of the Hebrew Bible. This approach is literary, not least, because it pays its attention primarily to the stylistic and structural qualities which mark 'texts' as 'compositions':

> I am interested in...understanding the nature of Hebrew literary composition, in exhibiting the structured patterns that are employed for the fashioning of a literary unit, whether in poetry or in prose, and in discerning the many and various devices by which the predications are formulated and ordered into a unified whole. Such an enterprise I should describe as rhetoric and the methodology as rhetorical criticism.[24]

I would rather call such an enterprise, centred on aesthetics, structure and unity, 'poetics'. Poetics in this sense is a welcome corrective to a historical exegesis obsessed with dissolving texts into sources, forms and traditions, but it is not the same as rhetoric.

C.C. Black II, "The Rhetorical Form of the Hellenistic Jewish and Early Christian Sermon: A Response to Lawrence Wills," *HTR* 81 (1988) 1–18, esp. 12f.; S.K. Stowers, "Social Status, Public Speaking and Private Teaching: The Circumstances of Paul's Preaching Activity," *NT* 26 (1984) 59–82; G.A. Kennedy, *New Testament Interpretation Through Rhetorical Criticism* (Chapel Hill, NC, 1984); J.I.H. McDonald, *"Kerygma" and "Didache": The articulation and structure of the earliest Christian message* (SNTSMS 37; Cambridge, 1980); W. Wuellner, "Greek Rhetoric and Pauline Argumentation," in *Early Christian Literature and the Classical Intellectual Tradition: in honorem Robert M. Grant*, ed. W. Schroedel and R.W. Wilcken (Théologie historique 53; Paris, 1979) 177–88; Thyen, *Homilie*, esp. 40–63.

[24] J. Muilenburg, "Form Criticism and Beyond," *JBL* 88 (1969) 1–18.

Historical rhetoric, deprived of immediate access to the performances and audiences of the distant past, must often make do with the text-linguistic data which it shares with poetics. Nevertheless rhetoric as I understand it has properly to do with a wider range of data and with a distinct basic question. Where the task of poetics is to investigate the conditions for symbolic, expressive unity in texts, the complementary goal of rhetoric is to study speech, including texts, as the instrument of persuasion and motivation. Consequently, rhetoric is never interested in texts *per se*, but only in texts as integral to larger rhetorical acts. That is, it deals with the whole linguistically, socially and historically mediated communication between speaker and audience within the framework of particular historical and social experiences. Rhetoric is as interested in performances, conventions and audiences as it is in scripts.

Literary-critical appeals to reader-response often borrow at least some of the technical vocabulary of rhetoric to think about the potential of some texts for perennial and cross-cultural influence. They often do so, however, without considering the generative influence of rhetoric on early Christian speech, its performers and audiences and without taking seriously the ancient rhetorical assumption that texts are meaningful within a carefully cultivated climate of verbal communicativeness.

Amos N. Wilder's *Early Christian Rhetoric: The Language of the Gospel* (1964) continues to inspire a New Testament rhetorical criticism which is significantly more concerned to address social and historical concerns than was Muilenburg's project. The sub-title, however, is still a fairer description of the book's approach than its title; in fact, the first United States edition happily reversed title and sub-title: *The Language of the Gospel: Early Christian Rhetoric*. Despite Wilder's breadth of vision and critical wisdom, "rhetoric" is, here too, a misnomer for what is more properly a "Poetics of Faith."[25] This confusion of the aesthetic and phenomenological discipline of poetics with the socially inclusive,

---

[25] A.N. Wilder, *Early Christian Rhetoric: The Language of the Gospel* (London, 1964; rpr. Cambridge, MA, 1971)=*The Language of the Gospel: Early Christian Rhetoric* (New York, 1964); W.A. Beardslee, ed., *The Poetics of Faith: Essays offered to Amos Niven Wilder*, 2 vols.=*Semeia* 12, 13 (1978); cf. V.K. Robbins and J.H. Patton, "Rhetoric and Biblical Criticism," *Quarterly Journal of Speech* 66 (1980) 327–50. Watson's note on the change of titles seems mistaken; D.F. Watson and A.J. Hauser, *Rhetorical Criticism of the Bible: A Comprehensive Bibliography with Notes on History and Method* (Biblical Interpretation 4; Lieden, 1994) 107 n.42.

historically and psychologically particular business of rhetoric is fundamental to much modern literary criticism. In the context of New Testament and Early Christian studies, where poetically complex texts are the only surviving echo of a once even more involved rhetorical history, confusion of poetics with rhetoric becomes too easily reduction of the latter to the former.

Wilder himself sought to define a poetics of early Christian language which could still influence social-historical reconstructions of Jesus' aims and impact on early Christianity. Jesus' movement and earliest Christianity are separated from each other and from the production of early Christian literature by rhetorical distances which, if not negligible, are still less than many such leaps documented in the Old Testament. Wilder therefore wisely refused to reduce his hybrid, but essentially aesthetic and literary poetics still further to a discussion of stylistics, semantics and text structures.

The benefit has been a rediscovery of biblical language, dialogue and story, myth and metaphor, with something of their original pointedness. Thus, for example, Wilder does recognize the complexity and import- ance of relating orality and literacy in ancient and, especially, early Christian rhetoric. Wilder gave whole generations of biblical scholars a welcome licence to engage early Christian texts as literature, yet without having to repudiate historical and theological curiosity.

One cost of Wilder's influence has been Jesus' misrepresentation as a kind of poetaster, and especially as the implied author of (tradition- historically reconstructed) parables. Jesus' parables can certainly be received as poems, subject to the specialized, often aesthetically and philosophically maximizing interpretation which poetry invites. It is historically more probable, however, that they were composed and performed as rhetorical linkages and illustrations (*paradeigmata*) within longer discourse and in contexts which we can only tentatively grasp in their complexity and specificity. There is no need to preclude poetic or, eventually, theological interpretation of parables and other sayings materials attributed to Jesus. Historically, however, their most authoritat- ive exegesis will be in terms of the rhetoricity and topicality which made them tempting points of departure for more speculative readings.

For New Testament criticism, certainly for historical Jesus research, the value of Hellenistic rhetoric is not primarily its interest in texts and their potential for meaning. Rather rhetoric is valuable because of its interest in whole communicative processes, comprising speaker, setting, message, medium and audience in all their social and historical particularity and ambiguity. Of course, Greco-Roman rhetoric is not above reproach in its pursuit of this inclusive task. Many modern tyrannies found inspiration in the cultural and political hegemony which took rhetorical Hellenism beyond critical analysis to determine the production and reception of texts and the formation of speakers and audiences. Nevertheless, the gospel, too, is both rhetoric and specifically Hellenistic.

The deliberate Greco-Roman imposition of Hellenizing rhetoric on the ancient world as an educational and political programme allows almost empirical analysis of rhetorical behaviour. In this historical and social context, it becomes possible to estimate the effects of texts even where evidence for their actual reception is lacking. This historical grounding also forces us to expect that the internationalist, imperialist rhetorical programme of Hellenism will often have been assimilated to local speech traditions: hence the cross-cultural importance of the gnomic sentence, practised expertly in near eastern rhetoric long before the imposition of Hellenistic theory and curricula. Still, Hellenistic rhetoric, especially its most popular educational and performance registers, is the one important intellectual heritage common to Galilean talkers, New Testament writers and Academic theorists.

Socio-rhetorical criticism (B.L. Mack and V.K. Robbins)

A new tendency in rhetoric-inspired New Testament studies is emerging in the "socio-rhetorical" criticism of Vernon K. Robbins, Burton L. Mack and their associates. Their work emphasizes argumentative purposefulness, social engagement and aggressive authority claims in Christian rhetoric.[26] These writers correctly see in Hellenistic rhetoric

---

[26] V.K. Robbins, *Jesus the Teacher: A Socio-Rhetorical Interpretation of Mark* (Philadelphia, 1984); Mack, *Myth of Innocence*; Mack, *Rhetoric and the New Testament*; Mack and Robbins, *Patterns*, sympathetically reviewed by J.D. Hester in *Rhetorica* 9 (1991) 179–85; Robbins "Rhetorical Discussions of the Chreia"; V.K. Robbins "Progymnastic Rhetorical Composition and Pre-Gospel Traditions" in *The Synoptic Gospels: Source Criticism and the New Literary Criticism*, ed. Camille Focant (BETL 110; Leuven, 1993) 111–147; B. Mack, *The Lost Gospel: The Book of Q and Christian Origins* (San Francisco, 1993).

an essential bridge between linguistic theory and practical influence on Christian beginnings. I am sympathetic with many of these goals. They mark an explicit shift from linguistic aestheticism toward social realism. They are consequently aware that the influence of speech and texts is structured by the overarching influence of rhetorical culture and its sub- and counter-cultures. They are also appropriately conscious that Greek rhetoric and Jewish/Christian mythical experience are related by mutual assimilation and competition, so that the fit of Hellenistic rhetorical categories to the various forms of gospel speech will be selective, occasionally ambiguous and therefore critically significant. Mack and Robbins have even begun to call attention to the specifically Hellenistic and rhetorical character of pre-Synoptic oral tradition associated with Jesus.

Notwithstanding the importance and sophistication of their contribution, however, Mack and Robbins have based their socio-rhetorical approach on the double fallacy of which I earlier accused modern philosophical rhetoric. First, overreacting against narrowly aesthetic and literary uses of rhetoric, they tend to reduce rhetorical persuasion to formal argumentation. In any rhetorical performance or text, persuasive effect depends on 'ornamental' qualities of personality and mood (*ethos* and *pathos*) as well as on argumentative strategies (*logos*). Although philosophical and scientific positivism often shames us into pretending otherwise, the perceived sincerity and authority of a speaker may well and even rightly move us more than any cogency of speech analysed as argumentation. This is doubly true of early Christian rhetoric in its transformation of rhetorical *pistis* into spiritual experience.

In addition, both Robbins, e.g., in his uncritical, foundational acceptance of G. Theißen's sociology of "the Jesus movement," and Mack, e.g., in his bold (though not single-handed) invention of the "Q people," fail to distinguish adequately between the rhetorical (usually argumentative) strategies of texts and their social-historical implications.[27] Robbins usefully summarizes Mack's history of Christian origins thus:

---

[27] Mack, *Lost Gospel, passim*; B.L. Mack, "Q and the Gospel of Mark: Revising Christian Origins," *Semeia* 55, ed. Kloppenborg and Vaage (1991) 15–39; Robbins, *Jesus the Teacher*, 7, 209–23; contra R.A. Horsley, *Sociology and the Jesus Movement* (New York, 1989); Mack, *Myth of Innocence*, 84–7 and nn. 6, 7; Kloppenborg, *Formation of Q*, 39; Kloppenborg, "Q People"; "Q: Recent Opinion"; Piper, *Wisdom in the Q-Tradition*, 184–92.

Burton Mack's analysis of Mark probes five different cultural subgroups in early Christianity. Each subgroup exhibits a distinctive use of language, a preference for a particular form of tradition, special social strategies, and a significant ideology.[28]

Yet each subgroup is no more than an uncontrolled inference from precisely those allegedly distinctive uses of language; rhetorical diversity, even within a document, equals cultural diversity organized into distinct communities. Mack's working maxim is always that linguistic differences within and between texts index different, indeed, competing and incompatible social normativities.

The socio-rhetorical project involves the methodical denial of the gap between the rhetorical normativity projected by texts and the actual social normativities interacting in the production and reception of texts. At the same time, socio-rhetorical criticism insists on the gap between different social normativities despite their presence side by side in the final redactions of such ideologically composite texts as Q, Mark and John. John Kloppenborg is, of course, right that,

> it is a priori no less probable that Q was associated with a discrete community than is the case with the canonical gospels, where it is quite unexceptional to speak of Matthew's church or the Markan community.

Within the form-critical model of early Christian writing as quasi-folkloric *Kleinliteratur*, it did, temporarily, make sense to regard the texts of the Christian subculture as reflexes of community identity and social history. We have noticed above the continuation of this expectation within the redaction-critical model of early Christian gospel-writing as confessional theology. Indeed, it is the shared a priori assumption that every text must have been "associated with a discrete community" that has left redaction-critically tutored historiography speechless before revisionist histories based on "the Q people" in opposition to Marcan and Pauline Christianities. Within a rhetorical critical horizon, however, "the premise that a homological relationship exists between the symbolic world of the social group and the formal and material characteristics of its documents" should be indefensible: there are rhetorical processes of metonymic selection and metaphoric projection

---

[28] Robbins, "Pre-Gospel Traditions," 147.

at work between even symbolic social normativity and the norms of particular texts or corpora.

A central goal of rhetorical production, interpretation and criticism is to identify a selective analogy between texts (rhetorical normativity) and social normativity. It is essential to the notion of rhetoric as publicly purposeful speech that there be an imaginable public in the speaker's social world. A degree of intentional, normative analogy between rhetorical text and real social life is indeed among the premises of rhetorical interpretation in its traditional forms. I have argued above, however, that rhetorical-social analogy in antiquity is consciously selective, reductive and prescriptive. This goes beyond conceding "that some documents may have been preserved precisely because they challenged rather than reflected community theology and practice." The essential task for rhetorical normativity is to reduce a plurality of linguistically and socially possible speeches and responses, first, to a finite list of topics and, then, to a binary dilemma. Selection of topics and definition of *stasis* are thus directed toward some aspect of social conditions; on the other hand, texts as rhetoric represent their speakers' calculated gambits in a game where both issues (types of *stasis*) and terms of reference (topics) are purposely abstracted from the social actualities they ostensibly presuppose.[29]

Rhetoric, like model-building, implies general social-material analogy. Still, a particular rhetorical performance or genre need not imply the existence of a correspondingly particular community any more than a particular model necessarily implies the existence of the possible system it models.

Materially, the rhetorics of the gospels and of their probable sources and redactional strata witness primarily to the brief activity of a few individuals able and motivated to write rhetorically complex and experimental works in passable Greek. The textual evidence is compelling, that these few writers worked in a network close enough to promote intense synoptic intertextuality and surprisingly little ideological conflict; each text blithely incorporates substantial material with which, redaction-critically, it ought to disagree. Indeed, any criticism which relies on distinguishing among social ideologies in early Christian texts should have to deal explicitly with the puzzling complacency of

---

[29] Kloppenborg, "Q People," 77, 79, 78.

the texts themselves, all of which are ideologically hybrid. Once again, the material evidence is that such gospel writers read each other before any of their works became anything like public or institutionalized within particular, ideologically or locally defined communities.

In view of recent assessments of Greco-Roman literacy rates and the use and circulation of rhetorically complex texts, there is a presumption worth testing that gospel writers, like other Greco-Roman authors, wrote in the first place for each other, for emerging cadres of abnormally educated Christians, rather than for ordinary believers and their actual communities as such. Through collection, canonization and liturgical reading the gospels did reach a mass audience, perhaps the second in literary history, after the Septuagint. Initially, however, Mark and Q reached Matthew and Luke. Perhaps their authors intended little more, though they do presuppose the existence of larger groups. Perhaps gospels are more nearly manuals for Christian rhetoric than representative samples of its achievements.[30]

In fact, the production, use and reception of texts is quite often ironically, even tragically distant from their rhetorically normative effect. Serious disjunction between normative tendency of rhetorical texts and social normativity before and after their production is particularly to be expected where, as in early Christian gospel-writing and epistolography, current rhetorical and literary conventions have been deliberately distorted.

Thus, for example, if it be granted that the "overall rhetorical form" of the Gospel of Mark centrally identifies "Jesus as Teacher," it does so with an intense irony which its author probably consciously meant—Jesus is the Teacher who scarcely teaches and whose disciples are models mainly of social malfunction. And the irony of Mark and the irony of any possible relationship between it and any actual discipleship community were sufficiently pronounced that Mark's earliest known readings, Matthew and Luke, both work hard to rescue Jesus' teaching and his ecclesiology. It might be challenging and valuable to construct a Marcan Christianity for the future; it ought to be more difficult to argue its existence in the past. For Mark and for most early Christian literature, I doubt the clean analogy between rhetoric and actual social organization which Robbins presupposes:

---

[30] Harris, *Ancient Literacy*, 3–24, 126–7; Gamble, *Books and Readers*, 65–66.

> The preservation of the Gospel of Mark was evidently linked with the sympathies of a significant sector of early Christianity.... [T]he Gospel of Mark appealed to Christians who perpetuated the ideals of itinerant disciples of the suffering, teacher-Messiah Jesus.[31]

In terms of Marcan rhetorical normativity, perhaps it ought to have been so. In terms of social normativity, however, the subtle, ironic Marcan rhetoric went immediately astray. It appealed instead, its rhetorically experimental qualities largely ignored, to the Christians who wrote Matthew and Luke-Acts, to those who gradually institutionalized a four-fold gospel canon and who attributed its anonymous texts to a hierarchy of apostolic authorities. Moreover, much the same might be said about social-historical receptions of Q, and of Pauline and Johannine rhetorics: they seem often to have exerted their greatest social and literary influence in directions quite unpredictable from the texts' rhetorically probable implications, or even contrary to them. At any rate, the almost universal supposition that Marcan, Q, Pauline and Johannine rhetorics must have emerged from and been preserved by theologically and/or sociologically distinct Christian parties is one of the least tested in the history of early Christianity. On the contrary, a future task for rhetorical, rather than theological or ideological, criticism of early Christian literature is to explain how its greatest texts failed at the outset to perpetuate or construct readerships worthy of themselves.

Still, if the dissociation of Marcan social normativity from Marcan rhetorical normativity is embarrassing for the socio-historical project, the continuity of gnomic rhetoric across early Christian oral and literary traditions may link social and rhetorical developments less speculatively. At least gnomic rhetoric is attested in all the early Christian sub-rhetorics and is analysed and exemplified in the larger world of Hellenistic theory and practice. Moreover, a key function of gnomic language is to assert a rhetorical normativity which can remain influential and survive reformulation in several possible settings.

In general, though, the problem remains that if we do not independently know the social context of speech, its rhetorical normativity can tell little about social normativity.

---

[31] Robbins, *Jesus the Teacher*, 197, 210–12.

This is not the same as Robbins' warning, in the words of Clifford Geertz, that "our data consists of 'our own constructions of other people's constructions of what they and their compatriots are up to'."[32] The function of rhetoric in Hellenistic antiquity was to equip speakers, audiences and critics alike to construct and to construe complex meaning within a standard technical and hermeneutical framework. The corollary, however, is that such standard rhetorical constructions need only seldom and schematically return to what both speaker and audience already know—the social setting, the stuff "of what they and their compatriots are up to."

One characteristic of early Christian rhetoric is its uncertainty about just who "they and their compatriots [sic]" are; its voices are uncertain of their audience, allegiance and social influence. Rhetorical normativity (myths, gospel, Christian pistis, even eschatology) and personal authority (the ethos of Jesus or of Paul) thus remain the controlling concerns of early Christian texts. As evidence for social conditions they are profoundly insecure, unrepresentative and marginal; however careful, imaginative and engaged, our constructions upon them cannot provide 'data' to match our social-historical questions. Little knowledge, historical or rhetorical, is gained by replacing Wilder's aestheticism or the folkloric assumptions of the classical form critics with a similarly positivist socio-rhetoric.

Burton Mack, in particular, is candid about one key aspect of the rhetoric of rhetorical criticism: its massive social location in the late twentieth-century United States.

> Social issues within the American context have raised questions about the many ways in which identities, loyalties, and motivations are generated in subcultural groups or classes. We know that there are many factors in human association....What we do not know or talk about is the mythic equation, how these factors are rooted in mythologies, and how a mythology works in return to inform and support a particular social configuration.

To the extent that "mythology" here means roughly the narrative part of social normativity, I hope it is clear that I remain suspicious of its presumed relationship to rhetorical normativity. For Mack, however, and

---

[32] C. Geertz, *The Interpretation of Cultures: Selected Essays* (New York, 1973) 9, cited by Robbins, *Jesus the Teacher*, 5.

for most socio-rhetorical critics, critical engagement with United States civil mythologies is a fundamental motive toward a revisionist history of early Christian rhetoric.

> [T]aking up a socio-rhetorical method is no guarantee against Christian bias in the imagination of social situations in early Christian history. The Christian investment in this literature is deep and pervasive in the field of biblical studies, as everyone knows. But just for that reason, the academic quest to understand the first-century issues of social and ideological moment apart from Christian evaluation should set the controls at every turn.[33]

The "academic quest to understand...apart from Christian evaluation" has a long and patchy history, "as everyone knows." The relationships among North American academic study of religions, changing United States social identities and the rhetorics of Christian heritage are much less clearly understood. I do not think that residual Christian bias is any longer the main distorting determinant in North American academic study of Christian origins. Mack hopes that rhetorical analysis may uncover the social locations of early Christian text-production. It is just as important and more urgent that an analysis of early Christian literature in terms of traditional rhetoric may promote discussion and nuancing of, e.g., anti-theological bias in North American academic text-production.

> Rhetorical critics, rhetors themselves, attempt to interpret and recreate the past rhetorical phenomena by showing their meaning for the critics' own cultural situations. The rhetorical critics must be cognizant of the rhetors' and their own hermeneutical situations, the parameters of rationality of both their cultures, and the actual and potential consciousness and receptivity in both audience situations...[34]

It is not wrong to expect that critical analysis of early Christian rhetorics should interact with critical analysis of contemporary Christian and post-Christian rhetorics, especially in North America where both

---

[33] Mack, *Lost Gospel*, 253; B.L. Mack, "Persuasive Pronouncements: An Evaluation of Recent Studies on the Chreia," *Semeia* 64, ed. V.K. Robbins (1993) 283–7, 286.

[34] B. Fiore, "NT Rhetoric and Rhetorical Criticism," *ABD* V (1992) 715–9, 715.

academic and biblicist readings of early Christian texts are busily seeking public influence. In practice, however, I know no rhetorical critical essay in which an even balance of critical horizons and transparency of ideological commitments has been achieved and explicitly maintained; the programmatic "both" of rhetorical criticism cannot be carried through in specialist academic publications. Mack's analysis of early Christian literature thus depends for its persuasiveness largely, but not transparently, on a prior analysis of "myth-making" rhetorics in North American religion and United States politics. Despite unusual ideological transparency, Mack's discourse seems in particular to veil the anxious relations among the social-scientific and comparative study of religious movements, historical-literary theology, and actual religious community formation in the United States and elsewhere.

The most urgent critical task and competence for Mack's readers is to that extent in socio-rhetorical criticism of North American academic rhetoric about religion, more than in ancient rhetoric or early Christianity. Above all, the reader of rhetorical criticism of early Christian literature must exercise a cunning insight into the tensions within academic religious studies and within popular practices of religion in North America. With the best of wills, such tensions and the interests they represent are almost impossible for any rhetorical critic adequately to declare and weigh.

Thus, for example, Mack finally lists four distinctive characteristics of early Christian rhetorics: "a large incidence of figurative language," "the relative lack of historical examples," "a high polemical quotient," and, above all, "the issue of authority." His inferences about the social implications of these alleged rhetorical distinctives are, on the historical level as description of early Christianity, banal. They read, however, less as social description and analysis of early Christianity than as speculative and patronizing diagnoses of future (even contemporary?) Christianities as mythological misappropriations of canonized rhetorics.

> One might extrapolate from this [*scil.* intensive use of analogical and figurative language] that Christian gatherings may have been lively occasions, and that part of the attraction may have been the intellectual stimulation occasioned by the social experimentation.
>
> [T]he absence of the paradigmatic example in early Christian argumentation is a very significant datum. By filling in the vacant space with

images of the impossible, early Christians may have been in danger of cultivating fantasies in place of this-worldly pieties and performances.

If winning an argument against a straw man were to become a favorite imagination, models for conversation with those of different persuasions would be woefully inadequate, and in-house Christian discourse also would be in danger of falling into self-deceptions.... The danger is that, taken up into the Christian myth of origins, these residues of an understandable but unfortunate rhetorical history may be read as originary and taken as paradigmatic for Christian discourse. We can see what a disaster it would be if they were to become paradigmatic for Christian pronouncements aimed at those outside.

[S]hould the rhetoric of assertion, pronouncement, and "speaking with authority" become a habit, social structures could be created that cancel out the courage of critique that gave rise to the discourse in the beginning.[35]

New rhetoric, old rhetoric and hermeneutics

R. Scroggs quotes an anonymous but symptomatic warning: "We do not know what Paul thought; we know only what he wanted the Corinthians to think that he thought."[36] Rhetorical analysis should help us grasp what history and theology should perhaps have told us already: As they disclosed themselves to their contemporaries, Jesus, Paul and their audiences did not "think" except rhetorically; they thought mainly in topics, in symbols and in public, not in rationalist abstractions. This should be enough, even for the modern reader: historically and theologically as well as rhetorically, the thought of Paul or of Jesus has meaning through its public articulation and reception. The impossibility of reading from the New Testament Paul's or Jesus' mind is a deficit only if we espouse a hermeneutic which, whether motivated by scepticism or by piety, presumes to reconstruct the intentions and influence of historic voices into personal or social essences. But texts do not contain people or communities from the past—nor do modern scholarly readings of old texts directly reconstitute or subvert the readerships of today, even when we wish they would. Such reconstruc-

---

[35] Mack, *Rhetoric and the New Testament*, 94–100.

[36] R. Scroggs, "Can New Testament Theology Be Saved? The Threat of Contextualisms," *USQR* 42 (1988) 17–31, 20.

tion may be worthwhile or even spiritually necessary, but it is not history—nor is it rhetorical criticism. These are disciplines which must assume the communicability, perspicuity, even collectivity of experience even as they challenge it ethically, which must therefore accept, though not uncritically, the claims of ancient rhetoric to mean pretty much what it says—and not too much more.

My concern with the various rhetorical criticisms current in New Testament and Early Christian studies is, therefore, not just technical. I disagree with the declared and implied views of many rhetorical critics about the desirable future as well as about the probable past of early Christian rhetorics. In particular, I am suspicious of simple connections between rhetorical criticism of ancient discourses and programmatically critical rhetorics for today. Even from a theological point of view, it is seldom clear how biblical rhetorics are normative for contemporary faith communities; from a more rhetorical point of view, the communicative interests behind new scholarly rhetorics about Jesus, the New Testament and early Christianity are so little understood and so seldom acknowledged as to make claims for the reinvention of rhetoric seriously misleading.

For a history of the influence of their public words, Jesus' and Paul's rhetorical purposes are the only relevant aspect of their historic intentions and thought. Historical rhetoric focuses more precisely and authoritatively than any other interpretative discipline on just that level of deliberate, public and rhetorical intention. But even more fundamentally, the project of Hellenistic rhetoric implies a hermeneutic within which early Christian rhetoric was produced and in relation to which it should be interpreted if historical understanding is even part of the goal. Such a hermeneutic seems to me necessary if balance is to be achieved in the hermeneutical melée of contemporary scholarship.

The great diversity of surviving rhetorical literature confirms that Hellenistic rhetoric for its part never achieved perfect uniformity on any point of theory or technique, not even on the school-book level of progymnasmatic rhetoric. And the rhetoricians were also deeply and consciously divided on hermeneutical issues. Still, their work cumulatively reflects a basic consensus about a range of hermeneutical possibilities and goals which is at once limited and subtly different from the hermeneutical horizons of modernity. It is on this level that classical rhetoric constitutes a distinctive whole. I think it is one from which modern readers, whether hermeneutically or sociologically oriented, should learn.

The hermeneutical relevance of ancient rhetoric is, I think, all the easier to discern when we acknowledge that ancient philosophy never developed a sub-discipline of hermeneutics. In the place of a general theory of interpretation (hermeneutics) the ancient world offered a general theory of persuasion and influence (rhetoric). This pre-empting of hermeneutics by rhetoric meant, however, not that hermeneutical questions were neglected, but that they were deliberately taken up under the tutelage of rhetorical theory and practice. The dramatic nineteenth-century displacement of rhetoric by hermeneutics is an important characteristic of modernity, over which the partial reinstatement of rhetoric in recent years raises an interesting, but still ambiguous question mark.[37]

The important point is that in the absence of—indeed, in preference to—a discipline of philosophical hermeneutics, antiquity cultivated rhetoric, and used rhetoric as the primary context in which to pose questions we might label as hermeneutical. What is more, this difference between antiquity and modernity in locating hermeneutical questions and constructing a general communicative theory is not accidental or hermeneutically neutral. Ancient rhetoric implies a hermeneutic which is not that implied by modern hermeneutics, or even by the modern revival of rhetoric in the wake of hermeneutics. Modernity is in no small part the rejection of rhetoric, a rejection which even post-modernisms and social contextualisms cannot heal.

The generative hermeneutic informing Hellenistic rhetoric should therefore not be regarded as pre-critically naive or even sub-conscious; nor is it a theological "hermeneutics of consent" (P. Stuhlmacher) or an "oral hermeneutic" (W. Kelber). Rhetoric (and with it any honest rhetorical criticism) accepts the ethical and political ambiguities of its universalist and imperialistic programme, ambiguities which are heightened into irony in gospel rhetoric. Rhetoric provokes criticism in the polemical (i.e., self-consciously rhetorical) forms of orthodoxy, heresy, enlightenment, liberation and deconstruction. In our present

---

[37] G.W. Most, "Rhetorik und Hermeneutik: Zur Konstitution der Neuzeitlichkeit," *Antike und Abendland* 30 (1984) 62–79; see Rickman, "Rhetoric and Hermeneutics"; Mailloux, "Rhetorical Hermeneutics."

context, appeal to ancient rhetoric as interpretive framework is an attack on both modern and post-modern hermeneutics as both of these depend on a reification of the text over against the experience of communication.

A rhetorical hermeneutic presupposes—and did in Jesus' and Paul's world—the conventional and ethical predisposition of speaker and audience (and, hence, of text) to communicative understanding—if not to sincerity or simplicity or clarity at any price, then to the conscious priority of those meanings of speech which are publicly possible in actual and remembered performance. Where rhetoric in no way presupposes dogmatic assent (and may therefore be of use to critical theology), it does demand the readiness of speaker, audience and critic to judge and act on the rhetorically presented merits of the case.

One strength of rhetoric is its studied superficiality. Texts have meaning not intrinsically, but as performed scripts. Performances have meaning as publicly shared experiences, not as private rites. Over against the special reading procedures which in most cultures accompany recognition of poetic texts, rhetorical criticism and reception of texts in performance do not seek to maximize and multiply textual meanings. Instead rhetorical criticism seeks to specify the predictable meanings of texts in performance before particular audiences. Rhetoric is about first, though tutored impressions.

A rhetorical hermeneutic also presupposes that texts are personally and socially purposeful, yet fallible, limited and two-edged, instruments. The literary dimensions of textuality as well as the historical dimensions of social and personal influence can thus be taken seriously, but without idolatry. Rhetorically, it becomes necessary and (at least within the sphere of Hellenism's influence) possible to talk about 'reader-response', for instance, in terms of the projected and actual responses of actual readers as well as in terms of the constructive potential of the text. In these respects, ancient rhetoric has much to teach about the nature of understanding texts.

Particular communications may authorize more suspicious readings, e.g., the supplement of comic, ironic or allegorical interpretations. The hermeneutics of historical criticism, however, as of its competitors and heirs, typically moves beyond the heightened curiosity rhetorically called for by the strangeness of, e.g., a Gospel of Mark. Instead, historical criticism, especially in its long-standing and still unresolved competition with confessional exegesis, has privileged suspicion and ideological critique and so countenanced essentially counter-rhetorical readings. The tradition of hermeneutic suspicion of early Christian rhetorics in academic exegesis is not really anchored in the subtle relationship of the gospel to Greco-Roman and Jewish (or any other) rhetorical culture. The long hold of historical criticism on biblical exegesis has had even more to do with the on-going reception history of scriptural texts in religious and anti-religious, revolutionary and anti-revolutionary polemic. But the persistence and periodic resurgence of methodic suspicion in scholarly readings of biblical Christianity has, I think, even more to do with a specifically modern nervousness about the significant, especially the Western Christian past. Such alienation should not be ignored, but should not be the determining criterion for interpretation.

In moments of hermeneutical doubt, it may be necessary to substitute an aggressive *Tendenzkritik* for received ways of understanding texts and hearing their rhetoric, but such reading transplants are an emergency operation, called for by the temporary collapse of rhetorical normativity in critical culture. Whether F.C. Baur's arbitrary but tenacious nineteenth-century division of early Christian texts and their rhetorics between presumed 'Jewish' and 'Gentile' Christianities, or Burton Mack's schematic opposition of a Marcan "Myth of Innocence" to the "Lost Gospel" of Q, or those other recent academic fantasies reading Jesus' movement into the Dead Sea Scrolls—such approaches say more about the rhetoric of modern criticism and its search for a post-Christian audience than about the criticism of ancient rhetoric.[38] The meaning of rhetorical criticism may be as a reminder that texts, even haunted old texts, are not primarily barriers to communication.

Rhetoric may also help us to understand why some texts have such haunted reception histories. Those aspects of early Christian texts which most seem to demand surgical or reconstructive interpretation do so because they rhetorically exaggerate normativity and authority over conceptual lucidity, *pathos* and *ethos* over *logos*—they abruptly break off argumentation and evidence (*pisteis*) to demand an assent (*pistis*) which the reader, ancient or modern, cannot so readily give. From a

---

[38] Mack, *Lost Gospel*; Mack, *Myth of Innocence*; B. Thiering, *Jesus and the Riddle of the Dead Sea Scrolls* (San Francisco, 1992); R. Eisenman and M. Wise, *The Dead Sea Scrolls Uncovered* (Shaftesbury, 1992).

rhetorical point of view, one legitimate function of subsequent critical methods (source criticism; tradition history; literary analysis) is to guard against the sort of uncritical rhetorical positivism which would insist on making every text clear. Non-rhetorical criticisms help define the textual limits within which the modern reader can identify with Jesus' or Paul's historical audiences (or opponents); only rhetoric, apart from theology itself, asks to what extent and under what conditions any reader could ever have done so.

The neo-orthodox protest against theological historicism may offer an analogy to the claims of rhetorical criticism against post-theological historicism. Karl Barth's epochal theological impatience with trivial historicism was surely justified; the historical critics must still become more comprehensively and comprehendingly critical. Now, when few critics can confidently intuit a surrogate rhetorical sensitivity either from a received theology of the Word or from an avowedly classical primary education, it is all the more essential that they should be critically disciplined in rhetoric proper. But in his [*sic*] *Epistle to the Romans* Barth wished not only to understand without reductionism what the text ultimately and permanently tends to say; he also wanted to become the speaking voice of its apostolic author.[39] Not content to be the rhetorician, he wanted to be the rhetor, and so to merge the text with his own and the Church's Spirit-given voice. For Barth, "the Word in the words" is sublimely theological rather than rhetorical, and the rhetoric of early Christianity is on his side, and yet he dramatizes the temptation to exaggerate the contemporary perspicuity of our ancient texts, a temptation to which rhetoric is no more immune than theology or history.

Even today Hellenism can fool itself on this point, but the hermeneutic underlying Hellenistic rhetoric is really not some universally, automatically valid hermeneutic which modern interpreters can simply borrow or sample at will, not even in its Jewish and Christian hybrid. Conversely, Hellenistic rhetoric in New Testament exegesis is not hermeneutically autonomous of modern critical concerns. My working assumption, however, is that the hermeneutics behind Hellenistic rhetoric are on the whole better understood, less parochial and less

---

[39] Karl Barth, *Der Römerbrief* (2d ed., München, 1922, rpr. 1929) xii.

inappropriate to biblical interpretation than late modern hermeneutics of suspicion and ideological revision.

The tension between ancient rhetoric and modern hermeneutics is often concealed under the topic of 'the new and the old'—especially in relation to a text for which as Scripture both antiquity and contemporaneity are claimed.[40] The topic is, however, a red herring; both new and traditional rhetorical categories have strengths and weaknesses for modern criticism of ancient texts. Both the modernity and the antiquity of any credible rhetoric are inevitable. It is impossible not to use modern categories, even if we dress them up in Greek or Latin. It is equally impossible to avoid the weight of (sometimes repressed) rhetorical tradition on our texts and on our critical tradition, especially where the latter is tempted to boast of its newness or power.

Ancient rhetoric and its categories have the advantage of permitting insight into the generative, formative rhetoric of texts written in ancient Greek or Latin. Such texts were all produced more or less within the influence of that particular rhetorical culture. By the same token, Greco-Roman rhetoric is a central part of a political and ideological movement of which the modern interpreter should be wary, lest the humanity and civility of Hellenistic rhetoric should desensitize us to the less exemplary values and motives of Athenian, Macedonian and Roman statecraft and society or of Jewish and Christian sectarianism.

In places, moreover, modern rhetoric has gone well beyond its classical sources, notably in the modern appreciation of narrative rhetoric and of the audience as active agents in the production of rhetoric. Key distinctions in my own discussion of gnomic rhetoric in Jesus' tradition are cast in terms which, if not wholly unanticipated in ancient theory, are essentially modern: the distinctions between rhetorical and social normativity, between oral and literary sensibility and between proverbiality and anti-proverbiality. On the other hand, application of distinctively contemporary categories, e.g., 'argumentative or rhetorical situation', often reflects the positivism and reductionism within modern philosophy and sociology, leading to oversimplified and overconfident conclusions about early Christian experience.

---

[40] The topic was especially current at the 1992 Heidelberg conference on Rhetorical Criticism of the New Testament; see Porter and Olbricht, *Heidelberg Conference*; Mack, *Rhetoric and the New Testament*, 9–20; Stamps, "Rhetorical Criticism."

The real question is therefore not whether ancient or modern categories may be used and combined; they must be. Instead, the urgent question is how best to exercise critical judgement over both sets of categories, that is, how to use each or both in ways which enhance the critic's responsibility to the past and to the needs of contemporary readerships. These questions are, of course, less technical than ethical, political and hermeneutical.

It is from this hermeneutical perspective, I believe, that the ancient categories of classical rhetoric deserve priority over those of contemporary argumentation and communications theories. Classical rhetoric and the long, continuous tradition which it inspired is not only separated from the modern renewal of rhetorical inquiry by the passage of time. Instead, modern rhetorical criticisms (argumentation theory, speech-act theory, discourse-analysis, etc.) attempt to begin, on alternative hermeneutical premises, the task of an ancient rhetoric which academic criticism largely repudiated in favour of romantic aestheticism and rationalist statistics.

The eclipse of rhetorical tradition and its replacement by alternative rhetorics has a double impact. First, the immediate background of most new rhetorics and of their application to the New Testament is not the tradition of antiquity, but its rejection in the ongoing explosion of media and propaganda in our own generations. It is as yet unclear to me whether there exists between our own prejudices and the newest rhetorical categories the critical distance necessary for discerning and responsible application to the present, let alone to the mythical past. Technically, there is no harm in re-inventing the wheel; a better wheel may result. Yet rhetoric, as the ancient rhetoricians (despite Aristotle's equivocal protest) recognized, is not "a morally neutral tool."[41] To re-invent rhetoric as though from nothing is to invent a future which is opposed to its past and not merely neutral toward it.

By partial contrast, intentional retrieval of the classical tradition has the advantage of a long continuity not only of use but also of searching criticism and periodic rejection; the rhetoric of the ancient world has long since been subjected to critique, revision and reappropriation. Like theology, rhetoric is a humbled and dethroned tyrant, not always to be believed, but never to be disregarded as a measure of the real changes

---

[41] Murphy, *Synoptic History of Classical Rhetoric*, 25.

in regimes. Almost all of us can see through the Emperor's new suit. As loyal courtiers, however, most of us are more candid about the wardrobes of orthodox Theology and classical Rhetoric than about the chosen garments of reigning monarchs of theory, monarchs who too often pretend to be defenders of the revolution.

A traditional rhetoric has not only its formative influence on the composition of the New Testament to recommend it over the new rhetorical tradition of the last half-century; traditional rhetoric also offers an attractive basic hermeneutical stance of communicative expectancy, chastened by a long history of criticism. It is the devil which from longest observation we may claim to know best. We are accustomed to searching out the hidden complicities and assumptions of ancient texts, thinkers and movements under our scrutiny; most of us are less expert, less sincere and less diligent in exposing the hidden motives of our own preferred hermeneutics and exegetical methods.

> A rhetorical criticism that is not radically self-reflexive can too easily be harnessed to an ideologically conservative program of reaffirming classical texts and values. What happens when a modern scholar, through a skilled practice of rhetorical criticism, demonstrates the persuasiveness of an ancient text? Where does he stand, where does he place his students, in relation to the truth of that text? The rhetorical effect—intended or not—may be to establish the truth of the classics.[42]

From a rhetorical point of view, which in my case is also a confessional theological point of view, there is no "truth of" the canonical texts as texts. Yet it remains for me ethically and politically challenging to respond to the communicative past of such ancient canonical rhetorics with self-critical loyalty and trust in a new rhetorical context (academic discourse) where such a response is anomalous. Rhetorical proof is never more or less than an invitation to assent (*pistis*), and rhetorical truth is likewise neither more nor less than moral plausibility (*doxa*). I am more confident of holding the "truth of the classics" within a rhetorical discipline, learned in part from re-reading the classics, than I am of successfully juggling the perceptions of late modern contextualisms and mercurial postmodernisms.

---

[42] Bible and Culture Collective, *Postmodern Bible*, 166 (quoted), 177.

Both Stamps and, more recently, the Bible and Culture Collective rightly fear that the revival of rhetoric may feed social and theological nostalgia. I am not immune to that spell. But the charms of liberal and postmodern rhetorics are also readily available to reinforce false consciousness of the rhetorical realities of our various and confused social relationships.

The diversity and vicissitudes of classical rhetoric make it clear that the New Testament conceived as rhetoric will not necessarily prove more manageable than did the New Testament as theology. At any rate, we are probably better equipped by historical experience to discern the dangers of the old tradition than those of its still speculative replacement. The rhetoric which was actually influential on the origins of the gospel may also inform a historically positive appreciation of the settings available for gospel speech, without literary-critical or sociological positivism and with a minimum of the "euphoria" which attends "new" methods.[43]

Above all, ancient rhetoric is not hermeneutically neutral, indifferent or naive. It may, nonetheless, be a relatively fair, inclusive and attentive mediator between modern critical questions and the communicative deposit of early Christian texts. The constraints and possibilities of such rhetoric, its massive influence and the enormity of even the earliest Christian rhetorical pretensions must narrow our options for historically responsible interpretation. Finally, the profound socialization of ancient rhetoric, its self-consciousness as political, ethical, legal and religious discourse, may provide just the corrective which the hermeneutical tradition requires, especially in the silence of theology and amid the noise of social-scientific and ideological reductionisms. Especially when ancient rhetoric is appreciated as an open speculative and theoretical enterprise and not only as a dogmatic system, it can usefully correct both the worn-out hegemony of anti-theological historicism and the delusory "radical rhetoric of revolution and reconfiguration."[44]

---

[43] C.J. Classen, "Ars Rhetorica: L'essence, possibilities, Gefahren," *Rhetorica* 6 (1980) 7–19, esp. 18 and n.29 on the excessive rhetorical optimism of New Testament critics.

[44] Stamps, "Rhetorical Criticism," 274.

Hermeneutics and style in antiquity

One important reason for particularly studying gnome in Greco-Roman rhetoric is that the tradition's hermeneutical concerns and predispositions surface clearly in the perennial question of how gnome can generate rhetorical conviction (*pistis*). The rhetoricians' general discussions of style are another sight-line along which rhetoric's hermeneutical underpinnings become visible.

The ancients approached style initially in formal terms. Against modern formalisms, however, rhetorical form is assessed by aptness for its occasion rather than by poetic originality, psychological individuality or even social relevance. The stylistic achievement of a Cicero or a Demosthenes was not that they shed light on personalities or on social values or that they produced aesthetically unified texts. Instead they were canonized as stylists because each of their speeches creates its own specific and impressive climate within which the speaker could choose and define his own *ethos*, the goals and issues of a unique case over against the emotional disposition and mental attitudes of a unique audience. Cicero and Demosthenes are model orators because they so often succeeded in applying typical forms to seemingly typical situations in a way that dramatized the atypicality of the speaker and of his case.

> In the developed theory of rhetoric, stylistic distinction was seen essentially in terms of types, rather than individuals; the *charakteres* and *genera* express shared qualities which are opposed to other shared qualities. As such they reveal a significant difference between ancient and modern outlooks.... [T]he fact that the Greeks thought about style as belonging to a group, rather than to an individual, makes it possible to trace their ideas over a period of time and through different genres.[45]

Consistent with this, Greco-Roman rhetoric in all its diversity always recognized the heuristic and provisional character of its own formalism. Thus the tradition of formally distinguishing three stylistic registers never became a uniform doctrine. It was variously and vaguely used to justify a formal mean or a judicious mixture or to make a tidy analogy

---

[45] N. O'Sullivan, *Alcidamas, Aristophanes and the Beginnings of Greek Stylistic Theory* (Hermes Einzelschriften 60; Stuttgart, 1992) 3, 5.

with three goals of formal speech (dicanic/judicial, epideictic/demon-strative and symbouleutic/deliberative) or with three ways to persuade (*logos, ethos* and *pathos*), but the idea of three levels of style never displaced more nuanced and open positions. Throughout Hellenistic rhetoric the strong impulse to formal classification yields on this question of style to explicit consciousness of hermeneutical questions: why language sometimes works well and sometimes badly and why the uncanny and elliptical is sometimes more forceful than the lucid.

For Cicero and Quintilian this emerges in the paradox of their rejection of Asiatic style—and their knowing acceptance of each of its characteristic techniques (especially gnome-use) duly moderated. So also Aristotle grudgingly recognizes that paradox, allusiveness, ellipsis and even equivocation can be integral to rhetorical success and even characteristic of one useful extreme of communicative style, preferring the effects and values of *ethos* and *pathos* over (even Aristotelean) *logos*.

As much as possible, Aristotle assimilates the formal means of persuasion (*pisteis*, including *paradeigma* and *enthymema*) to dialectical proof. But he is forced to admit that supposedly paradigmatic fables (*mythoi*) and supposedly enthymematic gnomai work by stirring popular imagination and not by arguing, even informally, from precedent and premise. Aristotle tries to compensate by chaining gnome, especially its paradoxical, laconic and enigmatic side, to reasonable clarification. Still, he recognizes that gnome is effective above all in establishing *ethos*, not in giving reasons (*Rh.* 2.20-21=1393a-95b; 3.17= 1417b-18b).

In much the same way, Aristotle's discussion of style (*lexis, Rh.* 3) opens rhetoric not only to common ground with poetics in linguistic and performance theories; it more profoundly admits that *pathos* is central to rhetorical conviction, again sharply qualifying analogy between rhetoric and dialectics. Transplanted from poetics into the pragmatic context of rhetoric, Aristotle's theory of metaphor (as moderately far-fetched) must account for more than the intrinsic economy of a text and the aesthetic response it invites. Rhetorical theory must also investigate the uses of story, analogy and metaphor to transform loyalties and to motivate decisions in specific settings.

Aristotle's frequent but still jarring tributes to the persuasive legitimacy of *pathos* and especially of *ethos* are telling, possibly late, concessions from a writer committed to relating rhetoric more closely, if possible, to dialectics than to poetics.[46] Although for Aristotle the irrational is a *phantasia* justified in rhetoric only by the depravity (*mochtheria*) of audiences, it remains essential to all but the most privileged discourse. Try as he might to save rational discourse from the affective realities of rhetoric, the best Aristotle can do is to assert (falsely, I hope) that "no one teaches geometry this way" (*Rh.* 3.1.6= 1404a). Aristotle's reluctant and equivocal mixture of a philosophical theory of argumentation with a properly rhetorical theory of influence, embracing style, emotion and personality as elements of meaning, is symptomatic of the unavoidability of hermeneutical issues in ancient rhetoric.

Certainly Aristotle's most explicit stylistic distinction, one which arguably underlies all later Greco-Roman stylistic theories, is inescapably hermeneutical in character. Aristotle and, less bluntly, Alcidamas and Isocrates contrast two main stylistic poles: the "written" (*graphike*) and the "competitive" (*agonistike*) (*Rh.* 3.12=1413b-1414a).

> I use the quotation marks advisedly. For they are, in a sense, purely nominal designations, indicating tendency rather than method of presentation: Alcidamas tells us that writers could use the unwritten style (*Soph.* 13), and Aristotle actually confirms this (*Rh.* 1413b16).[47]

Clearly this opposition corresponds only very loosely to the problematic modern dichotomies between 'oral' and 'literary' media, and between literate and illiterate (or pre-literate) societies. Instead the rhetoricians assumed a more nuanced opposition between the slow, reflective, critical styles made possible by written pre-composition and the

---

[46] See W.W. Fortenbaugh, "Aristotle's Rhetoric on Emotions," *Archiv für die Geschichte der Philosophie* 52 (1970) 40–70; W.W. Fortenbaugh, "Persuasion Through Character and the Composition of Aristotle's Rhetoric" *Rheinisches Museum für Philologie* 134 (1991) 152–56.

[47] O'Sullivan, *Greek Stylistic Theory*, 43; see D.K. Shuger, *Sacred Rhetoric: The Christian Grand Style in the English Renaissance* (Princeton, NJ, 1988) 14–41; I.H. Henderson, "Style-Switching in the *Didache*: Fingerprint of Argument?" in *The Didache in Context Essays in Its Text, History and Transmission*, ed. C.N. Jefford (NovTSup 77; Leiden, 1995) 177–209, 191–194; H.L.F. Drijepondt, *Die antike Theorie der "varietas"* (Hildesheim, 1979); A. Cizek, *Imitatio et Tractatio: die literarisch-rhetorischen Grundlagen der Nachahmng in Antike und Mittelalter* (Rhetorik-Forschungen 7; Tübingen, 1994) 64–81.

brilliant, grandiloquent, repetitive styles required in extempore debate. In Greco-Roman rhetorical theory, the latter presuppose literate education just as much as the former, but appeal to *ethos* and *pathos* more than to reason. These are all features of the literate, but agonistic (and gnomic) style of the sophist Gorgias which Aristotle condemned as too 'poetic' (*Rh.* 3.1.9=1404a26, 3.2=1404b4, 3.3=1406a32).[48]

Ultimately, the difference between oral and literate styles in ancient rhetorical theory, though vitally important, is not a difference between modes of production or between states of culture as in most modern orality theory. Instead the difference between literary and agonistic styles—with critical and fashionable preferences for one over the other—is one of sensibility rather than technology. Thus, both Aristotle and Isocrates prefer the literary style over the agonistic, poetic styles of the sophists, especially Gorgias and Alcidamas. Yet neither Aristotle nor Isocrates was finally able to marginalize the passionate styles of agonistic improvisation. Plato's *Phaedrus* ironically pointed beyond both literate and rhetorical technique toward the post-technical ideal of the sublime. Yet, as we shall see in a later chapter, both master styles remained permanent and competing options in rhetorical performance throughout antiquity.

Here the ancient theory of style can make a major contribution to modern discussion of orality and literacy in cultural production. The rhetoricians confirm the hermeneutical, stylistic importance of such distinctions. At the same time they make clear that, except in cultural comparisons so extreme as to be irrelevant to even the least literate classes in ancient society, such differences are in the order of conflicting and co-existing psychological and social sensibilities. In the Greco-Roman world, there was no orality—no oral tradition—innocent of the technical possibilities of literary rhetoric and scriptural wisdom. In that nuanced context, it is all the more important that there were also non-Greek scribal literacies and Greek sectarian oral traditions which dared to assert themselves within the hegemony of rhetorical hermeneutics.

Aristotle and the Romans sought to wed the passionate and uncanny as closely (and unequally) as possible to argumentative usefulness, to keep *pathos* and *ethos* as the means, or at most the partners, and not the ends of *logos*. The later Greek theorists of rhetorical style are more

---

[48] O'Sullivan, *Greek Stylistic Theory*, 10–14, 42–62; on Gorgias, 10–11, 20–21.

boldly oriented toward the primary communicative power of equivocation, obscurity and vehemence. Thus Hermogenes, *On Qualities of Speech* (*Peri Ideon*), culminates his taxonomy with a paradoxical and aporetic celebration of "intensity" (*deinotes*). Stylistically, Hermogenes associates intensity with figures of vehemence and compression. In the end, however, he insists that it is formally undefinable. Of the seven qualities of speech, only intensity includes and transcends all others—and so decisively that Hermogenes dramatically breaks off his climactic discussion as too difficult and, promising a further book, turns to define good style by the example of Demosthenes.

The treatise of Demetrius, *On Expression* (*Peri Hermeneias*), is well-known to New Testament scholars for its few remarks on epistolary style; their inclusion within a general theory of style is seldom noticed. For Demetrius, as for Hermogenes, the "intense style" (*deinos charakter*) is the pinnacle of rhetorical expression. Unlike Hermogenes' later discussion, Demetrius' analysis does not collapse under the pressure of relating formal and hermeneutical insights. Demetrius dares to exemplify the association between intensity and particular—often gnomic—effects: (Laconic) compression, allusion, vehemence, (Cynic) sarcasm and innuendo. For both Demetrius and Hermogenes, the point is primarily not stylistic, but hermeneutical: where, by whatever figural means, every stumbling block is placed in the way of facile understanding, the burden of meaning falls on the intensity of almost unspoken rapport: "By the gods, even obscurity (*asapheia*) is often intensity (*deinotes*)" (Demetr. 254).

This position and its essentially hermeneutical character are put most radically in the anonymous tractate *On the Sublime* (*Peri Hypsous*). Here we find the fullest articulation anywhere of essentially the Asiatic position on style and psychology, an appropriation for rhetoric of Plato's meta-rhetorical hermeneutic. Here the passionate and personal (*pathos* and *ethos*) are explicitly exalted over the discursive (*logos*) in selection of topics (*heuresis*), in style (*lexis*)—in the whole projected impact (*hermeneia*) of speech.

Historically, it is impossible to recreate Jesus' rhetoric. However, once we recognize it as rhetoric and as Hellenistic both in style and in spirit, we can interpret it and distinguish its specific, limited and sometimes erratic influence on early Christian rhetoric. Jesus' speech was influential enough to inspire a tradition and to some extent a literature, yet without founding a school. This rhetorical achievement is, however, qualified by Jesus' near silence, not only in Pilate's but also in Paul's court and by the extent and variety of rhetorical reconstructions needed to produce the gospel literature.

An approach to Jesus' speech-tradition through specifically gnomic rhetoric allows us to identify and evaluate one stylistic-hermeneutical key to his public language: its Asiaticism, its elliptical, vehement intensity (*deinotes*), its pre-christological immersion of *logos* in *ethos* and *pathos*. Rhetorically, the conceptual imprecision of 'Kingdom' or 'Son of Man' need not be a stumbling-block for interpretation. Instead, it is the mark, like a gnomic and parabolic style, of the interpersonal, evocative and confrontational burden of Jesus' self-expression.

Rhetoric, then, is more than a tool-box from which to borrow at will in order to fasten sociological, theological, political, or poetic and aesthetic concerns more securely onto New Testament criticism. It is an essential presupposition for the genesis and early interpretation of Christian rhetoric. It is also a necessary, though not a sufficient or unambiguous, presupposition for modern exegesis. It allows us to ask important social-historical, literary and theological questions without pretending to an unattainable command of the social and experiential backgrounds of early Christian speech-making. The modern interpreter should not only be obliged to appreciate and criticize the use of rhetorical forms in, before and around Christianity; it is equally important to come to terms with the innate struggle of ancient rhetoric to relate technical competence and communicative transcendence (or failure). The appeal to Hellenistic rhetoric can therefore not be made without consequences for our own contemporary hermeneutical stances. Certainly, its equivalence to newer rhetorics cannot be assumed.

Above all, rhetoric offers partial redemption from, in Scroggs' phrase, the "hermeneutics of paranoia" to which suspicion of theological and ideological consent increasingly condemns exegesis. Like apologetically motivated hermeneutics, rhetoric implies a priority of consent over the possibility of authoritative interpretation, but consent here is to a tradition of speech production and interpretation which is distinct from new and old contextualisms of hermeneutics, sociology, politics, poetics—and theology. Thus, in relation to Jesus, rhetoric assures us of the perspicuity and intentional significance of the repeated pattern; we can know how gnomic or parabolic rhetoric worked in Jesus' speech-world. On the other hand, the same gnomic and intensified (*deinos*) rhetoric advises us to search for the historical meaning, the *logos*, of

Jesus' allusive and vehement style precisely in the definition of Jesus' *ethos* and in its summons of an audience to personal adherence (*pathos*).

III

The rhetorical approach to Jesus and his influence which I am proposing is necessarily complex and often technical. It also often involves a clash between two historic ways of being technical, of speaking rigorously about complex skills. For much of antiquity, the discipline and jargon (*technologia*) of rhetoric exerted some of the ambiguous prestige and power which we associate with the different technology of scientific and quasi-scientific styles of argument.

I begin, therefore, by bringing together in Chapter One the discussions of gnomic language in the progymnasmatic textbooks with those of the theoretical rhetoricians. Against this background I reconsider recent scholarly notices of progymnasmatic elements— especially chreia—in early Christian literature. The goal of this first chapter will be to synthesize a definition of gnome which will do justice to ancient theory and practice, but which will also raise interesting questions from a modern critical, especially cross-cultural perspective.

For biblical scholars like myself, a sympathetic and responsible use of Greek rhetoric must also be grounded in a critique of the largely anti-rhetorical history of modern biblical exegesis. Chapter Two, therefore, criticizes the notion of 'wisdom sayings' in oral traditions and literary compositions in the context of Old Testament criticism and ancient near eastern wisdom studies generally. This context remains formatively, though ambiguously, influential on methods of New Testament study. The role of gnomic rhetoric as a bridge between Greek and non-Greek cultures is one key to the importance of gnome in Jesus-tradition and early Christian rhetorics. Genres and sub-genres of wisdom literature undeniably influenced early Christian writing. Moreover, wisdom tradition in its broader, less specifically literary sense is presumably a part of Jesus' intellectual heritage. Only it is gnomic and parabolic rhetoric and not the 'wisdom saying' which allows us to trace trajectories of Jesus' rhetorical influence through oral tradition in Greek into literary formalization.

In Chapter Three, I return to the problem of 'wisdom sayings' and 'aphorisms' in New Testament form criticism and in the aesthetic and hermeneutical movements which have inherited the 'saying' as a basic category. The constructive purpose is to use the concept of 'gnome' to articulate a model of gospel tradition as a coherent rhetorical process working in both oral tradition and literary composition and in both Jewish and Gentile milieux. This entails the more negative task of countering the dominant scholarly tradition of arguing about the authenticity of traditions—usually 'sayings'—attributed Jesus using anti-rhetorical, atomistic and reductive criteria.

The remaining chapters are more exegetical. Chapter Four discusses the relationship between gnome and the composition and redaction of literary gospels, asking whether gnomic sayings are indeed a privileged hinge between oral traditional, rhetorical technique and literary, authorial styles. Chapters Five and Six undertake to interpret Synoptic gnomai as members of a rhetorical set, that is, concentrating on those aspects of gnomic rhetoric—personally authoritative *ethos* and normative slant—which mark the set as a whole and which require no special knowledge of the social-historical settings of individual sayings. While no extensive social-historical application is possible on this basis, these categories of rhetorical personality and normativity do invite cautious correlation with the more social-historical categories of discipleship and eschatology.

The final chapter (Six) in particular takes up the difference, despite formal and topical likeness, between gnomic rhetoric and laws. The difference is an unused key to the problems of Synoptic and Pauline receptions of topically legal gnomai. In this way the model of pre-gospel oral tradition as rhetoric—and as gnomic rhetoric—can be tested by its power to explain the difference between Jesus' influence on the evangelists and that on Pauline writings.

Last of all come two appendices, one a list of Synoptic gnomai, the other the glossary of terms and conventions, to which I referred above. Let me say again that the glossary in particular is not meant as an impartial guide, but rather as part of the argument of the book itself.

CHAPTER ONE

DEFINING GNOME

I

GNOMIC SAYINGS IN GRECO-ROMAN RHETORIC

How does the tension between rhetoric and hermeneutics work out in reading early Christian literature and in assessing its relationship to Jesus? One key decision has already been offered as a direct conse-quence of my understanding of ancient rhetoric and of modern rhetorical criticism; the choice of gnomic or sententious rhetoric as a starting-place reflects not only my belief that gnomai are essential ligaments of both Jesus tradition and early Christian speech. I am also convinced that gnomic language is the best possible thread to guide us through the mazes of school-book rhetoric (progymnasmata), theoretical rhetoric (*technai*) and ancient rhetorical stylistics—and beyond into the realm of cross-cultural comparison of speech and tradition patterns.

Choosing between gnome and chreia

My option for gnomic rhetoric is not, however, the obvious rhetorical critical choice. Indeed, it has largely been preempted by the only movement so far in New Testament rhetorical criticism to attempt intensive analysis of gospel and pre-gospel rhetorics. Burton Mack's work on the "myth-making" rhetorics of the gospel tradition and Vernon Robbin's "socio-rhetorical" criticism are the culmination of more than a decade's work in the Chreia Project of the Institute for Antiquity and Christianity, Claremont, and in the Pronouncement Stories Group of the Society of Biblical Literature; this whole development has tended to canonize the chreia as *the* point of entry for rhetorical study of gospels. It is characteristic that chreia is the only technical term in Greco-Roman rhetoric to receive a separate article in a recent reference work on biblical studies.[1]

Apart from dark, deep hermeneutical motives, the chreia has an obvious advantage for New Testament critics—especially for ex-form critics—over any other ancient rhetorical category: it is easy to define. The very fact that chreia is far easier to define than the other basic school patterns (gnome, *mythos* or *diegema*) does have hermeneutical implications. It is above all important to notice that the chreia alone is a 'form' in the sense that, despite its formal flexibility, it is definitively marked by a formula of personal attribution. R.O.P. Taylor gives the consensus of the whole Greco-Roman tradition when he defines chreia as "a concise and pointed account of something said or done, attributed to some particular person."[2] Depending on whether the account is of "something said or done" or both, the ancients distinguished among sayings-, action- and mixed-chreiai. To exemplify the verbal and gestural categories, we may paraphrase two gospel chreiai: a little imagination will suggest several ways to mix them to make the hybrid type. What makes these chreiai is, formally, their syntactically explicit attribution to a particular person and, semantically, their pointedness.

Jesus asked, "Who is the greater: the one at table or the one who serves? Yet I am among you as one who serves!" (Luke 22:27)

Jesus got up from table, removed his outer garments and, taking a towel, wrapped it around his waist; he then poured water into a basin and began to wash the disciples' feet. (John 13:2–5)

Functions of chreia in rhetoric and research

Even for the classic form criticism of an earlier generation, the chreia and not the gnome was the obvious point of contact between form-critical categories and Greco-Roman rhetorical terminology, a point of contact which was at that time deliberately renounced. It is of fundamental importance for understanding form criticism (and its rhetorical

---

[1] R.F. Hock, "Chreia," *ABD* I (1992) 912–4.
[2] R.O.P. Taylor, *The Groundwork of the Gospels* (Oxford, 1946) 76; cited by Mack and Robbins, *Patterns*, 16.

critical revision) that the form critics consciously elected to study both chreia and gnome under other, less rhetorical, names. They did so, not accidentally, but in order to emphasize social function over linguistic form and, above all, to assert the perspicuity of social function in basic linguistic forms.

Ancient rhetorical categories, such as chreia and gnome, are valid primarily within the particular institutions and conventions of Hellenistic and Greco-Roman public life, notwithstanding that such conventions are by no means dead or neutral in modern theology, ideology and politics. Instead of locating Christian origins within Greco-Roman public life, however, the form critics and their heirs wished to situate Christianity between two interpretive horizons with even stronger pretensions to universal validity: on the one hand, a philosophical and social-scientific anthropology of 'folklore' and, on the other, the transcendent claims of Israelite prophetic experience. The hermeneutical interests of the form-critical (and redaction-critical) project required it to try to disembarrass itself of the hermeneutical implications of Greco-Roman technical rhetoric.

Socio-rhetorical criticisms preserve this hermeneutical imbalance toward social function, while no longer pretending that Hellenistic rhetorical categories can simply be finessed away. Thus, for example, socio-rhetorical criticism need not continue the form-critical exaggeration of the folkloric elements in early Christian rhetorics. Still, it will be a major burden of this chapter to show that socio-rhetorical selection of chreia over gnome (not to speak of *mythos* and *diegema*) unconsciously has one of the same hermeneutical effects as the form critics' conscious renunciation of rhetorical categories; either way, the move from form to social function is artificially facilitated by privileging misleadingly simple formal categories.

Both formally and functionally, chreia rhetoric is proving more complex and hermeneutically ambiguous than anticipated; both formally and functionally gnome rhetoric creates even greater complexity and imposes even greater nuances on hermeneutics which wish to turn quickly from the rhetorical to the social. Indeed, contrasting form versus function rarely helps us describe the purposefulness of rhetorical patterning; I suspect the dichotomy often conceals a basic gap between *linguistic* form and *social* function.

Socio-rhetorical criticism has the virtue of candidly recognizing itself as an ideologically motivated revision of form criticism. However, it has

not yet been made quite so clear that the socio-rhetorical privileging of
chreia rhetoric is also a major hermeneutical transformation of Greco-
Roman rhetoric; for its own reasons, socio-rhetorical criticism is almost
as uncomfortable as form criticism was with early Christian acceptance
of Greco-Roman rhetorical values. Form criticism had a basic need to
contrast Christian preaching (kerygma) with normal Greco-Roman
rhetoric. Socio-rhetorical criticism has an equally basic need to find a
plurality of pre-gospel rhetorics to affirm a plurality of sub- and
counter-cultural values. From the latter point of view, chreia rhetoric
looked more promising than gnomic or parabolic rhetorics.

In particular I want to show that gnome can guide us, as chreia
research cannot, into the whole range of Greco-Roman rhetorical theory
and practice, including stylistic criticism and philosophical reflection on
rhetoric. As a technical basis for comparing Greco-Roman rhetoric as
a whole with that part of it which is early Christian rhetoric, gnome is
at least as reliable as chreia. As a guide to the hermeneutical implications of such a comparison, gnome is even more important than chreia:
gnome rather than chreia is discussed in every category of ancient
rhetorical theory. Moreover, gnome, like *mythos*, has direct cross-
cultural analogues among the patterns of ancient near eastern wisdom.
Still, precisely because I want to use gnome to assert and exemplify the
integrity of Greco-Roman rhetoric as a whole system and of gospel
rhetoric as a coherent subsystem, I do not want to seem to deny the
importance of the chreia. The issue here is whether chreia rhetoric alone
can bear the weight being placed upon it in current rhetorical criticism
of the gospels.

It is no new observation that the original form critics, Martin
Dibelius and Rudolph Bultmann, consciously sought to minimize the
relationship between ancient rhetorical categories and form-critical

categories deduced from early Christian literature.[3] It is not so often noticed that they did so because they correctly perceived the hermeneutical clash between the universalist communication theory and practice of Greco-Roman rhetoric and the form-critical assumption that traditions about Jesus must reflect a counter-cultural, millenarian, oral, folk movement. The form critics' avoidance of progymnasmatic categories was no oversight; their decision was entirely consistent with their declared hermeneutic. Only with continued, intense study, especially of the pronouncement stories, did it become impossible to ignore consistently the current of conventional, specifically Hellenistic rhetoric in the gospel traditions.

This impossibility appears most explicitly in Dibelius' struggles to turn chreiai into "paradigms," but underlies also Bultmann's analysis of the "apophthegms." I shall return in later chapters to Bultmann's related sublimation of gospel gnomai as "logia" and "wisdom sayings." Dibelius' "constructive" form criticism began not with a formal analysis of gospel literary units, but with the hypothetical construction of one normative social-rhetorical situation for almost all pre-gospel rhetoric, the *Sitz im Leben* of preaching. The label "paradigm," then, focuses on the presumed rhetorical function of the gospel pronouncement stories in pre-gospel rhetoric. Dibelius conceded formal *analogy* between gospel "paradigms" and Hellenistic chreiai. The concession is vitiated, however, by an invidious contrast between "the *eutrapelia* [of, especially, the Cynic chreiai], the dexterity in jocular speech which Aristotle called educated insolence" and the eschatological intensity and forthrightness of the pronouncement stories. In truth, the gospel pronouncement stories are not merely analogous to chreiai, they *are* chreiai, within which wit and intensity are in dynamic tension. Yet for Dibelius the presumed paradigmatic function of the gospel stories in kerygmatic rhetoric justified concealing their formal identity with other chreiai.[4]

---

[3] Mack, *Rhetoric and the New Testament*, 12; Mack and Robbins, *Patterns*, 2–11, esp. 7 (n. 29) for Bultmann and 10 (nn. 44, 45) for Dibelius; K. Berger, "Hellenistische Gattungen im Neuen Testament," *ANRW* II 25/2 (1984) 1031–1432 and 1876–1885, 1104–7.

[4] M. Dibelius, *From Tradition to Gospel*, transl. B.L. Woolf (London, 1934; New York, 1935) 152–64, quoting 157.

Dibelius' arbitrary construction of the pre-gospel rhetorical situation and his arbitrary limitation of its possible rhetorical functions are nowadays universally rejected because of their transparently theological motivation. His procedure, however, is disquietingly analogous to that of socio-rhetorical criticism with its a priori construction of rhetorical situations and subgroups behind gospel rhetorical types. The motivations differ, but Dibelius' insistence on the priority of the kerygmatic task in all Christian public speech is very like the new socio-rhetorical insistence on the priority of argumentation over all other social functions of rhetoric and on the priority of that function over the form, the intrinsic rhetoricity of patterns. One key difference is Dibelius' clarity about the incompatibility between ancient rhetoric and the hermeneutic which he was constructing for early Christian language.

By contrast, it is only recently that chreia research has begun to notice the rhetoric in and of chreiai as distinct from their rhetorical use in composing more elaborated discourses. And even so, the "rhetorical qualities" of a chreia are still assumed to be reducible to its "argumentative figures":

> Even an abbreviated chreia may contain argumentative figures.... There has not been enough investigation of the rhetorical qualities of short statements themselves, but perhaps we are at a stage where this kind of investigation can move forward.[5]

Chreia-centred rhetorical criticism is fundamentally more interested in how chreiai can be varied for use in essentially non-chriic contexts than in how chreiai work in themselves. Only from such a perspective could it come as a late surprise that chreiai at their briefest and least distinct from gnomai ("short statements") are intrinsically, formally rhetorical: they do not merely *become* rhetorical by virtue of their use in argumentative contexts. This intrinsic rhetoricity of even the most basic patterns in ancient rhetorical education and practice is the premise of the present book as it seeks to balance intrinsic and contextual analysis of rhetorical patterns; the same premise informs the intensive investigation of gnomic rhetoric in the advanced theoretical and philosophical literature from Aristotle and Anaximenes onward.

---

[5] Robbins, "Rhetorical Discussions of the Chreia," vii–xvii, xii–xiii.

Ironically, the chreia became prominent in gospel exegesis just because a new generation of form critics sought formal categories more appropriate to texts in ancient Greek and less compromised by the form critics' functionalist quest for community settings, the fabled *Sitze im Leben*. Too often rhetorical critics seem to be replacing the kerygmatic functions presupposed by form criticism with supposedly universal functions of argumentation. This willingness to accept new functional presuppositions suggests that the rebellion against form criticism was more anti-theological than anti-functionalist.

Be that as it may, the intensity of interest in the chreia, rather than in gnome, *mythos* or *diegema*, is evidence of the continuation, after all, of form-critical functionalism into the new rhetorical criticism. For the new interest in chreia has above all been an interest in its developmental, contextual possibilities, its availability for expansion and elaboration. That is, the main topic of research has not been the astonishing versatility of the chreia itself and the astonishing variety of chreiai actually attested. Instead the focus of study has been the undeniably important possibilities of modifying and contextualizing a given chreia. Even this focus on expansion and elaboration has been narrowed to reflect the functionalist equation in the New Rhetoric between rhetoric and argumentation; only argumentative functions are rhetorical.

> Since a chreia is a rhetorical form, one of its major characteristics is its potential for modification. A chreia can be adapted to function in very different ways—beginning an argument, ending an argument, winning a person to a particular side of an argument, separating allies from one another, uniting divided groups, or furnishing amusement for one purpose or another.[6]

From a socio-rhetorical perspective, "one purpose or another" must always come back to argumentation. This forces on chreia research its basic confusion between (linguistic) form and (social) function. Primary school teachers in antiquity naturally liked chreia for its formal clarity and they naturally emphasized its usefulness for argumentation, since argumentation is one of the greatest challenges for children learning to

---

[6] Robbins, "Rhetorical Discussions of the Chreia," xiii.

speak in public. But 'argumentation' has turned into a monster in recent rhetorical criticism.

It is, of course, a valuable insight of modern rhetoric that all public language, all rhetoric, is argumentative in the sense that it is intentional. The primary quality of all public speech is to persuade an audience toward seeing its social situation as a concrete dilemma and to convince the audience to choose one option. This insight is reduced to nonsense, however, if we slip from saying that all rhetoric is argumentative to saying that all rhetoric is argumentation. Socio-rhetorical criticism needs to impose a misleading ambiguity on the words 'argument' and 'argumentation'. On the one hand, they are stretched to designate the whole intentional aspect (and social function) of rhetoric. On the other hand, the same words continue to denote those particular parts of discourse which most explicitly present an implied dialectic.

Ancient rhetoric differentiates systematically between the universal, intentional function of rhetoric—persuasion and conviction—and the particular job of selecting and organizing the most appropriate arguments, which is done in the form of argumentation. This job also includes that of suppressing arguments which would be imaginable to the speaker but not appropriate to the chosen audience or not appropriate for explicit utterance. A "text is meaningful not only in virtue of what is but also in virtue of what might have been."[7] Such consciously suppressed arguments, both those deemed too risky and those thought too banal for performance, are often closer than any actual argumentation to the social and cultural norms which the socio-rhetorician would like to expose.

> The eye and ear of the socio-rhetorical critic is on argumentation and its social and cultural meanings in the context in which it emerged. Exploration of the contexts of utterance, reference, and culture of argumentation in the gospels begins to exhibit various kinds of subcultural and countercultural movements in early Christian tradition.[8]

---

[7] M.A.K. Halliday, "Linguistic Study of Literary Texts," in *Proceedings of the Ninth International Congress of Linguists*, ed. H.G. Lunt (The Hague, 1964) 302–7, 302.

[8] Robbins, "Pre-Gospel Traditions," 147.

It is often the task of the public speaker to gloss and confuse incompatible "social and cultural meanings." Detecting the reasons consciously
hidden by argumentation involves more than just "reading between the
lines" or "against the grain" of the text; it requires from the socio-
rhetorical critic a competence in the rhetorical conventions of the text's
cultural matrix greater than the competence of its primary performer,
who is consciously trying to conceal the social and cultural agendas and
risks which the critic wishes to discover. At least we must stop using
the same two terms to designate interchangeably (1) the universal
function of rhetorical intentionality, (2) the particular form of claiming
logicality in a speech and/or (3) the speaker's agenda whether consciously or unconsciously hidden or expressed in a speech.[9]

Socio-rhetorical study of chreia expansion and elaboration in the
gospels as a pattern in argumentation has greatly illuminated early
Christian argumentation. It is crucial that modern readers be trained to
notice when early Christian texts are formally undertaking argumentation. It is perhaps even more important for us to realize that in its day
gospel argumentation formally made sense, even to its enemies.

Nevertheless, an account of the rhetoric of the gospel tradition and
its use of chreiai must also do justice to those aspects of intention in
speech (notably characterization and rapport) which are not formally or
exclusively part of an argumentation. In this widened rhetorical critical
context it also becomes urgent to consider the internal economy of the
chreia's own rhetoric. As we shall see, however, in antiquity this last
consideration always involved intensive comparison with the rhetoric of
the gnome.

Moreover, the danger of subordinating all rhetorical forms/patterns
to a single function is aggravated by the basic socio-rhetorical assumption that rhetorical function (argumentation) is in turn a direct index of
social function. If rhetorical form does not always index unique
rhetorical function, if rhetorical function is not essentially reducible to
argumentational function, or if rhetorical/argumentational function does
not always directly index social function, "the appropriateness of the

---

[9] See Robbins, "Pre-Gospel Traditions," 123; Mack, "Persuasive Pronouncements,"
284.

'socio' in *socio*-rhetorical" becomes, in B.B. Scott's word, "problematic."[10]

"The complete argument(ation)"

The problem of establishing a fully reversible relationship between
chriic forms and argumentational function (always with social function
in the background) can be illustrated by the labour Mack and Robbins
expend to construct a unitary pattern for "the complete argument(ation)"
in Greco-Roman rhetoric. The strategy is to construct a composite of
prescriptions for the argumentation section of a speech in the Latin
Rhetorica ad Herennium and elsewhere. This construct is then coordinated with at least one of the several school-book patterns for elaborating
chreiai and gnomai, that of Hermogenes' *Progymnasmata*. It is surely
an exaggeration to suppose that something like this modern construct
"had come to be known [*sic*] as 'the complete argument'"[11] in antiquity, for the analogy implied in this construct is quite loose. Nevertheless Mack's construct has considerable heuristic value: It shows the
reciprocity between basic Latin and Greek schooling and the argumentational conventions of Greco-Roman elites and their retainers. In this
light it is clear that as far as argumentation forms are concerned early
Christian rhetoric, whatever its topical eccentricities, is Greco-Roman
rhetoric.

But what does this do to the socio-rhetorical premise that there "are
specialized forms of argumentation in subcultures and minicultures?"
Mack lists "a large incidence of figurative language," "relative lack of
historical examples" (paradigms), sharply polemical attitude with
"bifocal address (to two audiences at once)" and, above all, intense
struggle with "issues of authority" as the distinguishing features of early
Christian discourse.[12] Among Greco-Roman rhetors, Jews, Christians
and their opponents used the *topic* 'Law' and related topics of authority

---

[10] B.B. Scott, "A Response: The Chinese Box: Method within Method," *Semeia* 64,
ed. Robbins (1993) 275–81, 276.

[11] Quoting Mack and Robbins, *Patterns*, 52; see Cizek, *Imitatio*, 57–58.

[12] Quoting respectively Robbins, "Pre-Gospel Traditions," 123 and Mack, *Rhetoric
and the New Testament*, 94–100, see also 50.

in special ways. Within such topics use of historical examples (*para-deigmata*) posed special problems for a new and hybrid movement.

A certain Bohemian casualness about argumentation fits with the initially exotic quality of gospel literature, but this is above all a reminder that good rhetoric is more than argumentation. In general though, early Christians and their neighbours kept any "specialized forms of argumentation" pretty much out of the texts they all wrote in Greek, while making obvious topical adjustments to the common repertoires.

I will return in a later chapter to my hunch that peculiarities of social rank, ethnicity and religious experience in early Christian literature will be voiced not so much in specialized forms of argumentation as in a specialized repertoire of topics. For the present, as regards the preeminence of argumentation theory in socio-rhetorical criticism, it is important to notice that Robbins and his immediate colleagues are not only beginning to notice their relative neglect of the intrinsic, formal rhetorical qualities of basic rhetorical patterns. They are also emphasizing increasingly that the varied models for school elaboration of gnomai, chreiai and other basic patterns do not all equally fit the construct of "the complete argument(ation)": ancient rhetoric was more complex than social-argumentational analysis of chreia-use anticipated. While querying Robbins' reference to two main types of elaboration as "levels," Mack himself observes that the unitary construct of "the complete argument(ation)" is in trouble:

> [Robbins] apparently has in mind something like the level of complexity or degree of approximation to the "complete argumentation." I suppose I should be satisfied with that, having made so much of "the complete argument" pattern in my own studies. But Robbins' work on the many ways in which the chreia could be turned into a small unit of argumentation is compelling and has the effect of dethroning "the complete argument" as a standard for judging a degree of rhetorical achievement.[13]

Pressed too far, the notion of "the complete argument(ation)" becomes a caricature both of Greco-Roman rhetorical theory and of early Christian practice. Moreover, the throne on which socio-rhetorical

---

[13] Mack, "Persuasive Pronouncements," 284; Robbins, "Rhetorical Discussions of the Chreia," xi–xiv.

criticism set "the complete argument(ation)" was its preference for the elaboration of the chreia over the rhetorical use of the other basic rhetorical school patterns—gnome, *mythos* and *diegema*. Interest in aspects of rhetoric other than argumentation and interest in aspects of the chreia other than its potential development into "the complete argumentation" eventually should threaten the argumentation-theoretical stance itself as the cornerstone of socio-rhetorical theory.

Chreia as character and story, not deed

Thus far, I hope to have shown that chreia study in gospels research is implicated in a series of questionable hermeneutical choices in form criticism and, even more powerfully, in its socio-rhetorical successor. It might be useful now to anticipate some aspects of the survey of ancient sources below. Chreia and gnome have different, discordant associations in contemporary biblical interpretation, but even in antiquity—and from a modern linguistic point of view—the two patterns were never equivalent. As regards their intrinsic rhetoricity, however, the two patterns are intimately related in ways that have not yet been adequately understood in chreia research. Indeed, recognition of the rhetorical qualities of chreiai and gnomai has been hampered by too much insistence on their argumentational and (for some chreiai) gestural aspects.

In ancient school texts, chreia usually receives greater attention than gnome, so that the socio-rhetorician can point to one important school-writer (Theon) who treats gnome only in his chapter on chreia. Still, it remains true that chreia was never discussed in antiquity without reference to gnome. Furthermore, the advanced theoretical, technical and critical writers usually discuss gnome but rarely refer to chreia. In every discussion of gnome at least some examples of gnomai are given in the form of sayings-chreiai. Likewise, historical or mythological example-stories (*paradeigmata* or *exempla*) are often performed as sayings- or action-chreiai in the advanced treatises. This makes sense not only because 'gnome' and '*paradeigma*' gained a technical rhetorical sense before 'chreia' did, but also because chreia and *paradeigma* are rhetorically simpler than gnome, despite the fact that a chreia can formally frame a gnome or *paradeigma*. That is, from the point of view of the advanced theoretical texts, chreia is the simplest way to perform a gnome or a *paradeigma*.

The formal mark of a chreia is its explicit and immediate attribution to a named personality or to a stock character (e.g., "a Laconian"): chreia is a narrative form, marked by a formula attributing significant speech or action to a significant personage. The salient rhetorical qualities of a chreia are thus attribution and pointedness along with the resulting topic of how character (not personality in any modern sense) relates to pointedness in word or deed. Chreia research has focused on the potential of this narrative form for including further topics and becoming explicitly argumentational; certainly ancient schoolmasters taught argumentational use of chreiai. Not enough emphasis has been placed, however, on the way that even the most elaborate, argumentational chreia presentation retains the definitive, narrative topic of character expression.

Throughout the history of the chreia in Greco-Roman rhetoric and education, the narrative topic of characterization has defined the form, notwithstanding intense interest in its potential also for argumentational topics. It is difficult not to associate the definitive topic of character in the chreia form with its immense popularity in Hellenistic and Greco-Roman literature: the chreia fundamentally addresses the "first century fascination with, and fear of, the power of words [and, I might add, gestures] to form [and express] character." We have already noticed with Peter Brown how the "emphasis on the 'care of the self' that flourished in the first two centuries A.D. was in many ways the reaction of thinking persons to their own bleak perceptions of Roman society as one in which heightened self-control was the only, frail guarantee of humanity to others."[14] The chreia form in collections and in all kinds of rhetorical performance offered gestural and verbal models for projecting character in a normatively constrained universe. Projecting character without creating alienation was the fundamental challenge for all Greco-Roman public speakers—and *a fortiori* for the alternative voices of early Christianity.

Chreia is not only a narrative about character, it is also definitively a *third-person* narrative about character. It is consistent with the growing anxiety about self-characterization in middle antiquity that so

---

[14] Mack and Robbins, *Patterns*, 43; Peter Brown, *Power and Persuasion* (Madison, WI, 1992) 50.

many of the boldest turns of characterization in Greco-Roman rhetoric are emphatically attributed by their speakers to others. Rhetorically a chreia is a report, carefully distancing the reporter from the agent of the reported words and/or deeds. A speaker in the fraught ethical-political universe of middle antiquity could dare to risk pointedness more freely within a form which attributed pointedness to the salient characteriz-ation of a named hero. In a world where idiosyncrasy was not only rhetorically dangerous, a speaker could nonetheless realize some of the benefits of pointedly projecting a salient characterization, by rhetorically projecting the socio-linguistic risk onto a carefully chosen chreia protagonist.

This formally encoded distance between speaker and protagonist in chreia poses problems if rhetorical criticism is to explore not only the surface, third-person narrative of the gospels, of which chreiai are so clearly constitutive. To assess the probability that Jesus and his earliest interpreters said things in public, we must take seriously the formal tension between narratives in chreia form *about* Jesus and traditions of speech *from* Jesus. The rhetorical effect of the third-person form in the chreia is precisely to locate chreiai in the rhetoric of a speaker who is not the chreia's named protagonist; if we are interested in the rhetoric of the protagonist for its own sake and not only as a construct of the reporter, the chreia form as such is an obstacle.

Chreia was chosen and gnome rejected as the focus of gospel rhetorical criticism largely through ambivalence toward the form-critical heritage: positively, chreia study has revitalized form-critical study of pronouncement stories. At the same time chreia research is a conscious rejection of another aspect of form criticism: Bultmann tried to look through the undeniably chriic rhetoric of the gospel "apophthegms" to focus behind them on the more gnomic rhetoric of "logia" which he assumed would mark pre-gospel rhetoric. Scholarly disquiet about this aspect of Bultmann's form-critical project is an increasingly important motive for intense chreia study. This negative, anti-Bultmanian slant in chreia study is especially crucial as rhetorical criticism begins to tackle the reconstruction of pre-gospel, traditional rhetorics.

Bultmann's hunches are often worth more than his own or others' reasoning; I agree with him that pre-gospel rhetoric was more often structured by gnomai than by chreiai.[15] Still, Bultmann's global

---

[15] I.H. Henderson cited in Sanders and Davies, *Synoptic Gospels*, 143–5.

presumption that simple sayings will always be genetically prior to more complex narrational or argumentational patterns is now clearly indefensible. Robbins is right about the hermeneutical imbalance in Bultmann's approach:

> Bultmann began to determine if the saying in a literary unit originally existed as an isolated saying (*gnome* or *sententia*) or an "organic *apophthegma.*" The apophthegms [=chreiai] are especially pertinent to his analysis, since they contain both narrative and speech, and his approach to the apophthegm established the model for his analysis of the other forms. For Bultmann, the saying is the primary phenomenon in the apophthegm. Any information in the narrative is subsidiary to the saying. Thus, a saying in an apophthegm may originate with Jesus or it may be a secondary saying that someone later developed from another saying in the tradition. In either case, however, the narrative depends on the saying.... This procedure pervades the entire program of interpretation. Only sayings have a natural potential for being primary. Actions, if necessary in the setting of the saying, may be genuine. Otherwise, actions are contrived or derived.[16]

The movement toward rhetorical study of New Testament chreiai rightly doubts Bultmann's unargued assumption of the general priority of sayings over contexts and of abbreviated over elaborated and expanded units. The work of Mack, Robbins and their associates has shown that both relations, between words and deeds and between brief and long forms, change in response to the rhetorical requirements of particular performances and not as a product of one way genetic evolution. Thus Greco-Roman chreia-use shows equal and highly flexible interest in words and deeds, in short and long formulations; the competent speaker can move back and forth as occasions for speech demand.

The socio-rhetoricians, however, are not only troubled by Bultmann's untenable model of linear development in tradition, they also challenge the underlying hermeneutical conviction that speech is interpretatively more important than action and that 'pure' forms are more important than 'hybrid'.

> The privileging of speech over action and situation in pre-gospel tradition is an ideological bias of traditional interpretation that must be revised.

---

[16] Mack and Robbins, *Patterns*, 7; compare Robbins, "Pre-Gospel Traditions," 134.

New Testament interpreters have shown more interest in ideological culture than social culture—a privileging of word over action and situation, of mind over body, of cognitive issues over practical issues. But both aspects are present, and both are being dealt with creatively and interactively in recitation.

The social energy emerges in the recitation of various situations and actions.... The nurturing of ideological culture occurs in the various sayings that recitation generates.[17]

I doubt, however, that chreia study should support the revision Robbins has in mind, or the presumption that goes with it of hermeneutical superiority over form criticism. Again, the only stable, definitive quality of the chreia for the ancients is that it is pointedly third-person narrative. A chreia is someone's speech about someone else's pointed speech and/or action. Bultmann may have been wrong to privilege speech over action in life generally, but a chreia is always irreducibly speech, even when it is ostensibly about action.

Bultmann was certainly wrong to assume that sayings as such were always older than narratives or argumentations. But the form critics and the socio-rhetorical critics both err—though they compensate in opposite directions—by failing to take seriously enough that narration and argumentation are also speech. The form critic neglects narrative and argumentation in a misguided attempt to privilege 'pure' speech forms; the socio-rhetorical critic privileges narrative and argumentation in an equally misguided attempt to balance action and speech as vectors in speech tradition.

In oral tradition and in rhetorical tradition, and above all in texts, speech is indeed irreversibly privileged over action and situation because, after all, action and situation can only be recited as speech; in recitation, word really is hermeneutically prior to deed. Conversely, whatever Robbins means by "ideological culture," it must be just as dominant in a story about a deed as in a story about a saying, since both are nothing but speech.

Thus in the case of the two chreiai cited at the opening of this chapter, about Jesus washing his friends' feet (John 13:2–5) and about Jesus describing himself as a servant (Luke 22:27), it would be folly to insist on the chronological priority of either word or deed. Yet it is not

---

[17] Robbins, "Pre-Gospel Traditions," 134, 135.

a mere ideological bias on my part to suppose that if Jesus actually made the Johannine gesture he probably also said something about his dramatic servanthood. The reverse supposition—that if Jesus spoke of himself as servant he must have washed his friends' feet—is considerably less consistent with the expectations of rhetorical culture and verbal tradition. At any rate the tradition actually seems to share the ideological bias toward speech: In the first place the tradition—or Luke—bothered to retell Jesus' self-characterization as a story about a gesture. Above all, though, the tradition's core, the topic of leadership as servility, appears also in several well attested gnomai.[18]

The point is not at all to deny the significance of actions in the gospel tradition, from table fellowship and healing miracles to the sign against the Temple and the Cross itself. Prophetic, therapeutic and liturgical gestures by Jesus and his followers were not at all incompatible with the public practice of speech. But only speech can be systematically analyzed from the standpoint of Greco-Roman rhetoric, only speech is embodied in chreiai. The pre-gospel tradition and the gospels themselves are rhetoric not just in the modern sense of being argumentative, but also in the ancient sense of being public speech, structured by traditional topics.

Robbins rightly worries about the fragmentary preservation of pre-gospel spoken rhetoric: "many different things may have been said, and the sequence of statements is often as important as the statements themselves."[19] The same is true, of course, of the deeds of Jesus and his successors. Indeed it must be granted to Bultmann that some of the "situations and actions" in gospel chreiai (e.g., the Pharisees in the Sabbath fields [Mark 2:23–28]) do sound decidedly contrived if we forget that they are just as rhetorical—just as idealized—as the adjacent, highly artificial "sayings."

Studying gospel chreiai therefore brings us no closer to the actual deeds behind pre-gospel tradition than studying 'sayings.' Rhetorical criticism is moving—as it should—from studying the rhetoric of the gospels to studying also the rhetoric of the "pre-gospel traditions" and of Jesus himself. The further we move toward a rhetorical model of pre-gospel oral tradition as public speech, the more the socio-rhetorical

---

[18] Mark 9:35 par Luke 22:26; Mark 10:43–4 par Matt 20:26–8, Luke 22:26 (Matt 23:11); Matt 23:12 par Luke 14:11, 18:14; Matt 18:4.

[19] Robbins, "Pre-Gospel Traditions," 134.

topic of revising the interpretative relationship between speech and action becomes a red herring; in ancient texts, there is nothing but speech for rhetorical criticism to study. Studying chreiai under the illusion that they might somehow help revise the hermeneutical imbalance between speech and action ignores the basic fact that chreiai in ancient rhetoric are irreducibly speech, whether they talk about actions or not.

E.P. Sanders[20] has made a programmatic attempt to interpret the strongest evidence of the public behaviour of Jesus and his immediate followers as a way out of the impasse of literary-historical preoccupation with 'sayings.' Sanders' heuristic list of "facts" is not impeccable, but it does press beyond fragmentary accounts of actions to integrative categories of action. Sanders' suggestion is that we read Jesus and his followers as responsible agents. The task of rhetorical criticism is to complement that part of Sanders' programme which comes close to a materialist reconstruction of Jesus' social agency. This means extending the hypothesis to assume that Jesus and those who began to recount his actions and words were rhetorically competent enough to generate a significant tradition of chreiai, gnomai, *mythoi* and (rather fewer) *diegemata*. Because the tradition is in Greek and the setting is the first-century eastern Mediterranean, the generative hermeneutical horizon is that of basic Greco-Roman rhetoric, a horizon not easily reconciled with that of North American socio-rhetorical criticism.

The error of form criticism, therefore, is not that it paid too little attention to sayings about actions (though this minor charge is true). More seriously, both form criticism and socio-rhetorical criticism so far have failed to coordinate ancient and modern hermeneutical horizons closely enough to allow criticism of an integrated rhetoric behind the fragmentary literature of gospel 'sayings.' The contribution of rhetorical criticism to historical Jesus research should be to imagine public speech behind fragmentary narrative and quotation. Greco-Roman rhetoric offers, in fact, protocols for doing some of that work; in their intense discussions of how to make, remake and use gnomai, the rhetoricians

---

[20]   *Jesus and Judaism*, (London, 1985); see R.A. Horsley, "'Like One of the Prophets of Old': Two Types of Popular Prophets at the Time of Jesus," *CBQ* 47 (1985) 435–63; R.A. Horsley, *Sociology and the Jesus Movement* (New York, 1989) cited in H.W. Attridge, "Reflections on Research into Q," *Semeia* 55, ed. Kloppenborg and Vaage (1991) 223–234, 233.

come closest to addressing the problem of transmitting and reintegrating fragmented speech.

The primary resource for reimagining hopelessly fragmented 'sayings' as an integrated gnomic (and parabolic) rhetoric is not the verbal quotation mark of the chreia form, but rather the basic rhetorical concept of topicality. Durable insight into the rhetoric of Christianity and of Jesus will not be won from analysis of the tensions between action and word or between abbreviated/pure forms and elaborated/ expanded/hybrid forms in the composition of the gospels. Instead, an approximate assessment of pre-gospel rhetoric can only be made beginning with a topical analysis of the internal rhetorical economy of those speech patterns which rhetorical conventions expected to be intentionally 'fragmentary': gnome and *mythoi* (parable).

I argued above that chreia is formally simpler than gnome, because of the chreia's explicit, indispensable formal marking by attribution to a named protagonist. Moreover, although both chreia and gnome can invoke a wide range of topics, chreia always formally invokes the narrative topic of character. The third definitive rhetorical quality of chreia is not so simply discussed, however. "Pointedness" (*eustochia*) is hard to define, but I guess it is a sociolinguistic category, neither purely linguistic nor purely social, a judgement of markedness or salience in relation to speech norms. How is such deliberate unconventionality compatible with the conventionality and formality of chreia pattern?

In part, as we have seen, the risk of pointedness is controlled by the strict formal convention of attribution to a heroic protagonist. As a narrative form, the chreia discreetly emphasizes the safe distance between speaker, as narrator, and chriic protagonist, as actor, and between social and rhetorical normativities generally. Yet, even more fundamentally, the rhetorical quality of the chreia itself as reported action or speech allows for a linguistically wide range of topical, stylistic and figurative means for achieving 'pointedness': it is always rhetorically possible to be verbally pointed without being socially offensive.

That is, the linguistic, rhetorical pointedness of good chreiai may not be a unitary phenomenon for the purpose of social analysis. As with the punchlines of jokes, the pointedness of chreiai will usually have some reference to background social normativities. Such social normativities will in themselves be complex and ambiguous enough. Yet the pointed chriic reference to them will, in addition, be directly controlled by linguistic, poetic factors. Finally, rhetorical normativity abstracts and revalues social normativity for its usefulness in rhetorical contexts where the speaker is not the protagonist and the audience are not characters in the narrative. The chreia in Greco-Roman rhetoric was thus explicitly a container for managing the risqué while avoiding, concealing or controlling the real social and personal risks in speech.

It is easier, therefore, to specify how chreia as such controls and contains pointedness than to specify how pointedness is achieved at all. For this second question, only just now being broached in chreia research, the theoretical discussions of gnome in advanced technical, philosophical and stylistic manuals are far superior to the prescriptions and taxonomies for chreia- and gnome-use in the school texts. The rhetoricians recognized in gnome an even more subtle and versatile envelope than chreia for managing rhetorical pointedness across the whole spectrum of rhetorical normativity, from provocation to domestication. The pointedness which speakers risked in the name of another in chreia is ultimately a special case of the pointedness which they could also risk in their own names in the more personal and confrontational styles of gnome.

Robbins' call for "investigation of the rhetorical qualities of short statements themselves" is thus overdue. Even in terms of the progress of research on chreia in argumentation, it is now high time to reassess the postulated trajectory from chreia elaboration to "complete argument(ation)."

> Even an abbreviated chreia may contain argumentative figures.... [A]ny rhetorical figure may be present in an abbreviated chreia...A chreia is a rhetorical form. This means that it contains some kind of language that has an attractive, authoritative, or logically persuasive quality. There has not been enough investigation of the rhetorical qualities of short statements themselves, but perhaps we are at a stage where this kind of investigation can move forward.[21]

Yet in so far as character, pointedness and arm's length third-person narration are central to the rhetoricity of chreiai, the bias of socio-

---

[21] Robbins, "Rhetorical Discussions of the Chreia," xiii.

rhetorical criticism toward analyzing argumentation and toward divining social location is bound to deflect such forward movement.

I propose, therefore, to begin reassessing the rhetoricity of "short statements themselves" by locating chreia more clearly in relation to its undisputed next of kin, gnome. In part, this is the logical next step even within the socio-rhetorical project. In general, however, a turn from argumentation-theory toward rhetorical qualities like pointedness and character marks a fundamental difference of perspective over against socio-rhetorical criticism. It is not only time to go beyond and behind chreia; it is time to turn away from a narrow understanding of chreia as a matrix for argumentation. By turning instead toward gnome I am attempting to take seriously not only the pointedness of gospel rhetorics, but also the tensions between fragmentation and homogeneity and between anonymity and Christological characterization in the oldest Christian rhetorical traditions.

Greco-Roman rhetorical theory and education expected gnome to have a quasi-fragmentary formal character, what I will call 'resistance'. The rhetoricians knew that such linguistic resistance could be heightened by pointedness and especially by pointed characterization. Such resistance and the resulting memorability and versatility encouraged exceptionally thick preservation of pre-gospel gnomic rhetoric in the literary composition of early Christian texts. Qualities of resistance, characterization and pointedness figure prominently in theoretical discussions of gnome, certainly more prominently than argumentational figures within gnome. The advanced theoretical discussions are therefore an essential complement and corrective to the progymnasmatic school-books. It is thus historically justified to reassess pre-gospel tradition as gnomic rather than as chriic rhetoric because of the sheer thickness of gnomic rhetoric in early Christian texts. We are guided in this reassessment by the intense theoretical and practical engagement with gnome in ancient rhetoric even beyond the progymnasmatic school-books.

The priority of chreia and the priority of Theon

Some knowledge of chreia and of the *Progymnasmata*, the books of early secondary-school exercises, is increasingly common among technically trained readers of early Christian literature. Such acquaintance is limited, however, by its source: Naturally enough, knowledge of the chreia and its place in ancient schooling has been limited as well as fostered by socio-rhetorical interest in argumentation. Published discussion of the *Progymnasmata* is often confined to their chapters on chreia, despite routine use of other progymnasmatic patterns in early Christian rhetoric.[22]

It is not only the focus on chreia which has narrowed awareness of the *Progymnasmata*. As school texts, the *Progymnasmata* have often lain neglected, below the threshold both of Classical and of Biblical scholarly canons; accurate, accessible editions, translations and studies of the *Progymnasmata* have not been forthcoming. The main, though still partial, exception is the work ascribed to Aelius Theon, which is probably the earliest (late first century AD), but certainly the most idiosyncratic of the extant progymnasmatic handbooks. In its original form (reconstructible from internal evidence and from the Armenian version) Theon's work was quite unlike later *Progymnasmata*. Even truncated as it is in the extant Greek manuscripts, it is far longer and articulates a more ambitious pedagogical programme.[23]

All *Progymnasmata*, including Theon's, outline a curriculum designed to take students beyond passive literacy to effective rhetorical performance. They begin with a gradually more challenging series of basic patterns, to each of which in turn is applied a series of analytical, variational and compositional exercises. The "progression from more mimetic and analytical exercises to those that required compositional skills" is a basic principle behind this pre-rhetorical curriculum.[24]

The progression was not smooth, however, but tended to divide the progymnasmatic cycle in two: the early patterns are forms (*mythos, diegema*, chreia and gnome) and invite formal drills, while later patterns are speech types or discursive strategies which demand exercises in

---

[22] Hock and O'Neil, *Chreia in Ancient Rhetoric*; Hock, "Chreia"; Robbins, "Pre-Gospel Traditions," 121–2, 118–20; Watson and Hauser, *Rhetorical Criticism*, 115–20, 158–60; though see Berger, "Hellenistische Gattungen," 1296–8 on the genre, *Progymnasmata*; and the exhaustive survey, Cizek, *Imitatio*, 227–319.

[23] J.R. Butts, *The Progymnasmata of Theon: A New Text with Translation and Commentary* (Ph.D. diss., Claremont Graduate School, 1987); I. Lana, *Quintiliano, Il "Sublime," e gli "Esercizi Preparatori" di Elio Teone* (Torino, 1951); I. Lana, *I Progimnasmi di Elio Teone* vol. I *La storia del testo* (Torino, 1959); Professor Rossella Granatelli also projects a critical edition and translation of the *Progymnasmata* including the Armenian textual evidence. For useful introductions, see Hock and O'Neil, *Chreia in Ancient Rhetoric*, 3–22, 63–74; Mack and Robbins, *Patterns*, 31–51.

[24] Mack and Robbins, *Patterns*, 35.

composition and performance. Because the pedagogy aims to be cumulative, it is massively repetitive; in most *Progymnasmata*, for example, *enkomion* is taught first as an exercise on gnome and chreia, only to return later as a pattern in its own right, the object of its own exercises in topical versatility rather than formal variation.

Theon's curriculum also spirals from passive reading through formal analysis toward topical composition, but Theon differs attractively from later progymnasmatists because he is systematically and explicitly conforming educational practice to the goals implicit throughout the progymnasmatic and rhetorical traditions; after completing Theon's syllabus, the student is ready for full-scale practice declamations (Theon, *Prog.* 1,146 Spengel 59). Theon's list of primary exercises, those which would come to be known as progymnasmata proper, is structured to produce, perhaps, a more even gradient of difficulty than in normal *Progymnasmata*. Theon prescribes a shorter list of secondary exercises, structured in pairs, the first of which (recitation/inflection) is mechanically formal while the rest (approval/disapproval + topics; expansion/abbreviation; refutation/confirmation + topics) open quickly to the whole repertoire of argumentative and narrative topics.

Theon insists on these exercises only in relation to his first three basic patterns, chreia, *mythos* and *diegema*; the approach in the second half of Theon's curriculum is controlled by topical rather than by formal analysis. Behind this rapid movement toward real rhetoric is, moreover, a uniquely meticulous formal and rhetorical taxonomy of the possible subpatterns of especially the early more formal patterns. Theon thereby emphasizes even more than later *Progymnasmata* an alternation at first of formal analysis with topical development, yielding eventually to an almost wholly topical approach to rhetorical composition and perform-ance.

In concluding chapters removed from the Greek manuscript tradition by a later editor—who was trying to conform Theon to the more uniform later handbooks—Theon consolidates with another concurrent series of exercises (reading; listening; paraphrase; elaboration; rebuttal). These are not, for Theon, "extra exercises."[25] The first three in particular give practical expression to Theon's unique insistence on reading, writing and classical literacy and are to be practised from the

---

[25] R.F. Hock, "General Introduction to Volume I," in Hock and O'Neil, *Chreia in Ancient Rhetoric*, 3–60, 17.

beginning (Theon, *Prog.* 1,158 Spengel 65). Theon shares the consensus of Greco-Roman tradition that education is to equip students with the rhetorical and social *savoir faire* to be publicly influential, a rhetorical socialization to which reading and imitating classical literature are ancillary though never incidental; "Reading is the nourishment of speech" (*Prog.* 1,150 Spengel 61). Theon stands out among the progymnasmatists in the extent of his emphasis on serious reading and writing not only as a means, but even as one goal of rhetorical education (e.g., *Prog.* 1,152 Spengel 62; 2,168 Spengel 70).

Overreading Theon, Vernon Robbins concluded that the progymnasmata "[a]lso...influenced the oral skills of the student, since the student was asked to express the exercises orally as well as to write them." In fact, the actual relation between writing and oral performance skills among the goals of progymnasmatic education was precisely the reverse, even in Theon's elitist treatment of the curriculum: progymnasmatic exercises were primarily taught and practised orally, not only because a school-child's wax tablets afforded little scope for extensive written composition, but above all because the central educational goal was public-speaking proficiency.

Theon's uniqueness within the progymnasmatic tradition shows particularly in his handling of chreia and gnome. Theon alone puts chreia first in the order of basic patterns and subsumes gnome under the more narrative form; all later *Progymnasmata* place chreia later in the curriculum and treat gnome separately. Given his insistence on the priority of chreia (1,157 Spengel 64) and his acknowledgement that others had compiled pre-rhetorical textbooks before him (1, 146/7 Spengel 59), there is a strong presumption that this arrangement is Theon's own idea. Moreover, Theon devotes far more space to work with the chreia than any other ancient educationist, a fact which in itself contributes to the dominance of Theon as a source for chreia research.

The priority of chreia is, however, a tribute to its pedagogical rather than its rhetorical importance in Theon's eyes. Painstaking taxonomy and inflection of the chreia mark the threshold from primary literacy schooling to real rhetorical education. Theon makes fairly modest claims for the importance of chreia-use in real public speaking, as it were, after graduation: it "imparts not only a certain force of words, but also a certain favourable characterization when we are conversant in the apophthegms of the wise" (1,148 Spengel 60).

We should note one more characteristic of Theon's work and especially of his attitude to the earlier, formal patterns led by chreia. Mack underlines Theon's expressed preference for "approved" or at least contextually appropriate chreiai and relates it to a general movement in the first century AD toward moralism and classicism in philosophy and literary taste.[26] Theon himself lets the criterion of high moral tone cramp his selection of examples only a little; what matters more is that the alleged source (and style) of a chreia be suitably prestigious and canonical. For modern sensibilities it is problematic that ancient rhetoric (and culture in general) should so centrally concern itself with character projection, and that characterization in turn should be conceived of so largely in terms of stylish handling of respectable voices of authority (even of respectably shocking voices). Rhetorical *ethos*, expressible in well crafted or well chosen chreiai, is not personality—and antiquity found the former more interesting than the latter as a verbal means for asserting, nuancing and challenging social identity.

Mack may be right to detect a shift in first-century sensibility among the literary classes and Theon's moralism may be one symptom of this; but Theon's rhetorical moralism is not morality or ethics in any modern sense. Theon's rhetorical moralism and classicism are above all a programmatic educational assertion of rhetorical normativity over against social normativity. Theon does represent rhetoric as virtual morality more than most prior rhetoricians and more than most later progymnasmatists. This should, however, be associated closely with Theon's equally unusual insistence on literary training and practice in rhetorical education: the goal is to enable the student to use canonized characters and their texts to assert solidarity, real or fictional, with a social elite.

Patrick Sinclair has captured this *arrivisme* of rhetorical moralism in his study of *sententia* (i.e., gnome) in the Latin *Rhetorica ad Herennium*, which prescribes a similarly careful, but in modern terms ethically inconsistent, selection of authorities, topics and styles:

> Rhetoric at Rome was not only a means of persuasion, it was also an opportunity for self-invention for the would-be statesman, for the newcomer who could convincingly "speak the language" of his social superiors, who

---

[26] Mack and Robbins, *Patterns*, 41–44; see Mack, *Lost Gospel*, 198–201.

could incorporate the general views and opinions that were canonical to their class, who could successfully reproduce their patterns of speech and language, who, in short, could "act out" their own image of themselves.[27]

For Theon this means quoting the right authorities and their sentiments; for the writer *ad Herennium* it means echoing their sentiments and rhetoric, while stylishly avoiding vulgar direct quotations.

Theon's work goes well beyond the scope of ordinary (later) *Progymnasmata*. Its extensive reflections on pedagogy and rhetorical self-characterization and internal hints at innovation, especially in its treatment of chreia and non-treatment of gnome, give the work experimental and theoretical dimensions which make it more interesting, but less representative. In terms of literary genre, Theon's work falls somewhere between the later school-book genre and that of the older philosophical-technical manuals, whether or not it was ever actually called a *techne peri progymnasmaton*.[28]

Theon's uniqueness raises two related and central questions for rhetorical criticism of gospel traditions. First, does the critics' natural choice of Theon, as earliest and longest source for progymnasmatic rhetoric, contribute to the bias of rhetorical criticism toward chreia and away from gnome? Second, what is the relationship between the textbook genre, *Progymnasmata*, and the educational tradition of pre-rhetorical exercises, progymnasmata, between primary literacy and advanced rhetorical practice? The uniqueness of Theon dramatizes the tension between *Progymnasmata* and progymnasmata as vividly as the uniqueness of John or of Q or of Paul raises the question of the relation between gospel and Gospels.

Genre and tradition in the *Progymnasmata*

At the same time that rhetorical criticism of the gospels has tended to canonize the chreia at the expense of other basic rhetorical patterns, it has also tended to canonize Theon's unique approach to the chreia.

---

[27] P. Sinclair, "The *Sententia* in *Rhetorica ad Herennium*: A Study in the Sociology of Rhetoric," *AJP* 114 (1993) 561–80.

[28] R.F. Hock and E.N. O'Neil, "The Chreia Discussion of *Aelius Theon of Alexandria*," in Hock and O'Neil, *Chreia in Ancient Rhetoric*, 61–78, 63.

Rhetorical critical studies of the chreia have interpreted Theon's uniqueness over against the rest of the progymnasmatic literature as a sign that Theon is more representative of an earlier situation, closer to the composition of early Christian literature. The key assumption has been that Theon is more representative of rhetorical and educational practice at the time of Christian origins than are the later *Progymnasmata*. That is, the probably early date of Theon's idiosyncratic work is assumed to prove its greater authority than that of later *Progymnasmata* as a guide to progymnasmatic tradition.

> [W]hile the contents of the *Progymnasmata* eventually became rigidly standardized, Theon's textbook reminds us that in the earlier period variety in the number and nomenclature of exercises may have been the standard.... To sum up: The contents and function of the *Progymnasmata* varied early on, as the evidence from Quintilian and especially from Theon shows. But from the time of Aphthonius and later variety gives way to standardization.[29]
>
> Theon's *Progymnasmata*, written in Greek and directly contemporary with the gospels, is a central document for our new understanding.... The...*Progymnasmata*...and the *Rhetorica ad Herennium* are the most important ancient documents for helping us to develop this new approach. The rhetorical perspective of Aelius Theon of Alexandria, which comes from our earliest extant *Progymnasmata*, reveals three basic aspects of culture-transmitting tradition.... Theon's discussion of the chreia reveals these aspects most vividly.... The chapter on the chreia...in the *Progymnasmata* of Aelius Theon of Alexandria gives special insight into the rhetorical nature of culture-transmitting tradition.[30]

Actually, neither the date nor the authorship of Theon's work is all that secure.[31] But the very expectation that the earliest surviving written document should be the best source for a tradition is doubtful. Gospel historians in particular should long since have been inoculated against it. One dubious fruit of the recent flowering of Q research, in a scholarly milieu closely overlapping with that engaged in chreia study,

---

[29] Hock, "General Introduction," 17–18, 21.

[30] Robbins, "Pre-Gospel Traditions," 111, 118–9.

[31] Hock and O'Neil, "Theon," 64 and n.11; Easterling, "Books and Readers in the Greek World," puts Theon's *Progymnasmata* in the second century A.D.; Butts, *Theon*, 1–5 expresses the majority view that Quintilian is at least indirectly dependent on Theon's *Progymnasmata*.

has been the reinstatement of the fallacy that literary priority should bestow interpretative primacy.

Clearly scholars who promote a rhetorical criticism of gospel traditions centred on Theon's treatise and especially on its chapter on chreia also intensively consult later *Progymnasmata*, especially that attributed to Hermogenes (end of the second century AD?). They also rely heavily on one of the earlier theoretical manuals (*technai*), the Latin *Rhetorica ad Herennium* (c. 86–82 BC). Robbins, Mack and others do, however, derive exclusively from Theon master components of their approach: notably the hermeneutical and tradition-historical centrality of chreia and the negligibility of gnome.

Theon and the "approved chreia"

More subtly, Burton Mack builds provocatively but, I think, misleadingly upon Theon's exceptionally intense emphasis on the authority of "approved" chreiai, of approved chriic protagonists and of approved literary sources for chreia selection. Mack finds a key to the interpretation of gospel sayings-traditions and of the genre of the sayings gospel, Q, in Theon's emphatic, moralizing deference to accepted canons of literary authority. Theon, of course, prescribes systematic adaptation of received tradition for new rhetorical contexts, but the skill to adapt tradition is taught within the framework of imitation (*mimesis*) in rhetorical self-characterization (*ethos*).

> There are hints in the educational literature of the first century that this shift in sensibility [*scil.*, toward embodiment of *ethos* in 'sayings'] was widespread and had pushed educators into serious reflection about the role of classical education in a period of cultural transition.... This mentality was taken for granted throughout the hellenistic world, and it gives the proper cultural context for understanding the way in which the Jesus movements treated Jesus' sayings.... Thus the genre of a collection of sayings was not a weak or insufficient foundation for a movement of followers in Jesus' name.[32]

---

[32] Mack, *Lost Gospel*, 199, 201; see Mack and Robbins, *Patterns*, 41–44.

I have already expressed my scepticism that any "collection of sayings" ever provided the "foundation for a movement of followers in Jesus' name." For the present, it is enough to note that the "hints" of literary classicism and ethicism (in the rhetorical sense of character projection) align Theon with the earlier—and socially elite—literary-ethical conservatism of Plato's critique of immoral fables in education, of the philosophical *technai*, of Aristotle, Anaximenes, and the *Rhetorica ad Herennium*, as well as of Quintilian's massive digest of philosophical and pedagogical theory.

The "shift" which Mack notes here may thus be a difference in the social prestige claimed for their readers by different documents, as much as a shift across time. No doubt Theon, like other writers for the aspiring elite is expressing a new "fascination with, and fear of, the power of words to form character." Two centuries on, the rhetorical self-confidence of the *novus homo* which inspired the emphatic ethical pragmatism of the *Rhetorica ad Herennium*[33] is giving way in tutored society to a classicist anxiety to consolidate the cultural aspects of elite identity and legitimacy—perhaps in response to the more dangerous and exclusive political markers of elite status. From the first century on, elite norms of taste, education and characterization increasingly reflect anxiety about rhetorical performance and rhetorical identity (*ethos*). Theon is right that rhetorical risk-taking is not always a better strategy than careful identification with conventional values, if a speaker's goal is social mobility or stability near the top of a highly traditional society.

The relative lack of moralistic "hints" in the *Progymnasmata* after Theon may thus have more to say about the social prestige claimed by Theon and Quintilian than about changing ethical frameworks; Theon aspires to a readership more like that sought by Quintilian or Seneca than the readerships sought by later *Progymnasmata* or by early Christian literatures. Mack interprets Theon's chreia rhetoric in terms of the transfer from rhetorical theory into literary criticism and appreciation of the rhetorical expectation that a culture-hero's words should be the ideal medium for conveying his chosen *ethos*, his rhetorical character and philosophical authority.

As rhetorical theory came to be applied to literary criticism, the scholars of antiquity apparently transferred this dictum about *logos* and *ethos* from the

---

[33] Sinclair, "*Sententia* in *Rhetorica ad Herennium*."

oral speech situation to the speeches and sayings of speakers encountered in literature.[34]

From this point of view, the later, *déclassé Progymnasmata* may be more relevant for comparison with the rhetorics of gospels, rhetorics ascribed to a judicially executed Galilean Jewish villager, barely credible even as a Cynic anti-hero. Even within Theon's work, if discriminating selection of examples is an attempt to coin literary taste as a negotiable currency of rhetorical and social prestige, the mass of Theon's own examples of chreia nevertheless do not fit the advertised moralistic criteria:

> We have now explored the moralistic concerns and rhetorical-literary theories which determined that only helpful chreiai be chosen for exercises in confirmation.... We are on the way to the second sophistic and the cultural domestication of rhetoric.... What, then, are we to make of the many other examples of the chreia in Theon that are not moralistic? What of those chreiai that are examples of clever, terse, and telling rejoinders by speakers who set a situation on its ears? This kind of anecdote is actually predominant in Theon's chapter...[35]

Theon's evidence is thus disarmingly ambiguous: much as he professes a decorous, tasteful, discriminating rhetorical repertoire, he cannot bring himself to reject the weight of tradition—and continuing relevance— behind a more free-wheeling practice of speech. Theon prescribes a Platonic programme of pedagogical censorship which he shows no intention of actually carrying out (cf. Plato *Resp.* 2.376e– 3.392d). At any rate, I have trouble finding Theon's elitist, moralizing theory of literary-rhetorical characterization (often belied by the pointedness of his actual examples) in gospel rhetorics of Jesus' sayings. In so far as Theon's rhetorical decorum differs from that of the later *Progymnasmata*, it is the latter which are relevant to gospel rhetorics.

---

[34] Mack and Robbins, *Patterns*, 43.
[35] Mack and Robbins, *Patterns*, 45.

Theon, Quintilian and the origins of progymnasmatic schooling

Certainly Theon, though early and elaborate, is deeply idiosyncratic compared with both earlier and later progymnasmatic tradition. It was simply a mistake on the part of R.F. Hock and E.N. O'Neil to suppose from Theon that in the first century the "number and sequence" of exercises in the progymnasmatic curriculum varied widely from teacher to teacher and that only after the second century the curriculum "became rigidly standardized" in written *Progymnasmata*. This misestimation of Theon's (and Quintilian's) significance sadly dominates the most accessible and widely cited source-book for rhetorical criticism of chreia-use—and reinforces bias toward chreia-centred rhetorical criticism. Nonetheless, I have shown elsewhere that Theon and his approximate contemporary, the great Latin educationist Quintilian, both responded more or less independently to a progymnasmatic tradition which was already practically fixed in number and order, though not rigidly fixed in presentation.[36]

Theon's treatise and the later *Progymnasmata* are initially by-products of a wider tradition of teaching with the progymnasmata. That wider progymnasmatic tradition was mediated more by schoolmasters and their pupils than by textbooks. Like gospel tradition, progymnasmatic tradition was a mainly oral tradition, though one which worked with older, canonical texts and which produced its distinctive literary genre as a later by-product. Theon characteristically urges daily writing (1,152 Spengel 62), but the obvious way to practice the progymnasmata is aloud. Theon's insistence on writing practice reflects the very real possibility of teaching the progymnasmata without much emphasis on written composition. Very few in antiquity owned a *Progymnasmata*, but no one in antiquity learned to express more than a few sentences in Greek or Latin, without mastering at least the first, more formal progymnasmata.

---

[36] Hock, "General Introduction," 17–18, 21–22, quoting 21 and 17; E.N. O'Neil, "Discussion of Preliminary Exercises of *Marcus Fabius Quintilianus*," in Hock and O'Neil, *Chreia in Ancient Rhetoric*, 113–43; I.H. Henderson, "Quintilian and the *Progymnasmata*," *Antike und Abendland* 37 (1991) 82–99, esp. 87–94; see also B.L. Mack and E.N. O'Neil, "The Chreia Discussion of *Hermogenes of Tarsus*," in Hock and O'Neil, *Chreia in Ancient Rhetoric*, 153–81, 162; R. Granatelli, "M. Fabio Quintiliano *Institutio oratoria* II 1–10: struttura e problemi interpretativi," *Rhetorica* 13 (1995) 137–160.

We must reckon at all periods with considerable variety in pedagogical practice: there was in antiquity nothing remotely approaching a school system or an accredited primary school teacher. Even the word 'school' is a misnomer for informally-housed, parentally-funded group tutorials, very small businesses run by self-declared teachers.

> It is necessary here to think not of a single, integrated track of primary and secondary schools,...but of different types of schools serving different segments of the population. The population at large, massively illiterate, was served (however ill) by the "schools of letters"..., institutions of low prestige that provided general, utilitarian literacy. But others, those who had access to the liberal schools of grammar and rhetoric, would receive the rudiments of instruction at home or from teachers assigned to impart the first elements in the grammarian's school; they thus would meet the grammarian as their first teacher.[37]

These facts make it all the more astonishing and significant that from the first to the sixth centuries a basically stable curriculum of studies bridged the gap between basic literacy and advanced rhetoric. The progymnasmatic curriculum is even more significant because it straddles, indeed internalizes, the gap between basic literacy acquired at home or at a street-corner tutorial and the public, prestigious and exclusive cultivation of higher rhetoric. The *Progymnasmata*, here including Theon, provide an intermediate curriculum in a society where nothing so tidy as a middle school could be counted upon except by the highly privileged. In fact, the continuity and ubiquity of the progymnasmatic tradition is the most impressive evidence in existence for a common educational experience available even to some with few social pretensions; the progymnasmatic tradition was earlier and more widely disseminated than the few textbooks which now attest it.

Internally, as we noticed above, the progymnasmata in all sources are divided between early, formalistic exercises (*mythos*, *diegema*, chreia and gnome with their exercises) and later assignments which move quickly toward composing and performing whole speeches. More outwardly, the Quintilian explicitly raises a question implied in Theon's placement of chreia first and by his assignment of such grindingly

---

[37] Kaster, *Guardians of Language*, 24; see also R.A. Kaster, "Notes on 'Primary' and 'Secondary' Schools in Late Antiquity," *TAPA* 113 (1983) 323–346.

inflectional exercises to chreia (with gnome), *mythos* and *diegema*. Quintilian discusses the first few exercises (*fabella*, probably some form of *narratio, sententia, chria* and something he calls *aetiologia* or *ethologia*) with frustrating brevity in a context which is really about dividing the progymnasmatic curriculum between two classes of teacher, the *grammaticus* and the *rhetor*.

Quintilian recognizes that these early exercises, the *primordia dicendi*, first elements of public speaking, are so basic as to be harmlessly allowed to the primary teacher (*Inst.* I 9,1–6), while the remainder of the patterns discussed in the later *Progymnasmata* are reserved by Quintilian to the *rhetor* and are discussed later and at much greater length (*Inst.* II 4,2–40). If the progymnasmata all together define "the minimum formal rhetorical equipment of any literate person,"[38] Quintilian's *primordia dicendi* are the shared formal rhetorical equipment of many less literate persons, unable to afford more than Quintilian's *grammaticus*, but able, after all, to read and write complex gospels.

On one point, we may confidently correct a basic error which has misled chreia studies into taking Theon as evidence of an early period in progymnasmatic education, before the canon and order of exercises was fixed. Unlike his contemporary, Quintilian discusses almost all of the patterns which appear in the later Greek *Progymnasmata* ascribed to Hermogenes (late second century?), Aphthonius (fourth century) and Nicolaus (fifth century). Quintilian does so, moreover, not in some idiosyncratic order, indicative of an unfixed tradition, but in essentially the order which would be recognized as normal also in Hermogenes, Aphthonius and Nicolaus.

It is generally at least possible that Quintilian was indirectly aware of Theon's work.[39] There is no doubt, however, that Quintilian's discussion of the *primordia dicendi* and later of the rest of what would later be called progymnasmata is substantially independent of Theon and responds to an older, pre-Theonic tradition which resembles that of Hermogenes, Aphthonius and Nicolaus.[40]

---

[38] Cairns, *Generic Composition*, 72.
[39] See Butts, *Theon*, 1–6; Hock and O'Neil, "Theon," 64; Lana, *Quintiliano*, esp. 141–2.
[40] O'Neil, "Quintilianus," 118, 132–4.

Quintilian's central importance for understanding progymnasmatic rhetoric in the period of Christian origins has been ignored because of rhetorical criticism's triple obsession with chreia, with formal analysis and with Theon. Quintilian's discussion of the *primordia dicendi* (*Inst.* I 9) is extremely brief and is primarily about regulating the aspirations of lower-class teachers (*grammatici*) to encroach on the advanced rhetorical parts of the progymnasmatic curriculum. The result is difficult to read and uninformative for anyone interested mainly in chreia, and in formal analysis of chreia. It is, moreover, true that Quintilian has only passing interest in the *primordia*. In so far as he does discuss them in I 9, it can look as though Quintilian "devoted much more space to the chreia than to any other of the *quaedam dicandi [sic] primordia*" and, therefore, that chreia "stood in a position of special importance in [his] limited set of elementary exercises."[41]

In fact, Quintilian's set of elementary exercises is less limited than Theon's and is more closely related to tradition from before and after Theon.

> [Quintilian] discusses each standard *progymnasma* somewhere, often repeatedly and usually at considerable length, especially once II 4 is seen to be a resumption of I 9.... In fact, among the *primordia dicendi*, only *chria* receives no further exposition, hardly a sign of special importance.

Not only does Quintilian discuss the more advanced exercises elsewhere (II 4), he returns to each of the *primordia* except chreia. Instead of returning to the chreia, Quintilian gives a massive discussion of *sententia* or gnome (VIII 5), a discussion in which most examples of gnome/*sententia* are presented, without comment, in chreia form, i.e., with an attributive formula. That Quintilian so tacitly subsumes chreia under gnome/*sententia*, is a good indication of his estimate of their relative rhetorical importance.[42]

Focusing exclusively on chreia, it becomes possible, though not pardonable, to ignore Quintilian's extensive discussion of the more rhetorical progymnasmata (II 4) and his massive discussion of *sententia* (=gnome) (VIII 5) later on. Only from such a constricted point of view could anyone conclude that "we should consider Quintilians's discussion

---

[41] O'Neil, "Quintilianus," 135–36.

[42] Henderson, "Quintilian and the *Progymnasmata*," 95.

little more than an historical curiosity" in comparison with Theon's demonstrably unrepresentative work.[43]

On the contrary, Quintilian is the earliest witness to the standard order and canon of pre-rhetorical exercises (later to be labelled progymnasmata). In addition, Quintilian has the virtue of observing the early progymnasmatic tradition from outside.

> Quintilian remains by far the most detailed and authoritative discussion of *progymnasmata* (exercises) outside the *Progymnasmata* (textbooks); he is also the only witness from antiquity to discuss *sententia* [i.e., gnome] and related forms both as progymnasmatic exercises and as topics in advanced theory.[44]

An important and unique aspect of Quintilian's work is that it explicitly evaluates traditional rhetorical education (beginning with the progymnasmata) in terms of the tradition of theoretical, technical and philosophical, reflection. The integrity of the progymnasmatic curriculum is respected except in order to bring prescriptive, educational categories into closer connection with the descriptive and critical aspects of Quintilian's Rhetoric: hence his strong emphasis on *sententia* (and on *narratio*) rather than on chreia as pivotal in primary and advanced practice and in theoretical analysis.

> The three passages, on the *primordia dicendi* (I 9), on the later *progymnasmata* (II 4) and on *sententia* (VIII 5), are the most articulate link available between the *Progymnasmata* and the rest of ancient Rhetorical theory and practice.[45]

What we may learn from all this is, above all, that Theon and Quintilian witness a phase in progymnasmatic tradition prior to the establishment of a literary genre of textbook, called *Progymnasmata*, but well within the period of a fixed series of basic patterns. Among these especially the *primordia dicendi* (*mythos/fabella*, *diegema/ narratio*, gnome/*sententia* and chreia/*chria*) are a powerful common denominator between unpretentious literacy, rhetorical education and technical/philosophical theory. Both Theon and Quintilian emerge as critical and

---

[43] O'Neil, "Quintilianus," 138.

[44] Henderson, "Quintilian and the *Progymnasmata*," 89–90.

[45] Henderson, "Quintilian and the *Progymnasmata*," 99.

idiosyncratic observers of prevenient tradition. Of the two, however, it is Quintilian who with all his complexities represents the impressive continuity of progymnasmatic tradition from the first century on.

Reading Theon in the light of Quintilian and reading both in their entirety, not just selecting chreia excerpts, suggests that the pedagogical importance of the chreia was never so total as to obscure the practical and theoretical importance of gnomic rhetoric. Recognizing Theon's eccentricity and Quintilian's threefold interest, in basic education, in advanced technical rhetoric and in broad philosophical reflection on rhetoric, suggests wider horizons in which to ask ourselves about the relation of rhetoric to tradition.

By underlining *sententia*/gnome rather than chreia, Quintilian opens us to the technical and philosophical literatures, since among the *primordia dicendi*, only *sententia*/gnome is directly considered in the several registers of theoretical rhetoric. On the other hand, both Theon and Quintilian implicitly remind us that neither chreia nor gnome was created by educationists; both patterns have roots and uses in non-technical speech and tradition, roots which elite cultivation of education and rhetoric did not seek to sever.

The importance of the progymnasmatic tradition and of gnome-use in particular, is as a convergence of prestigious liberal rhetoric and still-popular speech forms. The gospel tradition, unlike early Christian epistolography, can be described in terms of these *primordia*. In this respect the gospels present a chosen rhetorical decorum, a rhetorical normativity, on the threshold between liberally-cultivated rhetoric and daily conversation. This liminal condition can best be described in its various aspects through study of gnomic rhetoric.

Gnome, chreia and **mythos** in rhetoric before progymnasmatic tradition

Gnome, chreia and *mythos* (fable) have long pre-rhetorical histories in the Greek-speaking world and beyond it; an important task for later will be to model an approach to gnome which will do justice both to its specifically Hellenistic, rhetorical qualities and to its cross-cultural influence. It would be impossible here to attempt a full history of any of these. It is essential, however, to note that all these patterns were already ancient—and were already cultivated for use in public speech—before the period of Christian origins, indeed before the period of progymnasmatic education. All three provided material for relatively homogeneous literary collections, so that they can in part be treated as sub-genres for collection-literatures (*Sammelgattungen*). All three also figured, no doubt, in training the young to speak well and to pass verbal judgement on the behaviour of others. Yet rhetorical theory and actual texts confirm that each was also used in every genre of rhetoric, at every educational and social level throughout antiquity.[46]

The Greek fable-tradition presents particular challenges: its antiquity is attested by close parallels with near eastern stories and its continuity in Greek is evident from inclusion of such tales in literary texts from Hesiod on. Nevertheless, the oldest extant collections are from the first or second century AD; surviving collections mostly owe their preservation to the lasting influence of progymnasmatic education on Byzantine and Renaissance taste. The older, lost collections seem to have been made "mostly for practical reasons: for use by writers and speakers."[47] Easterling notes

> that in our earliest examples the fable is normally addressed to a particular person and is used as a means of remarking on his behaviour.... More often than not there is a marked element of wit in the way the story is formulated, and fables were clearly used for attacking opponents as well as for light entertainment.[48]

Plato's ambivalent, sometimes ironic fascination with *mythos* is well known: Plato's Socrates dabbles in versifying prose fables; theological myths are subjected to ethical critique; yet demythologizing by scientific allegory is also rejected; early pedagogical use of myths is presupposed

---

[46] Berger, "Hellenistische Gattungen," 1049–74 (Gnome, Hypotheke, sententia); 1074–5 (Ainos, Fabel); 1092–1110 (Chrie, Apophthegma, Anekdote), treats these under symbouleutic rhetorical genres; in his later synthesis, K. Berger, *Formgeschichte des Neuen Testaments* (Heidelberg, 1984) 40–59 (Gleichnisse); 62–67 (Sentenzen); 80–93 (Chrie, Apoftegma), he treats them instead (with Argumentation) under *Sammelgattungen*. On *mythos*, see also A. Hausrath, "Fabel," *PW* VI (1909) 1704–36; B.E. Perry, *Aesopica* I (Urbana, IL, 1952); on *gnome* and gnomic collections, see K. Horna and K. von Fritz, "Gnome, Gnomendichtung, Gnomologien," *PWSup* VI (1935) 74–90. For a list of edited gnomologia and *chreia*-collections, see J.S. Kloppenborg, *Formation of Q* (Philadelphia, 1987) Appendix I 337–41.

[47] W.M.A. Grimaldi, *Aristotle, "Rhetoric" II: A Commentary* (New York, 1988) 252, on *Rh.* II 20=1393a 30–31; see Easterling, "Fable," 142.

[48] Easterling, "Fable," 141.

and reformed, preparing the way for Plato's massive experiments in political and metaphysical myth-making.[49] Aristotle recognized, as Plato dramatized, the rhetorical usefulness of fables as one species of *paradeigma*.[50] For both Plato and Aristotle, fables are a basic part of rhetorical practice and theory and never primarily a didactic instrument. Plato, in addition, attests their early pedagogical use and criticizes it from a point of view which, indeed, subsumes pedagogy under political rhetoric.

The history of chreia and related anecdotal styles is more densely attested, but the terminological problem is greater; there is much overlap of meaning among chreia, gnome, *apophthegma*, and *apomnemoneuma* as species of pointed saying and/or anecdote. The latter two categories were long and extensively used, but never closely defined as technical terms; hence the attractive imprecision of "apophthegm" for Bultmann. The chreia pattern, though not the name, is easily recognizable in the philosophical literature of the Socratic milieu.[51] The plural title, '*Chreiai* of X,' with the related titles '*Apomnemoneumata...*' and '*Diatribai...*', rapidly became common to name a philosophical collection-genre; the singular, chreia, to designate the individual formal units may have been an innovation of the progymnasmatic tradition as it adopted a pre-existent style of philosophical propaganda (i.e. rhetoric) for the training of adolescents.

> The term *chreia* does not provide any information concerning the form, but seems to be used originally as a collective term for the different types already mentioned, stressing their usefulness.... It is commonly held that the use of the term *chreia* for shorter items originated in the Cynic school, but even if this is doubtful, there is a strong connection between the *chreia* and

---

[49] See *Phd.* 60c–61c; *Euthphr.* 6a–c; *Phdr.* 229c–230b; *Resp.* 2.377b–392d, 3.414b–415d.

[50] *Rh.* 2.20=1393a, 22–1394a 18; see Plato *Resp.* 2.376e; Aristotle calls fables *logoi* rather than *mythoi*, though he can speak of *mythologein*, 2.21=1395a 5; see Theon *Prog.* 3,174 Spengel 73.

[51] Plato *Resp.* I 329b–c, noted by Theon *Prog.* 2,158–159 Spengel 66; Xenophon *Mem.* [=*Apomnemoneumata*] *passim*.

the Cynics.... The first known collector of *chreiai* is also a Cynic, Metrocles (Diog. Laert. VI 33).[52]

Again, the point for the moment is that the chreia, closely associated with critical and activist rhetorics in the Cynic, Stoic, Christian and Rabbinic traditions, entered the progymnasmatic repertoire not just because it was a didactic style, but because it was an effective rhetorical tool, especially for dramatizing relatively radical philosophical traditions. Hence in part Theon's ambivalence, interpreted by Mack as part of a "shift in sensibility," calling for censorious selection of approved characterizations, but pragmatically exemplifying every kind of rhetorical "pointedness."

Theon and the later progymnasmatists prescribe for chreia not only "pointedness," but also, by way of etymology, "usefulness" and "helpfulness": at least for education, one should prefer, though not even Theon really does, chreiai which are *chrestos* or *chreiodes* (or *biopheles*). Nonetheless, the usefulness which really characterizes chreia both in the rhetoricians' examples and in the philosophers' collections (Diogenes Laertius *passim*) is seldom the usefulness of an exemplary moral; instead, the essential usefulness of the chreia is the rhetorical usefulness of versatility and memorable pointedness.[53]

Greek politics, philosophy, literature and rhetoric and, hence, Greco-Roman pre-rhetorical pedagogy took to *mythos* and chreia because of their usefulness in argumentation, dramatization, illustration and characterization—not because of their moral utility. The same is true of gnome which was also the earliest of these patterns to become a technical term, normatively defined in the same way for philosophical, juridical, rhetorical and pedagogical contexts.

---

[52] J.F. Kindstrand, "Diogenes Laertius and the '*Chreia*' Tradition," *Elenchos* 7 (1986) 217–43, 223; see also useful overviews of *chreia*-literature in Hock, "General Introduction," 1–9; H.A. Fischel, "Transformation," 376ff.

[53] Against F. Trouillet, "Les sens du mot Χρεία des origines à son emploi rhétorique," *Formes brèves: De la* γνώμη *à la pointe: métamorphoses de la "sententia"=La Licorne* 3 (1979) 41–64, and R.A. Spencer, *A Study of the Form and Function of the Biographical Apophthegms in the Synoptic Tradition in the Light of their Hellenistic Background* (Ph.D. diss.; microfilm Ann Arbor, MI, 1979) 90, 158–60, cited by J.D. Crossan, "Kingdom and Children: A Study in the Aphoristic Tradition," in *Kingdom and Children: Aphorism, Chreia, Structure*, ed. D. Patte=*Semeia* 29 (1983) 75–95, 77.

> *Gnome* indicates a short saying, in poetry or prose, with a general
> application and a moral intention, the Latin equivalent being *sententia*. We
> know the word with this technical meaning at least from Xenophon,
> Isocrates and Aristotle.[54]

As with *mythos* and chreia, we shall have to ask what "general
application" and "moral intention" meant in rhetorical practice, and how
they attached to actual gnomai. But the evidence for gnome-use and
reflection on gnome-use in antiquity permits an exceptionally nuanced
answer.

Gnome (and chreia) in rhetorical theory

Unlike chreia and far more extensively than *mythos*, gnome received
critical attention before incorporation into the tradition of the
progymnasmata. Gnomic rhetoric is prominent in at least three
distinctive levels of rhetorical tradition, in technical manuals, in
philosophical rhetorics and in the *Progymnasmata*. Of these, only the
Progymnasmata document anything like a direct influence on early
Christian literature, so that we may say with moral certainty that anyone
able to write or read out a gospel would have come into contact with
at least the *primordia dicendi* of the progymnasmatic curriculum. The
more advanced manuals of rhetoric (*technai rhetoricai*), written under
Sophistic or philosophical influence, remain indispensable, however,
precisely because they are theoretical and descriptive. Such texts
provide—from the side of antiquity—a theoretical basis for crossing the
gap between ancient rhetorical culture and modern rereading of early
Christian texts.

Any attempt to interpret early Christian rhetoric, especially gospel
and pre-gospel rhetoric, in the light of progymnasmatic tradition will be
obliged not only to interpolate between the *Progymnasmata* and the
gospels. It will also be necessary to abstract a theoretical model for
rhetorical tradition to guide and interpret comparison with a reconstructed tradition of rhetoric about Jesus. Mack and Robbins have not
been unaware of this constructive necessity; they recognize that their
work has "positioned the elaboration pattern as a bridge from the larger

---

[54] Kindstrand, "Diogenes Laertius," 221; see Horna and von Fritz, "Gnome," 74.

field of advanced rhetorical theory to the rhetoric of gnomic and biographic compositions."[55] For them the key theoretical construct is that of the "complete argument(ation)," under which the "pattern of elaboration" is subsumed. Mack and Robbins use the complete argumentation to bridge a general understanding of the "rhetorical culture" of antiquity and the socio-rhetorical argumentation theory of late modernity. That is, the progymnasmatic patterns of expansion, elaboration, abbreviation and so on are interpreted as instances of a higher order rhetorical pattern.

I have complained above that Mack and Robbins' "complete argument(ation)" distorts ancient rhetorical culture in the direction of modern argumentation theory and cultural anthropology[56] and that elaboration and other basic patterns cannot be understood solely from the point of view of argumentation. They are quite right, however, to look for patterns also in the use of patterns: the patterns which govern progymnasmatic elaboration may well also inform Hellenistic notions of completeness and persuasiveness in the argumentational sub-genre (*absolutissima et perfectissima argumentatio* [*Rh. ad Herennium* 2.18]) and in the standard format for whole speeches. Within such patterns, recurring at every level of rhetorical composition and appreciation, forms, topics and turns of speech could combine and recombine at the leisure of speaker and audience.

The *rapprochement* of progymnasmatic and gospel rhetorics therefore demands more than knowledge of the *Progymnasmata* and of the gospels, more even than critical candour about contemporary scholarly loyalties and interests. It is necessary somehow to do justice to the pervasive quality of Greco-Roman rhetorical culture as a whole. Among the *primordia dicendi* (chreia, gnome, *mythos* and *diegema*) and their progymnasmatic elaborations, only gnome designates such an explicit, continuous and comprehensive strand in rhetorical theory, performance and education, especially if we at all distrust ancient or modern tendencies to reduce rhetoric to argumentation.

Yet even gnome must be studied as a paradigmatic part of the larger and organically developing whole of Greco-Roman rhetorical culture. Moreover, it will still be necessary to relate ancient gnomic rhetorical patterns to the categories of modern cross-cultural and sociolinguistic

---

[55] Mack and Robbins, *Patterns*, 200.
[56] See Robbins, "Pre-Gospel Traditions," 113–115.

theory as a critical corrective both to the universalist pretensions of
Hellenism and to those of modern argumentation theory. Our eventual
definition of gnome will thus be in some respects no less a modern
construct than Mack and Robbins' "complete argument(ation)," though
a modern construct which may better claim to represent and interpret
ancient theoretical rhetoric, progymnasmatic rhetoric and gospel
rhetoric.

Thus from an argumentation-critical point of view, the absence of
the chreia from the advanced handbooks before Quintilian can only be
an accident of date: the *technai* predate the progymnasmatists' reception
of the literary chreia form as a model for primary oratorical instruction
and argumentative elaboration. But the difference between the interests
of the *technai* and those of the progymnasmata is no mere accident of
chronology. As far as it is possible to reconstruct such origins, gnome
and not chreia had a special role in the fifth-century BC transition from
social admiration for gifted public speech and its speakers to technical
cultivation.

Gnome in the transition from orality to liberal rhetoricity: the Sophistic
techne (Gorgias and Anaximenes)

Often too much has been made of the revolutionary shift from cultural
orality to a new mentality conditioned by unprecedented literacy in
Athenian society. The issue remains doubly unavoidable, however: the
invention of rhetoric and the florescence of literature are both characteristic symptoms of deep changes in sensibility between archaic and
classical Athens, changes which proved decisive for western culture.
And the issue is equally central to the development of a rhetorical
model to connect early Christian literary production with early
Christian, especially pre-gospel, oral tradition and propaganda. Indeed
an important task for rhetorical criticism is to debate the extent of
analogy between early Christian transition from oral tradition to literary
production and canonization and the classical transition in earlier Greek
experience.[57] Athens and Jerusalem have at least this in common, that

---

[57] The seminal works are: Eric A. Havelock, *Preface to Plato* (Cambridge, MA,
1963); Havelock, *Origins of Western Literacy* (Ontario Institute for Studies in Education
14; Toronto, 1976); Havelock, *The Literate Revolution in Greece and Its Cultural*

each in turn used Greek literacy to effect an ideological-rhetorical-literary revolution.

The first documented steps toward distinguishing rhetoric from either inspired poetry or naturally gifted talk are those of the older Sophists, Protagoras (c. 480–c. 420 BC), Gorgias (c. 480–c. 375 BC), Critias (c.460–c.403 BC), Alcidamas (fl. c. 390 BC) and Anaximemes (c. 380–c. 320 BC).[58] The Sophistic project of defining and marketing a teachable system (*techne*) of effective public speaking is best characterized by Gorgias' pioneering attempt to adapt verse effects to produce a new quality of public prose. The first technical rhetoric was thus a systematically, consciously 'poetized' prose applied to public discourse. This novel rhetoric was defined by intense exploitation and virtuosic control over a limited range of hitherto verse figures of contrast, balance or parallelism:

isocolon—clauses of equivalent syllabic length;
parison—syntactical parallelism;
antithesis—semantic contrast in syntactical parallelism;
alliteration;
homoioteleuton—corresponding words or word-series with like endings, especially at the ends of clauses;

Consequences (Princeton, NJ, 1982); Havelock, *The Muse Learns to Write: Reflections on Orality and Literacy from Antiquity to the Present* (New Haven and London, 1986); W.J. Ong, *Interfaces of the Word: Studies in the Evolution of Consciousness and Culture* (Ithaca and London, 1977); Ong, *Orality and Literacy: The Technologizing of the Word* (London and New York, 1982). More specifically see J. Poulakos, *Sophistical Rhetoric in Classical Greece* (Columbia, SC, 1995); O'Sullivan, *Greek Stylistic Theory*; S.C. Jarratt, *Rereading the Sophists: Classical Rhetoric Refigured* (Carbondale, IL, 1991); T.M. Lentz, *Orality and Literacy in Hellenic Greece* (Carbondale, IL, 1989); J. de Romilly, *Magic and Rhetoric in Ancient Greece* (Cambridge, MA, 1975); R. Thomas, *Oral Tradition and Written Record in Classical Athens* (Cambridge, 1989); Harris, *Ancient Literacy* 45–115. For the gospel tradition see W.H. Kelber, *The Oral and the Written Gospel: The Hermeneutics of Speaking and Writing in the Synoptic Tradition, Mark, Paul and Q* (Philadelphia, 1983); L.H. Silberman, ed., *Orality, Aurality and Biblical Narrative=Semeia* 39 (1987); P.J. Achtemeier, "*Omne verbum sonat*: The New Testament and the Oral Environment of late Western Antiquity," *JBL* 109 (1990) 3–27; I.H. Henderson, "*Didache* and Orality in Synoptic Comparison," *JBL* 111 (1992) 283–306; Robbins, "Pre-Gospel Traditions," 116–8.

[58] English translations in R.K. Sprague, ed., *The Older Sophists* (Columbia, SC, 1972); texts, H. Diels and W. Kranz, eds., *Fragmente der Vorsokratiker* 3 vols. (7th ed.; Berlin, 1951–54).

polyptoton—repeating root-words with variation by inflection[59]

Hypnotic use of such 'Gorgianic' figures is typical of the extant fragments not only of Gorgias' but also more or less of Antiphon's and Alcidamas' speeches. Their stylistic repertoire corresponds tantalizingly to twentieth-century characterizations of "oral style"[60]—and of ancient near eastern literary poetry and wisdom. The Gorgianic style and related Sophistic styles constituted an 'oral style' only in the most relative and manneristic sense. The sophists were deliberately transplanting conventions of oral verse for intense, literate cultivation in the new soil of public rhetoric and technical training. In this way their rhetoric may helpfully be seen as intermediate between the valued speech of gifted councillors and the literary discourse of classical philosophy.

Certainly within a generation of Gorgias' death the style he successfully modelled and taught sounded bizarre, vulgar, mannered and dated (Aristotle *Rh.* 3.1.9=1404a; 3.3=1406a-b)—as indeed it appears to modern tastes. It is important to remember therefore, that in its own brief day it was sensationally powerful; both its proponents and its critics agree that it worked and that its effects were magical and narcotic. Unlike Aristotle and later writers, Isocrates and Plato do not attack Gorgias and the other sophists for stylistic excesses. Instead, both Isocrates and Plato treat the sophists as dangerously successful rhetorical wizards whose spells can be broken only by a new, philosophical, self-critical rhetoric—a new rhetoric which not incidentally expressed itself in written, not performed, prose. Throughout the dialogues with or about the sophists, Plato's Socrates thus opposes the white magic of the dialectic to the bewitchment of the sophistic *techne*, a bewitchment which is acknowledged even when Socrates himself practises it.[61]

The Socratics thus sought to modify the threefold relation of orality-rhetoricity-literacy by inserting and privileging a fourth term, logicality.

---

[59]   G.A. Kennedy, "Sophists and physicians of the Greek enlightenment," *Cambridge History of Classical Literature* I,3 (1989) 60–65, 62; J.J. Murphy, *A Synoptic History of Classical Rhetoric* (Davis, CA, 1983) 10–12.

[60]   See Ong, *Orality and Literacy*, 40; Kelber, *The Oral and the Written Gospel*, 38; Berger, *Einführung*, 109–11; M. Jousse, *Le style orale: rythmique et mnemotechnique* (Paris, 1925); Lentz, *Orality and Literacy in Hellenic Greece*, 139–40.

[61]   *Menex.* 235a-c; *Prt.* 315a-b, 328d; *Euthd.* 289–90; *Soph.* 233a, 234c, 255a; and *Phdr.* 238–41; see R.J. Connors, "Greek Rhetoric and the Transition From Orality," *Philosophy and Rhetoric* 19/1 (1986) 44–54.

Apart from its historic influence, Gorgianic and Sophistic rhetoric may thus have a special relevance for literature produced on the threshold between oral tradition and literary canonization. In early Christianity, too, we may discern analogous movement in the mediation of orality and literacy through rhetoricity (prophecy and gospel) and logicality (theology and canonicity). In both instances, change in rhetorical taste and attitudes to oral tradition seem more than coincidentally allied with the florescence of literary production.

Be that as it may, Gorgianic and Sophistic rhetorics cannot be understood in terms of stylistics alone; the Socratics attacked and vilified 'sophistry' instead for its bewitching preference for emotional effects (*pathos*) over argumentation as the dominant means of persuasion. The enchanting, incantatory style of sophistic rhetoric was calculated to impress more than to convince. For Gorgias, "Speech is a powerful lord...; it can stop fear and banish grief and create joy and nurture pity" (*Encomium of Helen* 8).[62] It is vitally suggestive, then, that 'gnome' first became a technical term among the Sophists and is a leading feature of their surviving fragments; at least in its originating rhetorical use, gnome is clearly not a specialized sign of formal argumentation.

The first attestation of gnome as a technical term in rhetoric is in Aristophanes' parody of Sophistic discourse in the *Clouds*.[63] The overheated gnome-use which Aristophanes attributes to the sophist—labelled "maxim-forming" (*gnomotypos*) or even "maxim-formative" (*gnomotypicos*)—[64]is no mere repetition of time-honoured wisdom; on the contrary, the Sophists' pupil is taught to use and to create gnomic maxims to manipulate and subvert traditional norms.[65] The same process is elegantly lampooned at the climax of Socrates' pseudo-sophistic discourse in the *Phaedrus* (241d), but it is massively embodied in the actual speeches of the Sophists, e.g., in the probably pseudo-Isocratean *To Demonicus*, in which gnomic and antithetical language

---

[62] Sprague, *Older Sophists*, 52.

[63] *Nub.* 896, 924, 948, 1037, 1045, 1084, 1314.

[64] Sinclair, "*Sententia* in *Rhetorica ad Herennium*," 564 n.12.

[65] J.P. Levet, "'ΡΗΤΩΡ et ΓΝΩΜΗ, Présentation sémantique et recherches isocratiques," in *Formes brèves: De la γνώμη à la pointe: métamorphoses de la "sententia"=La Licorne* 3 (1979) 9–40, 34.

provides an important compositional device which at the same time surrounds the sophistic new man in an aura of aristocratic nostalgia.

Sophistic rhetoric, like its Platonic and Aristophanic parodies, was typically punctuated with gnomai, working neither as argumentations nor as mere ornaments. In addition, the Sophistic *techne* itself found typical expression in distinctive, counter-traditional gnomai, most famously in the maxims of Protagoras, but also in the lists which seem to have preceded the Sophists' composition of the first written manuals of rhetoric (*technai*).

> The Sophists applied writing's ability to preserve maxims to the collection of stylistic devices, with the result that a revolution had begun.... [T]his use of poetic devices and maxims, which taught through the oral tradition of memory, still relied upon writing. The ancients preserved in written form the discourses that the students learned as well as the devices and antithetical maxims that they practised.... [W]e find extemporaneous speech itself is reliant upon written collections of topics and maxims.[66]

The Sophists' interest in gnome is thus an essential part of their invention of rhetoric as a *techne*. Technically, gnomai aided impromptu, virtuosic speech, the ancestor of progymnasmatic elaboration, and facilitated also retention of technical rhetorical principles. Thus Protagoras' gnomai constitute a virtual rhetorical *techne*: "There are two sides to every question"; "Man is the measure of all things"; "Make the weaker argument stronger." Substantively, gnomai embodied the sophistic subversion of traditional wisdom and that appeal to style and emotion over reason which the Socratics resented.

This is the context in which we should read the oldest extant rhetorical manual, the so-called *Rhetorica ad Alexandrum*, a fourth-century BC compendium of "'ready-made' phrases or tricks" in the Sophistic spirit "probably originally the work of Anaximenes of Lampsacus (ca. 380–320 B.C.)."[67] The reference to progymnasmatic

---

[66] Lentz, *Orality and Literacy in Hellenic Greece*, 137, 140; see Murphy, *Classical Rhetoric*, 7–11; R. Barilli, *Rhetoric* (Theory and History of Literature 63; Minneapolis, 1989) 3–6.

[67] Quoting Lentz, *Orality and Literacy in Hellenic Greece*, 138 and G. Kennedy, *Classical Rhetoric and its Christian and Secular Tradition from Ancient to Modern Times* (London, 1980) 22; see also Murphy, *Classical Rhetoric*, 78–80.

exercises (28.4=1436a 25) may be a later gloss.[68] It is quite clear, however, that only gnome among the *primordia dicendi* is treated, and in a way quite in keeping with the sophistic heritage. Gnome is therefore not treated as a literary allusion or as a commonplace of traditional morality, but as "the expression of an individual opinion on general matters" (11=1430b). The writer's assumption is clearly that most gnomai will be the orator's own, usually antithetic, formulations. The key distinction is thus not between traditional and new gnomai, but between gnomai which should be generally acceptable (*endoxos*) and those which are counter-intuitive (*paradoxos*) enough to risk alienating an audience. The latter should be accompanied with reasons.

This main treatment of gnome is among the rhetorical proofs (*pisteis*): "...probabilities, examples [*paradeigmata*], evidences, enthymemes, maxims [gnomai], signs and refutations" (7.2=1428a 20). It is important therefore to say something about ancient rhetorical expectations of 'proof' especially because, even at their most dialectic, these differ from modern expectations of argumentative, quasi-objective evidence. Modern conventions of logicality strongly favour material evidence (e.g., fingerprints, statistics) over either of the ancient rhetorical categories of proof: atechnical (witnesses, documents, oaths, confessions) and technical (issues of law and fact, emotions, prejudices and character of persons speaking and of the audience). This is not only because decisive material evidence is sometimes available in modernity as it almost never was in antiquity, but also because we think of proof as a corrective to that fallenness of human nature which makes courts and councils susceptible to technical rhetoric.

Ancient rhetoric begins from that susceptibility, though not always without protest. Here proof is anything which may dispose its hearer, intellectually or emotionally, toward the speaker's preferred option, especially if such proof is distilled into one of a few, brief conventional patterns (paradigm, enthymeme, gnome).

> For the persons who are to make the judgement after deliberation are individuals, each possessed of emotions, feelings, a certain character, and an intellect. Therefore, any effort to enable such an auditor to make a judgement must address itself to the whole person who is being asked to

---

[68] M. Fuhrmann, ed., *Anaximenis Ars Rhetorica* (Leipzig, 1966) 59.

attend to the evidence, and who then, in the light of it, will make an assertion for the truth of *this* rather than *that*.[69]

The semantic distance between rhetorical and theological senses of *pistis* is thus not so great as might appear,[70] and the relation between proof and argumentation is less exclusive. The *Rhetorica ad Alexandrum* recommends gnome as an impromptu technique for meeting interruptions and heckling and as an attractive way to mark the conclusion of a section.[71] In addition, gnomai and truncated enthymemes are recommended to make a speech elegant and to vary its length; gnomai are to be attached to every division of the speech and for reasons having little to do with argumentation.

The Socratic rectification of rhetoric (Aristotle)

Both Isocrates and Plato were critical of the Sophistic rhetorical *techne*. Both these admirers of Socrates called for an alternative, philosophical, ethical, and critical rhetoric, though each modelled this ideal distinctively in his own writings. Both rhetorical philosophers are aware of the sophistic use of gnomai and of gnome as a technical category, but show themselves reserved toward it.

Isocrates expresses an interesting ambivalence toward culling technically (*technicos*) refined gnomai from the poets (Isoc. *To Nicocles* 44), yet throughout the same composition freely expresses his own gnomai. It may be that Isocrates objected to the separation of technical ('maxim') and general ('personal opinion') meanings of 'gnome' which occurs when speakers, like the writer *To Demonicus*, borrow stock gnomai as well as composing their own.[72]

Plato's Socrates invents a gnome, deployed with other Gorgianic features to close his own pseudo-sophistic speech, but goes on to repudiate his speech and its concluding flourish as a blasphemous,

---

[69] Grimaldi, *Aristotle*, *"Rhetoric"* I, 349–56, "Appendix: The Role of the ΠΙΣΤΕΙΣ in Aristotle's Methodology."

[70] J.L. Kinneavy, *Greek Rhetorical Origins of Christian Faith* (New York, 1987).

[71] *Rh. Al.* 18.4=1432b 26; 18.10 =1433a 26. Also 32.6, 8=1439a 20, 35; 35.12, 15, 16=1441a 20, 39, 1441b 11.

[72] Levet, "Recherches isocratiques," 39.

intoxicated approximation of the authentic manic/mantic inspiration (*Phdr.* 241d–242e, *cf.* 267c).

Isocrates' programme for a responsible rhetoric became the norm for all higher education in Greco-Roman antiquity. It fell to Aristotle, however, to attempt the reconciliation of the Socratic dialectic to the Platonic vision of a psychagogic rhetoric. Wherever possible Aristotle's *Rhetoric* assimilates rhetoric to dialectic. Such is the influence of the sophistic achievement, however, that full assimilation is impossible: rhetoric remains the worthy correlative (*antistrophos*, *Rh.* I 1=1354a) of dialectic, distinguished not only by regrettable concessions to the illogicality of vulgar audiences, but also by the proper influence of (often gnomic) appeals to emotion, personal character and social solidarity. The Aristotelean project explicitly rests not only on initially assimilating as far as possible rhetoric and dialectics, but also on eventually distinguishing as far as possible rhetoric and poetics (*Rh.* III 1–4=1403b–1407a). Yet the three remain for him overlapping and complementary, yet distinct *technai* of discourse criticizing its communicative, argumentative and imaginative aspects.

Like Anaximenes, Aristotle treats gnome among rhetorical *pisteis*.[73] Unlike Anaximenes, Aristotle does not discuss gnome in other contexts as well. Because of Aristotle's agenda of dignifying rhetoric by coordinating it more closely with dialectics, it is all the more important to acknowledge that, even for him, rhetorical *pisteis* are 'proofs' in the pragmatic rhetorical sense that they usually, conventionally, work on audiences.[74] For Aristotle, "the general proofs are two in kind, example (*paradeigma*) and enthymeme, for a gnome is part of an enthymeme" (II 20,1=1393a). Enthymeme in turn is the rhetorical analogue to the syllogism in dialectics (I 2,8=1356b; II 21, 2=1394a; 22=1395b).

Aristotle thus locates gnome-use at the centre of his rhetorical project and at the same time confines it, as the sophists did not, by more rigorous subordination to enthymeme and *pistis*. This step not only attests Aristotle's ambivalence toward the non-probative uses of gnomai, it also betrays a latent ambiguity in Aristotle's definitions of proof forms. Aristotle's lengthy discussion of gnome does not in

---

[73] *Rh.* I 2,8=1356b; II 20–22=1393a–97a; see Anaximenes *Rh. Al.* 7,1–3=1428a; 11=1430b.

[74] Grimaldi, "ΠΙΣΤΕΙΣ."

practice succeed in treating gnomai as shorthand evocations of an implied enthymeme; indeed, the very fact that he must give gnome a long and independent chapter belies its equation with enthymeme.

More fundamentally, Aristotle never quite makes clear the limits of analogy between enthymeme (including gnome) and real syllogism. He is unwilling to say either that gnome and enthymeme are only vulgar or abbreviated expressions of syllogisms or that they are essentially unlike syllogisms after all. An enthymeme is not "simply a syllogism having a suppressed premise or conclusion."[75] A syllogism in rhetorical performance need not be formally deficient; at the same time, its rhetorical effects cannot be reduced to the logical force of any syllogism.

Aristotle candidly preferred virtual dialectics. Yet even in his hands rhetoric resists reduction to argumentation, enthymeme resists interpretation as syllogism, and gnome resists assimilation to enthymeme. A more illuminating topic in Aristotle's discussion is one which he inherits from the sophists, the relation between gnome and prior literary or proverbial tradition. This relationship between rhetoricity and traditionality (or, intertextuality) is, of course, also an essential topic for any rhetorical criticism of pre-gospel rhetorical tradition.[76]

I noted how Anaximenes insisted on "individual opinion" rather than tradition or allusion as the essence of gnome; each speaker's personal character is recognized behind the proverbial or quasi-proverbial tone of his gnome-use (*Rh. Al.* 11,1=1430b). So also the possibility of deliberately counter-intuitive (*paradoxos*) and hyperbolic gnomai is emphasized. And Isocrates shows his nervousness about mining gnomai from the poets (*To Nicocles* 44).

For Aristotle the probative quality of gnome is more definitive than it was for Anaximenes, because of the controlling analogy between rhetorical and dialectical proof. Aristotle therefore defines gnome as a generalization, distinct from, but analogous to, an axiom in geometry (21,2=1394a; 21,15=1395b). Even so, he clearly recognizes that gnome-use (*gnomologia*) is not an impersonal or straightforward appeal to traditional authority, be it popular, proverbial or classical. Aristotle says there are four types of gnome. Two are either (1) so familiar or (2) so clear as to require no explanation. Another type (3) includes an

---

[75] L. Bitzer, "Aristotle's Enthymeme Revisited," in *Aristotle: The Classical Heritage of Rhetoric*, ed. K.V. Erikson (Metuchen, NJ, 1974) 141–55, 149, 142–45.

[76] Robbins, "Pre-Gospel Traditions," 119–121.

explanatory clause (*epilogos*) which is clear enough to make a complete or almost complete enthymeme. The last type (4) also has some sort of *epilogos*, but is only implicitly enthymematic. These are the most esteemed. He twice insists that gnomai which are counter-intuitive (again, *paradoxos*) or debatable should have such a more or less explicit *epilogos* (*Rh.* II 21,3–8=1394b).[77]

Clearly, Aristotle anticipates not only traditional, but also personal, even *anti*-traditional gnome formulations. He recognizes that some gnomai may come from the proverb-tradition and actually prescribes directly contradicting such proverbial wisdom if it will help assert the speaker's chosen *ethos* or convey strong emotion (21,13–14=1394b). Because gnome-use reflects on the character of the speaker, Aristotle warns (*Rh.* II 21,9=1395a) that gnomic style must accord with the dignity and experience of the speaker: excessive gnome-use will make the young sound foolish and rustic. On the other hand, the main advantage of gnome-use is in establishing the character of the speaker and his rapport with the audience (21,16=1395b). Thus in the context of advising against overuse of enthymemes, Aristotle warns:

> Nor when speech is about character (*ethikon ton logon*) is it right to try for an ehymeme, for rhetorical demonstration can express neither character (*ethos*) nor judgement. It is appropriate to gnomai, however, both in narration and in proof (*pistis*), for gnome-use is about character (*ethikon*). (*Rh.* III 17,9=1418a)

The tension in Aristotle between the interpersonal quality of gnome and its alleged probative function is thus dramatically unresolved. If gnome is a proof (*pistis*) even in the qualified rhetorical sense, its stated advantage over other kinds of proof, enthymematic and paradigmatic, is its capacity for building speaker-audience rapport and for heightening emotion. Similarly, Aristotle emphasizes generalization in gnome. His treatment makes it clear, however, that the rhetorical effectiveness of gnomai, even as proof/argument, does not come from their real or perceived validity as generalizations, but from their pragmatic relevance to topics of general interest. An effective gnome may be obviously false, counter-intuitive or anti-traditional. Nor is gnome for Aristotle primarily a means of invoking tradition: some of his examples are

---

[77] Henderson, "Quintilian and the *Progymnasmata*."

literary quotations, some are proverbial and some are ad hoc compositions. Whatever it means to list gnome among the conventional proofs
(*pisteis*), the force of gnomic rhetoric in Aristotle does not depend on
its logicality, traditionality, or morality, but on its usefulness for
expressing and creating a speaker's self-characterization and audience
rapport.

Gnome and *sententia* (*Rhetorica ad Herennium*)

There are undeniable differences between classical Greek rhetoric and
its transplantation into Latin culture. On the technical and theoretical
level, however, the continuities are more striking. Moreover, the
difference between Classical and Greco-Roman is more important for
our enquiry into early Christian rhetoric than the difference between
Greek and Latin; the *Progymnasmata*, the Latin rhetoricians and early
Christianity are on the same side of this divide.

Both the differences and the continuities between Athenian
Enlightenment and its Greco-Roman institutionalization can be briefly
illustrated by comparing *sententia* in the *Rhetorica ad Herennium* with
gnome in Anaximenes' *Rhetorica ad Alexandrum*. Anaximenes includes
gnomai among the rhetorical *pisteis*, though without making
Aristotelean claims for the almost dialectic status of *pistis*. Moreover,
unlike Aristotle, the sophist freely refers to gnome in contexts having
little to do with argumentation. Above all, the gnomai of Anaximenes
and the other sophists, are means of imposing personal self-characterization and opinion on still (literally) unsophisticated audiences.

The audiences foreseen by the Rhetorica ad Herennium are no longer
rhetorically unsophisticated, but they retain a specifically Roman loyalty
to sententious aristocratic conventionalism. In this Roman, late
republican context, the writer *ad Herennium* is motivated by a sophistic
pragmatism to adopt an attitude toward gnome-use which looks
superficially quite unlike those of either the sophists or the
Aristoteleans. Patrick Sinclair's model study illustrates this paradoxical
relation, so I shall quote him extensively:

> Of his two most important Greek forerunners whose treatments of the
> *gnome* are still extant today, Aristotle and Anaximenes, the general attitude
> [of the Auctor *ad Herennium*] toward rhetoric is closer to the more "goal-

driven" spirit that animates and motivates the sophist. The portrait of the Auctor that emerges from *Rhetorica ad Herennium* is that of a man spurred mainly by social ambition and proudly self-reliant, in short, a late Republican *novus homo*.

The Auctor's pragmatic view of rhetoric actually eschews the moral and philosophical dimension of oratory...He is more concerned with admonishing his reader not to appear to overstep the bounds of social propriety by seeming to dictate morality or by exhibiting too much enthusiasm for philosophy. For this reason it is significant that his examples of *sententiae* draw upon the formal aspects of generally accepted and objectified statements of Roman morality, especially the laws, rather than being original formulations of his own personal code of moral beliefs.... The Auctor's treatment of the *sententia* brooks no scruples about sincerity; rather, it provides an ideal "*in nuce*" model for the rhetorical strategy of a practical-minded Roman with a career to make in the Sullan period.

It is against this background of antiphilosophical and anti-intellectual posturing among the educated elite that we should set the Auctor's cautionary precept for using *sententiae* only with discretion....[78]

The greatest difference between the author *ad Herennium* and his predecessors is thus the former's goal of conformity to the sententious-ly-stated values of a rhetorically-educated social elite, whereas the sophists and Anaximenes sought to create and then reform such a rhetorical matrix in their own image. Aristotle's advice against the young and inexperienced affecting a gnomic style (II 21,9=1395a) is amplified by the Latin writer into a warning against any frequent use of *sententiae*, lest the speaker sound too pretentiously moralistic (*Rh. ad H.* 4,25)—like a Greek professor.[79]

If a use of gnomai in the sophistic manner as a basic building block of discourse is thus excluded, an Aristotelean use of gnomai as basic argumentation forms is even less countenanced. Unlike Anaximenes and, surely consciously, against Aristotle's basic premise, the writer *ad Herennium* barely alludes to argumentational uses of *sententia* (4,25). Instead he treats *sententia* under "style" (*elocutio*) dwelling at length on its usefulness for "embellishment" (*exornatio*, 4,24–5, *cf.* 4,18), especially of discourse in the "middle style" (4,11–16).

---

[78] Sinclair, "*Sententia* in *Rhetorica ad Herennium*," 565, 562, 564–5.
[79] Sinclair, "*Sententia* in *Rhetorica ad Herennium*," 564 n.12.

Analysing the examples of *sententia* in the *Rhetorica ad Herennium*, Sinclair shows how closely they reflect "the style of Roman legal formulae."[80] Notwithstanding this emphatic conventionality, the writer fiercely denounces writers on rhetoric who borrow examples—especially examples of *sententia*—from literature rather than composing their own illustrations as he does (4,1–10, esp. 6–7).

> While many of the examples the Auctor uses are identifiable as adaptations from other orators, [and] writers,...his insistence on a speaker's originality is not for that reason fraudulent...[T]he Auctor anticipates winning the reader's admiration with his ability to inject new life and vigor into a cliché or a familiar notion.... [T]his sort of "creative quotation" is intended to demonstrate the soundness of his education and the integrity of his social and ethical values. The Auctor thereby reinforces his connections with the reader by implying that both are thoroughly erudite—that they are essentially "graduates of the same school."[81]

As for the sophists so for the *ad Herennium*, gnomai work primarily as vehicles for rhetorical *ethos*, for self-characterization and for establishing or adjusting audience rapport. Argumentation and the expression of any actual moral or social loyalties are secondary. The sophists used gnomai to revolutionize public speech; the writer *ad Herennium* uses *sententiae* rather to identify himself with an exclusive educational and political elite. Theon and the *Progymnasmata* seem, by the way, to use gnomai to bridge the growing gap between educational and political elites. My guess is that behind the production and success of progymnasmatic curricula lies the agenda of using education to access and assert an often fragile solidarity among local, regional and imperial elites.

All agree, however, in using gnomic rhetoric to project a sometimes fictional rapport between a speaker and his hoped-for audience within some larger imagined public milieu. This "ethical" function controls the relation of gnome-composition, selection and variation to argumentation and to traditions of public language, whether literary, proverbial or legal. In terms of an earlier distinction between rhetorical normativity and social normativity, gnomic rhetoric in the *ad Herennium* is a surprisingly important way for the writer to create a rhetorical normativ-

---

[80] Sinclair, "*Sententia* in *Rhetorica ad Herennium*," 576.
[81] Sinclair, "*Sententia* in *Rhetorica ad Herennium*," 567–8.

ity which will mimic the perceived social normativity of a social elite to which the writer wishes to assimilate himself. The sophists made a more revolutionary use of the rhetorical normativity in gnomic rhetoric to transform social consciousness. In these differing cases, however, the use of gnomai to sketch a programmatic, rhetorical normativity is radically similar.

The imperial synthesis (Quintilian)

By far the richest source for locating gnome-use in the theory and practice of Greco-Roman rhetoric is Quintilian's *Institutio Oratoria* ("Training of an Orator") written before the end of the first century AD under imperial patronage. As its title implies it embraces the whole training of an orator and synthesizes along the way all the major strands of rhetorical education, practice, and criticism, Greek and Latin. Quintilian's work is particularly important for historical criticism of early Christian rhetoric because he explicitly and fairly transparently links the history of technical and philosophical rhetoric with less exalted levels of contemporary education and performance practice. Quintilian is the only author in antiquity who systematically connects all the different registers of rhetorical theory, training and performance. In particular, his *Institutio Oratoria* is the only text to discuss both the progymnasmata and the topics of the technical manuals. In so doing, he underlines the centrality of gnomic speech to both educational and technical rhetoric by discussing *sententia* twice: in *Institutio Oratoria* I 9 it appears among other basic progymnasmata, while in VIII 5 Quintilian deals exclusively with *sententia* in technical and philosophical tradition and in contemporary performance vices.

I have already argued above for the primacy of Quintilian over Theon as a general guide to progymnasmatic tradition as it was usually practised in the period of Christian origins—and I present the case elsewhere in greater detail.[82] Quintilian's most important testimony about the progymnasmata is his early attestation (I 9; II 4) of the order which, with minor variations reappears in all the Greek *Progymnasmata* except Theon.[83] In addition, his *primordia dicendi* (*fabella* [=*mythos*],

---

[82] Henderson, "Quintilian and the *Progymnasmata*."
[83] Henderson, "Quintilian and the *Progymnasmata*," 90–4, esp. 93, table 1.

sententia [=*gnome*], *chria*, *aetiologia* [whatever that is!] and
narratiuncula [=*diegesis*?]) demarcate a level of schooling which would
have been accessible and affordable at the social and regional margins
of elite culture. This is, in fact, why Quintilian can so briefly scan this
part of the curriculum (I 9,1); he mentions the *primordia* only to
indicate precisely the outer threshold of the more prestigious education
which really interests an imperial professor of rhetoric. It is no
coincidence that Quintilian's *dicendi primordia* precisely describe the
rhetorical competence demanded of their readers by the Christian
gospels.

We noticed above that Quintilian returns to discuss each of the
primordia, except chreia, in later, more theoretical contexts. Of these
reprises, the discussion of *sententia* (*Inst.* VIII 5) is by far the most
extensive and important. In it Quintilian seeks to draw together the
sophistic tradition of enchantment with gnome, the Aristotelean
argumentational tradition and the still problematic role of *sententia* in
Roman oratory. Quintilian's general approach is always to seek a
middle way between extremes. This strategy is nowhere more apparent
than in his discussion of *sententia*.

Quintilian thus initially sets up two extremes, the modern fashion of
excessive use of *sententiae* and an old-fashioned renunciation of such
frills (*Inst.* VIII 5,25). Quintilian is unwilling to condemn globally
either fashionable or conservative attitudes to *sententia*. Instead he
strongly opposes overuse and abuse of gnomic language generally as
vices prevalent in the rhetoric of his day. The extreme of rhetorical
austerity seems largely a myth of the Roman past; the extreme of
sententious mannerism seems more real in Quintilian's experience (*Inst.*
VIII 5,13–14. 30–34).

At any rate, Quintilian favours moderate use—and lively formulation—of *sententiae*. But such a position requires him, like the *Rhetorica
ad Herennium*, to treat *sententia* under embellishment (*ornatus*) rather
than with elemental forms of argumentation as in Aristotle: if *sententia*
were really one of a very few basic, compulsory argumentation forms,
overuse could hardly be a modern vice and avoidance could hardly be
a sign of honourable, if old-fashioned, austerity.

At the same time, Quintilian discreetly shifts away from contrasting
excessive gnome-use and avoidance of gnome-use, toward a less
absolute contrast between old-style gnomai and newfangled gnomai. In
general, Quintilian prefers the old-style gnomai, but sees good also in

the new—used with restraint (*Inst.* XII 10,48; VIII 5,32–33). There are good and bad in each style (5,19). Thus the vice of too frequent and too facile use applies to both styles (see 5,14) and both styles can benefit from livelier formulation (5,6. 15–19).[84]

All this equivocation is interesting in itself. It is not only typical of Quintilian's harmonizing tendency; it reflects the fact that in Quintilian's day the handling of gnome/*sententia* was still an important and apparently controversial criterion for evaluating style. The dispute between 'Atticists' and 'Asianists' in Greek and Roman rhetoric around the beginning of the Christian era is notoriously muddled: 'Asianist' is an all too adaptable term of abuse. It is important, however, that elite political-rhetorical culture could marginalize as exotic—non-Roman or non-Attic—any style marked by gnomic and epigrammatic mannerism and by stylistic, personal or emotional effects. Thus both Cicero and Quintilian must work hard to defend the occasional propriety of an Asianic reliance on sententious balance and liveliness.[85]

Some aspects of Quintilian's analysis, moreover, go beyond his pose as mediator between extremes of contemporary practice. In keeping with his semi-official status as encyclopedist of rhetoric, Quintilian does not explicitly mark his personal contribution. His taxonomy of sub-types of *sententia* is not especially interesting except for the general principle that *sententiae* should be varied by means of the whole repertoire of rhetorical figures and that such figuration enhances the force of gnomic rhetoric (VIII 5,5–6).

For the very first time in rhetorical literature, Quintilian takes the further step of discussing *sententiae* in which personality is explicitly emphasized and approved. Having set *sententiae* free from the constraints of Aristotelean argumentation theory by moving it into *ornatus*, Quintilian goes on to canonize the turn away from pseudo-generalization to explicit personal characterization, the turn *a communi ad proprium* or *ad personam*. It is one thing for someone to say, "It is easy to harm, hard to help." It is quite another thing—significantly more powerful (5,5–8)—for Ovid's Medea to say, in character, "I was able to save him; do you ask whether I can lose him?" Still other examples

---

[84] Henderson, "Quintilian and the *Progymnasmata*," 83–4.

[85] Cic. *Brut.* 95, 325–7, *concinnitas illa crebretasque sententiarum*; *Orat.* 49, 165; Quint. *Inst.* VIII 4, 29; 5, 15–34; XII 10,48.

are *ad personam* because they specifically comment on one of the Caesars (5,3. 7. 15–16. 18).

These latter styles, by the way, account for the rhetorical usefulness of the sayings-chreia, though Quintilian does not bother to say this. The sayings-chreia allows a speaker to borrow another speaker's self-characterization. What is more important by far is that Aristotle would not even have recognized Medea's passionate self-assertion as a gnome. Aristotle's reductive concern for argumentation forms is in this respect a rhetorical blind alley from which Quintilian delivers us.

> In fact we have seen, from Aristotle to Quintilian, this type of gnome or *sententia* regain little by little the autonomy which it had lost.... *Sententia* remains a general form, but it is above all the privileged and unique point of contact between the individual and the universal.[86]

Certainly, the Jesus of gospel gnomic tradition resembles Ovid's Medea more than either resembles Aristotle's orator. That is, it is often (not always) decisive for understanding gnomai in early Christian contexts to ask whether Jesus is or is not the putative speaker. A very few gnomai ("Let the dead bury their dead") make little sense any other way.

Quintilian does not explicitly acknowledge his undoing here of the Aristotelean revolution, but he leaves no chance of overlooking his correction of Aristotle. Quintilian warns that highly personal *sententiae* should be used mainly by those whose stature (*auctoritas*) is such that their character assertion will add weight to their case (*...ut rei pondus etiam persona confirmet* [*Inst.* VIII 5,8]). Quintilian's language recalls Aristotle's warning (*Rh.* II 21,9=1395a) that gnomic style is only appropriate to the aged and experienced speaker. Yet Quintilian applies the warning solely to his own anti-Aristotelean category of *sententia ad personam*.

In addition, Quintilian goes on from his discussion of strongly personal *sententiae* to discuss the Aristotelean topic of the relation of gnome, enthymeme and syllogism. The Latin writer agrees with his predecessor that *sententia* and enthymeme and syllogism often overlap: an enthymeme is the rhetorical performance or imitation of syllogistic

---

[86] F. Delarue, "La sententia chez Quintilien," *Formes brèves: De la γνώμη à la pointe: métamorphoses de la "sententia"=La Licorne* 3 (1979) 97–124, 105–6.

argument (V 14; *cf.* I 10,38; IX 4,57), so it may be part of a syllogism (V 14,24) or it may be a pseudo-syllogism (V 10,3). A *sententia* in turn may be a compact enthymeme or part of one, as in Aristotle (*Inst.* VIII 5,4; *Rh.* II 21,6=1394b).

Few ancient rhetoricians other than Aristotle cared much about analogy between rhetoric and dialectics or, consequently, about analogy between enthymematic argumentation and syllogistic reasoning. Quintilian points out that he has already discussed enthymeme under argumentation, but that an enthymeme is not always used argumentatively; its relation to *sententia* proves that enthymeme is sometimes decorative. For Quintilian, as for Anaximenes and Cicero, enthymeme can be a form of argumentation or a figure of speech, depending on context. What is practically essential is that enthymeme plays with some sort of opposition.[87] In the un-Aristotelean context of ornamentation, an enthymeme may even be said to be strictly (*proprie*) a *sententia ex contrariis* (*Inst.* V 5,9). In such *sententiae* the effective opposition need not be syllogistic; it is more often the sort of contrast the old sophists rejoiced in: "The wretch, though he could not speak, could not shut up" (V 5,18).

In at least two respects, then, Quintilian's digest of the tradition of technical and philosophical rhetoric achieves unprecedented clarity with regard to gnome/*sententia*. Quintilian makes explicit two key insights which Aristotle's influence somewhat clouded: gnomic rhetoric often succeeds by characterizing the (actual or imagined) speaker or addressee (*ad personam*) and/or by juxtaposing (logical or semantic) opposites (*sententia ex contrariis*). It is important to remind ourselves that, while Quintilian is more explicit and more approving of these qualities of gnomic rhetoric, they are central to the whole tradition from the sophists on, so that even Aristotle must make room for them. Quintilian's formulations can thus provide the basic framework for a historically responsible, rhetorical definition of gnome. The categories of personal (*ad personam*) and contrastive or analogical (*ex contrariis*) *sententiae* will be especially fruitful for analysing early Christian gnome-use.

By way of qualification, however, it must also be recalled that the *ad personam* and *ex contrariis* qualities are not present, or equally present, in every gnome/*sententia*. For Quintilian and, more or less, his

---

[87] *Ex contrariis*, see *Inst.* V 10, 2; Cic. *Top.* 13,55–6; Anaximenes *Rh. Al.* 10 =1430a.

predecessors such qualities define gnomic rhetoric by characterizing its most striking and successful effects. Quintilian and ancient rhetoric generally are at their best where they define by example, prescriptively and critically, rather than by exhaustive definition. We should not leave Quintilian, however, without noting several more general, descriptive comments he makes.

It is perhaps typically Roman[88] that Quintilian likens gnomai/ *sententiae* to public resolutions and decrees (*similes sunt consiliis aut decretis* [*Inst.* VIII 5,3]); the observation does, however, balance the personal with the public character of gnomic language throughout antiquity. It also, of course, directly raises the ambiguous relationship between gnomic rhetoric and laws, a topic of definitive importance for early Christian rhetorics. The public quality of gnomic language, notwithstanding its highly personal aspects, is more positively characterized by Quintilian as its universal appeal (*vox universalis* [VIII 5,3; I 9,3]). This is the aspect of gnomai which allows them to be useful and interesting even apart from any particular contextualization (*etiam citra complexum causae...laudabilis* [VIII 5,3]).

As J.D. Crossan rightly saw, such a *vox universalis* does not mean proverbial, folkloric anonymity:[89] Quintilian's *sententiae* are either quotations from known personalities or the speaker's own *ad hoc* formulations. In this Quintilian speaks for the whole rhetorical tradition down to his day, Greek as well as Latin. Because of their universal appeal, some gnomai may be or become proverbial (or legal), but all gnomai are the responsibility of the speaker who invents or reinvents them in a particular speech. In the case of quotations from known authorities, the speaker deliberately links his own responsibility and character with the responsibility and authority of an earlier putative speaker.

Crossan is right, therefore, about Quintilian, but wrong about the rest of the rhetorical tradition, specifically "the later grammarians" as he calls the progymnasmatists, when he says that

---

[88] Sinclair, "*Sententia* in *Rhetorica ad Herennium*," 562, 576.

[89] J.D. Crossan, "Aphoristic Tradition," 79–80; see M. Winterbottom, *Problems in Quintilian* (BICS 25; London, 1970) 68; Henderson, "Quintilian and the *Progymnasmata*," 97.

while they clearly distinguish the gnome, as being an anonymous saying of universal application (a proverb), Quintilian considers it an authored saying but of universal application (an aphorism).[90]

The critical distinction for rhetoricians and progymnasmatists alike is not between "attribution [in chreia]...and anonymity [in gnomai]," but between explicit, formally required attribution (chreia) and formal independence (gnome). A few gnomai in the ancient sources are proverbial; far more are either invented by their speaker or quoted from a known authority. In all cases, the speaker is free, indeed required, to adapt precise wording to suit his immediate needs. Chreia differs from gnome, not because gnome is occasionally anonymous, but because chreia is defined by its compulsory, explicit narrative formula of attribution.

Gnome in the *Progymnasmata*

The foregoing provides an essential context for comparing gnome in the *Progymnasmata* with gnome in early Christian tradition. The rhetoricians from Gorgias to Quintilian can hardly be thought of as direct influences on pre-gospel tradition. But it is Quintilian who, after all, makes it clearest that the first few progymnasmata, his *primordia dicendi*, provide *the* formative conventions for the composition of typical gospel episodes.

Moreover, the tradition from the sophists to Quintilian, even including Aristotle, offers an interesting checklist of qualities against which to study gnomic language in early Christian literature:

1) Even in Aristotle it proved impossible to reduce gnomai to their argumentational, quasi-syllogistic uses; on the contrary, all analyses attest their usefulness for characterization (*ethos*) and for adjusting rapport. Gnomai also provide elegant embellishment and punctuation (e.g., they often mark the end of a larger unit).

---

[90] Crossan, "Aphoristic Tradition," 80.

2) Gnomai are not necessarily proverbial or anonymous; indeed, they can be sharply personal (*ad personam*), both in origin and address, and can be aggressively anti-proverbial.

3) Gnomai are often structured as oppositions or as analogies (*ex contrariis*); they resemble public laws; sometimes they do use proverbial language. In at least these ways they do express a universal appeal which refers beyond any particular context (*vox universalis...citra complexum causae*).

By comparison Theon's *Progymnasmata* can tell us little about gnome, which is mentioned only to differentiate chreia from it (Theon *Prog.* 5,202 Spengel 96–7). Thus, unlike chreia gnome is never attributed to a named authority, since a gnome explicitly attributed to someone *is* a chreia. This clearly does not mean that Theon thought gnomai were anonymous proverbs; his one example of a chreia expressed "gnomically" is attributed to Bion (5,207 Spengel 99). Unlike chreia, gnome is always general (*catholou*) and always practical (*biopheles*), though Theon goes on to say that chreia, more than other progymnasmata, is "useful for life" (*chreiodes to bio* [5,202 Spengel 97]). Last, chreia differs from gnome in that the former may recount a saying or a deed, while the latter is always a saying.

Another set of *Progymnasmata* is very doubtfully ascribed to Hermogenes of Tarsus. Even the evidence usually adduced to date it in any case to roughly his period (late second century AD) is unconvincing. Burton Mack and E.N. O'Neil cite differences in order and content from Theon as evidence of Hermogenes' later date, but Quintilian (*Inst.* I 9 and II 4) shows that the (pseudo-?)Hermogenean order was already normal in the first century AD. Hugo Rabe instances some close verbal parallels between Theon and Hermogenes' *Progymnasmata*, but the very nature of the progymnasmatic tradition makes such parallels inconclusive.[91] Nonetheless, the Hermogenean *Progymnasmata* is the oldest extant textbook to embody the general order of exercises attested as normal by Quintilian.

---

[91] B.L. Mack and E.N. O'Neil, "The Chreia Discussion of *Hermogenes of Tarsus*," in Hock and O'Neil, *Chreia in Ancient Rhetoric*, 153–181, 159–160; Henderson, "Quintilian and the *Progymnasmata*," 90–4; H. Rabe, ed., *Hermogenis Opera* (Rhetores Graeci VI; Stuttgart, 1913, rpr. 1985) v–vi.

Like all later *Progymnasmata*, Hermogenes (for lack of a better name) has separate, consecutive chapters on chreia and gnome (*Prog.* 3 and 4 respectively). As in all discussions of chreia, Hermogenes' third chapter distinguishes between chreia and gnome, though not exactly in the same terms as Theon. For Hermogenes, gnome differs because it is spoken as a "bare assertion" whereas chreia is often in question-and-answer format. The remaining two points agree with distinctions in Theon's catalogue: that gnome is a saying only without any direct reference to actions and without explicit ascription.

Hermogenes tells us in passing that "ancients" divided chreiai into assertive and interrogative types; both in its brevity and in the types chosen, this resembles Quintilian's note on *chria* much more than Theon's much more complex taxonomy.[92] Hermogenes spends most of his space exemplifying the elaboration (*ergasia*) through a much simpler set of topics than those demanded by Theon. Hermogenes' example chreia is one which contains a gnome (and two more gnomai are cited in the course of *ergasia*):

Isocrates said: "The root of education is bitter; its fruit sweet."

Because the chapter on chreia is immediately followed by one on gnome, the latter needs only a brief definition to introduce further examples: a gnome is a summary saying in the form of a general statement used to dissuade, commend or clarify (4 Rabe 8). This definition is admittedly too Aristotelean for my taste; more to the point, it would include many statements which no one would ever call gnomai. The elaboration exercises set for gnome are the same as those for chreia. They begin with a brief encomium of the putative original speaker. Once again, it is clear, whatever "general statement" means, that gnomai are not expected to be anonymous folklore. In fact, Hermogenes' example is a famous Homeric tag (*Iliad* II 24) also closely associated with Alexander the Great.[93] It is clearly up to each speaker whether to perform such Homeric and Isocratic tags as gnomai or in chreiai. Few people able to read a text as complicated as a gospel would miss such allusions to schoolmasters' favourite gnomai: even before

---

[92] Herm. *Prog.* 3 Rabe 7; Theon *Prog.* 5,202–206 Spengel 97–99; Quint. *Inst.* I 9,4–5.

[93] Hock and O'Neil, *Chreia in Ancient Rhetoric*, 314–5.

beginning the progymnasmata, school children practised handwriting on gnomai and Homeric tags.[94]

The two later *Progymnasmata* attributed to Aphthonius (fourth century AD) and to Nicolaus the Sophist (fifth century), and a third-century Oxyrhynchus papyrus defining chreia, attest the continuity of the progymnasmatic tradition. Aphthonius relies on examples of each progymnasma and its elaboration rather than on careful definition or taxonomy. The resulting simplicity and clarity assured Aphthonius' lasting influence as a school-book. The few words which he does give to defining gnome are almost identical to Hermogenes' except that Aphthonius omits the word "general." Nicolaus, by contrast, is much more expansive and leans more heavily on the usefulness of both gnome and chreia for moral advice and for argumentation. Nicolaus' gnome is accordingly a means of "enthymematic demonstration" (*enthymematice apodeixis*) and of "general advice" (*catholice parainesis* [Nicol. *Prog.* 4 Spengel 464]).

Thus the *Progymnasmata* generally tend to differ in emphasis from the technical and theoretical rhetorics: the pedagogical orientation of the former is compatible with, and probably responsible for, a slightly patronizing insistence on the morally edifying use of such forms as chreia, gnome and *mythos*. In practice, the progymnasmatic patterns were above all cultivated as steps toward compositional fluency. The rhetoricians observe, criticize and prescribe mature use of gnomai in terms of characterization, rapport and style. In the progymnasmatic textbooks, model gnomai are almost always quotations, adaptations or allusions to famous, though unnamed, authorities; among the rhetoricians, the option for a mature speaker to invent his own gnomic formulations is just as important.

In either corpus, it is clear that gnome is ill-served by translation as 'proverb' or 'maxim': both proverbs and maxims may serve as gnomai or as models for gnomai, but there are maxims and proverbs which are not gnomai, and most gnomai are not proverbs in any modern or folkloric sense of the word. 'Maxim', I think, evokes especially an argumentational context, which perhaps explains its currency for

---

[94] See the listings in R.A. Pack, *The Greek and Latin Literary Texts from Greco-Roman Egypt* (2d ed., Ann Arbor, MI, 1965) 2642–2751, 2643, 2707, 2712, 2713, 2729, 2731, 2737, 2746, 2750; E. Ziebarth, *Aus der antiken Schule* (Bonn, 1910) for illustrations.

'gnome' in argumentation-theoretical rhetorical criticism.[95] 'Proverb',
at least since the romantic rebellion against classicism, has tended to
imply anonymous and popular oral tradition. 'Proverb' is unfortunately
offered for 'gnome' in the most widely available translation of any
complete *Progymnasmata*, R. Nadeau's translation of Aphthonius; an
inadequate definition of gnome is thus made even worse:

> A proverb is a concise expression in the form of a statement promoting
> something, or opposing it.[96]

In Greco-Roman rhetoric, however, gnome, whether invented or
borrowed from Homer, celebrates the character of its speaker and his
rapport with a selected audience, within the framework of elite cultural
affinity. A major goal of progymnasmatic education was virtuosic
adaptability. In that context, gnome-use was deliberately taught as a
prestigious substitute for vulgar proverbiality. Few graduates of the
progymnasmata would have read the classics, but they could all imitate,
adapt and elaborate their gnomai—and even quote a few.

II

TOWARD AN ANALYTICAL DEFINITION OF GNOME

Primary schooling was only minimally organized in Greco-Roman
antiquity; nonetheless, the progymnasmatic tradition was a powerful
culture-transmitting institution. Like rhetorical culture in general, it was
ultimately oriented toward performance. In both progymnasmatic
pedagogy and rhetorical theory, performance and example take
precedence over definition. Neither in principle nor in practice,
moreover, was such rhetoric democratic or popular. On the contrary,
gnome-use is an exclusive, elite surrogate for proverb-use in the same
way that cultured rhetoric generally both replaces and extends naturally
and supernaturally gifted speech. Another side of this relationship
appears in the imitation of Roman legal maxims in the gnomai of the

---

[95] E.g., Robbins, " Pre-Gospel Traditions," 119.
[96] Aphthonius *Prog.* 4 in R. Nadeau, "The Progymnasmata of Aphthonius: in
translation," *Speech Monographs* 31 (1952) 264–85, 267.

Rhetorica ad Herennium and in the way it condemns as uncultured (*rudis* and *ineptus* [4,4]) the use without adaptation of literary tags. The use of vulgar adages is not even on the horizon of *ad Herennium*'s would-be genteel rhetoric, though Aristotle admitted that a proverb could sometimes become a gnome and gnomic rhetoric was especially useful addressing an uncultivated audience.

The relationship between gnomic rhetoric and proverb is even more challenging, given early Christianity's cross-cultural situation. Gnomai, chreiai and mythoi attested in Greek appear also in Rabbinic and near eastern sources. Moreover, there are analogies as well as differences between near eastern wisdom and Hellenistic rhetoric, each with its collection genres and educational traditions. In early Christian rhetoric this becomes more than an analogy as Jewish scriptures in Greek often fill the place vacated by the gnomai, chreiai, mythoi and diegemata of Homer and the classics in Greco-Roman educated culture.

The first flowering of Christian literature is remarkable for its unequivocal adoption of Greek, a fact which is even more interesting if bilingualism was widespread in Palestinian or early Christian speech communities.[97] The gospels defy all attempts to reconstruct a non-Greek pre-Synoptic oral tradition. "And virtually all recent studies of Q hold that it was composed in Greek." This is especially important if, as I doubt, Q represents Galilean groups with a living memory of Jesus' own rhetoric and engagement.[98] Q as a (series of) Greek text(s) strikingly recalls both Israelite prophecy and wisdom and the language of the Cynics. Still, though at home only a few kilometres from Sepphoris, Jesus of Nazareth was no Theodorus of Gadara (fl. 33 BC), who Quintilian tells us preferred to be called Theodorus of Rhodes (*Inst.* III 1,18). Nor was Jesus a Flavius Josephus. Jesus' influence is distinctly Greco-Roman, yet Jesus' unanimously Greek-writing interpreters insist on his local, class, ethnic and cultic interests.

---

[97] Henderson, "Style-Switching," 177–209, 190–191, 201–204; J.A. Overman, "Recent Advances in the Archaeology of the Galilee in the Roman Period," *Currents in Research: Biblical Studies* 1 (1993) 35–57, 44–45; Millar, *The Roman Near East*, 352–366.

[98] Kloppenborg, "Q: Recent Opinion," quoting 10 which cites H.O. Guenther "The Sayings Gospel Q and the Quest for Aramaic Sources: Rethinking Christian Origins," *Semeia* 55, ed. Kloppenborg and Vaage (1991) 41–76.

From the point of view of social history, the absence of the three Galilean cities (Sepphoris, Tiberias and Schythopolis) from the gospels is striking and important.[99]

The special urgency of defining gnome for early Christian rhetorics has several other aspects. First, gnomai in early Christian literature are rarely marked as such. The modern critic cannot begin with a list of New Testament gnomai; a list must be abstracted with the help of a working definition. But the definitions of the schoolmasters and rhetoricians are not meant to function apart from the canon of examples in textbooks and performances.

In addition, a rhetorical analysis of early Christian gnome-use is deeply interested in the issue of socially specific tradition. The rhetoricians presuppose and greatly strengthen a classist view of culture and therefore keep quiet about how ordinary people talk (e.g., in proverbs).

This silence is only obliquely challenged by early Christian sectarianism as it struggles to connect private conversation, mythical narrative and an alternative public rhetoric. Progymnasmatic tradition and synoptic tradition are both rhetorical, in that they turn a cultural minority into a self-conscious public and in that they define a relationship between oral performance and canonical literacy. Our knowledge is patchy when it comes to the institutions (city, class, household, school) within which progymnasmatic tradition must have worked. Still, it greatly exceeds what we really know about the institutional locations of synoptic tradition.

To risk another contrast, George Kennedy is wrong, though suggestively wrong, about the relationship between gospel rhetorics and Jesus:

Behind the rhetoric of the two evangelists in these sermons [*scil.* on the Mount and on the Plain] stands their perception of the rhetoric of Jesus, and behind that perception stands the actual rhetoric of Jesus. The last of these, first in chronological sequence, cannot be objectively determined, but it

---

[99] E.P. Sanders, *Jewish Law from Jesus to the Mishnah* (London and Philadelphia, 1990) 40; Overman, "Archaeology of the Galilee," 45–49; Millar, *The Roman Near East*, 342–343.

may be possible to make some suggestions about the evangelists' perception
or preconceptions of the rhetoric of Jesus.[100]

I wonder about objective determination in rhetoric, religion, literature
and history. But we are not actually that ignorant of Jesus' rhetoric: he
cultivated a double reputation, for speaking in parables and for supernatural healing—and he got himself publicly executed in Jerusalem.
Moreover, we know incomparably more about the cultural, religious,
political and economic contexts in Galilee and Judaea in which Jesus
spoke and acted publicly than we do about the circumstances in which
the gospel-writers wrote.

It is a deeply entrenched maxim of New Testament studies that the
gospels are primarily evidence for the early Christian communities in
which they were presumably written and only secondarily evidence of
Jesus' activity a generation earlier. This is a better maxim for theological than for historical exegesis, however.

Historically, the gospels have proven almost opaque to questions
about the circumstances of their production. By contrast, they document
from a unique social perspective one part of the Greco-Roman world,
the world of "villages and small towns of the Jewish region, Galilee and
its neighbouring territories above all." With Josephus they also document the busy emergence of alternative leaderships, counter-elites,
within that world.

> [A]lthough we cannot state when, where, by whom or for whom any one
> of them was written, it is beyond question that they emerged out of the
> same world, the Jewish life of Galilee, Judaea and Jerusalem itself, as do
> the works of Josephus...The fact that [the Gospels] do genuinely reflect this
> world with its social divisions and its religious disputes, as it was in the 20s
> and 30s, does not mean that they were written either there or then. But they
> remain authoritative testimony to the concerns, and the historical conscious-
> ness, of Jewish society, in Galilee and Jerusalem above all, before the fall
> of the Temple.[101]

This deliberate repression of the gospel-writers' rhetorics shows itself
in their literary frameworks. The gospels are extended narratives and/or

---

[100] G. Kennedy, *New Testament Interpretation*, 67, cited in Watson and Hauser,
Rhetorical Criticism, 116 n. 85.

[101] Millar, *The Roman Near East*, 342.

sayings-collections, literary forms for which (unlike the epistle) ancient rhetoric had no explicit theory.[102] In ancient terms, the evangelists' rhetorics are at least as far below the narrative and discursive surfaces of their anonymous gospels as Jesus' rhetoric is.

In fact, neither Jesus' rhetoric nor the evangelists' rhetorics can be understood without a connecting model of tradition to coordinate public speech with less public book production: the form critics rightly perceived this necessity. The value of progymnasmatic rhetoric is not only that it was directly influential on the production of gospels, providing basic literary sub-genres. The progymnasmata are also an instance of a tradition which spans oral performance, cultivation of an exclusive cultural identity and the production of books. But this is not a critical interest which the rhetoricians themselves foresaw or which their shorthand, prescriptive definitions accommodate.[103] Schoolmasters surely used progymnasmatic exercises to inculcate culturally significant tradition, such as plots, characters and gnomai from Homer. What the progymnasmata as such teach, however, is facility in variation and adaptation of conventional patterns, and an identification with others who share such facility.

In relation to the historical problem of synoptic pre-gospel tradition, this rhetorical emphasis on virtuosic variation and adaptation of tradition assumes a new significance. Quintilian is representative in his recognition that *sententiae* may be varied through all the figures (*per omnes enim figuras* [*Inst.* VIII 5,5]). Thus the same *sententia* may and should be performed quite variously, depending on the speaker, audience, and context *and* on the possibilities of language:

Death is not wretched; the entrance to death is wretched.

Is it so wretched, then, to die?

This priority of variation in performance over tradition is doubly important for gospel studies; the tension between variation in performance and continuity in tradition must figure more prominently in a

---

[102] Watson and Hauser, *Rhetorical Criticism*, 116.
[103] Robbins, "Pre-Gospel Traditions," 120; Mack, "Persuasive Pronouncements," 284.

definition of gnome for analysing synoptic tradition than in a definition
constructed for school children and lawyers.

Gnomic core and variation in tradition

J.D. Crossan is one of very few New Testament scholars to consider
even in passing the relation between gnome and synoptic sayings
tradition. Apart from acknowledging the centrality of Quintilian's
evidence for the rhetorical tradition, Crossan makes two distinctions
which I think are helpful for connecting ancient rhetorical patterns and
modern critical categories. The first distinction is between "aphoristic
structure" or "core" and "aphoristic saying"; the second is between
"performantial" and "hermeneutical variation."[104] Both are grounded
in a basic distinction between actual rhetorical performance and remembered tradition. In that context, gnomic core is the memorable gist
behind a potentially rich variety of gnomic performances. Thus
Quintilian's two examples above clearly share one gnomic core: the
contrast between death and wretchedness. They perform that core
differently, however. The ancient rhetorical tradition encourages us to
dare to interpret such core, family similarities and differences even
when we cannot know much about their contextualization in particular
occasional speeches.

To talk in this way of a gnomic core which facilitates recollection
and controlled variation has the advantage of bypassing the form-critical
obsession with original or pure forms. Neither of Quintilian's *sententiae*
about dying is more original or authentic than the other; they are
deliberate variants of a single gnomic core. They are both rather
effective versions of a gnomic core that could, after all, be botched.

Crossan's notion of "core" is, moreover, grounded in an assumption
that pre-gospel traditions were informed by a positive "oral sensibility"
which favoured attention to core structures over attention to particular
options for their performance.

---

[104] Crossan, "Aphoristic Tradition," 75–95; J.D. Crossan, *In Fragments: The Aphorisms of Jesus* (San Francisco, 1983) 37–66.

> [O]ral memory retains a linguistic structure rather than a syntactical sequence. One could even define oral sensibility as the victory of structure over sequence.

> In oral sensibility one speaks or writes an aphoristic saying, but one remembers and recalls an aphoristic core.[105]

The kind of structure Crossan seems to have in mind over against syntax is that which the rhetoricians describe as figures (*schemata*) of thought and speech. In these terms, the rhetoricians' and progymnasmatists' prescriptions for gnome-variation clearly embody a relatively oral sensibility: though highly literate, they are centrally concerned with teaching speakers to adapt gnomic core to the requirements of each particular performance. They feel free to adapt gnomic cores from literary tradition, but accurate textual reproduction is irrelevant or even, as in the *ad Herennium*, inelegantly blunt.

As a psychological, linguistic and social phenomenon Crossan's "oral sensibility" clearly differs from the pristine orality of some lost, illiterate tribe. It is the real orality of most traditional societies, in which literacies or mnemonics of one sort or another play important roles in limited contexts, but in which talk and memory are in practice and in value systems the dominant public communication mode. Greco-Roman rhetoric and its Christian mutations are extraordinary only in the extent to which they self-consciously embody a return to such oral sensibility in the continuing light of elite and ethnic-sectarian experiences of intense, canonical literacy.

Crossan's further distinction between performantial and hermeneutical variation is by no means absolute: the differences among performances are sometimes hermeneutically motivated by a speaker's more or less conscious development of argument, character or mood. At times, however, an oral indifference to textual reproduction or a carefully inculcated rhetorical habit will invite variations which are not determined by the particular occasion of speech. Such "performantial variations" are not, of course, hermeneutically insignificant. But they say more about general cultural background than about particular hermeneutical options within a tradition. The differences between Quintilian's two versions of the gnomic core on death and dying would

---

[105] Crossan, "Aphoristic Tradition," 95; *In Fragments*, 67.

usually, though not necessarily, be more obviously performantial than hermeneutical: at least Quintilian himself is not interested in the hermeneutical possibilities of the two examples.

Redaction criticism, by contrast, assumes that variation among the synoptic gospel-writers is either hermeneutical—indexing the conscious theological sensitivities of the writers—or merely stylistic—part of their personal, irrepressible, often unconscious styles.[106] This distinction between the evangelists' theological changes to tradition and their stylistic changes to tradition in literary redaction is fundamentally different from Crossan's distinction. Crossan is really distinguishing between memory and performance, whether in oral or literary rhetoric. He is therefore led to think of oral tradition in the way the rhetoricians think of their performance craft: because performance was the norm even for written texts, variation was also normal, conventional and conscious—and might have a specific hermeneutical function. But such variation is impossible without discernable patterns, patterns like gnome, which the rhetoricians researched and which schoolmasters taught—patterns which aid and condition speaker and listener, writer and reader to remember the gist and the core rather than the text.

Fascinated by multivalence in texts, modern criticism tends to treat the studious reader's perceptions of difference as hermeneutically decisive. Because, for rhetoric, texts are aids to oral performance, they are not so polyvalent; the competent speaker can make sure the audience gets his gist. The rhetor experiences the hermeneutical problem more acutely in terms of the linguist's principle of equivalency or synonymity: there is always more than one way of saying (almost) "the same thing," from which the speaker must efficiently choose. In this way hermeneutical variation is a specialization of performantial variation. Each student of the progymnasmata must learn to expand, contract, paraphrase and transpose in performance according to the conventions of relative synonymity. The assumption, linguistically quite correct, is that mastery of such performantial variation will be the precondition for deliberate, occasional hermeneutical variation. How many different ways are there of saying (almost) the same thing? What are the relatively stable, conventional topics and patterns on which variations are to be wrought?

---

[106] Henderson, "Style-Switching," 179–85, 187–90.

The shared orientation toward performance brings modern orality theory and conversation analysis close to ancient rhetoric. Indeed, they are closer here to ancient rhetoric than modern argumentation theory is. To the extent that pressures of performance are more urgent in extempore oral situations than in writing, oral theorists might plausibly expect performantial variation to predominate over hermeneutical variation in non-writing tradition. At any rate, rhetorical theory and education suggest that performantial variation may be more prevalent even in gospel literary composition than we modern print-literates might expect. The acceptability and inevitability of performantial variation in an orally performed tradition is one of the conditions which temporarily encouraged slightly more hermeneutical variation in gospel literary production.

Above all, the tension between core in tradition and memory, and variation in performance puts to rest the older, form-critical discrimination between saying and episode. In terms of the psychology of memory, the relation between gnomic core and gnomic performance is essentially like that between episodic core and story-telling, whether *mythos* or *diegema*, except that gnomic core consists of words where episodic core may be visual. (Chreia, of course, may be either gnomic or episodic or both.)

Protesting the older form-critical view, "that sayings were primary, and situations and actions were created out of and for sayings," V.K. Robbins goes overboard in the other direction:

> Regularly, one's memory of a situation and of action in that situation is more precise than one's memory of words that were spoken.... There are, to be sure, special circumstances when a person said something that was striking, like "Ask not what your country can do for you; ask what you can do for your country."[107]

A major goal of trained speaking and listening in the Near East and in the Greco-Roman world was to create, wherever possible, such "special circumstances." It may be (I am not sure) that a "simple test of one's memory of an episode from the past will raise questions about" the old form critics' greater confidence in verbal over episodic memory. In any society, memory is a complex, culturally and linguistically as well as

---

[107] Robbins, "Pre-Gospel Traditions," 134.

psychologically conditioned behaviour. Both ancient near eastern wisdom and Greco-Roman rhetoric warn us, however, to reckon with speakers and even vulgar audiences conditioned to mark and inwardly digest a phrase which is both well-turned and topically relevant. The rhetoricians and progymnasmatists were well aware of the power of narrative and visual memory. They also insist, however, on the ability to recall and adapt the gist of a good gnome as one of the basic skills of public speech.

Rhetoric and conversation, gnome and proverb

It has been clearly acknowledged that ancient rhetoric did not undertake the analysis of extended narratives, though episodic narratives (*mythos, diegema,* and chreia itself) are basic to Greco-Roman rhetoric. The task of analysing epic and dramatic stories was left to poetics, though antiquity readily acknowledged that such narratives *contained* rhetoric and were pervasively informed by its conventions. This division in itself raises valuable questions for criticism of gospel narrativity.

It is even more important that ancient rhetoric did not undertake the analysis of ordinary conversation. In the *Phaedrus* Plato famously distinguishes between the technical, eristic rhetoric of his day and the project of a real, psychagogic rhetoric (269d–274b). For Aristotle, however, the latter task led to dialectics, to the analysis of conversation under the control of Socratic interrogation (*elenchus*), rather than to demagogic rhetoric. Dialectics thus becomes not only the analysis, but also the ideal rectification of conversation, its assimilation to a Socratic and Platonic model of dialogue.[108]

In consequence, ancient rhetoric provides tools and a historically generative hermeneutic for reading gospel texts. This is more than any other theoretical construct can now do. Yet ancient rhetoric does not provide direct models for narrative literary criticism or for analysis of dialogue as such. In principle, it should be possible to apply ancient rhetoric to the analysis of the conversational elements in gospel and pre-gospel rhetorics. Gnome with its ambiguous relationship to proverb, and

---

[108] Barilli, *Rhetoric*, 9–10.

indeed all the basic progymnasmata, are patterns in dialogue as well as in monologue.

The challenge and legitimacy of such an extension of ancient rhetorical criticism may be illustrated from a passage to which we will return in later chapters. Luke's story of Jesus' rejection in Nazareth (Luke 4:16–30) is emphatically Lucan rhetoric. In it, moreover, Jesus is portrayed as a prophetic, habitual public speaker; programmatic rhetoric is directly attributed to him. On the other hand, the episode is a narrative, not the script of a rhetorical performance. Only a suggestive sample of Jesus' putative words is offered. Moreover, the key speech is in the form of an enigmatic exchange between the audience and a suddenly confrontational Jesus. Luke's Jesus puts one gnome/ proverb (*parabole* Luke 4:23) on his hearers' lips. Luke follows it with one in Jesus' own name.

The gnome, "Healer, heal yourself!", and the gnome about a home-town prophet (4:24) are surely more or less proverbial, but this is not implied in the description of the first as *parabole*, "analogy." In Luke's wider narrative horizon both sayings foreshadow the coming rejection in Jerusalem. But in their immediate context, the gnomai are used by Jesus in ways which Aristotle could easily appreciate: Jesus is character-izing himself by analogy with the dual roles of healer and prophet. Luke's Jesus expects the former, but affirms the latter. And he is adjusting—shockingly rejecting—his rapport with his audience, thereby changing the whole genre of the rhetoric from ceremonial (epideictic) to juridical (dicanic).

Luke's rhetoric strikingly presents Jesus as prophetic, provocatively gnomic rhetor. Behind this presentation, there is also a tantalizing probability of Jesus' actual, historic rhetoric, or at any rate of pre-gospel tradition. The literary gospels give us four different performances of the gnome of the prophet rejected at home (Mark 6:4; Luke 4:23; John 4:44; *Gos.Thom.* 31, see POxy. 1.6). The Lucan (4:24) and Egyptian versions associate the prophet-gnome with different performances of the healer-gnome. Moreover, the Marcan, Lucan and Johannine narrative contextualizations are all odd enough to suggest both complex pre-gospel tradition and redactional variation.

This group of gnomic passages will have to be taken up again in more detail. It illustrates very well, however, the usefulness of thinking in terms of gnomic core traditions undergoing variation in oral and written performance. Clearly here, looking for an 'original' form of either gnome is a waste of time; the four versions should be studied as a single gnomic complex.

In addition, this case suggests a relation between gnomic and episodic memory which confirms a nuanced "privileging of speech over action and situation in pre-gospel tradition." It would be difficult to argue for the detailed historicity of any of the gospel stories of Jesus' home town rejection. It is plausible that Jesus did experience such rejection at some key point; it is credible that Jesus himself or early tradition should relate that rejection to Jesus' prophetic, more-than-therapeutic role. But that general impression is fully conveyed in the gnomai of the prophet and the healer. Without prejudice to the question whether anything really happened or not, no sharp divide between 'saying' and 'actions' is justified in this case.

On balance, however, Bultmann's prejudice that sayings will be prior to stories, since the latter must be secondary to the actions they report, holds up well. The gnomai imply the deed and its interpretation. It seems unnecessary to insist with Robbins that "one's memory of a situation and of action in that situation is more precise than one's memory of words that were spoken."[109] In this case, someone may have preserved an accurate memory that Jesus was rejected at home. But this possibility is most probably attested by the tradition's varied use of one or two gnomic cores, sometimes in narrative contextualizations, sometimes alone.

Toward a comparative definition of gnome

There is no good reason not to apply Greco-Roman rhetorical theories of gnome-use to gospel narratives and dialogues or to pre-gospel tradition. The boundaries between public rhetoric and private conversations, between Jesus' self-representations and early Christian memories are not fixed or sacred. But ancient rhetorical definitions of gnome were intended for classroom use. They should be supplemented and refined if possible from the perspective of our modern critical interests, especially our interest in speech communities which seem to challenge or qualify the rhetorical hegemony of perceived elites.

---

[109] Robbins, "Pre-Gospel Traditions," 134.

A useful approach to defining comparatively and systematically something like "gnomic core" is available in modern attempts to define 'proverb' for cross-cultural and semantic study. Precisely because this line of research is comparative and cross-cultural, it cannot presuppose speech conventions with anything like the normative, prescriptive status of the basic progymnasmata in the Greco-Roman world. The best inductive and comparative definitions from modern paroemiology are quite compatible with the prescriptive definitions, examples and advice about gnome-use in ancient rhetoric. Synthesizing these two approaches to definition will help us to take seriously not only the Greco-Roman rhetorical surface aspect of (pre-)gospel tradition, but also its exotic, cross-cultural, sectarian and class-conscious aspects.

The work of A. Jolles on "simple forms" has strongly influenced both modern paroemiology and biblical form criticism. Jolles declined to offer any systematic definition of proverb. He did, however, reject descriptions of proverb which depended on notions of its 'popular' origins. Jolles also denied that the proverb's supposed didactic, moralistic function is definitive. Proverb is not essentially a teaching or argumentational form. On the contrary, it evokes quite particular, not generalized experiences.[110] The romantic refusal to define is even more pronounced in the work of A. Taylor. Since "an incommunicable quality tells us that this sentence is a proverb and that one is not," the best attainable definition of proverb is itself gnomic: "the wisdom of many and the wit of one."[111]

In an essay toward semiotic analysis of proverbs, Algirdas Greimas emphasizes the connotative character of proverbs, that is, the equivocal relationship between the syntactical dimensions of proverbs and the actual communicative meaning of proverb performances. The definitive structure at work in the proverb, but also elsewhere, is an implicit "binary modulation" often, but not always, underlined by explicit verbal antithesis.[112]

---

[110] A. Jolles, *Einfache Formen* (Tübingen, 1930, rpr. 1968) esp. 153, 158; see H.-J. Hermisson, *Studien zur israelitischen Spruchweisheit* (WMANT 28; Neukirchen-Vluyn, 1968) 29–32 for application to biblical forms.

[111] A. Taylor, *The Proverb and an Introduction to the Proverb* (Copenhagen, 1962) 3, cited by O. Blehr, "What is a Proverb?" *Fabula* 14 (1973) 243–46, 243; A. Taylor, *The Wisdom of Many*, ed. W. Mieden and A. Dundes (New York, London, 1981).

[112] A.J. Greimas, "Les proverbes et les dictons," in *Du sens: Essais sémiotiques* (Paris, 1970) 309–314.

The temptation to define proverb by syntax can be illustrated from a series of essays by G.B. Milner. Milner describes proverb in terms of a four-part sentence structure, each part of which carries in context a negative or positive socio-linguistic value. It is the veiled interplay of negative and positive valuations which makes proverbs interesting. Milner's procedure is frustratingly arbitrary: four-fold structure excludes too many potential proverbs, while socio-linguistic valuations of key terms are not stable, unambiguous, unequivocal or even uncontroversial. In "Render unto Caesar what is Caesar's, unto God what is God's," "Caesar" must be less positively valued than "God," but "Caesar" is not unequivocally or invariably negative in socio-linguistic valuation.[113] Milner's emphasis on socio-linguistic valuation of gnomic imagery is helpful in the end because it exposes the riddling, evaluative ambiguity of many proverbs. The meaning of proverb-use thus lies often in its ability to gloss conflicting valuations of key terms. In conversation, use of proverbs, especially of metaphorical, connotative proverbs is often related to speakers' anxiety to control (sometimes to exploit) the "social cost" of communicating value judgements in highly-charged situations.[114]

P. Crépeau has undertaken a definition of proverb which would be useful across cultural and linguistic barriers and which would select proverbs from among other speech types. Crépeau's definition is built upon a large, multilingual and predominantly oral sample; it also works well with the majority of examples of gnomai in ancient rhetoric.

By comparison with the rest of the spoken performance, proverbs are marked by syntactical peculiarities (e.g., brevity, archaic style, verse rhythm, unusual vocabulary), but it is not special syntax alone which definitively gives proverbs their "special status in the spoken chain." Crépeau thus echoes Greimas' insistence on the connotative quality of proverb and yet also, more than Greimas, focuses on the tension

---

[113] G.B. Milner, "Quadripartite Structures," *Proverbium* 14 (1969) 379–383 ; "What is a Proverb?" *New Society* 6 (1969) 199–202; "De l'armature des locutions proverbiales: Essai de taxonomie sémantique," *L'Homme* 9 (1969) 49–70.

[114] B. Kirschenblatt-Gimblett, "Toward a Theory of Proverb Meaning," *Proverbium* 8 (1967) 821–827; A. Dundes, "On the Structures of the Proverb," *Proverbium* 25 (1975) 961–973, 963–5; N.A. Barley, "A Structural Approach to the Proverb and Maxim with Special Reference to the Anglo-Saxon Corpus," *Proverbium* 20 (1972) 737–750, 743; P. Crépeau, "La Définition du proverbe," *Fabula* 16 (1975) 285–304, 289–91; Blehr, "Proverb?" 243–6.

between proverb and context in actual performances. One criterion of proverbiality for Crépeau is syntactical distinctiveness ("autonomy") over against any particular contextualization, what I will call separability.[115]

Crépeau, too, criticizes Milner's mechanical criterion of four-part syntactical form; instead Crépeau suggests a four-fold logic, often only implied in the syntax of a particular proverb. Describing proverbs as analogies, that is, as comparisons of relationships (A:B::C:D or A:B::C:B), not only allows for the formal variety and performantial variation of proverbs. It also takes the interpretative emphasis off Milner's speculative valuations of bits of syntax and places it instead on the comparative valuation of relationships. Proverbs are "analogical in structure and not in form." Even where all four elements of analogy are more or less explicit in four-part syntax ("Render unto Caesar..."), the key to their interrelationship may not be syntactically explicit or stable between performances. The second criterion of Crépeau's definition of proverb is thus analogical structure. This criterion of analogy relates closely to the rhetoricians' interest in gnomai structured by oppositions of apparent contraries.

> Analogy does not constitute an approximate resemblance among objects.... It forges an equality of relation among differing, dissimilar, opposed objects.... Analogy is based on opposition of contraries or on relative opposition.[116]

Crépeau's analysis of proverb-use in several speech communities suggests a third defining dimension. The structuralist approaches to proverb of Greimas and Milner have little to say about proverb-use, about the functions of proverbial language in social communication. On the other hand, traditional paroemiologies (including ancient collection literatures) tend to emphasize uncritically the supposed popular, practical and didactic functions of proverb. Crépeau recognizes that the normative dimension of proverbs is an indispensable condition of their actually observed uses in speech. At the same time, Crépeau discerns considerable variety in the normativity of proverbs. He thus describes proverbial normativity along two axes: intensity and range.

---

[115] Crépeau, "Définition," 286–7.
[116] Crépeau, "Définition," 290–297, 303, quoting 303 and 295.

Intensity varies from observation, through prescription to command. Intensity is far from unambiguous. "A stitch in time saves nine" is ostensibly only an observation; in public speech it is seldom employed without stronger normative implications. Range has to do with the ostensible (often ambiguous) social address of a proverb: "Healer, heal yourself!" is not universal in range, since it focuses on the socially regulated role of healer. In Crépeau's terms, it may, however, be read as "specific" in range (referring to recognized practitioners) or "optional" (referring to do-gooders generally).

It is clear, however, that proverbial normativity is an instance of what I earlier called rhetorical normativity rather than social normativity. That is, neither "Healer, heal yourself!" nor "A stitch in time..." directly expresses a social norm. Instead both invoke one or more complexes of language about social rights, topics and obligations. Proverb-use is prescriptive rather than descriptive and is, moreover, more directly conditioned by its linguistic context than by its speaker's social setting. If anything, Crépeau's analysis of normativity in proverbial sayings is still too syntactical. Rhetorical normativity in proverbs is more complex and more ambiguous than the rather explicit clues upon which his taxonomy depends. Because proverbial normativity is expressed as analogy, a proverb's normative impact can seldom simply be read off its imagery. Thus exactly the same proverb can be performed in different contexts with quite different normative implications.

Finally, Crépeau does remark in passing on one aspect of the relationship between proverb and rhetoric. He notes as something specific to French culture since the seventeenth century the devaluation of proverbs as vulgar. He explains this as a reaction against the vulgarity of French medieval proverbs. By contrast,

> in China, in Japan, among the Arabs and the Bantu peoples, "speaking in proverbs" is part of the art of speaking well [i.e., of rhetoric classically defined].... It is necessary therefore to eliminate from the definition of proverb the epithet "popular."[117]

The tension between vulgar proverb and elite rhetoric has, however, as we have seen, a longer history in Western rhetoric. It was Aristotle who

---

[117] Crépeau, "Définition," 287.

pointed out that some (not all) proverbs and riddles were also gnomai (*Rh.* II 21,8=1394b; 21,12=1395a) and that one advantage of gnome-use in rhetoric was its accessibility to uncultivated audiences (21,15=1395b). Aristotle is even said to have made a collection of proverbs (Diog. Laert. 5,26) and certainly such collections were common. On the other hand the *ad Herennium* (4,4) rejects as vulgar any *sententia* which quotes too directly, whether from literary or proverbial tradition. In practice, the distinction between classical gnomai and vulgar proverbs only partly subsumes the more universal distinction between tasteful and vulgar proverbs. In early Christian texts, on the margin of Greco-Roman rhetoric, some aspects of this distinction are heightened and others put into question, an adjustment which may, indeed, bring us close to social normativity.

The essential point is that there is a positive but problematic relation between gnome and proverb. It is not, therefore, arbitrary to adopt a single definition for gnome and proverb. In the context of early Christian rhetoric such a unitary definition makes special sense as Christian social locations limit and partly challenge the essentially classist, though dynamic, division between elite and vulgar. The difference between gnome and proverb is rather precisely analogous to the difference between advertising slogan and proverb today. Indeed, modern advertising and ancient rhetoric are significantly analogous. Both sets of public communication conventions have a great deal to do with class definition; yet both rhetoric and advertising define permissible avenues of social mobility rather than static class identities. Christians of unclear social standing were thus able to apply and adapt the possibilities of progymnasmatic rhetoric and those of biblical tradition to produce a strikingly effective hybrid medium.

In what follows, therefore, Crépeau's definition of proverb will be applied to gnomic rhetoric in two ways: to identify gnomai in early Christian texts and to analyse the structure and intrinsic normativity of gnomai. The definitions, advice and examples provided by the technical and progymnasmatic traditions in ancient rhetoric provide a control on the first, selective application of Crépeau's criteria. It is far more important, however, that ancient rhetoric fills out the functional analysis of gnome-use and of rhetorical normativity in gnomai. It is ancient rhetoric which provides the key analytical concepts of topic, character (*ethos*), rapport (*pathos*), and variation in performance. Crépeau's definition, moreover, crystallizes themes already met among the rhetoricians: analogy (often of contraries and often metaphoric) is the structure of gnomic cores; normativity (including relation to tradition, social role, class, proverb and law) is essential to gnomic rhetoric, yet also ambiguous and variable; formal independence combined with analogical structure accounts for much of the memorability and adaptability of gnomic cores. The criteria of analogy, normativity and independence or separability in fact exclude some items, context-bound conceits, which Quintilian still treats as (inferior) *sententiae* (*Inst.* VIII 5,12–14); the Latin term always retained a wider and less technical sense than the Greek.

Conclusion

What does it mean to define gnome as an analogical, normative and separable speech pattern? This definition allows us to select a sample of items from synoptic tradition and elsewhere to compare with the examples of the ancient rhetoricians and school masters. It provides a good, shorthand synthesis of the defining features of gnomai among the rhetoricians, without replacing the rhetoricians' fuller insights and prescriptions for the use of gnome in communication. It may be helpful to reconsider briefly a double example from Quintilian (*Inst.* VIII 5,5–6), with one from synoptic tradition (Matt. 8:22):[118]

Death is not wretched; the entrance to death is wretched.

Is it so wretched, then, to die?

Let the dead bury their dead.

These are normative in the double sense that they take up the socially significant topic of death and that they implicitly require something from their audiences in relation to the topic. This is true despite the separability and relativity of the gnomai: the relationship between these gnomai and any particular contextualization is quite flexible, but would in any case involve the imposition of a requirement on the hearer. The

---

[118] For a characteristically clear summary, see Sanders and Davies, *Synoptic Gospels*, 143–4.

examples are syntactically separable from their various contextualizations. They are also semantically autonomous in that they permit only
a fairly narrow range of hermeneutical and performantial variations
before they would cease to be recognizable or memorable—or gnomic.
Much in these gnomai is left implicit, but the missing, implied elements
are not supplied by the surrounding context, but by the culturally
competent reader.

Analogy may be the most difficult aspect of these gnomai to
understand. The essential point is that they imply or state a comparison
of two relations. Often, as in these cases, analogy is complicated and
energized by symbolism and probable metaphor as well as by weight of
normative implication; death, dying and wretchedness are in themselves
evocative and multivalent. For many gnomai, especially those which
invoke risky topics, there may be several ways of diagramming the
analogical relationships involved. The essential insight that prov-
erbs/gnomai are self-contained comparisons of relations holds well in
the available examples of gnomai.

In the first example above, the relationship between death and
wretchedness is fairly explicitly contrasted with the relationship between
dying and wretchedness: though death and dying are closely related, on
the common denominator of wretchedness, they differ normatively. The
second example from Quintilian gives nearly the same gnomic core in
a more implicit performance. Here death and dying are not distinguished
and a more open contrast is implied: the relation between death/dying
and wretchedness is contrasted with a range of possible relations
between aspects of life and wretchedness.

The synoptic example is by far the most complex. Its complexity
arises in part from its different normative topicality. Death and burial
is a riskier topic than death and dying in Greco-Roman antiquity. This
is underlined by the synoptic gnome's imperative form. In addition,
however, the gnome implies two different ways of being "dead." The
gnome imposes an unwelcome analogy of similarity--not contrast as
above--between its hearer's relationships with the conventionally dead
and with those with the rhetorically dead. Few synoptic and even fewer
classical gnomai are normatively as intense or analogically as complex
as this gnome of burial; the presence in synoptic tradition of such
gnomic intensity will occupy the concluding chapters of this book. First,
however, it is necessary to relate gnomic rhetoric more precisely to
older, form-critical models for studying biblical wisdom sayings.

CHAPTER TWO

GNOME AND WISDOM SAYING

The last chapter was largely concerned with justifying an approach to gospel tradition centred more on its gnomic rhetoric than on its chreiai. Now it is time to differentiate the study of gospel gnomai from a third approach, which, even more than chreia research, has influenced New Testament studies. Ironically, the monopoly of chreia research over rhetorical criticism of gospel traditions originates directly from a protest against the older dominance of 'wisdom sayings' in form criticism.[1] Gnome is an important critical category in large part because it permits a direct confrontation of the weakness of the 'wisdom saying' as a category. Apart from the imprecision of 'wisdom saying', there is no necessary formal difference between it and 'gnome'. The essential difference between 'gnome' and 'wisdom saying' is in the double cultural context which each invokes: 'Wisdom saying' recalls the ancient Near East, especially as imagined before the middle of this century; 'gnome' recalls distinct interests in speech in the Greco-Roman world and in the late twentieth century. It has thus been possible to define gnome in terms designed to facilitate cross-cultural comparison with proverbs.

'Proverb' is indeed often used as a synonym for 'wisdom saying'. This use, though ancient, is tendentious: it glosses over the difference between the use and repertoire of proverbs in speech and the uses of canonized proverbs in specialized literary wisdom. Whether from Crépeau or from Aristotle, a proverb would seem best understood as a special kind of gnome; a proverb is a gnome which most members of a given speech community might be expected to know. My assumption that readers will know "A stitch in time..." is thus an assumption not only about this gnome as a proverb, but also about my own extended speech community.

---

[1] Mack and Robbins, *Patterns*, 6–11; Robbins, "Pre-Gospel Traditions," 134.

Some proverbs are literary in origin, especially if that origin is not always recognized ("Neither a borrower nor a lender be"). Such proverbs might be used or taught as gnomai, but the rhetoricians assume that many gnomai will instead be their speakers' own ad hoc formulations, indirectly modelled on memorized school-tags. In rhetorical performance, different types of gnomai, proverbs, literary tags and ad hoc gnomai, represent different, sometimes conflicting, sometimes complementary colourings of *ethos*. In the Greco-Roman world gnomai and proverbs were collected in scholastic, didactic and parenetic compilations, as indeed they had long been collected in non-Greek and Greek pre-classical literatures. Such specialized books of collected 'proverbial' wisdom are often also marked as poetry or verse and associated with sagely culture heroes and with scribal or aristocratic class prestige. Greek rhetorical theory recognized, however, that gnome was not essentially a pedagogical or didactic or sapiential or scribal pattern. Indeed, by recognizing that gnome is far more than a simple tool for pedagogy and for wisdom verse, the rhetoricians anticipated the results of modern proverb-studies. One basis for modern paroemiology has been André Jolles' vehement protest against exaggerating the importance of the didactic over the many other functions of gnomic language.[2]

Thus gnomai were appreciated more as a smart way to talk than as items in a list of the Sayings of the Wise. Such lists certainly remained in undiminished favour in the Greco-Roman world—and they have exercised an inordinate influence on gospel studies.[3] In addition, we have seen that the progymnasmatic school teachers were not averse to teaching chreiai, gnomai, *mythoi*, and the rest as moral as well as rhetorical models. The fact remains, however, that virtuosic facility at inventing, selecting and adapting gnomai in actual rhetorical performance takes absolute priority both in the theoretical manuals and in the *Progymnasmata*. Personal moral appropriation of the conflicting messages of famous gnomai is, at most, only a desirable byproduct of progymnasmatic education. The Greek-speaking world was thus quite aware of specific literary conventions like those governing near eastern

---

[2] *Einfache Formen*, 158.
[3] See the seminal, J.M. Robinson, "LOGOI SOPHON: On the Gattung of Q," in *Trajectories through Early Christianity*, ed. J.M. Robinson and H. Koester (Philadelphia, 1971) 71–113.

wisdom poetry; it is all the more important, then, to see with the Greco-Roman rhetoricians that the actual use of gnomai in public discourse was not controlled by poetic or pedagogical motives.

For biblical scholars and for theologians the most obvious field of comparison for New Testament gnomai is not Greco-Roman rhetoric. More visible on the horizon is the wisdom literature of the Old Testament and the ancient Near East. This makes sense, indeed, not only in terms of the history and shape of the Christian canon, but also because the translations of the Septuagint and the new writings of the New Testament are characteristic of the universalization of Greek language and rhetoric in imperial antiquity. The Greek Bible is a monument to the two-way flow of cultural assimilation. Comparison of New Testament gnomai and Old Testament proverbs is made problematic, however, by the nature of wisdom literature itself and by the kinds of critical approach which have been made to it.

The wisdom collections, like Hellenistic and Greco-Roman gnomologies, recall the direct speech of primary rhetoric in their sub-units: they try to be, as it were, collections of sound-bites. They do so, however, without the important supplements of contemporary theoretical reflection like that provided by Greek rhetoricians and progymnasmatists. Biblical categories like *mashal* and *parabole* are thus heuristic and informal compared with the rhetoricians' categories.

Comparing non-Greek proverb collections with gospel oral and written tradition, we are also hampered by the lack of an extensive non-Greek performance literature. That is, Old Testament narrative and prophecy present surprisingly few gnomic or proverbial performances to balance the wisdom literature's collections and compilations.[4] Like classical gnomai and everyday proverbs, most gospel gnomai are presented in conversational or dialectic contexts, however artificial; most Old Testament maxims are parts of poems.

Gospel gnomai are readily comparable with analogous forms in the Old Testament and elsewhere, but the rhetorics of wisdom collections and compilations are not likely to be representative of the public speech

---

[4] For examples see below and C. Fontaine, *Traditional Sayings in the Old Testament* (Bible and Literature 5; Sheffield, 1982) 5, 74–138; C. Fontaine, "Proverb Performance in the Hebrew Bible," *JSOT* 32 (1985) 87–103; Hermisson, *Spruchweisheit*, 38–52; O. Eißfeldt, *Der Maschal im Alten Testament* (BZAW 24; Gießen, 1913) 45–46.

even of their actual writers. No doubt the wisdom literatures attest the importance of proverbs and similar patterns in the rhetorics of traditional cultures; there is no need to underestimate the overlap between wisdom and rhetoric or the similarity among conversationally driven cultures. But there is every reason to doubt that anyone spoke like the wisdom literatures. By contrast, the gospels and the rhetoricians are in relatively privileged contact with uses of gnomic language in actual oral communication. There is every reason to suppose that the overuse of dramatic gnomai which Quintilian condemns as modern and exotic ('Asiatic') really was available as a model to self-taught Greco-Roman 'sophists' like Jesus and the gospel writers.

Modern critical study of Hebrew, Egyptian and related wisdom literatures poses an even greater obstacle to successful comparison of gospel gnomic rhetoric with wisdom literary conventions. Such study too often uncritically accepts the identity of 'wisdom sayings' with actual speech-forms. To the extent that wisdom is a profoundly literary movement, 'wisdom saying' is an oxymoron. Even more prejudicial, however, has been the obsession with determining the date, social origins and original syntactic forms of sub-units of wisdom literature.[5] In scholarly eyes, the mood and style of wisdom-literary compositions has often seemed ill-matched with the rest of Israelite literature; the perennial interest in abstracting the 'essence' of wisdom is a rhetorical as well as a theological problem.[6] 'Wisdom' themes are an attractive principle of unity through Israelite, Jewish and early Christian literatures; the temptation is to overstate the continuity and specificity of sapiential forms and styles in order to detect hidden wisdom influences.

Wisdom influences have in practice been detected everywhere in the biblical literatures, not least in law, historiography, prophecy and apocalyptic. Wisdom is everywhere, though not uniformly. Some critically differentiated history of sapiential forms and motifs must therefore be undertaken. But the 'wisdom saying' and 'wisdom

---

[5] Fontaine, "Performance," 91.

[6] W. Zimmerli, "Zur Struktur der alttestamentlichen Weisheit," ZAW 51 (1933) 177–204; G. von Rad, *Weisheit in Israel* (Neukirchen-Vluyn, 1970) trans. J.D. Martin, *Wisdom in Israel* (London, 1972) 1–8; E.G. Bauckmann, "Die Proverbien und die Sprüche des Jesus Sirach: Eine Untersuchung zum Strukturwandel der israelitischen Weisheitslehre," ZAW (1960) 33–63; J.L. McKenzie, "Reflections on Wisdom," *JBL* 86 (1967) 1–9; J.T. Collins, "Proverbial Wisdom and the Yahwist Vision," in *Gnomic Wisdom*, ed. J.D. Crossan=*Semeia* 17 (1980) 1–17.

epistemology and christology' as the formal and ideological signs of sapiential influence, seldom seem to mix. There is undoubtedly a convention in wisdom literature which associates wisdom themes with proverbially-styled language, but the association is not always reciprocal; wisdom writers clearly like to sound proverbial up to a point, but it does not follow that every gnomic form indexes wisdom influence, especially in Greek texts.

We must beware of seeking biblical wisdom or "an educational or pedagogic quality" in every gnomic turn of early Christian Greek.[7] It seems straightforward to assert modestly that a

> good deal of the speech attributed to Jesus is cast in a form which has obvious affinities with proverbial forms of speech found principally in the wisdom literature.[8]

Yet however obvious the affinities, it is important to question whether "forms...found principally in" a particular kind of *"literature"* are likely to be "forms of *speech*" (my emphasis). Greco-Roman rhetoric expects that gnome will be heard principally in conversation and rhetorical performance and will therefore appear in all types of literature. Gnomai will only secondarily be concentrated in specialized handbooks, collections and compilations.

One of the few studies of proverb performance, as distinct from proverb collection and poetry, begins with the observation that "wisdom literature seems to engender a particular failure of method rather more often than other texts."[9] This failure, all too easily duplicated in relation to New Testament 'wisdom sayings', can be illustrated by the two controlling distinctions in Hebrew wisdom studies: between 'folk proverb' (*Volkssprichwort*) and literary aphorism or 'wisdom saying'

---

[7] Quoting P.J. Nel, *The Structure and Ethos of the Wisdom Admonitions in Proverbs* (BZAW 158; Berlin and New York, 1982) 1; in general see H. von Lips, *Weisheitliche Traditionen im Neuen Testament* (WMANT 64; Neukirchen-Vluyn, 1990) 5–6, 15–28.

[8] A.P. Winton, *The Proverbs of Jesus: Issues of History and Rhetoric* (JSNTSup 35; Sheffield, 1990) 27.

[9] Fontaine, "Performance," 88, citing J.L. Crenshaw, "Method in Determining Wisdom Influence Upon 'Historical' Literature," *JBL* 88 (1969) 129–142 and R.E. Murphy, "Form Criticism and Wisdom Literature," *CBQ* 31 (1969) 475–483.

(*Kunstspruch* or *Weisheitsspruch*) and between imperatival 'admonition' (*Mahnung*) and indicative 'maxim' (*Aussage* or *Sentenz*).

Folklore and wisdom poetry (Otto Eißfeldt)

The first of these distinctions is fundamentally confused. Folklore and artistic sophistication (*Kunst*) are vague notions at best; as opposites in a distinction which claims to be *form*-critical, they hide basic ambiguities.

Attempts to pick out folk sayings using formal criteria are best represented by Otto Eißfeldt's study of *mashal* in the Old Testament.[10] This study is typical of a much wider and controversial interest in 'folklore' in biblical studies.[11] Eißfeldt began from a very short list of sayings explicitly identified in their biblical contexts as *meshalim*.[12] To these might be added a few sayings with apparently formulaic introductions (e.g., Gen 10:9; 2 Sam 5:8; 20:18). It is also possible that the words attributed by the prophets to a self-deceiving Israel (*Disputationsworte*) may indirectly tell us something about folk conventions of proverb-use.[13] The riddles of the Samson cycle have an even better claim at least to parody folk usage (Judg 14:14, 18). Finally, a range of proverbial-sounding units may be noticed.[14] From all of these, the

---

[10] Eißfeldt, *Maschal*, 45–46; see J.M. Thompson, *The Form and Function of Proverbs in Ancient Israel* (Studia Judaica 1; Paris and The Hague, 1974) 59 n. 1; R.B.Y. Scott, *The Way of Wisdom in the Old Testament* (London and New York, 1971) 63–70; J. Schmidt, *Studien zur Stilistik der alttestamentlichen Spruchliteratur* (Münster, 1936); J. Hempel, *Die althebraische Literatur und ihr hellenistische-jüdisches Nachleben* (Potsdam, 1930); J.G. Williams, "The Power of Form: A Study of Biblical Proverbs," *Semeia* 17, ed. J.D. Crossan (1980) 35–58, 47–49.

[11] See P.G. Kirkpatrick, *The Old Testament and Folklore Study* (JSNTSup 62; Sheffield, 1988).

[12] Ezek 12:22; 18:2=Jer 31:29; 1 Sam 10:12=19:24; 24:14; Ezek 16:44 (not mentioned by Eißfeldt). See Hermisson, *Spruchweisheit*, 41 and references there.

[13] Isa 40:27; Zeph 1:12; Ezek 9:9; 18:25, 29; 33:10, 17, 20; 37:11—add Isa 5:19; Jer 5:12, 13; and Ezek 8:12 not mentioned by Eißfeldt; Hermisson, *Spruchweisheit*, 40, 44 n. 4.

[14] E.g., Judg 8:2, 21; Jer 8:20; 12:13; 51:58=Hab 2:13; Isa 22:13; 37:3; 1 Sam 16:7; 1 Kgs 20:11—with Job 2:4; Ezek 11:3; Hos 4:11 and 14 not mentioned by Eißfeldt. W. Rudolph, *Hosea* (KAT 13/1; Gütersloh, 1966) 112; Hermisson, *Spruchweisheit*, 44 n. 4; Fontaine, *Traditional Sayings*, 80–81.

optimistic critic might plausibly hope to abstract formal criteria for detecting nuggets of pure folklore buried in the predominantly elite literary wisdom collections.[15]

Eißfeldt's basic position was that the sententious *meshalim* (and anything strongly resembling them) represent an earlier, original stratum or style of pre-poetic wisdom. The evidence of proverb-performances in the Old Testament apart from legal or sapiential collection-forms is thin, though suggestive. There are more accounts of rhetorical or conversational gnome-use in the gospels than of spoken proverb-use in all the Hebrew scriptures. Eißfeldt's belief that a core of authentic Hebrew folk proverbs could be retrieved from otherwise artificial literary wisdom collections has therefore been generally rejected.[16]

It has proven more difficult, however, to lay to rest his supposition that folk sayings must be formally distinguishable from the *bon mots* of the learned, literate few, even in the collections of that few. Even if we had an adequate sample of Israelite folk speech, formal resemblance of a wisdom aphorism to folk proverbs could not in principle prove its actual *origin* in popular, presumably oral usage. It is impossible to define an original, oral sayings-form on the basis of slim and itself literary evidence for non-writing use of proverbs.

What is striking in Eißfeldt's approach, critically re-examined by Carole Fontaine, is the slimness of the proverb performance literature beside the massive scale and long tradition of the wisdom collection literature. The few stories of proverb performances suggest that the passion for proverbs was not as prominent in public rhetoric as it is in more private, courtly and scholarly collections. And in their biblical performances even Eißfeldt's most convincing folk proverbs are spoken in courtly/diplomatic contexts,[17] though I can imagine less glamorous applications.

The parallels between the few known performed proverbs and a few of the collected aphorisms confirm a limited but significant continuity among narrative, prophetic and wisdom literary rhetorics; there is no consistent generic difference between folk proverb and elite aphorism, however different their literary contextualizations. On the other hand,

---

[15]   Eißfeldt, *Maschal*, 45–49; Fontaine, "Performance," 90 (table); Hermisson, *Spruchweisheit*, 18ff.

[16]   Fontaine, *Traditional Sayings*, 7 n. 14; Collins, "Proverbial Wisdom," 4.

[17]   Fontaine, "Performance," 100.

the literary stories of oral proverb performance do relate selectively to a formal and thematic subset within the wisdom collections proper. It may therefore be legitimate to suggest tentative, heuristic differentiations which are not about basic genre, date or social origin, but about style. Thus, for example, James Williams proposes a distinction between collective and individual voices in proverbs/aphorisms. Such a distinction recalls Crépeau's study of "normative range," but has no necessary implications about the social locations in which any particular gnome might be used.[18]

A more significant distinction is the literary difference among narrative, prophetic and collection books as contexts for biblical gnomic rhetorics. In general, the first two are no doubt just as imaginative and stereotyped as the third genre. Prophetic and wisdom literatures also overlap significantly, so that oracles are almost as likely as wisdom instructions to be in verse and to be gathered into collections. As witnesses to typical ways of performing gnomic rhetoric, however, narrative and prophetic texts probably presuppose conventions of rhetorical verisimilitude far more than do sapiential poems. In the narrative and prophetic literatures, gnomai play the familiar gnomic/proverbial roles of audible punctuation; in the wisdom literature gnomai function as formal sub-units in the construction of poetry.

Formally, Eißfeldt's most plausible instances of 'folk' gnomai are single-line sentences (with the partial exception of 1 Samuel 24:(13), 14[19]). He further observed that his presumed folk proverbs showed less reliance on the verse rhythms and parallelism common in collection aphorisms. Eißfeldt therefore assumed that the 'one-line' (monostich) prose saying is the evolutionary precursor of the 'two-limbed' (distich) poetic, verse aphorism.[20]

The evolutionary inference is invalid, but the observations are still important: the verse, distich aphorism *is* characteristic of the literary genres of the wisdom collections. By contrast, prose, monostich gnomai are not essential to any of the literary genres in which they occur.

---

[18] J.G. Williams, *Those Who Ponder Proverbs: Aphoristic Thinking and Biblical Literature* (Sheffield, 1981) 80; "Power of Form," 40.

[19] Eißfeldt, *Maschal*, 47 and n. 1.

[20] Eißfeldt, *Maschal*, 48–9.

If the popular proverb already reveals a tendency to linguistic refinement in that it happily exists in elevated language, then the literary proverb which comes from the schools differs from it by an essentially still stronger cultivation both of language and of content. This is what we find in the Solomonic book of Proverbs, for the idea which used to be widespread, namely that its sentences are to be traced back to popular proverbs, can no longer be maintained.[21]

To the extent that the wisdom collections are characterized by gnomai and especially by more or less versified distichs, those collections are an unpromising basis for analysing oral transmission and performance of gnomai in conversation and public rhetoric. Formally, the aphorisms in collection literature often show signs of adaptation to their specialized poetic contexts. Gnomai elsewhere in biblical literature just as precisely reflect the requirements of their literary contextualizations in narrative or prophecy, but the latter contexts require evocation of explicitly rhetorical settings. In other words, formal differences between gnomai in descriptions of rhetorical performance and gnomai in poetic collections are just enough to suggest a certain tension between gnomic rhetoric and gnomic poetry.

This matters for any attempt to transfer insights from Hebrew biblical studies to synoptic gospel studies; the gospel tradition presupposes basic progymnasmatic conventions and an oral conversation tradition, but it also mediates the influence of literary collection wisdom.[22] Gnomai in stories, gnomai in speeches and gnomai in poems reflect the same range of formal possibilities, but the first two categories tend to prefer monostich variants embedded in non-gnomic texts, while the last tends to favour distich variants as a basic convention of wisdom poetry. All three options for performing and contextualizing gnomai exist in the synoptic literature and may have existed in pre-gospel oral tradition. None of these literary traditions directly reproduces the rhetorical and conversational conventions of any actual speech community. On the other hand each of these literary conventions evidences gnome-use along a wide stylistic continuum from prosaic to

---

[21] Von Rad, *Wisdom*, 26, citing Hermisson, *Spruchweisheit*, 52ff.

[22]   Since Robinson, "LOGOI SOPHON," see especially J.S. Kloppenborg, *Formation of Q*.

formally versified; this unanimity is presumably anchored in a marked rhetorical use of gnomai in early Christian public speech.

The phenomena of collection and versification in wisdom literature invite special understanding as well as special caution—especially with regard to formative influences on early Christian writing. In most languages poetry is linguistically as well as conceptually marked for special processing by listeners or readers: poetry is marked by verse. In the languages of Mediterranean antiquity, this distinction between poetry (with verse) and normal prose is more fundamental than any distinction between oral and literary language. Part of the interest of gnome is that both in Greco-Roman rhetoric and in biblical tradition, gnomai may be in verse or in prose. Unlike wisdom poetry, gnomic rhetoric straddles the border between poetry and prose.

Contemporary analyses of Hebrew poetics differ as to the relative importance of stress-metre, formulaic word-pairs, syntactical line-forms, and various kinds of parallelism.[23] All these features exist in ordinary speech, but are heightened and condensed in verse—and in gnomic sentences. In gnomai and in poetry, metre, parallelism and the rest emphasize the play of symmetry and asymmetry and make a demand for special attention: they provide techniques for linguistically marking analogy. In poetry, written or oral, the same techniques permit the extension of analogy into longer and more complex texts, sacrificing gnomic normativity and separability, but gaining magnitude and drama.

Dissolving the muddled distinction between simple, folk gnome and poetic, elite gnome has, therefore, a double advantage. The distinction between folk and elite idioms, though probably intuitively sound, is also presumably only relative. It is unverifiable from the gnomai preserved in extant (elite) texts; it is hard enough to discern the notes of class identity and aspiration to mobility in Greco-Roman rhetoric. The distinction between prose and verse is at least partly a linguistic (e.g., stylistic and thematic) distinction in the biblical texts. Within this

---

[23] W.G.E. Watson, *Classical Hebrew Poetry: A Guide to its Techniques* (JSOTSup 26; Sheffield, 1984) 97–159; J.L. Kugel, *The Idea of Biblical Poetry: Parallelism and its History* (New Haven, 1981); J.L. Kugel, "Some Thoughts on Future Research into Biblical Style: Addenda to *The Idea of Biblical Poetry*," *JSOT* 28 (1984) 107–117; P.D. Miller Jr., "Meter, Parallelism, and Tropes in the Search for Poetic Style," *JSOT* 28 (1984) 99–106.

distinction gnome mediates between prose and verse both formally and hermeneutically, though not chronologically.

Some Hebrew poetry is not gnomic (Psalms); some gnomai—most of Eißfeldt's presumed "folk proverbs"—are not demonstrably verse, though they are usually somehow odd prose. The particular conventions of Hebrew poetry ('parallelism') relate it even more closely to the analogical structure of gnomai than is the case with Greek poetry. The same Hebrew conventions are also strikingly easy to translate or imitate in Greek, a factor of incalculable importance for the formation of early Christian rhetorics and poetics.

Such insights have no necessary bearing on the priority of one form or one text over others. Attention to the differing poetics of texts which use gnomic rhetoric may, however, have some useful bearing on questions of relative orality and literacy.[24] The relative predominance of individual poetic techniques in particular documents may thus indicate differences, not of date, but of compositional or transmissional mode. Other things being equal, heavy use of formulaic word-pairs in a text (e.g., Psalm 54) is consistent with strong influence of oral improvisational techniques.[25] Where poetic structure is marked mainly by stress-metre—without precluding less intensive use of word-pairs—as in Micah 3:9–12, the less improvisational possibility of memorizing a metrically fixed text must be considered.[26] By contrast, a probable mark of a relatively literate sensibility would be repeated use of enjambment, deliberately letting sense slip away from verse line-forms, magnifying the tension between rhetoric and poetics in the same text (e.g., Ps 119[27]). Yet no biblical text goes as far in this direction, twisting together the conventions and techniques of versification and gnome formulation to create an exotic new rhetorical style, as did the sophists of the Greek enlightenment, whose performances created the necessity of a critical theory of rhetoric.

---

[24] Henderson, "*Didache* and Orality."

[25] Watson, *Hebrew Poetry*, 136–142, esp 137 and n. 61; R.C. Culley, *Oral Formulaic Language in the Biblical Psalms*, (Near and Middle East Series 4: Toronto, 1972).

[26] Watson, *Hebrew Poetry*, 101 and n. 51, 113.

[27] G.S. Kirk, "Formular Language and Oral Quality," *Yale Classical Studies* 20 (1966) 153–174.

Refinements in oral and poetic theory have traditionally moved from Old Testament to New Testament criticism.[28] Rhetorical study of the gospel traditions as a crossroads of differently oral and literate cultures may in fact yield strategies for reformulating and illuminating some of the problems of Hebrew poetics (for example, the relation between popular proverb and poetic parallelism).[29] The interpretive juxtaposition of folk orality and poetic literacy in relation to Old Testament wisdom has massively influenced similar treatment of New Testament sayings-tradition. It is vitally important that studies in wisdom literature span linguistic and chronological boundaries (Egyptian; Hebrew; Greek).[30] On the other hand, discussion of 'wisdom sayings' and 'proverbs' among new Testament gnomai ought to be greatly restrained by the collapse of strong formal distinctions between folk proverbs and units of composition in wisdom poetry.

Gnomai attributed to Jesus are stylistically more like the monostich sayings selected by Eißfeldt than like the sentences of wisdom poetry generally. Parallelism, regular line forms, accentual and semantic patterning have been applied at every level of wisdom literature, including parts of the gospel literary tradition, to produce the extended incantatory effect of versification; the same formal means are used more sparingly in Eißfeldt's sayings and synoptic gnomai to emphasize analogical structure and syntactical separability.

Imperative and indicative normativities

The second thematic distinction in Old Testament proverb studies, between imperative 'admonition' (*Mahnung*) and indicative 'maxim' (*Aussage* or *Sentenz*), has even more directly determined research into gospel 'wisdom sayings'. Indeed, the classification of wisdom sayings into maxims, commands and questions (*Grundsätze/Aussagen, Mahnworte* and *Fragen*) informed Rudolph Bultmann's standard

---

[28]   See R.C. Culley, "Oral Tradition and the Old Testament: Some Recent Discussion" in *Oral Tradition and Old Testament Studies*, ed. R.C. Culley=*Semeia* 5 (1976) 1–33, 20; E. Nielson *Oral Tradition* (SBT 11; London, 1954) 11–17.

[29]   D. Greenwood, "Rhetorical Criticism and Formgeschichte: Some Methodological Considerations," *JBL* 89 (1970) 418–426, 419.

[30]   Kloppenborg, *Formation of Q*.

discussion of "Jesus as Teacher of Wisdom." Since this distinction is at least grounded in verifiable syntactical differences, it is harmless enough if not taken too seriously; in fact, Bultmann uses it only as a convenient descriptive framework.[31] The simpler two-fold division (for most purposes questions may be included with *Aussagen*[32]) has become general enough in Old Testament criticism to be assumed almost without comment also in the neighbouring field.[33]

Too frequently, however, judgements of historical development are based upon this descriptive typology of supposed wisdom sayings. H.-J. Hermisson, for example, combined the imperative-indicative distinction with A. Jolles' wise insistence that proverbs are essentially not didactic. Hermisson decided that imperative admonitions *were* didactic and therefore could not be real folk proverbs. They must instead have originated in wisdom schools.[34]

Soberer attempts to attach the two formal types to different historical origins begin, however, from two observations: Particular imperative admonitions often seem to depend logically upon particular indicative maxims.[35] In addition, the ratio of maxims to admonitions varies greatly among wisdom writings.[36] In the climate of modern biblical studies, the obvious explanations for such a state of affairs were all

---

[31] R. Bultmann, *Die Geschichte der Synoptischen Tradition* (5th ed., Göttingen, 1961) 73–113; von Lips, *Weisheitliche Traditionen im NT*, 18–19; M. Küchler, *Frühjüdische Weisheitstraditionen: Zum Fortgang weisheitlichen Denkens im Bereich des frühjüdischen Jahweglaubens* (OBO 26; Freiburg, Switzerland and Göttingen, 1979) 158–9; E. Schick, *Formgeschichte und Synoptikerexegese: Eine kritische Untersuchung über die Möglichkeit und die Grenzen der formgeschichtlichen Methode* (NTAbh 18/2–3; Münster, 1940) 160.

[32] Bauckmann, "Proverbien," 43; Fontaine, *Traditional Sayings*, 80 n. 28.

[33] Hermisson, *Spruchweisheit*, 36 and n. 1; von Lips, *Weisheitliche Traditionen im NT*, 18–19, 197–214, esp. 204; H. Greßmann, "Die neugefundene Lehre des Amen-em-ope und die vorexilische Spruchdichtung Israels," *ZAW* 42 (1924) 272–96; H. Gese, "Weisheitsdichtung," *RGG* VI (1962) coll. 1577–81; H. Gese, *Lehre und Wirklichkeit in der alten Weisheit: Studien zu dem Buche Hjob* (Tübingen, 1958) 5–6; Murphy, "Form Criticism and Wisdom Literature."

[34] Jolles, *Einfache Formen*, 158; Hermisson, *Spruchweisheit*, 28–9, 36–52, 187–9; Fontaine, *Traditional Sayings*, 10–13.

[35] E.g., Prov 22:14a upon 23:27; 13:9b upon 24:20; and, according to Zeller, 20:66 upon 22:27 and 21:17 upon 23:31. Zimmerli, "Struktur," 184; D. Zeller, *Die weisheitlichen Mahnsprüche bei den Synoptikern* (FB 17; Würzburg, 1977) 23 n. 74.

[36] Zimmerli, "Struktur," 185–6.

evolutionary. Greßmann, Hempel, Zimmerli and others deduced the historical priority of the indicative maxim from its preponderance in early literary collections. E. Gerstenberger conversely declared the imperative admonitions, like the prohibitions of apodeictic law, to be the early products of tribal and clan normative speech.[37]

The temptation to cross the imperative-indicative distinction with Eißfeldt's monostich-distich distinction has proven particularly irresistible—with predictably complicated results. In terms of strictly *literary* history, it does seem that the imperative, distich admonition was the dominant gnomic form in the oldest Egyptian wisdom literature, with monostich gnomai more prominent only under later Hellenistic influence.[38] This early, cosmopolitan and elite literary influence, of course, settles nothing about oral gnome-use unless one already knows, like Eißfeldt and Hermisson, that the indicative monostich is "the genuine form of authentic folk proverbs."[39]

Wolfgang Richter has sought to break the form-critical isolation of the imperatival distich admonition as a product of international literary influences on Israelite wisdom. Without minimizing literary influences from Egyptian wisdom, Richter seeks evidence for specifically Hebrew styles of speech with which international wisdom presumably interacted in the production of an Israelite wisdom literature. Richter identifies two forms which he relates to legal and ethical settings respectively, though the two forms mingle in later sapiential collections. That is, his study concerns itself with possible relationships between different sayings forms and different kinds of prescriptive normativity not only in wisdom collections, but ultimately throughout classical Hebrew literature.

---

[37] Greßmann, "Spruchdichtung," 298; Hempel, *Literatur*, 175; Zimmerli, *Maschal*, 186; E. Gerstenberger, *Wesen und Herkunft des "Apodiktischen Rechts"* (WMANT 20; Neukirchen-Vluyn, 1965).

[38] J.S. Kloppenborg, "The Formation of Q and Antique Instructional Genres," *JBL* 105 (1986) 443–462, 458–460; Kloppenborg, *Formation of Q*, 267–272; W. McKane, *Proverbs: A New Approach* (London and Philadelphia, 1970) 3–10; K.A. Kitchen, "The Basic Literary Forms and Formulations of Ancient Instructional Writings in Egypt and Western Asia," in *Studien zu altägyptischen Lebenslehren*, ed. E. Horning and O. Kee, (OBO 28; Freiburg, Switzerland and Göttingen, 1979) 235–282; P. Nel, *Wisdom Admonitions*.

[39] G. von Rad, "Die ältere Weisheit Israels," *KD* 2 (1956) 54–72, 63.

Richter acknowledges the distinction between admonitions (*Mahnwort*) and maxims (*Aussage*), but substitutes for the former his own narrower definition based on exclusively syntactical and grammatical analysis of Proverbs 22:17–24:22. This substitution is interesting not least because it underlines the fact that the distinction between imperatival admonition and indicative maxim, prevalent since Zimmerli, is more a semantic distinction of *perceived normativity* than of verbal mood. Richter tries to define many of the same items, but without systematic reference to the semantic aspect. He therefore distinguishes among admonition (which he prefers to call *Mahnspruch*), prohibition and command as much as possible on grammatical-syntactical grounds. One consequence is concentration on the grammatically more varied negative forms, the legal-sounding prohibitions and negative admonitions.

At the same time Richter's admonition (*Mahnspruch*) often incorporates a maxim in the Aristotelean role of quasi-logical premise; for Richter's purposes, the admonition-form requires at least two non-parallel line-forms, one 'line' (the *Mahnung*) including a verbal mood of warning and one (the *Begründung*) giving a rationale or motive. This motive-clause is often, though not always, a proverbial-looking indicative maxim.[40] A Greco-Roman reader would easily recognize Richter's admonition-form as a species of enthymeme and would discern gnomai in many of its warnings and motive-clauses.

Richter usefully recognizes that all of the forms he defines—admonition, prohibition and command—reflect the tastes and interests of the "schools"—which I take to mean of the text-writing elites. Here he is trying to have his argument both ways: the admonitory saying is a hybrid product of popular speech forms, of specialized scholastic legal, ethical and prophetic styles, and of international literary influences. Thus, even imperatival prohibitions are not to be classed as law in anything like the strong sense of more narrowly cultic commandments.[41] Richter's position on the changing, nuanced and often mixed ways of expressing normativity in biblical Hebrew is too complicated to persuade. His work should, however, weigh heavily against simplistic positions, e.g., that the indicative maxims were originally folk proverbs

---

[40] W. Richter, *Recht und Ethos: Versuch einer Ortung des weisheitlichen Mahnspruches*, (SANT 15; München, 1966) 39.

[41] Richter, *Recht und Ethos*, 120, 144–6.

(Zimmerli) or that admonitions, but not the maxims which now accompany them, preserve the forms of pre-literary clan-wisdom (E. Gerstenberger[42]). The strength of Richter's complex position is the implication that, despite the pervasive literary tension between distinguishable folkloric and sophisticated tones in wisdom, both kinds of influence are at work behind every wisdom sentence and in the whole history of biblical wisdom.

Richter's detailed form-critical analyses and complicated results are highly specific to Hebrew syntax and grammar. His method is, moreover, partly tautological: the reception of international sapiential literary influences into Israelite writing was not a mechanical process of translation, but rather a gradual and discerning process of assimilation which necessarily drew on forms of speech with long prehistories in Hebrew. The origins of 'form' in this grammatical-syntactical sense can hardly fail to be found among the possibilities of everyday language.[43]

As A.J. Bjorndalen has shown, such indispensable elements of Richter's definition of the admonition-form as "warning" and "motive" or "rationale" are still semantic rather than grammatical-syntactical. This brings the problem of defining wisdom sayings back to mainly semantic and rhetorical questions about analogy, separability and—for Richter, especially—normativity:

> What is lacking in Richter's description of the *Gattung* of the admonitory saying is a description of the deictic peculiarity of the admonitory saying as a saying...[44]

Richter's work is of special interest here because, for better and for worse, its framework has been adopted for Dieter Zeller's landmark study of "wisdom admonitions in the synoptic gospels." The sophisticated interpretation of admonitory wisdom by Richter and Zeller has thus directly influenced reconstruction and interpretation of the Q tradition and of post-biblical Jewish wisdom generally. Even A.P. Winton's discussion of *The Proverbs of Jesus* explicitly stakes its own territory

---

[42] Gerstenberger, *Wesen und Herkunft*, 89–130; see Hermisson, *Spruchweisheit*, 82–4.

[43] Hermisson, *Spruchweisheit*, 84–6.

[44] A.J. Bjorndalen, "'Form' und 'Inhalt' des motivierenden Mahnspruches," *ZAW* 82 (1970) 347–361, 361 (abstract).

in terms of Zeller's survey: "Proverbial sayings" "as opposed to the
Wisdom Admonition, Question or longer sections of discourse."[45]

Zeller adapts Richter's definition of the admonition, eliminating
many specifically Hebrew definitional elements and distinctions:

> The characteristic of the admonition is a verb which, by its grammatical
> mood, indicates that some particular behaviour is to be prescribed. In
> Proverbs the admonition is expressed throughout in the second person
> singular. The warning-clause (*Mahnsatz*) is almost never without a motive-
> clause (*Begründung*), the form of which is basically variable.[46]

Zeller thus retains Richter's emphasis on grammatical/syntactical form
(imperatival/optative mood) and on 'two-line' semantic construction
(warning + motive-clause), though in the new context of Greek texts,
Zeller cannot be as precise in the application of, especially, the
grammatical criterion. Consequently, Zeller locates his admonition-form
within a much more open continuum of proverbial language. Thus both
imperatives and indicatives express normative intentions, only the
former do so explicitly and more aggressively.

> It is not as though indicative maxims (*Aussagen*) are irrelevant to normative
> direction—most bring deed and consequence into relation or poetically
> formulate some principle. But where with maxims it only emerges from the
> context (*aus der Textpragmatik*) that something is being demanded from the
> hearers, this comes in admonitions in the grammatical form of expression.
> With their combination of imperative or prohibition with motive-clause,
> they offer the best chance to clarify the background of Jesus' directives.[47]

Moreover, the imperatival admonition shares with the gnome a less
readily defined semantic economy and autonomy, what, following
Crépeau, I have called analogical structure and separability.

---

[45] Zeller, *Mahnsprüche*; Kloppenborg, *Formation of Q*; Küchler, *Weisheitstraditio-nen*, 16–20; Winton, *Proverbs*, 31–6.

[46] Zeller, *Mahnsprüche*, 22.

[47] Zeller, *Mahnsprüche*, 11.

The linguistic resistance (*sprachliche Resistenz*) of the admonition seems therefore to imply that, like the gnome (*Sentenz*) in origin, it is a sub-category of the proverb (*Spruch*).[48]

The attempt by Zeller to contextualize the admonition within a wider range of gnomic language has led him to qualify Richter's highly specific literary form-critical approach with a much more general and intuitive semantic interest. It is not clear that these two are compatible. Richter was interested in everyday language only as one partial but necessary (because authentically Israelite) background of the admonition.

Zeller, however, needs to speak of admonitions in Jesus' public speaking and in its oral tradition and not only in learned books written under wisdom influence.[49] He must show that the *literary* admonition-form had the same characteristic place (*Sitz im Leben*) in oral tradition and in the conversation of Jesus as Richter thought it might have had in the oral prehistory of Israelite wisdom. Hence, for example, Zeller's need to insist—rather against the evidence—on the continuity of the specialized admonition-form in rabbinic tradition.[50] For Zeller the assimilation of near eastern wisdom and Greco-Roman rhetoric is unimportant beside the hope of locating specialized wisdom literary forms in non-writing, pre-gospel tradition.

It is to accommodate such tradition that Zeller compromises the apparent grammatical/syntactical rigour of his working definition derived from Richter. Zeller's umbrella definition embracing both admonitions and maxims is radically incommensurable with his working definition of the admonition alone. This more general definition of proverb is a familiar enough list of frequent, not definitive, semantic or syntactical features: separability from any particular literary context, speaker or rhetorical situation (often marked by parataxis or asyndeton); stylistic distinctness; metaphoric, symmetrical and/or binary structure.

---

[48]   Zeller, *Mahnsprüche*, 23.

[49]   Zeller, *Mahnsprüche*, 147ff.

[50]   Zeller, *Mahnsprüche*, 41: "The admonition, of which the classical form appears in Proverbs, is also living in post-exilic times right through to rabbinic Judaism.... The special setting (*Sitz im Leben*) of the admonition is impressively documented in the fact that *Abot* commands a special place in the *Mishna* and that only two extra-canonical collections [Qohelet and Sirach] preserve to any extent the admonition's proper character."

The paradoxical result is that Zeller's analysis of the admonition as distinct from the maxim was (I would add, until the work of Klaus Berger) "the best description in the exegetical literature of both these two sayings-types." Zeller's work remains more influential than Berger's in the English-speaking world.[51]

Zeller epitomizes the attempt to (con)fuse a deliberately exclusive and formalist definition of the admonition with a deliberately inclusive and semantic definition of proverbial language. The greatest, though illusory, advantage of such a confusion is that it glosses over the question of how Jewish and Christian—and Greco-Roman—rhetorics related to the production of Jewish and Christian—and Greco-Roman—wisdom books. One necessary middle term between rhetorical perform-ance and literary production in Greek is Greco-Roman rhetorical theory, practice and education about gnome-use.[52] It is not only Jesus and his tradition to whom admonitions are attributed: as a species of enthymeme, the combination of a second person singular imperative-clause with a motive-clause is, for example, densely exemplified by Isocrates (twenty times in *To Nicocles* 13–38).

Moreover, throughout the rhetoricians the postulated form-critical gap between imperatival and indicative gnome is routinely bridged. Zeller's study, though focused on imperatival admonitions, should have had the second advantage of qualifying the interpretive distinction between imperative admonitions and indicative maxims. Zeller fundamentally equivocates between Richter's formalism and a more pragmatic analysis of gnomic rhetoric. That element of pragmatism deserved, even from him, more respect as it relativizes the gap in normativity between admonitions and maxims and emphasizes their basic commonality in a shared "linguistic resistance."

All admonitions and maxims reflect the "paradigmatic function of the proverb."[53] The imperative mood of the admonition is one way to include in this function an assertion of higher social rank. Zeller's

---

[51] Zeller, *Mahnsprüche* 16–20; quoting Küchler, *Weisheitstraditionen*, 163; for influence see Winton, *Proverbs*, 33–36; L.G. Perdue, "The Wisdom Sayings of Jesus," *Forum* 2 (1986) 3–35, 18; Kloppenborg, "Formation of Q," 456; see Berger, "Hellenistische Gattungen," 1049–74; Berger, *Formgeschichte*, 62–74, 155–220.

[52] Berger, "Hellenistische Gattungen," 1056.

[53] Zeller, *Mahnsprüche*, 17, see also 31–2; J. Thomas, *Der jüdische Phokylides: Formgeschichtliche Zugänge zu Pseudo-Phokylides und Vergleich mit der neutestament-lichen Paränese* (NTOA 23; Freiburg, Switzerland, and Göttingen, 1992) 27 n. 3.

selection of the admonitions depended largely on his intuition that, in their emphatic normativity, they represent Jesus' own rhetorical *ethos*. This is the right reason for the wrong choice: the normativity which attracts him to the admonitions is also rhetorically basic to all other gnomai, when they are imagined in any possible rhetorical performance. Above all, such rhetorical normativity is not essentially defined by the grammatical mood of a verb, as is clear when Zeller distances himself from Richter's influence.

> [For Zeller] the proverb has a "paradigmatic function"(17); the admonition is its non-indicative "variant"(21): the proverbial saying's lightly veiled normative function (*Anweisungsfunktion*) becomes a grammatical form in the admonition, without the "sapiential perceptiveness" being lost.[54]

It is true that variation between imperative and indicative forms is not merely performantial: the imperatival insistence on social distance as a basis of normative authority is a significant hermeneutical variant, especially when it is reinforced by father-son, master-disciple, divinity-mortal metaphors. But Zeller's equivocal approach both invites and frustrates raising relative difference in rhetorical normativity into an assumption of different developmental and social trajectories (*Sitze im Leben*) for the two kinds of gnome.

On one hand the obvious, though misleading, inference frequently drawn from Richter and Zeller is still that the imperative is normative while the indicative is not:

> Unlike the proverb, the admonition is didactic in intentionality, for it seeks to persuade its hearers to pursue an action, while its opposite, the prohibition, attempts to dissuade.

Or again,

> Unlike what happens with the purely descriptive, indicative *sententia* (*Einzelsentenz*), in the admonition, in literary sayings collections and in the instruction-form the communicative dimension receives an authoritative force.[55]

---

[54] Küchler, *Weisheitstraditionen*, 163.

[55] Perdue, "Wisdom Sayings," 18 and n. 30; Thomas, *Der jüdische Phokylides*, 26 and 25 n.1.

On the other hand, Zeller concedes in advance that the 'admonition' *is* a 'proverb' and that they share their persuasive, normative, paradigmatic function.

It is in the Greco-Roman rhetorical tradition that this radical and practical continuity between styles of gnome is most consistently explained and taught. Early Christian gnome-use and Greco-Roman gnome-use are not at all limited to teaching settings; rhetorical performance has a much wider range of normative interests. By contrast, the association of gnomai, indicative or imperative, with wisdom and teaching is a conventional fiction of both Greek and non-Greek wisdom poetry.

From this rhetorical point of view, variations in verbal mood can still be significant. Zeller is mistaken, however, to assume verb-forms are a sufficient criterion for choosing a sample from which to re-create the normative *ethos* of Jesus' rhetoric or of the pre-gospel tradition. If any sub-category of gnomai has a special claim to historical relevance it should not be those sayings marked by a grammatical imperative, but those touching most clearly on controversial or atypical normative topics; Richter was right to raise the issue of normativity in proverbial language in relation to prophetic and legal speech.

Both rhetorical theories of gnome-use and modern paroemiological study of proverb-use in non-print societies confirm the importance of gnomic language in legal contexts and the close topical and formal relationship between laws and other maxims. In many societies and institutions there is no systematic distinction among normative styles and topics of law, rhetoric and wisdom, all of which can be expressed in gnomai.[56] Even in the modern nation-state the legal maxim has remarkably retained its influence as a rhetorical meta-law. But this kind of normative directness in the sense of, at least potential, casuistic relevance has little to do with the grammatical directness of second person singular which defines the admonition. The example gnomai of the rhetoricians and progymnasmatists conspicuously include, and without much comment, both imperative and indicative forms.

Moving away from studying the admonition to studying gnomai involves more than just abandoning the exaggerated and formalistic distinction between imperative and indicative. The admonition as

---

[56] P.R. Callaway, "Deut 21:18–21: Proverbial Wisdom and Law," *JBL* 103 (1984) 341–352, esp. 345–6.

defined by Richter and Zeller is a compound form. In Greco-Roman terms, the admonition is a kind of enthymeme which may include one or more gnomai. The compound "classic form"[57] defined by Richter and Zeller is, moreover, irreducibly derived from literary study of Proverbs 10–29 and related collection-poems. Moreover, "the great major[i]ty of admonitions among the sayings of Jesus are found in instructions";[58] that is, they belong to the even more clearly literary genre of wisdom instruction (*Lehrrede*), the sapiential analogue of the rhetorical argumentation-form. Indeed, the extremely doubtful relation of Zeller's admonitions to 'sayings' as oral communication or as independent elements of oral tradition led Klaus Berger to seek a less prejudicial name for the literary admonition (*begrundete Mahnrede* instead of *Mahnspruch*).[59] Wide variation in the density of admonitions in wisdom collections and other texts is therefore likely to be an index of literary-poetic tradition, of argumentational form or of authorial stylistic decisions, rather than of textual openness to oral traditions and styles.

But Zeller (like most scholars interested in Q as a wisdom collection) wants to study not only literary influences on the composition of the gospels; Zeller wants to find admonitions in rabbinic and pre-gospel oral traditions. Such strongly literary categories as the admonition and the larger, composite unit, the instruction, are doomed to prove inconclusive for the history of oral tradition and performance. In keeping with their form-critical heritage, both Richter and Zeller are essentially confused about how to relate literary forms (admonition) to spoken idioms and conversational, rhetorical traditions. Greco-Roman rhetoric is much less perplexed by the use of gnomai in both written and spoken performance.

Gnomai in non-Greek wisdom rhetorics

Are there gnomai in biblical and related non-Greek texts? Does a definition of gnome derived from Crépeau and from the rhetoricians

---

[57] Zeller, *Mahnsprüche*, 47.

[58] Perdue, "Wisdom Sayings," 19; he notes the following exceptions: Mark 7:27 par; Mark 12:17 par; Luke 12:15; Matt 7:6; Matt 5:16.

[59] Berger, *Formgeschichte*, 157.

work better than definitions from Eißfeldt or Richter as a middle term between synoptic rhetoric and its non-Greek backgrounds?

Nothing like a complete answer can be attempted in the space available here. Some samples may, however, be taken, with the help of surveys by Max Küchler and John S. Kloppenborg.[60]

Of twenty-nine sayings in thirty-nine instances isolated by Eißfeldt in narrative and prophetic literature, about sixteen would readily be picked out using Crepeau's structural model. That majority of Old Testament sayings-in-contexts, however, more nearly resembles Synoptic gospel sayings than either set resembles typical wisdom texts. The remainder are mostly items which seem too closely dependent on their particular contexts (e.g., Jer 8:20; 12:13; 23:28). That is, they do not satisfy the criterion of separability. The clichéd metaphors of Genesis 16:12 and 1 Samuel 24:15 (see 2 Sam 9:8; 16:9) are both grammatically and logically dependent upon their contexts, but these may be shorthand evocations of a separable analogy like "an Attic neighbour" (Arist. *Rh. II 21, 12=1395a*) or "a stitch in time"—virtual gnomai.

Analysed in Crépeau's terms, Eißfeldt's sayings do confirm the centrality of analogy and normativity (including personal *ethos*) for the analysis of actual (or here realistically represented) speech. By comparison, distinctions among grammatical forms, among folk, scribal and courtly origins and even between prose and verse styles are relatively unhelpful.

Is Saul, too, one of the prophets? (1 Sam 10:12, royalist; 19:24, anti-royalist)

Days pass and visions fade. (Ezek 12:22)

Out of the wicked: wickedness. (1 Sam 24:13)

One who puts on armour should not brag like one who takes it off. (1 Kgs 20:11)

---

[60] Küchler, *Weisheitstraditionen*; Kloppenborg, *Formation of Q*, 263–316, 329–341; for comparison with Greco-Roman collections see Berger, "Hellenistiche Gattungen," 1059–74 and Table I "Systematischer Analyse gnomischer Sammlungen und vergleichbare Texte."

Literary versification in Old Testament and Gospel wisdom

Almost all of Eißfeldt's proverbs and especially the sixteen most independent sayings among them are formally as well as semantically marked in relation to their contexts. Still an important aspect of this sample of gnomai from narrative and prophetic texts is their notable poetic informality by the standards of Hebrew sapiential, lyric and psalmic poetry. Thus, for example, most of the extra-sapiential sayings are one-line (monostich) whereas distichs are the norm for near eastern wisdom poetry before the Hellenistic period.[61] Eißfeldt's sample gnomai, gnomai from the Synoptic gospels and gnomai in Greco-Roman rhetoric have in common that they are somehow linguistically heightened above other normal speech. They need not be in verse, however.

If a verse-prose distinction is not critical for gnomai as such, it does seem to be a critical distinction for literary collection genres. Many Hellenistic gnomologia are uniform verse compositions; I do not know any gnome collection in which verse and prose gnomai are freely mixed. The situation is even clearer in Hebrew wisdom poetry: such writings are not only poetic in an aesthetic sense, they are recognizable as verse, however debatable (and variable from text to text) the fine points of Hebrew verse conventions may be. In Old Testament narrative and prophetic texts, verse constraints are less consistently evident and have much less impact on gnomic forms. And this is true also of the gospel literature and its gnomai. Despite the (often exaggerated) influence of "semitic poetic features" on gospel composition and the presence in the gospels of liturgical pastiches and of instructional forms reminiscent of wisdom poetry, the gospels and their gnomai are essentially in prose.[62]

Even the identification of Q as basically (or originally) a sapiential collection composed of typical sapiential instructions must raise the question of how this macro-generic classification relates to the less obviously sapiential qualities of its gnomic micro-rhetoric. To the extent that Q really was a wisdom book, it was an anthology of poems, not a

---

[61] Kloppenborg, "Formation of Q," 458 and n. 60.

[62] S. Segert, "Semitic Poetic Structures in the New Testament," *ANRW* II 25/2 (1984) 1433–62; Kloppenborg, *Formation of Q* and "Formation of Q"; Piper, *Wisdom in the Q-Tradition.*

collection of sayings; the move from J.M. Robinson's *Logoi Sophon* to John Kloppenborg's book of instructions is not quite so straightforward an evolution as Robinson himself suggested.[63]

Robinson's influential articles sought to establish a "trajectory" of collected "sayings of the wise" from such collections as Aramaic Ahiqar, Egyptian Amenemope and biblical Proverbs 30, 31 and 22:17–24:22. The other end of this trajectory Robinson located especially in the mishnaic collection *Abot*, in the "Wisdom Gospel" Q and in the *Gospel of Thomas*. As Kloppenborg emphasizes, Robinson's achievement lay in his recognition "that the transition from oral to written stages of the Jesus tradition was enabled by the mediation of literary genres." Kloppenborg goes beyond Robinson (and Zeller) in defining the literary genre which is supposed to have promoted the assimilation of oral tradition of Jesus' sayings to wisdom literature. More specific than Robinson's *Logoi Sophon* yet more inclusive than Zeller's admonition form, Kloppenborg identifies the wisdom instruction as the formative, generic convention governing Q.

The very precision of Kloppenborg's proposal (like Zeller's, though on a grander scale) makes the relationship between literary genre and oral tradition once again problematic. Robinson had assumed that the *literary* genre of sayings-of-the-wise had a privileged relationship to the patterns in which Jesus' followers transmitted oral tradition about the way he talked. Kloppenborg's more refined analysis of the literary instructional genre behind Q makes this assumption look much less plausible:

> It must be recognized that almost all of the examples which Robinson adduces are, from a form-critical and history-of-traditions standpoint, much more homogeneous than Q. In fact Q is a composite of not only wisdom sayings, but chriae, prophetic and apocalyptic words and the temptation story. Is such variety compatible with its inclusion in the genre of *logoi sophon*?...I think, yes.
>
> That the genre [*logoi sophon*] functioned in a situation of oral transmission of sayings is not clear.[64]

---

[63] J.M. Robinson, "Forward" to Kloppenborg *Formation of Q*, xi–xiv.

[64] Kloppenborg, *Formation of Q*, 30–31.

Kloppenborg's greatest contribution is to make the genre behind Q look even more specifically bookish; he recognizes more clearly than his teacher the "careful *literary* stylization which is present in Q." As a result, it is harder than ever to imagine how that book-type could have significantly mediated "the transition from oral to written stages of...tradition." To press the metaphor of trajectories, if the instruction-form is the projectile launched by classical wisdom literature, it remains unexplained why that bullet should have been stopped by the gospel-writers' traditions about how Jesus talked and by the proto-rabbinic traditions behind *Abot.*

Kloppenborg suggests that the "presence of wisdom sayings among Jesus' sayings no doubt [*sic*] accounted for their organization in the *Gattung logoi sophon.*"[65] But no one has ever suggested that anyone, let alone Jesus, actually spoke in the literary genre of sapiential instruct-ions. There is no necessary, let alone demonstrable, trajectory from a gnomic personal or traditional style of rhetoric to the composition of instruction-books.

My own suspicion is that the presumed association between literary instruction forms and oral tradition is ultimately grounded in an uncritical acceptance of the "authorial fiction" of classical wisdom literature, that it presents parental instruction: both wisdom literature and oral tradition are assumed to be didactic, so that the tension between written and spoken performances can be smoothed over. But there is nothing harder to pin on Jesus than a didactic intention.

> [W]hy is there so little teaching material within the Gospels that can be carried back to Jesus himself[?]...If Jesus was a teacher, what—to put it crudely—was the syllabus within his school?[66]

At any rate, Kloppenborg is right to worry about the claims of M.E. Boring and W. Kelber that Q was less sapiential than prophetic, less literary than oral, in its formative conventions—despite the excesses of both Boring's and Kelber's positions. The issue is not whether 'wisdom' or 'prophecy' is a better hermeneutical key to gospel sayings material;

---

[65] Kloppenborg, *Formation of Q*, 36, 30, 29.

[66] P.S Alexander, "Orality in Pharisaic-Rabbinic Judaism at the Turn of the Eras," in *Jesus and the Oral Gospel Tradition*, ed. H. Wansbrough (JSNTSup 64; Sheffield, 1991) 159–184, 183.

I see even less use than Kloppenborg in quarrelling about whether "a given saying" should be designated "as prophetic or sapiential."[67]

Kloppenborg acknowledges that there is a problem for 'trajectory' theories in the "form-critical heterogeneity" of Q, compared with classical wisdom books. But the force of the analogy between Q and biblical prophecy is not solely derived from the formal and thematic diversity of the Sayings Gospel. Rather the truth of saying that Q "is closer to Jeremiah than it is to Proverbs," has to do with the closer imitation of actual speech-forms in prophetic and gospel literatures.[68]

This is also the relative insight in Werner Kelber's muddled assertion that "Q represents an oral genre," notwithstanding that Q clearly was a book, crafted with considerable (Greek) literary skill, and under at least some biblical influence. As Kloppenborg notes, "the 'oral' nature of the genre resides," for Kelber, "in the fact that it was intended for 'oral performance'." But such an intention links virtually all the literature of antiquity, except for narrowly scribal manuals, records and lists; the whole of ancient literature is in this sense 'more oral' than print literature. For the present purpose, however, I think there is another, more significant indicator of relative orality: By comparison with the classics of ancient near eastern sapiential literature, Q and the other gospels—like Old Testament narrative and prophecy—are generically committed to representing speech with some verisimilitude. Q and Jeremiah are more 'oral' than Proverbs in that they are more explicitly rhetorical, less consistently poetic, less countably versified.

This is not to say that the units of composition in gospels are less stylized than those in sapiential poetry, but they are differently stylized. The rhetoric of the prophets and the rhetoric of the gospel traditions were no more 'natural rhetoric' than were the experimental rhetorics of the sophists. Still, the units of composition in the gospels, the units within which poetic conventions are constant, are more often the units of public speech and progymnasmatic education than the units of wisdom versification—the couplet, the quatrain and the instruction. It is surely true that there is a strong influence of wisdom poetry upon the writing of Q. Kloppenborg may be right, though I do not know how to

---

[67] Kloppenborg, *Formation of Q*, 37; but see M. Sato, "Wisdom Statements in the Sphere of Prophecy," in *The Gospel Behind the Gospels: Current Studies on Q*, ed. R.A. Piper (NovTSup 75; Leiden, 1995) 139–158.

[68] Kloppenborg, *The Formation of Q*, 34–6.

test this, that successive editions of Q underwent a change of literary influence from wisdom literature toward apocalyptic.

All this has no bearing, however, on how Jesus tradition found its way with such density into the gospel genre. The missing link between oral tradition about what Jesus said and books about Jesus is not found in the intensely literary (I would say, scribal) conventions of wisdom poetry. "Popular, proverbial rhetoric underlies the rhetoric of poetry, and in a dead language they are hard to distinguish."[69] There is every reason to believe, however, that in the wisdom-literary models of admonition and instruction applied by Zeller and Kloppenborg to gospel literature, we are dealing with "the rhetoric of poetry" rather than with conventions which were ever used to define a genre or a style of public speech. On the other hand, it is also clearly naive to assume that the gospels and related literature (e.g., *Did.* or *m.Abot*) immediately reflect "popular, proverbial rhetoric." They all reflect in their own ways "careful...stylization" of oral traditions which were in themselves never just popular or proverbial.

Theorists of orality and literacy have long since begun to speak of an intermediate sensibility characterized socially by craft-literacy, the use of writing systems by an exclusive class or profession of retainers. Most studies of sapiential poetry locate its production and readership in such scribal milieux, and the nature of the poetry, grounded in list-making is consistent with such a character. It would be out of place here to attempt a history of Israel's scribal wisdom from the earliest collections of Proverbs to the hellenized (and therefore relatively gnomic) wisdom of Greek Sirach, Wisdom of Solomon and pseudo-Phocylides.[70] Suffice it here to suggest that such a literary history ought to be structured by the tension between verse and prose conventions and between scribal list-making and literary, argumentative poetry—and to note that these tensions are not decisive for gnomic rhetoric outside collections or for gospel rhetorics on the whole.[71]

---

[69] P. Levi, *The Lamentation of the Dead* (Poetica 19; Oxford, 1984) 10.

[70] For convenient reference see von Lips, *Weisheitliche Traditionen im NT*, 29–35; Kloppenborg, *Formation of Q*, 263–316; Thomas, *Der jüdische Phokylides*.

[71] An exception which proves this rule is identified in I.H. Henderson, "Gnomic Quatrains in the Synoptics: An Experiment in Genre Definition," *NTS* 37 (1991) 481–498.

A distinctive, mnemotechnical variation of this axis between scribal and literary qualities is suggested by internal economy of much rabbinic literature and in particular of the sayings collections, *Abot* and *Abot de Rabbi Nathan*, which Robinson claimed for his *Logoi Sophon*. To the extent that such literature is mnemotechnical, it is to be described as a consequence of the production and transmission of scribal, documentary *texts*, yet initially without writing. It owes little to any trajectory of literary development and influence from Proverbs and Job, through Qohelet, Hebrew Sirach and Tobit to Greek Sirach, Wisdom of Solomon and pseudo-Phocylides. Because proto-rabbinic literature probably responds in writing to the traditions of an originally non-writing movement, I will return to it in some detail to compare its mnemotechnical sensibility (suspicious of writing, yet insistent on textuality) with the rhetorical sensibility of pre-gospel tradition and gospel literature.

Rhetorical criticism suggests yet another pole of sensibility in the production of texts, that of public rhetoricity. A rhetorical sensibility is more grounded than literacy and scribality in oral performance, yet at the same time more grounded than orality in critical and textual self-consciousness and official, public, collective recognition. Such rhetoricity characterizes many of the texts of Greco-Roman literature, though, of course the Roman world carried on producing scribal and mnemotechnical texts as well. Kelber's description of Q as representing "an oral genre" is thus conceptually ambiguous. Greco-Roman rhetorical texts are globally informed by the expectation of a public audience, and not only a private readership. Yet some rhetorical texts, and no doubt some rhetorical performances, showed more influence of the ambient literary rhetoric of progymnasmata and *technai* than others; it might be useful to argue that Q was more or less oral or scribal or literate in its overall rhetoricity compared with other selected (e.g., gospel) texts.[72]

It is, of course, confusing to postulate such a plurality of sensibilities in the use of texts and in speech. This is the place not to sort out the confusion, but to exploit it.[73] I want to insist on the complementarity—and historical accumulation—of the several sensibilities over against all tidy contrasts between written and spoken tradition. Conversational

---

[72] Henderson, "*Didache* and Orality," 293–8, 305–6.

[73] I.H. Henderson, "Rhetorical Determinacy and the Text," in R.B. Robinson and R.C. Culley, eds., *Textual Determinacy: Part 2= Semeia* [forthcoming].

orality, mnemotechnical oral scribality, writing scribality, rhetoricity and literacy are all more or less implied in the production of the surviving texts of antiquity; such varied sensibilities presumably blended also in spoken, unwritten performances and their reception and transmission.

The whole study of wisdom literature from Eißfeldt and Richter to Zeller and Kloppenborg has centred on the problem of "the precise relationship of the document to the oral performance." Much the same has been true of modern study of the gospel tradition. But the question cannot be approached by simply labelling some written genre, 'saying', without identifying the institutions within which literary genre and rhetorical pattern were analogous. For most of biblical history we actually know next to nothing about the conventions and institutions of "oral performance" and their relation to literacies which were quite varied and quite unlike typographic literacy. Analogy with complicated interactions of various styles of orality and various modes of literacy in such areas as the Balkans and East Africa suggest, on balance, a cautious, flexible and sceptical approach to 'sayings' in ancient collection genres.

Greco-Roman rhetoric, especially including progymnasmatic education, provides unique critical control over the conventions and institutions which related public speaking and writing in the Greek-influenced world of Christian origins. To some extent we must anticipate that the socially marginal, regional, cross-cultural and sectarian origins of Christianity will have distorted its aspirations and attainment of 'public' quality in its rhetorics; we should expect an element of conscious or unconscious parody of the prescribed conventions and institutions of Greco-Roman rhetoric. But Vernon Robbins is right to emphasize the primacy of progymnasmatic rhetoric as the key mediating sensibility among conversational and kerygmatic oralities and gospel literacies in pre-gospel tradition.[74]

> Literary-historical criticism presupposes a polarity between oral culture and scribal cultural [*sic*] for its context of analysis. In contrast, socio-rhetorical criticism presupposes that rhetorical culture dominated Mediterranean society during the first half of the common era and that rhetorical culture provided the environment in which early Christians produced their first literature. One of the primary characteristics of a rhetorical culture is lively

---

[74] Robbins, "Pre-Gospel Traditions," 116–118.

interaction between oral and written composition.... Our challenge is to
understand the kind of scribal activity that does not refrain from progymnasmatic rhetorical composition, that is, the level of rhetorical composition
that reperforms written and oral sources and traditions in the manner we see
in the *Progymnasmata*.

When Robbins points to the mediating role of rhetoricity between
orality and literacy in gospel tradition, he is trying to nuance what he
sees as W. Kelber's and J.D. Crossan's anachronistic tendency to
interpose a homogeneous scribal culture between oral culture and print
culture. Robbins has in mind particularly a scribality conditioned by the
economy and mentality of monastic copyists reproducing already sacred
scriptures. This is surely not the scribality of Jewish priests, courtiers
and proto-rabbis.

Robbins himself is only beginning the necessary movement toward
a theory of multiple sensibilities of language; it is, in fact, not enough
even "to distinguish between an oral culture, a rhetorical culture, and a
scribal culture." When, for instance, he says that "an oral culture has no
written literature in view" he inadvertently ignores the half-chosen
oralities of communities, classes and sects for whom illiteracy is a
strategy of resistance as well as a sign of marginality. He does better to
describe scribality as focusing "on 'copying' and 'editing' either oral
statements or written texts," though here he probably underestimates the
differences among differently organized scribal institutions: The scribal
culture of the classical wisdom movement, the mnemotechnical oral
scribality of the pre-mishnaic rabbis and the scribality of monks
produced noticeably different texts.

The complications which Robbins introduces are, therefore, equally
applicable to the different and diverse scribal institutions (including
Wisdom herself!) behind and within the wisdom collection genres. The
powerful approaches to gospel tradition associated with Zeller and
Kloppenborg are seriously compromised by their presumption of a
special affinity between the oralities of pre-gospel traditions and the
scribal genres of classical wisdom literature. By contrast, a rhetorical
critical model of the transition from spoken to spoken-and-written
tradition about Jesus suggests that progymnasmatic rhetoricity was more
influential than biblical, sapiential scribality in mediating among
conversational orality, quasi-public sectarian rhetoric, Greco-Roman
public culture and gospel literacy.

It is not proven that the continuing influence of classical wisdom literature in Jewish and Christian antiquity has anything to do with continued institutions for talking in sapiential instructions or in 'wisdom sayings'—any more than the cultivation of apocalyptic literature implied the activity of groups—still less communities—of apocalypticists.[75] Indeed the emergence of proto-rabbinic tradition and of rabbinic literature suggests that even before AD 70 the need was felt for alternative institutions and genres for transmitting scribal wisdom without wisdom literature in its classical forms.

The task is still ahead, and can only be anticipated here, of surveying the canons and genres of ancient literature from the standpoint of how sensibilities mingle in texts and performances and of how they respond to the basic technical opportunities of language, e.g., verse and prose, speech and writing. What I hope is clear is that any binary opposition of orality and literacy, no matter how carefully applied, will only distort our understanding of the prehistory and beginnings of Christian literature.

It must also be clear that any use of the concept 'wisdom saying' to analyse gospel texts both enshrines and obscures such an orality-literacy dichotomy. Handy sayings are 'wisdom' because the scribes write them down in collections; the scribes' aphoristic scribbles are 'sayings' because wisdom literature conventionally, paradoxically claims to be speech. There is, of course, nothing wrong with such paradoxical conventions; it is, after all, the modern critics who have invented the oxymoron 'wisdom saying' and thereby specified the range and ambiguity of the Bible's native categories (*mashal, matla, parabole*) in terms of an oversimplified oral-literary confusion.

In this way it is the fault of modern criticism rather than of ancient literature when we invoke the 'wisdom saying' to gloss over the tensions between biblical, scribal literacy and the various ways people conventionally spoke and wrote in Greco-Roman antiquity generally or specifically in Jesus' following. In so far as the composition of gospels was facilitated by examples of wisdom admonition and wisdom instruction forms, the gospels are unlikely to resemble speech. Moreover, to the extent that the wisdom admonition is defined by the grammatical category of imperative and prohibitive form, it obscures the

---

[75] See P.R. Davies, "Eschatology at Qumran," *JBL* 104 (1985) 39–55.

central problem of normative meaning across a variety of speech and text types.

Conversely, since the gospels do show signs of dependence on a specific oral tradition which itself recalled Jesus as, among other things, a public speaker, they demand analysis in terms of a sensibility which freely moved between speaking and writing. Such movement is a declared goal of Greco-Roman rhetoric and of progymnasmatic education within it. Such rhetoric was public and artificial in relation to the continuing relative orality of most everyday conversation, but at every level of rhetorical culture, people were taught to talk the way they wrote and vice versa. Whatever the production and redaction of the "Sayings Gospel" Q show about reception of sapiential and apocalyptic literary influences, the process of writing Q proves that the milieu in which pre-synoptic tradition developed was not afraid of using Greco-Roman literacy, not least, to reinterpret the traditions of biblical wisdom.

Literacy and orality in the Ahiqar-tradition and in rabbinic tradition

If there is not room here for a history of ancient literature based on comparison of sensibilities, it may still be useful to mention two examples of non-Greek gnomic texts. Aramaic *Ahiqar* and Mishna *Abot* are, like the gospels, strong cases of texts with prehistories in some sort of oral tradition. They also figure prominently in theories about trajectories of wisdom-literary influence in oral tradition, because they both claim to report the collected sayings of named wise men: presumably in 'wisdom sayings'. On the other hand, neither *Ahiqar* nor *Abot* can easily be located along a single trajectory of instructional literary genres, running from Egypt to biblical and post-biblical wisdom collections.

The *Ahiqar* sayings-material with its probably later narrative framework is extant in a famous fifth century BC Aramaic manuscript from Elephantine and in much-expanded versions from the Christian period. Both the narrative and the sayings materials of the *Ahiqar*-tradition widely influenced Jewish and Greek as well as Syrian literatures. The tradition presents many linguistic and traditional-critical questions which I am not competent to treat. Clearly, however, Max Küchler's conclusion that the sayings are "the most mobile element" of the *Ahiqar* tradition is justified in virtually all respects: dissemination, expansion, variation and edition through time, space and cultural barriers.[76]

The several extant versions provide widely separated benchmarks showing just how massively the sayings tradition has transformed itself by substitution as well as by accretion; against this background, specific instances of the continuity of sayings and/or of gnomic cores between Elephantine and the much later versions are particularly interesting.[77] Such mobile gnomic cores suggest, according to Küchler, that although the later versions, like the varying recensions of Tobit, are linked by literary relationships, the sayings in the Elephantine manuscript and those in later versions are linked in oral not written tradition. Moreover, isolated and textually imprecise parallels with Aramaic *Ahiqar* are scattered through Jewish literature from canonical Proverbs to Sirach, Tobit (including the Qumran Aramaic fragments), Talmud, Midrash and perhaps the New Testament. They would seem to imply that the name of *Ahiqar* illuminates only a few of many possible trajectories through the cloud of sayings circulated orally and in writing in near eastern antiquity.[78]

For the most part the older *Ahiqar* material seems to have exerted an oral, not a written, literary influence on Jewish literature. And while aspects of the *Ahiqar* story have been influential, it is the gnomic aspects of the tradition which have been busiest. Later non-Jewish versions do give evidence of written transmission, and they also show signs of a relatively scribal sensibility, especially the increasingly homogeneous presentation of sayings as admonitions within instructions marked by introductory formulae ("my son..." [Syriac]; "O my boy..." [Arabic]; "Son..." [Armenian]).[79]

---

[76] Küchler, *Weisheitstraditionen*, 403–410, quoting 411; J.M. Lindenberger, "Ahiqar," in *The Old Testament Pseudepigrapha*, ed. J.H. Charlesworth, vol. II (London, 1985) 479–493 (introduction), 494–507 (translation); J.M. Lindenberger, *The Aramaic Proverbs of Ahiqar* (Baltimore and London, 1983) esp. 19–20; I. Kottsieper, *Die Sprache der Ahiqarsprüche* (BZAW 194; Berlin and New York, 1991) esp. 175.

[77] For a conservative selection, see Küchler, *Weisheitstraditionen* 358–363 and Lindenberger, "Ahiqar," 498–507, notes.

[78] Küchler, *Weisheitstraditionen*, 365, 411.

[79] See R.H. Charles, ed., *The Apocrypha and Pseudepigrapha of the Old Testament in English*, 2 vols. (Oxford, 1913, rpr. 1963) II 715–784 for a convenient synoptic presentation.

Aramaic *Ahiqar* looks comparatively oral in sensibility not only in its lack of such formulae but in the greater formal variety and independence of sayings. In addition, Aramaic *Ahiqar* lacks the noticeable regularity of line-form or parallelism which marks even the least bookish collections of biblical proverbs as verse. Moreover, the variation of single core structures within Aramaic *Ahiqar* itself without obvious redactional purpose suggests an oral mindset, open to performantial variation (e.g., logia 39, 41, 93, or 40, 42)—though the repetition of already fixed pairs of unrelated logia (39 and 40, 41 and 42) implies some degree of textual determination, whether by writing or memorization.

The ambiguities of the designation 'wisdom saying' are readily visible in the contrasts between the formal and topical variety and ephemeral textuality of the *Ahiqar*-sayings and the standard verse-forms, increasingly thematic organization and stable growth of the Hebrew wisdom literature. Especially in Aramaic *Ahiqar*, a higher proportion of *Ahiqar*-sayings is readily describable in terms of Crépeau's normativity, analogy and separability, than is the case in the classical biblical wisdom books (though the longer animal fables are parables (*mythoi*) rather than gnomai for present purposes).

We can examine its documents, so the *Ahiqar*-tradition is obviously literary. Yet it shares with the Jesus-tradition, though on a vastly different time-scale, a continuing openness to oral sensibilities and techniques of transmission and composition. The analogy is useful not only because it captures much of the difference between Synoptic gnome and the styles of Old Testament wisdom poetry, but also because it warns of the continuous co-opting of new gnomai into tradition.

Even more than the *Ahiqar*-tradition, rabbinic literature paradoxically emphasizes in writing the spokenness and relative independence of gnomic sayings from their literary contexts. For the rabbinic literature generally, the "saying, whether a proverb current in popular speech or the popularized dictum of a sage,"[80] lags only behind story-telling and Scriptural comment as a favourite pattern for *haggadah*. Among the rabbis, such proverb-like sayings are formally much more diverse than are the units of classical wisdom poetry—scriptural models of which the rabbis are, of course, not unaware. The rabbis' proverbial sayings are

---

[80] Zeller, *Mahnsprüche im NT*, 46.

more often describable as gnomai (i.e., as separate, normative analogies) than as 'wisdom sayings' or admonitions.

Independent analogical norms (gnomai) pepper halakic as well as haggadic contexts, although the only instances known to me of legal judgements actually couched in such independently analogical sayings are disavowals of halakic relevance rather than positive adjudications.[81] The role of gnomai in halakic contexts seems mainly to be that of making explicit the analogies behind related legal judgements (e.g., R. Meir's saying *m.Ned.* 9.3 or even Hillel's famous summation of the Torah *b.Shabb.* 31a[82])—such gnomai provide logical rather than legal principles.

The earliest strata and/or the earliest documents of rabbinic tradition are another sample of written sayings for which an oral background may be claimed—and which do not easily fit onto trajectories from biblical wisdom literature. Jacob Neusner's is by far the most celebrated attempt at a stratigraphy of proto-rabbinic traditions to date. His initial work isolated a selection of rabbinic materials which may plausibly claim rough contemporaneity with oral traditions about Jesus.

Distinguishing between "types" and "forms," Neusner pointed to laws and wisdom sayings as the "two important types [*sic*] of biblical literature that recur in rabbinic traditions about the Pharisees." Remarkably, in pre-rabbinic tradition, these two types are formally distinct not only from one another, but also from their respective biblical analogues. Thus, the "moral sayings" of Neusner's earliest rabbinic strata—most of them in *Abot*[83]—strongly contrast in form with the "proverbial sentence" of literary wisdom verse, "with its parallel sections, its rhythms," and its tendency to integration into "long and highly developed" instructions and poems. Except by way of contrast, formal comparison of Neusner's moral sayings with Eißfeldt's sample or with the *Ahiqar* materials would scarcely need to refer to the literary tradition from Proverbs to Sirach: a hypothetical trajectory from Eißfeldt's

---

[81] *m.B.Mes.* 91a and *m.B.Mes.* 97a, which adapts a saying in which Fischel detected influence from Epicurean *sententiae*, H.A. Fischel *Rabbinic Literature and Greco-Roman Philosophy* (SPB 21; Leiden, 1973) 36ff; see also A. Strikovsky, "Proverbs, Talmudic," *EncJud* 13 (Jerusalem, 1972) 1274.

[82] Küchler, *Weisheitstraditionen*, 207–8.

[83] J. Neusner, *The Rabbinic Traditions about the Pharisees before 70*, 3 vols. (Leiden, 1971) III 78, 84.

gnomai to Neusner's sample would not need to pass through classical wisdom literature.[84]

Neusner's form criticism also emphasized formal discontinuity between Pharisaic-rabbinic legal sayings within his sample and styles of biblical law. Over against the several legal forms of the Old Testament and the laws of Qumranic, Apocryphal and Pseudepigraphic writers, Neusner's "Pharisaic-rabbinic laws seldom use the imperative...; it is chiefly in M. Avot 1:1–18 that we find the imperative, in moral sayings." In the exemplary area of Sabbath rules, "one *never* finds the imperative." Proto-rabbinic laws avoid the imperative; gnomai do not.[85]

The Pharisaic-rabbinic wisdom sentences characterized by Neusner also differ from gospel sayings in ways which suggest that the sensibility of the pre-rabbinic traditions is neither that of literary wisdom nor that of oral pre-gospel tradition. Neusner's Pharisaic-rabbinic materials, and especially the *Abot* collections, differ significantly both from the scribal verse of classical wisdom poems and from any plausible estimate of pre-gospel orality. The rabbis' attribution of each individual saying to an individual master and a triplet-form quite unlike that used in Sirach[86] tend to confirm, even for the early stages Neusner is trying to reconstruct, that pre-rabbinic tradition is mnemotechnical in orientation. "Pharisaic sayings not in narrative setting do not seem to follow the model of Proverbs or BenSira" yet, nonetheless, "they do not exhibit the rich variations and full expression of the equivalent Jesus-logia."[87] It is no surprise, then, that *Abot* includes few classical wisdom admonitions as defined by Richter and Zeller.[88]

Ambitious questions about Pharisaic identities and the origins of rabbinic tradition initially kept Neusner cautious about exaggerated claims for the antiquity, scale and precision of pre-rabbinic memorizational oral tradition. Neusner rightly followed Morton Smith's rejection of Birger Gerhardsson's romantic vision of rabbinic tradition, to say

---

[84] Neusner, *Pharisees*, III 68–70, quoting 69 and 70.

[85] Neusner, *Pharisees*, III 78, 72; on the early rabbinic preference for participial over imperative laws see D. Daube, *The New Testament and Rabbinic Judaism* (London, 1956) 90–105; see also L.H. Schiffman, *The Halakah at Qumran* (SJLA 16; Leiden, 1975) 80ff.

[86] Neusner, *Pharisees*, III 70; Zeller, *Mahnsprüche*, 44–45.

[87] Neusner, *Pharisees*, III 84.

[88] Zeller, *Mahnsprüche*, 47.

nothing of Gerhardsson's attempt to assimilate pre-gospel traditions to the same memorizational model.[89] Ironically, the peculiar opacity of the rabbinic texts to historical inquiry partly saved Neusner from the temptation to write a form-critical "history" of rabbinic tradition.[90]

The result is that Neusner characterizes Mishna (and especially *Abot* and especially the wisdom sentences) as mnemonic, more with regard to its intent than to its largely inscrutable oral prehistory.[91] That is, it is possible—and interesting—to analyse the particular brand of oral sensibility which informs the oldest identifiable strands of the rabbinic literature even though we cannot be sure about the actual processes of its prehistory. There is still, moreover, a fairly strong probability that the largely gnomic material in *Abot* and in the two recensions of *Abot de Rabbi Nathan* give a privileged glimpse of the sensibility of a self-consciously non-writing, memorizational tradition comparable in date to pre-gospel traditions.[92] The peculiar rabbinic mnemonic literary sensibility is likely to be, in part, the consequence of a pre-rabbinic mnemotechnical oral sensibility. The gnomic material and especially *Abot* traditions are the decisive evidence for this limited continuity between pre-rabbinic, if not exactly Pharisaic, speech and rabbinic writing.

In that case, a double contrast emerges: one contrast between a pre-rabbinic, mnemotechnical tradition and scribal, wisdom literature and a second contrast between pre-rabbinic, mnemotechnical tradition and a pre-gospel oral tradition which was neither mnemotechnical nor scribal. The fact that the rabbis do not really fit onto alleged wisdom-traditional trajectories underlines an even more basic fact to which this chapter has been devoted: the affinity between a sensibility and a text-type is elective.

The wisdom tradition selected a scribal sensibility of list-making and versification, though it very gradually moved toward more literary and rhetorical elaboration. The rabbinic tradition chose to affect a mnemo-

---

[89] Neusner, *Pharisees*, III 146–7, citing M. Smith, "A Comparison of Early Christian and Early Rabbinic Tradition," *JBL* 82 (1963) 169–176; see E. Güttgemanns, *Offene Fragen zur Formgeschichte des Evangeliums* (BEvT 54; 2d ed., München, 1971) 119–153.

[90] Neusner, *Pharisees*, III 78–88, 312–364.

[91] Neusner, *Pharisees*, 161; J. Neusner, *The Memorized Torah: The Mnemonic System of the Mishnah* (BJS 96; Chico, CA, 1985) 9–28.

[92] Küchler, *Weisheitstraditionen*, 174–197, esp. 179 n.8.

technical sensibility precisely in the way that it was committed to writing. Furthermore, the choice of menemotechnical sensibility seems to have been made in a context where other writing and speaking traditions (Qumran, Christianity) were making different choices.

Discussions of Mishna published by Neusner since his ground-breaking work on the Pharisees have been criticized for their equivocations: in some contexts, Neusner has emphasized the oral character of the Mishna, while elsewhere recognizing its irreducibly written character.[93] It is, of course, not my place to harmonize Neusner's varied thought. 1 do think, however, that Neusner's approaches imply and require that orality is never just synonymous with 'not writing'. The two distinctions, between orality and literacy as sensibilities, and between writing and not writing as techniques, are not co-ordinate. Indeed, anything we know about pre-rabbinic, pre-gospel or any other oral tradition, we know because its orality was conserved in self-consciously odd writing.

Neusner's description of the Mishna becomes more convincing and useful for me when "oral," "memorized" or "mnemonic," and "written" are seen to describe different aspects of the same texts; these labels need not define mutually exclusive theories about original production techniques. Neusner is descriptively right that "the dominant stylistic trait of the Mishnah is the acute formalization of its syntactical structure" and that this "stylization and formalization testify to a mnemonic program." Historically, these characteristics of Mishna are at least compatible with the notion that the mnemonic program predates the writing of Mishna as a book, if not on anything like the Mosaic scale claimed by *Abot*.[94]

The position which I take as more or less Neusner's is thus that Mishna is mnemotechnical in sensibility, though it is obviously literate in the technique of its definitive stage. The selection of such a sensibilitiy was a deliberate one, conditioned by the cultural possibility—perhaps the availability—of a memorized tradition, but also deliberately and ironically contrasting mnemonics with the obvious fact of 'routine' technical literacy in Hebrew and in Greek. Within Mishna's choice of cultivating a memorizational mentality, moreover, *Abot* and its gnomai stand out; mnemonic sensibility is the topic more than the form of what

---

[93]   Sanders, *Jewish Law*, 110–115; see Alexander, "Orality in Judaism," 172–176.
[94]   Neusner, *Memorized*, 28, 111–112 (quoted).

Neusner calls "Mishnah's first and most compelling apologetic." The contrast between Mishna as a whole conceived mnemotechnically and *Abot* (with the two recensions of *Abot de Rabbi Nathan*) suggests that even memorizational sensibility must be differentiated: more than the gospels, *Abot* was written to be memorized, but not memorized as the rest of Mishna demanded to be.[95]

The essential interest of early rabbinic tradition for comparison with pre-gospel tradition is, therefore, not that *Abot* and the gospels jointly attest late developments in post-biblical sapiential tradition. Instead, the *Abot* traditions and the gospel sayings-traditions attest differing relatively 'oral' sensibilities, memorizational and dialectical respectively, both of which consciously differ from the scribal sensibility of classical wisdom books.

This impression of the distinctness of *Abot* and the gospels from each other and from any wisdom-literary trajectory is reinforced by synoptic intertextual relationships (e.g., among *Abot*, and *Abot de Rabbi Nathan* A and B).[96] These make it extraordinarily probable that each set of texts does actually reflect privileged contact with a tradition which had tried for a while to be 'oral' both in sensibility and in technique in a world where both (Greek) rhetorical and (non-Greek) scribal literacies were readily available.

At the same time the distinctness of Mishna and of the *Abot* traditions from the gospels makes it clear that the two literatures are not 'oral' in the same sense. If Neusner is roughly justified in calling traditions of Mishna and *Abot* memorizational, then the traditions of the gospels must be differently labelled, though their historical antecedents and their sensibility as texts are no less oddly oral. A theory of synoptic oral tradition must begin with the distinctness of the gospels from either biblical wisdom or the pre-rabbinic wisdom of *Abot*.

---

[95] Neusner, *Memorized*, 129.
[96] Küchler, *Weisheitstraditionen*, 174–197.

CHAPTER THREE

LOGIA, APHORISMS AND AUTHENTICITY

No analysis of gnomic materials in early Christian literature has escaped the baneful influence of the dichotomies between folk proverb and elite wisdom saying and between imperative and indicative norms. Neither distinction should be taken for granted in any rhetorical model of early Christian rhetoric and tradition. The prejudicial effects of such over-drawn polarities on New Testament criticism is, however, qualified in most twentieth-century criticism by another impulse, the impulse toward phenomenological study of sayings as logia or as aphorisms.

The idealistic and volatile blend of historical positivism and aphoristic phenomenology is presumably one legacy of academic scholarship's anti-dogmatic, but still residually confessional and devotional interest in early Christian texts and in Jesus words: There is a telling continuity from Albert Schweitzer's apocalyptic fascination with the words of Jesus "lying in the corner like explosive shells" to the "contemporary iconoclastic mysticism" which Amos Wilder attributes to J.D. Crossan.[1]

In every important writer on gospel sayings since Schweitzer, it is this aphoristic tradition of interpretation which more or less dilutes the dominant, formalist and sociological, ways of analysis. Since Schweitzer, and especially in the last decade, there have been a few serious attempts to come to critical terms with the fragments of gnomic rhetoric attributed to Jesus. These can suggestively be placed along a continuum from relatively strict formalist, Wisdom-literary historicism, haunted by premonitions of aphoristic complexity (D. Zeller) to an aphoristic and

---

[1] A.N. Wilder, *Theopoetic: Theology and the Religious Imagination* (Philadelphia, 1976) 77, cited by Winton, *Proverbs of Jesus*, 76.

"parabolic metaphysics," grounded in "intricately argued historical-critical study" (J.D. Crossan).[2]

Wilder's own "poetics of faith" is a uniquely self-conscious attempt to reconcile the phenomenology of aphoristic intuitions with the quest for an objective history of pre-gospel language. Such a reconciliation of history and intuition is, however, impossible without the mediation of theology and/or rhetoric between intuited aphorism and collected wisdom saying.

The uncomfortable interaction of aphoristic and sapiential approaches to the form criticism of sayings is nowhere clearer than in the work of Rudolph Bultmann. Indeed it has long been impossible to write about the speech materials of the gospels and their possible relation to pre-gospel rhetorics and traditions without reference to Bultmann's essay on "Logia (Jesus as Wisdom teacher)."

One result of Bultmann's pre-eminence is that his form criticism generally and his treatment of the logia in particular have been subjected to careful, insightful cross-examination in the light of subsequent scholarship.[3] As a result, we can focus here on the ambiguities of form-critical approaches to sapiential or aphoristic logia and on their relationship to the stricter categories of gnomic and parabolic rhetoric.

I am, of course, arguing in this book precisely that gnome is culturally and historically far more appropriate and analytically more rigorous than such commonly applied categories as admonition, proverb, saying, logion, aphorism and even chreia. That is why I have sought first to establish gnome as a category before introducing the standard approach to the tradition of Jesus' public speech. But that standard approach is undoubtedly determined by Bultmann's personal mixture of sapiential form criticism and phenomenological/eschatological appreciation of the gospels.

The trajectory from Bultmann to, especially, J.D. Crossan's studies of Jesus' speech-tradition raises the basic question of whether a

---

[2] Winton, *Proverbs*, 98, citing W. Kelber, review of J.D. Crossan, *In Fragments: The Aphorisms of Jesus* (New York, 1983) *JBL* 104 (1985) 716–19, 718; to fill out the continuum I am proposing, I might tentatively suggest: D. Zeller—R.A. Piper—C.E. Carlston—R. Bultmann—N. Perrin—W.A. Beardslee—A.P. Winton—J.D. Crossan.

[3] In general see Sanders and Davies, *Synoptic Gospels*, 123–197; in particular see Winton, *Proverbs*, 59–98.

compromise between historical positivism and romantic and existential-
ist poetics can adequately nourish and integrate the study of Christian
origins. As the title of Bultmann's essay on the "Logia" indicated, it is
from the standpoint of this hybrid hermeneutic that historical Jesus
research has approached the ambiguous question of authenticity. Can
synoptic literary (secular) Wisdom authentically relate Jesus' (eschatological) logia? In the chapters that follow, the double question of
authenticity will crop up more and more often: how did Jesus talk? If
we can answer that, what implications might Jesus' partially reconstructed speech-practice have for writing histories of Christian origins?

Sayings-types and forms

The gospel writers did not have, much less write, eye-witness accounts
of the events they narrate. It would be equally irresponsible, however,
to declare their writings the products of sheer literary fantasy. The
gospel writers sought faithfully—in most senses of the word—to
interpret Jesus. They do seem, moreover, to have had privileged access
to traditional information about Jesus, information transmitted orally for
some years.

> The first Christians, or rather some of them, could 'create' sayings by Jesus
> in numerous ways...On the other hand, they seem not to have been wildly
> creative.... The early Christians did not have professional or semi-pro-
> fessional schools of memorizers who meticulously passed down oral
> tradition. On the other hand, many things which Jesus said and did were
> striking and were remembered.[4]

Given this positive ambiguity of the gospel traditions of Jesus' words,
there are two possible ways to assess sayings-tradition as historical
evidence of Jesus' public self-expression. On the one hand, individual
items from the gospel literary tradition may be selected with a view to
reconstructing their history in pre-gospel oral tradition. On the other
hand, collective judgements may be made about types of text and types
of speech, and about individual items only as possible exemplars of

---

[4] Sanders and Davies, *Synoptic Gospels*, 145, see 36–46.

larger categories. Both approaches are attested in Bultmann's seminal work, which, indeed, always assumed their complementarity.

The first strategy, that of microscopically analysing individual units of literary tradition in the hope of discerning their oral pre-history, has dominated tradition-history since Bultmann. This is the approach which has been dramatized by the public work of the Westar Institute's "Jesus Seminar" in recent years.[5] The goal here is to deduce from the form and compositional history of gospel literary sub-units the history of the interests behind their invention, preservation and modification in oral as well as in literary tradition. Such analysis seems possible, especially when more than one variant of a single traditional core is attested in the documentary sources. It is, for example, reasonable to ask what Jesus really said about divorce or what he really said about cup, blood and covenant; it is even more reasonable to ask at the same time why subsequent tradition grew so confused about such interesting sayings.

Answers to such questions will always be at best relatively plausible. They will also always be arguments rather than stable, definitive conclusions, arguments in narrative form about conversations and situations in which Jesus and/or others might have talked and written. The argumentative character of such tradition-history is particularly embodied in the voting procedures of the Westar Jesus Seminar. The Seminar's voting statistics are a fascinating measure of political consensus and dissent in a civil community, but are hardly binding on Jesus or his admirers.

This tradition of micro-reconstruction of the 'original form' of and subsequent history of each individual saying is also the context for the endless literature of criteriology in Historical Jesus Research.[6] Criteria of authenticity and development for traditions, usually sayings, attributed to Jesus are never finally settled, above all because they represent conventions (topics) for argumentation rather than objective tests; the Jesus Seminar prefers to talk about "rules of evidence,"[7] invoking the possibilities of forensic rhetoric—in a case where virtually all physical evidence has long since vanished leaving mostly hearsay. In such a case, grand-sounding "criteria" are mostly rules of thumb,

---

[5] See Funk, Hoover and the Jesus Seminar, *The Five Gospels;* and the journal *Forum* (Sonoma, CA).

[6] Funk, "Unravelling the Jesus Tradition."

[7] Funk, Hoover and the Jesus Seminar, *The Five Gospels*, 16–34.

useful in balancing fairness and sharpness in cross-examining the
tradition—and each other. Optimum use of such criteria requires
rhetorical invention at least as much as historical judgement. There is,
therefore, scarcely any saying—perhaps Matthew 8:22[8]—attributable to
Jesus beyond serious dispute; in practice, sayings, even in multiple
variants, almost never carry enough socio-linguistic DNA to permit
definitive assignment of their individual ancestry.

Even so, this work of approximate and speculative genetic finger-
printing is, as E.P. Sanders has pointed out, largely inevitable. It does,
moreover, have a real, though negative value: to claim any historical
knowledge about Jesus or about the milieux between Jesus and the
gospel-writers, we have to propose a plausible model of oral tradition
and of oral influence on gospel-writing. But no model of oral tradition
and written composition is plausible unless it can account for significant
details of actual gospel texts, even if such hypothetical accounts of
particular details can seldom be verified.

> Sanders...has argued that secure information about Jesus cannot be obtained
> by rewriting individual pericopes, and that if by chance the rewriting were
> successful, there would be no way of proving it.... [H]ypothetical recon-
> structions do not lead to firm knowledge. But if we will not dig, we know
> less than if we do.[9]

We shall return to the mostly false assumptions which allowed
Bultmann and his imitators to make detailed hypothetical reconstruction
of oral traditional processes a standard practice in New Testament
argumentation; the fundamental irony is, of course, that "digging" and
"rewriting" presuppose mounds of paper and so beg the question
whether the gospel-writers were also good listeners who had good
informants. Following Sanders, I cannot quite renounce these exercises
in literary archaeology, in the hope that they will somehow make me a
more attentive listener to ancient rhetorics.

The progymnasmatists encourage me in that hope, for they thought
(and taught the gospel writers) that careful listening and effective public

---

[8] M. Hengel, *Nachfolge und Charisma: Eine exegetisch-religionsgeschichtliche
Studie zu Mt 8,21f. und Jesu Ruf in die Nachfolge* (BZAW 34; Berlin, 1968).

[9] Sanders and Davies, *Synoptic Gospels*, 134, citing Sanders, *Jesus and Judaism*,
3–5, 129–139.

speaking were promoted not only by intense live practice, but also by reading and writing. But it is of the utmost importance that the rhetorical study of gnome-use by Jesus and the gospel-writers does not depend upon reconstructing 'original forms' or on arguing the authenticity of individual gnomai. My goal instead is to understand through gnomic rhetoric the reciprocity of orality and literacy deliberately cultivated in ancient rhetoric.

Consequently, for a study of gnomai in Greco-Roman—including early Christian—rhetoric, the form critics' attempt to define linguistic types to link traditional speech with gospel composition is far more important than their work with individual 'sayings'. It is crucial to differentiate rhetorical concepts of type and pattern from the key form-critical concept of 'form'. In fact, much of the previous chapter anticipated such a differentiation: 'Wisdom sayings' in traditions which were sometimes unwritten cannot be defined by an appeal to grammatical mood (the imperative 'admonition' versus the indicative 'proverb') since grammatical mood does not solely determine rhetorical impact.

Bultmann's classic study of the synoptic 'logia' and subsequent studies of 'aphorisms' present an interesting ambiguity from this point of view. As we noticed earlier, Bultmann, like Zeller after him, borrowed a formal typology of sayings from current Old Testament form criticism, distinguishing maxims, commands and questions (*Grundsätze/Aussagen*, *Mahnworte* and *Fragen*).[10] In Bultmann's approach, however, these grammatical distinctions do not ultimately control the analysis. Semantic types, distinguished at a more abstract level of language, turn out to be more basic to Bultmann's analysis. Thus, for example, on a small scale, he distinguished between topically and personally formulated maxims. On a larger scale, he divided all sayings material according to a major hermeneutical distinction among wisdom, prophecy, apocalyptic and law.

In between these examples, the primarily semantic quality of Bultmann's criticism of the smaller units in gospel direct discourse is evident in his choice of "logion" over more specific formal categories like the admonition. As the sub-set of the "words of the Lord"

---

[10] Bultmann, *Geschichte*, 73–113; von Lips, *Weisheitliche Traditionen im NT*, 18–19; Küchler, *Weisheitstraditionen*, 158–9; Schick, *Formgeschichte und Synoptiker-exegese*, 160.

(*Herrenworte*) which show Jesus as "Wisdom teacher," Bultmann's logia seem synonymous with wisdom sayings.

> In Bultmann, Dibelius and others there is however a more general usage, in which "Logion" is employed as more or less synonymous with "Spruch" ("saying") or "Ausspruch" ("utterance").[11]

Thus even in the very discussion where Bultmann interprets the Logia of Jesus the Wisdom teacher in terms of the Wisdom literary form criticism of his day, his interpretation subtly dissociates logia, at least any authentic logia, from biblical or proverbial wisdom sayings on grounds having little to do with form. At the outset Bultmann complained that Old Testament form criticism failed to distinguish "constitutive" from "ornamental" aspects of wisdom sayings; the former appear in the "logical form of the sentence," which Bultmann loosely relates to grammatical form. Although Bultmann asserted, without argumentation, that the forms of synoptic logia were also those of Old Testament and Jewish wisdom sayings, his actual treatment turns the formal analogy into a more basic hermeneutical (I would say, rhetorical) contrast.

Bultmann began by formally distinguishing gospel logia, like biblical wisdom sayings, from prophetic, apocalyptic and legal sayings. Yet in the last (historical) analysis, Bultmann overrides the literary parallel between logia and wisdom-literary sayings: Jesus' authentic logia are distinguished from accretions of popular and secular (*profane*) wisdom in other logia not by any formal difference but by mood.

> One must see that the tradition has picked up many logia from popular wisdom and piety. We may also suppose that the tradition was now and then prompted to this by the fact that Jesus used or coined such an utterance.... Only in a few cases can any attempt to attribute one of the logia to Jesus be brought off: for those utterances which are spoken out of the exaltation of [Jesus'] eschatological mood (*Hochgefühl der eschatologischen Stimmung*).... All these utterances, though they no longer entirely have the proper character of logia, contain something characteristic, new, something going beyond popular wisdom and piety yet even less

---

[11] D. Lührmann, "Q: Sayings of Jesus or Logia?" in *The Gospel Behind the Gospels: Current Studies on Q*, ed. R.A. Piper (NovTSup 75; Leiden, 1995) 97–116, 102.

scribal-rabbinic or Jewish-apocalyptic. Thus here if anywhere must be found what is characteristic of Jesus' public speaking.[12]

In an earlier chapter we noticed how Bultmann preferred to speak of apophthegms rather than chreiai, probably because the vaguer category left him freer to define the form of the pronouncement story in keeping with his hermeneutical interest in defining Jesus over against his Jewishness. In relation to the smaller forms of direct discourse Bultmann likewise opted for the vaguest designation, logion, eclipsing not only sententia and gnome, but gradually also the wisdom saying of Old Testament form criticism.

For Bultmann, a few logia stand out from the crowd not on any formal criterion, but only as egregious expressions of that eschatological temperament which Bultmann believed to be pre-eminently Jesus' own. Conversely, those logia which make up the crowd—even if Jesus might have used them in his own way—define a rhetorical background of secular, popular and churchly static.[13] The result is that form and formal characteristics matter even less in Bultmann's treatment of the logia than in his discussion of apophthegms. It is subliminal, "characteristic" mood and personal *ethos* rather than syntactical form which determine the history of such language. Faced with the question whether the logia of Jesus actually have anything to do with Jesus, Bultmann virtually jettisoned his formal distinctions in favour of topical and hermeneutical distinctions. Here I think Bultmann, though for inadequate reasons, was right.

Everything I am trying to do in this book rests on a definition of gnome which is primarily semantic, oriented toward mood rather than formal syntax. It is also essential—against Bultmann—that such a definition of gnome is culturally appropriate to Greco-Roman sectarian rhetoric both as written and as spoken. The basic progymnasmata define categories in which any gospel-writer could not only write but also listen and speak. Moreover, many who could not have written a gospel in Greek would have been able to imitate the speaking and listening conventions of their school-literate neighbours, since the latter could

---

[12] Bultmann, *Geschichte*, 109–110; I have attempted to improve upon the often imprecise translation of J. Marsh, R. Bultmann, *The History of the Synoptic Tradition* (Oxford, 1963) 104.

[13] Bultmann, *Geschichte*, 92.

only assert the power of their modest rhetorical education by airing it among those less rhetorically literate. That is, the progymnasmata and Greco-Roman rhetoric generally are strong evidence for a continuum of basic patterns (including gnome) and attitudes between written and unwritten rhetoric.

Any attempt to analyse the sayings tradition of Jesus historically must define linguistic types which make sense both of the forms of literary, canonical tradition and also of the probable speech-types of the gospels' antecedents in primarily oral rhetoric. Especially where Jesus, early Christianity and the texts themselves are all objects of a single inquiry, categories must be found which are both text-types, representative of early Christian writing and its non-Christian influences, and speech-types, representative of real speech options and practices. Rhetorical criticism and form criticism differ in their methods for defining such text-cum-speech-types, types which can be interpreted with some precision for each stage and mode of tradition. In practice, however, the best form criticism was always ready to compromise its commitment to 'form' as a guiding category.

Bultmann and the subsequent form-critical tradition tried to project selected literary 'forms' into oral discourse by sociological sleight of hand: since Jesus, his audiences and the preservers of his tradition were ordinary folk, the tradition which they sustained and developed must have obeyed the laws of folklore. The gospels too were palpably sub-classical, non-elite, popular literature (*Kleinliteratur*); they too are folklore, not literature. Consequently the forms, processes and conventions of the gospels are oral, not literary. This meant not only that gospel literary forms could be read backwards into the oral tradition. It also allowed the form critics to imagine 'pure forms' in the oral tradition which were significantly different from the actual gospel forms, the latter presumably mummified by contact with letters.

Few conceits have been subjected to such conclusive criticism as that which consigned the gospels to a category of sub-literary writings (*Kleinliteratur*). Along with the notions of pure form and of formative life settings (*Sitze im Leben*) in tradition, the conception that the gospels were, in their day, non-literature was one of the three legs of the form-critical milking-stool, and the first to break. For Bultmann, it is basically all the same whether the tradition took place orally or in writing, since there is no essential difference between them with regard to the unliterary character of the traditional material.[14]

This assumption allowed Bultmann and his successors to concoct a model of conservation and development in pre-gospel oral tradition, based on observations about the behaviour of the gospel writers as sub-literary redactors of their written sources. It was not only the gospels as books which the form critics classed as unliterary and therefore virtually oral; the whole process of gospel literary tradition with its writers, redactors and readers became the model for a theory of oral tradition. This is the basis for Bultmann's deduction (wrong even on his terms) that development in the oral tradition of speech material must have been a linear movement from simple, brief sayings toward complex, discursive clusters and narratives.

Against Bultmann, subsequent study of the gospels has emphasized their modest, experimental and sectarian, but irreducibly literary qualities: the gospels are odd literature, but they are not *Kleinliteratur*. In addition, Bultmann claimed to know the "laws" of oral traditional development, deduced partly from (sub-)literary redaction of the gospels and partly from folklore studies in other culture areas. In fact, however, studies in Bultmann's day and later work on oral traditions do not confirm Bultmann's claims. Nor did a careful review of development and change in the use of gospel material in other early Christian (presumably sub-literary) literature. The form critics' model of oral tradition and its laws is not sustained by the evidence of early Christian literature itself or by analogy with better known oral traditions elsewhere; the oral tradition was not folklore, nor were the gospels *Kleinliteratur* as they imagined.[15]

---

[14] Bultmann, *Geschichte*, 7, see 50.

[15] Sanders and Davies, *Synoptic Gospels*, 127–137; K. Berger, *Einführung*, 13–18; *Formgeschichte*, 9–24; W.H. Kelber, "Mark and Oral Tradition," in *Perspectives on Mark's Gospel*, ed. R. Petersen=*Semeia* 16 (1979) 7–55; *The Oral and the Written Gospel*; W. Schmithals, *Einleitung in die drei ersten Evangelien* (Berlin and New York, 1985) 234–318; "Evangelien: Synoptische," *TRE* X (1982) 570–626; "Kritik der Formkritik," *ZTK* 77 (1980) 149–185; E. Güttgemanns, *Fragen*; E.P. Sanders, *The Tendencies of the Synoptic Tradition* (SNTSMS 9; Cambridge, 1969); E. Schick, *Formgeschichte und Synoptikerexegese*.

Despite this massive erosion of such key assumptions of classical form criticism, Bultmann remains partly convincing after all. For one thing, most alternative models of early Christian tradition have failed just as decisively to describe the relation between oral and written modes of gospel tradition. B. Gerhardsson's quasi-rabbinic, mnemotechnical or scribal models of pre-synoptic tradition are an instructive failure: it is really quite striking how little in the gospels is compatible with transmission by mnemotechnical or scribal specialists. Rabbinic literature may well reflect an oral tradition which was geographically and socially close enough to pre-gospel tradition to demand comparison. When the comparison is made, however, it becomes a contrast. Thus, if it is possible to imagine that the rabbinic texts were produced without writing and with a view to nearly verbatim memorization, the same cannot be said of the gospels' compositional units—even if we refused to recognize that the latter exemplify progymnasmatic rhetoric.[16]

Increasingly, the relationship between orality and literacy in classical antiquity has become a topic of research in its own right, reinforcing criticism of the form critics' insistence "on the irrelevance of a distinction between orality and literacy."[17] In fact, the problems of difference and continuity between writing and non-writing traditions are more complex and difficult than Werner Kelber's provocative studies would suggest. The weakness of non-rhetorical models of Synoptic development lies in their inability to appreciate that New Testament origins involve both more and less than a sudden, technical shift from not writing to writing. There were highly literate Christians before and beside the few who wrote gospels. There were also Christians actively engaged in the oral tradition of Christianity, who nevertheless did not habitually recite Jesus' pre-Easter words and deeds; the Last Supper narrative is the exception which proves this rule.

Modern studies suggest that "it takes only a moderate degree of literacy to make a tremendous difference in thought processes," but they

---

[16] Sanders and Davies, *Synoptic Gospels*, 129–133; J. Neusner, *Oral Tradition in Judaism* (A.B. Lord Studies in Oral Tradition 1; New York, 1987); J.D. Crossan, *In Fragments;* M. Smith, "A Comparison of Early Christian and Early Rabbinic Tradition," *JBL* 82 (1963) 169–176; *pace* B. Gerhardsson, *Memory and Manuscript*, (ASNU 22; Lund, 1961) esp. 111–2.

[17] Kelber, *The Oral and the Written Gospel*, 6, cited in Winton, *Proverbs of Jesus*, 63.

also make clear that a simple dichotomy of orality and literacy is almost never realistic, certainly not in classical and Greco-Roman antiquity.[18] In Jesus' world and in the slightly different worlds of the gospel writers, we must reckon with many hybridizations of orality and literacy: both Greek and non-Greek literacies; many registers of literacy, from classical and scriptural to bureaucratic, epigraphic and private; scholastic and sectarian mnemotechnical traditions; progymnasmatic rhetorical education, incorporating literacy as an aid to rhetorical practice; a busy round of civic and ceremonial rhetorical performance, made more urgent by the arbitrariness of real power; and perhaps social groupings where illiteracy and subversive parody of the dominant rhetorics became aspects of negative, marginalized identity. In such a context, oral and literary are not exclusive opposites, but at most poles on a continuum of mixed and changing sensibilities.

It is therefore still useful to ask where on such a continuum early Christian texts were produced and to test the relatively oral sensibility of gospel literature and of some gospels in particular. In this limited sense, Gerd Theißen is right to defend Bultmann's refusal to differentiate too sharply between oral tradition and the peculiar literacy of the Synoptics.[19] Criteria for detecting relative orality are only slightly stronger than criteria for determining authenticity of logia, though the former are at least an attempt to describe the sensibility of a text and not that of its distant ancestor.

[C]riteria [of orality] clearly differentiate some texts and sub-texts from others and generate at least plausible hypotheses of oral influence on the selected texts.... [T]hey are essentially relative criteria, useful for comparing texts within a continuum. This relativity is increased by the fact that our access to orality in antiquity is almost entirely through the literary medium.... Moreover, the complexity and importance of interaction between orality and literacy is liable to have been even greater in the cross-cultural, mobile and socially marginal matrix of early Christian text production. Criteria of orality, then, are not only promising, but actually necessary for

---

[18] Quoting W.J. Ong, *Orality and Literacy*, 50; on complexity and continuity between classical Greek orality and literacy see, *e.g.*, Thomas, *Oral Tradition and Written Record*; and Cizek, *Imitatio*, 39–41.

[19] G. Theißen, *Miracle Stories of the Early Christian Tradition*, trans. F. McDonagh (Edinburgh, 1983) 189; see H.C. Kee, *Christian Origins in Sociological Perspective* (London, 1980) 134.

measuring the "dynamic tension" between orality and literacy as a changing influence on the production and reception of ancient and especially early Christian texts.[20]

It is the particular poetic and rhetorical character of the Synoptic texts, their sensibility, which is the grain of intuitive truth in Bultmann's ultimately misleading allegation of unusual continuity between the forms of gospel literature and oral tradition. The Synoptics do show a mix of sensibilities, which recalls patterns of conversation and of literature from marginal communities. And yet the same texts are unmistakably, if ambivalently, related to Greco-Roman narrative and biographical genres and even more clearly rely upon the compositional conventions of progymnasmatic rhetoric.

The tension between speech and text in the gospels' hybrid sensibility motivates Werner Kelber's polemically, or else misleadingly, absolutized call for an "oral hermeneutic," a systematic interpretive opposition between gospel tradition and gospel literature. Such absolutism cannot, however, escape the fact that it is the texts themselves, technically written and ultimately literate in poetics, which conserve in their literacy other co-assertive sensibilities. The revolutionary sensibility of modernity has too much difficulty imagining the deliberate preservation and reconstruction of orality in the literary rhetoric of antiquity. It is the rhetorical competence, not the literary incompetence, of the gospel writers which allows modern critics to find in literary gospels challenging evidence of their relatively oral environment and (even technical) antecedents.

New Testament studies has only just begun to take seriously the inevitability of combining orality and literacy in ancient text production, and the possibility of doing so in any of several hybridizations. Vernon Robbins' socio-rhetorical study of the Gospel of Mark is particularly valuable in this regard as it recognized the complexity and intimacy of the relationships among biblical literacy, folkloric orality and Greco-Roman rhetoricity in the first narrative gospel. Nonetheless, his discussion of the "fusion of religious traditions, folklore, and ethical pronouncements in the Gospel of Mark" still clings to exaggerated

---

[20]   Henderson, "*Didache* and Orality," 294–5; quoting Havelock, *Literate Revolution*, 9–10; and *Origins of Western Literacy*, 21.

form-critical assumptions about the possibility of assigning "forms" to one or other of these categories and to specific, exclusive social settings.

In particular, the gospels' "minor forms," "proverbial sayings, parables, and aphoristic stories," are folklore which Robbins quite form-critically assumes to have "created a social cohesion within sectors of early Christianity." Robbins' difference from Bultmann here is not about whether a partly oral, partly written tradition should be analysed in terms of literary forms or in terms of rhetorical patterns. Robbins differs from Bultmann instead over which literary forms express the gospel books' privileged continuity with the social organizations of some pre-gospel Christians. I think that the text-linguistic data point to an even more intimate assimilation of folkloric, biblical and rhetorical sensibilities. From a rhetorical point of view less committed than Robbins to a Burkean sociology of culture, I guess that such intimate assimilation of sensibilities was possible for the gospel writers in part because they were not writing constitutions for particular sectarian congregations, but because they dared to produce publicly Greco-Roman and rhetorical gospels.[21]

The rhetorical compromise between conversational orality and classical literacy was also made possible—especially at the personal characterization—by the development and imposition of conventional categories more abstract than those of real dialogue yet less abstract than those required for the production of long texts. No one ever spoke (or acted) in the literary forms of the gospels as such. Yet, in the speech-conscious communities of the Greco-Roman world, people did speak (and literate people were taught to) in gnomai and *mythoi* (parables). Moreover, Jesus is represented as doing so to an unusual degree.

When Bultmann appealed to "mood" as final criterion of gnomic authenticity, he effectively conceded that the link between gospel rhetorics and Jesus' (real or fictional) speech habits is not in the specific forms of the gospels as books. Instead, the missing link is in the topics, styles and patterns of analogy and variation taught in the school of performance. The progymnasmata give us an unparalleled glimpse into that school. Rhetorical 'patterns' and literary 'forms' may differ least in the smallest-scale speech-types which make up the first few progymnasmatic exercises. Nevertheless, many aspects of the literary form of

---

[21] Robbins, *Jesus the Teacher*, quoting 5, 8.

gospel 'sayings' (e.g., imperative versus indicative) are often matters of indifference for rhetorical performance or traditional recollection.

The unique value of Greco-Roman rhetoric for understanding gospel orality is that the rhetoricians, school teachers, pupils, audiences and imitators all knew that they were engaged in such a hybridization of literacy and orality. Progymnasmatic rhetoric assumed a fairly high level of active Greek or Latin literacy and valued a (usually excerpted) canonical literature. Like Greco-Roman urban architecture and political institutions, progymnasmatic rhetoric promoted the assimilation of local, regional and inter-regional elites. Early Christian writers, readers and public speakers took conscious advantage of this assimilative power of Greek rhetoric. Cultural assimilation is always a two-way street.

Throughout antiquity, the primary stated goal of progymnasmatic education remained public speaking proficiency, though Quintilian and Theon also recognized and affirmed more literary, secondary teaching goals. As a hybrid of orality and literacy, combined under a distinctive political and cultural sensibility, Greco-Roman, progymnasmatic rhetoric is not only a precondition for the composition of written gospels, it is analogous to the gospel tradition as a whole. Both rhetoric and the gospel boldly and publicly experiment with the re-integration of potentially divergent oralities and literacies.

Another analogy—one from print literacy—may illustrate what I mean by hybrid sensibilities in texts and by relative orality in the critical comparison of texts. Boswell's great *Life of Johnson* is obviously literary and in ways quite unlike the gospels: it is overwhelmingly about writers, critical readers and performers of printed texts. Especially in the nineteenth century, however, it was sometimes received as nearly *Kleinliteratur*: its "primitive" compositional conventions attracted misconstrual of its characterizations, especially of Johnson and of Boswell himself.[22]

The biography's literacy is emphasized and at the same qualified, by frequent invocation of diaries, memoranda, letters and memoirs as sources: these are literary genres which often mimic or depend on oral and everyday conversation. The print literacy of "Dictionary" Johnson's *oeuvre* and of Boswell's *Life* is belied by the more personal and private conversational literacy which the *Life* publicizes. The *Life* scores high

---

[22] F. Brady, "Introduction" to J. Boswell, *The Life of Samuel Johnson*, ed. and abr. F. Brady (New York and Scarborough, ON, 1968) 7–17.

on the comparative criteria of orality current in modern orality theories; at the same time, the book is unusually crowded with "literacy events," references to books, reading, writing, etc.[23]

In such a context, Boswell's studious literariness, his chatty orality, and his candid yet moralistic characterizations must be taken together as deliberately exploring the tensions among conversational wit, compositional literacy and moral character. Boswell's distinctive blend of literary forms and conversational patterns and topics argues that literacy and orality are complementary sensibilities and that the former is at least as essential to civilized life as the latter. Moreover, the topic of tension and/or coexistence between various levels of oral and literate sensibilities is often explicit. Thus, for a double example, Boswell's Johnson, showing off his oral, conversational Latin, explicitly character-izes Voltaire as of the finest mind yet few letters ("*acerrimi ingenii et paucarum literarum*").

As an episodic patchwork of gossip, anecdotes and *bon mots*, the *Life of Johnson* is more oral even than its contemporary models of biographical narrative; it is at the same time literate and literary in ways that recall the rhetorical conventions of Greco-Roman lives of philos-ophers and sophists. The problem of being literary is the conscious subject of Boswell's work to a degree unparalleled in the gospels. Yet the *Life* and the gospels have in common their insistence on the constitutive power of conversation. Boswell's *Johnson* forces discussion not only of literacy and orality, but of differing kinds of literacy and different kinds of orality in the sensibility of a single writer.

Above all, however, comparison of the *Life* and the gospels on a long spectrum of many oralities and literacies makes sense for both works. In its strengths as well as its weaknesses the *Life of Johnson* presupposes a progymnasmatic as well as a belles-lettres rhetorical sensibility. By Boswell's day, the former was in retreat among readers of English print literature, but the *Life* is probably its greatest achieve-ment in English.

The *Life of Johnson* was even in the eighteenth century a literary anomaly. Like the gospels, it seemed to be a collection of fragments. Its adoption of the conventions of Hellenistic biography place it rather on the margins of the rhetorical tradition; Boswell's book is a collection of

---

[23] Henderson, "*Didache* and Orality," 294–5.

chreiai and of *apomnemoneumata* centred on the moral character, rhetorical *ethos*, taste and manners of its hero—as well as his books. From this perspective, the *Life* is anomalous in the intense, yet marginalized presence of its displaced Scottish author, self-parodied in the book's figure of Boswell of Auchinleck; Boswell the character, comic shadow of Johnson, both conceals and legitimates Boswell the author. This is a different technique, but a similar effect to that achieved in Mark by combining authorial anonymity with the apostolic incompetence of Jesus' companions. Both Boswell's *Johnson* and Mark's Jesus stand out in Western literature as unique, self-consciously rhetorical integrations of peculiar oralities and literacies.

The hermeneutics of gospel "proverbs" (R. Bultmann; W.A. Beardslee; C.E. Carlston)

Bultmann guessed that some logia attributed to Jesus are distinguished from other logia (ordinary proverbial sayings) by an exaltation of mood which was personal as well as eschatological. It was only these intensified and personalized logia which Bultmann assigned to the inspiration or authorship of the historical Jesus. This intuition seems to me probable on rhetorical grounds, even if it is indefensible on form-critical logic. Bultmann's hunch has been notably refined by W.A. Beardslee in the light of Bultmann's own later reflections on the theological rather than the historical relationship between proverbial language and gospel.[24]

Bultmann suggested that such expressions of general truths as ethical imperatives and proverbs give, in the first place, a reassuring sense of the continuity and intelligibility of existence. The same or similar formulations could, however, by eluding the hearer's confident grasp, become a forceful expression of the ambiguity of life. Even formally indicative declarations of general, natural, proverbial truth imply a

---

[24] W.A. Beardslee, "Uses of the Proverb in the Synoptic Gospels," *Interpretation* 24 (1970) 61–76; "Saving One's Life by Losing it," *JAAR* 47 (1977) 57–72; "The Proverb," in *Literary Criticism of the New Testament* (Philadelphia, 1970) 30–41; R. Bultmann, "Allgemeine Wahrheiten und christliche Verkündigung," *ZTK* 54 (1957) 244–254="General Truths and Christian Proclamation," *JTC* 4 (1967) 153–162; compare Winton, *Proverbs of Jesus*, 67–83.

selective demand aimed at the hearer. Proverbial (gnomic) truth "is precisely not 'enlightening,' but rather paradox, a provocation for the 'natural' human."[25]

It is thus in the nature of proverbial truth to belie itself and so move at least implicitly from general and conceptual to personal, existential address. No general truth can be performed in real discourse without becoming a concrete demand between speaker and hearer. It is this shift, not the formal illusion of stable meaning, which makes ethical imperatives and proverbs appropriate for Christian discourse. Bultmann's insight here into proverbiality in real communication is a rhetorical insight. It provides a stronger base than the belief that Jesus' eschatology was personal, distinctive and irrepressible for Bultmann's perception of exaltation of mood in a minority of gospel logia.

W.A. Beardslee sharpened Bultmann's characterization of the (rhetorical) function of proverb. For Bultmann, proverb expressed a general truth, but a general truth nonetheless addressed in every real performance to the concrete situation of its actual hearer. Beardslee emphasized more strongly the element of confrontation inherent in the formulation and/or selection of "even the most 'cracker-barrel' type of wisdom" for a particular occasion. That is, the rhetorical tension between apparent generalization and actual confrontation is always basic to proverb-use and not only to the appropriation of gnomic language for distinctively Christian proclamation. Thus proverb is only in a limited sense a 'generalization': it is always to some degree an unforeseen "challenge to insight and action."[26]

Turning to the proverb-like sayings of the Synoptic traditions, Beardslee found a minority in which the confrontational aspect has been heightened, primarily by the extension of antithesis into paradox (e.g. Luke 17:33) and by hyperbolic exaggeration of the forms of general statement (e.g. Matt 8:20 par; 8:22 par). At the same time, the presence at every level of Synoptic tradition of proverbs which have not been thus sharpened delineates the "field of intensification"[27] sayings in which the aspect of confrontation is formally concealed by the appearance of order.

---

[25] Bultmann, "Allgemeine Wahrheiten," 248.

[26] Beardslee, "Uses of the Proverb," 66.

[27] Beardslee, "Uses of the Proverb," 66–7, quoting 70.

Not every proverb is intrinsically "intense," nor should we suppose that Jesus or his imitators always performed proverbs 'intensely'. Use of proverbs in synoptic tradition is determined, according to Beardslee, by their ambiguous availability for asserting order or for confronting disorder. This ambiguity of function is always more or less felt at the rhetorical level of performance; in some instances it also appears in the actual form of a gnomic sentence. Enough Synoptic proverbs are intrinsically intensified to make intensification of proverbiality an inescapable issue for understanding rhetoric in Jesus' tradition.

The value of such an approach to the gospels' use of proverbial language is not least that it accounts at once for the usefulness of proverbial-sounding literary forms in Wisdom poetry and for the use of real proverbs in ordinary conversation. The greatest strength of Beardslee's analysis of the proverb is, however, that it exposes the intimacy and inseparability of confrontation and quasi-generalization, since the proverb is never a truly adequate summary of experience, but is always ad hoc or *ad hominem*. Once the fundamental artfulness and double-edgedness of proverb-use and proverb-formulation is recognized, the way has been prepared for moving beyond literary (sapiential) to rhetorical (gnomic) analysis.

In particular, Beardslee points to a better way of relating proverbial language as a category to Jesus' own way of speaking.

> If we could undertake a more detailed form-critical analysis we should show, despite all the judgements of probability involved, that the proverb, like the parable, comes into the tradition from its use by Jesus himself, and that the same is true of its intensification by paradox and hyperbole, which is the distinctive mark of the use of the proverb in the Synoptics.[28]

The characteristic shift in some Synoptic proverbs toward more intense confrontation can be referred to Jesus' inspiration, if not always to his authorship. At the same time, the tradition's inclusion of many quite conventional truisms cannot be dismissed as entirely the moralizing work of the Church: even Jesus' rhetoric needed conventional patterns sometimes to affirm conventional meanings.

Moreover, Beardslee, like Bultmann, relates intensification and reversal to eschatology in synoptic uses of proverbial style. There is,

---

[28] Beardslee, "Uses of the Proverb," 71.

however, nothing in Beardslee's case for the authenticity of Jesus' gnomic habit that demands appeal to a distinctive, personal "eschatological mood" as historical criterion. On the one hand, intensification need not be eschatological; on the other, Jesus is allowed to use topics other than eschatology. This essential point seems lost in Norman Perrin's treatment of "The Proverbial Sayings," which otherwise follows Beardslee closely. Perrin missed the essential importance of dealing with the history of the category as a whole and instead followed Bultmann into turning the notion of intensification—and of eschatological intensification—into an index of authenticating dissimilarity.[29]

Historically, the frequency and coherence of proverbial-sounding language ascribed to Jesus and the intensification of a sub-set of the whole category creates a strong presumption in favour of authenticity. This presumption of authenticity applies, however, not to any particular saying but to the whole manner of using (and sometimes intensifying) proverbial language. This point is absolutely fundamental to any credible examination of these sayings as evidence for Jesus. Bultmann's discussion of the logia was limited by the inevitably arbitrary use of a criterion of authenticity (in this case "eschatological mood") to select individual sayings. By contrast, Beardslee's analysis of function does not promise to authenticate any one, single saying but rather a habit of speaking in proverbs and especially of heightening their implicit tone of confrontation.

Beardslee's approach offers a direction toward meaningful discussion of Jesus' language without undertaking the hopeless project of isolating a corpus of authentic sayings.[30] C.E. Carlston[31] has sounded a similar warning against trying to authenticate fragments by criteria which require that Jesus be radically dissimilar from his environment and from his successors. Especially applied to materials which depend for their effect on apparently commonplace generalization, criteria of radical alienation are absurdly inappropriate. Carlston particularly exposes the futility of claiming uniqueness for the gospel materials in view of the

---

[29] N. Perrin, *Jesus and the Language of the Kingdom* (London, 1976) 48–54.

[30] Sanders, *Jesus and Judaism*, 1–18, 132–141; G. Schille, "Was ist ein Logion?" *ZNW* 61 (1970) 172–182.

[31] C.E. Carlston, "Proverbs, Maxims and the Historical Jesus," *JBL* 99 (1980) 87–105.

wide range of parallels available from antiquity and from traditional cultures generally.

It is therefore all the more necessary to deal with the proverbs ascribed to Jesus not piecemeal but as a category which links Jesus, his world and the world of Christian rhetoric. For Carlston, the very attribution of so large a group of sayings to Jesus by all the recognizable streams of gospel tradition must be in itself a significant fact for our understanding of their putative author. Moreover, Carlston undertook a thematic analysis of the Synoptic proverbs as a corpus, an analysis which indicated the absence of some (by no means all) typically sapiential themes: "education, personal character and habits, friendship, women and family relationships, ethnic matters, politics and prudence."[32] Whatever we make of this result, the procedure of comparison on a topical basis is an essential step toward rhetoric analysis.

Memory and performance in aphoristic tradition (J.D. Crossan)

I earlier acknowledged J.D. Crossan's exceptional contribution to the conceptual vocabulary needed for rhetorical criticism of Jesus' tradition and of synoptic gnomai in particular. It is to Crossan that we owe the psychological and social notion of sensibility in tradition as distinct from mechanically technical distinctions among oral, mnemotechnical and literary traditions. Crossan himself is less interested in the problem of complex cultural sensibilities than in the specific case of synoptic tradition. He does, however, refuse simply to confuse techniques (e.g., of writing, scholastic memorization, oral formulaic improvisation, or rhetorical performance using topics and prose patterns) with the collective mentalities which permit and limit application of techniques. It is Crossan's language of sensibility which allows us to appreciate the ironically Greco-Roman character of early Christian rhetoric: the intensive use of Greek literate and literary technique to reconstruct for wider Mediterranean publics the politicized orality of the city-state.

The persistence and mutation of oral sensibility in Greco-Roman rhetorical culture and in early Christian rhetoric is surely even more complex than Crossan anticipates. Still, noticing the tension between

---

[32] Carlston, "Proverbs and Jesus," 98–99.

oral sensibilities and literary techniques in rhetoric does make it possible to imagine early Christian tradition, both written and non-writing, as rhetorical, without arbitrarily inventing a special category of text such as *Kleinliteratur*.

Crossan is, moreover, the author of the most thorough investigation of the smaller elements of discourse attributed to Jesus in gospel literature. Identifying Synoptic tradition as strongly oral in sensibility has important implications about the tradition's usual priorities in memory and transmission. No matter how literate they undoubtedly were, the synoptists, readers and writers, seem to have been more interested in recollecting the emotional and argumentative gist of remembered speech than in syntactically faithful, verbatim iteration.

Crossan therefore concentrated attention on the transmission and creative variation of core structures in tradition rather than on sentence-editing in written format. Oral sensibility is interested in gist rather than syntax, even in written tradition. The use of literary technique gave the gospel writers much greater scope for systematic redaction; yet one evidence of persistent oral sensibility in gospel rhetoricity (and more or less in most ancient literature) is the writers' laziness as redactors, by typographic standards. Redaction criticism has underlined the extent to which the gospel-writers did imprint their own vision and tastes on received tradition. Even more regularly, however, the gospels blithely preserve from their sources every kind of stylistic, theological and narrative inconsistency, incongruity and redundancy.

The continuity of oral sensibility in literary technique can conveniently be illustrated by performantial variation between alternative versions of gnomai in Matthaean and Lucan receptions of the Sayings Gospel Q. Several Q gnomai (11:11–12; 12:6; 12:54–55) are embedded in material which strongly supports the theory of a non-Marcan documentary source used (in slightly variant forms) in Matthew and Luke. Yet these items vary gratuitously in ways inexplicable by theories of solely literary influence and redaction, unqualified by recognition of strong oral sensibility.

Do not two sparrows sell for a penny? (Matthew 10:29)

Do not five sparrows sell for two pence? (Luke 12:6)

Curiously, Crossan remains unusually, perhaps unduly, committed to the literary archaeology of source-critical stratigraphy and to reconstructing the traditional pre-history of individual fragments of text.[33] His basic model of the relationship between oral and written modes of tradition should have been more conducive to rhetorical analysis of larger patterns. It is rhetorical patterns, rather than individual items in some tradition-historical inventory, which connect book-writing to oral tradition about Jesus. Still, some inventory of possible examples of rhetorical variation and performance in written tradition is inevitable, as later chapters here attest; the necessary inventory is, however, negative, showing the irreducibility of the synoptic texts either to folkloric or to literary causes.

Crossan's very full inventory of synoptic aphorisms, indeed any list of gospel gnomic materials however defined,[34] underscores one of the paradoxes of form-critical analysis: this form is not a form, but a semantic pattern, perceived differently by different critics. Years before his work on gospel form criticism, Bultmann correctly noted Paul's uses of gnomai as evidence of diatribic style; it is hardly possible therefore that he was unaware of Greco-Roman interest in gnome and chreia when he chose instead the more heuristic, though still Hellenistic, categories of apophthegm and logion. Bultmann's choice certainly cannot be reduced to a preference for Hebrew categories.[35]

For his part, Crossan specifically discussed gnome and chreia, before instead merging them indiscriminately among his other aphorisms; we saw earlier how he mistakenly concluded that for most progymnasmatists gnome was synonymous with proverb. Crossan wrongly thought that only Quintilian (correctly) considered gnome "an authored saying but of universal application (an aphorism)."[36] Quintilian's position is,

---

[33] Crossan, *Historical Jesus*, xxvii–xxxiv, 427–450 "Appendix 1: An Inventory of the Jesus Tradition by Chronological Stratification and Independent Attestation"; Robbins, "Pre-Gospel Traditions," 117–118; Winton, *Proverbs of Jesus*, 75–79, 93–98.

[34] Von Lips, *Weisheitliche Traditionen im NT*, 198–203 and D.E. Aune, "Oral Tradition and the Aphorisms of Jesus," in *Jesus and the Oral Gospel Tradition*, ed. H. Wansbrough (JSNTSup 64; Sheffield, 1991) 211–265, 211–212, 242–258 for synopses of incommensurable, but heavily overlapping lists by Carlston, Crossan, Berger, Schulz, Kloppenborg, Zeller, Küchler, Sato, Schulz and Bultmann.

[35] Sanders and Davies let Bultmann off too easily on this score, *Synoptic Gospels* 136–137; see Bultmann, *Stil der Paulinischen Predigt*, 94.

[36] Crossan, "Aphoristic Tradition," 80.

in fact, normative for the whole progymnasmatic tradition in which almost all gnomai are by known authorities or by the speaker himself with only a few really anonymous proverbs.

Crossan's misreading of the progymnasmatists' discussions of gnome has unfortunately been influential, for example, on David Aune's false assumption that gnomai are anonymous proverbs and, consequently, very rare in Jesus' tradition.[37] But Crossan, like Bultmann, would probably have preferred in any case the vaguer, more heuristic and inclusive designation of aphorism to the rhetorical technical term. Extrapolating beyond Bultmann and Beardslee, Crossan is interested in the aphorism as a heuristic type understood in analogy with modern phenomenological readings of parable; the relatively precise and public conventions associated in antiquity with gnome-use do not serve this agenda any better than they serve wisdom-literary form criticism.

> [I]t is worth observing that Crossan's use of 'aphorism' is extremely broad.... His work covers the shorter sayings tradition as a whole, as opposed to parables or narrative material, and therefore includes the sayings which [Winton] would consider examples of proverbial wisdom.
>
> [Crossan] notes that the heuristic function of the aphorism is often connected with contradiction, and the more perplexing the contradiction, the more it teases thought and insight from the hearer or reader.... The distinction between proverb and aphorism becomes a question of the traditional and authoritative opinions of the proverb being treated paradoxically in the aphorism.[38]

In most language communities, the main distinction between proverbs and other witticisms (including literary wisdom sayings) is one of social convention rather than verbal form. Many, but by no means all, proverbs are formally marked by features associated with versification: special diction, rhythms or imagery. Yet in the plainest sense of the word, a proverb is an utterance familiar to all and usable by all speakers within a particular speech community or a particular public speaking institution.

Proverb, in this socio-linguistic sense, has not been of much interest to Crossan, Beardslee, Bultmann or anyone else in New Testament studies. Interest in the shorter discursive sentences of the synoptics is

---

[37] Aune, "Oral Tradition," 215–220, esp. 216 and 220 n.3.
[38] Winton, *Proverbs of Jesus*, 94; see Aune, "Oral Tradition," 211–212.

almost always focused on analogy with older wisdom books or with the phenomenology of reversal, surprise and paradox. At the same time, the tendency toward paradoxical intensification which Beardslee noted particularly among the proverbs of the Jesus-tradition is not confined to proverbs in the narrow sense; the possibility of intensification in formulation or in contextual deployment is in varying degrees charac-teristic of all parabolic, sententious and aphoristic language: ordinary discourse heightened by rigorous economy and poetic imagination. The curious equilibrium among the Synoptic logia between conventionality and intensification of meaning therefore demands a less prejudicial designation than 'proverb' or 'wisdom-saying'.

Greco-Roman rhetorical theories of gnome-use include together, but also distinguish among, genuinely proverbial gnomai, conventional though original gnomai, and intensely virtuosic or confrontational gnomai. The rhetoricians also provide a framework for recognizing that gnomai may be intensified (or domesticated) not only in the way they are formulated, but also in the way they are performed or contextualized. For key interpreters, however, 'aphorism' and 'logion' helped fill the need for terms other than 'proverb' and 'wisdom-saying' without invoking the troublesome technicality and cultural specificity of Greco-Roman rhetoric. Even more than the earlier form critics, Crossan is attempting rhetorical analysis of synoptic tradition, while shunning the tools provided by Greco-Roman rhetoric, for fear that they will limit his interpretative freedom. That is and was, of course, their purpose.

There is some point, therefore, to the complaint of Winton and others that the line of criticism from Bultmann through Beardslee to Crossan insists too exclusively on the rhetorical functions of shock and reversal—a criticism which could also justly be brought against most parable interpretation since Bultmann. If aphorisms, like parables, have the important "rhetorical function of disorientation or disordering" by means of paradox, hyperbole and reversal of values, they *must* also at times perform the complementary opposite rhetorical function. If structural analyses of aphorism like those of Beardslee, Perrin and, especially, Crossan show that the aphorism often seems rhetorically tailored to disorient, it is necessary also to ask how often and in what ways it is patterned to orient the hearer. At least it should be possible to ask with reference to what norms disorientation and orientation take place, a question about gnomic content which Winton has rightly championed.[39]

An important reason for talking about gnomai, chreiai and even mythoi in the gospels instead of about aphorisms and parables is that the rhetorical terms imply a normative universe within which talking about possible rhetorical functions and effects can be more than speculative anachronism. For Winton,

[t]he danger in Crossan's work is that it focuses attention on the rhetorical effect of the proverbial or parabolic material with little attention to the broader context of meaning. The broader context is literary and linguistic, involving the myth or symbol of the Kingdom of God; and also sociological, involving the praxis and setting of Jesus' activity.[40]

Somewhere between literary-linguistic and social contexts, however, is the "broader context" of Greco-Roman rhetoric itself, within which the outspoken aspects of Jesus' activity and that of his interpreters took place. Winton's legitimate concern for both the "content" and the "broader context" of aphoristic rhetoric is, in fact, met by rhetorical analysis of gnomic topicality and of the interaction of oral and literary sensibilities in gnomic rhetoric. Greco-Roman rhetoric of gnome-use provides many of the missing postulates needed to link the content and forms of particular gnomai in texts to the broader context of individuals and groups speaking, writing and reading in public.

The appearance of literary gospels may well mark an important shift in the balance between orality and literacy in early Christian rhetorics. Any shift at that point toward a more literary sensibility was certainly a less radical revolution than that canvassed by W. Kelber.[41] In fact, there is little evidence that the shift to writing about Jesus was traumatic. The shift from discursive and epistolary rhetorics also to include extended narrative is probably a more significant change than any change from relative illiteracy to literacy in synoptic rhetoric. The later reception of selected gospels into a gradually instituted canon does mark a basic shift in ancient Christianity toward a reconstructed scribal sensibility. Yet preservation, even in the canon, of a four-fold, largely

---

[39] Winton, *Proverbs of Jesus*, 77, 85.
[40] Winton, *Proverbs of Jesus*, 76–77.
[41] Kelber, *The Oral and the Written Gospel*; Silberman, *Orality*.

synoptic gospel is a monument to the Christian rhetoricity, both oral and literate, which preceded Christian canonicity.

The basic gap in early Christian rhetorics is therefore not between two radically different techniques of producing language (writing and speaking), but between two psycho-social sensibilities. By distinguishing between sensibility and technique, Crossan pointed toward the necessity of locating both oral and literary sensibilities in antiquity within an over-arching sensibility of rhetorical communication. Gospel oral tradition and the literary gospels it inspired share a sensibility anchored in the critical, secondary orality of Greco-Roman rhetoric. In both gospel orality and gospel literature the Greco-Roman rhetorical balance is displaced, but not replaced. That is, the gospels are deeply influenced both by the scribal sensibility of scriptural literacy and by the implied orality of the Gospel's intended rhetorical appeal to marginal as well as to elite audiences.[42]

One more aspect of Crossan's work should be mentioned here as a step toward the rhetorical model which I am proposing for early Christian tradition, oral and written. Crossan's distinctions between sensibility and technique and between performantial and hermeneutical variation are part of a generative model of tradition itself. Like the earlier form critics, Crossan has sought to develop a model of tradition which would respect both the continuity and the discontinuity between pre-gospel talk and gospel writing. Such a model of tradition must not be only descriptively adequate to the visible phenomena of the gospels, e.g., their synoptic relationships. A merely descriptive model can say little about pre-gospel oral traditions, except that they existed and that they were not mnemotechnical. (This much can be deduced from, e.g., the Lord's Supper, Anti-Divorce and *Hakel Dama* traditions.)

Crossan's contribution, beyond abandoning the older form critics' romantic notions of folklore, *Sitz im Leben* and *Kleinliteratur*, is to have made explicit a theoretical step which most interpreters of early Christian tradition leave implicit. Crossan makes it clear that behind his literary-historical analysis of the written tradition he has constructed a theoretical model of how early Christian tradition *might* have developed in such a way as to have produced oral performances and collective memories as well as, eventually, multiple written gospels about Jesus. Because Crossan's model is just that—a theoretical model—it includes

---

[42] Henderson, "Rhetorical Determinacy"; Gamble, *Books and Readers*.

possibilities for the development of tradition which, in fact, seem not to have been actualized in early Christian gospels (e.g., the possibility of "Aphoristic Chronicle").

Crossan is decisively right that one prerequisite for investigating pre-gospel oral traditions and, hence, for knowing anything about Jesus, is a generative model of tradition: one which will produce a finite range of options for how an initially non-writing tradition could have conditioned the literary production of sayings and other collections and then, quite suddenly, of several closely related narrative gospels. Such a "dynamic and generative model" must be flexible, comprehensive and credible enough to embrace both writing and non-writing phases of the tradition. Crossan's model, though heuristically centred on aphoristic tradition, explicitly relates aphoristic, dialectical, parabolic and narrative impulses in the generation of gospel tradition within a relatively strong and persistent "oral sensibility."[43]

Much in Crossan's hypothetically constructed generative model of aphoristic tradition is analogous to rhetorical-critical use of the categories and processes of Greco-Roman rhetoric. Greco-Roman rhetoric furnishes a model of tradition which is not unambiguous in its availability for understanding early Christian written and oral rhetoric. Precisely because the model is rhetorical it deliberately provides materials for diametrically opposed developments. Unlike Crossan's model, however, a rhetorical model of tradition can claim to be more than a hypothetical generative theory, grounded essentially in modern perceptions and only heuristically applicable to the behaviour of pre-gospel traditionists and gospel writers.

In progymnasmatic educational tradition and performance practice, Greco-Roman rhetoric was historically generative of early Christian rhetorics and exegesis. The progymnasmatic conventions for manipulating gnome, chreia, mythos, and the rest emphasize the kinds of performantial and hermeneutical variation envisioned by Crossan's model. The influence of the progymnasmata and their accessibility to us through the surviving textbooks make a concrete connection between our theoretical model and the practice of early Christian tradition in the Greco-Roman world. By conditioning the minority who spoke and wrote in public and, hence, in Greek, the progymnasmata also conditioned the majority who listened. At least as soon as traditions about

---

[43] Crossan, "Kingdom and Children," 76, 93–95; *In Fragments.*

Jesus were recalled in Greek—almost immediately—the progymnasmatic model became *the* model by which potential gospel-makers were
taught to speak, listen, read and write in public. The basic progymnasmata, blended with narrative influences—and a hint of scribal sensibility—from biblical literature, constituted the model which the gospel-
writers actually used to generate their written texts.

Crossan's work is often idiosyncratic, notably so in his combination
of an almost mystical phenomenology with demonstratively rigorous,
even aggressive historicism. There are, nonetheless, key lessons to be
drawn from Crossan if an authentically rhetorical and historical model
of Jesus' tradition is to be developed. First, Crossan's distinction
between sensibility and technique is a helpful way to make it clear that
literate, scribal and mnemotechnical sensibilities need not be opposed
as radical antinomies to orality; differentiation and interaction between
sensibilities is much less clear-cut than the technical distinction between
writing and non-writing traditions. If anything, the dominant sensibilities
of a tradition, its authors and audiences, influence the compositional
character of performances and texts even more directly than does
transmissional technique. The next step is to recognize in Greco-Roman
rhetoric, specifically in the progymnasmatic tradition, the self-conscious
and prescriptive integration of oral and literary sensibilities which
informed both the gospel-writers and their predecessors. This already
hybrid rhetorical sensibility is the matrix into which the gospel-writers
further incorporated selected narrative and scribal influences from the
biblical heritage.

Second, Crossan's inclusive discussion of gospel aphorisms
epitomizes the problem of interpreting the smaller discursive materials
attributed to Jesus. Crossan rightly perceives that they are central to any
credible model of tradition linking Jesus and the gospels. At the same
time, Crossan has abandoned those pretensions to a formal definition of
'saying', 'logion' or 'aphorism' which were already eroding in
Bultmann's pioneer essay. This has costs. Crossan's inventory of
aphorisms is long, unwieldy and formally heterogeneous. In addition,
Crossan's analysis of aphoristic structure rests too narrowly on his
perceptions of a few rhetorical turns: those characterized by semantic
reversal.

There are greater benefits, however, of dropping 'form' as even a
nominally controlling category in the criticism of sayings-tradition. In
principle and in his detailed studies Crossan makes it clear that the

specifically syntactical characteristics of gospel sayings, such as, for example, the use of imperative, conditional or relative formats,[44] must be regarded as among the least stable, least continuous aspects of a tradition which, even in literary form, retains strongly oral qualities. Crossan's emphasis on the persistence of cores rather than of texts in gospel tradition is foundational.

> Aphoristic Core is extremely important since the aphoristic tradition begins in oral not scribal transmission. Oral memory and oral sensibility operate with *aphoristic structure* rather than with *aphoristic saying*, that is, oral memory retains a linguistic structure rather than a syntactical sequence. One could even define oral sensibility as the victory of structure over sequence.[45]

Crossan's undefined category of 'aphorism' does not, however, allow him to define what sort of structures constitute cores or to show that such structures actually did constitute cores in the memory of ancient speakers, writers and audiences.

In this way, substituting gnomic cores for aphoristic cores is no mere adjustment of nomenclature. The rhetoricians' gnomai share the structure of analogy, sometimes intensified by figures of reversal, paradox, hyperbole and confrontation. The general coherence of the rhetoricians' examples and definitions and their prescriptions for the use and variation of gnomai in performance permit us to abstract a sample of gospel gnomai under the historical and socio-linguistic authority of the dominant generative sensibility of Greco-Roman antiquity. Looking for gnomai is not only less anachronistic, it is also more precise than looking for aphorisms, logia, wisdom-sayings or proverbs.

Because hermeneutical variation takes place in rhetorical tradition, it will never be possible to count gnomai with final objectivity. There is always a grey area between two variant performances of one gnomic core and two related but distinct gnomai. In Greco-Roman gnomic rhetoric as in radically non-literate oral traditions "[e]very performance is a premier and appreciated as such by the audience."[46] Even the most

---

[44] Crossan, *In Fragments*, 37–40; Barley, "Structural Approach," 741–750.
[45] Crossan, "Kingdom and Children," 95.
[46] J. Vansina, *Oral Tradition as History* (Madison, WI, 1985) 26.

fixed, traditional and proverbial gnome is hermeneutically new in every performance and therefore open to reformulation or replacement.

By the same token, however, gnomai are regarded by the rhetoricians and their audiences as countable, discrete items. The rhetorically trained (i.e., experienced) audience knows when it has heard one and the progymnasmatically trained speaker or writer knows when he deploys or invents one. Within the historical and cultural domain of progymnasmatic education, such basic rhetorical categories as gnome have a virtual objectivity. Texts and performances are expected to contain them, the question being to what degree and to what effect. Both the cause and the effect of this gnomic consciousness in Greco-Roman rhetoric is that gnomai are more reliably countable in Greek texts than are Crossan's aphorisms or Bultmann's logia. Gnomai are, by Greco-Roman convention, the most audibly and memorably structured aphorisms.

The special historical interest of early Christian gnomai lies largely in their exceptional integration of oral sensibility and rigorously structured expression; gnomai are designed to be memorable at first hearing, at least in their core images and analogies, without careful memorization. They are among the most textual of rhetorical patterns in that they invite repetition, yet they are among the most clearly oral in that they invite also free variation. The precise syntactical forms of particular aphoristic or gnomic performances, though form-critically interesting, is an unreliable guide to their history. Nevertheless, those aphorisms, mostly gnomai, which show the most definitely structured 'core' patterns, will be particularly promising indicators of the general character of pre-gospel oral tradition.

Crossan's work on aphoristic tradition between Jesus and the gospels thus takes us a long way, but not all the way toward a rhetorical analysis of gnomai attributed to Jesus. His heuristic but generative model of a tradition, both oral and writing, united by a strong residue of oral sensibility, is an immense improvement over lesser form critics' analysis of the syntax of 'wisdom sayings'. Crossan's model demands, however, the historical reality check of collation with progymnasmatic rhetoric.[47] It is only within that context of progymnasmatic rhetoric that Crossan's notions of variation of memorable cores become concrete in the prescribed uses of gnomic language. It is the correspondence and

---

[47] Robbins, "Pre-Gospel Traditions," 117–118.

tension among progymnasmatic prescriptions and synoptic performances which make a rhetorical model of gospel tradition uniquely powerful.

Form criticism in rhetorical reformation (K. Berger)

Despite the socio-rhetorical criticism of Vernon Robbins and the explosion of interest in rhetorics generally, the most comprehensive and systematic attempt so far to apply a rhetorical model to early Christian tradition and its texts is in the work of Klaus Berger. A rather extensive review of Berger's work is, I think, justified here for three reasons. First, almost none of Berger's work is available in English and he is consequently more often cited than studied in English-language scholarship.[48] In addition, his critical revision of classical form criticism is largely guided by an interest in both Greco-Roman and modern rhetorics which also differs critically from North American models of rhetorical criticism. Finally, he has explicitly studied the unique role of gnome in the rhetoric of early Christian texts; this side of his work is therefore the closest parallel to my own.

Berger's "orientation toward rhetoric" is essential to his project, if a renewed form criticism is to be more than just a chastened resuscitation of the old. Berger's approach depends upon the pre-eminence of ancient, indeed, progymnasmatic rhetoric for a generative model of New Testament forms. Appeal to Greco-Roman rhetorical conventions allows him to escape both the folklorists' pursuit of anthropologically universal forms and norms and the phenomenological aestheticism of some more recent critics.[49] The progymnasmata in particular were among the most widely and systematically disseminated aspects of Hellenistic culture.

> In ancient schooling appropriating certain literary types was so central that the latter were not only receptively, but also actively mastered.

---

[48] Berger, "Hellenistische Gattungen"; *Einführung*; *Formgeschichte*; *Exegese*; "Rhetorical Criticism"; Sanders and Davies, *Synoptic Gospels*, 133–4.

[49] Berger, *Formgeschichte*, 16.

In their role as historic pseudo-universals, e.g., percolating into the formulation of rabbinic tradition, they can guide interpretation without absolving modern critics of critical responsibility for our judgements.[50]

Berger recognizes that rhetorical categories are flexible communicative conventions unlike the originally 'pure forms' of the classical form critics. This has two vital implications. First, rhetorical patterns are always mixed or embedded in each other. Gnomai in particular are always distinct from their contexts and can be used in more than one context. Yet gnomai are never context-free. In early Christian rhetoric, gnomai overlap especially with parables and chreiai. Second, replacing 'forms' in the form-critical sense with rhetorical patterns involves renouncing naive form-critical schemes of linear evolution. In gnomic chreiai and other compound rhetorical units, the pre-existence of the 'punch-line' as an independent saying cannot be presupposed.[51]

At the same time, the Greco-Roman rhetorical tradition almost ignores private, psychological aspects of an author's choice of forms and instead concentrates upon the relation between speech forms and their predictable effect upon an audience.

> For the following reasons, form is a rhetorical element: (a) it is surface-oriented (*Sinnlichkeit*, sensuality), (b) it is to be seen *prima vista*, (c) it is almost always something known and allows easy identification. ...If we want to take advantage of rhetoric in establishing genres or text-types we have to look for those elements in a text which have a dominant influence on the effect.

The ancient rhetoricians identified and publicly institutionalized performance factors and techniques in speech. Their work points modern critics toward the key concern of Hellenism with the spoken effect of language, whether written or not. This means that ancient rhetoric is the source of first resort for critical categories relevant to the purposes and history of the New Testament documents. Berger does not hesitate to use modern categories or to abstract modern criteria for ancient categories, but he recognizes the central, generative role of Greco-Roman rhetorical conventions behind early Christian texts and he

---

[50] Quoting Berger, *Formgeschichte*, 23; "Hellenistische Gattungen," 1040, 1296–1299.

[51] *Formgeschichte*, 21–22, 63, 84.

acknowledges an increased burden of proof whenever he is forced to replace ancient rhetorical categories with ad hoc modern ones.[52] Consequently, Berger follows the rhetoricians in devoting important discussions to *sententia* and gnome as such rather than to some vague category of 'wisdom-saying', 'logion' or 'aphorism'.[53]

Because he focuses on "text-types" and their "goal-orientedness" (*Wirkaspekt*), their probable rhetorical effects, rather than on pure forms emanating directly from specific settings (*Sitze im Leben*), Berger takes only an opportunistic interest in the pre-textual origins of textual rhetorics. Berger is not globally sceptical about the possibility or legitimacy of reconstructing pre-gospel traditions "to get access to the historical Jesus."[54] Yet such reconstruction is at best an occasional by-product of Berger's form criticism, not its guiding star. Judgements about the historical relationship between gospel materials and Jesus himself are not impossible, but they are persuasive, not on the basis of reconstructed lines of evolutionary development, but on the basis of general, self-consciously rhetorical arguments of probability.

> It is therefore not always straightforward and also not vitally important to look here for the *ipsissima vox Jesu*. The only—admittedly imprecise—criterion which helps with the question of what derives from Jesus is, to the best of my knowledge, the criterion of 'historically plausible effects' ['*wirkungsgeschichtlichen Plausibilität*']: That is, does the broad history of early Christianity (the history of Jesus' influence [*Wirkungsgeschichte Jesu*]) become as a whole incomprehensible, or does it gain comprehensibility, if Jesus is supposed to have done or said this or that?[55]

The rare cases in which Berger does attribute special historical significance to a particular rhetorical pattern are therefore potentially paradigmatic for a rhetorical criticism which seeks to pay primary attention to probable effects of language claiming Jesus' influence. One such instance of exceptional social and historical transparency in Jesus'

---

[52] Berger, *Formgeschichte*, 16–22; "Hellenistische Gattungen," 1036–1038, 1056–1057; and quoting "Rhetorical Criticism," 390.

[53] "Hellenistische Gattungen," 1049–1074 on "Gnome, Hypotheke, *sententia*"; *Formgeschichte*, 62–74 on "Sentenzen."

[54] "Rhetorical Criticism," 391.

[55] *Formgeschichte*, 14–15, quoting 15.

speech tradition—an exception which Berger has repeatedly emphasized —is in early Christian uses of *sententiae* and gnomai.[56]

For Berger, the historical relationship between orality and literacy in gospel tradition is far more problematic than in the older form criticism. The old form critics were right that the relationship is crucial not only for understanding the processes of pre-textual transmission, but also for understanding the formation of the texts themselves. Both the form critics, however, and more recent advocates of a dehistoricized "oral hermeneutic" (W. Kelber) have misrepresented that relationship. The former overstated the sub-literary and impersonal folkloric character of the gospels as written oral tradition; the latter exaggerate the hermeneutical discontinuity between orality and literacy in Greco-Roman rhetorical cultures.

Thus Berger finds little evidence of extensive and immediate formal continuity between early Christian texts and units of pre-gospel oral tradition: the strong cases for pre-gospel oral tradition suggest non-formal, rhetorically variable transmission of sayings and narrative materials alike.[57] The choice between writing and not writing, like the more microscopic choices among variable communicative conventions, was calculated throughout the gospel tradition "to meet the requirements of an intended effect."

> This means that in this model the freedom of the text producer in his/her specific situation has to be estimated higher than in [classical form criticism].[58]

It is of extraordinary importance, then, that Berger identifies gnome-use as a uniquely transparent field of interplay among "the freedom of the text producer," the dominant communicative conventions of rhetorical and biblical culture, and the changing situations of early Christian speech and writing.

---

[56] Especially *Formgeschichte*, 13, 67; "Hellenistische Gattungen," 1055–7; also *Einführung*, 64, 120, 126–7; *Exegese*, 106, 110.

[57] Berger, *Formgeschichte*, 13–16; *Einführung*, 128; *contra* Schmithals, "Kritik der Formkritik."

[58] Berger, "Rhetorical Criticism," 392.

The *sententiae* have a special *historical worth* in that they are one of the few opportunities to get back with relative certainty to the *oral stages of the gospel tradition.*

To treat the 'wisdom sayings' of the gospels as Jesus' expression and thereby to leave out the whole field of Greek gnomic literature is a completely unjustified limitation.... Moreover, the closeness between literacy and orality [in gnomai] is an important bridge for crossing back from the literary pattern to everyday speech. Thus gnomai offer a unique and hitherto neglected opportunity to obtain the most representative information possible on those norms and attitudes which played a role in the daily life of the pagan hearers of the New Testament. It is necessary to deal at the same time with the basic situation for reception and with its tradition-historical preconditions.[59]

There are several important dimensions to Berger's privileging of gnomic language as a vector of historic tradition. Above all is the special proximity of orality and literacy in gnomai. Notwithstanding the variability of gnomic cores, many gnomai constitute remarkably fixed bundles of themes and imagery, effectively reproducible in written or spoken tradition. Spoken gnomai are more like fixed texts than most other rhetorical patterns; conversely, written gnomai recall the practices of ordinary speech, memory and tradition more invitingly than most other text-types. In this connection Berger repeatedly points to the so-called '*Wanderlogien*' to exemplify the relative textuality of gnomai in oral tradition.[60]

For Berger, gnomic language is not only important as a bridge between orality and literacy. Continuities in gnome-use are a key point of comparability across a wider variety of critical gaps:[61]

a) between rhetorical performance and text-production under progymnasmatic influence;
b) among Greco-Roman rhetorics and non-Greek, especially Jewish wisdom and poetry;
c) between popular and elite discourses;

---

[59] Berger, *Formgeschichte*, 67; "Hellenistische Gattungen," 1056–7, against Zeller, *Mahnsprüche*, 32.
[60] *Formgeschichte*, 13, 62–67; "Hellenistische Gattungen," 1077; *Einführung*, 120.
[61] "Hellenistische Gattungen," 1056–57.

   d) among differing larger speech- and text-types (chreia, apophthegm, parable, parenesis);

   e) between gospels and letters in Christian tradition.

It should be clear from all this that the peculiar historical relevance which Berger assigns to gnomai in early Christian discourse has practically nothing to do with whether Jesus actually spoke any particular gnome. Berger can on occasion argue persuasively for the virtual authenticity of a particular gnomic core and for its importance in understanding Jesus historically (e.g., "greatness=servanthood" Mark 10:35–45 par).[62] Berger is always concerned, however, not to reduce the cultural and historical significance of early Christian gnomai by letting gnome-use become just another topic in historical Jesus research. The unique importance of gnomai linking Jesus and a wide range of Jewish, Christian and pagan rhetorics, spoken and written, is that the conventions for inventing, selecting and deploying gnomai, and sometimes the gnomic cores themselves, are clearly shared across cultural, social and linguistic boundaries. Moreover, in general, within early Christian texts or more broadly, the bulk of similarities in gnome-use are simply not reducible to literary influence.

Berger devoted two discussions to gnomic language, both published in 1984; the differences between them raise important issues. In his slightly earlier treatment, of "Hellenistic text-types in the New Testament," Berger discusses gnome, *hypotheke* and *sententia* together as a single, indeed his first, category of deliberative (symbouleutic) rhetoric—with a brief supplementary discussion of "gnomic elements in letters" among miscellaneous "non-rhetorical," "pre-literary" types.[63]

In his more comprehensive handbook of New Testament form criticism Berger distinguishes between gnome and *sententia*. The distinction is initially syntactical: gnome are imperative or prohibitive, *sententiae* are usually indicative. This has functional implications, so that Berger treats *sententia* with parable, chreia and, surprisingly, argumentation among pre-rhetorical collection types (*Sammelgattungen*). Gnome is treated among symbouleutic types, specifically as a characteristic sub-unit of parenesis and instruction. *Sententia*, on the other hand, is more closely related to parable than is gnome.

---

  [62] *Einführung*, 227–240.
  [63] "Hellenistische Gattungen," 1049–1074; 1362.

The distinction is neither to be forced nor to be dismissed. Preference for imperative and prohibitive gnomai may be a necessary criterion for describing parenesis as a genre. Berger is also right to note the close functional and textual relationship between indicative gnome (*sententia*) and parable. Elsewhere it is clear that what Berger says about *sententiae* usually also applies to individual gnomai as his earlier discussion implied. In practice, Berger's distinction between imperative and indicative forms of gnome is a distinction within a basically unified rhetorical category.

Thus it is particularly to his (indicative) *sententiae* that Berger, in his second publication, attributes special "historical relevance"—because he regards these as relatively "fixed" in their core structures. Likewise, Berger is more likely to speak of the rhetorical turns to antithesis and reversal in relation to his indicative *sententiae*.[64] Nevertheless Berger also describes his (imperative) gnomai as an exceptional bridge between orality and literacy and between gospel and epistolary rhetorics.[65] Despite the greater importance of (imperative) gnomai in parenesis, parenetic material also includes (indicative) *sententiae* (e.g., Gal 5:25–6:19, Matt 6:1–24).

Berger defines (imperative) gnomai as symbouleutic specifically in relation to the larger genre, parenesis; in continuity with the biblical Wisdom instruction and its component imperative admonitions, parenesis as such requires a series of imperatives. In his earlier discussion, of imperative and indicative gnomai together, Berger was of course aware of this literary relation between parenesis and symbouleutic gnomai, but makes it clear that the grammatical imperative or prohibitive is less important than the normative implication: "not only formal imperatives are meant here."[66] On the other side of his *sententia*/gnome distinction, Berger recognizes that *sententiae* can function in symbouleutic, epideictic and dicanic contexts.[67]

In general, the literary convention associating parenesis with imperative gnomai should be treated as a specialization of the more open convention of Greco-Roman rhetoric as a whole, in which no systematic distinction is made between imperative and other gnomai and

---

[64] *Formgeschichte*, 13, 67.
[65] *Formgeschichte*, 156.
[66] "Hellenistische Gattungen," 1052 n. 10, 1059–62.
[67] *Formgeschichte*, 65–66.

in which gnomai are treated outside and prior to the ancient framework of three master rhetorical genres. This is implicit in Berger's own recognition that both his parenetic gnomai and his *sententiae* are described by the *Progymnasmata*, which certainly do not distinguish imperative from indicative gnomai or distribute gnomic forms among the three overarching rhetorical genres.[68] Regardless of verbal mood, gnomai can be used in all three kinds of rhetoric:

> texts intended to activate or admonish the reader (symbuleutic texts), texts intended to impress the reader (epideictic texts) and texts intended to explain a decision (dicanic texts).[69]

Imperative gnomai often answer legally relevant questions in gospel chreiai, an aspect of the complex, historically important relationship between gnome-use and Law. But as Berger rightly notes, (indicative) *sententiae* as well as (imperative) gnomai are used in this topically legal way (e.g., Mark 2:19–22; 27, 28).[70] In fact, as Berger makes obvious, imperative and indicative gnomai are used freely in gospel chreiai on all topics (e.g., Luke 4:23, 24; *Gos. Thom.* 31=POxy. I,6).[71]

In the previous chapter, I agreed that variations in verbal mood can be rhetorically significant even if they are not definitive for speech-types. No one would argue that "Healer, cure yourself!" and "No healer cures those who know him," are rhetorically equivalent: they imply critically different relationships among the putative speaker, audience and "healer." But, to invoke Crossan's terms, they are hermeneutical variants of the one gnomic core. Each variant embodies the linguistic resistance which gives the gnomic core the independent memorability which Berger notices. Imperative/indicative variation is not nearly rare enough in gospel tradition or in Greco-Roman rhetoric to justify a radical distinction (e.g., Luke 12:3 par (imperative); Mark 4:22 par (indicative)).

Neither in rhetorical precept nor in gospel practice is the (imperative) gnome a separate species from the (indicative) *sententia*. Rather, the imperative is one, often marked performance option over against what

---

[68] *Formgeschichte*, 19, 156.
[69] "Rhetorical Criticism," 391.
[70] *Formgeschichte*, 122 (on legal gnomai), 66 (on legal *sententiae*).
[71] *Formgeschichte*, 66, 82, 85, 89, 117.

Berger is probably right to perceive as the unmarked, default option of using the indicative. I shall continue to follow the rhetoricians (and the spirit of Berger's own double study) in calling both indicative and imperative forms gnome (*sententia* in Latin), without denying the importance of the imperative sub-type in Wisdom-literary and parenetic conventions.

CHAPTER FOUR

GNOMAI IN TRADITION AND REDACTION:
DISTRIBUTION AND DISTINCTNESS

A central lesson to be won from reading the gospels in the light of the Progymnasmata is an appreciation of the intimacy of tradition and redaction in the composition of Greco-Roman rhetorics. Classical form and redaction criticism has long been devoted to distinguishing received tradition from redactional innovation in the styles and outlooks of the gospel documents. Such criticism approaches questions of style and outlook in the gospels with arithmetic precision: statistics of word- and syntax-preferences are collated with lists of additions, subtractions and transpositions of material from known literary sources. The results are exegetically useful, but irreducibly literary sketches of individual gospel writers as authors, indeed, as theologians.

By contrast, classical rhetoric and, above all, the progymnasmatic tradition dramatize the fact that even the building blocks, the most common text-types and sentence-types in gospels, are neither folkloric nor sectarian in form, nor yet the inventions of the gospel writers. Saying, anecdote and parable are not specialized styles developed as responses to the peculiar life-settings, instutions and needs (*Sitze im Leben*) of distinctive proto-Christian groups. Instead gnome, chreia and *mythos* along with progymnasmatic models for their variation and adjustment are the dominant conventions in the Greco-Roman speech-world for blending tradition and originality into a dynamic and effective performance. These are the conventions which are adopted whole-heartedly by the gospel writers and which seem also to have structured their received sources and oral traditions.

But how does the continuity of gnome-use in pre-gospel oral tradition and in the writing of both epistles and gospels relate to the discontinuities of authorial, redactional styles in gospel literature? Gospel gnomai function in the argument—even betray the personal style—of particular gospel writers; otherwise particular gnomai would simply not have been used. Can the same gnomai simultaneously be held up as representative of meaningful continuity among Jesus, Paul and the gospel-writing milieu and also as representative of various distinct redactional styles? How many gospel gnomai are simply products of the authorial and redactional work of successive gospel writers, marked as such by their authors' stylistic and topical signatures?

In earlier chapters I noticed that intensive gnome-use was often seen as a mark of sophistic, Asianic, modern and/or Cynic rhetorics at their most agonistic. Such aggressive, agonistic, often improvisational gnome-use epitomizes the ambivalence of rhetoric toward both tradition and authorship. In Greco-Roman rhetoric, gnomai are neither universal 'proverbs' nor authorial 'aphorisms'. In fact, from the highest Aristotelean theory to the lowest common denominator of progymnasmatic elaboration, amplification and abbreviation, the extant documentary evidence insists that gnome-use was taught in terms of the speaker's liberty to play with the ambiguity between proverbiality and aphoristic individuality. This is why it is necessary to distinguish between gnomic cores in tradition and memory, and gnomai in actual, unique performances and texts. As one would expect from progymnasmatic and rhetorical precepts, not many gnomai occur in the same words in more than one text, but many gnomic cores are repeated in different texts and/or contexts among the gospels, in the Pauline literature and beyond.

The ambivalence between tradition and performance in gnome-use corresponds to rhetoric's general ambivalence toward writing and reading. Rhetorical *theory* would have been impossible without the peculiar developments in classical Athenian literacy. So too would the Greco-Roman educational programme of rhetorical hegemony and elite solidarity have proven impossible without the widely felt influence and prestige of minority literacy in Greek. Rhetoric, like epigraphy, was in many ways an officially supported semi-public institution; basic literacy in Greek or Latin was, by contrast, left to take care of itself at home and in the market place. Thus rhetorical education is the only educational tradition in antiquity we know much about and it is richly documented, not least in the extant written Progymnasmata.

The rhetorical educators themselves emphasize the importance of higher literacy, but in so doing suggest its limited place in the (rhetorical) project of ancient education. Among the progymnasmatists, as we have seen, Theon is singular in the extent to which he emphasizes both the importance of classicist reading and daily writing and also the usefulness of rhetoric for strictly literary pursuits, but he was not alone among elite educationists to urge the value of knowing the classics and imitating them in written exercises (*scriptio*).

As I argued earlier, however, such an emphasis in the most literary educationists suggests a less literate and less classicist practice further down the long scale of actual progymnasmatic education: the gospels were not written by pupils of Theon. Even at its face value, moreover, advice to practice selected reading and writing comes as preface (Theon *Prog.* 1,158 Spengel 65) or appendix (Quint. *Inst.* X 3), on the edges of a pre-rhetorical curriculum of which the primary goal is always articulate and effective speech: "The pen [*stilus*] is the best and foremost perfector and teacher of speaking" (Cicero *De Or.* I 150; Quint. *Inst.* X 3,1; Theon *Prog.* 1,150 Spengel 61). Just where it is most highly praised, classical reading and imitative writing are seen as a secondary parallel track shadowing the primary curriculum of rhetorical learning and performance and only occasionally emerging into full view.

Even this rhetorical ambivalence between orality and literacy is enough for Alexander Cizek to suggest that the "postulate of orality in ancient civilisation, so often assumed by moderns, must in many respects be revised."[1] In still more general terms, the long tradition of rhetorical stylistics also suggests that the impression of ancient rhetoric's bias toward orality be qualified though not reversed; rhetorical orality is always a secondary orality, ever mindful of the power of literacy, but consciously choosing the publicity of speech over that of texts.

Ancient rhetorical critics "liked to tie communicative virtues to specific congeries of figures, vocabulary and syntactical choices." They also liked the classicist idea that vicious or virtuous styles could be illustrated by opposing pairs of historic models. Essentially, however, ancient rhetoric never gave up locating "stylistic analysis within an aspiring general and inclusive theory of effective verbal communication."[2]

As a result, despite the clutter of invidious comparisons, inconsistent evaluations and differences between Latins and Greeks, two constants emerge: First, virtually the whole history of ancient criticism of rhetorical styles bears interpretation in terms of Aristotle's fundamental binary opposition between the stylistic poles of "written" (*graphike*) and

---

[1] Cizek, *Imitatio*, 40.
[2] Henderson, "Style-Switching," 194.

"competitive" (*agonistike*) rhetorics (*Rh.* III 12=1413b–1414a). This opposition already implies the necessary revision of modern theories which oppose orality and literacy too harshly, especially because it is the improvisational, agonistic style which conditions the favoured 'grand style' of Greco-Roman rhetoric.[3]

Aristotle's distinction between improvisational and textual styles of rhetoric is one of relative sensibility rather than of radically opposed or discontinuous modes of oral and literary production—every speaker/ writer should aim to master both styles, both in performance and in composition. Partly just because 'textual' and 'agonistic' are not intuitive opposites for modern rhetoricians, these poles provide a stylistic axis along which various Christian and non-Christian rhetorics, orally performed and/or written, can be cautiously yet fruitfully compared.

Second, and consistent with this, we noticed that in "the developed theory of rhetoric, stylistic distinction was seen essentially in terms of types, rather than individuals."[4] This too has massive implications for fresh ways New Testament rhetorical criticism should approach questions of style in tradition and authorship. In order to establish any genuinely rhetorical model of gospel tradition, it will be necessary to challenge received form- and redaction-critical notions of style, grounded as these are in romantic and positivist rebellions against rhetoric. Gnomai are rhetorically calculated to cross and even erase the boundaries between tradition and individuality. And because gnome-use also straddles whatever thin line may be drawn between style and argument, gnomic rhetoric will be particulary useful in working out a rhetorical-critical mean between reductive psychological and sociological assumptions.

Style in rhetoric and redaction

The dominant approach to thinking about style in Early Christian studies is that of redaction criticism. The surface style of gospel texts and their written sources was for form criticism an irrelevance except

---

[3] O'Sullivan, *Greek Stylistic Theory*, 42–62, esp. 59; Shuger, *Sacred Rhetoric*, 14–41.

[4] O'Sullivan, *Greek Stylistic Theory*, 3.

insofar as the evangelists' allegedly sub-literary style was part of the myth that gospel texts were open windows into pre-gospel Christian folklore. In form criticism gospel style, especially 'clumsy' gospel style, worked "negatively [as] an index of limited authorial competence and positively [as] an index of folkloric orality."[5] Redaction criticism, to its credit, convincingly returned critical attention to the work of the gospel writers as authors and thinkers and therefore as stylists. Characteristically, however, this redaction critical interest in gospel styles was essentially instrumental: stylistic analysis is still subservient to some other controlling interest, specifically the ecclesial and theological identity of each gospel author. As J.E. Botha has noted in his call for a new approach to style in New Testament studies, "individual style studies are mostly undertaken not with a view to style itself, but to provide stylistic data for some other purpose."[6]

The discipline of gospel redaction criticism is founded on the peculiarly close textual relationships among the Synoptic gospels. Such criticism is thereby also deeply committed to a working definition of style as a composite of authorially distinctive micro-stylistic features of diction and short syntax: of the several kinds of difference which nuance and qualify the general relationships of synoptic similarity, these are the most easily *counted*. At its best, then, redaction criticism works by collating lists of micro-stylistic and/or ideological peculiarities of individual gospels with more general (usually theological) observations about the architecture of each book. The stated goal is a better understanding of the distinctive authorial and social characteristics of each gospel, rather than an understanding of style specifically or of the impressive similarities and commonalities among the gospels. 'Redactional style' is thus at best a subset of the style of a whole text, a subset selected to emphasize stylistic distinctiveness over stylistic continuity.

Redaction-critical notions of 'style' are, however, more than just a reflex of the special requirements of synoptic logic. Redaction-critical notions about style strongly reinforce romantic and phenemenological presumptions about authors and texts. The contrast between redaction-

---

[5] Henderson, "Style-Switching," 188; see, e.g., J.C. Meagher, *Clumsy Construction in Mark's Gospel: A Critique of Form- and Redaktionsgeschichte* (New York and Toronto, 1979).

[6] J.E. Botha, "Style in the New Testament: The Need for Serious Reconsideration," *JSNT* 43 (1991) 71–87, 78.

critical and ancient rhetorical approaches to style is thus a key aspect of the anti-rhetorical bias in twentieth-century New Testament studies. A thorough study of rhetorical and sociolinguistic stylistics is very much needed in New Testament studies; for the time-being, however, the contrast as I see it between redaction-critical and rhetorical intuitions about style may be schematically laid out. For redaction criticism:

1) Style is individual and—often sub-consciously—specific to each author, text, or originating social group; style is psychologically and socially determined; style expresses distinctive identity.

2) Personal style is *literary*. Redactors, not oral traditionists, have one.

3) Style is therefore fixed within each redactional stratum of each text; Marcan style, e.g., is 'clumsy'.

3) Style is a congeries of small-scale 'features', syntactical and vocabulary preferences, analysed statistically.

4) Redactional differences between gospels should be divided between stylistic and theological, argumentative differences.

Rhetorical criticism thinks of style quite differently:

1) "Style has to do with the *choice* available to users of language."[7] Audiences consciously expect speakers/writers to choose among conventional stylistic patterns and registers. "Style corresponds to the rhetorical principle of the *aptum*, of appropriateness to the circumstances of the communicative relationship. The means of style are conventional, yet nonetheless always in this connection unexpected." All style is therefore simultaneously both 'redactional' and 'traditional'.[8]

2) Style varies within texts and within each author's work; audiences consciously expect speakers/writers to vary style deliberately within performances and within conventions.[9]

---

[7] Botha, "Style," 78.
[8] Berger, *Exegese*, 90 (quoted), cf. 208.
[9] Drijepondt, *"Varietas"*; Cizek, *Imitatio, passim.*

3) Style and its variations are determined by speakers/authors in relation to specific persuasive goals, perceived rhetorical opportunities, and anticipated evaluations of subject matter; style indicates the speaker's projected relationships with audience and subject.

4) Style therefore varies especially along an axis from improvisation to textuality depending on the degree of flexibility required in the central communicative relationships; style is improvisational, heterogeneous,[10] dynamic and elastic.

5) Style consists of both large- and small-scale contrasts within texts and within rhetorical conventions; style and argument are inseparable, though heuristically distinct aspects of rhetorical effect.

Sadly, 'stylistics' is something of a bad word in contemporary rhetorical criticism. The revival of rhetoric today is quite consciously a correction of the early modern subversion of holistic rhetoric in favour of a radical dissociation of poetics and scientific reason. Unfortunately, the corrective antidote has been applied more consistently to the individualist aesthetics of the romantics and phenomenologists than to the objectified, positivist logic of experimental and statistical science. Particularly in studies of early Christianity, rhetorical critics have challenged romantic and phenomenological aestheticism more effectively than they have challenged positivist historicism.

Ironically, the consequence is that in much rhetorical critical practice, the reduction of 'rhetoric' and 'style' to impressionistic judgements about the "reconstructed literary or stylistic coherence" of texts has been replaced by an over-compensating reduction of rhetoric to argumentation.

Rhetorical critics resist reducing rhetorical style to mere stylistics. If stylistic techniques are seen only as artistic devices or ornamentation, then their main function as argumentation will be diminished or discounted altogether. Wuellner calls for "the liberation from Babylonian captivity of rhetoric reduced to stylistics."[11]

---

[10] Bible and Culture Collective, *Postmodern Bible*, 172.

[11] Bible and Culture Collective, *Postmodern Bible*, 172, 154 quoting W. Wuellner, "Where is Rhetorical Criticism Taking Us?" *CBQ* 49 (1987) 448–463, 457.

Both pre-modern and postmodern rhetorics agree that the universal, defining goal of rhetoric is persuasion, that is, practically effective communication. Both pre-modern and postmodern rhetorics also agree in principle that affective and emotive appeal is, like reasonableness, central to persuasion. But ancient rhetoric did not treat style as subordinate and tributary to argumentation. On the contrary, it recognized style and argumentation as simultaneously developing, complementary aspects of effective rhetorical performance. Rhetorical persuasion is more than argumentation, and style is one index of how much more.

Restoring rhetorical stylistics to its rightful place beside argumentation theory is essential for historical Jesus research, because we will never recover or reconstruct Jesus' argumentation, except insofar as it may be known by analogy from his gnomic and parabolic style. Analysis of argumentation typically requires longer syntactical units than anything we can plausibly attribute to Jesus. The argumentative implications of Jesus' gnomic and parabolic argumentation are thus irretrievably damaged by fragmentation and re-contextualization— though in later chapters I shall argue that the urgent topicality implicit in many gnomai does tell us something, albeit skeletal, about Jesus' argumentative intentions. Nonetheless, the stylistic aspects of his gnomic and parabolic rhetoric are far more completely re-imaginable from the syntactically brief fragments available.

Rehabilitating a stylistic analysis which is reducible neither to poetics nor to argumentation theory is at any rate essential to the next step in the argument of this book. My goal in the following pages will be to argue that gnomai are so widely diffused throughout the Synoptic gospels and related literature that their presence in the tradition cannot be reduced to the work of a particular writer or a particular period in the redactional history of the gospels. Gnomai are attributed to Jesus within a wide variety of form-critical contexts and by virtually every recognizable literary source or redactor. My contention is therefore simply that gnomai are basic to synoptic tradition and that they are so basic because of the influence of Jesus' actual speaking habits.

Many gnomai certainly show stylistic and topical kinship with the redactional interests and habits of the texts in which they are presented. The fact that a good many gnomic cores are attested in more than one textual setting gives us some control over redactional creation of new gnomai and assimilation of older cores. In any case, the progymnasmata warn us to expect any trained writer freely to blend traditional and original gnomai and to perform them in a variety of styles ranging from the archaizing to the highly personal. Indeed, the rhetoricians prefer to distinguish between imitation and variation (*imitatio et tractatio*) rather than between redaction and tradition.[12]

Partly because a certain kind of stylistic analysis has been fundamental to redaction criticism and partly because contemporary rhetorical criticism too often represses its legitimate stylistic interests, a corrective attention to style has been forced on us. One of my declared tasks here is historically disciplined understanding of Jesus. I am therefore constrained by the fact that the stylistic aspect of Jesus' rhetoric is more credibly evidenced than the argumentative aspects, though the inseparability of style and argument makes me hopeful for a return to the latter. Both ancient and modern rhetorics perceive gnome to lie on the porous, imaginary border between style and argumentation. Recent argumentation theory rather shies away from gnomic rhetoric on that ground; my argument here is that the close integration of style and topicality in gnome is essential to the unique opportunity which gnomic tradition presents for historical understanding.

This then is at last the place to begin describing and evaluating more microscopically the particular conditions of written sayings attributed to Jesus in the New Testament literature by drawing out the implied oral pre-history of the Synoptic gnomai. My intention is to present samples of gnomic rhetoric from the gospels and related texts in two steps. In the first step I will try to illustrate, on the one hand, the diffusion of gnomai across all kinds of critical boundary and, on the other, the cohesion of gnomai attributed to Jesus as a rigorously definable category in spite of considerable stylistic, syntactical and topical variety. Because I want to highlight the semantic distinctness of gnomai within the process of tradition and literary redaction, the following survey focuses on gnomai which mark redaction-critical watersheds and on gnomai which exemplify at the same time traditional rhetoric and redactional style.

Two final chapters will take the further step of identifying gnomai and gnomic cores which suggest particular argumentative connections and topics which might have belonged in Jesus' rhetoric. In the previous chapter, I pointed out with approval the position of W.A. Beardslee and

---

[12] Cizek, *Imitatio, passim.*

C.E. Carlston arguing that the wide distribution and frequency of proverbs make an irresistible presumption in favour of the authenticity of the category as a whole in its ascription to Jesus. I have tried to show that their case works even better if we substitute the rhetorical and, therefore, traditional category of gnome for the misleading notion of 'proverb'. That general, collective assurance of gnomic authenticity and consequent historical relevance should be more persuasive than any claims for the authenticity and representativeness of individual 'sayings' attributed to Jesus.

Within this general presumption of collective historicity, however, some Synoptic gnomai show a particular historical topicality and/or a particular pattern of diffusion which should be co-ordinated more narrowly with specific problems in early Christian history and rhetoric. This second, topically more specific and historically more emphatic stage of enquiry will, however, only be a legitimate construction if it is clearly seen to depend upon the results and assumptions of this chapter's discussion of how gnomai relate tradition and redaction in the gospels.

Tradition, redaction and gnomic style (M. Goulder)

As part of his highly idiosyncratic proposal for solving the problem of inter-textual relationships among the Synoptic gospels, Michael Goulder attempted a major stylistic analysis of Matthew, Mark and Luke.[13] Goulder's goal was to prove that most of the "poetry"—largely gnomic sayings—which he found in the gospels derived from the specifically literary influence of one original writer, the author of Matthew. Goulder's revisionist position on gospel origins involved denying all non-textual influences on the composition of the first three gospels, which may explain why, more than more conventional redaction critics, Goulder has dared to sieze the gospel tigers by their stylistic tails. Stylistically, Goulder's central task is to show that the language of the supposed non-Marcan source, Q, is, in fact, irreducibly Matthaean and hence that the Q hypothesis is invalid: In the face of overwhelming source-critical evidence for the existence of a Sayings Gospel Q behind

---

[13] M. Goulder, *Midrash and Lection in Matthew* (London, 1974); see Sanders and Davies, *Synoptic Gospels*, 93–97.

Matthew and Luke, Goulder must find alternative topics on which to argue an alternative hypothesis.

Goulder has been astute enough to see that topics arising from large-scale stylistic analysis have been largely left to anyone wishing to advocate a maverick position in Synoptic studies. Goulder is right that mainstream New Testament studies have not yet adequately pre-empted the available opportunities for stylistic arguments to the same extent that they have succeeded in incorporating other kinds of evidence/ argument into the dominant Q hypothesis. That is, because form criticism and redaction criticism were both predicated on minimizing continuity between redaction and tradition, neither of these conventional approachs could fairly carry out the task of holistic stylistic analysis of their intimate interaction in gospel composition.

The stylistic analysis which Goulder actually carries out is as whimsical as his theory of gospel origins is quixotic. Like other redaction critics, Goulder treats rhetorical styles and gnomic rhetoric in particular as "poetry" and, indeed, as sub-conscious authorial reflexes. He is intuitively right, however, that stylistic analysis of what amounts to gnomai will dominate any global theory about possible relations between redaction and tradition in gospel texts.

What emerges from a critical reading of Goulder's analysis is therefore not his desired result: he fails to persuade that Matthew's poetry is brilliantly original and identical with the poetry of Q, that Luke's is a lame imitation and that Mark's is a pale shadow of biblical tradition with an outside chance of having something authentic to do with Jesus. Instead, each evangelist seems to have struck a more or less peculiar balance between the consistencies of a personal and literary style and the more fluid (oral) conventions of Greco-Roman rhetorical variation.

Re-examining instances of Goulder's "poetry" which are also gnomic cores performed at least once in each Synoptic gospel confirms that each evangelist has characteristic stylistic and/or topical preferences for literary performance of shared gnomic cores. Gospel redactors are, however, inconsistent in applying their own redactional preferences and are even less consistent in effacing the preferences of their sources. Varied performances of one gnomic core, moreover, show not only the diversity of redactional characters, but also the unity of their shared cores, as progymnasmatic rhetorical conventions might lead gospel readers to expect: the ratio of strictly redactional and strictly traditional traits in any performance of a gnomic core will be neither here nor there as regards whether the gnomic core itself is traditional or its speaker's immediate personal coinage. Take for example the widely-performed gnome of saving/losing life:

Whoever wishes to save his/her life will lose it; whoever loses his/her life for my [Mark: the gospel's] sake will save [Matt: find] it. (Mark 8:35 par Matt 16:25, Luke 9:24)

The one who finds his/her life will lose it; and the one who loses his/her life for my sake will find it. (Matt 10:38)

Whoever seeks to preserve his/her life will lose it and whoever loses it will revive it. (Luke 17:33)

The one who loves his/her life loses it; and the one who hates his/her life in this world will safeguard it. (John 12:25)

Any gospel performance of any gnome may be expected to show stylistic and thematic characteristics compatible with those of the gospel writer who uses it, wherever homogeneity suits that author's purpose. Conversely, gnomai may be expected to look more exotic, wherever a change of style or topic needs to be strongly marked. Progymnasmatically trained gospel writers will be perfectly capable of presenting traditional gnomic cores in redactional style, or of presenting their own newest coinage as timeless adage. Either way, the relation of redactional to traditional styles and topics in particular performances is rhetorically determined and not controlled by whether the actual origin of a particular gnomic core was traditional or redactional. Tradition and redaction are nowhere more intimately wedded than in gnome-use.

Tradition and redaction in gospel composition

The presence or absence of literary authorial style in synoptic gnome-performances is thus an indifferent measure of the influence of oral tradition on synoptic literary tradition. Still, synoptic literary variety and stylistic instability even in manifestly careful redaction *do* suggest in general a shared, relatively oral, rhetorical sensibility. The Greco-Roman rhetoricity of early Christian literature and the relative orality of that rhetorical culture remain, despite qualification, necessary postulates for understanding the synoptists' work and their relation to Jesus-tradition. This background is especially vital to understanding the gospels' gnomic rhetoric.

Recognizable literary-authorial style in a gnome or in a larger context does not imply the absence of oral traditional influence. Still less does the presence of redactional stylistic traces indicate the absence of received rhetorical patterns, stylistic or topical. In fact, as Philip Sellew candidly admits, there is, at least in Mark and John, a striking *"continuity of language"* between gospel redaction and pre-gospel traditions, a continuity more consistent with progymnasmatic conventions than with redaction-critical expectations of distinctive authorial styles.

> [T]here are considerable overlaps in vocabulary and mode of expression between Mark's source material and his own editorial and compositional work.... [T]his phenomenon causes problems that are more severe than are sometimes acknowledged by those attempting to separate tradition from redaction.... [T]he implication that arises, somewhat paradoxically, out of the success achieved throughout this century in the detailed and painstaking analysis of Marcan language patterns is that redaction critics can no longer discover and isolate a supposed pre-Marcan source text on the grounds of vocabulary usage or grammatical construction alone.[14]

As we shall see, the gospel-writers—and not only Mark—used gnomai at comparatively final levels of literary redaction. In the gospels gnome appears not only as an element in substantially independent units of tradition but also as an oral compositional technique still current and available to literary redactors. This double character of the Synoptic writers' interest in gnome, as the vector of a rhetorical tradition which includes models for its own performantial and hermeneutical variation, can best be shown from the nature and large number of synoptic gnomai which are the sole, or the essential, differentiae between otherwise parallel literary units.

The remainder of this chapter will therefore be a list of gnomai which are most clearly aspects of redactional activity. I begin with gnomai which are either added to or subtracted from what are otherwise

---

[14] P. Sellew, "Composition of Didactic Scenes in Mark's Gospel," *JBL* 108 (1989) 613–634, 614 (Sellew's italics).

triple tradition contexts, then I examine gnomai attached to or removed from Matthaean or Lucan reception of Q material. Finally I discuss those gnomai which seem to be embedded in material found in only one gospel. I proceed in this manner because I wish to move away from the question, "Is this gnome authentic, traditional or redactional?"

Recently—especially since the massive work of J.D. Crossan—the metaphor of archaeological "stratigraphy" has been applied to the move from redaction criticism to tradition history of gospel sayings tradition. Crossan, it must be admitted, relies not only on stratigraphy of Jesus materials, but also—rightly, in my view—on criteria of multiple independent attestation as evidence for rhetorical variation within pre-gospel oral tradition. Another article by Philip Sellew makes explicit the influence of specifically stratigraphic, essentially literary-redactional approaches on the study of speech tradition attributed to Jesus.

> The problem of locating authentic Jesus material in the Gospel of Mark can be defined as one aspect of identifying and separating tradition and redaction. In the heritage of classical form criticism, this sort of analysis has tended to presuppose a model of ever greater accumulations and accretions of material, as traditions about Jesus are transmitted and ultimately preserved in a written document. This accumulative metaphor has many analogies with the model of successive strata developed by geologists and adapted for archaeological analysis. The technique of "stratigraphy" is used to picture the successive layers of accumulated deposits at a particular site. The objective of a stratigraphic analysis of the Gospel of Mark, then, would be to clarify the relative age of its various individual units and sections, thought of as "deposits".... A guiding principle of stratigraphy is that *a stratum can be dated no earlier than its latest deposit.*[15]

Sellew expresses only a heuristic commitment to his stratigraphic approach. But to think like this at all as a model to account for the production of written texts within a public speaking tradition epitomizes much with which I disagree in the practice of historical Jesus research and much against which rhetorical criticism should warn us.

---

[15] Crossan, *Historical Jesus*, 427–452, "Appendix 1: An Inventory of the Jesus Tradition by Chronological Stratification and Independent Attestion"; P. Sellew, "Aphorisms of Jesus in Mark: A Stratigraphic Analysis," *Forum* 8 (1992) 141–160, quoting 141–142.

The justification for stratigraphic analysis in geological and archaeological contexts is that strata are often visible as distinct layers in a structure which is known to have been formed by cumulative deposit, whether of sediment or of refuse. Texts and performances are not formed this way. Rhetorical motifs, topics, arguments, turns of style, even written texts are regularly older than the latest element of any particular performance or entextualization. The only generally credible stratigraphic conclusion on the synoptic gospels might be that Mark (with reconstructed Q) is an older layer than (the rest of) Matthew and Luke. But even here the stratigraphic metaphor breaks down before the dynamics of progymnasmatic convention and synoptic intertextuality.

Texts and performances were certainly not conceived stratigraphically in Greco-Roman rhetorical culture, where the textual aspects of rhetorical performance are understood to be telescopic, dynamic and adjustable to fit the needs of varied performances and readings. Specifically, the oldest, most traditional elements of an oration and the newest, most redactional aspects may occur simultaneously. It still makes sense in a rhetorical critical context to analyse "individual units and sections" of written gospels, in this case to see how gnomai and the topics they express are used and varied. It does not, however, make sense to decide which of the fragments constituted in this way are older or more authentic in ascription to Jesus than others. The best we can do is to verify that gnome-use is unlikely to be an exclusively redactional, textual habit within gospel rhetorics. On the contrary, I believe what follows should establish that, insofar as we may know anything about the history of gospel rhetoric, heavy gnome-use (with certain topical characteristics) was among its original and salient features.

I wish to emphasize therefore the question of how gnomai implicate and knit together tradition and redaction, even in contexts where gnome-use is indisputably a redactional or rather authorial, compositional technique, whatever else it may also be. The key rhetorical assumption is that, especially in gnome-use, redaction and tradition are essentially inseparable, although the traces of each will be more or less visible in particular cases. The example gnomai in this chapter are all obviously redactional. My interest is in showing that it is by no means obvious that even these strong cases of redactional artifice are therefore stylistically or topically non-traditional. Nor are these gnomic redactional hinges fundamentally unlike gnomai which are less clearly pivots for redactional change.

Redactional gnomai in multiple literary tradition

(1) No one who has drunk old [wine] wants new, for he/she says: (2) "the old is best." (Luke 5:39)

Luke 5:39 provides a particularly straightforward example of two gnomai which have been redactionally added to otherwise triple literary tradition, derivative from Mark, but accepted almost verbatim by Matthew and Luke. These examples illustrate one typical Synoptic use of gnome, to conclude or supplement a larger unit, especially a parabolic saying.[16] This transparently redactional addition to Mark 2:22 cannot, however, be dismissed as merely Lucan redaction; the incongruity of the topic "old [wine] is best" with the context in Luke 5:33–39 and the existence of a close but plausibly independent parallel in *Gospel of Thomas* 47 suggest that even this rather banal gnomic core was available in pre-gospel tradition, already associated with Jesus.

Other cases are more involved, but the issue of relative gnomic incongruity with the style or argument of redactional contexts will emerge often. The sort of redactors imagined by redaction critics are unlikely to add gnomai which fit badly either with the style or the argument of the host context unless redaction is influenced by tradition.

No city set on a mountain can be hidden. (Matt 5:14b)

Thus, in the gnome of the prominent city (Matt 5:14b par *Gos. Thom.* 32) Matthew found only a fairly fitting complement to his pronouncement about the "light of the world" (14a), as the gnome changes metaphors from luminosity to visibility.[17] Once again, the suspicion of slight redactional incongruity is confirmed by a parallel in the *Gospel of Thomas* which lacks the Matthaean introduction. It is thus the topic of visibility which links the gnome of the unhideable city with the

---

[16] Berger, *Formgeschichte*, 65, 50–51.

[17] The incongruity may be less in view of ancient theories of light and vision, cf. D.C. Allison, "The Eye is the Lamp of the Body (Matthew 6.22–23=Luke 11.34– 36)," *NTS* 33 (1987) 61–83; H.-D. Betz, "Matthew 6:22–23 and Ancient Theories of Vision," in *Text and Interpretation: Studies in the New Testament Presented to Matthew Black*, ed. E. Best and R.McL. Wilson (Cambridge, 1979) 43–56, reprinted in Betz, *Essays*, 71–87.

gnome of the unhidden lamp in both Matthew and *Thomas* (Matt 5:14b–15 par *Gos. Thom.* 32–33). In terms of redaction-critical notions of style, Matthew 5:14b looks very Matthaean: it uses favourite turns of phrase and topical keywords.[18] Nonetheless, the pairing of gnomai, Matthew 5:14b–15, is almost certainly older—'more traditional'—than any extant text or known source.

This apparently traditional as well as redactional relationship between Matthew 5:14b and 15 forces upon us the question of traditionality and redactionality in several gnomic discourses in the synoptics, linked—and distinguished—by their diverse uses of a few *Wanderlogien*, dramatic instances of the performantial and hermeneutical flexibility of gnomic cores.[19] The gnome of the unhidden lamp (Matt 5:15 par Mark 4:21, Luke 8:16) thus links Matthew 5 to the quite different gnomic discourse in Mark 4:21–25 and its Lucan parallel (8:16–18). Matthew 5:15 (par Luke 11:33) also links Matthew 5 to the equally different discourse in Luke 11 (29–36), which presumably reflects the order of the Q source.[20]

There are three essential points here: The gnome of the unhidden lamp was handled in highly redactional—or, rather, progymnasmatic—ways by as many gospel writers as we know about. Secondly, it was clearly traditional for all of them, wholly invented by none. Finally, there is no intrinsic quality in the gnome of the unhidden lamp and other such *Wanderlogien* to distinguish them rhetorically from many other synoptic and Greco-Roman gnomai which happen to be less diversely attested in the surviving texts. From a progymnasmatic point of view the diverse, interlocking, yet rhetorically distinct contextualizations of the 'wandering' gnomai are the norm for gnome-use in rhetorical tradition and performance, though the norm for surviving attestation in texts is less lavishly abundant.

---

[18] U. Luz, *Das Evangelium nach Matthäus* (EKKNT I/1; 3d ed.; Braunschweig and Neukirchen-Vluyn, 1992) 35–55.

[19] On the importance of the *Wanderlogien* among gnomai see Berger, *Formgeschichte*, 64, 66–7; *Exegese*, 106.

[20] See J. Dupont, "La Transmission des paroles de Jésus sur la lampe et la mesure dans Marc 4, 21–25 et dans la tradition Q," in *Logia—les Paroles de Jésus—the Sayings of Jesus*, ed. J. Delobel (BETL 59; Leuven, 1982) 201–236.

Mark 4:21–25 par Luke 8:16–18

The gnome of the unhidden lamp and the four gnomai which follow in Mark 4 (verses 22, 23, 24 and 25) and (excepting Mark 4:23, 24) in Luke 8 were dispersed among "four different contexts" in the Sayings Gospel Q. "In addition, three of them show up in Thomas, again in separate contexts." It is hard to imagine a more vivid textual representation of the oral traditionality and semantic separability of these gnomai in association with Jesus' name. I do not think it follows that the "way the sayings are collected in Mark is therefore the work of Mark." H.-W. Kuhn argued on formal grounds Mark 4:21–25 was a Marcan gnome collection inserted redactionally into Mark's older parable-source. On the contrary, the gnomic discourse is sufficiently anomalous within Mark to be a strong case for a pre-Marcan source.[21]

The individual gnomai are, as Boismard points out, better contextualized in their separate Matthaean and Lucan settings derived from Q than in the discourses in Mark 4 and Luke 8.[22] Still, both discourses are the work of competent writers working within rhetorical conventions for gnome-use;[23] neither is simply "collected." It is quite true from a literary, or even an argumentation-critical point of view that the Marcan version coheres only very loosely around the theme of final revelation and reward. This topicality is underscored in the central gnome (verse 22) and the whole composition is divided by the gnomic formula (verse 23, repeated in Marcan redaction from 4:9?) and formulaic warning (verses 21 and 24a, "*kai elegen autois...*"[24]). Apart from such easily audible punctuation, however, the individual gnomai, especially those of the discourse's second sub-section (verses 24b, 25), are painfully discordant with one another.

Clearly the central topics have an important place in Marcan theology and narrative. The very discordance of Jesus' speech reinforces

---

[21] Quoting Funk, Hoover and the Jesus Seminar, *The Five Gospels*, 56; H.-W. Kuhn, *Ältere Sammlungen im Markusevangelium* (SUNT 8; Göttingen, 1971) 129–131 and n. 28; Boismard, *Synopse*, 190; Schmithals, *Einleitung*, 321–2.

[22] Boismard, *Synopse*, 190.

[23] Compare M. Mees, "Die Bedeutung der Sentenzen und ihrer Auxesis für die Formung der Jesusworte nach *Didaché* 1,3b–2,1," *Vetera Christianorum* 8 (1971) 55–76.

[24] On the redactional character of this formula see Sellew, "Didactic Scenes," 615–616 and nn. 6–11.

its function in this connection; Mark's Jesus needs to speak this way at this point in the story. Moreover, placing the emphatically central gnome of revelation (verse 22) and the climactic gnome of disproportionate reward (verse 25) around the gnome of measurement (verse 24b) serves to subordinate this last. Argumentative subordination—without grammatical subordination—is confirmed by the unparalleled Marcan redactional supplement which effectively subverts the gnome of reciprocal measure: "In the measure you measure it shall be measured to you—and more so [*kai prostethesetai humin*]!" (Mark 4:24b).

Source or no source, and discordance notwithstanding, Mark 4:21–25 is no mean achievement of Marcan redactional technique. At the same time, however, the discourse also unmistakably uses pre-Marcan gnomic tradition. The stylistic and semantic character of the discourse is unusually marked, but can be read in two ways. More than most sections in Mark this passage may be read as a text which is less than fully competent because of its vulgar orality. Micro-stylistic features such as paratactic use of "and" (*kai*) and "for" (*gar*) instead of more nuanced subordinating conjunctions, asyndeton between emphatic imperatives (verse 24a) and apparently clumsy repetition (for example, of "measure" [*metr-*] verse 24b and "have" [*echei*] verse 25) conform to modern notions of 'oral style'[25] and are common in Mark.

Yet much the same figures of style and superficially clumsy ways of relating topics also conform to ancient rhetorical expectations of emphatic or dramatized or revelatory discourse.[26] Moreover, this (rhetorical) explanation for the style and topicality of Mark 4:21–25 is consistent with the functions of the passage in Mark. At the same time, the conclusion that this gnomic discourse is rhetorically calculated to function as spontaneous revelation in its Marcan context is not finally incompatible with a recognition of its strongly oral, improvisational sensibility and of the oral traditionality of its gnomic elements.

---

[25] Henderson, "*Didache* and Orality," 294.

[26] F. Thielman, "The Style of the Fourth Gospel and Ancient Literary Critical Concepts of Religious Discourse," in Watson, *Persuasive Artistry*, 169–183, esp. 178; G. Lüderitz, "Rhetorik, Poetik, Kompositionstechnik im Markusevangelium," in *Markus-Philologie: Historische, literargeschictliche und stilistische Untersuchungen zum zweiten Evangelium*, ed. H. Cancik (WUNT 33; Tübingen, 1984) 165–203, esp. 180–181; M. Reiser, *Syntax und Stil des Markusevangelium im Licht der hellenistischen Volksliteratur* (WUNT 2/11; Tübingen, 1984) 138–161.

Explanations of Marcan redaction as either involuntarily clumsy or deliberately profound are difficult to reconcile on redaction-critical suppositions. Gnomic rhetoric and Greco-Roman stylistics provide a framework within which textual finish is not a necessary criterion for persuasiveness or profundity. Within a rhetorical framework, the Marcan redactor is allowed to use the roughness of improvisational orality to link the oral rhetoric of his source traditions and the expectations of moderately cultivated audiences. It is a moot question whether the author of Mark *could* have written Mark 4:21–25 more classically; he has certainly written it progymnasmatically[27] and in a strongly improvisational style.

The Lucan parallel collection (8:16–18) shows a different blend of oral-conversational, improvisational-rhetorical and literary sensibilities. Yet only a part of the rhetorical, stylistic effect of improvisational immediacy is sacrificed to greater literary argumentative nuance. Mark's improvisational spontaneity, intensity and numinosity are blunted in ways which defy separation into stylistic or argumentational/ thematic. The formulaic structure of the Marcan discourse ("*kai elegen autois,*" verses 21 and 24) is suppressed; the verb of seeing is, however, purposefully repeated (Luke 8:16b, 18a) giving the Lucan composition a more optimistic and not only a more literary quality. The dark, paradoxical qualities of Mark 4:22, 24 and 25 are further moderated by skillful hermeneutical changes to otherwise intact gnomic cores. The main conceptual dissonance is eliminated by relegating the gnome of reciprocal measure (Mark 4:24b) to the better integrated, ultimately less contradictory context of Luke 6:38.

Matthew 7:1–5 par Luke 6:37–42

In the measure you measure it shall be measured [Luke: back] to you [Mark: and more so!] (Mark 4:24b; Matt 7:2b par Luke 6:38b)

This particular gnome of reciprocal measurement was evidently central not only to the Marcan (and pre-Marcan?) discourse, Mark 4:21–25, but also to an otherwise unrelated Q gnomic discourse behind Matthew 7:1–5 and Luke 6:37–42. It is difficult to imagine a clearer indication

---

[27] Mack and Robbins, *Patterns*, 152–158; Robbins, "Pre-Gospel Traditions," 130–131.

of the importance of gnome in the birth and development of synoptic written tradition than this intersection of apparently separate redactional paths in slightly variant interpretations and contextualizations of a single impressive core. At the same time the saying provides a striking instance of gnomic independence and resilience even through intensive, perhaps successive, literary redactions.

Even more than Matthew 7:1–5, Luke 6:37–42 resembles Mark 4:21–25 in terms of basic rhetorical character—style and structure. All three gnomic discourses are composed within progymnasmatic principles of elaboration (*expolitio/ergasia*). In addition, however, Luke 6:37–42, like Mark 4:21–25, exemplifies authorial (and traditional) use of gnomai to mark a noticeably improvisational style (*varietas/poikilia*) within which arguments, mostly in the form of gnomai, are allowed to qualify each other by accumulation (*amplificatio/auxesis*) rather than by explicit logical subordination. In progymnasmatic terms, the elaboration here is kept relatively simple, a matter of addition and subtraction rather than of generic transformation, e.g., from gnome series into parabolic narrative or enthymematic argumentation.

In an exemplary article on *Didache* 1:3b–2:1, the *Didache*'s notoriously puzzling *sectio evangelica*, B. Layton argued that the "rhetorical figures and literary forms which occur in the passage [are] deliberate constructive formal devices." Layton found unusually heavy use in this particular section of *Didache*—more than in parallel gospel discourses—of small-scale figures of climax, parallelism, chiasmus, antithesis, refrain and proverb-quotation. He concluded that the pronounced rhetorical character of the discourse *Didache* implied its literary dependance on the synoptic gospels. This source-critical conclusion seems to me a bold *non sequitur*, rightly challenged by M. Mees. Accumulation of gnomai and small-scale figures, rather than sustained development of enthymematic induction, is a rhetorical sign of improvisational intensity. Such marks of rhetorical style have no necessary bearing on the relations among oral tradition, written sources and redactional liberty behind the production of gospel texts, though the production of such rhetorically oral discourses by early Christian writers in contact with Jesus-tradition is consistent with the modest social and educational pretensions of early Christian rhetorics.[28]

In both Matthew 7 and Luke 6 the meaning of the gnome about measurement is determined in a more ethically normative direction than the textually less integrated but clearly eschatological Marcan perform-ance. This difference is marked partly by the two Q-influenced gospels' omission of the Marcan redactional supplement, Mark 4:24b; more fundamentally, Matthew and Luke—and presumably Q—contextualize the gnome of measurement by surrounding it with pastoral imperatives and paradigms. The dominant rhetorical (and redactional) tactic is one of contextual specification by supplementing gnome with gnome to make a strong cumulative impression rather than to arrive at a closely argued conclusion.

The metric gnome was simply eliminated from Luke 8; in Luke 6, by contrast, the gnome of measurement is ethicized and domesticated within community relationships modelled on civil (Luke 6:37–38), discipular (verse 40) and fraternal (verses 41–42) orders. The potentially uncontrollable reciprocity of the gnome of measurement is controlled by the introduction of hierarchical relationships of judgement, beggary, discipleship and fraternity. Even more subtly, the reciprocity of measurement is concretized by reference to an ethical situation of unbridled reciprocity: the blind leading the blind (verse 39b). Eschatol-ogical reciprocity is bad news here; salvation is in the reciprocity of the passage's present ethical imperatives.

Formally, the opening verses (37–38a) and the second part of the discourse (verses 39–42) are emphasized at the expense of the gnome of measurement (verse 39b). Verses 37 and 38a are solemnized by massive, surely deliberate, repetition of "and" (six of twenty-two words are "*kai*": polysyndeton), of imperatives, of forms of the verb "give" (polyptoton) and of rhymed words qualifying "measure" (congeries, homoioptoton and asyndeton)—all before introducing the gnome of reciprocal measurement with its potential ambiguities and its own instance of polyptoton. Similar figures of repetition characterized the whole of Luke 6; they are less prevalent in Matthew 7.

---

[28] B. Layton, "The Sources, Date and Transmission of *Didache* 1.3b–2.1," *HTR* 61 (1968) 343–83, esp. 349–69, quoting 344; Mees, "*Auxesis*"; see Henderson, "*Didache* and Orality," 300.

This is not the only context in Lucan redaction marked by strongly moralizing (rather than eschatological) gnomai in the form of simple reciprocal proportions (cf. Luke 7:47; 12:28; 14:11; 16:10; 18:14). Tension among the individual gnomai is brought under rhetorical control by explanatory additions which are themselves gnomai (Luke 6:37b, 38b and 40b); in this way the difficult gnome of measurement is reduced to being one of several supplementary comments.

As in Mark 4:21–25, the main internal division of the Lucan discourse 6:37–42 is marked by a common redactional formula (*"eipen de kai parabolen autois..."* verse 39a).[29] Here and, indeed, in all its occurences the Lucan formula and its striking keyword, *parabole*, have more hermeneutical significance than the more performantially used Marcan analogue. The Lucan formula here breaks up the direct discourse ascribed to Jesus and emphasizes what follows rather than what immediately precedes (verse 38b). The two gnomai which follow (verses 39, 40) further qualify the (original?) gnome on just measurement: its horizons are not those of apocalyptic revelation, retribution or reward as in Mark 4:24, but rather those of secular society and of the fraternity of disciples in which Jesus alone (verse 39b) gives (verse 39a) and is (verse 40) the relevant paradigm.

Matthew's version of the Q discourse including the measurement gnome (Matt 7:1–5) is arguably less improvisational in style than either the Marcan or Lucan (Q) versions. Matthew has parallels to Luke 6:39 and 40 in quite un-Lucan and "clearly redactional" contexts.[30] Moreover, in Matthew 7 the connection between verse 1 (against judging) and verse 2b (on measuring) is made formally explicit in a hybrid gnome (verse 2a). It is difficult not to think that verse 2b is the product of reflection on the written words of verses 1 and 2b, to the extent of using unfamiliar materials in a strained setting (*en krimati*) in order to wed the vocabulary of one gnome to the syntax of another. The marriage is not entirely harmonious, as 7:1 is a global prohibition while 7:2b is a selective prescription of closely related behaviours. Matthew's redactional work here, though it too shows signs of topical incongruity, is nevertheless determined more by issues of large textual architecture than by the local, topical stylistic and arguemntative interests of the

---

[29] See Luke 5:36; 12:16; 13:6; 14:7; 15:3; 18:1,9; 21:29; Boismard, *Synopse*, 153.

[30] A.D. Jacobson, *The First Gospel: An Introduction to Q* (Sonoma, CA, 1992) 103; *pace* Boismard, *Synopse*, 153.

gnomic discourse itself: that is, Matthew's use of the gnome of measurement suggests more than Luke's or Mark's that the rhetorical unit is the whole gospel book.

Matthew's typical procedure is to redact individual gnomai into argumentatively integrated and subordinated contexts with fewer of the argumentative and stylistic figures (e.g., repetition, redundancy, serial contradiction, formulaic emphasis) which characterize both Mark 4:1–25 and Luke 6:37–42 as relatively improvisational rhetoric.

Begging many questions of redactional-critical method, it is still possible to offer Mark 4:24c, its parallels and developments as a particularly fair illustration of four essential points. In the first place, the gospel writers did select gnomai as instruments and focal points for redaction. Evident redactional interest in modifying, transferring, deleting, coining and interpreting gnomai confirms the relevance of the Hellenistic rhetorical category as I have synthesized it for application to Synoptic criticism.

In the second place, it seems clear that the treatment of gnomai by different redactors is an index of personal, authorial rhetorical sensibilities. These relative differences of sensibility seem to me best described in terms of deliberately chosen rhetorical styles ranging between improvisational and self-consciously textual. Such differentiation is qualified by the general tendency of the tradition of Jesus' rhetoric toward improvisational style—and, after all, by the decorum implied by the content of Jesus' story with its Jewish, peasant, biblical and biographical, rather than classical horizons.

In the third place, gnomic discourses like those around the measurement gnome confirm the indivisibility, but also the reciprocal irreducibility, of stylistic and argumentational analysis. In a later chapter of this book, I shall return to the legal topicality of the gnome on measurement, a topicality which is subverted in all the Synoptic performances. For now, it is vital to notice that the improvisational character of the gnomic rhetoric attributed to Jesus is encoded not in the stylistic features of gnomai or of progymnasmatically elaborated gnomic discourse, but also in their topical character, in theoretical terms, in the relationship between their implicit normativity and their analogical structure. Figures of thought and of speech, style and topic are simultaneously and equally basic to the way gnomic rhetoric works.

Finally, the gnome on reciprical measurement (Mark 4:24b par) is a good instance of a gnomic core which is largely respected through redactional processes of hermeneutical and performantial (e.g., Luke 6:38c, *antimetreo*) variation and elaborate contextual reinterpretation —even editorial omission. Mark 4:21–25 and Luke 6:37–42 and their parallels show that the category of gnome can be a useful index of redactional activity and style; the same categorization, however, also identifies a datum more basic than any identifiable literary redactor and a range of gnomic material which does not seem redactional, or necessarily literary in origin. Gnomai attributed to Jesus are typically clearly redactional in style and contextualization, but they are seldom merely redactional and include some of the strongest prima facie cases for very early entry into tradition about how Jesus spoke.

Similar points can be made in relation to the *Wanderlogien* of the first/last and of self-exaltation/humility—with the advantage that this gnomic core is contextualized in elaborated chreiai.

The First and the Last, etc.: Mark 9:35 par Luke 9:48c; Mark 10:43–44 par Matt 20:26b–27, Luke 22:26(–27); Matt 23:11; Mark 10:31 par Matt 19:30; Matt 20:16 par Luke 13:30; Matt 18:4 par Luke 14:11

Perhaps the simplest version of the gnome of the first and the last (Mark 9:35) is set in its context so curiously as to raise questions about Marcan redaction even if synoptic comparison were impossible: verse 35 and verses 36, 37 seem equally satisfactory but to that extent redundant conclusions to a single chreia. In fact Mark 9:33–37 with its three suspiciously similar transitional formulae (verses 35a, 36a, b) can be used to illustrate all three of the traditional subtypes of the progymnasmatic chreia: the introduction (verses 33, 34) with verse 35 makes a saying (*logike*) chreia; with verse 36a instead of verse 35, the unit becomes a gestural (*praktike*) chreia; with verses 36, 37 (and 35 for good measure) Mark gives us a mixed (*mikte*) and partly elaborated chreia.[31]

One of the roots of rhetorical criticism in New Testament studies was Vernon Robbins' influential essay on Mark 10:13–16 and Mark 9: 33–37 with their parallels. Robbins was quite correct to represent the redaction of these chreiai as exemplary of the progymnasmatic rules for elaboration and variation. Robbins' focus was, as it remains, on the

---

[31] See Berger, *Formgeschichte*, 82; Crossan, "Aphoristic Tradition," 78.

episodic rhetoric of the chreia-narratives and especially on Jesus' paradigmatic interest in children. Robbins tends to dismiss the gnome of the first and the last as "ideological culture," but in his initial study he did point to the structural importance of the gnome and of the *inclusio* created by its repetition (Mark 9:35; 10:31). It is to this observation that Robbins attached his conclusion that "Mark's composition of the story in Mark 9:33–37 is therefore an exercise in rhetorical composition." In addition, Robbins notes that Mark 9:35 and 8:34 share similar introductory formulae and conditional format ("If anyone wishes to...").[32]

It is clear even from this much that Marcan use of the first/last gnome is thoroughly redactional and rhetorical. We may go further, however, to note the hermeneutical variation of the gnome itself:

If anyone wishes to be first, let him/her be last of all and servant of all. (Mark 9:35)

Many shall be first who are last and last who are first. (Mark 10:31)

Whoever wishes to be great among you, let him/her be your servant and whoever wishes to be first among you, let him/her be the slave of all. (Mark 10:43–44)

The prophecy that many who accept the calling to be last of all will ultimately be the first, while many who now enjoy priority will face demotion, represents a variation in the normativity of the gnome, from optional prescription for the present ("if anyone..., let him/her...") to selective ("many") future indicative. Most important, however, these two normative dimensions are united in their relation to the story of Jesus (10:45). This connection is made explicit by the specification of the first/last opposition in terms of greatness versus servanthood and slavery (10:43–44). Clearly the variations and contextualizations of this gnomic core in Mark are close to the heart of Marcan redactional interests and style: this is how the author of Mark typically thought and wrote.

---

[32] Robbins, "Pre-Gospel Traditions," 134–7, quoting 135; Robbins, "Pronouncement Stories," 68–69, quoting 69.

On the other hand, the astonishing variety of versions and contextualizations throughout the Synoptics effectively rules out that any one
redactor attributed the core gnome to Jesus without traditional warrant.
Gospel performances of this gnomic core span every major source-
critical category; they also span most possible variations in normative
intensity and, especially, range—from universal, absolute, yet future
indicative norm (Matthew 20:16), through limited future indicative norm
(Matthew 19:30) and limited present indicative (Luke 9:48c), to strong,
deontic advice given to self-selecting hearers (Mark 9:35). Moreover,
within Mark imagery and hence topicality as well as normative range
vary from an analogy between the first and the last to a more precise
analogy between greatness and servanthood or slavery (Mark 9:35;
10:43–44). This process of fine-tuning is taken further in Matthew and
Luke, partly redactionally and partly under Q influence, and especially
in convergence with the topic of childhood and the kingdom (self-
promotion versus humility, Matthew 18:4; Luke 14:11).

Such hermeneutical variation and the fact that it was a rhetorically
prescribed way of handling gnomic tradition and performance make it
pointless to try to decide which variant is most authentic or representative in attribution to Jesus. Robbins concluded in relation to these same
gospel contexts that

> it is necessary to distinguish between free-floating maxims [i.e., gnomai]
> and maxims that have arisen through a rhetorical process in which a general
> statement has been created as commentary of a chreia tradition.[33]

That is, Robbins co-ordinates the distinction between "free-floating" and
commentary gnomai with another distinction between specific and
general gnomai. Some performances of the complex of gnomic cores
opposing first and last, etc., do indeed work in literary context as, in
Crossan's phrase, aphoristic commentary (e.g., Luke 9:48c or Matthew
8:4).[34] The progymnasmatists' interest in variation, elaboration and
contextualization of gnomai and related patterns warns that distinctions
in content, as between general and specific, or in contextualization, as
between text and commentary, may be rhetorically important, but are
probably inscrutable from the point of view of reconstructing or

---

[33] Robbins, "Pronouncement Stories," 73–74.
[34] Crossan, "Aphoristic Tradition," 88.

isolating an original, pre-redactional kernel of tradition. Even in a descriptive semantic sense it is often hard enough to tell which items in a series are commentaries and which are ground-texts without trying to guess the history of each element. The best we can say is that the fact that gnomic sayings—and certain gnomic sayings—figure prominently in the construction of varied argumentative complexes suggests that such sayings had a degree of early currency and normativity.[35]

The Jesus Seminar indeed tried to distinguish historically among versions of the first/last and related gnomai on a criterion of normative range: the version prophesying the most universal social reversal (Matt 20:16) was thought more authentic than versions directed selectively to aspiring sectarian leaders.

> [T]hese sayings [Mark 10:43–44 and their parallels] are so intimately bound up with the leadership struggles that ensued in the Christian communities that it is impossible to divorce the saying from the later situation.[36]

Jesus did, however, have disciples, including an inner circle called the Twelve. Aspirations to pre-eminence in such a group cannot be dismissed as an anachronistically Christian topic. No divorce is necessary here. As Klaus Berger has shown, once the tradition-historical goal of reconstructing and/or authenticating the original form of a saying is abandoned, the probability emerges very strongly that Jesus associated by word and/or by gesture the programmatic notions of servanthood, slavery and greatness. Apart from the gestures of table-service in Last Supper narratives (John 13:15–16; Luke 22:27b), this widely shared tradition seems to have lived as a widely varied gnomic core relating service and greatness.[37] Whether the language of first and last emerged from this tradition or converged with it, in Jesus' own rhetoric or in his recollected tradition, we are unlikely ever to be able to judge with certainty, though we may vote speculatively with the Jesus Seminar.

---

[35] J. Wanke, "'Kommentarworte' Älteste Kommentierungen von Herrenworten," *BZ* (1980) 208–233; for the "criterion of pregnant speech" see Westerholm, *Jesus and Scribal Authority*, 6.

[36] Funk, Hoover and the Jesus Seminar, *The Five Gospels*, 84, 95 (quoted) and 223–225.

[37] Berger, *Einführung*, 227–233.

Clearly the gnomai about the first/last, great/servant and humili-
ation/promotion have been attractive objects for intensive redactional
variation and reuse in ways that have everything to do with differing
authorial styles and topical preferences. Equally clearly, however, some
gnomai—and the tradition of gnome-use generally—have a life of their
own beyond the work of particular writers. Even the most busily varied
and elaborated gnome is never exactly free-floating; the range of topical
associations and normative variations, though impressive, is finite,
bounded by rhetorical and tradition-specific conventions. Above all, the
"rhetorical process" in which gnomai were attributed to Jesus does not
divide neatly into authentic and ecclesial or oral and redactional phases
since redaction was carried out within progymnasmatic conventions for
creating, varying and remembering tradition in oral performance.

Mark 9:42–50

Strong redactional interest in and freedom with gnome may again be
evidenced alongside a certain gnomic transcendence of literary redaction
in the complex of differences between Mark 9:42–50 and its partial
parallels. Mark 9:43–47(48) is among the longest of synoptic units
describable as gnome: both Matthaean parallels (Matt 5:30, 29; 18:8–9)
omit the ethically ridiculous, though literal, notion of one's foot causing
stumbling. In the more redactional of his two versions, Matthew makes
the unit into a double gnome (5:30a, 29a) with a double justification
("*sympherei gar soi...*" 5:30b, 29b), conforming to the Aristotelean rule
that difficult gnomai be accompanied by an *aitia*. Clearly, however,
Matthew recognizes the unit as rhetorically separable from its Marcan
context.

The saying, whether gnome or gnomic stanza, is conditional and
limited in normative range as the switch from third-person (Mark 9:42;
Matt 18:6–7) or second-person plural (Matt 5:27, 28) to second-person
singular redactionally underlines: the command is normative, but not for
everyone under all conditions. The normative intensity of the saying is
nonetheless strong, with an eschatological threat sanctioning the
imperative. The unit, though formally complex, does seem to be built
on a single analogy: physical wholeness and moral/spiritual integrity
respectively are differently related to eschatological destiny.

Matthew's two redactions also point out by contrast some stylistic
characteristics of the Marcan version. Mark's triple form shows a degree

of barely modified verbal iteration which goes well beyond the norms of either Hebrew verse parallelism or mnemotechnical triplet form as in *Abot*. The fact that both Matthew and Luke redactionally omitted the 'foot' variation and so reduced the Marcan triplet to a doublet suggests that even within the gospel tradition iteration could be seen as redundancy. What variation there is serves to highlight the basic symbols. Thus two amplifications underline the connection of *geenna* with fire (verse 43 and the biblical citation, verse 48), two variants describe how to get there (*apelthein*, verse 44, and *blethenai*, verse 45) and one variant makes the alternative more explicit (*basilean tou theou*, verse 47, for *zoen*, verses 43 and 45). Otherwise only the bare minimum of variation necessary to express the hand, foot, eye pattern (affecting ten words in a total seventy-nine) is allowed to modify strict verbal repetition.

This performantial development of a single gnomic form in three minimally differing variations seems calculated, if not to make a memorizable school-text, then certainly to given an aurally more memorable and impressive rhetorical effect. This Marcan text seems to epitomize—to an extent rejected by Matthew and Luke—the sorts of repetition and redundancy often characterized by modern orality theorists as oral style.

> The value of redundancy is axiomatic in ancient culture. Precisely what we literate people tend to shy away from, oral practitioners in antiquity and dominantly oral societies regarded as a great virtue.[38]

Stylistically as well as in content, Mark 9:43–48 is like a spell, curse or incantation. At the same time, these verses make a formal, rhetorically deliberate, link between biblical and Greco-Roman, gnomic conventions, above all, in the use of comparison figure.[39]

The next two Marcan sayings (Mark 9:49, 50) are connected to their context and to one another by argumentatively weak, though evocative, catchwords ("fire," verses 43, 48, 49; "good/better" [*kalon*], verses 42,

---

[38] W.H. Kelber, "Jesus and Tradition: Words in Time, Words in Space," in *Orality and Textuality in Early Christian Literature*, ed. J. Dewey=*Semeia* 65 (1994) 139–167, 150.

[39] Berger, "Gattungen," 1054, 1102; G.F. Snyder, "The Tobspruch in the New Testament," *NTS* 23 (1977) 117–126; Robbins, *Jesus the Teacher*, 161.

43, 45, 47, 50; "salt," 49, 50). These catchword links and the quite
dissimilar contextualization of both Matthew 5:13 and Luke 14:34–35
highlight the rhetorical independence of these two gnomai. In their
differing contextualizations and performances of this Marcan-and-Q
gnome Matthew and Luke are showing not only a typical pattern in the
use of Q materials, but also a typical pattern in their use of redactional
or traditional gnomai. About a quarter of all gnomai shared by Matthew
and Luke, whether from Marcan or Q material or both, are the essential
links between otherwise redactionally unrelated contexts. Nor is this
function confined to the composition (or dismemberment) of gnomic
collections in Mark 4 and Luke 6, as the next section, on gnomai in Q
material, will show.[40]

The exclusively Marcan verse 49 is especially interesting in the way
that it intensifies a biblical norm of sacrifice: because of its normative
range ("every sacrifice shall be salted"), Leviticus 2:13 is an important
commandment. In Mark 9:49 "fire" and "salt" become mixed and
undefined metaphors turning a non-analogical norm into a particularly
difficult gnome of rare intensity—without surrendering its universal
range. This verse is doubly important because it shares this relationship
of analogical extension from Mosaic norms with the one other Marcan
gnome not attested in Matthew and Luke, Mark 2:27; we shall return to
these two gnomai in later chapters discussing gnomic normativity and
the relationship between gnomic and legal rhetoric.

For now we need only note how both of these Marcan gnomai (2:27;
9:49) motivated later literary redactors to cut their Marcan source. Both
gnomai combine normative intensity with analogically universal range.
This challenging, yet vague topicality troubled Matthew and Luke as
readers and the rhetorical separability of both gnomai from their
contexts—from every possible context—permitted their redactional
excision. In other words the redactional processes here clearly vindicate
my use of the criteria of normativity, analogy and separability.

The gnome which follows in Mark (9:50) could plausibly be
described as a development from its preceding context; what is certain,
however, is that neither Matthew nor Luke sensed any such dependence.
Here as elsewhere significant differences between Marcan and Q

---

[40] Mark 4:21 par, 22 par, 24 par, 25 par; 9:50 par; 10:31 par; Luke 6:31 par, 39
par, 40 par, 44a par; 12:54 par; 14:11 par; 17:33 par; 22:26 par=14/58 Matthaeo-Lucan
gnomai (24%); the ratios for Marcan and Q gnomai are not significantly different.

instances of single gnomic cores make it difficult to reduce gnomic variation to a literary redactional phenomenon, though the comparison exposes "Salt is good" (Mark 9:50a) as probably Marcan redaction.[41]

The catchword architecture of the whole discourse and especially the transition from verse 49 to verse 50 make Mark 9:42–50 a tempting example of the agglomerative, "not particularly logical" style of oral tradition which orality theory expects to find just behind Marcan textuality.[42] Rhetorically, however, the move from Mark's universal salting with fire to the command to internalize "salt" in peaceful relationships is not so much illogical as elliptical and evocative; the argument is stylistically unnerving, but that effect is part of the point. Here again, it is more helpful to think in terms of the special effects of deliberately improvisational rhetoric in the gospels, especially in key speeches attributed to Jesus, than to worry about the orality of Marcan literacy.

Clearly, notwithstanding its improvisational style, Mark 9:42–50 has a vital redactional function in Mark's book: the whole section comprises Jesus' last words in Galilee and the climax of remarkably "direct positive teaching" on the nature of discipleship and its relation to Jesus' coming fate.[43] It is equally impossible to reduce individual gnomic items or the catchword discourse as a whole either to Marcan redaction or to mere catchword "oral" accretion. Nor is it possible satisfactorily to separate redaction from tradition in these gnomai: in its stylistic, dramatic (*ethos*) and topical values, the discourse is simultaneously characteristically Marcan and inescapably traditional. From a redaction-critical point of view this state of affairs is paradoxical; from a rhetorical point of view it is a remarkable achievement.

Gnomai and the redaction of "Q" material

Luke 16:13 is exactly paralleled in Matthew 6:24 except for a single word of, presumably, Lucan redaction ("servant" [*oiketes*]). The saying

---

[41] E.g., Mark 8:35 par cf. Matt 10:39 par Luke 17:33; Mark 9:40 par Luke 9:50b cf. Luke 11:23 par Matt 2:30; Mark 13:31 par cf. Matt 5:18 par Luke 16:17; See Jacobson, *The First Gospel*, 224.

[42] Funk, Hoover and the Jesus Seminar, *The Five Gospels*, 19.

[43] Robbins, *Jesus the Teacher*, 158–166, quoting 162.

about the servant of two masters is one of seven instances of "Gnomic Quatrain," a type of four-line verse beginning with a gnome (Luke 16:10–12 is another instance, also about "mammon").

No one [Luke: servant] can be a slave to two masters
for either s/he will hate the one and love the other
or s/he will be attached to the one and spurn the other.
You cannot be a slave to God and Mammon. (Luke 16:13 par Matt 6:24)

I have argued elsewhere that the rarity of the gnomic Quatrain form combines with the fact that the form occurs in Marcan, Q, special Matthaean and special Lucan material to make the gnomic Quatrain a probable instance of a pre-gospel, oral verse-form: a rare bird indeed.[44]

The two masters Quatrain is the sole point of contact between its Lucan and Matthaean contexts. J. Dupont has argued persuasively that the discourse on money with its catchword construction (*oikonomos*; *oikonomia* verses 1–9, *oiketes* verse 13, *mamonas* verses 9, 11, 13) is sufficiently atypical of Lucan composition to be probably the work of a pre-synoptic writer. At any rate the gnomic Quatrain is certainly redactional in at least one of Luke or Matthew; the Q context is irretrievable and another Lucan source may be involved.[45]

Luke 16:13 is thus at the same time evidence of Lucan redactional activity, pre-Lucan documentary sources (Q and another) and pre-gospel oral tradition. Collectively, the gnomic Quatrains of the Synoptics are, above all, interesting evidence for a very early pattern of formal poetic interpretation of gnomai. The gnomic Quatrain is a verse-form and not a progymnasmatic, rhetorical form; Quatrains seem to be formally more stylized and thematically more specific than the specimen gnome-expositions of the progymnasmatists. The existence of this highly specialized and uniquely synoptic form nevertheless attests an awareness

---

[44] Henderson, "Gnomic Quatrains"; see Matt 6:24 par Luke 16:13; Luke 16:10–12; Matt 6:22–23 par Luke 11:34–(36); Matt 7:6; Matt 10: 24–25 par Luke 6:40; Matt 10:26b–27 par Luke 12:23; Mark 2:21–22 par Matt 9:16–17, Luke 5:36b–39.

[45] J. Dupont, "Dieu et Mammon (MT 6,24 : LC 16,13)," in *Etudes sur les évangiles synoptiques* II, ed. J. Dupont (BETL 70/B; Leuven, 1985) 551–567; Jacobson, *The First Gospel*, 229; Boismard, *Synopse*, 297; S. Schulz, *Die Spruchquelle der Evangelisten* (Zürich, 1972), 459ff.

of the rhetorical character of the rather conventional gnome from which each Quatrain takes its hermeneutical start. The Quatrain of the two masters is typical of the genre in its gnome-use: the Quatrain as a whole interprets the opening gnome in a sense which intriguingly overturns gnomic proverbiality. The rhetorical turn from proverbial gnome to anti-proverbial insight is one which Aristotle foresaw and to which we will return in the next chapter.

For the moment, however, it is worth noting that the gnome at the beginning of the two masters Quatrain is itself semantically and quite probably traditionally independant, as its attestation without the Quatrain in the *Gospel of Thomas* shows (47:2). In addition, Dupont has made an extraordinarily strong case for the traditional proverbiality of the gnomic core about the impossibility of serving two masters.[46]

It is difficult to describe the balance of oral, rhetorical and literary sensibilities in Luke 16 and its two gnomic Quatrains. The fairly superficial catch-word organization of the chapter is compatible with either oral or mnemotechnical influence, but the verse-form of the gnomic Quatrains is something unique in early Christian literature. Luke 16 generally and its Quatrains in particular are less repetitive than, e.g., the rather strongly oral, probably not memorizational tricolon in Mark 9:43–47: Luke 16:10–12 and 13 offer only double repetition to compare with the tripling of Mark 9; secondly, the unit of repetition is the couplet in Luke 16 (though one couplet in verse 13 bisects the other) compared with the longer and less regular Marcan line-form; finally, the density of variation is much higher in the (pre-)Lucan passages. That is, the proportion of words affected by significant variation is much greater in the Lucan Quatrains (23/74 or 31%) than in the Marcan tricolon (10–14/79 or 13–18%). The Lucan stanzas are poems composed—rather more than the Marcan passage in our comparison—with a view to textual unity and/or verbatim memorization. In other (more rhetorical critical) words, the Lucan stanzas and the gnomic Quatrains generally seem significantly less improvisational in style than Mark 9.

At any rate, the balance of orality and literacy in Luke 16:10–12 and 13 and the other gnomic Quatrains, and the formality of their use of gnome are clearly not typical of Lucan redaction or of the Q material generally or of their immediate gospel contexts. Like gnomai, these little poems are equally adapted for oral performance and for literary

---

[46] Dupont, "Dieu ou Mammon," 552.

collection. Unlike gnomai, indeed as carefully specific applications of gnomai, they embody a drive away from performantially free variation of cores toward verbally fixed textuality, which requires us to think not of the most strongly oral virtually conversational tradition, or even of normal Greco-Roman progymnasmatic tradition, but rather of mnemo-technical or written design and use.

Still, the Quatrains reflect a recognized extreme in Greco-Roman rhetorical theories about gnome-use, the turn toward anti-proverbial-ity.[47] They also clearly reflect the power of gnomic material to knit together tradition and redaction. That is, these two stanzas and their Lucan, pre-Lucan and/or Q contexts show differing but strong redac-tional interest in gnome at the same time as they imply the prior independence of gnome-use generally and probably of individual gnomai like Luke 16:10 and 16:13a (par Matt 6:24a).

Gnome and antithesis: Matthew 5:38–42 par Luke 6:27–36

Redaction of a Q gnomic discourse into the antithesis discourse of Matthew's Sermon on the Mount also illustrates both the immediacy of redaction and tradition and the importance of gnomai as a means within the oldest tradition for constructing the newest redaction. Matthew's series of antitheses may have some pre-Matthaean antecedents, but the form is clearly fundamental to Matthew's redactional project. Perhaps some of the antitheses—those without Q parallels—preserve and correctly interpret "originally isolated words of Christ." Perhaps elements of the Matthaean antithesis are attested elsewhere in early Christian rhetorical tradition (Matt 7:10; 1 Tim 6:20[48]). Perhaps Matthew's antithetical manner after all captures "the impression which the teaching and attitude of Jesus conveyed."[49] The overwhelming presumption, however, must be that the Matthaean antithesis is an essentially Matthaean device.

---

[47] Something similar, but less compressed may be seen in the use of proverbial-sounding gnomai in prophetic *Disputationsworte* (Jer 31:29–30 par Ezek 18:2–4; Jer 51:58 par Hab 2:13), cf. A. Graffy, *A Prophet Confronts His People: The Disputation Speech in the Prophets* (AnBib 104; Rome, 1984).

[48] Berger, *Einführung*, 117–9 on antithetical pairs of biblical citations.

[49] R.J. Banks, *Jesus and the Law in the Synoptic Tradition* (SNTSMS 28; Cambridge, 1975) 184–186.

It is, of course, a rhetorically interesting and comprehensible device. One important aspect of progymnasmatic variation of gnomai is the careful introduction of supporting (or contradicting) judgements (*testimonia, martyriai, kriseis*) from the quasi-scriptural canon of Homer, Hesiod and subsequent classics (*hoi palaioi*). In the emerging context of Christian rhetoric this practice was problematic: Greco-Roman classical authorities had a negative social and religious value which for Christian rhetoric largely cancelled their authoritative value except in outward apologetic (Acts 17:28). Moreover, Christian self-definition over against Jewish religion and culture made biblical authority itself problematic. Early Christian proof-texting and prophecy-fulfillment citations are so needed to bolster Christians' ethical right to speak that little authority is left to bolster particular arguments. The best that early Christian biblical argumentation could hope for was to neutralize competing biblical rhetorics within and adjacent to Christian communities. Indeed most analyses of early Christian rhetorics remark on the ultimate—and in traditional antiquity surprising—reliance on immanent spiritual, rather than canonical, conventional authority.[50]

The antithesis form in Matthew's Sermon on the Mount thus does homage to both biblical and classical appeals to the authority of the canonical ancients. Matthew does so, however, in a form which dramatically emphasizes the orality (i.e., the rhetoricity and negotiability) of the biblical voices and Jesus' dominical voice: both Jesus and, especially, the biblical ancients (*hoi archaioi*, Matt 5:21) are emphatically represented as oral authorities, not texts ("[You have *heard* that] it was *said* {by the *ancients*}..." Matt 5:[{21}], [27], 31, [{33}], [38], [43] "...but/truly *I say* to you" verses 26, 28, 32, 39). The essential difference is the present immediacy of Jesus' speech and authority over the reported past speech of the ancients. Matthew self-consciously introduces a relatively strong oral sensibility in his use of authoritative texts here in a way which explicitly confirms the presumption that the choice between improvisational (in some sense "oral") and literary styles is a deliberate rhetorical decision among gospel writers.[51]

Matthew thus formally subverts classical and biblical normativity by balancing the rhetorical conventions of reverence for the ancients with the rhetorical convention of oral performance and relatively oral

---

[50] Mack, *Rhetoric*, 23, 96.
[51] Cf. Henderson, *"Didache* and Orality," 295, 301–304.

sensibility. Nonetheless, the gnomai of the Lucan and Q discourse are essential to Matthew's composition and are preserved as gnomai. Matthew's separate use of the Golden Rule (Matt 7:12) emphasizes both the topical and formal separability of the gnome from its earlier, equally redactional context. The Lucan parallel, chapter 6, verse 31 and the related (*kathos*) verse 36 (par Matt 5:48) are gnomai used in the fairly common Lucan and progymnasmatic role of marking transitions between discursive sections.

The pair of gnomai Luke 6:35b, 36 (par Matt 5:45b, 48) are not only positioned differently by the two gospel writers, they are a good example of hermeneutical and performantial variation of nevertheless recognizably continuous gnomic cores. It is contested to what extents Luke and the author(s) of Q are the architects of the discourse in chapter 6 (verses 27–36);[52] once again, the typical problem is that allegedly distinct redactional "strata" harmonize too well. Yet the Lucan forms of these gnomai nonetheless fit the style and ethos of Luke much better than would the contrasting Matthaean versions. Notably, the almost secular wisdom of Matthew 5:45b is ethically and theologically better controlled in the form and placement of Luke 6:35. This Lucan redactional piety in comparison with a Matthaean secular gnome is, moreover, repeated in the difference between Matthew 6:34 and Luke 12:32.

Where your treasure is, there shall your [Matt: singular; Luke: plural] heart be. (Matt 6:21 par Luke 12:34)

In Matthew 6:19–21 and Luke 12:33–34 the shared gnome about treasure has once more the function of transition between sections. This gnomic saying is not the object of significant redactional difference. Instead it is the hinge between strongly differentiated parallel redactions of the larger saying about treasures, rust and theives, set in quite different overall contexts. Even in so small an example, the real point of all these comparisons is clear: that the relationship between gnome and the redactional/compositional procedures of the gospel writers attests both the creative individuality and the formal independence and

---

[52] Funk, Hoover and the Jesus Seminar, *The Five Gospels*, 291–292; cf. Jacobson, *The First Gospel*, 102, citing D. Lührmann, "Liebet eure Feinde (Lk 6,27–36/Mt 5,39–48)," *ZTK* 69 (1972) 412–438, 415–422.

probable priority of many gnomai, even those most closely associated with redactional activity.

Again and again, gospel gnomai reflect the rhetorical assumption of the immediacy of tradition and originality in performance—and even in literary redaction.

Gnomai in special material

Gnomai (or gnomic performances) which are unique to the work of a single evangelist might be thought to show most unequivocally the creativity of the redactor/author. I have already pointed to the uncertain integration of Marcan gnomai (e.g., 2:27 and 9:49) into their respective contexts in order to suggest limits to authorial freedom in the selection or creation and deployment of gnomai. Mark's gnome-use is as distinctively Marcan as any other aspect of Marcan composition, but it also draws upon available rhetorical conventions of improvisational style as well as upon the conventions of a prevenient oral tradition of Jesus' speech.

Now I want to introduce a range of peculiarly Matthaean or Lucan gnomai, once again to show both considerable compositional liberty and yet also the resistance of even authorially introduced gnomai to complete contextual and redactional assimilation. It remains, moreover, at least part of my intention to illustrate the coherence of such presumably redactional gnomai with pre-Synoptic as well as more broadly gnomic tradition: Marcan, Q, special and progymnasmatic gnomai are all describable in terms of their definitive balance of normativity, analogy and semantic separability.

Do not give what is holy to the dogs. (Matt 7:6a)

In Matthew 7:6 as elsewhere in Matthew (Matt 5:14b; 6:34b; 7:6; 7:15; 10:8) a special Matthaean gnome is enclosed in or appended to Q material. Formally, Matthew 7:6 is another gnomic Quatrain. It shares with the other examples of the type the basic form of a gnome supplemented by parallelistic, but argumentatively pointed comments which focus interpretation of the opening gnome. Thematically as well, the Quatrain of the holy and the dogs typifies the Quatrains' almost dualistic interest in the oppositions of duty/self and of sacral/secular property and its faithful/unrighteous disposition.

The textual proximity of the Matthaean Quatrains (Matt 6:22–23; 6:24; 7:6) and of two of the three Lucan Quatrains (Luke 16:10–12; 13 —though see Luke 11:34–35), dramatically violates usual source-critical categories. It is to that extent doubly appealing to see in the Quatrains the influence of a remarkably specialized and, in Greco-Roman Christianity, marginal mnemotechnical (scribal) oral tradition. Such a specialized oral tradition differs not only from the textuality of written sources, redaction and rhetorical style, but also from less formal oral traditions and improvisational rhetorical styles. All traditions about Jesus' public speaking include gnomai; only the gnomic Quatrains make this rhetorical fact the basis for a unique verse genre. The gnomic Quatrains are concerned specifically with freezing the interpretation of a selected few gnomai; neither oral (progymnasmatic) performance tradition nor literary redactional tradition has anything else to compare. The norm for both oral and written traditions seems, by contrast, to be one of progymnasmatic (not "free") variation.

And yet the Quatrains, for all their poetic and mnemonic fixity, attest a deliberate reception of gnomic rhetoric and gnomic tradition. Thus the essential and less speculative point is that the opening gnome of Matthew 7:6 is traditionally as well as semantically separable from the mnemonic envelope of the Quatrain-form. The Quatrain is connected to the larger Matthaean context mainly by the notion of giving in the gnomic saying. Furthermore, even given the conventions of the Quatrain -form, which typically transcends or reverses any safe proverbial hearing of its opening gnome, the gnome of the holy and the dogs is strangely contextualized in Matthew 7:6. The Quatrain has proven a persistent pretext for flights of emendational and retroversional fancy.[53]

In this case, of course, the separability and quite likely the traditional independence of the gnome are indicated not only by tensions within

---

[53] Boismard, *Synopse*, 153; cf. J. Jeremias, "Matthäus 7,6a," in *Abraham unser Vater, Festschrift für O. Michel*, ed. O. Betz, M. Hengel, P. Schmidt (AGSU 5; Leiden and Köln, 1963) 271–275; F. Perles, "Zur Erklärung von Mt 7 6," *ZNW* 25 (1926) 163–164; M. Black, *An Aramaic Approach to the Gospels and Acts* (3d ed.; Oxford, 1967) 200–202; G. Schwarz, *'Und Jesus sprach': Untersuchungen zur aramäischen Urgestalt der Worte Jesu* (BWANT 118; Stuttgart *et alibi*, 1985) 236–244; J.A. Fitzmyer, "The Study of the Aramaic Background of the New Testament," in *A Wandering Aramean* (SBLMS 25; Missoula, Montana, 1979) 1–27, 14–15.

the gospel text. The gnome is cited without the Quatrain context and very explicitly as a saying of the Lord in *Didache* 9:5. The traditional, rhetorical and source-critical relations between *Didache* and the gospels, especially Matthew, are fiercely contested.[54] The Didachist's use of this gnome is in any case important, however, as its sense shows no necessary relation to either the development in Matthew 7:6 or the verse's larger context; the implied reference of "what is holy" in *Didache* 9:5 to consecrated food seems quite contrary to the metaphorically extended sense of the Matthaean performance.

Matthew 7:15–20

Matthaean redactional/authorial creativity can be seen relatively clearly in Matthew 7:15–20 as the passage combines and expands imagery and gnomai which appear in different combinations elsewhere in the same evangelist's work. Thus, in keeping with the Matthaean Wisdom-literary taste for animal fables and proverbs,[55] Matthew 7:15 takes up the rather conventional imagery of one-sided conflict between sheep and wolves, perhaps from the commonplace tradition, perhaps from Matthew 10:16a. The latter is itself surely a Matthaean redactional displacement from the Q context preserved in Luke 10:2–12.[56] Matthew 10:16b gives further evidence of the Matthaean redactional penchant for animal gnomai, not all of which can be referred to Q.

Even granting this Matthaean taste, however, similarity with Matthew 10:16/Luke 10:3 means that 7:15 is not redactional invention, but rather redactional, hermeneutical variation of a conventional, traditional gnomic core. In the Q performance the gnomic core is referred to relations between the members of the group and the outsiders to whom they are sent; in one Matthaean performance (10:16) this is retained and expanded (verse 16b), in the other Matthaean performance the core is applied to the relation between the faithful and pseudoprophetic infiltrators. In terms not only of imagery, but also of normative conflict and minority vulnerability, however, the gnomic core is preserved in variation.

---

[54] Henderson, "*Didache* and Orality," 284 n.7.

[55] Goulder, *Midrash*, 101–102; cf. Küchler, *Weisheitstraditionen*, 325ff on *Tierfabeln* in the Ahiqar tradition.

[56] Jacobson, *The First Gospel*, 67–69, 131–132, 137–149.

The larger part of Matthew 7:15–20 is, however, taken up with variations on the gnomic core about the correspondence between a tree and its fruit. This is imagery which appears in further mutations in Matthew 12:33–35 and Luke 6:43–45, as well as in parabolic and allegorical expansion (Matt 13:24–30, 36–43; Luke 13:6–9; John 15:1–17). The essential core of the analogy seems to be expressed in Matthew 7:16a (=7:20; 12:33b) and Luke 6:44a. Both gospel writers relate knowing plants by their fruit analogically to two distinctions: one distinction between unspecified qualities (*kalos* versus *sapros*, Matt 7:17–19 par Luke 6:43; Matt 12:33) and then also a more mixed distinction between unproductive species of plant (thorns/brambles) and those which yield desirable fruit (figs/grapes, Matt 7:16/Luke 6:44).

The organization of gnomic and other materials in Matthew 7:15–20 may be seen in part as an attempt to overcome this disparity of imagery by bringing it into a clearer argumentative relationship with the explicitly defined problem of verse 15: the essential conclusion of the Matthaean argument here, the solution to the problem of identifying pseudoprophets, is emphasized in repeated gnomic summary verses (16, 20). Within this frame, the order of Matthew 7:16–18 is the reverse of that in Luke 6:43–44. The Matthaean order reduces the incongruity between general (trees/fruits) and specific, perhaps biblically inspired imagery (thorns/figs, cf. Gen 3:18; Hos 10:8) by offering the latter first. Matthew's point is, after all, specifically against pseudophrophets, rather than generally in favour of good fruits.

Matthew's discourse therefore moves from specific warning (7:15) to recognition (verse 16) to punishment (verse 19) back to recognition (verse 20); Luke (Q) moves from generalization (6:43) to ethical application (verses 44–45). The Q gnome, Matthew 3:10 (par Luke 3:9), is brought forward to the climax of Matthew 7:15–20, verse 19. Matthew 7:19 and Matthew 3:10/Luke 3:9 are an interesting case of a gnomic core being attributed first to John the Baptist and then derivatively to Jesus. It is hard to imagine a more impressive indication of the redactional usefulness of gnome. The place of Matthew 7:19 in its context there is irreducibly redactional. Yet, by the same token Matthew's gnomic redaction here is far from arbitrary: instead, the gospel narrator is underlining a rhetorical continuity of gnomic cores from John the Baptist to Jesus which was already implied in Q tradition.

The redactional aspect of the gnome 7:19 is confirmed by its absence not only from Luke 6 but also from the closely parallel development of

Matthew 12:33–37. This time the relation with Matthew 3:7–10 and John the Baptist is asserted by repetition of the polemical address to John's and Jesus' opponents (verses 34–37).

Just as in Matthew 7:16–17 (par Luke 6:44, 43), Matthew 12: 34b–35 seems to reverse the order of a gnomic pair from Q (cf. Luke 6:45b) to make a more pointed opening address. Again, as in Matthew 7:19, a gnomic series in response to an initial problem of deceptive appearances (7:15; 12:34) concludes with an eschatological gnomic tour de force (7:19; 12:37).

Matthew 22:14; Matthew 26:52b

Two more gnomai will complete the list of Matthaean gnomai which mark redaction-critical watersheds. Matthew 22:14 "expresses his [i.e., the gospel writer's] point of view precisely."[57] Matthew 26:52b, too, is presumably Matthaean invention or a borrowed proverb—though Luke (22:51) and John (18:11) also show an interest in having Jesus resolve the abortive sword-play at his arrest. Affinities with Genesis 9:6 and Jeremiah 15:2 and with the problematic sayings, Matthew 10:34 (cf. Luke 12:51) and Luke 22:36, also suggest precedents in gnomic Jesus tradition. The main lesson is, however, that individual gnomai coined by a literate redactor are structurally indistinguishable from individual gnomai received from one kind of tradition or another; there is no generic difference between relatively redactional and relatively traditional gnomai in the Synoptics.

The one who is forgiven little, loves little. (Luke 7:47)

The history of the pericope Luke 7:36–50 is unclear, but formally the section grafts an anti-Pharisaic parable (verses 41–43, 47b) onto a narrative roughly parallel to that of Mark 14:3–9. Perhaps Luke retrieved the unit more or less from pre-Marcan texts or oral traditions. In any case the Lucan unit is rich in Lucan redactional interests (e.g., women, forgiveness) and has a powerful dramatic unity in the opposition of the women and the Pharisee. There is, however, a curious ambiguity of moral object-lessons: in the parabolic narrative and the gnome, love is a foreseeable consequence of being forgiven; in the

---

[57] Funk, Hoover and the Jesus Seminar, *The Five Gospels*, 235.

primary narrative, love is the ground of forgiveness. The actual historical process behind the Lucan composition hardly matters, except that it probably means that the incongruity between the gnome (verse 47b) and its setting (verse 47a) should be understood as the result not only of redactional laziness, but also of gnomic independence. That is, the whole story's contrasting formal and tonal aspects come into their most intimate and inescapable contact in the tension between gnome and setting in verse 47. The whole section is determined formally and quite possibly historically by reflection on and narrative inversion of a gnome which is at least not a derivation from the Marcan story.[58]

The too-familiar physician—and the prophet at home: Luke 4:23 (cf. Mark 6:4; John 4:44; Gos. Thom. 31)

The difficulty of distinguishing traditional from authorial gnomai—indeed an impossibility on redactional-critical grounds alone and an absurdity in rhetorical-critical terms—is illustrated in one last major example of redactional seam marked by gnome-use. Luke 4:23 is unusually explicit in its identification of a proverbial gnome: the physician gnome is cited as a *parabole* (for this sense of the word see also 6:39). Moreover, its ethopoetic attribution by Jesus to the Nazarenes marks this gnome as something of a proverb in the Lucan redactor's eyes, a currency confirmed by widespread classical and rabbinic parallels.[59] With the Q gnomai Luke 12:54–55, Luke 7:32b and the gnomic dialogue Mark 7:24–30 par, Luke 4:23 is the Synoptic equivalent to Eißfeldt's Old Testament proverb performances. Compared with those Old Testament proverb performances the proverbial gnomai performed within gospel stories are remarkable only for their less aristocratic social settings.

As in Luke 7:36–50, the poor motivation and rough transition from Luke 4:16–22 to Jesus' speech in verses 23–27, along with other hints of textual incoherence, have invited source-critical explanations beyond

---

[58] Schmithals, "Evangelien," 625; Schmithals, *Einleitung*, 366, 413; Boismard, *Synopse*, 178–9.

[59] S.J. Noorda, "'Cure Yourself, Doctor!' (Luke 4,23) Classical Parallels to an Alleged Saying of Jesus," in *Logia—les Paroles de Jésus—the Sayings of Jesus*, ed. J. Delobel (BETL 59; Leuven, 1982) 459–467; A.J. Fitzmyer, *The Gospel According to Luke I–IX* (AB 28; Garden City, NY, 1981) 535.

mere Lucan redaction of Mark 6. Such source-critical explanations seem to require at least a pre-Lucan composition for the peculiarly Lucan gnome of the too-familiar healer and for its setting in verse 23.[60] Certainly compared with Mark 6:1–6a (par Matt 13:53–58), Luke 4:16–30 is in some sense a hybrid story, a hybridization which makes the relations between story and gnome and between the two gnomai in verses 23, 24 all the more problematic. The situation is further complicated by the existence of a hybrid version of our gnomai preserved without narrative framework (POxy. 1.6=Gos. Thom. 31).

The ultimate complication is that, after all, the gist of the story, Jesus' home town rejection, is intrinsically plausible as historical memory. This complex of gnomic traditions (Luke 4:23–24; Mark 6:4; John 4:44; and *Gospel of Thomas* 31) is strong evidence against any rigid dichotomy between episodic tradition and speech tradition; if we had only these gnomai we would have to infer a narrative context like that so differently presented by Mark, Luke and John.

Whatever their value and probability, theories of source-conflation behind Luke 4 go only a very little way toward explaining how a literary redactor could allow so many aporias in so programmatic a composition. Another step may be taken by recognizing that the same juxtaposition of gnomai which divides the passage (and distinguishes it from the Marcan parallel) also gives it its greatest dramatic effect: within a minimal narrative, the reading from Isaiah and the discourse about Elijah and Elisha impressively frame a central dialogue which is further marked off by obtrusive introductory formulae (two each in verses 23 and 24). The result is a statement of the uneasy relation between prophetic mission and prophetic reception, an uneasiness which is effectively expressed in the uneasy balance of the writing— whether by rhetorical art or by chance.

The Marcan Nazareth story is also marked by inward tension between story and gnome; the initial similarities between Mark 6:1–6 and Mark 1:21–23, 27–28 are sufficiently striking to justify suspicions that the discontinuity of tone between 6:2 and 3 is not only a dramatic turn but also a trace of literary redactional development, turning the story toward the negative conclusion of verse 4 and its consequences.

---

[60] C.M. Tuckett, "Luke 4,16–30, Isaiah and Q" in Delobel, *Logia*, 343–354; R.C. Tannehill, "The Mission of Jesus According to Luke IV 16–30" in *Jesus in Nazareth*, ed. W. Eltester (BZAW 40; Berlin and New York, 1970) 51–75, 52–58.

The independence of the prophet gnome (verse 4) is suggested also by its expansion to include kin and household with home town in a narrative context which may mention also the first but condemns only the last of these. Needless to say, this falls far short of establishing the conclusion that Mark 6:4 was the fulcrum for the secondary reorientation of an originally more optimistic story.[61] It is enough, however, to underscore both the importance of the prophet gnome for Marcan redaction and also the gnome's probable independence—even without reference to the external testimonies of John 4:44 and *Gospel of Thomas* 31.

Decisions about the relation of John 4:44 to the Synoptic instances will usually be prejudiced by more general evaluations of Johannine literary (in)dependence. There can be no doubt, however, that the core of the prophet gnome was separable from whatever context the Johannine evangelist found it in and from the context of John 4. Once again, whether artfully or clumsily, the saying is sharply juxtaposed to its surroundings.

The Egyptian versions might be taken to represent a dependent conflation of Luke 4:23 and 24:56. Even in that case, however, they would indicate an early concurrence with the judgement that these gnomai are at least in principle separable from their Synoptic contexts and related to each other. In fact, the integration of the too-familiar physician gnome with the prophet gnome in *Gospel of Thomas* is quite unlike the juxtaposition of gnomai in Jesus' speech in Luke 4. A hint of tension with familiars as well as with compatriots is reintroduced, a tension explicit in Mark 6:4b but at most latent in Luke, where foreshadowing the Passion is the dominant interest. Any implied narrative in the second limb of *Gospel of Thomas* 31 is, moreover, more congruent with the Marcan story (see especially 6:5) than with the Lucan (see especially 4:18–22).

At any rate, there seems to be no compelling reason to assume the literary dependence of either the Johnanine or the Egyptian variants on our Synoptic witnesses. Moreover, the internal oddity of each of the gospel narratives of Jesus' rejection makes an exceptionally strong case for preferring to see Luke 4:23–24, Mark 6:4, John 4:44 and *Gospel of Thomas* 31 as literarily independent performantial variations of the

---

[61] Boismard, *Synopse*, 90–91, 212–213.

prophet gnome and, in Luke and *Thomas*, of a physician gnome which was early and orally associated with it.

Mercifully, we do not need what Bultmann thought form criticism could provide: a really satisfying history of individual items through Synoptic traditional and redactional development. What matters more here than the possibility that the narratives were redactionally shaped, reshaped and/or mixed on the basis of pre-existent gnomai is (1) the certainty that the gnomai Mark 6:4 and Luke 4:23 are separable sub-units in loosely integrated narrative contexts and (2) the probability that at least the former gnome circulated in Jesus-tradition independently of a textually fixed story of rejection at Nazareth. Both of these and especially the difficult move from semantic separability to the probability of independent tradition are supported by the dislocations which mark both the Matthaeo-Marcan and the Lucan narratives, dislocations which do most likely indicate development seams, and which seem to isolate the gnomai as items of consciously distinct interest to successive redactors. The Johannine and Egyptian evidence establishs the separability of these gnomai and adds greatly to the probability that separability in these cases meant traditional independence.

Gnome in redaction: conclusions

All these examples of proven redactional, i.e., literary authorial, interest in gnome show that gnome-use, including some pure invention, was an important compositional tool in the Synoptics. This is what progymnasmatic assumptions would lead us to expect, but the exercise was necessary to test the relevance of our gnomic category to actual Synoptic contexts. In addition, purely redactional gnomai are neither so numerous nor so varied as to make redactional activity an acceptable primary explanation for the prevalence of gnomai in the Synoptic Gospels. On the contrary, the redactional character of even the most demonstrably redactional gospel is not unequivocal: even Matthew 7:19 and Luke 4:23 are not without bases in more traditional gnomic material. Very few of the most 'redactional' gnomai are clearly reducible to impulses of authorial invention. A great many are related to their literary contexts in such a way as to make circulation in pre-literary Jesus-tradition relatively probable.

Some individual gnomic cores (e.g., the prophet at home, Mark 6:4; Luke 2:24; John 4:44; POxy. 1.6, *Gos. Thom.* 31) are well enough attested to allow us to recognize progymnasmatic processes of variation, expansion, elaboration and summation—and to prove that these processes were working in oral tradition as well as in literary redaction. Such individual instances are valuable, but their importance is as exceptional corroboration of processes which are normally less visible in the literary products of rhetorical tradition. Thus both Luke 4:23 and Mark 6:4 may claim with some probability to be associated with Jesus' tradition independently of redactional invention or episodic contextualization, but the probabilities in these two cases are by no means equally clear. The essential point relates not to the singularity of individual examples, but to the category as a whole, which is clearly not to be reduced to a function of literary redaction: redactional tastes do not adequately explain the gnomic quality of Synoptic tradition, though in the nature of the Synoptic evidence literary redaction has in all cases played a role.

Finally, these most obviously redactional, authorial examples of Synoptic gnome-use suggest something about the shared, though internally differentiated, stylistic and rhetorical decorum of the gospels. I have repeatedly pointed to the inconsistent integration of redactional gnomai into their literary contexts as a fallible but probable sign that the redactional gnome is nonetheless seldom an entirely free invention: more often it is a redactional performance of gnomic core tradition. This suspicion is borne out in the best-attested minority of gnomai, the only sample among which it can be tested.

At the same time, however, this redactional equivocation which betrays (or affirms) the general traditionality of gospel gnomai returns us to the question of stylistics with which this chapter began. The semantic tensions which surround the redactional contextualizations of so many gospel gnomai are from one point of view passive traces of the imperfect integration of traditions into texts. The same uneasy integration of even redactionally introduced gnomai in their gospel contexts is at the same time a defining aspect of the gospels' chosen rhetorical decorum. Stylistically, the gospel writers in their different ways all use gnomai to emphasize the traditionality of their rhetoric, a traditionality which belongs within biblical and classical gnomic traditionality, yet also differs authoritatively from them. The gospel writers' chose a deliberately oral-sounding, 'improvisational' and affective gnomic style—rather than the textual, 'graphic' and formally argumentational style which I think Mack and Robbins have led rhetorical critics to seek.[62] Only one reason for the gospel writers' choice of gnomic style is to be found in the fact that they did in fact write under the direct influence of a tradition of oral rhetoric. The numinous, oracular content[63] of that rhetorical tradition and its narrative references to the character, Jesus, and its exotic dramatic location in Jewish Galilee and Jerusalem are deeper reasons for the improvisational, gnomic quality of both written and oral gospel rhetorics.

Speech and episode in gnomic redaction

Any list of Synoptic gnomai will include many examples which are more or less thoroughly integrated into chreiai. Gnomic chreiai are the most challenging instance of the extension of gospel gnome-use well beyond the form-critical bounds of paraenetical collections. By comparison with the loose, though frequent and important association between gnome and parable,[64] gnome and chreia are far more intimately related. Because of this, the problem of the historical as well as structural cohesion of the category 'gnome' across form-critical frontiers may be treated as almost identical to the question of whether and how non-apophthegmatic and apophthegmatic gnomai belong together in their historical significance.

In order to define gnome, I have had to stress the relative independence (separability) of gnomai from their possible contextualizations. The other side of this, however, is that gnomai are never independent of actual performances or texts: every public speaker in antiquity was trained to use gnomai, but even the most gnomic style incorporated its gnomai into some less homogeneous discourse. A gnome could (though it need not) be remembered alone; it cannot be performed, i.e., transmitted orally or in writing, without at least a temporary context,

---

[62] Mack, *Rhetoric and the New Testament*; Mack and Robbins, *Patterns*; Robbins, "Pre-Gospel Traditions."

[63] Cf. F. Thielman, "The Style of the Fourth Gospel and Ancient Literary Critical Concepts of Religious Discourse," in Watson, *Persuasive Artistry*, 169–183.

[64] Berger, *Formgeschichte*, 50.

whether in a chreia, attached to a parable, or as part of a parenesis, a dialogue or a developed argumentation.

We saw in Chapter One how the form-critical tendency to ignore the complex integrity of gospel rhetorics has prejudiced understanding the historical relation between chreiai (apophthegms) and the often gnomic sayings which they frame. The form critics assumed without argument the prior independence of the logion against its literary setting. Still, if reaction against such overconfidently historicizing judgements is fully justified, the basic form-critical insight remains, that the pronouncement stories represent ideal, stereotyped scenes in which historical verisimilitude is compromised in favour of dramatic and rhetorical (polemical/apologetic/dogmatic) effect.[65] The intrinsic implausibility of many Synoptic chreiai/apophthegms as narratives of *events* is, I think not coincidentally, clearest in those chreiai which are most clearly centred on a rhetorically challenging gnome (e.g., Mark 2:23–28 par; Mark 7:1–23 par; Mark 3:1–6 par).[66]

Thus, as I argued earlier, the corrective position advocated by Robbins, that the form-critical "privileging of speech over action and situation in pre-gospel tradition...must be revised," contains within it the danger of privileging literary contexts over pre-gospel gnomic tradition: pre-gospel traditional rhetoric was speech, including speech about actions and situations, but also including gnomai which were rhetorically valued for their own sakes and not only as aspects of narration and argumentation.

Still, only a minority of gnomai—e.g., *Wanderlogien* like Mark 8:35 (cf. 10:43 par)[67]—are so broadly attested across source-and form-critical boundaries that we can identify beyond reasonable doubt gnomic cores which were transmitted in pre-gospel tradition without particular recurrent episodic or argumentational settings. In a few instances (e.g., the prophet at home, Mark 6:4 par) episodic memory seems, if anything, to have been borne by gnomic tradition, rather than the reverse; at any rate the event, Jesus' rejection at Nazareth, is tradition-historically more probably attested by the gnome than by the various (highly redactional) narratives surrounding some of its performances.

---

[65] Bultmann, *Geschichte*, 40; Berger, *Formgeschichte*, 84.

[66] Sanders, *Jesus and Judaism*, 264–267.

[67] Berger, *Formgeschichte*, 66–67; *Einführung*, 227–235.

It is far more significant, however, that the minority of gospel gnomai which can be proven to reflect independent pre-gospel gnomic tradition are indistinguishable from the less thoroughly attested majority either in their internal character or in their assimilation to written contexts. By and large, the canons of progymnasmatic rhetoric would lead us to expect wide variation not only in the formulation, but also in the contextualization of gnomic cores. This variation is present in multiple performances of the minority of most heavily used gnomic cores; it is also present, however, in the wide range of uses attested among that majority of gnomai which appear only in one Synoptic performance each. Moreover, the progymnasmatic tradition values not only the potential of gnomai for formal variation and for contextual adaptation. The progymnasmata prescribe gnomai for their core memorability: their aptness to express and/or influence tradition. From a progymnasmatic point of view, what is surprising is the scale of gospel gnome-use, the recurring tension between gnomai and their literary contexts, and some aspects of the topicality of gospel gnomai.

Gnomai occur in all kinds of contexts and in a variety of textual functions. A few individual Synoptic gnomai (apart from Johannine and other non-Synoptic parallels) are found in both apophthegmatic and non-apophthegmatic contexts (e.g., Matthew 7:13a par Luke 13:24). It is very difficult to count chreiai accurately as all definitions of chreia describe its formulaic beginning, but not its *end*. Still, fewer than half of all Synoptic gnome performances (96/228)[68] are part of *chreiai logikai* (e.g., Matt 8:20, 22)—although the Sayings Gospel Q may have had more chriic gnome performances than can now be known, depending whether Lucan attribution formulae are from Q (e.g., Luke 17:(22) 23–37). At any rate, other gnomai supplement or extend parables (e.g., Luke 18:14 or 16:8b).[69] Many are part (or extensions [e.g., Mark 10:31 par; Luke 10:42a]) of elaborated chreiai in ways which blur distinctions among narrative, dialogue and discursive forms (e.g., Mark 2:19a par,

---

[68] I have followed Berger's list of chreiai, to which I have freely added wherever I have found material introduced by an attribution formula ("Jesus/he said/says/answered/[gestured], etc."). Cf. Berger, *Formgeschichte*, 80–82; similar figures would be obtained from a list of apophthegms abstracted from Bultmann, *Geschichte*, 8–73, and H. Köster, "Formgeschichte/Formkritik II: Neues Testament," *TRE* XI (1983) 286–299, 291–293.

[69] Berger, *Formgeschichte*, 50–51.

21–22 par).[70] Other gnomai function in quite various ways in longer discursive compositions: parenetic series (e.g., Mark 4:21–25); apocalyptic discourse (e.g., Mark 13:13b); gnomic Quatrains (e.g., Luke 16:10). Some gnomai are closely—perhaps irreducibly— associated with the Son of Man mannerism (Mark 2:27; Mark 10:43 par; Matt 8:20 par; Matt 11:16–19 par).

Joachim Wanke has attempted to describe a genre of paired commentary-and-pretext sayings in the gospels. Wanke points to such commentary pairs as evidence of (1) the early normativity of even difficult sayings in Jesus' tradition and (2) the relative antiquity of at least the pretext saying (*Bezugswort*) compared with less directly 'commented' sayings material. In most of Wanke's fourteen examples, either the *Kommentarwort* (seven times) or the *Bezugswort* (five times) is gnomic—in three cases both. But here too the relation of gnomic tradition and variation/redaction is ambiguous: how can one limb of such small units be designated functionally or historically as 'commentary' on the other (e.g., Matt 12:34b, 35 par on 33 par; Matt 8:19–20 par on Matt 8:21–22 par; Mark 2:21–22 par on 2:18–20 par)?[71]

Forms, sources and and rhetorical topicality

Form-critically, the most noticeable concentration of gnome-performances is in chreiai (96/228=42%). This corresponds in part to a source-critical concentration: Marcan and derivative gnome-performances are even more likely to be contextualized in chreiai (59/113= 52%). By contrast, Matthaean and Lucan special tradition gnomai are rarely contextualized in chreiai (Matt, 1/13; Luke, 4/15). It is, of course, important to remember that what is being counted here is gnome-*performances*, not gnomic *cores*. Many gnomic cores are contextualized within different form-critical categories in different performances. Thus, for example, some gnomai which appear to have been performed within chreiai in Q (Luke 13:24; 16:17[?]) are not chriic when integrated in the Sermon on the Mount (Matt 5:18; 7:13). Likewise, some Marcan chreia-gnomai (Mark 4:21–25) are give mainly non-chriic discursive contexts

---

[70] Berger, *Formgeschichte*, 85, 89–90.

[71] Wanke, "Kommentarworte"; cf. T. Hildebrandt, "Proverbial Pairs: Compositional Units in Proverbs 10–29," *JBL* 107 (1988) 207–224.

in Matthew and Luke. Again, gnomai which are appended to chreiai in Mark (Mark 2:21, 28) are emphatically chriic in Luke (5:34; 6:5).

A further correlation may be mentioned as an impression, though I hesitate to produce even rough statistics for shrinking numbers of items based on inevitably heuristic judgements of "topicality." Still, gnomai contextualized in Marcan tradition within chreiai are also rather often rhetorically marked by especially strong intrinsic topicality. That is, the gnomai themselves invite reception in terms of urgent eschatology, rhetorical characterization (of the speaker, his hearer or opponent), legality or (anti-)proverbial normativity. Legal topicality, for example, occurs in about twenty percent (40/228=18%) of all Synoptic gnome performances, but in about twenty-eight percent of Synoptic gnomai performed in chreiai (19/74=26%; 16/19 are from Marcan or derivative material). The issue of gnomic topics will be taken up systematically in Chapters Five and Six. For now, however, it is proper to ask the question, how far such topicalities are a function of Marcan redactional, chriic gnomai. Indeed, it is necessary to ask how far Synoptic gnome-use generally can be reduced to Marcan chriic gnomai and other, marginalized uses.

There is fairly clearly a particular Marcan interest in topically striking gnomai contextualized in chreiai. This disproportionate—but not exclusive—interest might have been even more pronounced in a Marcan *Grundschrift*, if there was one, though Mark seems also blithely to have incorporated micro-sources which had no gnomai or chreiai at all (Mark 4:3–10, 13–20, 26–33).[72] Equally clearly there are many topically striking gnomai and many chriic gnomai outside Marcan influence: they occur in every major source- or redaction-critical category. Above all, some source-critical (i.e., redactional) specialization in gnome-use is to be expected within any rhetorically informed model of Synoptic tradition.

Aristotle carefully prescribed that puzzling or controversial gnomai—or gnomai toward which the speaker's attitude is unconventional—be accompanied by an *epilogos* (*Rh.* II 21=1394b–95a). In the argumentational contexts Aristotle imagines, the *epilogos* is presumably usually an *aitia*, an added reason bringing gnome closer to an enthymeme in form. In the context of a Sayings Gospel (Q) composed

---

[72] Schmithals, *Einleitung*, 410–421; Kuhn, *Sammlungen*.

as a mixture of wisdom and apocalyptic discourse genres, the Aristotelean injunction could be carried out directly: difficult gnomai could be
supplemented or contextualized with other gnomic or argumentational
material. Thus Matthew and Luke include twelve performances of
legally topical gnomai from Q, only three of which are in chreiai (Luke
9:60/Matt 8:22; Luke 16:17 [not Matt 5:18!]). Despite P. Vassiliadis'
attempt systematically to exclude sayings of a proverbial character from
Q precisely because he thought they might be due to the oral tradition,[73] there seem, in fact, to have been gnomai in each of the more
probable stages of Q's redactional development. Most Q gnomai,
however, including the most urgently topical subset, were not contextualized within chreiai. Matthaean and Lucan special tradition gnomai are,
by the way, even less likely to be integrated within chreiai; whatever
their origins, such gnomai are almost always redactionally contextualized as *epilogoi*, appended to forms inherited from Mark or Q.

Q did contain chreiai (Luke 4:1–13 par; 7:1–10 par; 18–23 par;
9:57–62 par),[74] probably more of them than the Matthaeo-Lucan
evidence unambiguously attests. J.S. Kloppenborg concluded that the
chriic element in the final redaction of Q was enough to justify giving
it the loose-fitting generic label of "chriae collection."[75] This will do
as a way of labelling Kloppenborg's distinction in literary genre
between the final redaction of Q and a more homogeneous earlier
version typified by instructional poems. In a progymnasmatically
informed enquiry, however, gnomai and chreiai cannot be treated as
rhetorically equivalent. In such a critical context, it is likely that gnome-
use is a more basic condition than chreia-use for bridging redactions of
Q and for balancing apocalyptic and sapiential aspects of the final
hybrid.

As C.E. Carlston insisted, the gnomic component in Q rhetorics is
also an important condition for asserting rhetorical continuity between
either the sapiential or the apocalyptic literacies of Q and the habits of
any actual speech community.[76] Q needed its gnomai to persuade its
intended readers (or its modern critics) that it represents a historically

---

[73] P. Vassiliadis, "The Nature and Extent of the Q Document," *NT* 20 (1978)
49–73.
[74] Berger, *Formgeschichte*, 81.
[75] Kloppenborg, *Formation of Q*, 322–325; cf. Jacobson, *The First Gospel*, 51.
[76] C.E. Carlston, "Wisdom and Eschatology in Q," in Delobel, *Logia*, 101–119.

representative sample of oral tradition about Jesus. Certainly, with regard to chreia frequency and gnome contextualization, Q was dramatically less chriic than, e.g., the *Gospel of Thomas*: *Thomas* is a strikingly homogeneous collection of chreiai, constructed without narrative framework, but entirely of narrative units.

In Mark, however, and to some extent in all subsequent gospels, the problem of providing a suitable *epilogos* for difficult gnomai is changed by the dominance of episodic narrative conventions and of discourse conventions rather than chreia for sayings blocks. Marcan rhetoric in particular seems to be structured by an extraordinary tension between episodic action and oracular speech, with the hermeneutical accent strongly on the former. This axis is especially important at the beginning of the gospel in which we find an astonishing series of mixed and gestural (miraculous) chreiai followed by mysterious parabolic and gnomic discourses (Mark 1–4). The gnomic chreiai of this strange introduction to Jesus' non-teaching not surprisingly include several gnomai marked by strong internal topicality (Mark 2:17, 19, 27; 3:4, 24; 4:21–25). Mark's ambivalence toward Jesus as public teacher and speaker coheres with his entombment of Jesus' most powerful gnomai within remorselessly stereotyped chriic narrative settings (e.g., Mark 2:23–28 par; Mark 7:1–23 par; Mark 3:1–6 par). In Mark at least (and, more gently, in derivative parts of Matthew and Luke) the rhetorical function of the chreia seems to be to confront quite specific topics, if not necessarily actual "congregational problems,"[77] with Jesus' anti-rhetorical authority in oracular word and gesture. Marcan use of gnome and chreia, together and separately, seems oriented toward eclipsing (especially Scriptural) argumentation with authority (Mark 2:23–28; 7:1–23; 10:2–12; 12:18–27):[78] Mark obstinately provides in his chreiai —and on a larger scale, in his gospel as a whole—narrative rather than argumentational *aitiai* for some of Jesus' perplexing words and gestures.

In other words, relative specialization in the topicality and contextualization of gnomai in different literary sources is strictly relative. Such relative specialization makes sense as part of the rhetorical strategy of each document. In particular, the relationship between gnome and chreia varies along with the relationship between narrative and discursive rhetorics. In Mark the relationship between gnome and chreia may have

---

[77] Berger, *Formgeschichte*, 86–87.
[78] Berger, *Formgeschichte*, 89–90.

something to do with Marcan rhetorical uses of controversial topicality. It is not surprising then that within R.C. Tannehill's typology of apophthegms,[79] all five sub-genres contain examples of apophthegmatic (i.e., chriic) gnome, although Tannehill's least confrontational class, the Commendation Stories, numbers only one definitely gnomic apophthegm (Luke 10:38–42) and no topically legal gnomai.

None of this means that individual gnomai or, rather, gnomic cores are authentic or inauthentic, but only that the gnomic habit is at the same time both irreducible to any function of literary, redactional practice and also profoundly attractive to literary redactors. Jesus (and his first interpreters) probably used gnomai as characteristically as he (they) used parable. But the historical importance of gnome-use is even more as "an important bridge" between oral and literary tradition and a link among differing genres, forms and topics in literary text production. "Gnomai belong to those forms which have no original *Sitz im Leben*. They can appear anywhere, but then fulfil a particular function."[80] This means that gnomai can and must be considered at the same time from the standpoint of their functional and formal integration into the rhetorics of particular performers and redactors and also from the standpoint of the resistance of gnomic cores to complete authorial and contextual appropriation: "Multifunctionality means also a certain strangeness over against any particular context," written or spoken.[81]

The variability and 'multifunctionality' of gnomai—and the compensating impressiveness and tenacity of gnomic cores in memory —make gnome a key bridge between different rhetorical styles and between tradition and redaction. Extensive gnome-use may be particularly typical of 'agonistic', improvisational styles, including most early Christian styles most of the time. Even relatively literary ('graphic') styles, however, proclaim their *relative* literacy in a more differentiated, subordinated gnome-use. Sensitivity to variation in gnome-use can,

---

[79]   R.C. Tannehill, ed., *Pronouncement Stories=Semeia* 20 (1981), esp. 1–13, "Introduction: The Pronouncement Story and its Types," and, 101–119, "Varieties of Synoptic Pronouncement Stories"; R.C. Tannehill, "Apophthegms in the Synoptic Gospels," *ANRW* II 25/2 (Berlin and New York, 1984) 1792–1829.

[80]   Berger, "Hellenistischen Gattungen," 1055–7 (quoted); *Formgeschichte*, 13, 67, 122, 156.

[81]   Berger, *Formgeschichte*, 63.

therefore, alert the gospel reader to the very wide spectrum of stylistic (oral versus literary) coloration available to speakers and writers in a cultural situation where active conversational, oratorical (prophetic, apologetic and polemical), mnemo-technical and professionally scribal, as well as more self-consciously literate traditions are only provisionally harmonized by the reigning conventions of technical rhetoric.

> [T]he distinction between orality and literacy is different from the distinction between *tradition and redaction*. For redactional style (*Sprachgebrauch*) says nothing about either the nonexistence of prior tradition or its possible form.[82]

Redactional performance of gnomai, some of which can nevertheless be shown to be traditional cores, i.e., gnomic cores used by more than one performer/redactor, does fundamentally relativize romantic distinctions between oral and literary tradition into a more pragmatic continuum of styles. Finally, this historic interest of the gospels' gnomic rhetoric as a richly differentiated whole and the historic interest of its most salient topics are independent of actual or foreseeable redaction- and source-critical results.

---

[82] Berger, *Formgeschichte*, 15.

CHAPTER FIVE

DISCIPLESHIP, ESCHATOLOGY AND THE PROJECTION OF CHARACTER IN SYNOPTIC GNOMAI

My proposal that gnome should occupy a far more decisive place in gospel criticism and in Synoptic oral-tradition theory, started from the attempts of Bultmann, Beardslee and Carlston to classify and understand a range of 'logia', not all of which could be inauthentic, and which seem sometimes to recall and sometimes to subvert proverbial and literary Wisdom. This form-critical project of defining and analysing the gospel 'sayings' has been increasingly preempted by more narrowly literary questions, e.g., of Q's use of sapiential and/or apocalyptic conventions, and of the use of chreiai in gospel composition.

Kloppenborg's reconstruction of the redactional history of the Q document, moving from sapiential to apocalyptic and chriic literacy, has encouraged recognition "that many of the sayings in these [sapiential Q] texts which are often described as prophetic need not be so understood."[1] At the same time, Robbins' concern to redress the imbalance of interpretive interest in sayings-reports over action-reports tends to diminish the perceived relevance of gnomic tradition: "Regularly, one's memory of a situation and of action in that situation is more precise than one's memory of words that were spoken."[2] Both herald a movement away from the form-critical procedure of seeking existential insight into individual sayings as the primary means of reconstructing pre-gospel tradition. Such movement is part of a broad though not universal or consistent movement away from the heritage of Schweitzer and Bultmann emphasizing eschatology and the phenomenology of language toward more social-scientific and ideological criticism.[3]

---

[1] Jacobson, *The First Gospel*, 49; Kloppenborg, *Formation of Q*.

[2] Robbins, "Pre-Gospel Traditions," 134.

[3] See, e.g., M.J. Borg, "A Temperate Case for a Non-Eschatological Jesus," *Forum* 2 (1986) 81–102.

In this climate it seems almost quaintly old-fashioned to champion the centrality of gnomic sayings for understanding continuity and variation in traditions influenced by Jesus. This impression may be aggravated by an analysis of gnomai and their receptions in terms of topics of eschatology and self-characterization (*ethos*), with its even less postmodern openings toward Christology!

Before Kloppenborg's studies on the literary evolution of Q, Q scholarship had to focus, albeit reluctantly, on the ultimate compatibility of 'wisdom' and 'eschatology' as they undeniably coexisted in the final form and Synoptic readings of the sayings document. In particular, R.A. Edwards, C.E. Carlston and, more recently, M. Sato have shown that sayings in Q which we would characterize together as gnomai, for example, the Q gnomai of weather change (Luke 10:2 par; Luke 12:54–55 par Matt 16:2–3), are the medium of both sapiential and eschatological expression.[4]

Recent relegation of urgent eschatology to a later stage in the development of Jesus tradition has been partly bolstered by the assumption not merely that many gnomai *need* not be read eschatologically, but also that gnomic language as such is non-eschatological.

> The eschatological understanding of Jesus has not been able to account adequately for the strong component of *proverbial wisdom* present in the teachings of Jesus (particularly in Q...).[5]

In fact, however, neither eschatological (apocalyptic) nor sapiential literary conventions explain the rhetorical variety, ambiguity and pointedness of Q gnomai. Today's exaggerated appeals to Cynic sagehood as a model for Jesus and his followers have the advantage of recognizing the rhetoricity of habitual gnome-use: first-century Cynics and Christians were mining similar veins in Greco-Roman rhetorical culture.[6] Such rhetoricity, however, is radically open to both eschatological and sapiential topics. The point may be extended beyond Q: certainly in their uses of gnomai, gospel writers seem indifferent to any

---

[4] Carlston, "Wisdom," 108–116, esp. 112–113; R.A. Edwards, "An Approach to a Theology of Q," *JR* 51 (1971) 247–269; Sato, "Wisdom Statements"; cf. Schmithals, *Einleitung*, 224–6, 384–404; on Luke 10:2 par see L.E. Vaage, *Galilean Upstarts: Jesus' First Followers According to Q* (Valley Forge, PA, 1994) 111–114.

[5] D.E. Aune, "Eschatology (Early Christian)," *ABD* II (1992) 549–609.

[6] Vaage, *Galilean Upstarts*; Mack, *Lost Gospel*.

ideological incompatibility of wisdom and eschatology. Moreover, Paul's uses of sapiential and eschatological motifs (and gnomai) do not arise from discrete ideologies or social settings, they arise from different argumentative moments within Paul's rhetoric.

Much of the work of New Testament and Early Christian studies in the twentieth century has been devoted to identifying sets of master conventions or institutions within which to contextualize the ambiguous fragments of pre-gospel sayings tradition. Robbins is, of course, right that at the origins of gospel speech traditions "many different things may have been said, and the sequence of statements is often as important as the statements themselves."[7]

In place of the irretrievable performance contexts of specific pre-gospel traditions, therefore, it has been necessary to seek wider ideological and social-linguistic contexts in which to re-integrate and distinguish fragmentary rhetorics. Folklore and urgent (apocalyptic) eschatology have been the main options, now challenged by more nuanced, less literary models of (e.g., Cynic) sageliness and sectarian organization. Robbins is right that progymnasmatic rhetoric provides a vital context within which not only the gospels, but also their prevenient traditions can be interpreted with some clarity and historical integrity. This is so because the progymnasmatic tradition provides us with precise and extensive conventions for the contextualization of basic gospel forms in both spoken and written performance.

If we agree that Jesus did speak in public and that he liked parabolic and gnomic rhetoric, it is clear that his discourse and that of his successors could not possibly have consisted of disembodied, free-floating sayings. It is equally clear, however, that we cannot know in any credible detail the specific contexts of his speaking (except, perhaps, on the night before his arrest [1 Cor 11:23 par]). In addition, the "relative multivalence of linguistic forms over against their social field of application (*sozialer Verwendungsbereich*) evidently applies particularly to the smaller forms."[8] Finally, the atomistic approach of Early Christian scholarship to reconstructing and authenticating sayings material has added to this real problem by systematically isolating sayings from one another as well as from any imaginable historical

---

[7] Robbins, "Pre-Gospel Traditions," 134.

[8] Berger, *Exegese*, 34–35 (Berger's italics).

context.[9] The general context provided by progymnasmatic rhetoric is therefore doubly necessary for any successful approach to 'sayings' traditions.

On the other hand, the variety and multivalence of gnomic cores should not be exaggerated into semantic indeterminacy. In the progymnasmatic context, gnomai are not only highly flexible, they are readily memorable and repeatable in their core structures. In particular performances they were impressive and understandable to audiences in ways which were not wholly determined by contextualization: gnomic cores do preserve and transfer finite ranges of meaning between performances. Progymnasmatic and technical rhetoric also strongly confirm that gnomic sayings are recognizably a significant family of sayings types. One function of the previous chapter's interest in gnomai which are redactionally (re)deployed in one way or another is to show that the gospel writers were as conscious of Jesus' gnomai as they were of his parables (both are sometimes called *parabolai*).

In the absence of historically reliable information about specific performances of specific gnomai in Jesus' tradition, rhetorical analysis must accept some limitations, especially as regards the "social field of application." It is, however, perfectly feasible and rhetorically legitimate to examine gnomai (and gnomic cores) for intrinsic topicality. In Chapter Three, I noted C.E. Carlston's observation that among Synoptic gnomai some topics which are well attested in Greco-Roman and near eastern gnomic texts are underrepresented in gnomai attributed to Jesus: "education, personal character and habits, friendship, women and family relationships, ethnic matters, politics and prudence."[10]

More positively, four important sub-sets of Synoptic gnomai invite collective analysis in terms of specific families of topics and tropes: legality, personal character (*pace* Carlston), discipleship and eschatology. These four topical sub-sets are particularly noticeable among the gospels' most "anti-proverbial," "intensified" gnomai (Beardslee). It does happen, after all, that some gospel gnomai materially transcend in one or both of two ways the limited perspicuity and historical relevance of their Synoptic contexts. A gnome may be marked by such strong imagery as to pre-determine all but the details of reception, variation

---

[9] See Bultmann, *Geschichte*, 103; Schille, "Was ist ein Logion?" 175–177; Sanders, *Jesus and Judaism*, 16–17.

[10] Carlston, "Proverbs and Jesus," 98–99.

and interpretation: it carries its context within it (e.g., Mark 6:4 par). Alternatively or in addition, peculiarities in receptions of a gnome may allow a more than usually confident guess as to the historic range of its meanings: hence the historical interest of the *Wanderlogien*. Even Robbins acknowledges these possibilities for the intensification of gnome-use:

> There are, to be sure, special circumstances when a person said something that was striking, like "Ask not what your country can do for you; ask what you can do for your country."

Both biblical tradition and progymnasmatic education trained speakers and listeners to make circumstances special by saying something strikingly gnomic. Robbins' welcome call for "investigation of the rhetorical qualities of short statements themselves" is overdue.[11]

In what follows I will therefore begin to analyse a selection of gospel gnomai which are intrinsically intensified and topical. But I will also explore gospel gnomai which intrinsically belong to what Beardslee called the "field of intensification," gnomai which are not salient in rhetorical intensity or topicality, but which early Christian texts receive topically. That is, I will use strong intrinsic topicality in some gnomai and strong contextual topicality around some others to give my sample some depth and to maintain its connection with the large number of gospel gnomai which are neither intrinsically nor contextually intensified or related to key topics.

Above all, it is necessary to evaluate both intrinsically topical and topically received or deployed gnomai because both belong equally to the general class of analogical, separable, normative sayings: 'intensified' and 'ordinary' gnomai have the same collective claim to reflect Jesus' rhetoric and reflect the same conditions of continuous traditional variation and invention. There is no generic or tradition-historical distinction between sub-sets of gnomai. And there are very few individual gnomai which can be at the same time authenticated and interpreted apart from the recognition of their gnomic character.

I have already often pointed toward the group of gnomai and gnome-receptions which reflect legal topicality. Such topics have strong

---

[11] Robbins, "Pre-Gospel Traditions," 134; "Rhetorical Discussions of the Chreia," xiii.

antecedents in the Sophistic and Greek political origins of Greco-Roman rhetoric, but they have special urgency in Greco-Roman Jewish and, hence, early Christian rhetorics. Legal topics are not only immanent in gospel gnome-use; they are, of course, central to Jewish and Christian self-definition. But both in Jewish texts and in Greco-Roman rhetoric legal topicality has a distinct, though ambiguous, affinity for gnomic language.[12] Chapter Six will be centred on questions arising from legal topicality and normativity.

In the present chapter, I will divide my attention among eschatological gnomai, gnomai which recall the topic of discipleship, and those gnomai which are most strikingly 'ethical' in the rhetorical sense, that is, which seem to reflect most directly on the characterization of speakers, opponents or audiences. Each of these fields of topicality is in its own way controversial in the present context of Early Christian studies. Debate about topics of discipleship are central to current discussion of the role of Q traditions (especially those of the "mission" instructions, Luke/Q 10:2–16) in the beginnings of Christianity.[13] One of the better questions for historical Jesus research is still why, if at all, Jesus wanted disciples.

As for 'characterization' as a field of gnomic topicality, I have already recalled that Carlston listed "personal character" among common sapiential topics underrepresented among gospel sayings. It is essential therefore to distinguish the parenetic topics of the sage/master/father advising his disciple/son on comportment from the different topics of a speaker's rhetorical self-characterization (*ethos*) and characterization of the other agents in rhetorical exchange. It is usually the Johannine Jesus who is accused of talking excessively and dogmatically about himself. In choice and deployment of gnomai, however, the putative—and at least partly historical—protagonist of the other gospels likewise reflects pointedly on himself as public agent. In this, Synoptic gnome-use confirms Aristotle's basic insight that gnome-use is essentially 'ethical', i.e., about rhetorical characterization (*Rh.* II 21,16 =1395a; III 17,9=1418a). Gnomic rhetoric in pre-gospel tradition thus emerges as an important, though ambiguous and unexpected antecedent of christological reflection.

---

[12] Berger, *Formgeschichte*, 121–124.
[13] Vaage, *Galilean Upstarts*, 17 and n. 3.

'Eschatology' and its false antinomy 'wisdom' remain the most difficult of the topical categories I propose to handle. Neither is easily defined in itself, so that 'eschatology' in particular oscillated vaguely since Schweitzer and Bultmann between connotations of existential ultimacy and intimations of critical futurity. It is easy to see why in the first half of the twentieth century apocalyptic eschatology should have seized European imaginations. But the appeal of eschatology is not merely to modern exegetical preferences for alienation and interim ethics.

Bultmann's detection of an authentically 'eschatological mood' and Beardslee's identification of paradoxical and hyperbolic 'intensification' among wisdom sayings attributed to Jesus reflect a recurring turn in gnomic rhetoric from 'normality' to something else. Wisdom literature and eschatology have in common an impulse toward authority and, perhaps hence, toward gnomai. It is not arbitrary to use 'eschatology' to describe gnomai and/or gnome-uses which go beyond rhetorical persuasion or characterization to become oracular. Greco-Roman antiquity recognized clearly that many gnomai were oracular; moreover, some surviving oracles are gnomic (e.g., Titus 1:12, quoted from Epimenides *On Oracles*).

> When he wished to apply a gnome with greater force, Seneca represented it as an oracular saying....We find the same tendency in the gospels when gnomai like "No prophet is accepted in his home town" (Luke 4:24) are introduced by *amen lego humin* as Amen-sayings and therefore marked as revelations.

The use of gnomai to claim quasi-oracular authority for scientific, medical and rhetorical maxims was typical of the Ionian philosopher-poets (e.g., Heraclitus) and of the Sophists (e.g., Protagoras). But, as D. Lührmann has lately pointed out, even the dominical '*logia*' of which Papias wrote his rhetorically self-conscious '*exegesis*' were 'oracles' rather than 'sayings'.[14] It may be rhetorically helpful to ask whether and why some gnomai seem more oracular than others in content and/or

---

[14] Berger, "Hellenistische Gattungen," 1056 (quoted); Lührmann, "Q: Sayings of Jesus or Logia?" in Piper, *The Gospel behind the Gospels*, 97–116; M. Black, "Use of Rhetorical Terminology in Papias on Mark and Matthew," *JSNT* 37 (1989) 31–41; cf. Eusebius *Hist. Eccl.* III 39,1.

reception as an indicator of 'eschatological' topicality. At any rate, I shall allow myself to speak of 'eschatology' wherever the topic of present-versus-future is treated in ways that augur the end of human agency.

Personality, discipleship and normativity in Matthew 8:22 par (M. Hengel)

In this chapter and the next, I try to show something of the relative distinctiveness of gnome-use attributed to Jesus by pointing to a few salient topical turns intrinsic to substantial minorities of Synoptic gnomai and/or implied by peculiarities in their receptions. The proposed strategy therefore is to narrow from defining Greco-Roman gnome, to Synoptic gnome and now to topically more specific gnomai in the Synoptic gospels while remaining basically oriented toward understanding categories of sayings rather than individual sayings. This is partly a response to the twin problems of authenticity and perspicuity in relations to individual small units; I am more confident of authenticating and interpreting gnome-use as a general and unusually continuous aspect of rhetorical tradition from Jesus to the gospels than I am of persuasively authenticating and interpreting individual gnomai. The thesis of this book is therefore not that some gnomai are authentic sayings of Jesus. It is instead that Greco-Roman rhetoric explains the preferential persistence of large numbers of gnomai in Synoptic tradition and that this gnomic habit in the gospels originates with Jesus. Individual gnomai, authentic or not, are therefore interpreted as examples of the general habit and its specific nuances within Greco-Roman gnomic rhetoric.

In principle such an approach complements movement from the other end, beginning with gnomic topical and formal particularity and moving, thence, toward generalization. In practice, however, arguments from individual sayings require coherent generic categories against which relative individuality can be defined. In the context of his well-known argument against overreliance on sayings tradition in historical Jesus research, E.P. Sanders mentions one impressive exception:

> Martin Hengel has argued that 'progress in Synoptic research to a great extent depends on...detailed analysis of small units', which is exemplified

by his own treatment of Matt. 8.21f.//Luke 9.59f. Every passage must be studied individually, employing 'redaction and form criticism, plus *Religionsgeschichte*'. It is hard to argue with Hengel's view, in light of the dazzling success of its application. I think Hengel's book is a masterpiece, possibly the best single treatment of a synoptic pericope ever done.... Hengel's remarkable success, unfortunately, does not show that the method will continue to pay off as one goes through the synoptics. Hengel picked the right passage.[15]

Matthew 8:22 and Luke 9:60 are clearly an egregious case, one in which the notorious 'criterion of double dissimilarity' actually works, and on a worthwhile fragment. Yet one pre-condition, not specifically recognized by Hengel, for the simultaneous uniqueness and interpretability of the gnome of the dead burying the dead is its use, after all, of familiar patterns of gnomic rhetoric.

Foxes have lairs and birds of the sky have dwellings, but the Son of Man has nowhere to lay his head. (Luke 9:58/Matt 8:20)

Leave the dead to bury their dead. (Luke 9:60/Matt 8:22)

No one who puts hand to plough and looks back is fit for the Kingdom of God. (Luke 9:62)

Matthew 8:22 is thus unique in the degree to which it combines so many strategies for gnomic intensification, but it does so within a strikingly conventional gnomic form—and within topics which are attested elsewhere in Jesus tradition. There are other gnomai which are urgently, imperatively normative (*aphes*); others are topically related to discipleship and/or legal duties, even in an apparently antinomian sense (e.g., Mark 2:27); others use similar imagery (e.g., Mark 12:27 par).

Matthew 8:22 stands out in its selection of a particularly universal and sacred norm (the burial of the dead) as the basis of analogy. The saying is, however, clearly not a new norm for community burial practice: although normatively imperative, its range is restricted to the individual auditor as an exception to existing norms. The topic 'burial' serves mainly to index the topic of 'law' itself. The gnome is therefore

---

[15] Sanders, *Jesus and Judaism*, 132–133; Hengel, *Nachfolge*, 3.

a norm about normativity itself. Its speaker is asserting a right to obedience which pre-empts basic duties of Law. The gnome is thus overwhelmingly 'ethical' in the rhetorical (nearly christological) sense. Because of this the gnome cannot be dismissed as metaphorical or hyperbolic: the 'dead' are spoken of in two senses, but the transfer of meaning is eschatological and personally oracular rather than metaphorical.

Hengel's unqualified insistence on the eschatological quality of Matthew 8:22 still reflects the unbridled influence of an eschatological hermeneutic in New Testament studies, as Leif Vaage has pointed out. This gnome, like most, can be read with historical credibility as reflecting an immediate social horizon even more than it reflects the supernatural, eschatological liabilities of being dead without burial. Still, Vaage has not persuaded me to abandon 'eschatology' as an exegetical category here. The gnome is not only about the absolute summons to discipleship and the absolute *ethos* of the summoner; it also ominously implies the consequences of non-obedience and suggests an expectation of miraculous reversal in social order as the consequence of leaving the dead behind.[16]

The peculiarity of this gnome of the unburied dead is the convergence in it of intensifying factors which in less imposing combinations also mark other gnomai. Hengel's exegesis of Matthew 8:22 is so uniquely persuasive precisely because he intuitively selected the saying which epitomizes gnomic intensification in the Synoptics. Luke 9:60 and Matthew 8:22 are the epitome of what Beardslee called 'anti-proverb'.[17]

I think that some recognition of this gnome's combined uniqueness and typicality is implied by its unusual reception in Synoptic contexts. The immediate context for the gnome of the dead is in a series of two (Matt 8:19–22) or three (Luke 9:57–62) sayings-chreiai. Formally, these are among the simplest, most obviously 'chriic', chreiai in the gospels. In the context of progymnasmatic rhetoric, it is clear that this need not have been the case: the gospel writers were not bound to any 'pure form'. Indeed, they and their listeners had been trained by experience

---

[16] Vaage, *Galilean Upstarts*, 90–93; cf. Sato, "Wisdom Statements," 141 n.10 "[P]rophets are also called 'eschatological' as long as they await or witness something decisively new for the destiny of the people."

[17] Beardslee, "Saving One's Life."

if not by schooling to expect considerable liberty in the expansion or elaboration of chreiai—or in their simplified presentation. That is, the authors of Q, Matthew and Luke chose the austerely thrifty presentation of these gnomic chreiai over against real options for either narrative or argumentative elaboration.

There are rhetorically good reasons for the minimal chriic framing of Luke 9:60 and, indeed, of the other two gnomai in the passage (verses 58 and 62). Above all, the gnome of the unburied dead implies with unusual clarity its own optimum narrative context:[18] the force of the gnome is qualified only by its application to following the speaker. The explicit mention of the unburied parent prevents any merely metaphoric reduction of the gnome. The chreia, Luke 9:59–60 and Matthew 8:21–22, thus helps the hearer contextualize the radical topic of Law within the minimally safer topics of discipleship and *ethos*. In other words, this remains a strongly gnomic chreia in which the narrative remains epexegetical, in progymnasmatic terms a minimal elaboration of gnome as chreia.[19]

Much the same can be said of the other chreiai in the series; they are rhetorically dominated by their gnomai. This is not the place to vote on whether the third chreia, Luke 9:61–62, was in Q or not.[20] In any case, both it and the chreia on homelessness, Luke 9:57–58 and Matthew 8:19–20, are like the gnome of the dead in their strongly gnomic character: all three are determined overwhelmingly by their gnomic punch-lines. The result is either a pair (Matt) or a triplet (Luke) of closely-matched chreiai. In Luke the overarching topic of discipleship is made even more explicit by the use of 'follow' (*akolouthein*) as "the first word of direct speech in three successive units" and by minimal designation of Jesus' interlocutors ('someone', verse 57; 'another', verses 59 and 61).[21] In both the Lucan and the Matthaean series, though, the extreme plainness of the chreiai highlights the distinctive rhetoric of the gnomai themselves. There is some performantial and hermeneutical variation between Lucan and Matthaean redactions of the

---

[18]   Hengel, *Nachfolge*, 5–6.

[19]   V.K. Robbins, "Foxes," in B.L. Mack and V.K. Robbins, *Patterns of Persuasion in the Gospels* (Sonoma, CA, 1989) 69–84, 74.

[20]   Jacobson, *The First Gospel*, 133; J.S. Kloppenborg, *Q Parallels: Synopsis, Critical Notes and Concordance* (Sonoma, CA, 1988) 64.

[21]   Robbins, "Foxes," 76.

chreia-contexts, but both the shared gnomai resist variation: there is no need to reconstruct any 'original form.'

Apart from its contextualization, the gnome (Luke 9:58 par Matt 8:20) of the introductory chreia in the series might have been read as a melancholic proverb of the human condition,[22] couched in the commonplace language of animal fables. Again, this is not the place to adjudicate on the relative authenticity claims of differing usages of that odd locution, '[the] Son of [the] Man'. Still, the minimum and only assured connotation of the Synoptic Son of Man mannerism is that it is exclusively placed on the lips of Jesus: the gnome of the fish and birds has an internal marker that designates Jesus. In Synoptic tradition, it is redundant to name the speaker of a Son of Man saying, as happens in the chreia attribution-formula (Luke 9:57, Matt 8:19). Jesus does not need to *be* the Son of Man, for only he gets to *say*, "the Son of Man." Whatever it means, the mannerism reflects on Jesus' unique rhetorical *ethos*.

At the same time, the generic plurals, 'foxes' and 'birds', make a collective, generic connotation of 'Son of Man' unavoidable here, despite the Synoptic formula's contrasting deictic singularity. Contextualized in Luke 9:20 and Matthew 8:20 this intrinsic ambiguity of the gnome between deictic peculiarity and generic collectivity is resolved by assigning the gnome, plausibly, to the topic of discipleship. Intrinsically, or rather in the broader context of a tradition in which only Jesus talks about the Son of Man, the saying is aggressively non-proverbial, that is, rhetorically ethical: the universal normative connotation in 'son of man' is retained and yet also turned into a much narrower, but more intense normative reference to Jesus and his imitators.

Strangely, it is only in the third chreia of the longer Lucan series that V. Robbins recognizes a gnome ("maxim"), Luke 9:62. Why does Robbins recognize a gnome in the ploughing-and-kingdom saying and not in the two preceding chreia punch-lines? Robbins refers to Aristotle's definition of gnome in terms of "generalization" (*Rh.* II 21,2 =1394a) and to his interest in the quasi-logical use of gnomai in enthymemes.

---

[22] Bultmann, *Geschichte*, 27 n. 3, 102.

In a rhetorical setting, then, it is customary to introduce the conclusion first, to provide a rationale in a maxim which follows, and to omit the second premise [of the implied syllogism].

In the sequence in Luke, the maxim in the third unit provides a general premise (a rationale) for the deliberative exhortations before it.... Prior to the maxim, the only basis for the exhortation was Jesus' authoritative *ethos*.... But the third unit introduces an argumentative reason why he should leave all attachments and go.... When Jesus' speech moves beyond the exhibition of *ethos*...in cleverness and exhortation to the exhibition of *ethos* in a maxim, it has interwoven inductive and deductive reasoning.[23]

Robbins here is more Aristotelean than Aristotle. Within ancient rhetoric Aristotle emphasizes gnomic generalization and enthymematic approximation of syllogism far more heavily than either his predecessors or his successors. The category of 'generalization' is problematic as a description of the use and appeal of proverbs and gnomai. Indeed, modern paroimiology is founded largely on Jolles' insight that proverbs are almost never generalizations, but are rather typical, topical, and therefore reusable specifications, presented in a quasi-generalized form.[24]

As we saw in Chapter One, even Aristotle repeatedly recognized not only the overwhelmingly 'ethical' quality of gnome-use, but also the limited analogy between rhetorical reasonableness (expressed in gnomai and enthymemes) and logical reasoning, deductive or inductive. Aristotle thus recommends against using enthymemes in passages dealing with character and recommends instead the use of gnomai in such 'ethical' arguments and narratives as Luke 9 (*Rh.* III 17,7–8= 1418a). In post- (and probably pre-) Aristotelean rhetoric *ad personam* formulation of gnomai was an important counterbalance to the appearance of generalization.

Certainly there is nothing in Luke 9:58 and 9:60 or in their use which would have prevented Aristotle from recognizing them as generalizations and as gnomai, though Aristotle would have recognized these as risk-taking gnomai. Luke 9:57–62 is thus clearly a series of gnomic chreiai and not formally an argumentation. When Robbins looks

---

[23] Robbins, "Foxes," 78–79.

[24] A. Jolles, *Einfache Formen* (Tübingen, 1930, rpr. 1968) esp. 153, 158; see H.-J. Hermisson, *Studien zur israelitischen Spruchweisheit* (WMANT 28; Neukirchen-Vluyn, 1968) 29–32 for application to biblical forms.

for a single "underlying syllogism," with only one gnome, verse 62, as its delayed premise and verse 60 as its anticipated conclusion, he is working harder than he should to assimilate the Lucan series to the model of "complete argument" as rationalizing "elaboration." Luke 9:61–62 is no more gnomic than the two preceding gnomic chreiai. In fact, the series of three brief, strongly gnomic chreiai linking topics of self-characterization and discipleship is remarkable for its rhetorical uniformity. It is therefore misleading to conclude that in the triple chreia series "we have the beginning steps of an elaboration."[25]

The ploughman gnome (Luke 9:62) is both like and unlike the preceding gnomai of the foxes and birds (verse 58 par) and of the unburied dead (verse 60 par) with respect to normativity and proverbiality. Both the earlier gnomai have internal clues suggesting a narrowed normative range: the second person singular address in the gnome of the dead and the Son of Man language in the gnome of the foxes and birds. Formally, Luke 9:62 rather suggests universal normativity ("No one who...") within the topic of the Reign of God. Robbins rightly implies that this last gnome in the series is normatively the least radical: it depends uncritically on the domestic proverbiality of the ploughman as a pan-Mediterranean byword for concentration.[26] There is, moreover, a strong element of intertextuality with the topics (prophetic discipleship) and perhaps the narrative of 1 Kings 19:19–21. Carlston is doubtless right that "many modern interpreters probably overinterpret Luke 9:62...because of its context," but it is surely overstating the point to say that "as an isolated saying it hardly goes beyond what everyone who has ever ploughed already knows."[27] The rustic imagery of ploughing is proverbial enough, but it is more than perverse urbanity and an awareness of the less inflexible calling of Elisha which suggest that the ploughman gnome deliberately exceeds proverbial good sense.

The two gnomai which frame Luke 9:60 use a similar strategy to bias reception away from proverbiality and toward topics of authoritative self-characterization by the speaker, discipleship and prophetic, if not eschatological urgency. That is, both Luke 9:58 and 9:62 use clichés associated indelibly with Jesus' speech habits to specify the normative range of the gnomai; formal, chriic ascription to Jesus and identification

---

[25] Robbins, "Foxes," 80–81.
[26] Robbins, "Foxes," 81.
[27] Carlston, "Proverbs and Jesus," 103.

of discipleship as the controlling topic in the chreia series and Luke's surely redactional reference to the Reign of God in verse 60b make the topicality of the gnomai only slightly more explicit and homogeneous. In fact, the use of 'Son of Man' and 'Reign of God' in two such closely related gnomai is a rare bridge over the chasm between two probably authentic, yet strangely segregated symbolic categories in Jesus' speech.

Regardless of the series' history, or of the authenticity or redactionality of the individual gnomai and their framing chreiai, Matthew 8:19–22 and Luke 9:57–62 have an unusual claim to represent the speech of Jesus. As Hengel's analysis showed, if any single saying is both authentic and representative of Jesus, it is the burial gnome (Luke 9:60 and Matt 8:22). But it is of even greater significance that it and the other gnomai here are gnomai: they are not reducible to "single sayings." Instead they are both typical and unique instances of a more widely attested rhetorical pattern and of the topics most often associated with its use under Jesus' influence.

The gnomai in Matthew 8:19–22 and Luke 9:57–62 are also a challenging problem for chreia-driven rhetorical criticism of the gospel tradition. They are, as Jacobson notes, "formally the best examples of chreiai in Q." Excepting Luke 9:62, they were likely elements of Q at a stage of its composition when formally simple chreiai were still relatively rare.[28] I think this suggests the pre-Q juxtaposition of the chreia of the foxes and birds with the chreia of the unburied dead. On the grounds of normative tensions among Luke 9:57 (on voluntary discipleship), verse 58 (on involuntary homelessness) and verses 59–60, Jacobson has reconstructed a plausible, though unverifiable pre-history of the Q antecedents to Matthew 8:19–22 and Luke 9:57–62.

> Thus it would appear that Q 9:59–60a represents the nucleus of the brief collection dealing with "discipleship." Q 9:58 was added later, and Q 9:57b was created as a means by which to insert 9:58.... But...Q 9:57b and 9:58 do not really fit together very well; this means that the context is artificial.[29]

From a rhetorical point of view, all contexts for gnome-performance are artificial and these are not that incongruous. But Jacobson may be right

---

[28]   Jacobson, *The First Gospel*, 51.
[29]   Jacobson, *The First Gospel*, 136.

about the developmental process, in which case the chreia series is older than Q and the gnomai, Luke 9:58 and 60a, are older than the chreia series. Certainly, these chreiai are semantically, rhetorically dominated by their gnomai. Moreover, at least in their rather long Synoptic literary tradition, the gnomai have undergone less variation than their chriic contextualizations. If Luke 9:62 is a Lucan redactional addition to the Q series, it must be granted that it is an addition in kind, a fine imitation of the preceding gnomai and not an arbitrary distortion or elaboration of their rhetoric.

Wisdom's children (Matt 11:19 par Luke 7:35)

Incidentally, it may well be that the chreia series in Q was linked to the preceding Q context (Matt 11:16–19 and Luke 7:31–35) not only by the topic of rejection (of Wisdom's children and Jesus' followers respectively), but also by the importance in the earlier, non-chriic passage of its concluding gnome (Matt 11:19 Luke 7:35).[30] The gnome of Wisdom's children is very like the gnomai of the chreia series, including Luke 9:62: like them it is highly 'ethical'; like them, its ethical quality regulates topics of personal religious adherence (family; discipleship); like them it explicitly, though ambiguously invokes an important symbol of religious normativity (Wisdom; Son of Man; burial; the Reign of God).

The significance which Hengel detected in Matthew 8:22 is therefore not confined to its unique qualities. In fact, the gnome of the unburied dead is typical of Synoptic gnomai except in the density of gnomic rhetorical qualities and topics which it dramatically combines. All gnomai use analogy and connotivity to express intrinsic normativity; many do so in relation to topics of self-characterization, legality and discipleship (or elective relationship); even more are read in relation to such topics. It is essential to interpret Matthew 8:22 and other exceptional gnomai as limit-stretching instances of a much wider rhetorical pattern in Synoptic tradition and in Greco-Roman rhetorical traditions. It is also important to see that the limit-stretching involved in such cases is not only a linguistic exploration of poetic possibilities; it is profoundly linked to issues of public (sectarian) normativity.

---

[30] Jacobson, *The First Gospel*, 130–131, 137.

Normativity and topicality

Clearly there is no possibility here of exhaustively analysing any, let alone every, gnome. It is still necessary, however, to review closely a large number of individual gnomai. The double task of rhetorical criticism involves balancing the intrinsic rhetorics of particular gnomai with the general, generic rhetoric of their reception, invention and variation as a category. I think this can be done by surveying the Synoptic gnomai under several sample headings, none of which is exhaustive, and each of which represents a line of tension amongst gnomai and in the sayings tradition generally.

My basic contention throughout this book has been that the category gnome is historically more significant for pre-gospel rhetoric than any rhetorically random sample of more or less probably authentic sayings. By the same token, however, it is also the category gnome which is ultimately central to Synoptic tradition, rather than any particular instance of gnome—even Matthew 8:22. The topical headings under which I will catalogue are therefore only partly abstracted from the internal rhetoric of the gnomai themselves and of their receptions. The topics of (anti-)proverbiality, discipleship (elective personal allegiance), eschatology (oracularity), specific *ethos* (individual particularity), and law also reflect both the conventions of Greco-Roman rhetoric and the peculiarities of early Christian rhetoric. That is, topical headings have been selected with an emphasis on the normative function of gnome. Topicality is the consequence of rhetorical normativity.

The normativity essential to gnome offers no pretext for rehabilitating a notion of a social setting peculiar to each speech pattern (*Sitz im Leben*): rhetorical normativity is related to social norms mimetically or even dialectically, with room for the play of wit in connotation and function. This means also that the topical headings which I am using to guide my analysis are not meant to designate mutually exclusive or commensurable sub-categories; their relevance is heuristic not taxonomic and depends in large part on their interaction. Two of these, 'eschatology' and 'proverbiality' refer less to topics than to normative moods, present more or less in any gnome, and provide an inclusive frame for the three more narrowly normative topical fields, 'discipleship', 'individual particularity' and 'legality'.

P. Crépeau's typology of proverbial normativity provides an appropriate vocabulary for describing some of the normative complexity of gnome-use. As we saw in Chapter One, Crépeau describes normative language in terms of normative intensity and range.[31] The main problem with normative intensity (observation, prescription or command) is that it need not correspond simply either to grammatical mood or to social norms: a grammatical indicative may encode a rhetorical command; the rhetorically mandatory norm may well, in turn, be ineffectual in the actual social settings where it is performed.

Range (universal, specific or optional) is also often formally ambiguous. Crépeau noticed that proverbs in many cultures often refer explicitly to specific socially recognized roles or categories of persons (e.g. by profession or craft). Gnomai in Greco-Roman antiquity and in the New Testament index similar roles (e.g., healer, prophet, ploughman, the dead). Such indices often help to define rhetorical *ethos* and individual particularity, but do not do so automatically or unambiguously. Crépeau classified normative range according to whether such marked role-designations were exclusive ('specific') or voluntary ('optional'). Frequently, though, they could be either, even both (e.g., the dead) within the analogical structure of a given gnome. All gnomai are analogical; moreover many are also marked by turns of metaphor, metonymy or hyperbole. Analogically, "Let the dead bury their dead" is about more than funeral practice, though its potential implications for funeral practice could not be ignored. In addition, though, the double reference to the "dead" forces the hearer to allow for another level of rhetorical normativity: the gnome is not reducible to "let someone else bury the dead." It thus combines the specific normativity of the summons to discipleship with the undefined (optional?) normativity of the "dead" grave diggers. Finally, normative role-designations in gnomai may refer to the speaker, addressee or others

Normative range exposes the often severe limitations of our insight into normativity in New Testament societies. In Roman Palestine, normative diversity and conflict allow only tentative and partial association of even the most explicit normative formulae with particular fields of regulation or social functions. Thus, for example, a gnome referring explicitly to the master/disciple relation is, by itself, only indirectly relevant to the history of discipleship or to the historical relationship between Jesus and the Twelve, as the parallel reception in some contexts of a lord/slave analogy shows (Matt 10:24; John 13:15;

---

[31] Crépeau, "Définition," 298–303.

15:20 cf. Luke 6:40). Still, attention to normative range in this case underlines that the master/disciple relation may be scarcely more optional than the lord/slave relation to which it is parallel.

Finally, the relative importance of intrinsic and extrinsic, receptional indications of topicality will vary among topical categories: 'Individual particularity' covers gnomai in which the speaker's *ethos* in relation to the hearer is defined with special precision; this can only be determined from the (intrinsic) form of the gnome itself, though contextualization may confirm the assignment. 'Proverbiality' by contrast is primarily an extrinsic, social quality: proverbs are proverbs only in relation to actual speech communities which recognize them. 'Anti-proverbial' intensification, however, may be marked by intrinsic, hermeneutical variation of the proverbial core: "A stitch in time costs extra." In general though, receptional, extrinsic considerations function as subsidiary or corrective indices of the topical and normative qualities of gnomai.

Intrinsic and extrinsic eschatology in gnomic rhetoric

I noticed above an increasing willingness to acknowledge the complementarity, even at times the simultaneity, of wisdom and eschatology in and among sententious sayings, especially in the Q material. Such an acknowledgement is not simply a defensive fudge by those of us who are reluctant to abandon 'eschatology' as a hermeneutical category. Gnome is neither essentially eschatological nor essentially sapiential; it comprises both and goes beyond both in its rhetorical normativity. Thus, its quasi-oracular, pre-contextual style makes gnome an attractive vehicle for both attitudes and indeed a natural common ground between them. Gnomic rhetoric is thus (along with parable) a valuable basis upon which to build a sensitivity to both fundamental moods in early Christian tradition, without being forced to choose between alleged sapiential (Wisdom) and eschatological (Apocalyptic) literary conventions.

> Jesus as a 'Teacher', who used so-called 'wisdom' forms and Jesus, as 'eschatological charismatic', as 'messianic' prophet, are thus not at all contradictions.[32]

---

[32] Hengel, *Nachfolge*, 53.

Eschatology in Jesus' tradition is too well-attested to be dismissed as fragmentary, yet too sharply differentiated to support collective exegesis as a unitary category. A gnomic approach to Synoptic tradition and its literature offers the most coherent and comprehensive perspective possible on eschatological rhetoric and on its basis in more ordinary argumentation and characterization.

> The relative disconnectedness of sacred teaching, future prophecy and ethics, i.e., of materials which present themselves as sapiential, apocalyptic and rabbinic in Jesus tradition, along with their tradition-historical segregation...would seem to justify the most divergent interpretative emphases.[33]

It is in this latter respect that 'eschatology' even more than 'wisdom' differs from gnome as an exegetical category: gnome is a coherent, however atomized, rhetorical category with a relatively unitary, continuous tradition-critical and cultural significance. Even 'wisdom saying' can be related to specific literary forms, admonition and instruction. 'Eschatology' is a congeries of topics and styles not specific to any particular rhetorical pattern or literary type (including apocalyptic). Bultmann was wrong to evoke eschatology as a virtual criterion of authenticity in logia attributed to Jesus; he was right, however, to speak of eschatology as a mood, and as a mood which cannot be ignored in the continuum of early gospel rhetorics.[34]

Gnome is rare among gospel rhetorical patterns as it is intrinsically connected with the discrete complexes of Son of Man language (Matt 8:20 par; Mark 2:27–28; 14:21 par; Matt 24:28) and with Reign of God symbolism (Luke 9:62; Matt 19:12, cf. Mark 3:24–25). At the same time, most gospel gnomai do not contain either mannerism; gnome-use thus provides a background against which those abstractly symbolic mannerisms of Jesus' rhetoric are recognizable as such, even if their specific connotations remain obscure. Gnome-use provides some of the otherwise lost 'connectedness' in rhetorical (including eschatological) tradition attributed to Jesus.

Comparison between gnome and parable (*mythos*) may help to clarify the relation which I see between gnomai and the eschatological

---

[33] G. Klein, "Eschatologie IV: Neues Testament," *TRE* X (1982) 270–299, 271.
[34] Bultmann, *Geschichte*, 110.

moods of the gospels and, with due reserve, Jesus. Not every parable is strictly about the Reign of God.[35] Indeed, almost none (the dialogue Matt 21:28–32 is the rule-proving exception) is intrinsically and explicitly about God's Reign, that is, beyond an introductory formula. Moreover, the Reign of God mannerism cannot wholly or uncontroversially be labelled 'eschatology'. Finally, although by no means every parable or every gnome is an authentic speech of Jesus, gnomic rhetoric is, like parabolic rhetoric, generically typical of Jesus' authentic speech habits as well as generically typical of progymnasmatic rhetoric.[36]

Apart from their shared claim to generic authenticity, both gnomai and parables are essential to any account of the literary rhetorics of the gospel written tradition and specifically to any account of gospel eschatology. At the literary level, it remains impossible to discuss the Reign of God without a rhetorical or poetic theory of parable to replace Mark's oracular parable theory. Gnome-use, however, is an even less dispensable witness to the singularity and flexibility of the Reign of God and Son of Man symbols in Synoptic eschatologies.

Eschatological variation within and among gnomic cores

In the measure you measure it shall be measured to you—and more so!
It shall be given to whomever has, and taken from whoever has not!
(Mark 4:24b–25)

Relatively few gnomai are strongly and intrinsically eschatological in the sense that they are dominated by an express normative tension between the present and an urgent, terminal future. The relation between these and the less eschatological majority is nicely caught in the dissonance between the aggravated reversal of the future in Mark 4:25 and the harmonious proportionality of present and future in the core gnome of 4:24 and its parallels and complements (Matt 7:1–2, 7 par and Luke 6:38), all of which are received as basically eschatological references in their Synoptic contexts.

---

[35] Berger, *Formgeschichte*, 41.
[36] Beavis, "Parable and Fable."

The doubly attested gnome of cross-bearing (Mark 8:35 par Q 14:27[37]) sets present and future even more strikingly over against each other—and within the topic of fitness for discipleship (cf. Luke 9:62). Or again, Mark 9:43–47 contrasts characteristically with the other triple gnome of self-mutilation, Matthew 19:12, in that the Marcan gnome presents a specific, oracular, eschatological norm while the Matthaean sentence gives an optional norm, extrapolated from natural and social order.

The two salt gnomai, the disturbingly oracular Mark 9:49 and Mark 9:50 (par Q 14:34), differ strikingly from one another, as do the Marcan and Q versions of the shared gnome. Both in Mark and in Q-influenced contextualizations, both sayings are both intrinsically and in their reception eschatological. Even the Q gnome is no mere prudential advice to disciples; it implies a unique crisis of membership which is forcefully underlined in the otherwise pointless receptional supplement, Q 14:35, with its bald threat of exclusion from the renewal community.[38]

A difference of eschatological intensity is also notable within a single gnomic core between Mark 9:35, 10:43 and their parallels on the one hand and Mark 10:31 and its parallels. The former group is more programmatic than eschatological in its pastoral normativity, though as expressions of Jesus *ethos* the positive valuation of images of servant-hood and slavery would have eschatological overtones in any Christian context we can document. In contrast, however, the plural norm, Mark 10:31 par (cf. Matt 22:14), has an inescapably temporal stress. Intrinsically, Mark 13:31 and its parallels are explicitly eschatological in imagery and in the expectation of a discontinuous future determined by Jesus' oracular rhetoric. Even in the Q gnome (Matt 5:18 par Luke 16:17) an eschatological horizon like that of the Marcan oracle is argumentatively presupposed, though without being unambiguously espoused or rejected as the normative horizon within which to receive the Law. Thus, as A.J. Dewey has argued, "it would not be necessary to argue that" Q 17:1 "presupposes an apocalyptic Jesus," but it is

---

[37] Cf. D. Seeley, "Blessings and Boundaries: Interpretations of Jesus' Death in Q," in *Early Christianity, Q and Jesus*, ed. J.S. Kloppenborg and L.E. Vaage=*Semeia* 55 (1991) 131–146.

[38] Jacobson, *The First Gospel*, 224.

clearly not possible to treat the gnome as a wisdom proverb without oracular, eschatological overtones:

> Q 16:17 goes beyond the immediately experiential in its vision.... The image of cosmic collapse is hardly an everyday sight.[39]

In one last example of this kind, (Matt 18:7 par Luke 17:1 versus Mark 9:42, 14:21 par, cf. *Gos. Thom.* 11), it is particularly clear that the rhetorically significant differentiation is not between eschatological and non-eschatological or between future and realized eschatologies. All performances of this gnome are intrinsically and receptionally eschatological, but they differ in normative range. This continuity and variation is especially clear if we follow Bultmann in presupposing a background of pre-Christian proverbiality, from which the gospel performances are dramatically distanced. Both Mark 14:21 and Q 17:1 are curses. They indicate specific, individual application, which even in Q at least permits a narrative reference to Jesus' betrayal as the element of non-proverbial analogy. The normative range of Mark 9:42 is more optional. Mark 14:21 is even more specific than the Q gnome: the Son of Man is opposed to "that man." Mark 9:42 and Q 17:1–2 share a supplementary indication of normative range in "these little ones." In contrast to a hypothetical proverb, however, all these synoptic performances are formally oracular and eschatological.

Not all unambiguously eschatological sayings (e.g., Mark 2:19b par; 13:13 par; Luke 15:8, 9; to some extent 23:31) can be so tidily paired with less intense yet still implicitly eschatological turnings of closely related gnomic core analogies. The strategy of pairing is useful, however, as an illustration of just how finely and variously tuned broadly eschatological language can be. Quite different accents of expectation may be given to closely related gnomic core performances. Like 'orality', 'eschatology' is most useful as a comparative category, with an uneven and uncharted gradient from sharply eschatological to timelessly proverbial-sounding gnomai.

This may be illustrated with reference to gnomai which, like many parables, draw upon the imagery of natural cycles. Late modern city-dwellers need to remember that such imagery indexes not only cyclical

---

[39] Quoting A.J. Dewey, "Quibbling Over Serifs," *Forum* 5/2 (1989) 109–120, 116; Bultmann, *Geschichte*, 155.

predictability and dependability, but also mortal weakness, urgency and hazard. Nature imagery stands in an archetypally rich relation to ultimate hopes and fears. The richness is in evidence in Synoptic practice: e.g., in the mainly, though variously eschatological receptions of the tree/fruit, tree/fire, and fire/salt relations (Matt 7:16 par, 12:33; 7:19, and 3:10 par, Luke 23:31; and Mark 9:49 and 50). Equally pregnant imagery of planting (Matt 15:13), harvest (Matt 9:37 par, cf. John 4:35), weather (Matt 16:2 and Luke 12:54–55, again cf. John 4:35!), death and burial (Matt 24:28 par; 8:22 par) is certainly received as eschatological.

Such images are also to some degree intrinsically eschatological in contrast with equally conventional animal imagery, which seems to require non-figurative specification for an eschatological reading: the false prophets in Matthew 7:15 or the Son of Man in Matthew 8:20 par (contrast Matt 10:16; 29 par). The central point is this question of degree, of the particular relativity and flexibility of the eschatological aspect of gnomic sayings marked in these cases by imagery which is intrinsically prone to eschatological reception, which indeed could hardly be attributed to Jesus without eschatological undertones, but which might also be heard more prosaically, even in Synoptic context.[40]

The seven gnomic Quatrains[41] present a special balance of eschatological undertones in the gnomai themselves with overtones in their poetic reception. That is, in each case the quatrain development of an initial gnome emphasizes its eschatological relevance. But such eschatological inferences come as a surprise: four of the basic gnomai (Matt 6:22a par; Luke 16:10; Mark 2:21 par; Matt 10:24 par) are among the intrinsically least eschatological in the Synoptics; the other three (Matt 6:24a par; Matt 7:6a [=*Did.* 9:5]; Matt 10:26b) are more available for eschatological interpretation, but *need* not be read in such a light. Clearly, ethical (e.g., Matt 5:36; 6:34; 10:8; Luke 5:39; 6:43; 7:47; Matt 5:39–48 par) and quasi-legal maxims (e.g., Mark 7:15; 10:9; 12:17;

---

[40] See Mark 3:24–25 par; 4:21 par, 22 par; 6:4 par; 10:27; 12:17; Luke 12:48; 16:15; 13:24 par; 7:32 par for such eschatological common sense; cf. J.S. Kloppenborg, "Symbolic Eschatology and the Apocalypticism of Q," *HTR* 80 (1987) 287–306.

[41] Mark 2:21–22 par; Matt 6:22–23 par Luke 11:34–36; Matt 6:24 par Luke 16:13; Luke 16:10–12; Matt 7:6; Matt 10:24–25 (par Luke 6:40; John 3:16, 15:20); Matt 10:26b–27 par Luke 12:2–3; cf. Henderson, "Gnomic Quatrains."

Matt 10:10 par) acquire in Jesus' rhetoric and developing tradition a
strong patina of eschatological urgency. The relationship between such
contextual acquisition, gradual or immediate, and the intrinsic characteristics of individual gnomai is, however, quite variable. Even allowing
for a more urgent emphasis on eschatological rhetoric in Marcan
tradition than in Q rhetoric(s), gnomic rhetoric attributed to Jesus has
often an intrinsically oracular interest in future, preternatural crisis.

Recent study of Jesus sayings tradition has tended to focus on the
providential (if not sapiential) nature of proverbial wisdom and, then,
on its anti-proverbial, aphoristic (if not Cynic) subversion.[42] I think
that Synoptic gnomai as a sample of Jesus tradition tends to vindicate
'eschatology' or, at least, oracular futurity as a comparative category.
In this limited sense, eschatology is at most a pervasive undercurrent
within the gnomic style generally in Jesus' tradition, a mood rather than
a coherent topical or speculative code comparable to those of apocalyptic literacy. But some reference to Bultmann's "eschatological mood"
remains useful as a partial account of the relative intensity of some
gnomai.

The promised and threatened vindication of Wisdom by all her
children (Luke 7:35 par) may be as Wendy Cotter asserts proverbial.
Such vindication is, however, sufficiently counter-intuitive, ultimately
future, and biblically prophetic to be eschatological oracle more than
Cynic irony.[43]

Gnome as proverb and anti-proverb (W. Beardslee)

'Proverbiality' or, more significantly from a normative point of view,
'anti-proverbiality' is not only the basis for W. Beardslee's
hermeneutically refined essays.[44] Reference to (anti-)proverbiality as
a hermeneutical complement or alternative to eschatology also provides
the implicit rationale for a notable range of discussions of individual

---

[42] E.g., Perdue, "Wisdom Sayings."
[43] W.J. Cotter, "Children Sitting in the Agora: Q (Luke) 7:31–35," *Forum* 5/2
(1989) 63–82, esp. 79–80.
[44] Beardslee, "Uses of the Proverb," 61–73; "Saving One's Life," 57–72.

Synoptic gnomai as 'proverbs' or 'aphorisms'.[45] Moreover, the use of Cynic wit as an alternative to eschatology in readings of Q has the effect of historicizing the hermeneutical distinction between anti-proverbiality and eschatology. At least as used by New Testament critics, 'proverb' and 'wisdom' are at least as ill-defined as 'eschatology' and 'apocalyptic'; the former are made even more speculative and tendentious in current usage by references to their 'subversion' into (Cynic) anti-proverbiality. The difficulty of speaking critically as well as speculatively about proverbiality and its use in gospel tradition is, of course, exacerbated by the overwhelming difficulty of controlling the tradition history of actual proverbs in the Greco-Roman world.

Nonetheless, the relation between gnomic rhetoric and Greco-Roman notions of proverbiality is important, and not only for the analogy between Cynic and Christian discourses. Aristotle recognized the usefulness of giving a deliberately anti-proverbial spin to a known commonplace in order to emphasize the speaker's character and strong emotion (*Rh.* II 21,12–14=1395a). Moreover, the turn toward paradox, hyperbole, intensification and subversion of normal values *is* an aspect both intrinsically, of the internal rhetoric of the most extremely intensified gnomai (e.g., Matt 8:22), and extrinsically, of the intensified reception of some intrinsically innocuous sounding gnomai (e.g., in gnomic quatrains).

Many Synoptic gnomai reflect Beardslee's concept of 'proverbiality' as positive, socially integrative normativity, adopting "the typical proverbial stance of making a continuous project out of our life."[46] Gnomai of 'impossibility' and antithetical gnomai are also familiar both in the Synoptics as in the wider world of traditionally attested proverbial norms.[47] Such sayings are the normative baseline or "field of intensification" in partial contrast to which Beardslee seeks to define the

---

[45] E.g., Dewey, "Quibbling Over Serifs"; Cotter, "Children Sitting in the Agora"; Vaage, *Galilean Upstarts*, 128–131 on Q 10:7b, 117 on "the divisive proverb," Q 11:23.

[46] Beardslee, "Uses of the Proverb," 69; cf. Mark 14:38b; 9:40 par; 10:27 par; Matt 6:34b; 7:15; Luke 5:39; 6:38; Matt 6:22 par; 10:10 par.

[47] Generally see Berger, "Hellenistische Gattungen," 1049–1074. Impossibility: Mark 9:50 par; Matt 5:14b, 36b; Luke 5:39; 6:43; Matt 15:14 par; 6:27 par; cf. Perdue, "Wisdom Sayings," 15–16; Dewey, "Quibbling Over Serifs," 115–118. Antitheses: Mark 10:9 par, 27 par; 12:17 par; Matt 11:17 par.

historically significant Synoptic tendency toward paradox and hyper-bole.[48]

The relative contrast between normal and rhetorically intensified proverbiality is complicated by the problem of relating the normative baseline of Synoptic proverb-use to the presumed baseline beyond early Christian discourse. In some cases, gospel gnomai can be directly compared with widely current, i.e., proverbial, Greco-Roman and near eastern gnomai. Such comparison as is possible bears out Beardslee's hypothesis that a non-negligible proportion of (pre-)gospel gnomai are rhetorically marked over against an unmarked norm of conventionality. The credibility of this comparison is, however, greatly enhanced by converting Beardslee's 'proverb' category into a category systematically described and practised in Greco-Roman rhetoric. It is probably impossible to know enough about Greco-Roman proverbs as such, i.e., about topical sentences familiar to most competent members of particular speech communities, in order to be able to compare public, proverbial meanings with private, sectarian meanings.

Beardslee's qualified generalization that Synoptic tradition collective-ly is relatively more paradoxical and hyperbolic than wider proverb-tradition is one basis for the present study.[49] Yet even this legitimate and deliberately collective judgement is ultimately based on comparison with a general tradition which in its scale, more-than-literary character and topical variety is never securely within our grasp. The definitions and examples of the progymnasmatists and rhetoricians are indispens-able here, first because they balance exemplification and analysis and also because they anticipate clearly the movement from proverbiality to more specialized rhetorical application.

Beardslee, in keeping with the form-critical heritage, is still trying to compare gnomic rhetoric with proverbial folklore, rather than with Greco-Roman rhetoric as such. Even Beardslee is therefore forced to become a collector not only of gospel fragments, but also of proverbial fragments in order to construct a comparative context for proverbs and anti-proverbs attributed to Jesus. Gospel rhetorics are, however, a sub-set of Greco-Roman rhetoric as their gnome-use shows even in its relative idiosyncrasies.

---

[48] E.g., Matt 5:39 par, 44 par; Mark 8:35 par; Beardslee, "Uses of the Proverb," 66–68; "Saving One's Life," *passim*.

[49] Beardslee, "Saving One's Life," 61–65.

Whoever tries to save their life shall lose it; whoever loses their life...shall save it. (Mark 8:35 par)

Beardslee's model treatment of an exemplary anti-proverbial, paradox shows that the *Wanderlogion* about saving and losing life (Mark 8:35 par) is representative, if not authentic. The comparison perhaps inevitably confirms the dissimilarity of the saying's paradoxical attitude. At the same time, Beardslee's comparative work inevitably relativizes topical dissimilarity against a background of aphoristic or proverbial affirmations of patriotic, principled or loyal self-sacrifice.[50] Beardslee's approach to such emphatically paradoxical gnomai as Mark 8:35, Matthew 8:22, Matthew 5:39 and 5:44[51] is inevitably equivocal in its results for understanding pre-gospel rhetoric because inevitably such strong cases only more or less resemble recoverable proverbial traditions.

It is not enough, then, to point to the multiple attestation of such cases as the life-saving gnome and, then, to the lesser intensity of any available extra-biblical parallels. The claim that such gnomic language is representative of Jesus' rhetoric must rest also on seeing that intensified and normal cases alike belong to a single, recognizable rhetorical pattern and exemplify the conventional limits for its use. It is hard enough to argue for the authenticity of individual sayings, without having to argue also their individual representativeness. Even the most clearly rhetorical individual case—Matthew 8:22 or Mark 8:35—cannot securely be said by itself to characterize Synoptic tradition as a whole over against other rhetorics of its day. Instead, rhetorical analysis of Matthew 8:22 or Mark 8:35 only gives persuasive insight into Synoptic rhetoric as a whole when such instances are cited as limit cases of a gnomic rhetorical pattern described, exemplified, analysed and prescribed by the progymnasmatists and rhetoricians. It is the rhetorical pattern, defined by baseline as well as limit cases, which is both authentic and representative of the rhetorical continuum between Jesus and the gospels.

In that practical and theoretical context the Synoptic limit-case gnomai may be seen to be relatively frequent compared with the standards of Greco-Roman rhetorical theory and decorum. In this

---

[50] Beardslee, "Saving One's Life," 62–64.
[51] Beardslee, "Uses of the Proverb," 68–69.

respect Synoptic gospel rhetorics are, indeed, rather analogous to Cynic rhetorics: we do not need to suppose that Cynics, and not only Pharisees, were lurking in the suburban Jewish villages of Herodian Galilee to recognize that Cynics and Jesus' followers faced similar communicative problems over against the polite elitism of ideal Greco-Roman rhetorics. Nor does this analogy between two marginal rhetorical situations necessarily imply much analogy in actual social normative projects: Christian and Cynic programmes may well have resembled each other precisely in their rhetorical marginality and, hence, in their "redeployment of standard figures and tropes from Greek culture."[52]

It is still true that gospel gnome-use, like Cynic gnome-use, is proportionately biased towards limit-cases of rhetorical intensification. Such gospel gnome-use is, however, radically continuous with normal Greco-Roman and progymnasmatic gnomic rhetoric, since gospel gnomai include not only a disproportionate number and quality of intensified gnomai, but also a baseline of conventional instances which fit ordinary Greco-Roman expectations. Moreover, those Greco-Roman norms are themselves treated by the progymnasmatists and rhetoricians since Aristotle and Quintilian as a baseline for more extreme anti-proverbial, personally assertive and confrontational performances. Thus Aristotle's interest in the occasionally anti-proverbial, anti-traditional possibilities of gnome is the corollary of the recognition throughout the rhetorical tradition of the 'ethical' quality of gnome-use (*Rh.* II 21,9–16 =1395a–b; III 17,9=1418a). Few speakers may claim the personal *auctoritas* which alone can justify and sustain an unconventionally intensified gnomic style (Quintilian, *Inst.* VIII 5,8).

The weakness of Beardslee's proverbs, then, is just that they are not recognized as gnomai, for which guidelines, if not rules, of usage can be found at the educational and practical roots of Hellenistic culture. As a result, gnomic intensification, anti-proverbiality and personal assertion are still treated in existential, poetic terms and not as publicly meaning-ful rhetorical declarations of alternative authority.

Other attempts to locate Synoptic gnomai in a spectrum of proverbia-lity-unconventionality are even more piecemeal than Beardslee's, though they may nonetheless produce an exegetically interesting contrast. When the notion of 'proverb' is used to describe a particular gospel gnome, the critical emphasis is seldom on the intrinsic rhetorical or poetic

---

[52] Kloppenborg, "Q: Recent Opinion," 18–20, 26–28, quoting 27.

character of the gnome (e.g. figures, tropes or normative topics). Instead, exegetically labelling a gnome 'proverbial' usually indicates either an unargued assumption that gnome functions as a quasi-logical generalization or a focus on an alleged difference or similarity between the gnome's gospel receptions and traditional receptions elsewhere.

At least some gospel gnomai do seem to have been proverbial, in more than the negative sense that they do not intrinsically imply eschatological or oracular urgency, outrageous personal authority or unbridled conflict. At least some gospel gnomai seem to be performances of gnomic cores which would have been common currency in speech communities wider than that of Synoptic tradition as such.

The measurement gnome (Mark 4:24 par) is a good example. Essentially the same gnomic core is attested in the prosaically juridical context of Ptolemaic grain exchanges. The gnome's reception in this context is as a straightforward universal ethical/legal maxim. The value of the parallel is not, however, that it establishes 'le sens primitif' of the proverb, but only that it provides a vivid contrast to the personal and eschatological reception of the gnome in the Synoptics. There is no reason whatever to suppose that Jesus' followers were either ignorant of or interested in the gnome's obvious applicability to ordinary business.[53]

Similarly G. Lindeskog saw the *Wanderlogion* Mark 4:25 and parallels as an instance of anti-proverbial reception (by Jesus) of a common, prudential proverb into a newly eschatological and personal context.[54] In a Greco-Roman rhetorical context, however, the tension between Mark 4:25 and proverbiality does not really depend on the shaky presumption that the pre-gospel gnomic core was actually proverbial. Instead, Mark 4:25 is recognizably anti-proverbial because it is recognizably a gnome and because none of its diverse Synoptic receptions seriously qualifies its implicit availability for oracular interpretation.

S.J. Noorda's investigation of classical parallels to Luke 4:23 is more ambiguous, despite the inviting Lucan citation formula ("you shall cite me this proverb [*parabole*]"). Noorda's search for parallels illustrates the difficulty of an approach to gnome through proverb: he finds two quite distinct *topoi* represented in the same gnomic core imagery. The

---

[53] Boismard, *Synopse*, 152.
[54] G. Lindeskog, "Logia-Studien," *ST* 4 (1951) 129–189.

better attested *topos* is ironic: don't blame others for your own failings. The less attested *topos*, roughly that charity begins at home, seems to be dominant in this case, though (against Noorda) the context of rejection and the quotation-form with its future tense (*eirete*) suggests tragic irony. Luke 4:23 may thus embody a recognizable proverbial *double entendre*. Rhetorically, I think it is more valuable to see this gnome as Luke does: as a highly personal oracle complementing Luke 4:24 and parallels and pointing to the two best known aspects of Jesus' public activity: his thaumaturgy and his death (Luke 23:35 par).[55]

Rather similarly, J. Dupont identifies two topics current in ancient literature for a proverb about the impossibility of serving two masters. Formally similar performances of such proverbial gnomic imagery seem to refer either to the shared slave's excessive work-load or to the slave's virtual independence under conflicting authorities. In Matthew 6:24 and Luke 16:13, however, the proverb is received in neither proverbial sense. Instead it is dramatically redirected toward existential/theological decision.[56]

Examples of this kind, more or less pointedly unexpected receptions of fairly certainly proverbial gnomai, could doubtless be multiplied, especially if we knew the proverb traditions better. In this case, though, the Synoptic gnome-reception is recognizably anti-proverbial in the more basic sense that it exploits gnome rather deliberately as a means of evangelical disorientation. Even if the hearers of Q, Matthew and Luke could not be counted upon to know that the traditional senses of an old gnome were being violated, the turn from "no servant can serve to masters" to "you cannot serve God and Mammon" is a formidable reach of meaning. In fact, the rhetorical essence of the Gnomic Quatrain form (Matt 6:24 par; Matt 6:22 par; Luke 16:10–12; Matt 7:6; Mark 2:21–23; Matt 10:24–25; 10:26b–27) is its movement from an apparently straightforward gnome to a startling theological and existential conclusion.

Among gnomic Quatrains, Matthew 6:22–23 and Luke 11:34–36 are also based on a gnome which is almost certainly proverbial (Matt 6:22a par Luke 11:34a). In this case there is no suggestion that the proverb's Matthaeo-Lucan reception deliberately runs against the grain of specific commonplace proverbial receptions as in the gnome of the servant of

---

[55] Noorda, "'Cure Yourself, Doctor!'" 459–467.
[56] Dupont, "Dieu et Mammon," 552.

two masters. Still, the application (verse 23) is surprisingly far from the gnome's obvious sense, as perhaps the Lucan variations attest (verses 35, 36).[57] In fact, studies by H.-D. Betz, D. Allison and M. Philonenko suggest that the gospel gnome of the eye as the body's lamp is not itself a proverb, but rather a hermeneutical transformation of ideas of vision in antiquity, ideas which were "prone to parabolic and gnomic formulation." Moreover, as Philonenko suggests, the Quatrain avoids—perhaps pointedly—the obvious proverbial possibilities of the soul as the lamp of the body.[58]

I do not suppose that the verse form of the gnomic Quatrain is authentic in its attribution to Jesus, but the Quatrains' self-consciously challenging use of gnomai *is* characteristic of the origins of Synoptic tradition.[59] If some Synoptic gnomai (including Matt 7:6; cf. *Did* 9:5) were indeed widely received proverbs in more prosaic senses, this effect would be all the more striking. The essential and historically interesting point is, however, that the Synoptics are marked *both* by gnomai which are intrinsically disruptive of the hearer's/reader's proverbial expectations *and* by a corresponding reception of more conventional sounding gnomai in evidently unconventional senses. The gnomic Quatrains are interesting as they made a pre-Marcan and pre-Q verse art form from what is more generally in the Synoptic tradition a rhetorical strategy.

Even constructing a *corpus* of proverbs (with commonly received interpretations and topical contexts) current in the Hellenistic world, though intrinsically desirable, would have only an equivocal bearing on gnomic rhetoric. Such a 'new Wettstein' would most naturally foster the pursuit of "invidious comparisons" against which Carlston warned.[60] The real point was one made already by the rhetorical theorists from the Sophists onward: gnomai may be modelled on proverbs or received as proverbs; precisely because of this kinship, gnomai may also be used or abused in anti-proverbial, conflictual and disintegrative modes.

---

[57] Boismard, *Synopse*, 278.

[58] Henderson, "Gnomic Quatrains," 485 (quoted); H.-D. Betz, "Matt 6.22–23 and Ancient Greek Theories of Vision," in Betz, *Essays*, 71–87; Allison, "The Eye is the Lamp of the Body"; M. Philonenko, 'La parabole sur la lampe (Luc 11 33–36) et les horoscopes qoumrâniens," *ZNW* 79 (1988) 145–151, esp. 146–147 and nn. 10–12.

[59] Henderson, "Gnomic Quatrains," 496–498.

[60] Carlston, "Proverbs and Jesus," 104; A. Ehrhardt, "Greek Proverbs in the Gospel," *HTR* 46 (1953) 59–60; J.B. Bauer in proemion to J. Wettstein, *Novum Testamentum Graecum* (Amsterdam, 1751, rpr. Graz, 1962).

The theoretical and practical background of Greco-Roman rhetoric behind pre-gospel rhetorics frees the modern critic to some extent from the haphazard and tendentious business of finding proverbial backgrounds for gospel gnomai piecemeal: anti-proverbiality as a rhetorical strategy does not depend upon subverting actual proverbs or their conventional receptions. It is enough to say something which recalls proverbial imagery and topics, but does so in strikingly personal (ethical), paradoxical or conflictual terms.

Such deconstructive use of gnomic language plays an even greater role in the Synoptics than Beardslee sensed. This gives the whole problem of Synoptic (and gnomic) normativity an even greater urgency and relevance. The tension between integrative and deconstructive normativity comes into question not only as a useful topic of historical-critical interest, but also as a problem intrinsic to the (gnomic and parabolic) style of the Synoptics. Thus the gospels know not only Beardslee's broad "field of intensification," but also a large minority of gnomai which are intrinsically paradoxical and conflictual. But the gospels also know a second large minority of gnomai which, though not obviously anti-proverbial in content, are nonetheless received in Synoptic contexts as pretexts for a reorientation away from merely integrative, proverbial normativity.

I am reluctant to turn rhetorical insights too directly into sociological hypotheses. In addition, I am wary of exaggerating the deconstructive anti-proverbiality in Synoptic gnomai and their receptions. Still, the tension between proverbiality and anti-proverbiality is a tension within rhetorical normativity; the relative prominence in Synoptic rhetorics of anti-proverbial formulations and receptions of gnomai contributes to a relatively conflictual ethos in rhetoric attributed to Jesus.

In Chapter One, we noticed the rather well attested use of proverbs in many cultures to give speakers a degree of control, or at least protection, in socially threatening communicative situations.[61] In this chapter and the next, the presumption emerges that pre-gospel rhetorics indeed used gnomai to manipulate the "social cost" of speech. They seem to have done so, moreover, in the direction of heightening "social cost" at least as often as in the interest of moderating rhetorical danger.

---

[61] Kirschenblatt-Gimblett, "Proverb Meaning," 821–827; Dundes, "Structures," 963–965; Barley, "Structural Approach," 743; Crépeau, "Définition," 289–291; Blehr, "Proverb?" 243–246.

At the same time, however, parabolic and gnomic expression of social aggression or alienation is different from, say, the adoption of violence. Parabolic and gnomic rhetorics may have raised the social stakes of speech, but they also indicate a movement away from direct social confrontation to the sublimated confrontation of even the most outlandish rhetoric. Like the Cynics, gospel writers and pre-gospel speakers radically accept the very rhetorical conventions which they radicalize; their dangerous, marginal rhetorics become safe, even therapeutic because they mirror the social conventions which they rhetorically challenge.

The paradox of gnomic normativity is an internalized tension within the Greco-Roman rhetorical universe of Synoptic gnome. Pre-gospel gnome users were not globally hostile to proverbial normativity nor do they reflect the dysfunctionality of a purely private, sectarian rhetoric, unintelligible to those outside.[62] Furthermore, this rhetorical tension, expressed sometimes in the very structure, sometimes in the reception of gnomai, is referable with great probability to Jesus' own as well as to Synoptic style. In view of this it becomes all the more important to distinguish the rhetorical normativity of gnomai in writing and speech from the normative functions of social institutions viewed as such.

Such intrinsically disintegrative gnomai as Matthew 8:22 and Mark 2:19 show that their direct normative influence was on Christian rhetoric more than on Christian burials, weddings and fasting practices. Likewise, a gnome can be applied to one context as deconstructive and to another as integrative, albeit sectarian (e.g. Mark 4:22 par Matt 10:26; Luke 12:2; 8:17, cf. Matt 10:27 par Luke 12:3). The urgent point here is that for both rhetorical and social normativity,

> there is no functionality as such, only in relation to a given whole. In history, however, this whole can never be as unequivocally defined as an organism in the natural world. The framework for a sociology of early Christianity is therefore the whole of Greco-Roman society. It is nonetheless reasonable now and again to select another framework...[63]

---

[62] G. Theißen, "Theoretischen Probleme religionssoziologischer Forschung," *Neue Zeitschrift für systematische Theologie* 16 (1974) 35–56, 40–41.

[63] Theißen, "Theoretischen Probleme," 41.

Thus the strongly gnomic aspect of Synoptic rhetoric functions both to distinguish and to integrate it within the very broad and self-conscious whole of antique rhetoric. Both the relative frequency and prominence of gnomic elements and also the relative importance of the disintegrative side of gnomic normativity distinguish Synoptic rhetoric within this broad field of comparison. These relationships are not anhistorical, but they do not directly inform us about which social conflicts formed gospel gnome-use. Not least in connection with Jesus himself rhetorical normativity is buffered from social representation by the self-consciously abstract and linguistic business of speaking well.

The selection of the remaining topical headings in this survey (personal reference, discipleship and, in the next chapter, legality) is therefore determined partly by opportunism: these topics are relatively well represented. But the choice of topics is also based on a perception of Christian rhetoric and, to some extent, origins as by and large "a phenomenon of social disintegration."[64] That Christian rhetoric and, indeed, Christianity itself remains a rhetorical phenomenon is shown at the same time by the new movement's growing integrative capacity, expressed, for example, in its increasingly canonical literacy as well as in its adoption, however critical, of Greco-Roman public language. I want to adopt a predominantly conflictive model primarily (against Theißen) as a model of pre-gospel rhetoric and only secondarily as a model of Jesus' movement as it formed communities.

The secondary motive remains, however, as I continue to look for opportunities to translate the disintegrative rhetorical aspect of Synoptics gnomai into sociological (and psychological) terms of normative conflict both with other groups manoeuvring in the same general environment and within the earliest movement itself.

Personally attributive gnomai

The most fragile of the remaining subcategories of gnome embraces those which, intrinsically or in Synoptic reception, refer to the tradition's central personality. The number of gnomai attributed to Jesus which also directly, intrinsically refer to the personality of the putative

---

[64] See G. Theißen, *Soziologie der Jesusbewegung* (4th ed.; München, 1985) 45 (quoted) and 89.

speaker is not large. Together with gnomai which are received in their literary contexts as Jesus' self-references the few intrinsically self-referring gnomai are, however, unusually clear witnesses to the primary contextual fact about the gnomai of the Synoptic tradition. With few and instructively partial exceptions (Mark 7:28 par; Matt 11:17 par; 16:2–3 par; 3:10 par, but cf. 7:19; Luke 4:23), gospel gnomai are attributed to Jesus. Cynicism and Rabbinic Judaism had many gnome-speaking heroes and Christianity did too eventually, but there is only one canonical speaker whose habitual rhetorical decorum is marked by parabolic and gnomic oracles.

The most striking examples of intrinsically personal gnomai attributed to Jesus as self-references are curiously but closely interrelated: Mark 2:17 and 2:19 belong to adjacent, form- and probably source-critically kindred literary settings. Shared 'physician' imagery links Mark 2:17 and Luke 4:23. The latter is, in turn, connected with Mark 6:4 by the shared context of the Nazareth rejection—and by the contrasting existence of the double gnomic core in a probably independent form, unrelated to an episodic narrative (POxy. 1.6; *Gos. Thom.* 31). The significance of this constellation, together with the 'Johannine Thunderbolt' (Matt 11:27 par Luke 10:22) and also with the nexus of more prescriptive teacher and master (*didaskalos/kurios*) gnomai (Matt 10:24–25 par), is that the range of imagery from personal roles applied directly to the gnome-speaker (Jesus) is self-consciously narrow.

The speaker as son and bridegroom

It would be rhetorically quite possible to perform the gnome of father-son intimacy (Matt 11:27 par Luke 10:22) as normatively 'optional' (i.e., elective on both sides) and as relatively unmarked (i.e., most gospel hearers are presumed, however unfairly, to identify somehow with son-father relationships). There is no need to assert the authenticity of the saying or the proverbiality of father-son knowledge.[65] In terms

---

[65] This seems to be the implication of C.H. Dodd's reasoning on John 5:19–20, *Historical Tradition in the Fourth Gospel* (Cambridge, 1963) 386; "A Hidden Parable in the Fourth Gospel," in *More New Testament Studies* (Manchester, 1968) 30–40; cf. M. Sabbe, "Can Mt 11,27 and Lk 10,22 be Called a Johannine Logion?" in Delobel, *Logia*, 363–371.

of gnomic rhetoric what is notable is in the negative formulation of the gnome ("no one knows...") is that the normativity is not primarily integrative ("like father, like son"). In keeping with the Matthaean contextualization, the father-son gnome refers to the speaker's conflicting claim to special dynastic identity and intimacy.[66]

The bridegroom (Mark 2:19) is only slightly narrower a normative image than that of the son: at the primary level of the gnome's reference, all its hearers have experienced weddings and half could remember or aspire to being bridegroom. The universal familiarity of these roles makes their use in the gospel gnomai so striking; their normatively specific use in these gnomai reflects on the speaker's peculiar authority and transcendent relatedness.

As a whole, Mark 2:19a (par) is normatively more definite than its central (bridegroom) image in two ways, to which it will be necessary to return later. In the first place, the topic of fasting brings us face to face with a new normative universality, of socially, even legally, institutionalized roles. Secondly, the categories of the 'bridegroom' and the 'sons of the wedding' have a singularly personal place (Matt 22:1–14, 25:1–13; John 2:1–11; 3:29) within the broad field of wedding imagery. Such nuptial imagery is more basic to commonly shared eschatology than even the more speculative notion of 'prophet' (e.g., John 4). On one side of the analogy, the imagery of the 'bridegroom' is as accessible as that of sonship; the gnome does imply another side of the analogy, however. In analogy the 'bridegroom' is more clearly metaphorical and less domestic than either the 'physician' or the 'prophet'.

Any one and no one, can become or describe the groom. This is also true of the groomsmen whose relationship to the groom is asymmetrical and elective (i.e., more or less optional on both sides). Moreover, this relationship is located within a changing temporal frame. Once again, the gnome is not only about the speaker's self-characterization (*ethos*), it is at the same time about conflict with the consequent (in this case temporally) divided characterization of the listeners. In this gnome the rhetorically implied normative conflict is less between groups (though there is a tension between the groom who departs and his groomsmen) than between temporally conditioned changes in the groomsmen's election.

---

[66] Carlston, "Wisdom and Eschatology in Q," 103 and n.16.

In spite of the usual historical implausibility of idealized Synoptic narrative contexts,[67] the literary reception of the gnome confirms this analysis: both intrinsically and in reception, the gnomic saying's primary point is with defining the issue in a concrete normative conflict in terms of the temporal presence or absence of the speaker. There is of course no way to prove that Mark 2:19a is an *ipsissima sermo Jesu*, but it would be irresponsible not to observe that the gnome is (a) not redactional, (b) not entirely at home in its literary context,[68] (c) not obviously churchly or (d) merely proverbial and (e) not readily intelligible as any one else's utterance. As the following verses (Mark 19b–20) also suggest, the bridegroom gnome is also hopelessly inadequate as a regulation within its legal topic of fasting, a typical instance of the gnomic non-legality to which I shall return in the next chapter.

Mark 2:19a (par) is also exemplary for an approach to the exegesis of Synoptic gnome in that it embraces the proposed topical sub-categories of eschatology, personal reference, discipleship and legality. Above all it is paradigmatic for an approach which does not need fully to "recover the original application of the saying"[69] in order to recognize the probable historical representativeness of gnomai which are normatively more conflictive than integrative and which also suggest an element of careful gnomic self-reference among Jesus' speech-habits.

The speaker as physician, prophet and teacher

Compared with the essential imprecision of the 'physician' and 'prophet', the more marked and 'specific' role-names (healer, prophet and teacher) are limited and coordinated by their connotative complementarity. None poses as an exclusively adequate description of Jesus' ministry. 'Bridegroom' and 'son' define the most stable content of the speaker's claimed rhetorical *ethos*, his right to speak and act for God. 'Prophet', 'physician' and 'teacher' contribute to this *ethos* only

---

[67] Bultmann, *Geschichte*, 17–18; Schille, "Was ist ein logion?" 177–180; Berger, *Gesetzesauslegung*, 576–578.

[68] Vv. 19b and 20 (par) seem effectively to reverse the normative implication of v. 19a.

[69] Sanders, *Jesus and Judaism*, 207.

contingently: the speaker must supplement his words with deeds not only to verify his ethical self-characterization, but even just to make that self-characterization publicly intelligible. Indeed, the patronal images of teacher and lord (Matt 10:24–25 par Luke 6:40 cf. John 13:16) and of prophet and physician (POxy. 1.6; *Gos. Thom.* 31; Luke 4:23–24) come juxtaposed in pairs: they are not self-explanatory roles. In literary context and also intrinsically, given the general context of ascription to Jesus, each direct rhetorical characterization in the gospel gnomai is a self-consciously understated metaphor or metonymy in the face not merely of unclarity, but of opposition.

In its immediate Marcan and derivative contexts Mark 2:17 is performed as a metaphoric analogy: the passage is about Jesus' preference for bad company not about his healing work. In the gospels or in relation to any attribution to Jesus, 'physician' cannot be confined within the bounds of metaphoric connotation. Jesus' social recognition as a healer is as fundamental a historical datum as his perception as a parable-speaker or his crucifixion.[70] The New Testament knows the difference between Jesus thaumaturgy and the craft of an *iatros*, but the difference is relative and negotiable (cf. Mark 5:26).

At the same time, though, the gnomic designation of Jesus as a physician is also clearly qualified by its primarily polemical internal rhetoric. That is, the gnome itself is intrinsically about the controversial distinction between the well and the ill and the specification of those groups rather than about the indeterminate technique of the 'physician'. The contextualization of the gnome in Mark 2:13–17 (par) consequently does not focus on Jesus' role as healer, though this is just below the horizon (cf. Mark 2:1–12; 3:1–6). Instead the gnome in literary context is about Jesus' contrasting relations with two conflicting groups and about the basis of their conflict in a difference of autodiagnosis. In fact, the gnome in itself expresses the basic normative clash more clearly and plausibly than does the literary context with its confusion of institutional discipleship (*akoloutheo* 2:14, 15; *kalesthai* 17b) and social fraterniz-ation (*sunanakeisthai/katakeisthai* 15 par).

In Crépeau's universal, specific or optional normative range, the 'sick' and the 'healthy' are optional group terms, either of which could, depending on the 'physician', be accepted "by any member of the

---

[70] See Sanders, *Jesus and Judaism*, 4–8, 157–173; M. Smith, *Jesus the Magician* (New York and London, 1978).

society."[71] That is, the gnome of the physician of the sick (Mark 2:17) is not only about Jesus' self-characterization; it is also about the elective self-identification of his hearers and opponents. In this Mark 2:17 resembles Matthew 8:22 (par) where the hearers must decide who the 'dead' are and who they themselves will be in relation to an audacious speaker. This means, however, that Mark 2:17 is, in terms of its internal rhetoric, recognizably not primarily about health care. Instead, it is about the projected *ethos* of an audacious speaker and the responding crisis of self-re-characterization in the attentive listener. 'Physician' is the metonymic emblem of a normatively more complete persona, even for hearers who do not have in mind the unprofessionally charismatic healing career of Jesus.

Similar conclusions may be drawn from the other Synoptic physician-gnome (Luke 4:23). As Noorda showed in terms of classical proverbial parallels, Luke 4:23 could be heard within two quite distinct *topoi*.[72] Despite this topical ambiguity, the gnome is clearly a sharply specific normative challenge; indeed, topical ambiguity here dramatizes the personal and oracular qualities of the gnome's ethical-rhetorical normativity. The oddities of the Lucan literary context accurately reflect the implications of bringing such a gnome within the field of Jesus' rhetoric while at the same time designating Jesus as its implied addressee: the gnome is about Jesus' perceived, in part chosen rhetorical identity. But the gnome is not only about Jesus' qualified, even sarcastic acceptance of the characterization as healer; the gnome intrinsically (not only contextually) implies its antagonistic, disintegrative function toward the optional categories of the healer's patients and challengers.

In the gospel traditional context, a suitably ambivalent and confrontational 'physician' is readily available, but not without the implication that the gnomic model gives an ironic characterization of its speaker.

Even without the parallel in *Gospel of Thomas* (31, POxy. 1.6) and the association of Luke 2:23 and 24, with all the consequent tradition-critical uncertainties and possibilities, the family resemblances between the physician gnomai and the gnome of the prophet at home (Mark 6:4 par) would be compelling. Within this broad similarity however, there, are differences. The designation 'prophet' in an Israelite context is

---

[71] Crépeau, "Définition," 300.
[72] Noorda, "'Cure Yourself, Doctor!'" 459–467.

normatively more significant and controversial than the designation 'physician'.[73]

This socially normative indefiniteness of the notion 'prophet' (like that of 'the dead' in Matt 8:22!) makes it difficult to dismiss the gnome as metaphorical. Still, there is a discernible margin of figurative distance between Jesus and the prophet-title in the gospels' receptions. In John 4:44, the gnome is part of a christological strand which is scrupulously dropped in the second half of the gospel; in *Gospel of Thomas* (31; POxy. 1.6) the gnome need not refer to Jesus at all and anyhow implies the distance of symbolism in the physician-prophet parallel, as does the Lucan juxtaposition (4:23–24). Even, or especially, the Marcan-Matthaean context places Jesus in a by no means unambiguously prophetic role (cf. Mark 6:2 par).[74]

Internally, it is not only 'prophet' which is ambiguous in Mark 6:4 and parallels: the notion of 'home town' (*patris*) is at least as problematic, as the variant receptions confirm. *Gospel of Thomas* and Mark ignore the problem, but Matthew (4:13), Luke (4:16) and John (4:44 cf. 7:52) resolve it in characteristic and incompatible ways: the indeterminacy of the gnome in this respect is older than its gospel receptions. But in the same way that the gnome was not designed rhetorically to give the speaker's address, so also the designation 'prophet' is not offered as an exhaustive professional self-designation however prestigious.

In the gnome, Matthew 10:24–25; Luke 6:40; 22:27; John 13:16; 15:20, personal self-reference is also subordinated to the topic of discipleship—or, rather, the biographical topics of the disciple's (voluntary or involuntary) imitation of the (good or bad) master. It might be tempting in this case to fall back upon one of the strategies of 'anti-proverbial' exegesis discussed above.[75] Even viewed as a proverb, however, this gnome cannot be confined to the institutional *Sitz im Leben* of mnemotechnical pedagogy. Certainly the content of the gnome refers to a cultural view of discipleship as a means of preserving didactic tradition; the gnome is a classic statement of the traditional

---

[73] R.A. Horsley, "Popular Prophets."

[74] See E. Gräßer, "Jesus in Nazareth (Mc 6, 1–6a): Bemerkungen zur Redaktion und Theologie des Markus," in *Jesus in Nazareth*, ed. W. Eltester (BZNW 40; Berlin and New York, 1972) 1–37.

[75] Cf. K.E., Dewey, "*Paroimiai* in the Gospel of John," in *Gnomic Wisdom*, ed. J.D. Crossan=*Semeia* 17 (1980) 81–100, 96.

ethos of rote learning and imitative apprenticeship. As the supplementary imagery of the slave/master (Matt 10:24: John 13:16) and the anti-model of the blind leading the blind (Luke 6:39) confirm, however, the gnome's uses do not hinge upon affirmation of that view of discipleship. The nearest approach to a direct affirmation of imitative, memorizational discipleship would be Luke 6:40 where there is considerable scope for multiple intensions[76] and where the tradition to be kept is ironically the negative one of refraining from judgement. Once again it would be tempting to hear the teacher/disciple and master/slave gnomai as anti-proverbial rejections of relationships which in antiquity were often positively valued in proverbial maxims of loyalty and kindness —but I see no sign of such a reception.[77]

In fact, our gospel receptions of the gnome ignore the essential difference between conventional discipleship and household relationships in the gnomai and the actual conditions of following Jesus. Instead the conventional model of discipleship is affirmed only as the basis for normatively limited analogy. Thus the general gap between gnomic model and social institution is unusually well defined, in Matthew by associating the disciple/teacher and slave/master analogies and in John 13:16 by linking the slave/master and messenger/sender analogies. Beyond that, there are hints of awareness that discipleship was a different and conflictual social institution as practised by Jesus: Luke sees the catastrophic possibility of following the wrong teacher, Matthew thinks of the likelihood of sharing the master's fate, to which John adds the possibility of betrayal. The sharply disintegrative implications of discipleship for the socialization of Jesus' movement are not implicit in the gnome itself.

Other personally attributive gnomai

There are in the Synoptic gospels only a few further gnomai which intrinsically (as well as receptionally) depend for their imagery upon individual personality. Matthew 12:30 (par) with Mark 9:40 (par) and Mark 13:31 (par) with Matthew 5:18 (par) make interesting interpretive

---

[76] I.H. Marshall, *The Gospel of Luke* (Grand Rapids, MI, 1979) 269–270.

[77] M.G. Steinhauser, *Doppelbildworte in den synoptischen Evangelien* (FB 44; Stuttgart, 1981) 187 and n.16.

pairs. The former pair is the most explicit Synoptic instance (cf. Matt 10:8b, 10 par) of the *sic et non* widely tolerated, indeed cultivated in wisdom literature and classical rhetoric.[78] Only Luke gives both versions (11:23; 9:50), but their reception as a virtual pair in Synoptic tradition may be implied in the extreme topical similarity of their separate contexts. At any rate the Marcan and Q variants differ hermeneutically in two respects: the Marcan versions are more conciliatory ("whoever is not against...") and are addressed to the community ("us/you"); the Q variant is positively, exclusively centred on being "with" a rhetorical "me." In the rhetorical sense, therefore, the Q variant is both normatively and ethically more intense, although both variants presuppose normative conflict.

Between the other two rhetorically matched gnomai, the more personal version (Mark 13:31 par Matt 24:35; Luke 21:33) is remarkable because it is a normative saying about normative sayings ("my words" [*logoi*]). Moreover, the gnome places Jesus' rhetoric (for Matthew and Luke explicitly) in normative tension between the speaker's personal and oracular authority and scriptural authority. This is in sharp conflict with the less novel affirmation of the Q gnome (Matt 5:18 par Luke 16:17). Yet the normative tension within the Marcan gnome is expressed in a true paradox rather than in a bald opposition: symbols not only of permanence but also of totality will vanish in the face of apparent ephemera and fragments attributed to Jesus. Not only the eschatological quality, but also the personal authority (*ethos*) of Jesus as speaker is made emphatic by the oracular amen-formula ("Amen *I* say to *you*" Mark 13:30 par; Matt 5:18) in the Marcan versions and in the Matthaean variant of the Q *nomos* gnome.[79] Yet even in Marcan tradition, Jesus' oracular *ethos* is not absolute (Mark 13:32 par Matt 24:36).

---

[78] See Prov 10; 26:4,5; Cic. *Lig.* 32; for contextually detached pairs (e.g., Prov 16:32/17:1) see T. Hildebrandt, "Proverbial pairs: Compositional Units in Proverbs 10–29," *JBL* 107 (1988) 207–224, 209.

[79] Dewey, "Quibbling over Serifs"; Berger, "Hellenistische Gattungen," 1056.

*Gnomic **ethos**: interim conclusions*

Especially the first examples above (Mark 2:17a par; 2:19a par; Luke 4:23a; Mark 6:4 par; Matt 10:24–25 par; Matt 11:27b par) constitute a small and diverse, but still coherent gnomic sub-group. In these six and the two examples in which the speaker's self-reference is by pronoun (Mark 13:31 par; Matt 12:30 par) the intrinsic gnomic rhetoric combines putative self-designations by the speaker with predominantly disintegrative normative expressions. Rhetorical self-characterization is not gratuitous self-expression; it serves the normative goals of communication between speaker and listener.

Physician, prophet, teacher, even master, bridegroom and son are not in (self-)reference to Jesus strictly metaphoric (though the last two have special symbolic independence). Instead, these images are metonymic and partial, with some note of irony. Significantly, the designations and the gnomai do in fact cumulatively give a surprisingly good, theologically and historically plausible description of the public image of Jesus of Nazareth.

Each of these gnomai implies a not entirely sympathetic dialogue (see Mark 6 or Luke 4) between the speaker's self-characterization and the categories and perceptions of this audience. These gnomai, despite their often oracular qualities, and Greco-Roman gnomic style generally are not meant to represent esoteric speech. Rather they are a publicly nuanced distillation, often in normative conflict, of personally asserted, socially disputed authority. Thus, although they are strongly conflictive in implication, their normative tone is moderated by their analogical, connotative turns of language: even at their most oracular, they are neither bluntly polemical nor *ipse dixit* pronouncements. In this even the most personally referential gnomai (e.g. Mark 13:31 par and Matt 12:30 par) are rhetorically far from such direct metaphorical predications as Matthew 5:14 or John 8:12.[80]

Perhaps the most important historical characteristic of the 'personal' gnomai is therefore that they attribute to Jesus sayings which depend directly upon the character of their speaker for their authority without portraying him as an unreasoning mystagogue. The gnomai reviewed so far express serious normative conflict from that personal authoritative

---

[80] Berger, *Formgeschichte*, 38–39.

standpoint without assuming the official, objective forms of legal codification.

Can the small number of personally referential gnomai in the gospels be accepted as evidence of an authentic speech habit of Jesus, or is it still only the Johannine Jesus who talks about himself? My general claim that gnomai, like parables, authentically represent Jesus' marked rhetorical preferences depends in part on their massive attestation in the tradition. The small group of gnomai attributed to Jesus (in Luke 4:23 sarcastically as an imaginary hostile imitation!) in which the speaker is syntactically represented is not, however, rhetorically isolated from the rest of Synoptic gnome-use. Thus for the rhetoricians too only a minority of gnomai or gnome performances refer more or less explicitly to the speaker, addressee or a third party, but all gnome-use was understood (Aristotle, *Rh.* II 21,16=1395b; III 17,9=1418a) to be 'ethical', that is, to contribute heavily to the speaker's self-characteriz- ation in rapport (or conflict) with the audience. What is distinctive about gnomai attributed to Jesus is therefore not that his alleged gnomai are implicitly or—more rarely—explicitly personal. Instead, gnomai attributed to Jesus, like gnomai attributed to some Cynics, stand out *relatively* (e.g., against Aristotle's advice, II 21) for their conflictual and abrasive rather than ingratiating *ethos*.

In fact, the personal gnomai in the Synoptic gospels illustrate well the usefulness of gnomic rhetoric for dramatic, yet nuanced personal characterization. On the one hand, gnomai conventionally and seman- tically promote vivid characterization. On the other hand, the analogical, connotative aspects of gnome deny the gnomai their textual autonomy from a controlling performantial presence of the speaker.

Ethos and *Son of Man gnomai*

In this respect an appreciation of gnomic *ethos*-projection can guide us into other aspects of (e.g., symbolic) self-characterization (and charac- terization of others) in the gospel tradition—certainly these have proven frustrating or inscrutable for non-rhetorical criticism. E. Fuchs found the core of Jesus' rhetoric in his analogical representation of his relation to his followers:

[W]hat is special in Jesus' teaching proclamation is the analogical power by which Jesus implicitly makes himself, his obedience, into the standard for his disciples' awareness.[81]

The implied roles of narrator and audience in parable performance has not gone unnoticed in historical exegesis, though without reference to rhetorical *ethos*.[82] The Son of Man language in the Synoptics presents more resistant problems, but from a rhetorical point of view a large part of the problem is the gospel tradition's unanimous insistence that the Son of Man mannerism was (in any reconstructible pre-gospel context) both a rhetorical self-characterization, part of Jesus' distinctive *ethos*, and a symbol by which the speaker pointed normatively away from himself. The same thing happens, though more intelligibly, in every gnome performance, since gnomic *ethos* is not psychological self-expression, but communicative bridge or weapon. Indeed, in one gnome (Matt 8:20 par) the Son of Man mannerism is used both in self-characterization and to indicate the optional normative community of his followers. Notoriously the Son of Man mannerism does not define any rhetorically unified set of sayings comparable with gnome or parable. Still, like gnome and parable, the Son of Man materials embody a haunting mixture of authoritative self-revelation, proverbial anthropology and higher eschatological symbolism.

If the Son of Man sayings are authentic they also indicate that Jesus' proclamation was very much bound up with his character.[83]

Foxes, birds and the speaker: Matthew 8:20 (par)

The gnome of the foxes and birds is the only gnome which invariably refers to the Son of Man, but there are other gnomai in which Son of Man language marks one Synoptic variant. I discussed earlier the semantic tension and unclear tradition-critical relationship between the personal Mark 14:21 (par Matt 26:24; Luke 22:22) and the universal Matthew 18:7 (par Luke 17:1). Both the specific Marcan Son of Man

---

[81] E. Fuchs, *Hermeneutik* (2d edn., Bad Cannstatt, 1958) 226.

[82] E. Schweizer, "Jesus Christus I: Neue Testament," *TRE* XVI (1987) 671–726, 716.

[83] G.N. Stanton, *Jesus of Nazareth in New Testament Preaching* (SNTSMS 27; Cambridge, 1974) 156, cf. 165.

version and the somewhat more universal Q version of the scandal gnome reflect strongly on the normative stance of the speaker over against his hearers in a situation of conflict so profound that *skandala* and betrayal are inevitable. Even in Q, the agent of scandals (Matt 18:7b par) is emphatically singular. Conversely, in the Son of Man form, Jesus adopts a symbolic self-characterization not for its own sake alone but rather to sharpen the ironic analogy between the Son of Man's fate and that of his betrayer. That is, the explicitly personal version is still symbolically personal, with analogical implications beyond Jesus' biography, while the less personal Q version still characterizes the referee, if not explicitly the speaker.

Lord of the Sabbath: Mark 2:27 and 28 (par)

We may compare the next clearest case of a gnome attested in both a Son of Man and a less emphatically self-referential version. As in the preceding example, so also in Mark 2:27 and 28 (par) the tradition-historical connection between Son of Man saying and more general logion is not at issue. For the present it is the rhetorical relationship between the two which is of interest as an indication of the balance of personality and (in this case clearly legal) normativity in each. There is no simple equivalence between the two versions, as the Matthaean and Lucan texts fairly pointedly imply: introduction of the normatively specific '*kurios*' in verse 28 (par) made it the more acceptable qualification of the Sabbath norm.

The more universal gnome, Mark 2:27, is plainly not personal in the strongly self-referential sense of the examples treated above. It is to that extent all the better as an illustration of the essentially 'ethical' basis of gnomic normativity in personal authority even where no outspoken personal reference is made. Thus, argumentatively, Mark 2:27 is not presented even loosely as the logical outcome of the foregoing discussion, but instead as an authoritatively independent assertion relying ultimately on the authority of the speaker. Rhetorical self-characterization by the speaker is not the topic of the gnome, but its strongly implicit normative presupposition.

Servanthood and the Son of Man: Mark 10:43–44 (par)

The rhetorical link between Mark 10:43–44 (par) and the Son of Man saying, verse 45 (par), is not quite so close. The proximity of gnomic and Son of Man oracles, however, conveniently illustrates my main point in this section: the rhetorical difference between explicit self-reference and implied *ethos* is not that great. A self-referential aspect is explicit in the Son of Man formulation, but still very strongly implicit in verses 43 and 44—and would be in any context which attributed them to Jesus. As ever, it is not possible to tell surely whether the gnome was brought into the context of Jesus' rhetoric by Jesus himself or in subsequent imitation of his gnomic style. The theoretical distinction diminishes in historical significance, however, before the coherence of the gnomic category. It is important to notice, here again, the organic, rhetorical relationship of conflictive normativity, personal authority (explicit or implicit) and a preference for analogical connotivity which veils, asserts and blends normativity and *ethos*.

It is nonetheless also worth pointing out that Mark 10:43–44 and 45 belong together within a tradition-historical as well as rhetorical complex in which Klaus Berger has persuasively identified a common, orally transmitted gnomic core. Moreover the common verbal analogy (*diakonos/doulos; megas/meizon*) which Berger finds behind Mark 10, Luke 22 and John 13 is both traditionally and historically linked to Jesus' exemplary gesture of table service.

> The...sentence, "Who serves is great," presupposed for the background (*Vorstufe*) of Mark and Luke, is in fact the first formally (*gattungsmassig*) demonstrable common element of the tradition (Luke 22, 26f.; Mark 10, 43b. 44a), since—despite all the differences in detail—it deals with guidance for conduct in particular cases (for the great or leaders and for those who would be great).

Berger emphasizes the interrelation of gnomic and episodic memory and tradition. The same relation between gesture and word underlines the ethical character of both, even if the explicit self-reference of the speaker as Son of Man is tradition-historically the least secure aspect of the gnomic tradition. Not only are word (Mark 10:43, 44a) and gesture (John 13) rhetorically inseparable, both exemplify the inseparability of characterization (*ethos*) and persuasion (*pistis*) in gnome-use.

Wisdom's children: Matthew 11:16–19 par Luke 7:31–35

The remarkable discourse, Matthew 11:16–19 (par Luke 7:31–35) again combines gnomic and gestural or episodic elements. The discourse in general is also an interesting challenge to scholarly notions of authenticity: both gnomai (Matt 11: 17 and 19b) look proverbial, but are not therefore uncharacteristic of Jesus' or pre-gospel rhetorics. Likewise the relationship between Jesus and John the Baptist sketched in verses 18 and 19 is historical, even if the saying looks like reflecting a later rivalry of movements. In the context of the relation between Jesus and John—and their respective relations with the sayings' audience and their wider community—the gnomai (verses 17 and 19b) are clearly strongly self-characterizations by the speaker. But again, the speaker's self-characterization is in rhetorical relation (again in a quite complex normative conflict) with characterizations of others.

Carrion and the parousia: Matthew 24:27–28 par Luke 17:24 (cf. 17:37b)

In a final example of a gnome in which the putative speaker appears to characterize himself by association with a Son of Man saying, the association is more problematic. Matthew 24:27–28 brings the parousia of the Son of Man and the gnome of the corpse and carrion-birds together. Luke, however, gives them separately (17:24, 37b respectively). In defence of the Matthaean treatment it may be said that Matthew 24:26–27 are in some sense about location—and catastrophic, sky-borne signs of direction-whereas Luke must reintroduce the question of direction (17:37a), unmotivated after 17:22–35(36). The greatest difficulty is that of the gnomic imagery itself which recalls in assertive inappropriateness the offensive challenge of Matthew 8:22 (par). Luke seems to solve the difficulty by isolating the gnome. In Matthew the problem is not so much solved as aggravated in a reception which may well be redactional, but which even as such gives insight into gospel reception of gnomic rhetoric as personal as well as normative disclosure.

Above all, the relationship between the Matthaean verses 27 and 28 emphasizes the connotative incompleteness of both disclosures: it is not even clear whether the ominous attraction of the birds of prey and the portentous career of the lightening are positively compared. Perhaps the association is by way of contrast and the weirdly stable location of the 'corpse' signifies rather the parousia of the false prophet than the elusive and sudden revelation of the Son of Man. Even as antitype of Jesus, though, the dead body carries an ironic self-reference to his eminently foreseeable fate. Even in anticipation, such a fate may quite authentically have stood in puzzling tension with some of the expectations associated by Jesus with Son of Man symbolism.[84] In Jesus' situation the corpse is no more metaphoric than the contrary expectation of a celestial parousia or than the other unburied dead of Matthew 8:22. At any rate, Matthew 24:27–28 typify the implicitly self-assertive, personal and aggressively conflictual nature of Synoptic gnomai.

In all, the eight occurrences of Son of Man symbolism in, or close to gnome is an important bridge between explicit, yet normatively oblique self-characterization of the speaker in a comparative few gnomai and the self-assertive normativity of the bulk of Synoptic gnomic sayings. The explicitly self-characterizational gnomai and gnomai associated with the Son of man mannerism express rather clearly the disintegrative, conflictive tendency of early Christian rhetoric. These gnomai also reflect the fact that, because gnomai are analogical, even the most explicit expressions of rhetorical *ethos* remain elliptical. For the same reason the relation of rhetorical topicality and normativity to actual social normativity remains ambiguous. We may say, however, that the focus of normativity in gnomai is the specific or optional relationships of the community of discipleship around the gnome-speaker; Synoptic gnomai are seldom genuinely universal norms, even when, like Matthew 24:28 (par), they appear "simply" to "state a fact."[85]

Gnomai on the norms of discipleship

It can hardly be surprising that many of the gnomai which most expressly invoke the authority of the speaker are also among those which most clearly address the topic of discipleship. It makes sense that in normative rhetoric the speakers's personal authority to speak

---

[84] See Sanders, *Jesus and Judaism*, 145–146, the second most important argument in Sanders' case.

[85] Funk, Hoover and the Jesus Seminar, *The Five Gospels*, 249, 368.

commandingly should emerge often beside the normative requirements of a community of personal, discipular allegiance—especially with the third rhetorical ingredient, of conflictive self-definition beside other, ideologically more mature and homogeneous identities. The natural obverse of a rhetoric of normative self-assertion is a model of community, especially a model of community held together by rhetorical personality more than by coherent ideology.

Servanthood and subordination: Mark 9:35 (par); Mark 10:31 (par); Matthew 10:24 (par)

Among the most obvious examples of gnomai in which both the topic of discipleship and the paradigmatic authority of the speaker are relatively directly addressed are the *Wanderlogien* Mark 9:35 (par) and its analogue Mark 10:31 (par). Such a gnomic core could hardly function normatively at all unless informed (at least putatively) by the authority of a speaker who is both *protos* and *diakonos* (cf. the association of Mark 10:43–44 (par) with the Son of Man saying, v. 45 par). At the same time the norm presupposes a context within which primacy and servility could be concretely and symbolically practised (cf. John 13). Above all, this complex of gnomai and gestural chreiai and the shared, distinctive topic of leadership as servanthood in community are vital evidence for the norms of discipleship around Jesus. Against the superficial sense of Matthew 10:24a (par), Jesus' disciples were in no sense his apprentices; analogically, this gnome is about ethical rather than disciplinary imitation. In the servant gnomai the servants' function as disciples remains radically obscure, even irrelevant, compared with their emphatically evoked relationship to Jesus and to the discipleship community.

Discipleship and apprenticeship: Luke 9:57–62 (par) versus Matthew 10:24 par Luke 6:40 (cf. Luke 6:39 par Matthew 15:14; 23:16, 24)

As we saw at the beginning of this chapter, both modern critical[86] and Synoptic receptions of the series of gnomic chreiai, Luke 9:57–60 (par Matthew 8:19–22), emphasize their specific normative relevance to discipleship. These sayings concentrate on the call to discipleship and on its social and material cost. They are therefore more relevant evidence for the meaning of discipleship in Jesus' circle than the gnome (Matt 10:24 par) which actually uses the word 'disciple', but does so in a purely conventional, scholastic sense.

Matthew 10:24 (par) closely and uncritically reflects a social norm of discipleship which rhetorical normativity in Jesus' tradition elsewhere repudiates or contradicts (e.g., the polemical gnome of the blind leading the blind, Luke 6:39 par Matt 15:14; 23:16, 24). In gospel rhetoric, the norm of ethical assimilation of the disciple to the master is oriented toward radical renunciation of potentially conflicting, normal relationships, even life itself, rather than toward educational apprenticeship.

This normative conflict between the rhetoric of following Jesus and the social norms of apprenticeship discipline is, moreover, not only to be located in Jesus' career. Christian formation (e.g., prescriptive imitation of Paul) is more like conventional discipleship than like the summons of Luke 9:57–62. Q scholarship is still labouring hard to construct a Galilean community in which the rhetorical normativity of these three gnomic chreiai would be continuous with actual social norms as was clearly not the case in most Christian milieux. In this key respect a much greater normative continuity is postulated between the rhetoric of the Sayings Gospel Q and its presumed user community "Q people" than is postulated between other texts about Jesus and their user groups; to the extent that the "Q people" are theoretically supposed to have enacted Q discipleship rhetoric socially, they are qualitatively unlike Marcan or Pauline communities.[87] If Q is rhetoric and not social description, "social critique" rather than "social reform," then the "Q people" are out of a job.[88] Jesus' aggressive ethos of himself as

---

[86] Hengel, *Nachfolge*; G. Theißen, "Wanderradikalismus: Literatursoziologische Aspekte der Überlieferung von Worten Jesu im Urchristentum," *ZTK* 70 (1973) 245–271, 249–250; Vaage, *Galilean Upstarts*, 89–93; Jacobson, *The First Gospel*, 130–137.

[87] On the problem, see Kloppenborg, "Q People," 77–81; "Q: Recent Opinion," 12–28. Since Theißen, *Wanderradikalismus*, emphasis on itinerancy has declined, with growing interest in ideological (e.g., Cynic) critique, cf. Vaage, *Galilean Upstarts*.

[88] Cf. Kloppenborg, "Q: Recent Opinion," 19 on Mack, *Lost Gospel*.

speaker and of his followers may actually have been socially normative for a few people for a few years. There remains, however, a significant normative hiatus between the rhetorical normativity of these sayings in gospel literature and any actual community of readers and listeners.

Prophet and disciple: Mark 6:4 (par); Luke 9:62 (1 Kgs 19:20)

A similar hint of discontinuity between rhetoric and even sectarian society may be detected behind Mark 6:4 (par) and Luke 9:62: no doubt these gnomai should have been specifically relevant to Christian prophets, but there is no sign of this hypothetical interest in the texts.[89] Neither gnome makes Jesus the originator of a prophetic school. And positively, as in Mark 2:19a (par) or Matthew 11:27 (par), the relationship between Jesus and his disciples is defined in terms of personal intimacy and oracular premonition rather than scholastic or partisan adherence.

Eunuch and disciple: Matthew 19:12

Matthew 19:12 may well reflect one side of a homelessness (*Wanderradikalismus*) shared by Jesus with his immediate companions. Certainly Matthaean reception emphasizes the gnome's reliance upon the authority of Jesus' word, somewhat in contrast to the more complicated argument about marriage to which it is appended. As with many gnomai, it is a question here of "how far the logion is to be taken literally,"[90] but the question is one of social rather than physical realism, since those made eunuchs for the Reign's sake are distinguished not only from biologically natural but also from artificial eunuchs. Here as generally it is unwise to speak too quickly of metaphor: it is no poetic conceit to call someone a eunuch, who is deprived of normal family connections and succession in order to ensure undivided loyalty to his prince. The gnome is, however, normatively conflictive, in self-conscious opposition to the values of the wider society, as it envisions self-castration as an optional norm. Finally, like Luke 9:62, the eunuch-gnome mobilizes a commun-

---

[89] Theißen, *Wanderradikalismus*, 250 and n.14; cf. Gräßer, "Jesus in Nazareth," 13 and n.65.
[90] Theißen, "Wanderradikalismus," 250 n.13.

ity which is not simply that of technical discipleship, but which is nevertheless radically (i.e., conflictively) oriented to the Reign.

Disciple as labourer: Matthew 10:10b par Luke 10:7b; Matthew 9:37
par Luke 10:2

One of the least figurative, most widely attested and, by the way, most
proverbial-sounding Synoptic gnomai is "the proverb about the worker
and his wage," (Matthew 10:10b par Luke 10:7b).[91] Here once more,
gnomic analogy mixes metaphor and non-metaphoric normativities:
Jesus' adherents as such are not labourers, but they did need to eat, so
that it is labour which must be normatively redefined to include
whatever it is that Jesus' followers are supposed to do. Even so, the
notion of 'workers' here and in the more figurative and eschatological
Matthew 9:37 (par Luke 10:2a) is optional not universal in normative
range: a differentiation of roles is implied even within the movement,
toward goals which more or less disintegratively define it over against
the otherwise neglected field of labour.

Gnomai received within the topic of discipleship

Beyond those gnomai which signal relevance to discipleship in their
internal rhetorical use of role designations (disciple, eunuch, slave, etc.),
there is also a number of gnomic sayings which though topically less
precise are received by the Synoptics as norms for Christian
discipleship. Many more of the sayings gathered into Matthew 10 figure
here, notably Matthew 10:26, 27. Similarly in Mark 13:31b (par,
including Matt 10:22) something which looks intrinsically like a
universal eschatological indicative is received in all its gospel performances as an implicit imperative applicable to the experience of the
persecuted circle of discipleship. More than expressing a mere topical
ambiguity, such gnomai embody the fact that analogy (a comparison of
relationships) can be extended into metaphor, though it need not be
intrinsically metaphoric: "A stich in time saves nine," can be cited
normatively outside sewing contexts, but it does, by the way, imply
some indirect memory of sewing technique.

---

[91] Vaage, *Galilean Upstarts*, 128 (quoted)–131; Vaage is puzzled about the
proverb's function in Q.

Losing and finding life: Mark 8:35 par

Mark 8:35 (par) is the most impressive Synoptic reception of a gnome which is intrinsically more widely applicable as being about discipleship:

> There is no doubt that the tradition remembered the saying about losing and finding life in the definite context of the challenge to become a disciple. Mark (8:34–35) and most probably Q as well (Matt 10:38–39; Luke has a different order) associates this saying with the one about taking up one's cross.[92]

The gnome's conflictive aspect as a corporate norm is documented in Beardslee's survey of the motif of (roughly) immortality through self-sacrifice: such language functions most typically in crises of community survival. The normative self-assertiveness of Synoptic gnome, that is, the inherent problem of personal or social authority behind so challenging a rhetorical norm, surfaces not only in the self-reference discerned by post-Easter hindsight, but also more intrinsically in the saying's paradoxical logic, especially vivid in contrast with the more consistent message of Mark 13:13b (par). Beardslee (characteristically) overstates the tension between this 'phenomenological' emphasis on the paradox and the historical-comparative result which identifies similar motifs elsewhere.[93] In the parallels which he cites a metaphorical wedge is always readily available with which to prise apart the terms of an apparent paradox. In Mark 8:35, by contrast, although there is room for difference between the life that is lost and that to be gained, there is no reason to suspect any rhetorically intentional metaphor.

---

[92] Beardslee, "Saving One's Life," 60.
[93] Beardslee, "Saving One's Life," 61–66.

Discipleship, ecclesiology and soteriology

A further small group of gnomai raise the probably insoluble question of the relationship between discipleship and the wider renewal or recreation of Israel.[94] Thus in the minimal context of association with Jesus' conversation, the gnome about the City (Matt 5:14) is not simply a visual metaphor, but rather far more an essentially non-figurative extension of the symbolic, paradigmatic centrality of Jerusalem (cf. Isa 2:2–4; Mi 4:12),[95] the topographical correlative of Jesus' own self-assertion and destiny.

The few and the many: Matthew 22:14; 7:13 par Luke 13:24

This is the context also, not just eschatological but incipiently ecclesial, of the gnomai of the few and the many, Matthew 22:14 and Matthew 7:13 (par Luke 13:24), though variation of forms and reception points to differences of normativity. Thus Luke 13:24 relates the gnome apparently to Jewish obstinacy, while the Two Ways (and Two Cities) of Matthew 7:13 make a more universal application. Whatever the saying's original normative scope, its separation of the few is clearly agonistic (Luke 13:24) and disintegrative.

The sons of the light: Luke 16:8b

Something of the nuance given to this separation for renewal is captured in the gnome Luke 16:8b, appended to the Parable of the Unjust Steward. The normative opposition of the Sons of the Light to those of this age, which recalling the sectarian self-definition of the Qumran society, is filled with an irony which often seems to have been characteristic of Jesus' attitude:[96] the sons of this age as such are positively paradigmatic for the Sons of the Light. This saying is not strictly paradoxical, nor is it hyperbolic: the sons of this age really are smarter...It is, on the other hand, sharply conflictive as well as essentially self-assertive in the idiosyncratic light in which it discloses

---

[94]   Cf. Sanders, *Jesus and Judaism*, 47–49, 95, 116–119, 222–241; Theißen, *Soziologie*, 9, 104–106.

[95]   Boismard, *Synopse*, 132–133.

[96]   Sanders, *Jesus and Judaism*, 174–211 on "The Sinners."

the eschatological conflict. This gnome is normative and authoritative not as the distillation of a common-place view, but as the expression, authentic in its content and style, of an intensely personal revelation.

The children, the holy and the dogs: Mark 7:27 (par); Matthew 7:6

Like the complex, yet compelling discourse Matthew 11:16–19 (par Luke 7:31–35), Jesus' dialogue with the Syro-Phoenician woman is impossible to authenticate *in toto*, but impossible to dismiss in detail. Here, as elsewhere among strongly gnomic chreiai, the arguments which cast doubt on the authenticity of the whole do not bear with equal relevance on the central gnome. In this case the slight and equivocal results (basically Matt 8:5–13 and Mark 7:24–30) of the evangelists' efforts to bring Jesus into positive contact with Gentiles suggest that the gospel writers were impressively unprepared simply to fabricate the required material.[97] Jesus' "atrocious saying" (Mark 7:27 par) particularly is at least traditional and prior to the Synoptic story.[98] The point is not that the gnome is prior to any chriic framing, since the association of two gnomai (vv. 27 and 28) already implies episodic recollection in dialogue and narrative. But especially with Matthew 7:6, Mark 7:27 must be taken seriously as evidence that Jesus could at least sharply invoke the sacral distinction between Israel and the Gentiles, a stance which, if authentic, would not have precluded, but would scarcely have facilitated a subsequent Gentile mission. We shall have to return to the legal topic of the Gentiles in pre-gospel rhetoric

Conclusions

Before taking up the complex question of 'legal' topicality in and around gnomic normativity, it will be in order to draw together a few intermediate conclusions. As well, it may be helpful to clarify the exegetical logic at work in both the preceding and the following examples. In view of the Synoptics' massive attribution of a gnomic

---

[97] Sanders, *Jesus and Judaism*, 218–221 esp. n.36.
[98] F.W., Beare, *The Gospel According to Matthew* (Oxford, 1981) 343, he invents a bigoted Christian prophet to take the blame for Jesus, 344; cf. Luz, *Matthäus* I, 435 and n.59: a "topos."

rhetorical habit to Jesus, an approach to individual gnomai should begin from the special possibility of their authenticity or representativeness. The presumption is that gnomai collectively represent authentic aspects of Jesus' rhetoric, his stylistic decorum, *ethos* and preferred topics. This is clearly not convertible into a criterion of individual authenticity, though some gnomai are strong cases for authentication even apart from their cohesion with the gnomic pattern generally.

Roughly, then, since Jesus very probably did speak in gnomai often and memorably enough to bias his subsequent tradition, it is fair to ask what individual Synoptic gnomai might have meant, if Jesus had indeed used them. Applied to isolated sayings, this procedure would usually be exegetically and historically tendentious; applied to gnomai as instances of a wider rhetorical pattern, I think the problem is less acute. Some gnomai (Matt 8:22 par) can usefully bear atomistic study. For the most part, however, I have tried to examine aspects (*ethos*, topicality, oracularity) which are attested by a plurality of Synoptic gnomai and which are attested both in the intrinsic rhetoric of at least some gnomai and in gospel receptions of others.

The sayings themselves are, indeed, not quite as intractable as might be expected. Though gnomai make themselves memorable and evocative by a richness and flexibility of connotation, this is sensibly bounded in most cases by a balancing of figurative with more concrete and circumstantial topical or ethical references. Because gnomic connotivity is ultimately at the service of rhetorical normativity, its scope is never unlimited.

The most prevalent, though still not universal, aspect of Synoptic gnomai is the conflictive, disintegrative tendency of their normativity. Their frequent implicit or explicit reliance on characterization and assertion of the speaker's personal authority is therefore not merely a gratuitous assertion of identity, but is rather an integral part of the rhetorical rapport between an exceptional speaker and the exceptional audience he is trying to create.

Yet if the strikingly projected *ethos* of the gnomai so far is subordinate to rhetorical rapport and conflict, so too all other topicalities (eschatology, proverbiality, discipleship) normatively secondary to the relationship between speaker and audience. Eschatology and proverbial wisdom are both to a degree constitutive of gnomic normativity, but neither is essential to it in the Synoptic sample.

Furthermore, if the problems of authority and of normative conflict would seem to underlie the choice—by Jesus—of a gnomic as well as parabolic style, the analogical character of gnomai also offered a useful indirectness. Although Synoptic gnomai do not quite achieve "that worry-free atmosphere" of the parables,[99] the marriage of connotation to normative outspokenness does temper the arbitrariness and inflexibility of Jesus' *ethos*.

The relatively concrete normative fields of discipleship and communal renewal confirm that connotivity is cultivated in Jesus' rhetoric in order to express a nuanced, magisterially authoritative but not authoritarian normativity: discipleship and other communal institutions are vital to Jesus' movement, but neither the content of the gnomai nor the technical informality of a sayings-tradition which is so heterogeneous in even its most consistent aspects (gnome and parable) supports the assumption of a scholastic or mnemotechnical discipline. Allowing that Jesus should have had some practical programmatic motive for gathering disciples,[100] the Synoptic gnomai permit only its negative description.

In two essentials—conversationally informal, but ethically radical discipleship and strongly conflictive gnomic rhetoric—by far the best available analogy is from Cynicism,[101] although systematic comparison is hampered by the much wider popularity and longevity and unrestricted literary diffusion of more-or-less Cynicizing gnome traditions in antiquity.[102] Cynicism is, moreover, important not only as the least limited analogy to discipleship and gnome-use in Jesus' circles but also as one medium for the oral percolation of rhetorical culture beyond the literate minorities, though, in contrast with Rabbinic borrowings, individual gnomai ascribed to Jesus do not seem directly dependent upon gnomic cores from Cynic tradition.[103] In his study of Hebrew, Rabbinic adaptations of Greek chriic traditions, H.A. Fischel concluded with astonishment "that the gnomic parts of the Hillel *chriae* still show

---

[99] Theißen, *Soziologie*, 98.

[100] Hengel, *Nachfolge*, 80–94; Sanders, *Jesus and Judaism*, 224–228.

[101] Hengel, *Nachfolge*, 6, 31–32, 35, 37; Theißen, "Wanderradikalismus," 255–256; Downing, "Contexts;" Vaage, *Galilean Upstarts*; Kloppenborg, "Q: Recent Opinion," 18–20, 26–28.

[102] Downing, "Contexts," 446 and n.21.

[103] Fischel, "Transformations," 373 n.4, 409 and n.4.

so many traces of the original Greek patterns" to the extent that Cynic gnomic core-patterns are preferred even where suitable Old Testament gnomic models are readily available.[104]

Still, in his most thoroughly worked-out example of a Cynicist gnomic chreia ascribed to, among many others, Hillel, Fischel is embarrassed by the unique seriousness of the Hebrew version and specifically by "the heavy" (i.e., legal and eschatological as well as stylistically sombre) "terms of the gnome."[105] Gnomai which touch on the sensitive topics of social normativity—areas often regulated by legal and eschatological sanctions—are more common and less metaphoric in Jesus' tradition than in Cynicizing (including Hillel's) tradition.

Thus, for example, the Cynic, "Men were not created for the sake of horses, but horses for the sake of men,"[106] shows its rhetorical kinship with the Marcan Sabbath-gnome and its Son of Man complement (2:27–28, cf. 1 Cor 6:13). At the same time the normative stakes are clearly higher and the threateningly unsarcastic demand for actual normative adjustment all the more imperative in the saying attributed to Jesus.

Finally, the Synoptic reception of gnomai on discipleship raises again the question of continuity in gnomic normativity. That is, the repeated normative dissonance between the intrinsic rhetorical possibilities of gnomic sentences and their receptional applications suggests, rather ambiguously, both normative change through time and space and also normative dissonance between received or projected rhetoric and actual social groups.

That gnome is a medium of continuity and variation in pre-gospel normative tradition, makes it an all the more useful opportunity to detect and interpret discontinuities in reception and practice. In addition, the phenomenon of normative shift between receptions of gnomic sayings confirms their frequent tradition-historical priority. In relation to those gnomai which show a degree of 'legal' topicality, recognition of normative dissonance between gnome and reception may, moreover, provide a strategy toward more nuanced assessment of Jesus' relation to Jewish legality.

---

[104] H.A. Fischel, "Studies in Cynicism and the Ancient Near East: The Transformation of a *Chria*," in *Religion in Antiquity: Essays in Memory of E.R. Goodenough*, ed. J. Neusner (Leiden, 1988) 372–411, 409.

[105] Fischel, "Transformation," 398 n.4, 399.

[106] A.J. Malherbe, ed., *The Cynic Epistles* (Missoula, MT, 1974) 75 (#24).

CHAPTER SIX

GNOMIC NORMATIVITY AND LAW IN SYNOPTIC AND IN PAULINE RECEPTION

Balancing and testing a gnomic approach to Jesus' spoken tradition

A good hypothesis should not only explain convincingly the data at hand from the start; it must also suggest probable and testable connections beyond or behind its initial problems and it must indicate the relevance of otherwise wasted evidence. A good historical explanation must have both descriptive 'scope' and persuasive 'force', the power to generate unforeseen possibilities and to risk being tested by them. From this point of view, the impressive scope of the old form criticism could not compensate for its embarrassing lack of force at key junctures (e.g. the correspondence of form to generative social setting).[1]

An approach to Jesus' tradition through its gnomic rhetoric gains both scope and general force from the extensive distribution and intensive, conscious cultivation of gnome throughout Hellenistic rhetoric and education and across every sort of critical boundary in early Christian literature. Still, at this stage in an argument which claims such a scope and which depends upon a cumulative impression from many small textual sub-units, it is important to pay some specific attention to "the ratio of 'scope' to 'force'."[2] This means treating topically legal gnomai in some detail, as the best chance to test the persuasive force of a gnomic approach to Jesus' tradition on a narrower range of texts and on an exegetical problem with implications well beyond the Synoptic Gospels.

The most important consequence of recognizing the gnomic element in Synoptic literature is the evidence which it provides for basic continuity between Synoptic tradition and the rest of Hellenistic rhetorical and educational culture. The scope of this claim is very great.

---

[1] Downing, "Contexts," 439.
[2] Downing, "Contexts," 440.

Its power is in its testable potential for describing Jesus' sayings tradition, without appealing either to the ill-defined folkloric model of older form criticism or to the more consistent, but doubtfully relevant scholastic, memorizational model of oral tradition. A tradition of oral rhetoric, laced with gnomai (gnomai with other sayings types in argumentative discourses, gnomai with parables, gnomai with episodic memories and narratives) is a more probable alternative to the 'wild-sprouting folkloric tradition' required by form criticism. We may rightly think of such a tradition of gnomic rhetoric as 'carefully cultivated' without having to commit ourselves either to reductionist folkloric models of tradition or to scribal, memorizational models of teaching, seldom evidenced in the gospels.[3]

Because gnome is so prominent both in Synoptic literature and in the most accessible (and oral) levels of educational and rhetorical practice, an oral-traditional hypothesis is available for the first time which really fits the facts of early Christianity: Jesus' movement and its successor churches were never a folk and never a school, but from their beginning, they were engaged in vigorous, public, oral propaganda. Indeed, among Palestinian Jewish movements, Jesus' sect is distinguished not least by its early and spirited adoption of Greek, and of its rhetorical and literary possibilities. The uniquely demonstrable continuity of gnomic style and of at least some gnomai throughout Synoptic oral and written tradition is thus not only evidence (scope), it is the essential prerequisite for a theory of oral tradition which can do justice both to the gospels' distinctively oral sensibility and to their Greek literacy (force).

There are two dimensions of gnomic continuity in Synoptic tradition: quantitatively, Synoptic gnomai greatly outnumber parables; qualitatively, Jesus, early Christian rhetoric and gospel composition are more convincingly linked by gnome-use than by the social settings presumed by form critics and socio-rhetorical critics alike. These two dimensions make Synoptic gnomai the best available sample of sayings tradition as

---

[3] See the short list of examples, 1 Corinthians 11:23–25; 15:3–8 and the *gnome* Acts 20:35 in B. Gerhardsson, "Der Weg der Evangelien-tradition," in *Das Evangelium und die Evangelien*, ed. by P. Stuhlmacher (WUNT 28; Tübingen, 1983) 79–102, 80; cf. R. Riesner, *Jesus als Lehrer: Eine Untersuchung zum Ursprung der Evangelienüber-lieferung* (WUNT 27; Tübingen, 1981) 502 (quoted); see also Henderson, "Gnomic Quatrains," on the mnemotechnical possibilities of the Quatrains.

a continuous process linking Jesus and the evangelists. The importance of the gnomic sample is thus not only its broad coverage of the sayings material, but also its coherence as a semantic category in varied reception, formulation and application.

Social-historical interpreters rightly claim a degree of both contextual and personal continuity between Jesus and his tradition, between pre- and post-Easter situations and between discipleship circle and apostolic movement. Such general continuities help put questions about the individual authenticity of normative sayings in some sort of perspective.[4] Among the normative styles in Synoptic sayings material, however, only gnome-use is both demonstrably continuous from Jesus to the gospel-writers, and well-defined in its rhetorical functions. This makes it possible to keep some perspective on the generally impressive historicity of gospel traditions, while still making specific historical judgements wherever possible about particular developments of socially influential speech in Jesus' circle. The result is a stronger hypothetical basis for interpreting community relationships in Jesus' movement, wherever continuity and tension between rhetorical and social norms can be traced in differing receptions of similar gnomai.

The real test for a credible gnomic approach to Synoptic rhetoric is its ability to account for important Synoptic phenomena by relating them constructively to problems which go beyond the gospel literature. Thus gnome provides a specific ground for comparing Synoptic tradition with both Semitic (sapiential and prophetic) and Hellenistic (rhetorical) traditions. Even more urgently a gnomic approach should facilitate comparison between the Synoptic Gospels and other early Christian literatures (Pauline, Johannine, etc.), as well as between canonical and extra-canonical and between gospel and epistolary literatures.[5] The 'scope' of such comparisons is almost unlimited: in principle gnome should prove a useful basis for comparison between any Hellenistic texts.

---

[4] Downing, "Contexts," 440; Theißen, *Soziologie*, 12 and n.4.
[5] Berger, *Formgeschichte*, 156 (e) and (f).

Pauline gnome-use and Synoptic legal gnomai

Paul's letters were written prior to the composition of the surviving gospels and apparently without influence from any of the gospels' written sources (especially Q); Paul had clearly been in contact, first hostile, then reluctant and competitive, with the sort of circles in which any development of pre-Synoptic tradition would have been hard to ignore (Galatians). Comparison of Pauline with Synoptic gnome-use is therefore crucial either to verify or to falsify the hypothesis that pre-gospel sayings tradition was rhetorical—and in that sense deliberately, indelibly oral and gnomic. The comparison is also essential for assessing continuity and discontinuity in early Christian rhetoric generally. A new perspective on Pauline rhetoric and tradition-use may be the most persuasive collateral benefit of a gnomic approach to Synoptic tradition.[6]

At any rate, the problem of continuity between rhetoric and conflicting social norms and the problem of continuity between Jesus' rhetoric and that of his successors are key for both Synoptic and Pauline studies. The double problem of normative and of traditional continuity is also regularly discussed in connection with Pauline allusion or non-allusion to Synoptic sayings. Furthermore, many of the Synoptic sayings most plausibly reflected in Paul belong to the subcategory of topically legal gnomai, to which we return presently.

Paul's possible allusions to Jesus' sayings and authority have been intensively studied.[7] This adds greatly to the value of Pauline gnome-use and Pauline legality for testing a gnomic account of Jesus' tradition and of its quasi-legal normativity. Paul may well have known and

---

[6] On Johannine gnomology see Dewey, "*Paroimiai*," 81–99.

[7] F. Neirynck, "Paul and the Sayings of Jesus," in *L'Apôtre Paul: Personalité, style et conception du ministère*, ed. A. Vanhoye (BETL 73; 1986) 265–321; N. Walter, "Paulus und die urchristliche Jesustradition," *NTS* 31 (1985) 498–522; A.J.M. Wedderburn, "Paul and Jesus: The Problem of Continuity," *SJT* 38 (1985) 189–203; "Paul and Jesus: Similarity and Continuity," *NTS* 34 (1988) 161–182; S.J. Patterson, "Paul and the Jesus Tradition: It Is Time for Another Look," *HTR* 84 (1991) 23–41; H. von Lips "Paulus und die Tradition: Zitierung von Schriftworten, Herrenworten und christlichen Traditionen," *VF* 36 (1991) 27–49; see also the collection ed. by P. Richardson and J.C. Hurd, *From Jesus to Paul: Studies in Honour of F.W. Beare* (Waterloo, ON, 1984) esp. S.G. Wilson, "From Jesus to Paul: The Contours and Consequences of a Debate," 1–21.

echoed more sayings of Jesus than he actually cites; he certainly cites few enough and quotes only one, liturgical, saying (1 Cor 11:24–25). But the starting point for studying the apostle's relation to Synoptic tradition must be the odd combination of reverence for dominical authority with revision of dominical norms evident in his two definite citations, both in 1 Corinthians (7:10 and 9:14). This combination has only the sparsest analogues elsewhere in Pauline literature.[8]

Although "investigation of Paul's gnomic sentences remains a *desideratum* of New Testament scholarship,"[9] general similarity in gnome-use between Jesus and Paul and some of its limitations are not difficult to sketch.

Paul too permits himself to scatter sharply formulated gnomic sentences among his discourses. Examples of such sententious compositions are Rom 14:7f–17f, 1 Cor 5, 6, 8:2f, 10:24, 13:13 (which only becomes intelligible with attention to this sort of formulation), 14:33, 2 Cor 4:18b, 7:10, 9:6f, 13:13, Gal 2:6, 5:9, 6:7f, 1 Thess 5:7. Among these, sometimes no longer recognizable to us, are surely some then-current proverbial turns, as, e.g., Gal 5:9.[10]

A few Pauline gnomai are explicitly eschatological and at least some of the apostle's gnomai are almost certainly proverbial.[11]

On the other hand, though Paul is almost over-fond of strong, almost paradoxical juxtapositions (e.g. Gal 6:7b), there is little to approach Synoptic anti-proverbiality and self-assertion, except perhaps intensely personal, experiential, yet also christological gnomai like Galatians 2:21, Philippians 1:21 or the oracular 2 Corinthians 12:9. Correspondingly, the topics of discipleship and legality have largely converged into the

---

[8] Perhaps 1 Thess 4:14–15; 1 Cor 7:25; Rom 14:14; see Wilson, "From Jesus to Paul," 7–9; J.C. Hurd, "The Jesus Whom Paul Preaches (Acts 19:18)," Richardson and Hurd, *From Jesus to Paul*, 73–89, esp. 87–88.

[9] Betz, *Galatians*, 291 n.5; cf. K. Berger, "Die implizierten Gegner," in *Kirche: Festschrift für Günther Bornkamm*, ed. D. Lührmann and G. Strecker (Tübingen, 1980) 373–400, 374, n.12, and bibliography, 395–400; Berger, "Hellenistiche Gattungen," 1056–57.

[10] Bultmann, *Stil der Paulinischen Predigt*, 94; cf. Betz, *Galatians*, 291–311; Berger, "Hellenistiche Gattungen," 1059–1066.

[11] Eschatological: e.g., 1 Cor 15:42b–44a, cf. Gal 6:7b; 1 Thess 5:7; Rom 13:12. Proverbial: e.g., Gal 4:16, 18; 5:9; 6:7 *bis*. See Betz, *Galatians*, 26.

more universal norms of (typically gnomic) ethical parenesis.[12] This shift in gnomic normativity and topicality has conflicting normative consequences for the new topic of apostleship.[13]

Indeed Paul's Corinthian correspondence impressively documents the conflictive potential of gnomic rhetoric. Significantly, Paul seems to distance himself from those gnomai in his own Corinthian letters which come closest to the challenging tone of the most distinctive Synoptic gnomai; in fact, critics most often attribute such to Paul's correspondents or opponents.[14] Whatever the origin of the more radical gnomic slogans creeping into Paul's arguments, the balance in each context of radically disintegrative and irenic gnomai dramatizes the author's passionate, but perhaps contradictory and self-defeating desires for personal respect and church peace. Though the gospels share Paul's equivocal preference for peace with authority, the balance of rhetorical normativity among Synoptic gnomai alone is less irenic: perhaps in their original anonymity the gospel-writers could afford to risk their (borrowed) authority more than Paul could.

Paul's desire to gain or regain control over the conflictual possibilities of gnomic rhetoric is confirmed by the speculative and inferential rather than personally authoritative logic of his Corinthian gnomai (e.g. 1 Cor 6:13; cf. Mark 2:27). It is dangerous to reconstruct in any detail the actual historical situation behind Paul's Corinthian letters from their dramatic balance of conflictual and irenic gnome-use. Still, the Corinthian documents must reflect a social collision of powerful rhetorical traditions competing for normative influence, a collision which makes a variety of tradition-historical trajectories momentarily visible.

That is, the Corinthian material gives the clearest indications anywhere that the similarities and dissimilarities of gnomic style in Paul and in the Synoptics result not only from phenomenological (rhetorical) relationship but also from tradition-historical influences and conflicts. In the strong case of 1 Corinthians 9:5–14, a uniquely explicit reference

---

[12] E.g. Gal 5:25–6:10, see Betz, *Galatians*, 291–311; Rom 12:9–21, compare Luke 6:27–31.

[13] See 1 Cor 9:2, 9, 14; G. Theißen, "Legitimation und Lebensunterhalt: Ein Beitrag zur Soziologie urchristlichen Missionare," *NTS* 21 (1975) 192–221.

[14] 1 Cor 6:12/10:23; 6:13; 6:18b; 7:1, 8:1,4; 8:8. See J.C. Hurd, *The Origin of I Corinthians* (London, 1965) 67–68; Berger, "Gegner," 374 and n. 12.

to (and characteristic non-citation of) a dominical saying is strikingly linked to normative conflict and apostolic self-legitimation in gnomic style (cf. 9:2, 7, 9, 10,14). But the implied dominical gnome also confounds personal, legal and ethical normativities in its other appearances in early Christianity.[15] This collision of gnomic style and legality is at least as typical of Synoptic gnome-contextualization as it is of Pauline dominical allusion; in each it goes well beyond both the general reluctance of New Testament epistolary literature to cite sayings tradition[16] and the general Hellenistic interest in gnome.

Paul actually gives his readers no right to expect many references to sayings attributable to Jesus (Gal 1:11–24). It is another story, however, with the extreme allusiveness of the few references there are, their confinement to rhetorical contexts of normative conflict and their tendency toward topically legal Synoptic gnomai. Paul's own frequent gnome-use is in tension with his skittish, allusive relationship to Jesus-traditions which, in the gospels, are also gnomic. This tension feeds back into leading questions of Synoptic gnome-study: about oral traditional processes, about normative dissonance between Jesus' situation and that of his earliest interpreters, and about Law. The subcategory of gnomai on legal topics divides Jesus from Paul and Jesus from the Synoptists, but with telling ambiguities. These make possible a new consideration of Pauline analogues to Synoptic gnomai.

Gnome, law and Torah distinguished

Legal gnomai are marginalized in Paul's writing, both by his repudiation of (opponents'?) slogans and by his extreme allusiveness toward traditions in Jesus' name which look suspiciously like Synoptic gnomai. This raises again, however, the question of what is meant by legal or virtually halakic topicality in Synoptic gnomai. In the first place, notions of legal normativity in the ancient world correspond only loosely to modern concepts of law. Differentiation amongst sacral, civil,

---

[15] Matt 10:10 par Luke 10:7; 1 Tim 5:18; Jas 5:4; *Did.* 13:1,2.

[16] P. Stuhlmacher, "Zum Thema: Das Evangelium und die Evangelien," in *Das Evangelium und die Evangelien*, ed. P. Stuhlmacher (WUNT 28; Tübingen, 1983) 1–26, 18–19.

and ethical law, or amongst politics, religion and law cannot be pressed.[17] Less obviously, the single term 'law' in antiquity covers many competing or complementary normative systems. Among these, Jewish legality in the period of the Second Temple was obliged to adapt to a variety of situations and was itself a deeply variegated and controversial mixture of changing sectarian, partisan and ethnic relations. The very possibility of translating Torah with *nomos* betrays the breadth and fluidity of the two symbolic terms and their irreducibility to practically legal categories.[18] Law everywhere is rhetoric; in the ancient world it was less necessary to conceal this fact than to discover the normative boundaries between human and superhuman rhetorics.

In a discussion of Synoptic gnomai, the overlap between biblical and legal language is inescapable: the former gives the latter its urgency for the study of Christian origins. Still, I expect legal topicality wherever there is talk of defining and controlling practical disputes about rights and duties, without prejudice to the relationship of such law to the Law, i.e., to Torah.[19] Even in a Rabbinic literary context, legality admits of only provisional definition, though to the following I would add some reference to formal, linguistic specialization and normative clarity in laws:

> A legal, or halachic tradition is a saying or story about the way something is to be done, a statement intended to have practical effect and carry normative authority, or an inquiry into the logic or legal principle behind such a rule.[20]

Given the importance of the Law as a source of topics and as a religious and social symbol in ancient Judaism, our knowledge of actual legal speech is soberingly modest. It is still easy, with the best will in the world, to misrepresent anachronistically the 'Constraint of Law'[21] in ancient Jewish life. In the period of Christian origins, 'Law', 'Torah'

---

[17] Berger, *Formgeschichte*, 121–124.

[18] K. Berger, *Die Gesetzesauslegung Jesu*, Teil I: *Markus und Parallelen* (WMANT 40; Neukirchen-Vluyn, 1972) 32–55.

[19] Berger, *Formgeschichte*, 121–123.

[20] Neusner, *Pharisees* III 5; cf. 43 on "aggadic tradition."

[21] See Harvey, *Constraints*, 36–65 for a still problematic survey; also Downing, "Contexts," 441–442.

and 'halakah' were significantly open–ended symbols, enough so to generate fundamental conflict; as categories for modern understanding of ancient behaviour and speech, they must remain strictly heuristic. It is important, for instance, not to assume that distinctively Rabbinic styles and terms—the term 'halakah' itself—were normative for Jesus' and Paul's world, though they may authentically distil selected earlier developments.[22]

Still, rhetorical use of gnomai is specifically "intended to have practical effect and carry normative authority," though the normative effect is based on the rapport between a speaker and an audience and *not* on the clarity of the formula itself. The rhetoricians recognized that it is characteristic of gnomai to be law-like rather than to be laws (e.g., Quint. *Inst.* VIII 5,3: *similes...consiliis aut decretis*). The rhetorical versatility of gnome rests upon its aptness for symbolizing a diversity of relations among speaker, audience and topic; by contrast, a 'law' as text seeks to objectify speaker and topic and so to impose a political unity upon all its possible audiences. Laws as texts are no more socially normative than gnomai, but they generically express a rhetoric of coercion alien to gnomic language.

Thus, the rhetoricians regularly distinguished between even law-like gnomai and actual laws. Moreover, the rhetoric of biblical laws, of Rabbinic *halakot* and of the like at Qumran[23] is essentially not gnomic: such 'laws' may be based on analogical reasoning, but they are almost never formulated as analogically autonomous sentences.[24] Gnomai in Jewish texts can embody legal principles (e.g. *Jub.* 6:7; cf. Gen 9:4,9), so that Rabbinic tradition can occasionally produce legally topical gnomai, such as the "quasi-legal" gnome which disturbed Fischel's analysis of the Hillelite transformation of a Greek chreia.[25] However, such quasi-legal sayings are not only rare, especially among the Rabbis, they are also normatively marginal: Rabbinic legal sayings are normatively less ambiguous than legal-sounding gnomic sayings. Rabbinic rules are also often formally specialized, and not as gnomai.

---

[22] P.S. Alexander, "Midrash and the Gospels," in *Synoptic Studies: The Ampleforth Conferences of 1982 and 83*, ed. C.M. Tuckett (JSNTSup 7; Sheffield, 1984) 1–18, 11.

[23] Schiffman, *The Halakah at Qumran*, 80–83.

[24] Cf. Zeller, *Mahnsprüche*, 45–46.

[25] Fischel, "Transformation," 398–402, "The Greek bon mot in our *chriae* is witty throughout.... Only the Hebrew item seems to be totally serious" (398).

In Jewish Greek, where this departs from Hebrew biblical forms, the
Pauline practice is typical, in which legal topicality appears in gnomai
mainly where the topic is Law as a whole (Gal 2:21; Matt 5:18 par) or
in apologetic or moralizing epitomes of Torah.[26] Thus, for example,
the metrical sentence-collection written under the name of Phocylides
includes many biblical, legal references. In spite of the collection's title,
however, many of these items are not gnomai: they are either not
syntactically separable in their contexts or not analogically structured.
Instead they simply adopt the forms of Jewish biblical law to Greek
verse and taste. Among the actual gnomai in pseudo-Phocylides, legal
topicality appears as ethicizing summary or paraphrase: no autonomous,
self-assertive normative authority is implied.

Legal topicality in Synoptic gnomai

Some Synoptic gnomai stand out dramatically against this background.[27] Normally, either gnomic and legal normativities are formally
distinct, or else gnomic elements are incorporated with laws into
instructional or apologetic collections. In these Synoptic gnomai, by
subtle contrast, legal topics are subordinated to the connotative quality
of single gnomai in rhetorically more ambiguous narrative and
argumentative contexts. Because of its exclusively topical character this
subordination is not in itself antinomian, since gnomai in general are
argumentative rather than legislative or judicial. These gnomai, because
of their topicality, resemble public resolutions and decrees more than
most, but they, too, are functionally and formally not laws. This sub-
group among Synoptic gnomai, however, by being about law and
(rarely) the Law, seems calculated to exploit both this similarity and the
nuance of difference in style, content and implication between gnome
and law.

---

[26] Berger, *Formgeschichte*, 123; *Gesetzesauslegung*, 38ff; see Gal 5:14 (Betz,
Galatians, 274–276); Matt 7:12 par; Mark 12:28–34 par (less gnomic); Joseph. *Ap.* 2,
190–219 (Küchler, 207ff, esp. 219); Philo *Hypothetica* in Euseb. *Praep. Evang.* 8.7, 1–9
(Küchler, 222ff); *de Specialibus Legibus, passim*; Ps-Phocylides *Sententiae, passim*
(Küchler, 236ff).
[27] Notably Mark 2:19 par, 27–28 par; 7:15, 27; 12:17 par; Matt 7:6; 19:12; 6:24
par; 10:10 par.

The labourers deserve their food/to be paid. (Matt 10:10/1 Tim 5:18b)

You shall not muzzle an ox while it is treading out the grain. (1 Cor 9:9; 1 Tim 5:18a; Deut 25:4)

The wages of the labourers...cry out. (James 5:4)

As an example, the Synoptic gnome of the worker's hire or keep (Matt 10:10 par; 1 Tim 5:18b; *Did.* 13:1–2; see 1 Cor 9:14) may be compared in its connotative use of legal imagery and topicality with other more or less gnomic, more or less legal formulae in Ps-Phocylides (*Sent.* 19), Deuteronomy (Deut 25:4; 1 Cor 9:9; 1 Tim 5:18a) and James (5:4). All are legal in topic: the verses from Ps-Phocylides and Deuteronomy are relatively legal in form (apodeictic) and normative clarity, though the normative scope of the biblical injunction can be metaphorically (or casuistically[28]) extended (1 Cor 9:10). James 5:4, on the other hand, is primarily symbolic: implied social normativity, let alone legality, is secondary to eschatology. The peculiarity of the Synoptic gnome is its association of the specificity and perspicuity of law (neither the worker nor his hire/keep is metaphorical) with the connotivity of gnome (the audience is not merely being invited to pay their employees fairly): "You shall not muzzle an ox while it is treading out the grain" can be a law in a way which "the worker is worthy of his hire" cannot be.

Everyone will be salted with fire. (Mark 9:49)

Every sacrifice will be salted with salt. (Lev 2:13)

An even clearer idea of the difference between law and gnome may be gotten from a comparison of the strange gnome, Mark 9:49, and the biblical injunction to which it may refer, Leviticus 2:13. Formally and in content the latter is clearly legal: "Every sacrifice will be salted with salt" is a future tense of biblical command, giving a simple liturgical instruction without which correct sacrifice would be impossible. Mark 9:49 is not nearly so clear in its normative goal; Matthew and Luke sensibly replace it with a clearer 'salt' saying, while several manuscripts

---

[28] D. Instone Brewer, "1 Corinthians 9.9–11: A Literal Interpretation of 'Do Not Muzzle the Ox'," *NTS* 38 (1992) 554–65.

of Mark gloss it by quoting Leviticus. "Everyone will be salted with fire" takes the language of sacrificial law and turns it analogically into a dark oracle of eschatological experience.

In other words, Synoptic legal gnomai are seldom 'laws' in the sense of enforceably authoritative texts (for which they often lack perspicuity) or even 'legal principles' (for which most are at once too connotative and too specific). On the other hand, Synoptic gnomai turn surprisingly often to legal or potentially legal topics which are not typically gnomic in adjacent literatures. Nor are they simply borrowing unconventional imagery: Synoptic quasi-legal gnomai do seem to be assuming an authority tantamount to jurisdiction. Moreover, there is surprisingly little competition for gospel gnomai in this function, for there are practically no laws in Jesus' tradition.[29] Certainly, the separation between gnomic and legal rhetoric is not absolute: they share a continuum of normativity, especially where 'law' is defined more pragmatically than formally. But the fact that gnomai appear *instead* of laws in much Synoptic tradition, corresponds to a more general impression of gnomic language in Jesus' tradition; gospel gnomai deliberately introduce the speaker's informal, personal authority into public normativity. The peculiar frequency of controversial legal topics in gnomai attributed to Jesus makes it even more likely that intense normative conflict has a historic as well as poetic focus in Jesus' gnome-use.

The notion of quasi-legal gnomai thus focuses on a peculiarity of normative authority as well as of formal styles in the literature of Jesus' tradition, certainly when compared with Qumran and the Rabbis. Formally specialized legislative and casuistic material in Synoptic tradition is rare and late: instead, Synoptic tradition and literature prefer and generally ascribe to Jesus the special pleading of self-assertive gnomai.

---

[29] Synoptic and Pauline pericopae about divorce, Mark 10:2–12 par; Matt 5:27–32; 1 Cor 7:10–16, and about comportment of missionaries, Matt 10:5b–42 par; 1 Cor 9:5–14, are among the few and partial exceptions important for gnome-study. For formally specialized legal texts, see Matt 5:21; 18:15–18; cf. Berger, *Formgeschichte*, 214–216.

Gnomic rhetoric and oral dispute management

It is not fair to take the children's food and throw it to the dogs. (Mark 7:27)

On one level of explanation the difference between a gnome and a law may be related to a difference of oral and literary sensibilities. The Synoptic Jesus' use of gnomai in relation to legal topics should be compared to the use of proverbs in trials, suits and controversies, especially in societies or social classes where 'law' is principally an oral complex of rhetorical and social conventions, rather than a written or memorized body of verbatim reproducible, professionally controllable texts.[30] Such dramatized gnomic dialogues as Matthew 11:16–19 and its parallel, Mark 6:1–6 and parallels, 7:24–30 and parallels and Luke 12:54–56 and its parallel nicely illustrate the appropriateness of gnomai, including topically legal gnomai (e.g. Mark 7:27), for what I might call popular litigation.

The conflictual tone of Synoptic gnomai is by no means confined to those which show legal topicality, but such gnomai may suggest something important about Galilean conflict-management under the eyes but not the jurisdiction of elites of pen, school and sword. The mixture of conflictual self-assertion and connotative elusiveness in Synoptic gnomai generally corresponds closely to one widely observed role of proverbs even in higher rhetoric: as a means of managing and manipulating dangerous conflicts, legal, diplomatic or personal.[31] Many communities negotiate situations of legal, diplomatic, political or familial tension with a good measure of gnomic repartee. Even more important for comparison with the Synoptic Jesus' self-assertive and conflictual use of gnomai is that, face to face, proverbs may be used

---

[30] See R. Finnegan, *Oral Literature in Africa* (Nairobi, 1970) 408-413; S. Roberts, *Order and Dispute: An Introduction to Legal Anthropology* (Oxford, 1979) 147–153, 174; J. Blenkinsopp, *Wisdom and Law in the Old Testament: The Ordering of Life in Israel and Early Judaism* (Oxford, 1983) 80. Several of the 'proverbs' isolated by Eißfeldt in the Old Testament are intrinsically (2 Sam 5:8; 20:18) or receptionally (Judg 8:21; 1 Sam 24:13, 14) legal, while a large number of prophetic sayings extend juridical proverb-use into the Covenant-relationship; see Fontaine, "Performance," 5.

[31] Finnegan, *Oral Literature*, 408–413; Fontaine, "Performance," 94; P. Seitel, "Proverbs: A Social Use of Metaphor," *Gnome* 2 (1969) 143–161.

just as effectively to provoke conflict as to mollify it (Judg 8:21; 1 Kgs 20:11; 18:21).

Thus the unusual aspects of Synoptic legal gnome-use may be partially explicable in social-psychological terms of the relatively oral sensibility of the Jesus-movement. It may be helpful to interpret in this way the dissimilarity of legal normativity in pre-Synoptic gnomic rhetoric compared with Rabbinic, Qumran and biblical texts: Jesus' movement freely addresses legal topics while adducing or producing a shockingly small number of distinctly and specifically legal texts. Such legal topicality in Synoptic gnomai seems closer to the practice of rhetoric and of law in markets and in the semi-public spaces of the household or the edge of town than to rhetorical performance in the more constrained venues of the classical rhetorical definitions, official councils (deliberative and honorific), courts (forensic) and schools (didactic). The Synoptic Jesus addresses legal topics more as a vendor than as a lawyer or statesman, Greco-Roman or Jewish. In rhetorical and physical terms the distance among various competing elites and alternative movements may seem small by the standards of modern, highly segmented social life, but spatial and technical proximity may here be heightening the significance of what we might pass over as stylistic difference. The conflictual but coded rhetoricity of Jesus' movement and its relative orality warn against overreading gnomic legal topicality as a self-conscious attitude to the Law as a whole.

The characteristics of Jesus' rhetoric as they are emerging here—gnomic to the point of 'Asiatic' rhetorical excess, personal to the point of shamelessness, topical to the point of insolence toward cultural and legal authorities, whether Jewish or Roman—may permit one more step toward social location of Jesus as a provincial Jewish alternative public figure. Sociological or anthropological classification of Jesus and his circle is as questionable as it can be illuminating, as most notably in J.D. Crossan's "life of a Mediterranean Jewish peasant."[32] This characterization of Jesus is more persuasive as a way of exposing our ignorance of Galilee than as a description of Jesus' motives or audience.

The rhetorical strategies and values of Jesus' tradition of gnomic rhetoric suggest on the one hand seminal contact with the practice of rhetoric in the leading milieux of Greco-Roman and Jewish Galilee; on the other hand, the same evidence indicates a subtle but deliberate

---

[32] Crossan, *The Historical Jesus.*

insubordination and abandonment of decorum. That is, the gnomic rhetoric attributed to Jesus *mirrors*, I think critically, the rhetoric of tasteful and learned manuals, of Aristotle or Quintilian or Theon and the distant, Galilean products of their cultural influence. The manuals and theoreticians can guide us convincingly through the technical and hermeneutical implications of Jesus' rhetoric and its early Christian receptions. They are, however, incapable of imagining, except with indignation, the successful ascription of such a rhetoric of confrontation and personality to a crucified, Aramaic-speaking, Galilean, non-priestly, non-scribal Jew of doubtful birth. Jesus of Nazareth does not even pose as a proper Cynic, well-bred and well-educated and therefore acceptable in his or her professed insolence and indecency.

At the same time, an account of Synoptic quasi-legal gnome-use just in terms of oral sensibility, rhetorical genre and possible social location would still be incomplete. It needs to be extended by a recognition that the gnomic style and gnomic legality of the Synoptics, like their relatively oral poetics, are not accidental characteristics of that literature and its formative tradition. Nor are they simply the products of conflicting communicative (=communal?) sensibilities. Gnomic legality also fits into the wider pattern of Christian rhetoric explicitly ascribing personal normative authority (what we might call charisma) to Jesus. Given that Jesus and the gospel-writers could have adopted or adapted specialized, unambiguously legal and legal-exegetical forms, their heavy use instead of somehow legal yet disconcertingly informal gnomai must be treated as a founding decision in Jesus' tradition.

The rest of this chapter, then, is not merely intended to extend the descriptive scope of a gnomic approach to sayings tradition, but also to confirm its explanatory force as the way to reformulate key problems in early Christianity: the problem of unstable relationships among gospel rhetoric, legal normativity and social norms; the problem of Paul's normative language and his ambivalence toward dominical normativity; the problem even of Jesus' own "attitude to the Law." Linking Synoptic gnome with Synoptic legality generates a hypothesis which can be tested exegetically, especially with reference to Pauline parallels and analogues. In brief, the hypothesis is that gnomai gave Jesus and those close to him a rhetorical medium for asserting personal authority in controversial legal topics without adopting a specifically legal rhetoric or an attitude to the Law. In church tradition, this rhetorical strategy, on the one hand, invited christological reception and, on the other, established a frustrating normative ambiguity. This sort of frustration is expressed not only in Synoptic 'domestication',[33] but also in Pauline sublimation of topically legal gnomai.

Legal topicality and the interpretation of gnomic rhetoric

It would be unproductive to attempt a full-scale exegesis of each topically legal gnome in the three Synoptic Gospels. The comments which follow will try only to illustrate the rhetorical character of the gnomai themselves and to compare them rhetorically and, as much as possible, tradition-historically with their various contextualizations. Longer comments will mark gnomai which seem tradition-historically and/or rhetorically most interesting. I especially emphasize gnomai to which Paul may allude, that is, those with close topical analogues in places where Paul seems to be invoking dominical authority. The argument therefore mainly rests upon two overlapping groups of gnomai, those from Marcan controversy-stories and those with Pauline analogues: Mark 2:19, 27; 3:4b; 7:15 (Rom 14:14); 10:9b (1 Cor 7:10); 12:17 (Rom 13:7); Matthew 10:10 (1 Cor 9:1–14); 19:2 (1 Cor 7:6, 25).

Until heaven and earth pass away, not one letter, not one stroke of a letter, will pass from the law. (Matt 5:18 par)

Do to others as you would have them do to you. (Matt 7:12 par)

The sub-category of topically legal Synoptic gnomai has messy edges. On one margin are the two gnomic reflections about the Law as a whole, Matthew 5:18 (par) and 7:12. They are negatively quite important: their rarity testifies that although Jesus' tradition frequently refers to legal topics, it does not adopt anything like the global positions on the Law which Paul (by abandoning Jesus' rhetoric) and the gospel-writers (by reconstructing it) would take.

Matthew 5:36 is another marginal case of legal topicality, the only instance I have noticed of an intrinsically non-legal (and non-biblical) gnome being used as though legal in the Synoptics.

---

[33] Mack and Robbins, *Patterns*, 204 and *passim* on Synoptic 'domestication' of (often gnomic) chreiai.

You cannot make one hair white or black. (Matt 5:36)

This solitary exception proves the important rule that only intrinsically legal gnomai are accorded legal reception in the Synoptic Gospels. Elsewhere in ancient literature, intrinsically non-legal gnomai were freely used in juridical situations or legalizing contexts (see 1 Sam 24:13, 14). The uniqueness of Matthew 5:36 as a gospel attempt to find legality in a non-legal gnome therefore suggests that Jesus' tradition very early established a privileged, perhaps paradoxical or ironic, relation between quasi-legal gnomai and legalizing inference.

The theoretical notion of 'legal topicality' as intrinsic to some gnomai is therefore not just something I am making up. It does seem to be an active, though perhaps unconscious, principle in early Christian reception of Jesus' tradition: the gospel-writers by and large chose legal gnomai for topically legal contexts. More curiously, in topically legal contexts Paul seems most likely to echo (yet pointedly not to cite) sayings from Jesus-tradition which are both topically legal and gnomic in the Synoptics.

Do not judge, so that you may not be judged. (Matt 7:1–2 par)

In passing judgement on another you condemn yourself. (Rom 2:1b)

The gnome against judging, Matthew 7:1–2 (par), is a good instance of the normative flexibility of 'legal' gnomai in comparison with properly legal forms such as, in this case, the Church Order in Matthew 18:15–20. I can't prove that the opening of Romans 2 alludes to our gnome, but it is worth noticing that such extreme allusiveness would fit Paul's argument, in which a direct command from Jesus would be pointless. A veiled allusion to Jesus-tradition may be positively indicated by the normative tension between the Pauline gnome (Rom 2:1b), which like Matthew 7:1–2 (par) is interested in neighbourly forbearance, and the argument of 2:1c–11, which is rather about the inevitability and universality of eschatological judgement. Paul's use of a gnome on reciprocal judgement generates enough tension in this context to have been called a gloss.[34] Such normative tension or

---

[34] E. Käsemann, *Commentary on Romans*, transl. G.W. Bromiley (London, 1980) 54.

relative inappropriateness is a more plausible ground than mere verbal similarity for suspecting a common (gnomic) tradition.

The measure you give will be the measure you get. (Mark 4:24 par)

The closely related gnome of measurement, Mark 4:24 (par), is an instance of cited legality. That is, a saying with proverbial currency (at least in Ptolemaic Egypt) as a legal/commercial formula[35] took on additional eschatological and ethical weight in Synoptic reception (and probably in pre-Synoptic rhetoric). Intrinsically the saying is, exceptionally, a true law, the only gnome I can think of in or around Synoptic tradition which is in itself a fully coherent legal prescription. Synoptic reception, however, emphasizes its wider connotations, so that Matthew actually treats it as a legal principle rather than a free-standing rule; commercial parity is related to judicial parity (Matt 7:2) in order to temper the absolute and anarchical prohibition of judging in Matthew 7:1 (par). In Mark and Luke the gnome of measurement, though presumably remaining an active commercial and legal norm, also becomes an ethical and eschatological rather than legal principle.

No one [slave] can serve two masters. (Matt 6:24 par Luke 16:13)

In the quatrain, Matthew 6:24 (par), another legal proverb,[36] i.e., neither a law nor a general legal principle but a typical case, is extended metaphorically into a theological warning which is only very generally ethical, let alone legal. Despite its poetic reception in the quatrain form, the gnome itself is typical of our 'legal' sub-category: clearly intended to affect legal relationships, but indifferent to means and ends or to identification with a recognizably legal authority or corpus.

---

[35] Boismard, *Synopse*, 152.
[36] See Henderson, "Gnomic Quatrains."

Do not give what is holy to dogs. (Matt 7:6)

It is not fair to take the children's food and throw it to the dogs. (Mark 7:27 par)

The quatrain Matthew 7:6 is a similar poetic reception of a gnome, exploiting its legal topicality. The gnome itself is a more or less intrinsically legal norm, like Leviticus 2:13 or Deuteronomy 25:4. At the same time, it is too connotative to function simply as a 'law', even in its more specifically legal reception in *Didache* 9:5: the realm of the 'holy' is too unstable.

Comparison of Matthew 7:6 with Mark 7:27 (par) casts considerable light on why it is wise to talk of 'quasi-legality,' 'virtual' or 'topical' legality, and not of socially normative law in gnomai. Both gnomai are inescapably relevant to the strong normative—sacral and eschatological—distinction between Israelite and Gentile. They are not, however, a sufficient basis for reconstructing a complete and coherent legal, political or even social attitude toward Gentiles. In fact, despite the sharp mood which these gnomai share, some typically gnomic ways of escape are left open. Thus the references to "what is holy" (Matt 7:6) and "the children's food" (Mark 7:27) are not fully specified; there is also room in Matthew 7:6a and *Didache* 9:5 for eventual redefinition of the "dogs" and in the Marcan saying (even without stressing "let the children be fed *first*") for the doggies' eventual domestication. This combination of a sharply conflictual tone with the bare possibility of (eschatological) adjustment probably brings us as close to an "attitude to the Gentiles" as the pre-Easter movement itself came,[37] but such gnomic hints are far from being legislation.

All who take the sword will perish by the sword. (Matt 26:52)

The context of Matthew 26:52 is 'legal' only in a peculiar narrative and ironical sense: for the evangelist, we are at the scene of several crimes where the only innocent man is being arrested. The context is not argumentatively legal, it is not about law(s), but it does make a powerful normative contrast between Jesus' prophetic word and the

---

[37] See Sanders, *Jesus and Judaism*, 212–221 on 'The Gentiles' in which, curiously, these sayings barely figure.

depravity of the ostensibly legal narrative situation. Matthew 26:52 is intrinsically more than the restatement of a universal legal and sacral principle (Gen 9:6): in any context where pre-Synoptic tradition could have used this sentence, the topic of the sword would have had unavoidable legal and political resonances. The primary impact of the gnome is, however, not legal but biographical and oracular, in short, gnomic. It does not establish an attitude to violence so much as it asks its earliest hearers, "Who *did/*does live by the sword? Jesus, Judas, Peter, Paul...first-century Palestine as a whole?"

Let the dead bury their [own] dead. (Matt 8:22 par)

You received without payment; give without payment. (Matt 10:8b)

Labourers deserve their food/to be paid. (Matt 10:10 par)

There are eunuchs who have been so from birth, and
there are eunuchs who have been made eunuchs by others, and
there are eunuchs who have made themselves eunuchs
for the sake of the kingdom of heaven. (Matt 19:12)

Four further gnomai have a common structure: each applies imagery from one legal topic to a another, also basically legal topic. That is, Matthew 19:12 is not about eunuchs; 8:22 (par Luke 9:60) is not about burial; Matthew 10:8b (in Matthaean reception, though see Acts 20:35) is not about alms-giving; and Matthew 10:10 (par Luke 10:7) is not about labour justice (in Synoptic and Pauline receptions, though see James 5:4). All four are about discipleship, an institution which, even in the non-scholastic form associated with Jesus, might be expected to be a focus of legal or analogous regulation. In fact, even the least figurative and least authoritatively personal of the group, Matthew 10:10b and parallels, leaves the identity and function of the "worker" and the conditions and sources for receiving his keep open and dependent on the authority and context of the gnome-user.

Matthew 10:10, Luke 10:7, cf. 1 Cor 9:1–14; (1 Tim 5:18b)

Comparison between Matthew 10:10 (par) and the Paul's language in 1 Corinthians 9:1–14 tests with unusual precision the usefulness of identifying Jesus' sayings-tradition as largely gnomic rhetoric. The comparison is also a good illustration of the paradoxical relation between the non-legal character and the frequently legal topicality of gnomai attributed to Jesus. It may well have been hard for Paul's correspondents to give unequivocal answers to the rhetorical questions in 1 Corinthians 9 about his apostolic status. The legal character of the central question and of the closing appeal to dominical authority (verse 14) are, however, clear. It is unsurprising for a gnomic-rhetorical model of oral tradition that the obvious reference in Synoptic sayings material would be to a gnome. It is much more surprising from this point of view that Paul does not simply quote the gnome when he is willing for once to signal clearly a dominical allusion, but Paul is taking the uncomfortable risk here of admitting to the normative irregularity of his already challenged apostleship. He is probably wise not to cite the potentially embarrassing traditions in full.

The problem of Paul's extreme allusiveness relative to the, in principle, revered authority of dominical sayings is, of course, a standard topic in New Testament studies. It is attractive to conclude, above all for the Corinthian correspondence,[38] that such sayings were "largely, at that time and in Paul's eyes, 'in enemy hands'."[39] I noticed above that Pauline gnomai come closest to the Synoptic mood of gnomic challenge where the apostle seems to mimic ethopoetically the rhetoric of his correspondents and/or opponents.[40] In 1 Corinthians 9:1–14 Paul is almost his own opponent: he is securing for himself an apostolic privilege, in order grandly to lay it aside (verse 18). But from Paul's own gnomic references to law (verses 9, 13) and from his own legalizing citation of a dominical order (verse 14), it would have been easy to draw (from his point of view) the wrong conclusion. It would have been easy for even a sympathetic listener to suppose that the norm in question was not an optional privilege, which Paul could waive without losing credibility: it might instead define an indispensable attribute of real apostles, as indeed it seems to do in Matthew and Luke.

The conflict implied in 1 Corinthians 9, the riskiness of Paul's position and their background in received normative language can, however, be clarified on the assumption that the tradition of dominical

---

[38] See Nierynck, "Sayings," n.51 for bibliography.
[39] Wedderburn, "Problem of Continuity," 190.
[40] Betz, *Galatians*, 291–311.

pronouncement common to Paul and his correspondents is gnomic in style, and in its quasi-legality. In view of Matthew 10:10 and parallels and its wider attestation (1 Tim 5:18; Jas 5:4; *Did.* 13:1–2), this seems an exceptionally probable assumption. If Paul and other parties influential in Corinth all attributed to Jesus a saying unquestionably relevant to the support of missionaries, but also equivocally 'legal', attempts to apply the gnome as legally normative could only exacerbate conflict. If 10:10 and parallels represents even generally the kind of common normative tradition alluded to by Paul here, there is ample room for bona fide differences of opinion and practice: as multiple attestations show, this particular gnome is ambiguous both in normative intensity and in normative range.[41]

Even in this crucial instance of the centrality of gnomai to Jesus' tradition (especially on legal topics) it is not possible confidently to reconstruct the positions of individual parties. Gnomic rhetoric does, however, clarify the resources available in spoken tradition for talking about a particular case of social normative conflict. And a gnomic-rhetorical model of oral tradition does account for Paul's baffling willingness simultaneously to reject and assert the normative relevance of a dominical saying:[42] We may *guess* that this has grounds in (Paul's understanding of) the Corinthian situation and in social normative differences between Corinth and Jesus' Palestine; but we can *know* that the particular rhetorical quality of dominical tradition on this topic invited such normative ambivalence.

Dominical tradition in gnomic style would, on the one hand, be recognizably non-legal. On the other hand, it would still be topical enough to be used and feared on all sides "in a legalistic way."[43] Paul's reluctance to quote Jesus and his substitution of more plainly legal formulations (verses 8–12, 13, 14) are tendencies not confined to 1 Corinthians 9. They may in the end reflect frustration not just with

---

[41] On normative intensity and range see Crépeau, 300–3: the intensity might be *imperative* as in Matt and Luke or *directive* (Paul's qualified tendency in 1 Cor 9; cf. 1 Tim 5:18); the range might be *specific* to a particular class of 'worker' or (Jas 5:4) of employer, *optional* for 'workers' of various kinds, or *universal* to all people or to all disciples. On 'workers' see Theißen, "Legitimation," *passim.*

[42] On this paradox in Paul's use of gnomai from Jesus-tradition in 1 Cor 7:10 and 9:14, see D. Dungan, *The Sayings of Jesus in the Churches of Paul* (Philadelphia, 1971) 33–36, 76–80, 100–101, 132–135.

[43] Wedderburn, "Problem of Continuity," 190.

opponents, but also with the limited regulatory perspicuity of a speech-tradition which nevertheless retains its charismatic authority. Certainly there is evidence apart from Paul for the existence and normative ambiguity of such a gnomic tradition, which is more than can be said for reconstructions of Paul's opposition.

There are eunuchs who have been so from birth, and
there are eunuchs who have been made eunuchs by others, and
there are eunuchs who have made themselves eunuchs
for the sake of the kingdom of heaven. (Matt 19:12 /1 Cor 7:1–40)

At first sight, the treatment together of marital separation and celibacy in Matthew 19:3–12 and in 1 Corinthians 7 would seem to hold little promise for the identification of shared, putatively dominical tradition in a gnome like Matthew 19:12. In the first place, Paul and possibly the Corinthians have another gnome, 1 Corinthians 7:1b, 26b, which gives much the same gist rather more clearly and without the daunting imagery of the "eunuch." Secondly, if Paul was as unusual among "apostles" in upholding one clear dominical norm (Matt 19:12) as he apparently was in ignoring another (Matt 10:10 par), we might expect at least an allusion to the fact. Finally, Paul himself explicitly denies having a dominical precept about celibates (1 Cor 7:25 cf. verse 6).

In fact, the very forcefulness of Paul's denial requires clearer explanation; in 1 Corinthians 7:6 and 25 he particularly emphasizes that what he does not have is a *legal* tradition on dominical authority on the topic of celibacy. What he doesn't have, a "command," *epitage*, is in this sense unique to verses 6 and 25 in Paul's writings. The term is in sharp contrast with Paul's own guidance presented as a "concession," *syngnome* (verse 6) or an "opinion," gnome (verse 25). This contrast is not quite the same as that in 1 Corinthians 7:10–16 on marital separation, to which we turn shortly; on the latter topic Paul neither claims nor denies having a "command" (*epitage*), but simply joins the Lord's voice to his own ("I command—not I but the Lord"). Consequently, though he makes clear in verse 12 that he "and not the Lord" is making a concession on separation, Paul does not identify his concession as such: Paul rightly saw his permission of certain separations as ungrounded in the tradition of Jesus' opposition to divorce.

But if Paul lacked not only legislation but tradition of any kind in favour of the marital separation he permits, he does seem to me to have

had a tradition of sorts, just not a law, in favour of celibacy. In my
view, Paul's emphasis on his lack of a legal model (*epitage*) for his
counsel on celibacy suggests, as mere silence about dominical tradition
would not, that his apostolic opinion (*syngnome*) is consciously inspired
("as one who by the Lord's mercy is trustworthy") not only by his
personal experience, but also by a tradition which was intrinsically
inappropriate as a source of congregational law—which indeed, because
of its gnomic formulation, legal topicality and attribution to Jesus, may
have been open to legalizing misuse.[44] 1 Corinthians 7:25 may not
only indicate that Paul knew well "the difference between halakhoth of
the Lord and his own";[45] it may also show his awareness that the
Lord's sayings, even those on legal topics, were not *halakot* at all. The
attestation of an appropriate oracular gnome in Matthew 19:12 accords
this supposition a real measure of probability.

The Matthaean gnome also fits the Pauline requirements in being
plausibly pre-Matthaean, at least to judge from the slight emphasis it
receives and its loose (catchword) integration into a basically non-
Matthaean context.[46] In itself and in its Matthaean contextualization
the gnome has two rather different senses: for Matthew, the one who
makes himself a eunuch for the kingdom's sake is the husband who
obeys the gospel's (redactional) law by separating from his adulterous
wife (verse 9, cf. Matt 5:32) and then refraining from remarriage to
avoid adultery on his own part; no such casuistic definition of 'eunuch-
hood' can be intuited from the gnome itself, which seems to be the sort
of normative radicalization of prophetic and sapiential tradition which
we should expect from discipleship in Jesus' movement.[47] This looks
therefore like another instance of normative dissonance between a
gnome which is topically but not formally legal and its narrowly
legalizing Synoptic context.

A similar dissonance can be felt between the gnome, by itself or in
Matthaean context, and the normative rhetoric of the Corinthian

---

[44] *Pace* Q. Quesnell, "'Made Themselves Eunuchs for the Kingdom of Heaven'
(Mt 19,12)," *CBQ* 30 (1968) 335–358, 341 n. 10.

[45] Dungan, *Sayings of Jesus*, 100.

[46] Boismard, *Synopse*, 308–309; Berger, *Gesetzesauslegung*, 572–573.

[47] Isa 54:1–10; 56:2–7; Sir 16:1–3; Wis 3:13–14; Matt 8:22 par; Mark 10:29–30
par. See Boismard, 309, following Quesnell, "Made Themselves Eunuchs," esp.
341–347; Berger, *Gesetzesauslegung*, 573.

correspondence. The hyperbolic image of the "eunuch" and the triplet form of the gnome mark it clearly as a non-legal text in spite of its practical implications: the saying just is not a "command" (1 Cor 7:6, 25 *epitage*). Moreover, the paradoxically negative cultural value of 'eunuch-hood' as a metaphor for a positively valued state of discipleship, though imaginably in Jesus' style, is imaginably not such as to commend it to Paul, to his audience or to his opposition. Finally, if the gnome implied to Paul (as it did to Matthew) that the motive for celibacy should be the radical avoidance of ritual impurity,[48] Paul's unwillingness to use the saying to describe his own state would be fully understandable. The recurrence in and around Matthew 19:12 of normative tensions like those surrounding many Synoptic gnomai and Paul's sensitivity to the same tensions enormously strengthen the probability that Matthew's gnome and the fact or fear of its abuse underlie Paul's language in 1 Corinthians 7:6, 25. This complex gnome is more than just one which Paul ought to have known, but did not; it is another which might well have elicited from the him the delicacy of allusion rather than quotation.

What God has joined together, let no one separate. (Mark 10:9 par /1 Cor 7:10–11)

The children of this age are more shrewd in dealing with their own generation than are the children of light. (Luke 16:18 par)

A gnomic approach to Synoptic sayings also sheds light on the nature of traditional continuity amongst Paul, the Synoptics and Jesus in the (for Matthew and Paul) adjacent subject of marital separation. Paul's allusion in 1 Corinthians 7:10 to dominical authority is comparable only to that in 7:25 for explicitness. It is all the more challenging, then, that it too is an allusion, especially in view of the richness of comparable (and formally legal) discussion in the Synoptic texts (Mark 10:2–12 par Matt 19:3–9; Luke 16:18; Matt 5:27–32). As we have seen, even in 1 Corinthians 7:10 Paul does not claim to have a command from the Lord; rather he asserts that when he speaks on this topic (and not on others) it is the Lord who speaks. This unique intensity and specificity of Paul's allusion would seem to demand an extraordinary normative

---

[48] Berger, *Gesetzesauslegung*, 572ff.

continuity with Jesus; given the gospel traditions of Jesus' opposition to divorce it is nowhere more reasonable to look for verbal, oral traditional continuity. On the other hand, the scale and argumentative complexity of the Synoptic material combines with Paul's allusiveness to make identification of common verbal tradition difficult.[49]

The most conspicuous point of commonality among the Synoptic materials on divorce is an equally conspicuous point of discontinuity with Paul: "All the synoptic passages...are determined by the view that divorce leads to adultery."[50] This means that Mark 10:11–12 is unlikely to be the bridge between Synoptic and Pauline receptions of tradition, especially since Paul's primary interest is in the possibility of the wife initiating separation, a possibility which is an afterthought in Mark 10:12 and absent from both Matthew 19 and Matthew 5:32 (par). In itself this does not entail the inauthenticity of the Synoptic saying relating divorce to adultery. Its secondary character in at least the central pericope, Mark 10:2–12 (par Matt 19:3–9), is confirmed, however, by normative dissonance between the concluding saying, prohibiting remarriage as adulterous, and the preceding scriptural argument, prohibiting separation as against the nature of marital union.[51]

The latter argument is expressed in two scriptural citations (verses 6–8: Gen 1:27 and 2:24) and a culminating gnome (verse 9). The logic and one each of the biblical quotations are paralleled in the *Covenant of Damascus*, CD 4.21 (Gen 1:27), and in 1 Corinthians 6:16 (Gen 2:24). It is not fanciful, then, to notice that the only distinct verbal parallel between 1 Corinthians 7:10 and the Synoptic analogues is with the extraordinary vocabulary ("separate," *chorizein*) of the gnome, Mark 10:9 (par), which evokes the traditional argument linking marriage to creation, rather than that linking divorce to adultery.

---

[49] Sanders, *Jesus and the Jews*, 14–15, and Sanders and Davies, *Synoptic Gospels*, 324–29.

[50] Sanders, *Jesus and Judaism*, 256.

[51] Boismard, *Synopse*, 307; Berger, *Gesetzesauslegung*, 534–535, 574–374.

It is to this logion from Matt 19:6b and Mark 10:9 that Paul alludes in 1
Cor 7:10f, as to an order received from the Lord (same verb "separate"),
and not to the logion from Matt 19:9 par.[52]

This probability confirms an important hypothetical expectation: if
gnomic rhetoric is a major factor in structuring Jesus' sayings tradition,
it should illuminate both Synoptic and Pauline ways of receiving that
tradition. It does so in this difficult case by providing a model of Jesus'
normative rhetoric which *ought* to have produced varied and ambivalent
reactions among Christians seeking coherent family law.

E.P. Sanders and M. Davies have neatly expressed the challenge of
the anti-divorce tradition to historical method: retrojecting the most
widely-attested literary common denominator into tradition-history
suggests that Jesus prohibited remarriage after divorce (divorce leads to
adulterous remarriage). Broad developmental ("intrinsic") probability
suggests to the contrary that a global opposition to divorce is more
likely to have engendered the Pauline and Synoptic developments
(divorce violates creation).[53] Only the latter position is expressed as a
gnome (Mark 10:9). This does not, of course, clinch the question, but
it adds to the developmental case a mechanism (gnomic tradition) by
which the radical position could be transmitted and a motive (the
unhelpfulness of gnomai as non-laws) for plurality, complexity and
improvisation in the saying's normative influence. If Mark 10:9 is not
the root of the anti-divorce tradition, something like it should have
been: something memorable, radical, legally confusing and gnomic.

Citation from classical authority (Scripture) and use of gnomai are
often closely associated in argument. If my understanding of Jewish and
early Christian anti-divorce rhetoric is persuasive, then the argument
against divorce as contrary to created order is a case in point: early
Christian rhetoric (perhaps Jesus himself) added Mark 10:9 to a debate
in which Genesis 1:27 and 2:24 were already current—leaving the
tradition to work out responses to separation and remarriage when, after
all, marriages fail. Certainly, gnomai and Scripture citations are related

---

[52] Boismard, *Synopse*, 307; *pace* Westerholm, *Jesus and Scribal Authority*,
119–133.

[53] Sanders and Davies, *Synoptic Gospels*, 328.

contextually in the Synoptics and topically in 1 Corinthians 6 and 7.[54]
As well, Genesis 1:27 in Mark 10:6 (par) and Genesis 2:24 in 1
Corinthians 6:16 are actually cited as (again non-legal) gnomai in their
own right.

This interchange of scriptural and gnomic voices is a vital reminder
that a mainly gnomic tradition can transmit quite complicated argumentation, just as in other contexts (e.g. Mark 6:1–6 par) gnomic tradition
may be the peg on which to hang plausibly authentic episodic memory.
On a rhetorical model of tradition, the use of an authoritative literary
citation to supplement a gnome or a chreia would be routine. It is
prescribed by the Progymnasmata (e.g. Hermog. *Prog.* 8.7–11, 10.3, 20
(Rabe)). The oddity of Synoptic gnomic and chriic rhetoric is rather that
such gnome-quotation associations are so rare, that in Jesus' tradition,
or at least in gospel composition,[55] gnomai and chreiai are usually
supplemented by further gnomai rather than by classical or biblical
authority.

Furthermore, if it is probable that a gnome, particularly Mark 10:9b
(par), underlies Paul's allusion in 1 Corinthians 7:10–11, we may be
enabled to lift a little the veil of his allusiveness in relation to sayings
tradition generally. The particularity of this allusion in the Corinthian
context is that there is no hint of self-justification. Paul himself is
unthreatened by the norm and ideologically unreserved as to its
validity—though he hastens to provide legally for its circumvention!
Still, Paul's general allusiveness and the unseemly haste with which he
and the Synoptics independently turn from gnomic prohibition of
divorce to formally legal regulation of its consequences suggest again
the essential non-legality of gnome. Paul's allusiveness, even in
exceptionally outspoken appeal to Jesus' authority, even here where
such an appeal is ideologically and personally least likely to draw fire
onto Paul himself, is most understandable in this light.

If Paul's tradition was in fact the gnome, Mark 10:9b (par), we may
credit him for distinguishing between the normativity of an unenforce-
able ideal and that appropriate to the written pastoral judgements which
it inspires. On the one hand, Paul's puzzling compositional practice and

---

[54] Cf. Sanders, *Jesus and Judaism*, 257. (I assume that the quotation of Lev 2:13
in some MSS of Mark 9:49 is a gloss, albeit an interesting one.)

[55] Mack and Robbins, *Patterns*, 203–208, tentatively and, in my judgement,
prematurely suggest that this develops first in Church rhetoric.

attitude to Jesus' authority in contexts of normative regulation and, on the other hand, the gospel-writers' manifest efforts to surround the trickiest gnomai with more practical argumentation are newly explicable; we need only recognize that any writer capable of producing such texts in Greek had been schooled not only to use and like gnomic language, but also to seek out and use its very normative ambiguities, its typically paralegal tone. When such writers move from advocacy, proclamation and characterization of Jesus to become legislators, judges and rulers of the church, they know to alloy the rhetorical quicksilver of formally non-legal, gnomic tradition from Jesus on legal topics requiring serious regulation.

Apart from 1 Thessalonians 4:15–17 and 1 Corinthians 11:23–25, both of which are as exceptional from a Synoptic point of view as from a Pauline, these comparisons with Synoptic quasi-legal gnomai exhaust Paul's notoriously few explicit allusions to words attributed to Jesus. There may, of course, be more hidden references,[56] but the foregoing are not only Paul's most probable references to Jesus-tradition, they are also the points of closest contact between Pauline normative language and Synoptic quasi-legal gnomai. Paul's ambiguous, possibly ambivalent allusions to Jesus' normative authority are the closest analogues anywhere to the Synoptics' often incongruous legal contextualization of legal-sounding gnomai.

The legal gnomai still to be discussed are all Marcan and all lack compelling Pauline parallels, though I shall argue in at least one case (Mark 7:15 par /Rom 14:14) for the possibility of deliberate Pauline non-allusion. The examples which follow are, still, typical of Synoptic quasi-legal gnomai both in the internal tension between legal topicality and gnomic style and in the corresponding tensions and ambiguities in their gospel contexts.

Whoever wants to be first must be last of all and servant of all. (Mark 9:35)

Whoever wishes to become great among you must be your servant and whoever wishes to be first among you must be slave of all. (Mark 10:43)

---

[56] Dungan, *Sayings of Jesus*, 146–150.

The greatest among you must become like the youngest, and the leader like one who serves. ...who is greater, the one who is at the table or the one who serves? (Luke 22:24–30)

Slaves are not greater than their master, nor messengers greater then the one who sent them. (John 13:1–17)

The *Wanderlogion* Mark 9:35, 10:43 and parallels is notable for the degree to which it spans our exegetical sub-categories of personal reference, discipleship and legal topicality. Like Matthew 10:10 (par), the gnomai of this cluster are received as a practical model for leadership and rank within the community of discipleship, far more than as a prophetic model for wider social transformation. But as a typically gnomic, non-legal framework for resolving incipiently legal problems of leadership hierarchy, the saying about primacy depends concretely on Jesus' personal as well as verbal authority.

This is confirmed by K. Berger's exemplary investigation of "shared tradition" behind Mark 10:35–45, Luke 22:24–30 and John 13:1–17. Berger detects behind Mark 10 and Luke 22 a shared, orally transmitted double tradition consisting of a gnomic core and a complementary episodic core. He argues that a sentence on the (gnomic) pattern, "Great is the one who serves," was traditionally associated with an (authentic) episodic recollection of Jesus' practical example of servant-leadership. He emphasizes the impossibility and illegitimacy of formally defining the continuum of rhetorically flexible oral tradition beyond this double, gnomic and episodic, core. Mark 10:43 is, like Mark 6:4, a key instance of a gnomic core which, despite its semantic separability and distinctiveness, was closely associated in pre-gospel oral tradition with a particular episodic memory. Berger's discussion of the gnome represented in Mark 10:43 and parallels also underlines the expression of personal authority as the origin of normative force: Mark 10:43 presupposes the kind of narrative characterization which John 13 delivers.[57]

---

[57] Berger, *Einführung*, 227–233.

There is nothing outside a person that by going in can defile, but the things that come out are what defile. (Mark 7:15 par /Rom 14:14)

In relation to the gnome, Mark 7:15 (par), an entire literature has grown up around questions which should be standard for gnomic exegesis: "Could Jesus have said this?" and (especially, but not only, if "yes") "What could it have meant?"[58] As with every other gnomic saying in the Synoptics, so here, I want to contribute one basic insight: in Synoptic literature and tradition, gnomic sayings are a distinct rhetorical class, so that their cumulative profile (e.g. their frequently personal and quasi-legal aspect) matters more than the (in)authenticity and (limited) perspicuity of the individual examples.

This single insight, though fundamental for understanding Synoptic tradition and the literature under its influence as an argumentative, rhetorical process, is not likely to sever cleanly the Gordian knot binding tradition and criticism in Mark 7:1–23. The tangle may be loosened, however, by connecting the question of historically possible meanings not only with the endless pursuit of an 'original wording', but more especially with the saying's generic character as gnome.

Stephen Westerholm has shown that the most authentic aspects of topically legal sections in the Synoptics are not statutory, i.e., not formally legal. Furthermore he specifically recognizes that the *"mashal"* ("parable," *parabole*, verse 17), Mark 7:15, belongs to a non-legal order of normative rhetoric.

> Hence the "rule" which Jesus stated here with regard to true purity is left open, paradoxical, capable of providing guidance but lacking the precise applications of halakhah.[59]

That is, the vocabulary of defilement and purity which gives the saying its undeniable legal topicality also invests it with a legally intolerable ambiguity: the same gnomic core could be cited in illustration of

---

[58] For bibliography and intensive discussion see R.P. Booth, *Jesus and the Laws of Purity: Tradition History and Legal History in Mark 7* (JSNTSup 13; Sheffield, 1986); also J. Lambrecht, "Jesus and the Law. An Investigation of Mk 7,8–23," *ETL* 53 (1977) 24–83.

[59] Westerholm, *Jesus and Scribal Authority*, 81–84, quoting 84.

opposite attitudes to purity (inward *and* outward[60] versus inward *instead* of outward).

Synoptic contextualization, moreover, does little to resolve the inner normative ambiguity of the gnome; the Marcan and, to a moderated extent, the Matthaean contexts are argumentatively and topically so fragmented as effectively to isolate the gnome for historical exegesis. No amount of tinkering can make the gnome a sensible response either to the initial challenge about unwashed eating or to the subsequent excursus about *Korban*. As verse 15 stands it is clearly about the third distinct topic, food.[61] Even stripped of language relating unequivocally to food ("what goes in/comes out"), the gnome is about the possibility of incurring impurity through deeds, a possibility of which the disciples' accusers are already aware.[62] What follows in Mark 7:17–23 commits the passage to the basic contradiction of a question about handwashing and an eventual answer contrasting food with immorality as sources of impurity. As Berger has noticed, Mark 7:15 (on impurity) and 10:9 (on marital separation) are related in the same way to their respective contexts:[63] they are both instances, albeit unusually complicated, of the normative dissonance which often arises between intrinsically non-legal, though topical gnomai and their more or less plausibly legalizing Synoptic context(s).

This tradition-critical as well as semantic separation of Mark 7:15 from its Synoptic context does not, however, establish the saying's authenticity. Any argument that Mark 7:15 is pre-Marcan, let alone from Jesus, must explain the saying's silence outside the gospels. Even on the unsupportable supposition that the gnome originally excluded specifically food-related language,[64] its relevance to questions of Torah observance should have made it a focus of debate well beyond the readership of Mark 7.

---

[60] Cf. Philo *de Specialibus Legibus* 3.108–209.

[61] Sanders, *Jesus and Judaism*, 266.

[62] *Pace* Booth, *Jesus and the Laws of Purity*, 67–68, 215.

[63] *Gesetzesauslegung*, 534.

[64] Cf. H. Räisänen, "Zur Herkunft von Markus 7,15," in *Logia—les Paroles de Jésus—the Sayings of Jesus: Mémorial Joseph Coppens*, ed. J. Delobel (BETL 59; Leuven, 1982) 477–484, 478.

The problem remains that, if Jesus is the source of the *mashal* in v.15, it is difficult to understand the controversies in the early church related to table fellowship with Gentiles...and the eating of meat offered to idols.[65]

The point of the saying, in fact, is so clear that the positions of the false brethren, Peter and James become impossible to understand if the saying be considered authentic.[66]

The simplest explanation of Mark 7:15 thus assumes its inauthenticity as a saying of Jesus.[67] From the point of view of the saying's inclusion among Synoptic quasi-legal gnomai, however, a more comprehensive account is available without unacceptable complexity. Certainly a better explanation is desirable for a saying which, apart from assumptions about its original meaning and background, has a plausible claim to authenticity.[68] Sanders concedes that "if we provide a new context for the saying, it can be saved as an authentic logion," but it is only really clear "that as it is intended in Mark 7 it is inauthentic."[69]

In fact, a non-Marcan, pre-Marcan contextualization follows from interpreting Mark 7:15 as a gnome, since it belongs to a gnomic, quasi-legal sub-type well attested in Synoptic tradition and often marked by normative tension with its evolving gospel contexts.

One preliminary point is clear; unlike the church, Jesus and his associates can have had little or no occasion radically to question, let alone to abrogate or violate biblical food-laws as such.[70] The saying's only imaginably authentic context is in relation to projects for the clarification, harmonization and completion of biblical purity norms. In Jesus' day such projects for extending the normative intensity and scope of selected laws were still nascent and probably unsystematized, the largely private concern of minorities, against whose normative pretensions a gnome like Mark 7:15 might be directed without justifying antinomian inferences. Under such circumstances the speaker of our gnome could be upholding a perfectly respectable—indeed majority—position of fairly conscientious but ideologically unpretentious observ-

---

[65] Westerholm, *Jesus and Scribal Authority*, 81 and n. 114.
[66] Sanders, *Jesus and Judaism*, 266 and n.79.
[67] Räisänen, "Zur Herkunft von Markus 7,15," 482–483.
[68] Westerholm, *Jesus and Scribal Authority*, 80–81.
[69] Sanders, *Jewish Law*, 28.
[70] Harvey, *Constraints*, 39–40.

ance.[71] If it is generally true that our gnome "gives a thoroughly Torah-critical impression"[72] in its Marcan, and our modern libertarian, context, it does so much less in Matthaean reception. It may in fact have produced an even less abstract and more personally authoritative impact in a Jewish environment like that of Jesus' Galilee, to which principled, calculated rejection of biblical Torah as a whole must have been largely alien.

In the end, the impression given by Mark 7:15, identified even in its Marcan context as a relatively independent "parable" (verse 17), is not exactly that of Torah-criticism: either it rejects Torah absolutely (and scatologically) or it is essentially about something else, with no practical relevance at all to questions of law. The hypothesis that legally topical gnomai including Mark 7:15 are, as gnomai, generically, recognizably non-legal despite their topicality takes the latter option seriously: while the saying clearly is about some sort of problem of attitudes toward food and purity, it absolutely does not tell anyone what they should or should not eat, whether or how much they should care about purity or, above all, what rules or what approach to legal exegesis to follow. This gnome, like the other legal gnomai reviewed thus far, is neither legislation nor a coherent principle for legislation. Thus Mark is wrong to suppose (verse 19b) that in Jesus' religious and rhetorical milieu it could abolish anything except a caricature of pre-Rabbinic Jewish attitudes to purity laws. The cutting edge of this gnomic judgement is not so much its implied 'attitude to the Law', as its implied presumption of authority for the gnome-speaker whose bare and non-legal opinion (gnome) intrudes without apology upon sacred topics.

Viewed in this way Mark 7:15 coheres with other quasi-legal sayings and with the rhetoric of gnomai generally in Jesus-tradition. It is not a coherent critique of food laws, with implications for an 'attitude to the law', but an assertion of personal authority and a topically controversial expression of *latent* conflict between Jesus' mission of renewal and programmes for Israel's systematic, gradual purification. The gnome's potential authenticity as (1) representative of Jesus' rhetoric and (2) not demonstrably inauthentic, is indicated not just by its tradition-critical

---

[71] This characterization is fair even if we follow Sanders in greatly broadening Neusner's portrayal of the Pharisees as specifically, even exclusively interested in extending *priestly* purity in relation to *food*-laws: Sanders, *Jewish Law*, 97–254.

[72] Räisänen, "Zur Herkunft von Markus 7,15," 439.

detachability from its legalizing reception in Mark 7, but more especially by its gnomic resistance to legal application. Attribution of Mark 7:15 to Jesus is historically possible and interesting not because it abolishes laws, but because it gnomically confounds even sympathetic jurisprudence. If Mark 7:15 was spoken in Jesus' world, it was not to attack Torah as such, but rather to invite an audience to assess the authority and purpose of so legally impertinent a speaker.

This example, like Mark 10:9, is an actual instance of a possibility I have repeatedly invoked to help explain Paul's reticent use of gnomai attributed to the Lord. In such cases, the gospel-writers are actively abusing legally topical gnomai as directly legal texts, despite their intrinsic unsuitability and with chaotic consequences. Thus Mark 7:17–23 in the strongest terms represents Jesus' *mashal* as an effective and general abolition of biblical food laws, though even the Marcan context acknowledges the saying's legal unclarity in the disciples' need for clarification. Mark 7:15 is the most striking, but not the only instance of a general Marcan attempt to force the round peg of gnomic legal topicality into the square hole of concrete legal application. Since gnomai seldom work as positive laws, the only way to turn their legal topicality into something legally and ideologically concrete is to stress their antinomian possibilities. It is significant, then, that Matthaean redaction seems to moderate the misappropriation of gnomic authority by presenting a sanitized version of the gnome itself (Matt 15:11) and, above all, by omitting Mark's antinomian conclusion (Mark 7:19).

This brings us once again to Paul. Doubts about the potential authenticity of the food-purity gnome are founded on the apparent contradiction between its topical importance for post-Easter Church politics and its striking neglect by all parties.[73] The neglect may not be total, since Paul's remarkable insistence on dominical authority in Romans 14:14 may conceal an allusion to sayings tradition.[74] Any attempt to relate Romans 14:14 to Mark 7:15 must overcome the general but, I think, diminishing difficulty of Paul's allusiveness and/or ignorance in relation to Jesus' sayings. In this case, however, it is also necessary to address the apostle's failure (even more than in relation to Matt 19:12) to exploit a gnome which, if even plausibly authentic,

---

[73] Westerholm, *Jesus and Scribal Authority*, 80–81; Sanders, *Jewish Law*, 28.

[74] Booth, *Jesus and the Laws of Purity*, 99–100; Westerholm, *Jesus and Scribal Authority*, 81; contra Räisänen, "Zur Herkunft von Markus 7,15," 480–81.

should have allowed him instant triumph in a deeply divisive Church fight. Finally, an appeal to Jesus-tradition behind Romans 14:14 must satisfactorily explain his use there of a formula of inner spiritual conviction rather than of objective verbal allusion.[75]

I know and am persuaded in the Lord Jesus that nothing is unclean in itself; but it is unclean for anyone who thinks it unclean. (Rom 14:14)

I have argued in earlier cases that Paul's refusal to quote Jesus' words does not stem only from limited knowledge and interpretive competition from other authoritative bearers of tradition. Paul was a sufficiently accomplished Greek rhetor and a sufficiently deft Jewish interpreter of Law to be uncomfortably conscious of the legal ambiguity of the gnomai which make up most of the ostensibly legal sayings in Jesus' tradition. His reticence toward Jesus' sayings should therefore also be related to an elemental tension in Paul's own argumentative requirements. On the one hand, his doctrinal and practical argumentation required, if possible, reference to plausibly dominical and topically relevant norms, especially if these were familiar to his audience. On the other hand, Paul's own abnormally charismatic authority-claims militated against a straightforward normative appeal to a dominical rhetoric which could not easily persuade, coming from lips other than Jesus'.

If I am right that the available dominical tradition consisted for Paul (even more than for the gospel-writers) of gnomic sayings, then the tradition will have been directly topical for many of his controversial needs, yet dangerously indeterminate in its normative implications. Paul seems to have written in a double conundrum: caught between the need for norms which could function in his (epistolary) absence and the need to assert his apostolicity against such norms; caught also between the topicality of some available traditions and their intrinsic normative instability. This reconstruction of the tradition-historical situation in which Paul produced his written rhetoric is the best way to account for his complex attitude to Jesus' tradition: near silence, qualified, where reference to tradition was topically unavoidable, by diffident allusion to the volatile mix in gnomic speech of legal topicality and non-legal personal authority.

---

[75] Räisänen, "Zur Herkunft von Markus 7,15," 480–1 and n.21.

In this case, the loaded ambiguities of Mark 7:15—*either* internalizing observance without abrogating its biblical demands *or* abrogating law radically in its most Jewish aspect—make a plausible background for the peculiar nuance of Paul's appeal to Jesus' authority in Romans 14:14. This is especially so if we assume that a relatively conservative, observant reception of the food-gnome must have become less and less persuasive as the Church moved beyond its origins in Jesus' situation toward large-scale incorporation of Gentiles; Matthew's redactional disavowal (Matt 15:11, 17) of Mark 7:19 was already a rearguard. Even so Paul's own rhetorical position in Romans 14 as in 1 Corinthians 8 is that of an arbitrator[76] and not that of an openly committed advocate of the radical cause. Paul gives only concessionary and qualified acceptance to (his closest opponents' ?) formulae relevant to food-laws (Rom 14:20; 1 Cor 6:13; 10:23 cf. 6:12), formulae also on the border between law and gnome. If Paul knew Mark 7:15, he would probably have understood it in similar terms, much less absolute than those of Mark 7:19.

In general, then, Romans 14:14 fits my hypothetical expectation that Paul, diatribist and professed ex-Pharisee, should be more than usually sensitive—more than Mark—both to legal normativity and to the connotative possibilities of gnome as a rhetorical means for transcending argumentative, especially legal, rigour. Recognizing Mark 7:15 as a gnome, and as a gnome which, typically, confounds legal reference, non-legal ambiguity and implicitly personal authority, helps clarify Romans 14:14 by recognizing also Paul's good grounds for wariness toward so tempting a tradition.

In fact two such grounds are provided. First, is the serious possibility, confirmed in both Romans 14 and 1 Corinthians 8–10, that a gnome such as ours would become a football for competing interpreters addressing Paul's constituency.[77] Second, though, is the intrinsic difficulty of Mark 7:15, particularly for Paul himself, caught between the gnome's ambiguous demand, either for internalization of law or for its abrogation. In Matthew 7:15 Paul may well have had a command, on the highest authority, not to worry about food-laws. But the same gnome by itself (and tradition-criticism of Mark 7 suggests that the

---

[76] Harvey, *Constraints*, 39; Käsemann, *Romans*, 374.
[77] Käsemann, *Romans*, 374.

saying was originally transmitted in hermeneutical isolation[78]) or with the explanatory formula (Mark 7:19/Romans 14:20[79]) does not yield Paul's delicately nuanced positions in Romans 14 and 1 Corinthians 8–10. Any but the most careful allusion to Mark 7:15 would leave Paul exposed to authoritative contradiction from abrogationist and cautious tendencies alike. That is, the gnome could not tell him *how* not to worry about the (im)purity of foods.

Here again, it is impossible positively to demonstrate Pauline knowledge of a dominical gnome. It is important, however, to notice once more in this case the correspondence between the intrinsic difficulty, indeed dangers, of a Synoptic quasi-legal gnome and Pauline diffidence in citing the Lord's authority for his own legal rulings. Indeed the particular difficulty and topical urgency of Mark 7:15 correspond well to the tone of Romans 14:14, a tone of inner conviction in personal identification with Jesus' authority, not one of objectively confident citation.[80] More than most sayings, though not uniquely, Mark 7:15 is mute or offensively equivocal except to the interpreter who knows already its speaker's mind. Paul identifies himself as such an interpreter at just the juncture where he speaks of personal internalization of impurity ("unclean," *koinos* Rom 14:14, cf. Mark 7:15) and, less positively, of its outright abolition ("everything is clean," *panta kathara* 14:20, cf. Mark 7:19). The likelihood of a deliberately cautious reference to gnomic tradition is therefore impressive.

Either accidentally or (I think) deliberately, Pauline non-allusion to Mark 7:15 exactly illustrates the non-legality of such topically legal *gnomai* and their coherence with other Synoptic *gnomai* in a rhetoric of personal authority (e.g., Rom 14:14 "in the Lord Jesus"). As well, the intelligibility of a deliberately cautious allusion to Mark 7:15 in Romans 14 as a reasonable response to the saying's normative instability greatly weakens doubts about the gnome's authenticity. Recognizing the saying's characteristically gnomic difficulty allows us to see Paul's non-deployment of an apparently irresistible weapon as tactical forbearance, not ignorance.

---

[78] Berger, *Gesetzesauslegung*, 463ff; *pace* Booth, esp. 74, 83–90, hermeneutical isolation seems to me to be the consequence even of regarding our saying and the handwashing question (v.5) as the original unit of tradition.

[79] Räisänen, "Zur Herkunft von Markus 7,15," 481.

[80] Räisänen, "Zur Herkunft von Markus 7,15," 481.

The same recognition places the purity-gnome in a social context of radically personal, yet relatively controlled (i.e., symbolic, connotative and, mainly, verbal) normative challenge. The historical Jesus as speaker and as actor was at home in such a context. Within it, the present gnome may be seen to be in some sense, "a Hellenistic saying of sapiential type in apocalyptic tradition" without being therefore inauthentic or unrepresentative of Jesus.[81]

As Klaus Berger has noticed, all four remaining Marcan legal dispute -passages have the same literary and tradition-historical character as Mark 7:1–23 and 10:2–12: in each of these an older, gnomic, quasi-legal and potentially authentic saying (Mark 2:19, 27; 3:4b; 7:15; 10:9; 12:17) is set in an idealized, if not wholly imaginary, biographical frame.[82] In each, dissonance between the intrinsic non-legality of gnome and the evangelist's need for normative clarity probably reflects a difference of tradition-history between gnomic sayings and gospel settings.[83]

The wedding guests cannot fast while the bridegroom is with them. (Mark 2:19)

Normative dissonance is relatively near the surface in Mark 2:18–22.[84] In its immediate narrative context, the gnome forbids fasting. However, a further, dissonant and ambiguous eschatological setting is also implied, to which the non-legality of the gnome is central. Dissonance is slightly moderated in Matthew and Luke by the absence of a parallel to Mark's verse 19b, but in all three Synoptics incongruity is under-scored by the implication of the concluding parabolic material (verses 21 par) that the normative innovation of verse 19a is neither reversible nor compatible with the old order. For the present it scarcely matters whether the dissonance is to be put down, as verse 20 suggests, to normative shift over time or to diversity within the movement.[85] It is

---

[81] *Pace* Berger, *Gesetzesauslegung*, 465ff, quoting 469.

[82] Berger, *Gesetzesauslegung,* 576–580.

[83] Berger, *Gesetzesauslegung*, 578 (§ 10).

[84] Berger, *Gesetzesauslegung*, 578 (§ 11); Schille, "Was ist ein Logion?" 177–180; Bultmann, *Geschichte*, 17; J.B. Muddiman, "Jesus and Fasting (Marc 2,18–29)," in *Jésus aux origines de la christologie*, ed. J. Dupont (BETL 40; Leuven, 1975) 271–281.

[85] Schille, "Was ist ein Logion?" 178; Sanders, *Jewish Law*, 83–84.

sufficient here to notice once more that the equivocation of the whole pericope is grounded in the ambiguity and positively non-legal, incipiently christological character of its central gnome.

Against Gottfried Schille's well-meaning proposal that both Mark 2:19a and the contrary, Matthew 6:17–18, "simplify the issue,"[86] the Marcan saying embodies the whole scope of the problem of relating Jesus' authority to the practice of fasting (though reference could be made to the complementary gnomic tradition of Matthew 11:16–19 par). Thus no privileged, legally abstract or generally valid criticism or abrogation of fasting is implied, despite fasting's slim warrant in biblical law.[87] Instead, the normal order is unconditionally transcended and thus equivocally affirmed by the joyful demands of the Bridegroom's immediate presence. But such transcending presence was hardly unconditionally available, even to Jesus' pre-Easter adherents.

The sabbath was made for humankind, and not humankind for the sabbath. (Mark 2:27)

Certainly, gnomic assertion of personal rather than of legal authority is clear in the Bridegroom saying; it is almost as clearly expressed in the association of gnome and Son-of-Man saying in Mark 2:27, 28 and parallels. Without absolutely ruling out an authentic episode behind Mark 2:23–28, the implausibility and unclarity of its scenario,[88] the suspiciously ecclesial role of the disciples[89] and the doubtful relevance of the Davidic *exemplum* (verses 25–26 par)[90] once again tend to isolate the concluding gnomic sayings from their context for historical exegesis. Normative dissonance in this context is so complete as to be almost unnoticeable: neither the gnome nor the biblical *exempla* (Mark 2:25–26 and Matt 12:5–6) excuse the disciples' alleged misbehaviour, but the gnome does so least of all. By itself, verse 27 emphasizes the contribution of revealed law to human nature: This could just as easily fuel apologetic argument in favour of Sabbath-observance, as polemic

---

[86] Schille, "Was ist ein Logion?" 181.

[87] Sanders, *Jesus and Judaism*, 401 n.85; *Jewish Law*, 81–84.

[88] Sanders, *Jesus and Judaism*, 265.

[89] Sanders, *Jesus and Judaism*, 266; Bultmann, *Geschichte*, 16.

[90] Cf. F Neirynck, "Jesus and the Sabbath," in *Jésus aux origines de la christologie*, ed. J Dupont (BETL 40; Leuven, 1975) 227–270, 259ff.

against it. The replacement of Mark 2:27 with Matthew 12:7 seems to acknowledge this two-edgedness of the Marcan form.

As very notably in relation to Mark 7:15, so also here, isolation of the gnomic saying as historic tradition has led to conflicting judgements about (in)authenticity and—intimately, though inconsistently linked—(dis)similarity.[91] From a viewpoint in gnomic rhetoric, continuing disagreements about the meaning and background of the gnome probably indicate that the saying's ambiguity was originally intended—perhaps even by Jesus. Like most gnomai Mark 2:27 was meant to raise an issue and not to settle it.

> It has been shown that the radical meaning is not the only possible and that the logion could function in more than one direction. This reservation remains true with regard to objections raised against the authenticity of Mark II,27.[92]

Hearing this saying, too, as one of a set of gnomai which are topically but not functionally legal opens a wider horizon of "coherence with other sayings of Jesus."[93] Above all, the question of dissimilarity is related less to the individual saying than to the larger category to which it belongs. Gnomic styles are very common in Jewish, Christian and other Hellenistic rhetoric; gnomai on legal topics are, however, quite rare outside the gospels and may well reflect a specialized application in Jesus' usage. This saying, like the others reviewed here, must be interpreted and evaluated as a gnome and not as a would-be law. In this respect it is representative of Jesus' earliest tradition whether it is authentic or not.

Certainly it is not structured to guide the perplexed conscience toward either Torah observance or non-observance; the gnome's essential function, doubtless most striking in contexts where observance is normal, is to exploit and preserve normative perplexity as an opening to the more-than-legal authority of the speaker. This example, like the other quasi-legal gnomai, does not tell, as a properly legal rule would, how Jesus' circle actually should have behaved or, indeed, how they did

---

[91] Over against an unusually interesting range of parallels, see *Mek.* Exod 31:13, 14; *2 Apoc. Bar.* 14:18b; 2 Macc 5:19; cf. chap. 5 at n. 126 and Neirynck, "Jesus and the Sabbath," 246ff.

[92] Neirynck, "Jesus and the Sabbath," 269.

[93] Neirynck, "Jesus and the Sabbath," 270.

behave. Instead the gnome places the whole weight of concern about Sabbath norms on the urgent demand for understanding between speaker and audience.

In this regard the Matthaean formula (Matt 12:6) and the Marcan Son of Man saying (Mark 2:28 par) are impressively accurate receptions of the force of the gnomic norm, though they soften the urgency of its language. The Son of Man question has so effectively sabotaged tradition criticism of the sayings involved as to preclude any guess about the pre-Synoptic relationship between Mark 2:27 and 28. But verse 28 at least expresses the ultimate dependence of gnomic rhetoric upon the personal credibility of its supposed speaker. Such personal authority is not asserted in either gnome without impinging upon other, impersonal sources of normativity, notably biblical Sabbath norms, which are implicitly affirmed, yet profoundly relativized. Mark 2:27, 28 are, above all, sublimely unhelpful as directives for Sabbath behaviour or as models for an attitude to Law in relation to other sources of social or religious normativity. Like other gnomic sayings, these gnomai subject even the most sacred norms to the unpredictable, uncodifiable demands of the Kingdom in Jesus' voice.

Is it lawful to do good or to do harm on the sabbath, to save life or to kill? (Mark 3:4b)

Many of the same remarks might be made concerning the next context in Mark's order (3:1–6) and its central gnome (3:4). Once more, normative dissonance and the artificiality of the story show themselves in the poor fit of the presumed infraction, legally trivial and historically contrived, to the absurdly high tone of the gnomic double question. Once again, Matthaean sensitivity betrays the incongruity. In Matthew, Mark's double question becomes a single statement preceded by formal argumentation (Matt 12:11–12), surgery which succeeds only partially in making laws from Sabbath-gnomai. The Matthaean truncation of the Marcan gnome also alerts the synoptic reader to a singularity of Mark 3:4 among Synoptic gnomai: the second gnomic question actually presents an applicably coherent legal consideration, that life-saving takes priority over Sabbath-observance, a consideration which the Matthaean pericope rightly leaves out as irrelevant to the context of elective healing.

More important in an analysis of the functional non-legality of topically legal gnomai is the analogical juxtaposition of life-saving/killing to doing good/ill. These are not comparable alternatives in relation to Sabbath duties. Life-saving might excuse what otherwise would be a violation, but a non-laborious and divinely sanctioned miracle could not in any case violate Sabbath.[94] In defiance of the legalism of its Synoptic contexts, Jesus' word in Mark 3:4 points toward the wholly non-legal possibility that a more ordinary good work or a more laborious miracle, such as might constitute a trivial violation, could acquire salvific, life-saving meaning and so transcend the legitimate demands of Sabbath-rest. This comparison of good behaviour generally with the exceptional urgency of life-saving is legally pointless. In non-legal rhetoric, however, it makes good sense, as the collapse of ordinary legal or ethical normativity into transcendent, almost soteriological and christological categories corresponds precisely with the rhetorical function of gnomai generally in Jesus' tradition. Despite its unusual questioning tone, then, Mark 3:4 is typical of its gnomic kind in its non-legality and strong assertion of Jesus' personal authority.

Give to the emperor the things that are the emperor's, and to God the things that are God's. (Mark 12:17)

Pay to all what is due them. (Rom 13:7)

The last Marcan dispute-passage (12:13–17) and its climactic gnome (verse 17) are remarkable in several ways. First of all, there is none of the normative dissonance so often noted between Synoptic context and gnomic saying. The legal question is serious, controversial and dangerous enough to elicit the cunning response of the gnome. The pericope as a whole depends clearly upon the riddling non-legality of the gnome. In this typically gnomic ambiguity, Mark 12:13–17 is in telling contrast with the episodic equivocation of Matthew 17:24–27.

In addition, the saying, alone among those reviewed here, actually does express an 'attitude to the Law' and in terms which might have legally practical consequences (contrast Matt 5:18 par; 7:12c par). Despite the saying's implications for taxation and related topics, its only intrinsic legal topic is the whole normative system of Roman *imperium*.

---

[94] Sanders, *Jesus and Judaism*, 266 and n.82, 83.

For most purposes of New Testament study this is, of course, the wrong Law.[95] That Jesus or his immediate tradition could so succinctly express an attitude to it underscores by contrast the piecemeal and elusive bearing of Synoptic quasi-legal gnomai, including this one,[96] on Jewish Law as a whole.

Topically legal gnomai in the Synoptics offer a plausibly representative sample of legal topics in Judaism, but an attitude of Jesus to Torah can only be very imperfectly inferred from rhetorical topics which may be metaphorically quite distant from the various social situations they could address. If, as I have suggested above, Matthew 10:10 does not represent its putative speaker's attitude toward employment, nor Matthew 19:12 his attitude to eunuchs, they cannot—even together— yield an attitude to the Law as a whole. A partial attitude might be inferred from the two Law-gnomai, Matthew 5:18 (par) and Matthew 7:12c (par), but the result would be reflection on the specifically non-legal aspects of biblical Torah as revelation. Judging from the bulk of Jesus' language as it is reflected in Synoptic gnomai even this inference was not drawn: even the circumspectly critical stance of Mark 12:17 toward Imperial law as a source of actual normative demands does not reappear in relation to biblical Law working in Jesus' own Judaism.

Notwithstanding its clarity of attitude toward an alien legal system, Mark 12:17 is entirely typical in its non-legal ambiguity: do the taxes get paid or not? Neither gnome nor pericope really tells. Instead the saying embodies the more-than-legal question of the relationship between social, political norms and the prior but indeterminate claims of God. It is of historical and not only homiletical significance that the gnome (unlike the story) does not even hint at what God might leave to Caesar, or Caesar to God.[97] Instead, the saying advertises Jesus' prerogative authority precisely where such apparently idiosyncratic self-assertion would seem to be most jealously excluded, both by God and by Caesar.

Mark 12:17 combines non-legal, personally assertive ambivalence, typical in Synoptic gnomai, with a more unusual critical distance. This

---

[95] Harvey, *Constraints*, 36–7.

[96] Cf. F.F. Bruce, "Render to Caesar," in *Jesus and the Politics of His Day*, ed. E. Bammel and C.F.D. Moule (Cambridge, 1984) 249–263, 254–257.

[97] Bruce, "Render to Caesar," 259–262.

combination is mirrored in the curiously free-standing[98] parenesis of Romans 13:1–7 and its concluding gnome. It is not only the topic of Romans 13 and Mark 12:13–17 which have historically made them into weather-vanes of political folly;[99] the danger of their shared topic is aggravated by the typical non-legality of both gnomai, Romans 13:7 and Mark 12:17 and parallels. Each expresses and, deliberately, neither overcomes the perennial disproportion between the ruler's due and the subject's duty; both define the question to which neither prescribes a legally binding answer.

This parallel between the duty-gnome in Romans 13 and the Synoptics' Caesar-gnome is limited by the latter's dramatic reference to the emperor's personal authority. The advice to the Romans is naturally more nuanced, but the two gnomai are alike not only in their shared imperative ("pay," *apodote*) but also in its qualification by an unavoidable but impossible task of calculating how to pay what is due.

Whether Paul is aware of a parallel with Jesus-tradition or (more probably) not,[100] the independent character of Romans 13:1–7 within the composition of Paul's letter suggests a closer connection with generally Jewish (especially Diaspora) tradition than with Jesus. Paul is clearly not wrestling in Romans 13:7, as he seems to at other points of contact with gnomic tradition, with Jesus' sheer unquotability.

Likewise, as we have seen, although Mark 12:17 and parallels is impressively conflictual (contrast Matt 5:18 par; 7:12 par), it is not in conflict with its gospel context. The Pauline parallel underscores, then, the unique absence of normative dissonance in this case. Among topically legal gnomai ascribed to Jesus, only the Caesar-gnome asserts its speaker's authority over a virtual Jewish consensus of practical and theological ambivalence toward Roman rule.

This is the unique exception to a key rule of gospel rhetoric: topically legal gnomai in Synoptic tradition are in a problematic relation to the normative requirements of the texts which incorporate them—especially if we include Pauline texts here. Paul and the evangelists have an understandable need to assert church order and, if possible, to fashion a coherent and unifying attitude to the Law. Instead,

---

[98] E. Bammel, "Romans 13," in *Jesus and the Politics of His Day* ed. E. Bammel and C.F.D. Moule (Cambridge, 1984) 365–383, 366; Käsemann, *Romans*, 350–359.

[99] Käsemann, *Romans*, 352.

[100] Bammel, "Romans 13," 366–367.

gnomic sayings set the trap of rhetorical, personal self-reference and
bait it with provocative legal topics. In this respect, the gnomic style in
Synoptic tradition, like parable, looks forward to soteriological and
christological rationalization without developing an attitude to revealed
religion or legality as such. In principle, Jesus' gnomai say much more
about the character of the covenant relationship than about the status (to
that extent sharply relativized) of law and rhetoric inspired by it.

Conclusions: the non-legality of gnomic rhetoric in Jesus-tradition

All this, of course, begs the questions of practical (il)legal behaviour.
It is rhetorically and, probably, psychologically futile to ask about
Jesus' attitude to the Law as an abstract whole: he didn't need one.
Speaking in a profoundly Hellenistic world of public discourse, he could
invoke legal *topics* in a gnomic rhetoric without intending to convey
any such global analysis of Law. Rhetoric aside, however, the question
remains whether Jesus' and his immediate disciples' (non)observance
of Jewish custom was an issue for their original Galilean milieu (or for
Jerusalem party-elites). Did Jesus' practical example match his gnomic
rhetoric on legal topics? If so, how?

In the first place, Jesus' public behaviour and spoken prescriptions
cannot have been so decisive as to prejudice or obviate the normative
struggles of the apostolic movement: at least much of the time, Jesus'
behaviour did not seem egregiously antinomian.[101] Even more clearly,
the memory of his example and words did not immediately determine
early Christian practice or controversial rhetoric on legal issues. This
lack of direct influence probably does not mean that Jesus neither did
nor said anything legally interesting. As to his public speech, it is best
explained in terms of gnomic rhetoric and gnomic reliance on current
topicality, either as a source of characterization and rapport or as a
source of proof by analogy to a less topical issue. On available
evidence, such gnome-use must be interpreted as a deliberate and
impressive aspect of Jesus' speaking style.

In Jesus' historical context, Jewish covenantal and legal themes were
an important source of conflictual, controversial topicality; their use
need not imply, however, that Jesus talked much about Covenant and

---

[101]   Sanders, *Jesus and Judaism*, 268 and nn.86, 87.

Law as such, though he could hardly disown the emotions which his handling of such loaded symbols would surely evoke. Thus the quasi-legal gnomai document an aggressive willingness in Jesus' tradition to address controversial, emotive and practical topics in law, but they were probably never meant to determine anyone's law observance or non-observance. One key aspect of topically legal gnomai is their refusal simply to prescribe behavioral norms; by pointedly selecting legal topics Jesus emphatically projected this refusal into the most important areas of Law-observance. These gnomai deliberately and pointedly beg the question of what to do, in order to assert instead the normative authority of Jesus' word and presence. Thus, whatever the tradition-historical relationship between Romans 14:14 and Mark 7:15 (par), the Pauline formula of intuitive normative certainty "in the Lord Jesus" perfectly expresses the more-than-legal response called for by the gnomic quasi-legality of much of Jesus' tradition.

Bringing the legally topical gnomai exegetically and historically together lowers the stakes of questions about the real-life normative applicability of gnomai by relativizing their apparently antinomian overtones. Even these radical-sounding traditions are parts of a larger rhetorical category with collectively strong claims to authenticity. It is therefore possible to ask under what conditions and within what normative limits they might actually have exerted normative influence, without having to prove the authenticity of each example.

The topically legal gnomai look surprisingly suitable for the rhetorical task of claiming personal, charismatic authority as a radical alternative to more legitimate powers, without also destroying the legitimacy of the covenant itself. Taken together and with other gnomai, the very ambiguities which mark their inapplicability as laws suggest their openness to reception both to affirm legal norms and to declare the legal autonomy of the new Kingdom. In the previous chapter I argued that "anti-proverbial" gnomai subvert "the typical proverbial stance of making a continuous project of our life"[102] without implying a negative, or even a conscious general attitude to proverbial wisdom. In the same way, without entailing a distinctive or consistent response to the Law, quasi-legal gnomai subvert the project, underway at Qumran and

---

[102] Beardslee, "Uses of the Proverb," 69.

probably in Pharisaic rigour (*akribeia*),[103] of building a coherent legal system out of biblical Law.

Against Berger's otherwise persuasive study of the most important quasi-legal gnomai in Mark, their frequently alleged 'dissimilarity' is not such as to demand "an early post-Easter, Hellenistic origin."[104] If the quasi-legal gnomai imply a frustrating and aggressive hostility to someone else's attitude to the Law, the *ad hominem* hostility is much less the sayings' point than the assertion of Jesus' supra-legal authority. At any rate, none of this is obviously inauthentic.

Finally, there are aspects of gnome and of some quasi-legal gnomai which do suggest consequences for Jesus' and his followers' public activity. The rhetorical strategy of gnomic brinkmanship, especially in quasi-legal gnomai, where the 'brink' is well-defined in the possibility of saying something really blasphemous, disloyal or antinomian, does have a behavioral counterpart. This is most conveniently illustrated in Mark 12:17 and parallels; rhetorically, Jesus' nearness to the brink is implied as strongly as possible in the Marcan context and in the accusations of Luke 23:2.[105] Still, I suspect that it took more than a few gnomic sayings to attract ultimately fatal police action. An action against the Temple (Mark 11:15–19 par), isolated and individual enough to be more symbolic gesture than programmatic initiative, may have brought out some of the more dangerous possibilities of talk about God and Caesar.

In less dangerous normative fields, the relationships between gnomic sayings and Jesus' behaviour are less speculative. Berger's discussion of Mark 10:43 and 9:35 and parallels convincingly emphasizes the saying's tradition-historical as well as logical correspondence with Jesus' symbolic behaviour in the concrete situation of the meal (Luke 22:24–30; John 13:1–20).[106] Other aspects of Jesus' gnomic language presuppose behavioral adjustments.[107] Of these, only the attack on filial piety demands actual violation of biblical law and might have

---

[103] A.I. Baumgarten, "The Name of the Pharisees," *JBL* 102 (1983) 411–428; "The Pharisaic Paradosis," *HTR* 80 (1987) 63–77.

[104] Berger, *Gesetzesauslegung*, 576, see 461–496, 506–507, 576–592, 586–590.

[105] Bruce, "Render to Caesar," 262–263.

[106] Berger, *Einführung*, 233–235.

[107] Mark 2:19 par; Matt 11:16–19 par on not fasting, Matt 19:12 on celibacy; Matt 8:20 par on homelessness and 8:22 par on filial impiety.

marked Jesus or his imitator as "only one more 'am ha-arets among many."[108]

Combined with such behaviour, such rhetoric would, however, imply that Jesus' actions were grounded not in necessity or selective observance of the minimal or central obligations of biblical law, but in the private, legally unargued authority of Jesus' word and example. Again, such talk and such behaviour need not represent either a critical attitude to the Law or any substantial violation of biblical norms; they do, however, seem to involve a deliberate exploitation of the sacral character of social and legal norms in Judaism and of the ambiguity between voluntary social marginality and illegality.

Furthermore, Synoptic gnomai, very much including those which express legal topicality, construct their normative brinkmanship not only from general tensions latent within Palestinian society at the turn of the eras. Above all, they develop the particular tension between legal and social institutions and Jesus' personal authority and example. That is, gnomic normativity in Synoptic tradition depends on Jesus' presence. Only this presence and immediate call lend the hearer the authority and insight to 'obey' gnomic norms. As usual the extreme cases are clearest: Jesus' call in Matthew 8:22 (par) and the breach of legal duty which it demands from the hearer simply have no obvious normative force apart from Jesus' presence; so also in Mark 2:19 and parallels the freedom to omit customary fasts is directly tied to the presence of the Bridegroom.

In the nature of gnomic rhetoric—conflictual, connotative and highly personal—it will seldom be possible to deduce Jesus' behavioral standards from gnomic tradition. On the other side, however, it is also not possible to deny that the quasi-legal gnomai had some practical relation to Jesus' and his followers' behaviour. They do attest a general strategy of brinkmanship and social marginality, a willingness to redefine latent conflict in non-legal terms of personal response to himself. They suggest a certain knack, rhetorical and probably practical, for managing the consequences. Such an assessment is unavoidably speculative; here, however, it is at least informed by the intense cultivation in Jesus' immediate tradition of the haunting gnomic combination of topical, connotative and conflictual elements.

Much less speculative is the perception of normative dissonance, variable in kind and degree, but almost always there, between legally

---

[108] Sanders, *Jesus and Judaism*, 252–255, 267–269, quoting 291.

topical gnomai recorded in Jesus' name and the texts which incorporate them. W.D. Davies' generalization may well be re-applied to such gnomai in the Synoptics and Paul:

> [T]hese *radical* words begin to take on a *regulatory* character, that is, they become used as guides for the actual business of living, the *point d'appui* of an incipient Christian casuistry.[109]

The dissonance between intrinsic gnomic normativity and Synoptic or Pauline receptions of Jesus' sayings underlies the tradition-historical importance of this chapter's main thesis, that topically legal gnomai attributed to Jesus were functionally non-legal. Indeed, Paul and sometimes Matthew[110] seem to have discerned the limitations and dangers of applying gnomai in Jewish legal contexts.

In speech attributed to Jesus, legal topics are dominated by such gnomai. This explains how his followers could so early and so radically disagree about the basic issues of Torah-normativity and incorporation of Gentiles. Many gnomai in Jesus' name and especially many quasi-legal gnomai are poetically brilliant, provocative and easily memorable; they also cohere with one another as the preferred medium for a difficult message. Their persistence and influence in tradition needs no further explanation. A largely gnomic, essentially non-legal sayings tradition also explains the all but complete absence outside the gospels of appeals to particular sayings of Jesus to resolve practical conflicts.[111] Instead, we find the quasi-legality of ethicizing parenesis, strongly linked to pagan and Jewish gnomic tradition and—anonymously—to the many less topical, less fiercely personal gnomai attributed with some cumulative authenticity to Jesus.[112]

Behind the semantic fact of normative dissonance in literary contexts which incorporate or allude directly to legally topical gnomai lies the high probability that nearly all quasi-legal gnomai in the Synoptics are

---

[109] W.D. Davies, *The Setting of the Sermon on the Mount* (Cambridge, 1964) 387.

[110] Matt 12:5–8 versus Mark 2:27–28; 12:12 versus 3:4; 15:11 versus Mark 7:15.

[111] P. Stuhlmacher, "Das Evangelium und die Evangelien," 18–19.

[112] Rom 12:14, 21; Matt 5:44, 39 par; Rom 13:8–10; Gal 5:14; Jas 2:8; Mark 12:30 par; Berger, *Formgeschichte*, 121–124.

tradition-historically older than their gospel contextualizations.[113] It is less probable, but still impressively likely that the clearest Pauline references and most probable non-allusions to Jesus' words are to such gnomai. The scarcity of the Pauline evidence limits it to the subsidiary role of a test case for hypotheses generated by Synoptic studies.

The test hypothesis includes the expectation that Paul's knowledge of Jesus' sayings, however limited, should reflect both the importance of gnomai in Jesus tradition and also their rhetorical non-legality. This expectation is borne out by the topicality and form of the apostle's most probable references to Jesus as normative speaker. In addition, the peculiarities of Paul's appeals and non-appeals to Jesus' verbal authority are greatly illuminated if what was available to Paul in Jesus' name was an authentic, dangerously non-regulatory and controversial, yet topically legal tradition. If Paul's tradition, like pre-Synoptic tradition, was substantially gnomic, his extreme allusiveness was justified, at least in legalizing contexts, by the nature of his material and perhaps by its actual normative abuse.

In this way it is clear that gnomic language is interpretively basic to Jesus' tradition and not just its lowest common denominator. Quasi-legal gnomai (and their problems) are central to better explanation of Paul's attitude to Jesus, and of Jesus' self-understanding as a public speaker. They, and gnomai generally, are, moreover, fundamental to their literary contexts, contexts which seek not only to domesticate and institutionalize, but also authentically to recreate Jesus' challenging conversational orality. The retention of the non-legal language of gnome with all its difficulties complicated and enriched New Testament normativity by placing at its heart strategically and collectively authentic echoes of Jesus' disturbing personal rhetoric.

Thus the relative preponderance of the Marcan witness to legally topical gnomai need not unbalance our findings: whatever their attraction for the gospel writer, precisely these sayings stand over against their Marcan contexts as tradition-critically prior.[114] In addition we may notice argumentative and topical parallels between Marcan and non-Marcan gnomai on legal topics, parallels which strengthen the

---

[113] See esp. Berger's convincing conclusion in favour of the historical priority of the gnomai in the Marcan dispute-passages (Mark 2:16–17; 18–20; 23–28; 3:1–4; 7:1–23; 10:1–12; 12:13–17) *Gesetzesauslegung*, 576.

[114] Berger, *Gestzesauslegung* 576ff, and *Einführung*, 233–235.

claim for the traditional as well as literary cohesion of the legal sub-
category. Argumentatively, Mark 4:24 and parallels and the quatrain
Matthew 6:24/Luke 16:13 have in common the selection of a proverbial
gnome from economic life and its dramatic reapplication to the
transformed normativity of the community of discipleship. Topically
and for dourness of mood, we may further compare Mark 7:27 (par)
with another quatrain-gnome, Matthew 7:6, or again Mark 10:9 (par)
with, as the Matthaean composition implies, Matthew 19:12. It is not
unfitting that the "Gospel of secret epiphanies" (Martin Dibelius) should
show a special affinity for the elusive challenge of topically legal
gnomai. Still, whatever its importance for interpreting Mark, the Marcan
predominance in quasi-legal gnomai is tradition-historically only one
aspect of a pre- and supra-Marcan phenomenon.

Paul's probable use of quasi-legal gnomai from pre-Synoptic,
including pre-Matthaean, tradition is also important because it clarifies
some conditions under which a gnomic model of oral tradition might
theoretically be falsified: Paul's half- and nonallusions to Jesus' rhetoric
are better explained on the assumption that Paul knew the quasi-legal
gnomai without determining argumentative contexts than on the counter-
assumption that he knew their larger Synoptic argumentative and/or
narrative contexts. If the reverse were true, it would be less likely that
gnomai were structurally fundamental to oral tradition from Jesus.
Gnomai are not to be radically dissociated from more extended
argumentative or episodic recollections.[115] Gnomic cores are, nonetheless, the most widely shared and the most independently interpreted
elements of pre-Synoptic oral tradition. Their transmission and
interpretation in oral tradition is therefore likely to have been determined more by the public conventions of gnomic rhetoric than by the
often redactional conventions of the gospels' narrative and argumentative texts about Jesus.

If it is unlikely that gnomai were remembered in verbally fixed
contexts, it is probable that at least some were traditionally associated
with simple slogans or non-verbal traditions. Among legally topical
examples, the gnome Mark 7:15 may well have been associated in oral
tradition with a radically and legally less ambiguous interpretive slogan
like that of Romans 14:20b (cf. Mark 7:19b). It is a lot simpler and
orally more plausible to guess that both Mark and Paul knew such a

---

[115] Cf. Berger, *Formgeschichte*, 65–66, 121–123.

pairing of gnomic core and antinomian slogan in shared oral tradition than to argue that both knew "the whole context."[116] Similarly it is quite possible that the gnome against marital separation (Mark 10:9 par) was associated in oral tradition with the rather gnomic and quite non-legal citations of Genesis 1:27 and 2:24.[117] Finally, there is a good case for thinking that Mark 10:43 and parallels was traditionally associated with concrete memories of Jesus' servanthood at the Last Supper (Luke 22: 24–27 cf. John 13:1–20).[118]

But this picture of an oral tradition structured primarily around gnomai and their various argumentative, episodic, verbal and gestural associations is far from form-critical or mnemotechnical models in which verbal transmission of whole contexts is imagined. If Paul (or anyone else outside the gospels) cited in Jesus' name topically legal units as elaborate as Synoptic pericopes, the validity of a primarily gnomic model of oral tradition would be seriously qualified. In fact, this is never the case.[119] Furthermore, almost all topically legal texts in the Synoptic Gospels have at their heart and most probably at their tradition -historical origin textually and normatively unassimilated gnomai (though there are topically legal parables, e.g., that of the Good Samaritan Luke 10:29–37).

Moreover, if my interpretive emphasis on the deliberate, calculated non-legality of gnomai is correct, then gnomai are not only a basic rhetorical and transmissional device in Jesus' tradition, they are also the principal, almost exclusive vehicle for expressing Jesus' views on legal topics. This is a point of striking and well-attested dissimilarity between Jesus' rhetoric and other Jewish and early Christian rhetorics. It furthermore explains the unavailability of authentic Jesus-tradition as a basis for apostolic canons of Church order.

---

[116] Räisänen, "Zur Herkunft von Markus 7,15," 481.

[117] Sanders, *Jesus and Judaism*, 14–15, 257.

[118] Berger, *Einführung*, 233–235.

[119] The nearest approach is in Paul's discussion of divorce (1 Cor 7:10–11) and his presentation of the Lord's Supper tradition (1 Cor 11:23–26). While these passages prove Paul's access to dominical traditions on these topics, comparison with Marcan parallels shows precisely no verbal, textual commonality, only a non-legal gist for the former (perhaps expressed in the non-legal gnome, Mark 10:9, perhaps accompanied by Gen 1:27 and/or 2:24) and a liturgically incomplete gist for the latter ([bread-body-?]cup-blood-covenant); see Sanders, *Jesus and Judaism*, 14–15, and Sanders and Davies, *Synoptic Gospels*, 325–329.

   The picture of Jesus which emerges from the topically legal gnomai
is thus continuous with that provided by the overlapping sub-categories
of self-referential gnomai and gnomai about discipleship discussed in
the previous chapter. In addition, the quasi-legal gnomai show us a
Jesus who is not shy about addressing controversial, even dangerous,
topics in Law. The canniness of Jesus' gnomic language is not aimed
at concealing its topical relevance but rather at asserting Jesus'
sovereignty and autonomy over against the ideological coherence of
legal conventions and legal traditions. Such gnomic self-assertion is not
itself an 'attitude to the Law', however; instead, it is an effective protest
against the pretensions and ultimate (eschatological) dubiety of all such
'attitudes'. Certainly the prevalence of gnomai in Jesus' tradition attests
not so much his failure to establish a legal or scholastic tradition, as a
conscious and repeatedly expressed refusal to do so.
   This refusal is, at any rate, not based in an abstract critique of Law
or the Law. Rather the refusal to express mere legality is the consequence of Jesus' rhetorical assertion of a personal authority undisguised
as Law or as Wisdom. On the other hand, the authority asserted in
gnomai and especially in topically legal sayings is not simply bald
egoism. Instead it is an authority qualified by the assumption of
unlimited freedom and insight in the gnome-audience as well as in the
gnome-speaker, a freedom to respond to the immediacy of Jesus' word
in the controversial situations of legal topicality, without the clarification of legal or proverbial tradition. Gnomic authority is the authority
of linguistic immediacy between speaker and hearer, to which legal and
controversial topicality adds urgency and seriousness.
   The immediacy of gnomic address, the speaker's reliance upon at
least some of his hearers to accept his concrete but unargued authority
claim is perhaps the final argument against misrepresenting Jesus as in
any programmatic sense a Teacher. That Jesus' rhetoric is not didactic
is nowhere more clearly shown than his quasi-legal gnomai.

WHAT DID JESUS SOUND LIKE?

For generations Historical Jesus Research has asked above all the question, "What did Jesus say?" Because rhetoric concerns itself with the entire communicative process and not only with the words as virtual texts, and because rhetoric is interested in typical patterns of communication, rhetorical criticism would rather ask the question, "What did Jesus sound like?"

Socio-rhetorical analysis, especially of Q, suggests that Jesus perhaps sounded like a Cynic. Progymnasmatic analysis suggests that Jesus impressed his best listeners as someone who affected parabolic and gnomic rhetoric to an unusual degree and with unusual intensity. This has led me from time to time to suggest that Jesus exemplified some of the excesses which Greco-Roman rhetoricians usually condemned as 'Asianism.' This depends on what aspects or definitions of Asianism are selected: like most labels of marginalization (e.g., 'Cynic'), 'Asianism' can be adapted to fit its victim. In some relatively sophisticated contexts, 'Asianism' suggests an excessive mannerism of elaboration, the rhetorical equivalent of the architectural baroque-ism of, say, the great temple complexes at Baalbek, Damascus, Palmyra and Jerusalem. In more marginal contexts, however, 'Asianism' is most concretely related to the sporadic but incoherent and inconsistent flashiness of excessive and shallow gnome-use.

Recently Vernon Robbins has asked,

> Did Jesus copy in a scribal manner or compose in a progymnastic rhetorical manner? All of our evidence suggests that he did not.

Earlier in the same response Robbins asked, without answering,

> Did Jesus participate in rhetorical culture? This is a question that raises the
> issue of Jesus' imitation of written text in his speech.[1]

I do not think that Jesus imitated written text, except perhaps the
prophets, in his speaking; I certainly don't think that he copied in a
scribal manner. I do, however, think that the evidence of gnomai and
parables (*mythoi*) suggests that he did compose or, at any rate, perform
using the basic progymnasmata, brilliantly articulated, but perhaps not
elaborated according to the rules of the progymnasmatic text-books
which, I suppose, only a minority of progymnasmatic teachers would
ever have seen.

A leading new study of marginality has identified one set of local,
marginal rhetorics as more or less conscious parodies of selected aspects
of the regionally dominant rhetoric—which may, of course, itself mimic
and distort imperial rhetorical norms. Anna Lowenhaupt Tsing's *In the
Realm of the Diamond Queen: Marginality in an Out of the Way Place*
can help us imagine how Jesus of Nazareth could have performed
locally powerful rhetoric on the margins of Greco-Roman rhetorical
culture. Tsing's central informant, Uma Adang, a woman shaman in up-
country Indonesia, may be a bizarrely far-fetched analogue for Jesus;
they have in common their relative marginality and creative rhetorical
agency in relation to the haphazard encroachments of a distant
state—and in relation to more conventional leaders in their own milieux.
Like Jesus, Uma Adang travels intensively in her region. Like Jesus she
cultivates a ceremonial and prophetic rhetoric which more than mimics,
more than parodies the rhetorics of (Indonesian) statehood and (Islamic)
religious culture. Uma Adang speaks of past and future divine King-
doms, including the Reign of the Diamond Queen who provides Uma
Adang with "a role model" for her own alternative leadership and
rhetorical *ethos*.

> In a regional political climate of state symbolism, Muslim piety, and
> bureaucratic order, what could be more intriguing than Uma Adang's
> inspired fake-Koran readings, pompous "government" speeches full of

---

[1] V.K. Robbins, "Oral, Rhetorical, and Literary Cultures: A Response," in *Orality
and Textuality in Early Christian Literature*, ed. J. Dewey=*Semeia* 65 (1994) 75–91,
81, 80.

unintelligible patriotic verbiage, and eerie pronouncements about the political intersections of the past and the future?

I assume that Jesus spoke by preference in Aramaic, though he seems to have been heard in Greek. I also assume that he had no serious inside access to the progymnasmatic education he imitated. Jesus was perhaps less marginal in relation to the Greco-Roman and Israelite traditional rhetorics which shaped and distorted his experience than Uma Adang is in relation to the Indonesian and global rhetorics of power which she confronts. Jesus succeeded in impressing his words, or his style and *ethos*, very quickly on a new tradition which was both Greco-Roman and Israelite. Like Uma Adang, however, I think he knew how to turn modest rhetorical resources to good effect in sounding both biblical and official, while going well beyond the biblical and official rhetorics in his determination personally "to tie a great past to a small present and to unknown futures."[2]

Is it credible to think of a Galilean, Jewish, primarily Aramaic-speaking, village-based lay leader speaking in ways which would substantially determine not only the lives and deaths of his followers, but also a progymnasmatically structured, Greek language tradition like that which informs the gospels? This is a rhetorical problem, rather than a tradition-critical problem. It is greatly simplified by the recognition of an appropriate register of rhetorical culture in the basic progymnasmata, Quintilian's *primordia dicendi*. But the rhetorical problem can only be adequately defined with the aid of a more positive theory of cultural marginality and rhetorical alternativity, in which the integrity and creativity of marginalized agents is fully appreciated. Jesus can help us with that task.

---

[2] A. Lowenhaupt Tsing, *In the Realm of the Diamond Queen: Marginality in an Out-of-the-Way Place* (Princeton, NJ, 1993) quoting 278, 11, 281.

A CATALOGUE OF SYNOPTIC *GNOMAI*

The following handlist of Synoptic *gnomai* could doubtless be added to, but is inclusive enough to reflect the proposed criteria of separability, analogy and normativity. As a partial check on arbitrary selection, each instance of *Gnome/Sentenz* clearly identified as such by K. Berger (*Formgeschichte*; "Hellenistische Gattungen") has been examined and, in the event, included (Berger's examples are marked here by a preceding 'b'), along with all of C.E. Carlston's 'maxims' and most of his "Wisdom material not sententious in form [*sic*]" ("Wisdom and Eschatology in Q," 108–111). The selection below has also been compared with M. Küchler's list "*die weisheitlichen Logien Jesu bei den Synoptikern*" (*Weisheitstraditionen*, 572ff) of which it has been found to be a subset: *gnomai* figure in Küchler's list as parts of larger, specifically sapiential, units. Finally, all of the non-Q *gnomai* (*Sentenzen*) listed by H. von Lips (except Luke 12:47–8) have been included (*Weisheitlichen Traditionen im NT*, 228–229). Von Lip's comparative catalogue of eight lists of Q 'Wisdom sayings' (198-203) is valuable though it does not adjudicate among the lists surveyed. See also L. Perdue's form-critical catalogue "The Wisdom Sayings of Jesus" ("Wisdom Sayings," 3–35) and P. Sellew's "Aphorisms of Jesus in Mark" (150–157).

Mark alone and Mark par

Mark	Matt	Luke	
2:17a	9:12	5:31b	
2:19a	9:15	5:34	*Gos. Thom.* 104
2:21	9:16	5:36	*Gos. Thom.* 47:4
2:22	9:17	5:37-8	*Gos. Thom.* 47:5
2:27			
2:28	12:8	6:5	
3:4	12:10b	6:9, 14:3	

Mark	Matt	Luke	
3:24			
	12:25	11:17	
3:27	12:29	(11:21–2)	*Gos. Thom.* 35:1–2
4:21	5:15	8:16	*Gos. Thom.* 33
		11:33	
4:22	b10:26	b12:2	
4:24			
	7:2	6:38b	(Rom 2:1–3)
b4:25		8:18	*Gos. Thom.* 41
	b13:12		
	b25:29	b19:26	
b6:4	13:57		bJohn 4:44
		4:24	*Gos. Thom.* 31:1
b7:15	b15:11		*Gos. Thom.* 14:5
			(Rom 14:14)
7:27	15:26		
8:35	16:25	9:24	John 12:25
	10:39	17:33	
b8:36	b16:26a	b9:25	
8:37	16:26b		
9:23			
9:35		9:48c	*Gos. Thom.* 4:2
10:43–44	20:26b–27	22:26(–27)	
	23:11		
b10:31	b19:30		
	b20:16	13:30	
	18:4	14:11	
b9:40		b9:50b	POxy. 1224
b9:43–47	18:8–7		
	5:29–30		
9:49			(Lev 2:13)
b9:50			
	b5:13	b14:34	
b10:9	b19:6b		(1 Cor 7:10–16)
10:15	18:3	18:17	*Gos. Thom.* 22
10:23b	19:23b	18:24b	
10:27	19:26	18:27	
b12:17	b22:21b	b20:25	*Gos. Thom.* 100
			(Rom 13:6–7)

Mark	Matt	Luke	
12:27a	22:32b	20:38	(4 Macc 7:18; 16:25)
13:13b	24:13 10:22b	21:19	
13:31	24:35	21:33	
14:21	26:24	22:22	
b14:38b	26:41b		
15:31b	27:42a	23:35	

Matt (alone)		Luke (alone) see also Acts 20:35	
5:14b	Gos. Thom. 32	4:23a	Gos. Thom. 31:2
5:36b		5:39	Gos. Thom. 47:3
b6:34b		6:38a	
7:6	Did. 9:5	6:43	
	Gos. Thom. 93	7:47b	
	(2 Pet 2:22)	9:62	(1 Kgs 19:19–21)
7:15		b10:42a	
7:17		12:15b	
10:8b		12:48b	
10:16b	Gos. Thom. 39:3	16:8b	(1 Kgs 19:19–21)
12:37		b16:9	
15:13	Gos. Thom. 40	16:10	
19:12		16:15b	
b22:14		22:27	
b26:52		b23:31	

Matt par Luke only

Matt	Luke	
5:18	16:17	
5:39	6:29a	Did. 1:4
5:42	6:30	Did. 1:5
5:44	6:27–28	POxy. 1224; Did. 1:3 (Rom 12:14)
5:45	6:35	
5:46–7	6:32–3	
5:48	6:36	
6:21	12:34	
6:22a	11:34a	
6:24	16:13	Gos. Thom. 47:1–2
6:25b	12:23	Gos. Thom. 36

Matt	*Luke*	
6:27	12:25	*Gos. Thom.* 36
7:1	6:37a	(Rom 2:1; Jas 4:12)
7:3	6:41	*Gos. Thom.* 26
7:7–8	11:9–10	*Gos. Thom.* 2; 92:1; 94
b7:9–10	11:11–12	
b7:12a	6:31	*Gos. Thom.* 6:3; *Did.* 1:2; Tob 4:15)
7:13a	13:24a	
7:16a, 20	6:44a	*Gos. Thom.* 45
12:33		
7:16b	6:44b	*Gos. Thom.* 45
7:19		
(3:10b	3:9)	
b8:20	9:58	*Gos. Thom.* 86
b8:22b	9:60	
9:37b	10:2a	*Gos. Thom.* 73 (John 4:34)
10:10b	10:7b	(1 Tim 5:18; 1 Cor 9:5–14; 2 Thess 3:9; Jas 5:4; *Did.* 13:1)
b10:24	b6:40; 22:27a	John 13:16; 15:20
10:27	12:3	*Gos. Thom.* 33:1
10:29	12:6	
10:30	12:7; 21:18	
(11:17	7:32b)	
11:19b	7:35	
11:27b	10:22b	(John 3:35; 13:3)
b12:30	b11:23	
b12:34b	6:45b	*Gos. Thom.* 45
b12:35	b6:45a	*Gos. Thom.* 45
15:14	6:39	*Gos. Thom.* 34
(16:2–3	12:54–55)	
18:7	b17:1	
b23:12		
	b14:11	
	b18:14	
b24:28	b17:37b	
(27:42a	23:35c)	

BIBLIOGRAPHY

Principal Editions

Anaximenes, <Aristotle>
  M. Fuhrmann, ed., *Anaximenis Ars Rhetorica...ad Alexandrum* (Leipzig, 1966).
Aristotle
  R. Kassel, ed., *Aristotelis Ars Rhetorica* (Berlin and New York, 1976).
<Cicero>
  F. Marx, ed., *De Ratione Dicendi ad C. Herrennium* (Leipzig, 1894).
Hermogenes
  H. Rabe, ed., *Hermogenis Opera* (Rhetores Graeci VI; 1913, rpr. Stuttgart, 1985).
Progymnasmata
  L. Spengel, ed., *Rhetores Graeci* 3 vols. (Leipzig, 1853–56), vol. 1 revised and ed.
  C. Hammer (Leipzig, 1894).
Quintilian
  M. Winterbottom, ed., *M. Fabi Quintiliani Institutio Oratoria* 2 vols. (Oxford, 1970).

Other Works Cited

Achtemeier, P.J., *"Omne verbum sonat*: The New Testament and the Oral Environment of Late Western Antiquity," *JBL* 109 (1990) 3–27.
Alexander, P.S., "Midrash and the Gospels," in *Synoptic Studies: The Ampleforth conferences of 1982 and 83*, ed. C.M. Tuckett (JSNTSup. 7; Sheffield, 1984).
____. "Orality in Pharisaic-Rabbinic Judaism at the Turn of the Eras," in *Jesus and the Oral Gospel Tradition*, ed. H. Wansbrough (JSNTSup 64; Sheffield, 1991) 159–184.
Allison, D.C., "The Eye is the Lamp of the Body (Matthew 6.22–23=Luke 11.34–36)," *NTS* 33 (1987) 61–83.
Attridge, H.W., "Reflections on Research into Q," in *Early Christianity, Q and Jesus*, ed. J.S. Kloppenborg and L.E. Vaage=*Semeia* 55 (1991) 223–234.
Aune, D.E., "Oral Tradition and the Aphorisms of Jesus," in *Jesus and the Oral Gospel Tradition*, ed. H. Wansbrough (JSNTSup 64; Sheffield, 1991) 211–265.
____. "Eschatology (Early Christian)" *ABD* II (1992) 549–609.
Bammel, E., "Romans 13," in *Jesus and the Politics of His Day*, ed. E. Bammel and C.F.D. Moule (Cambridge, 1984) 365-383.
Bammel, E. and C.F.D. Moule, eds., *Jesus and the Politics of His Day* (Cambridge, 1984).
Banks, R.J., *Jesus and the Law in the Synoptic Tradition* (SNTSMS 28; Cambridge, 1975).

Barilli, R., *Rhetoric* (Theory and History of Literature 63; Minneapolis, 1989).

Barley, N.A., "A Structural Approach to the Proverb and Maxim with Special Reference to the Anglo-Saxon Corpus," *Proverbium* 20 (1972) 737–750.

Barth, K., *Der Römerbrief* (2d ed., München, 1922, rpr. 1929).

Barthes, R., "L'ancienne rhétorique: aide mémoire," *Communications* 16 (1970) 172–229.

Bauckmann, E.G., "Die Proverbien und die Sprüche des Jesus Sirach: Eine Untersuchung zum Strukturwandel der israelitischen Weisheitslehre," *ZAW* (1960) 33–63.

Baumgarten, A.I., "The Name of the Pharisees," *JBL* 102 (1983) 411–428.

———. "The Pharisaic Paradosis," *HTR* 80 (1987) 63–77.

Beardslee, W.A., *Literary Criticism of the New Testament* (Philadelphia, 1970).

———. "Uses of the Proverb in the Synoptic Gospels," *Interpretation* 24 (1970) 61–76.

———. "Saving One's Life by Losing it," *JAAR* 47 (1977) 57–72.

———. Ed., *The Poetics of Faith: Essays offered to Amos Niven Wilder*, 2 vols.=*Semeia* 12, 13 (1978).

Beare, F.W., *The Gospel According to Matthew* (Oxford, 1981).

Beavis, M.A., "Parable and Fable," *CBQ* 52 (1990) 473–98.

Berger, K., *Die Gesetzesauslegung Jesu*, Teil I: *Markus und Parallelen* (WMANT 40; Neukirchen-Vluyn, 1972).

———. "Die implizierten Gegner," in *Kirche: Festschrift für Günther Bornkamm*, ed. D. Lührmann and G. Strecker (Tübingen, 1980) 373-400.

———. *Exegese des Neuen Testaments* (UTB 650; Heidelberg, 1984).

———. *Formgeschichte des Neuen Testaments* (Heidelberg, 1984).

———. "Hellenistische Gattungen im Neuen Testament," *ANRW* II 25/2 (1984) 1031–1432 and 1876–1885.

———. *Einführung in die Formgeschichte* (UTB 1444; Tübingen, 1987).

———. "Rhetorical Criticism, New Form Criticism, and New Testament Hermeneutics," in *Rhetoric and the New Testament: Essays from the 1992 Heidelberg Conference*, ed. S.E. Porter and T.H. Olbricht (Sheffield, 1993).

Betz, H.-D., *Essays on the Sermon on the Mount* (Philadelphia, 1979).

———. *Galatians* (Hermeneia; Philadelphia, 1979).

———. *2 Corinthians 8 and 9: A Commentary on Two Administrative Letters of the Apostle Paul* (Hermeneia; Philadelphia, 1985).

Bible and Culture Collective, *The Postmodern Bible* (New Haven and London, 1995).

Bitzer, L., "The Rhetorical Situation," *Philosophy and Rhetoric* 1 (1968) 1–14.

———. "Aristotle's Enthumeme Revisited," in *Aristotle: The Classical Heritage of Rhetoric*, ed. K.V. Erikson (Metuchen, NJ, 1974) 141-55.

Bjorndalen, A.J., "'Form' und 'Inhalt' des motivierenden Mahnspruches," *ZAW* 82 (1970) 347–361.

Black, C.C., "The Rhetorical Form of the Hellenistic Jewish and Early Christian Sermon: A Response to Lawrence Wills," *HTR* 81 (1988) 1–18.

Black, M., *An Aramaic Approach to the Gospels and Acts* (3d ed.; Oxford, 1967).

———. "Use of Rhetorical Terminology in Papias on Mark and Matthew," *JSNT* 37 (1989) 31–41.

Blehr, O., "What is a Proverb?" *Fabula* 14 (1973) 243–46.

Blenkinsopp, J., *Wisdom and Law in the Old Testament: The Ordering of Life in Israel and Early Judaism* (Oxford, 1983).

Boismard, M.-E., *Synopse des quatre évangiles en français* vol.2 *Commentaire*, ed. P. Benoit and M.-E. Boismard (2d ed.; Paris, 1972)

Booth, R.P., *Jesus and the Laws of Purity: Tradition History and Legal History in Mark 7* (JSNTSup 13; Sheffield, 1986).

Borg, M.J., "A Temperate Case for a Non-Eschatological Jesus," *Forum* 2 (1986) 81–102.

Boswell, J., *The Life of Samuel Johnson*, ed. and abr. F. Brady (New York and Scarborough, ON, 1968).

Botha, J.E., "Style in the New Testament: The Need for Serious Reconsideration," *JSNT* 43 (1991) 71–87.

Brinton, A., "Situation in the Theory of Rhetoric," *Philosophy and Rhetoric* 14 (1981) 234–48.

Brown, P., *Power and Persuasion in Late Antiquity: Towards a Christian Empire* (Madison, WI, 1992).

Bruce, F.F., "Render to Caesar," in *Jesus and the Politics of His Day*, ed. E. Bammel and C.F.D. Moule (Cambridge, 1984) 249-263.

Buchanan, G.W., "Chreias in the New Testament," in *Logia—les Paroles de Jésus—the Sayings of Jesus: Mémorial Joseph Coppens*, ed. J. Delobel (BETL 59; Leuven, 1982) 501–5.

Bultmann, R., *Der Stil der paulinischen Predigt und die kynische-stoische Diatribe* (Göttingen, 1910).

_____. "Allgemeine Wahrheiten und christliche Verkündigung," *ZTK* 54 (1957) 244–254, translated as "General Truths and Christian Proclamation," *JTC* 4 (1967) 153–162.

_____. *Die Geschichte der Synoptischen Tradition* (5th ed., Göttingen, 1961).

Butts, J.R., "The Chreia in the Synoptic Gospels," *BTB* 16 (1986) 132–8.

_____. *The Progymnasmata of Theon: A New Text with Translation and Commentary* (Ph.D. diss., Claremont Graduate School, 1987).

Cairns F.W., *Generic Composition in Greek and Roman Poetry* (Edinburgh, 1972).

Callaway, P.R., "Deut 21:18–21: Proverbial Wisdom and Law," *JBL* 103 (1984) 341–352.

Carlston, C.E., "Proverbs, Maxims and the Historical Jesus," *JBL* 99 (1980) 87–105.

_____. "Wisdom and Eschatology in Q," in *Logia—les Paroles de Jésus—the Sayings of Jesus*, ed. J. Delobel (BETL 59; Leuven, 1982) 101–119.

Charles, R.H., ed., *The Apocrypha and Pseudepigrapha of the Old Testament in English*, 2 vols. (Oxford, 1913, rpr. 1963).

Cizek, A., *Imitatio et Tractatio: die literarisch-rhetorischen Grundlagen der Nachahmung in Antike und Mittelalter* (Rhetorik-Forschungen 7; Tübingen, 1994).

Classen, C.J., "Ars Rhetorica: L'essence, possibilities, Gefahren," *Rhetorica* 6 (1980) 7–19.

_____. "Paulus und die antike Rhetorik," *ZNW* 82 (1991) 1–33, translated and updated as "St. Paul's Epistles and Ancient Greek and Roman Rhetoric" *Rhetorica* 10 (1992) 319–344, and in *Rhetoric and the New Testament: Essays from the 1992 Heidelberg Conference*, ed. S.E. Porter and T.H. Olbricht (Sheffield, 1993) 265–291.

Collins, J.T., "Proverbial Wisdom and the Yahwist Vision," in *Gnomic Wisdom*, ed. J.D. Crossan=*Semeia* 17 (1980) 1–17.

Connors, R.J., "Greek Rhetoric and the Transition From Orality," *Philosophy and Rhetoric* 19/1 (1986) 44–54.

Consigny, S., "Rhetoric and Its Situations," *Philosophy and Rhetoric* 7 (1974) 175–186.

Cotter, W.J., "Children Sitting in the Agora: Q (Luke) 7:31–35," *Forum* 5/2 (1989) 63–82.

Crenshaw, J.L., "Method in Determining Wisdom Influence Upon 'Historical' Literature," *JBL* 88 (1969) 129–42.

Crépeau, P., "La Définition du proverbe," *Fabula* 16 (1975) 285–304.

Crossan, J.D., ed., *Gnomic Wisdom=Semeia* 17 (1980).

____. *In Fragments: The Aphorisms of Jesus* (San Francisco, 1983).

____. "Kingdom and Children: A Study in the Aphoristic Tradition," in *Kingdom and Children: Aphorism, Chreia, Structure*, ed. D. Patte=*Semeia* 29 (1983) 75–95.

____. *The Historical Jesus: The Life of a Mediterranean Jewish Peasant* (San Francisco, 1991).

Culley, R.C., *Oral Formulaic Language in the Biblical Psalms*, (Near and Middle East Series 4: Toronto, 1972).

____. "Oral Tradition and the Old Testament: Some Recent Discussion," in *Oral Tradition and Old Testament Studies*, ed. R.C. Culley=*Semeia* 5 (1976) 1–33.

Daube, D., *The New Testament and Rabbinic Judaism* (London, 1956).

Davies, P.R., "Eschatology at Qumran," *JBL* 104 (1985) 39–55.

Davies, W.D., *The Setting of the Sermon on the Mount* (Cambridge, 1964).

Delarue, F., "La sententia chez Quintilien," *Formes brèves: De la γνώμη à la pointe: métamorphoses de la "sententia"=La Licorne* 3 (1979) 97–124.

Delobel, J., ed., *Logia—les Paroles de Jésus—the Sayings of Jesus: Mémorial Joseph Coppens* (BETL 59; Leuven, 1982).

Dewey, A.J., "Quibbling Over Serifs," *Forum* 5/2 (1989) 109–120.

Dewey, K.E., "*Paroimiai* in the Gospel of John," in *Gnomic Wisdom*, ed. J.D. Crossan=*Semeia* 17 (1980) 81–100.

Dibelius, M., *From Tradition to Gospel*, transl. B.L. Woolf (London, 1934; New York, 1935).

Diels, H. and W. Kranz, eds., *Fragmente der Vorsokratiker* 3 vols. (7th ed.; Berlin, 1951–54).

Dodd, C.H., *Historical Tradition in the Fourth Gospel* (Cambridge, 1963).

____. "A Hidden Parable in the Fourth Gospel," in *More New Testament Studies* (Manchester, 1968) 30–40.

Doty, W.G., *Letters in Primitive Christianity* (Guides to Biblical Scholarship; Philadelphia, 1973).

Downing, F.G., "The Social Contexts of Jesus the Teacher," *NTS* 33 (1987) 439–451.

Drijepondt, H.L.F., *Die antike Theorie der "varietas"* (Hildesheim, 1979).

Dundes, A., "On the Structures of the Proverb," *Proverbium* 25 (1975) 961–973.

Dungan, D., *The Sayings of Jesus in the Churches of Paul* (Philadelphia, 1971).

Dupont, J., "La Transmission des paroles de Jésus sur la lampe et la mesure dans Marc 4,21–25 et dans la tradition Q," in *Logia—les Paroles de Jésus—the Sayings of*

Jesus: Mémorial Joseph Coppens, ed. J. Delobel (BETL 59; Leuven, 1982) 201–236.

———. "Dieu et Mammon (MT 6,24 : LC 16,13)," in *Etudes sur les évangiles synoptiques* II, ed. J. Dupont (BETL 70/B; Leuven, 1985) 551–567.

Easterling, P.E., "The Fable," *Cambridge History of Classical Literature* I,4 (1989) 139–142.

———. "Books and Readers in the Greek World: the Hellenistic and Imperial Periods," *Cambridge History of Classical Literature* I,4 (1989) 169–97.

Edwards, R.A., "An Approach to a Theology of Q," *JR* 51 (1971) 247–269.

Eißfeldt, O., *Der Maschal im Alten Testament* (BZAW 24; Gießen, 1913).

Ehrhardt, A., "Greek Proverbs in the Gospel," *HTR* 46 (1953) 59–77.

Finnegan, R., *Oral Literature in Africa* (Nairobi, 1970).

Fiore, B., "NT Rhetoric and Rhetorical Criticism," *ABD* V (1992) 715–9.

Fischel, H.A., *Rabbinic Literature and Greco-Roman Philosophy* (SPB 21; Leiden, 1973).

———. "Studies in Cynicism and the Ancient Near East: The Transformation of a *Chria*," in *Religion in Antiquity: Essays in Memory of E.R. Goodenough*, ed. J. Neusner (Leiden, 1988) 372–411.

Fitzmyer, J.A., "The Study of the Aramaic Background of the New Testament," in *A Wandering Aramean* (SBLMS 25; Missoula, MT, 1979) 1–27.

———. *The Gospel According to Luke I–IX* (AB 28; Garden City, NY, 1981).

Fontaine, C., *Traditional Sayings in the Old Testament* (Bible and Literature 5; Sheffield, 1982).

———. "Proverb Performance in the Hebrew Bible," *JSOT* 32 (1985) 87–103.

Fortenbaugh, W.W., "Aristotle's Rhetoric on Emotions," *Archiv für die Geschichte der Philosophie* 52 (1970) 40–70.

———. "Persuasion Through Character and the Composition of Aristotle's Rhetoric," *Rheinisches Museum für Philologie* 134 (1991) 152–56.

Fuchs, E., *Hermeneutik* (2d ed., Bad Cannstatt, 1958).

Funk, R.W., *Language, Hermeneutic, and Word of God* (New York, 1966).

———. "Unraveling the Jesus Tradition: Criteria and Criticism," *Forum* 5/2 (1989) 31–62.

Funk, R.W., R.W. Hoover and the Jesus Seminar, *The Five Gospels: The Search for the Authentic Words of Jesus* (New York, 1993).

Gamble, H.Y., *Books and Readers in the Early Church: A History of Early Christian Texts* (New Haven and London, 1995).

Gerhardsson, B., *Memory and Manuscript* (ASNU 22; Lund, 1961).

———. "Der Weg der Evangelien-tradition," in *Das Evangelium und die Evangelien*, ed. P. Stuhlmacher (WUNT 28; Tübingen, 1983) 79-102.

Gerstenberger, E., *Wesen und Herkunft des "Apodiktischen Rechts"* (WMANT 20; Neukirchen-Vluyn, 1965).

Gese, H., *Lehre und Wirklichkeit in der alten Weisheit: Studien zu dem Buche Hjob* (Tübingen, 1958).

———. "Weisheitsdichtung," *RGG* VI (1962) cols. 1577–81.

Goodman, M.D., *The Ruling Class of Judaea: The Origins of the Jewish Revolt against Rome AD 65–70* (Cambridge, 1987).

Goulder, M., *Midrash and Lection in Matthew* (London, 1974).

Gräßer, E., "Jesus in Nazareth (Mc 6, 1–6a): Bemerkungen zur Redaktion und Theologie des Markus," in *Jesus in Nazareth*, ed. W. Eltester (BZNW 40; Berlin and New York, 1972) 1–37.

Graffy, A., *A Prophet Confronts His People: The Disputation Speech in the Prophets* (AnBib 104; Rome, 1984).

Granatelli, R., "M. Fabio Quintiliano *Institutio oratoria* II 1–10: struttura e problemi interpretativi," *Rhetorica* 13 (1995) 137–160.

Greenwood, D., "Rhetorical Criticism and Formgeschichte: Some Methodological Considerations," *JBL* 89 (1970) 418–426.

Greimas, A.J., "Les proverbes et les dictons," in *Du sens: Essais sémiotiques* (Paris, 1970) 309–314.

Greßmann, H., "Die neugefundene Lehre des Amen-em-ope und die vorexilische Spruchdichtung Israels," *ZAW* 42 (1924) 272–96.

Grimaldi, W.M.A., *Aristotle, "Rhetoric": A Commentary* (2 vols.; New York, 1980, 1988).

Grube, G.M.A., transl., *A Greek Critic: Demetrius on Style* (Toronto, 1961).

Guenther, H.O., "The Sayings Gospel Q and the Quest for Aramaic Sources: Rethinking Christian Origins," in *Early Christianity, Q and Jesus*, ed. J.S. Kloppenborg and L.E. Vaage=*Semeia* 55 (1991) 41–76.

Güttgemanns, E., *Offene Fragen zur Formgeschichte des Evangeliums* (BEvT 54; 2d ed., München, 1971).

Halliday, M.A.K., "Linguistic Study of Literary Texts," in *Proceedings of the Ninth International Congress of Linguists*, ed. H.G. Lunt (The Hague, 1964) 302–7.

Harris, W.V., *Ancient Literacy* (Cambridge, MA, 1989).

Harvey, A.E., *Jesus and the Constraints of History* (London, 1982).

Hausrath, A., "Fabel," *PW* VI (1909) 1704–36.

Havelock, E.A., *Preface to Plato* (Cambridge, MA, 1963).

_____. *Origins of Western Literacy* (Ontario Institute for Studies in Education 14; Toronto, 1976).

_____. *The Literate Revolution in Greece and Its Cultural Consequences* (Princeton, 1982).

_____. *The Muse Learns to Write: Reflections on Orality and Literacy from Antiquity to the Present* (New Haven and London, 1986).

Heath, M., transl., *"Hermogenes" On Issues* (Oxford, 1995).

Hempel, J., *Die althebraische Literatur und ihr hellenistische-jüdisches Nachleben* (Potsdam, 1930).

Henderson, I.H., "Gnomic Quatrains in the Synoptics: An Experiment in Genre Definition," *NTS* 37 (1991) 481–498.

_____. "Quintilian and the *Progymnasmata*," *Antike und Abendland* 37 (1991) 82–99.

_____. "*Didache* and Orality in Synoptic Comparison," *JBL* 111 (1992) 283–306.

_____. "Style-Switching in the *Didache*: Fingerprint or Argument?" in *The Didache in Context: Essays in Its Text, History and Transmission*, ed. C.N. Jefford (NovTSup 77; Leiden, 1995) 177–209.

_____. "Rhetorical Determinacy and the Text," in *Textual Determinacy: Part 2*, ed. R.B. Robinson and R.C. Culley=*Semeia* [forthcoming].

Hengel, M., *Nachfolge und Charisma: Eine exegetisch-religionsgeschichtliche Studie zu Mt 8,21f. und Jesu Ruf in die Nachfolge* (BZAW 34; Berlin, 1968).

Hermisson, H.-J., *Studien zur israelitischen Spruchweisheit* (WMANT 28; Neukirchen-Vluyn, 1968).

Hester, J.D., review of B.L. Mack and V.K. Robbins, *Patterns of Persuasion in the Gospels* (Sonoma, CA, 1989) in *Rhetorica* 9 (1991) 179–85.

Hildebrandt, T., "Proverbial Pairs: Compositional Units in Proverbs 10–29," *JBL* 107 (1988) 207–224.

Hock, R.F., "General Introduction to Volume I," in *The Chreia in Ancient Rhetoric: Volume I. the "Progymnasmata,"* ed. R.F. Hock and E.N. O'Neil (Texts and Translations 27; Greco-Roman Religion 9; Atlanta, 1986) 3–60.

_____. "Chreia," *ABD* I (1992) 912–4.

Hock, R.F. and E.N. O'Neil, *The Chreia in Ancient Rhetoric: Volume I. The "Progymnasmata"* (Texts and Translations 27; Greco-Roman Religion 9; Atlanta, 1986).

Hock, R.F. and E.N. O'Neil, "The Chreia Discussion of *Aelius Theon of Alexandria*," in *The Chreia in Ancient Rhetoric: Volume I. the "Progymnasmata,"* ed. R.F. Hock and E.N. O'Neil (Texts and Translations 27; Greco-Roman Religion 9; Atlanta, 1986) 61–78.

Horna, K. and K. von Fritz, "Gnome, Gnomendichtung, Gnomologien," *PWSup* VI (1935) 74–90.

Horsley, R.A., "'Like One of the Prophets of Old': Two Types of Popular Prophets at the Time of Jesus," *CBQ* 47 (1985) 435–63.

_____. *Sociology and the Jesus Movement* (New York, 1989).

Hurd, J.C., *The Origin of 1 Corinthians* (London, 1965).

Hyde, M.J., and C.R. Smith, "Hermeneutics and Rhetoric: A Seen But Unobserved Relationship," *The Quarterly Journal of Speech* 65 (1979) 347–63.

Instone Brewer, D., "1 Corinthians 9.9–11: A Literal Interpretation of 'Do Not Muzzle the Ox'," *NTS* 38 (1992) 554–65.

Jacobson, A.D., *The First Gospel: An Introduction to Q* (Sonoma, CA, 1992).

Jarratt, S.C., *Rereading the Sophists: Classical Rhetoric Refigured* (Carbondale, IL, 1991).

Jeremias, J., "Matthäus 7,6a," in *Abraham unser Vater, Festschrift für O. Michel*, ed. O. Betz, M. Hengel, P. Schmidt (Arbeiten zur Geschichte des Spätjudentums und des Urchristentums 5; Leiden and Köln, 1963) 271–275.

Jolles, A., *Einfache Formen* (Tübingen, 1930, rpr. 1968).

Jones, A.H.M., *The Greek City from Alexander to Justinian* (Oxford, 1940).

Jousse, M., *Le style orale: rythmique et mnemotechnique* (Paris, 1925).

Judge, E.A., "A state school teacher makes a salary bid," in *New Documents Illustrating Early Christianity* 1, ed. G.H.R. Horsley (1981) 72–8 (#26).

Käsemann, E., *Commentary on Romans*, transl. G.W. Bromiley (London, 1980).

Kaster, R.A., "Notes on 'Primary' and 'Secondary' Schools in Late Antiquity," *TAPA* 113 (1983) 323–346.

_____. *Guardians of Language: The Grammarian and Society in Late Antiquity* (Berkeley and Los Angeles, 1988).

Kelber, W.H., "Mark and Oral Tradition," in *Perspectives on Mark's Gospel*, ed. R. Petersen=*Semeia* 16 (1979) 7–55.

_____. *The Oral and the Written Gospel: The Hermeneutics of Speaking and Writing in the Synoptic Tradition, Mark, Paul and Q* (Philadelphia, 1983).

_____. Review of J.D. Crossan, *In Fragments: The Aphorisms of Jesus* (New York, 1983) in *JBL* 104 (1985) 716–19.

_____. "Jesus and Tradition: Words in Time, Words in Space," in *Orality and Textuality in Early Christian Literature*, ed. J. Dewey=*Semeia* 65 (1994) 139–167.

Kennedy, G.A., *Classical Rhetoric and its Christian and Secular Tradition from Ancient to Modern Times* (London, 1980).

_____. *New Testament Interpretation Through Rhetorical Criticism* (Chapel Hill, NC, 1984).

_____. "Sophists and physicians of the Greek enlightenment," *Cambridge History of Classical Literature* I,3 (1989) 60–65.

Kindstrand, J.F., "Diogenes Laertius and the '*Chreia*' Tradition," *Elenchos* 7 (1986) 217–43.

Kinneavy, J.L., *Greek Rhetorical Origins of Christian Faith* (New York, 1987).

Kirk, G.S., "Formular Language and Oral Quality," *Yale Classical Studies* 20 (1966) 153–174.

Kirkpatrick, P.G., *The Old Testament and Folklore Study* (JSNTSup 62; Sheffield, 1988).

Kirschenblatt-Gimblett, B., "Toward a Theory of Proverb Meaning," *Proverbium* 8 (1967) 821–827.

Kitchen, K.A., "The Basic Literary Forms and Formulations of Ancient Instructional Writings in Egypt and Western Asia," in *Studien zu altägyptischen Lebenslehren*, ed. E. Horning and O. Kee (OBO 28; Freiburg, Switzerland and Göttingen, 1979).

Klein, G., "Eschatologie IV. Neues Testament," *TRE* X (1982) 270–299.

Kloppenborg, J.S., "The Formation of Q and Antique Instructional Genres," *JBL* 105 (1986) 443–462.

_____. *The Formation of Q: Trajectories in Ancient Wisdom Collections* (Studies in Antiquity and Christianity; Philadelphia, 1987).

_____. "Symbolic Eschatology and the Apocalypticism of Q," *HTR* 80 (1987) 287–306.

_____. *Q Parallels: Synopsis, Critical Notes and Concordance* (Sonoma, CA, 1988).

_____. "Literary Convention, Self-Evidence and the Social History of the Q People," in *Early Christianity, Q and Jesus*, ed. J.S. Kloppenborg and L.E. Vaage=*Semeia* 55 (1991) 77–102.

_____. "The Sayings Gospel Q: Recent Opinion on the People Behind the Document," *Currents in Research: Biblical Studies* 1 (1993) 9–34.

Kloppenborg, J.S. and L.E. Vaage, eds., *Early Christianity, Q and Jesus*=*Semeia* 55 (1991).

Koskenniemi, H., *Studien zur Idee und Phraselogie des griechischen Briefes bis 400 n.Chr.* (Helsinki, 1956).

Köster, H., "Formgeschichte/Formkritik II: Neues Testament," *TRE* XI (1983) 286–299.

Kottsieper, I., *Die Sprache der Ahiqarsprüche* (BZAW 194; Berlin and New York, 1991).

Küchler, M., *Frühjüdische Weisheitstraditionen: Zum Fortgang weisheitlichen Denkens im Bereich des frühjüdischen Jahweglaubens* (OBO 26; Freiburg, Switzerland and Göttingen, 1979).

Kugel, J.L., *The Idea of Biblical Poetry: Parallelism and its History* (New Haven, 1981).

_____. "Some Thoughts on Future Research into Biblical Style: Addenda to *The Idea of Biblical Poetry*," *JSOT* 28 (1984) 107–117.

Kuhn, H.-W., *Ältere Sammlungen im Markusevangelium* (SUNT 8; Göttingen, 1971).

Lambrecht, J., "Jesus and the Law. An Investigation of Mk 7,8-23," *ETL* 53 (1977) 24-83.

Lana, I., *Quintiliano, Il "Sublime," e gli "Esercizi Preparatori" di Elio Teone* (Torino, 1951).

_____. *I Progimnasmi di Elio Teone*, vol. I *La storia del testo* (Torino, 1959).

Lanham, R.A., *A Handlist of Rhetorical Terms* (2d ed., Berkeley and Los Angeles, 1991).

Layton, B., "The Sources, Date and Transmission of *Didache* 1.3b–2.1," *HTR* 61 (1968) 343–83.

Lentz, T.M., *Orality and Literacy in Hellenic Greece* (Carbondale, IL, 1989).

Levet, J.P., "'ΡΗΤΩΡ et ΓΝΩΜΗ, Présentation sémantique et recherches isocratiques," in *Formes brèves: De la* γνώμη *à la pointe: métamorphoses de la "sententia"=La Licorne* 3 (1979) 9–40.

Levi, P., *The Lamentation of the Dead* (Poetica 19; Oxford, 1984).

Lindenberger, J.M., *The Aramaic Proverbs of Ahiqar* (Baltimore and London, 1983).

_____. "Ahiqar," in *The Old Testament Pseudepigrapha*, vol. II, ed. J.H. Charlesworth (London, 1985) 479–507.

Lindeskog, G., "Logia-Studien," *ST* 4 (1951) 129–189.

Lips, H. von, *Weisheitliche Traditionen im Neuen Testament* (WMANT 64; Neukirchen-Vluyn, 1990).

_____. "Paulus und die Tradition: Zitierung von Schriftworten, Herrenworten und christlichen Traditionen," *VF* 36 (1991) 27–49.

Lüderitz, G., "Rhetorik, Poetik, Kompositionstechnik im Markusevangelium," in *Markus-Philologie: Historische, literargeschictliche und stilistische Untersuchungen zum zweiten Evangelium*, ed. H. Cancik (WUNT 33; Tübingen, 1984) 165–203.

Lührmann, D., "Liebet eure Feinde (Lk 6,27–36/Mt 5,39–48)," *ZTK* 69 (1972) 412–438.

_____. "Q: Sayings of Jesus or Logia?" in *The Gospel Behind the Gospels: Current Studies on Q*, ed. R.A. Piper (NovTSup 75; Leiden, 1995) 97–116.

Luz, U., *Das Evangelium nach Matthäus* (EKKNT I/1; 3d ed.; Braunschweig and Neukirchen-Vluyn, 1992).

Mack, B.L., *A Myth of Innocence: Mark and Christian Origins* (Philadelphia, 1988).

_____. *Rhetoric and the New Testament* (Guides to Biblical Studies; Minneapolis, 1990).

_____. "Q and the Gospel of Mark: Revising Christian Origins," in *Early Christianity, Q and Jesus*, ed. J.S. Kloppenborg and L.E. Vaage=*Semeia* 55 (1991) 15–39.

_____. *The Lost Gospel: The Book of Q and Christian Origins* (San Francisco, 1993).

_____. "Persuasive Pronouncements: An Evaluation of Recent Studies on the Chreia," in *The Rhetoric of Pronouncement*, ed. V.K. Robbins=*Semeia* 64 (1993) 283–7.

Mack, B.L., and E.N. O'Neil, "The Chreia Discussion of *Hermogenes of Tarsus*," in *The Chreia in Ancient Rhetoric: Volume I. the "Progymnasmata"*, ed. R.F. Hock and E.N. O'Neil (Texts and Translations 27; Greco-Roman Religion 9; Atlanta, 1986) 153–81.

Mack, B.L. and V.K. Robbins, *Patterns of Persuasion in the Gospels* (Sonoma, CA, 1989).

Mailloux, S., "Rhetorical Hermeneutics," *Critical Inquiry* 11 (1985) 620–41.

Marshall, I.H., *The Gospel of Luke* (Grand Rapids, MI, 1979).

Martin, J.P., "Towards a Post-Critical Paradigm," *NTS* 33 (1987) 370-385.

McDonald, J.I.H., *"Kerygma" and "Didache": The articulation and structure of the earliest Christian message* (SNTSMS 37; Cambridge, 1980).

McKane, W., *Proverbs: A New Approach* (London and Philadelphia, 1970).

McKenzie, J.L., "Reflections on Wisdom," *JBL* 86 (1967) 1–9.

Meagher, J.C., *Clumsy Construction in Mark's Gospel: A Critique of Form- and Redaktionsgeschichte* (New York and Toronto, 1979).

Mees, M., "Die Bedeutung der Sentenzen und ihrer Auxesis für die Formung der Jesusworte nach *Didache* 1,3b–2,1," *Vetera Christianorum* 8 (1971) 55–76.

Meier, J.P., *A Marginal Jew: Rethinking the Historical Jesus*, vol I: *The Roots of the Problem and the Person*, (AB Reference Library; New York, 1991); vol. II: *Mentor, Message and Miracles* (1994).

Millar, F., *The Roman Near East: 31 BC—AD 337* (Cambridge, MA and London, 1993).

Miller, P.D., Jr., "Meter, Parallelism, and Tropes in the Search for Poetic Style," *JSOT* 28 (1984) 99–106.

Milner, G.B., "De l'armature des locutions proverbiales: Essai de taxonomie sémantique," *L'Homme* 9 (1969) 49–70.

____. "Quadripartite Structures," *Proverbium* 14 (1969) 379–383.

____. "What is a Proverb?" *New Society* 6 (1969) 199–202.

Most, G.W., "Rhetorik und Hermeneutik: Zur Konstitution der Neuzeitlichkeit," *Antike und Abendland* 30 (1984) 62–79.

Muddiman, J.B., "Jesus and Fasting (Marc 2,18-29)" in *Jésus aux origines de la christologie*, ed. J. Dupont (BETL 40; Leuven, 1975) 271-281.

Muilenburg, J., "Form Criticism and Beyond," *JBL* 88 (1969) 1-18.

Murphy J.J., ed., *A Synoptic History of Classical Rhetoric* (Berkeley, 1972; 2d ed. Davis, California, 1983).

Murphy, R.E., "Form Criticism and Wisdom Literature," *CBQ* 31 (1969) 475–483.

Nadeau, R., "The Progymnasmata of Aphthonius: a translation," *Speech Monographs* 31 (1952) 264–85.

Neirynck, F., "Jesus and the Sabbath," in *Jésus aux origines de la christologie*, ed. J Dupont (BETL 40; Leuven, 1975) 227-270.

____. "Paul and the Sayings of Jesus," in *L'Apôtre Paul: Personalité, style et conception du ministère*, ed. A. Vanhoye, (BETL 73; 1986) 265-321.

Nel, P.J., *The Structure and Ethos of the Wisdom Admonitions in Proverbs* (BZAW 158; Berlin and New York, 1982).

Neusner, J., *The Rabbinic Traditions about the Pharisees before 70*, 3 vols. (Leiden, 1971).

____. *The Memorized Torah: The Mnemonic System of the Mishnah* (BJS 96; Chico, CA, 1985).

____. *Oral Tradition in Judaism* (A.B. Lord Studies in Oral Tradition 1; New York, 1987).

Nielson, E., *Oral Tradition* (SBT 11; London, 1954).

Noorda, S.J., "'Cure Yourself, Doctor!' (Luke 4,23) Classical Parallels to an Alleged Saying of Jesus," in *Logia—les Paroles de Jésus—the Sayings of Jesus: Mémorial Joseph Coppens*, ed. J. Delobel (BETL 59; Leuven, 1982) 459–467.

O'Neil, E.N., "Discussion of Preliminary Exercises of *Marcus Fabius Quintilianus*," in *The Chreia in Ancient Rhetoric: Volume I. The "Progymnasmata,"* ed. R.F. Hock and E.N. O'Neil (Texts and Translations 27; Greco-Roman Religion 9; Atlanta, 1986) 113–43.

W.J. Ong, *Interfaces of the Word: Studies in the Evolution of Consciousness and Culture* (Ithaca and London, 1977).

____. *Orality and Literacy: The Technologizing of the Word* (London and New York, 1982).

O'Sullivan, N., *Alcidamas, Aristophanes and the Beginnings of Greek Stylistic Theory* (Hermes Einzelschriften 60; Stuttgart, 1992).

Overman, J.A., "Recent Advances in the Archaeology of the Galilee in the Roman Period," *Currents in Research: Biblical Studies* 1 (1993) 35–57.

Pack, R.A., *The Greek and Latin Literary Texts from Greco-Roman Egypt* (2d ed., Ann Arbor, MI, 1965).

Patte, D., ed., *Kingdom and Children: Aphorism, Chreia, Structure=Semeia* 29 (1983).

Patterson, S.J., "Paul and the Jesus Tradition: It Is Time for Another Look," *HTR* 84 (1991) 23–41.

Perdue, L.G., "The Wisdom Sayings of Jesus," *Forum* 2 (1986) 3–35.

Perles, F., "Zur Erklärung von Mt 7 6" *ZNW* 25 (1926) 163–164.

Perrin, N., *Jesus and the Language of the Kingdom* (London, 1976).

Perry, B.E., *Aesopica* I (Urbana, IL, 1952).

Petersen, N.R., *Rediscovering Paul: Philemon and the Sociology of Paul's Narrative World* (Philadelphia, 1985).

Philonenko, M., 'La parabole sur la lampe (Luc 11 33–36) et les horoscopes qoumrâniens," *ZNW* 79 (1988) 145–151.

Piper, R.A., *Wisdom in the Q-Tradition: The Aphoristic Teaching of Jesus* (SNTSMS 61; Cambridge, 1989).

Pogoloff, S.M., "Isocrates and Contemporary Hermeneutics," in *Persuasive Artistry: Studies in New Testament Rhetoric in Honor of George A. Kennedy*, ed. D.F. Watson (JSNTSup 50; Sheffield, 1991).

Porter, S.E., and T.H. Olbricht, eds., *Rhetoric and the New Testament: Essays from the 1992 Heidelberg Conference* (Sheffield, 1993).

Poulakos, J., *Sophistical Rhetoric in Classical Greece* (Columbia, SC, 1995).

Quesnell, Q., "'Made Themselves Eunuchs for the Kingdom of Heaven' (Mt 19,12)," *CBQ* 30 (1968) 335-358.

Rad, G. von, "Die ältere Weisheit Israels," *KD* 2 (1956) 54–72.

____. *Weisheit in Israel* (Neukirchen-Vluyn, 1970) transl. J.D. Martin, *Wisdom in Israel* (London, 1972).

Räisänen, H., "Zur Herkunft von Markus 7,15," in *Logia—les Paroles de Jésus—the Sayings of Jesus: Mémorial Joseph Coppens*, ed. J. Delobel (BETL 59; Leuven, 1982) 477-484.

Reiser, M., *Syntax und Stil des Markusevangelium im Licht der hellenistischen Volksliteratur* (WUNT 2/11; Tübingen, 1984) 138–161.

Richardson, P. and J.C. Hurd, eds., *From Jesus to Paul: Studies in Honour of F.W. Beare* (Waterloo, ON, 1984).

Richter, W., *Recht und Ethos: Versuch einer Ortung des weisheitlichen Mahnspruches* (SANT 15; München, 1966).

Rickman, H.P., "Rhetoric and Hermeneutics," *Philosophy and Rhetoric* 14 (1981) 100–11.

Riesner, R., *Jesus als Lehrer: Eine Untersuchung zum Ursprung der Evangelienüberlieferung* (WUNT 27; Tübingen, 1981).

Robinson, J.M., "LOGOI SOPHON: On the Gattung of Q," in *Trajectories through Early Christianity*, ed. J.M. Robinson and H. Koester (Philadelphia, 1971) 71–113.

V.K. Robbins, "Pronouncement Stories and Jesus' Blessing of the Children: A Rhetorical Approach," in *Kingdom and Children: Aphorism, Chreia, Structure*, ed. D. Patte=*Semeia* 29 (1983) 43–74.

——. *Jesus the Teacher: A Socio-Rhetorical Interpretation of Mark* (Philadelphia, 1984).

——. "The Chreia," in *Greco-Roman Literature and the New Testament: Selected Forms and Genres*, ed. E. Aune (Sources for Biblical Study 21; Atlanta, 1988) 1–23.

——. "Foxes, Birds, Burial and Furrows," in B.L. Mack and V.K. Robbins, *Patterns of Persuasion in the Gospels* (Sonoma, CA, 1989) 69–84.

——. "Introduction: Using Rhetorical Discussions of the Chreia to Interpret Pronouncement Stories," in *The Rhetoric of Pronouncement*, ed. V.K. Robbins= *Semeia* 64 (1993) vii–xvii.

——. "Progymnastic Rhetorical Composition and Pre-Gospel Traditions," in *The Synoptic Gospels: Source Criticism and the New Literary Criticism*, ed. Camille Focant (BETL 110; Leuven, 1993) 111–147.

——. ed., *The Rhetoric of Pronouncement*=*Semeia* 64 (1993).

Robbins, V.K. and J.H. Patton, "Rhetoric and Biblical Criticism," *Quarterly Journal of Speech* 66 (1980) 327–50.

Roberts, R., *Order and Dispute: An Introduction to Legal Anthropology* (Oxford, 1979).

Romilly, J. de, *Magic and Rhetoric in Ancient Greece* (Cambridge, MA, 1975).

Rudolph, W., *Hosea* (KAT 13/1; Gütersloh, 1966).

Sabbe, M., "Can Mt 11,27 and Lk 10,22 be Called a Johannine Logion?" in *Logia—les Paroles de Jéus—the Sayings of Jesus: Mémorial Joseph Coppens*, ed. J. Delobel (BETL 59; Leuven, 1982) 363–371.

Sanders, E.P., *The Tendencies of the Synoptic Tradition* (SNTSMS 9; Cambridge, 1969).

——. *Jesus and Judaism* (London, 1985).

——. *Jewish Law from Jesus to the Mishnah* (London and Philadelphia, 1990).

Sanders, E.P., and M. Davies, *Studying the Synoptic Gospels* (London and Philadelphia, 1989).

Sato, M., "Wisdom Statements in the Sphere of Prophecy," in *The Gospel Behind the Gospels: Current Studies on Q*, ed. R.A. Piper (NovTSup 75; Leiden, 1995) 139–158.

Schick, E., *Formgeschichte und Synoptikerexegese: Eine kritische Untersuchung über die Möglichkeit und die Grenzen der formgeschichtlichen Methode* (NTAbh 18/2–3; Münster, 1940).

Schiffman, L.H., *The Halakah at Qumran* (SJLA 16; Leiden, 1975).

Schille, G., "Was ist ein Logion?" *ZNW* 61 (1970) 172–182.

Schmeller, T., *Paulus und die "Diatribe"* (NTAbh 19; Münster, 1987).

Schmidt, J., *Studien zur Stilistik der alttestamentlichen Spruchliteratur* (Münster, 1936).

Schmithals, W., "Kritik der Formkritik," *ZTK* 77 (1980) 149–185.

____. "Evangelien: Synoptische," *TRE* X (1982) 570–626.

____. *Einleitung in die drei ersten Evangelien* (Berlin and New York, 1985).

Schulz, S., *Die Spruchquelle der Evangelisten* (Zürich, 1972).

Schüssler Fiorenza, E., "Rhetorical Situation and Historical Reconstruction in 1 Corinthians," *NTS* 33 (1987) 386–403.

Schwarz, G., *'Und Jesus sprach': Untersuchungen zur aramäischen Urgestalt der Worte Jesu* (BWANT 118; Stuttgart *et alibi*, 1985) 236–244.

Schweizer, E., "Jesus Christus I: Neue Testament," *TRE* XVI (1987) 671–726.

Scott, B.B., "A Response: The Chinese Box: Method within Method," in *The Rhetoric of Pronouncement,* ed. V.K. Robbins=*Semeia* 64 (1993) 275–81.

Scott, R.B.Y., *The Way of Wisdom in the Old Testament* (London and New York, 1971).

Scroggs, R., "Can New Testament Theology Be Saved?   The Threat of Contextualisms," *USQR* 42 (1988) 17–31.

Seeley, D., "Blessings and Boundaries: Interpretations of Jesus' Death in Q," in *Early Christianity, Q and Jesus*, ed. J.S. Kloppenborg and L.E. Vaage=*Semeia* 55 (1991) 131–146.

Segert, S., "Semitic Poetic Structures in the New Testament," *ANRW* II 25/2 (1984) 1433–62.

Seitel, P., "Proverbs: A Social Use of Metaphor," *Gnome* 2 (1969) 143-161.

Sellew, P., "Composition of Didactic Scenes in Mark's Gospel," *JBL* 108 (1989) 613–634.

____. "Aphorisms of Jesus in Mark: A Stratigraphic Analysis," *Forum* 8 (1992) 141–160.

Shuger, D.K., *Sacred Rhetoric: The Christian Grand Style in the English Renaissance* (Princeton, NJ, 1988).

Sieveke, F.G., transl., *Aristoteles Rhetorik* (UTB 159, München, 1987).

Silberman, L.H., ed., *Orality, Aurality and Biblical Narrative=Semeia* 39 (1987).

Sinclair, P., "The *Sententia* in *Rhetorica ad Herennium*: A Study in the Sociology of Rhetoric," *AJP* 114 (1993) 561–80.

Smith, M., "A Comparison of Early Christian and Early Rabbinic Tradition," *JBL* 82 (1963) 169–176.

Snyder, G.F., "The Tobspruch in the New Testament," *NTS* 23 (1977) 117–126.

Sprague, R.K., ed., *The Older Sophists* (Columbia, SC, 1972).

Stamps, D.L., "Rethinking the Rhetorical Situation: the Entextualization of the Situation in New Testament Epistles," in *Rhetoric and the New Testament: Essays from the 1992 Heidelberg Conference,* ed. S.E. Porter and T.H. Olbricht (Sheffield, 1993).

_____. "Rhetorical Criticism and the Rhetoric of New Testament Criticism," *Journal of Literature and Theology* 6 (1992) 268–79.

Steinhauser, M.G., *Doppelbildworte in den synoptischen Evangelien* (FB 44; Stuttgart, 1981).

Stowers, S.K., *The Diatribe and Paul's Letter to the Romans* (SBLDS 57; Ann Arbor, MI, 1981).

_____. "Social Status, Public Speaking and Private Teaching: The Circumstances of Paul's Preaching Activity," *NT* 26 (1984) 59–82.

Strikovsky, A., "Proverbs, Talmudic," *EncJud* XIII (1972) 1273–1276.

Stuhlmacher, P., "Zum Thema: Das Evangelium und die Evangelien" in *Das Evangelium und die Evangelien*, ed. P. Stuhlmacher (WUNT 28; Tübingen, 1983) 1-26.

Tannehill, R.C., ed., *Pronouncement Stories=Semeia* 20 (1981).

_____. "Introduction: The Pronouncement Story and its Types," in *Pronouncement Stories*, ed. R.C. Tannehill=*Semeia* 20 (1981) 1–13.

_____. "Varieties of Synoptic Pronouncement Stories," in *Pronouncement Stories*, ed. R.C. Tannehill=*Semeia* 20 (1981) 101–119.

_____. "Apophthegms in the Synoptic Gospels," *ANRW* II 25/2 (Berlin and New York, 1984) 1792–1829.

Taylor, A., *The Proverb and an Introduction to the Proverb* (Copenhagen, 1962).

_____. *The Wisdom of Many*, ed. W. Mieden and A. Dundes (New York and London, 1981).

Taylor, R.O.P., *The Groundwork of the Gospels* (Oxford, 1946).

Theißen, G., "Wanderradikalismus: Literatursoziologische Aspekte der Überlieferung von Worten Jesu im Urchristentum," *ZTK* 70 (1973) 245–271.

_____. "Theoretischen Probleme religionssoziologischer Forschung," *Neue Zeitschrift für systematische Theologie* 16 (1974) 35–56.

_____. "Legitimation und Lebensunterhalt: Ein Beitrag zur Soziologie urchristlichen Missionare," *NTS* 21 (1975) 192-221.

_____. *Urchristliche Wundergeschichten: Ein Beitrag zur formgeschichtlichen Efforschung der synoptischen Evangelien* (Gütersloh, 1974); transl. F. McDonagh, *Miracle Stories of the Early Christian Tradition* (Edinburgh, 1983).

_____. *Soziologie der Jesusbewegung* (4th ed.; München, 1985).

_____. *Lokalkolorit und Zeitgeschichte in den Evangelien: Ein Beitrag zur Geschichte der synoptischen Tradition* (NTOA 8; Göttingen and Freiburg, 1989); transl. L.M. Maloney, *The Gospels in Context: Social and Political History in the Synoptic Tradition* (Minneapolis, 1991).

Thibeaux, E.R., "Rhetorical Criticism as an Integrative Paradigm for New Testament Studies," presented to the Society of Biblical Literature, Mid-Atlantic Region, 27 February, 1992, unpublished.

Thielman, F., "The Style of the Fourth Gospel and Ancient Literary Critical Concepts of Religious Discourse," in *Persuasive Artistry: Studies in New Testament Rhetoric in Honor of George A. Kennedy*, ed. D.F. Watson (JSNTSup 50; Sheffield, 1991) 169–183.

Thomas, J., *Der jüdische Phokylides: Formgeschichtliche Zügange zu Pseudo-Phokylides und Vergleich mit der neutestamentlichen Paränese* (NTOA 23; Freiburg, Switzerland and Göttingen, 1992).

Thomas, R., *Oral Tradition and Written Record in Classical Athens* (Cambridge, 1989).

Thompson, J.M., *The Form and Function of Proverbs in Ancient Israel* (Studia Judaica 1; Paris and The Hague, 1974).

Thyen, H., *Der Stil der Jüdisch-Hellenistische Homilie* (Göttingen, 1955).

Trouillet, F., "Les sens du mot Χρεία des origines à son emploi rhétorique," in *Formes brèves: De la γνώμη à la pointe: métamorphoses de la "sententia"=La Licorne* 3 (1979) 41–64.

Vaage, L.E., *Galilean Upstarts: Jesus' First Followers According to Q* (Valley Forge, PA, 1994).

Vansina, J., *Oral Tradition as History* (Madison, WI, 1985).

Vassiliadis, P., "The Nature and Extent of the Q Document," *NT* 20 (1978) 49–73.

Vatz, R.E., "The Myth of the Rhetorical Situation," *Philosophy and Rhetoric* 6 (1973) 154–61.

Vickers, B., *In Defence of Rhetoric* (Oxford, 1988).

Walter, N., "Paulus und die urchristliche Jesustradition," *NTS* 31 (1985) 498-522.

Wanke, J., "'Kommentarworte' Älteste Kommentierungen von Herrenworten," *BZ* 24 (1980) 208–233.

Watson, D.F., ed., *Persuasive Artistry: Studies in New Testament Rhetoric in Honor of George A. Kennedy* (JSNTSup 50; Sheffield, 1991).

Watson, D.F. and A.J. Hauser, *Rhetorical Criticism of the Bible: A Comprehensive Bibliography with Notes on History and Method* (Biblical Interpretation 4; Lieden, 1994).

Watson, W.G.E., *Classical Hebrew Poetry: A Guide to its Techniques* (JSOTSup 26; Sheffield, 1984).

Wedderburn, A.J.M., "Paul and Jesus: The Problem of Continuity," *SJT* 38 (1985) 189-203.

____. "Paul and Jesus: Similarity and Continuity," *NTS* 34 (1988) 161-182.

Westerholm, S., *Jesus and Scribal Authority* (ConBNT 10; Lund, 1978).

Wettstein, J., *Novum Testamentum Graecum* (Amsterdam, 1751, rpr. Graz, 1962).

White, L.M., "Sociological Analysis of Early Christian Groups: A Social Historian's Response," *Sociological Analysis* 47 (1986) 249–66.

Wilder, A.N., *Early Christian Rhetoric: The Language of the Gospel* (London, 1964; rpr. Cambridge, MA, 1971)=*The Language of the Gospel: Early Christian Rhetoric* (New York, 1964).

Williams, J.G., "The Power of Form: A Study of Biblical Proverbs," in *Gnomic Wisdom*, ed. J.D. Crossan=*Semeia* 17 (1980) 35–58.

____. *Those Who Ponder Proverbs: Aphoristic Thinking and Biblical Literature* (Sheffield, 1981).

Wilson, S.G., "From Jesus to Paul: The Contours and Consequences of a Debate," in *From Jesus to Paul: Studies in Honour of F.W. Beare*, ed. P. Richardson and J.C. Hurd (Waterloo, ON, 1984) 1-21.

Winterbottom, M., *Problems in Quintilian* (BICS 25; London, 1970).

Winton, A.P., *The Proverbs of Jesus: Issues of History and Rhetoric* (JSNTSup 35; Sheffield, 1990).

Wooton, C.W., transl., *Hermogenes' On Types of Style* (Chapel Hill, NC, 1987).

Wuellner, W., "Toposforschung und Torahinterpretation bei Paulus und Jesus," *NTS* (1978) 463–483.

____. "Greek Rhetoric and Pauline Argumentation," in *Early Christian Literature and the Classical Intellectual Tradition: in honorem Robert M. Grant,* ed. W. Schroedel and R.W. Wilcken (Théolgie historique 53; Paris, 1979) 177–88.

____. "Where is Rhetorical Criticism Taking Us?" *CBQ* 49 (1987) 448–463.

____. "Hermeneutics and Rhetorics: From 'Truth and Method' to 'Truth and Power'," *Scriptura S* 3 (1989) 1–54.

____. "Rhetorical Criticism and its Theory in Culture-Critical Perspective: The Narrative Rhetoric of John 11," *Text and Interpretation: New Approaches in the Criticism of the New Testament,* ed. P.J. Martin and J.H. Petzer (Leiden, 1991) 171–85.

Zeller, D., *Die weisheitlichen Mahnsprüche bei den Synoptikern* (FB 17; Würzburg, 1977).

Ziebarth, E., *Aus der antiken Schule* (Bonn, 1910).

Zimmerli, W., "Zur Struktur der alttestamentlichen Weisheit," *ZAW* 51 (1933) 177–204.

BIBLE REFERENCE INDEX

Genesis:
1:27   378-80, 405
2:24   378-80, 405
3:18   277
9:4,9   361
9:6   277, 372
10:9   161
16:12   178

Leviticus:
2:13   266, 363, 371

Deuteronomy:
25:4   363, 371

1 Samuel:
10:12   161, 178
16:7   161
19:24   161, 178
24:13,14,15   163, 178, 369

2 Samuel:
5:8   161
9:8   178
16:9   178
20:18   161

1 Kings:
18:21   366
19:19-21   306, 343-4
20:11   161, 178, 366

Judges:
8:2,21   161, 366
14:14   161
14:18   161

Isaiah:

2:2-4   347
5:19   161
22:13   161
37:3   161
40:27   161

Jeremiah:
5:12,13   161
8:20   161, 178
12:13   161, 178
15:2   277
23:28   178
31:29   161
52:58   161

Ezekiel:
9:9   161
11:3   161
12:22   161, 178
16:44   161
18:2,25,29   161
33:10,17,20   161
37:11   161

Hosea:
4:11,14   161
10:8   276

Micah:
3:9-12   166
4:12   347

Habakkuk:
2:13   161

Zephaniah:
1:12   161

Psalms:
54, 119   166

Job:
2:4   161

Prov:
22-24   170, 180

Matthew:
2:30   267
3:7-10   277, 315, 326
4:13   332
5:13   266
5:14   251-2, 273, 335, 347
5:15   252
5:18   267, 286, 288, 313, 333-4, 362, 368, 394-5
5:21   271
5:27-32   377
5:27-28   264, 271
5:29-30   264
5:31   271
5:32   376, 378
5:33   271
5:36   315, 368-9
5:38-42   270-2, 315, 319
5:43   271, 315
5:44   319
5:45   272, 315
5:48   272, 315
6:1-24   233
6:17-18   391
6:19-21   272
6:22-23   274, 315, 322
6:24   267-270, 274, 315, 322, 370, 404

6:34   272, 273, 315
7:1-5   255-259, 312, 369, 370
7:6   273-5, 315, 322, - 347-8, 371, 404
7:10   270
7:12   272, 368, 394-5
7:13   285, 286, 347
7:15   273, 276
7:15-20   275-7, 280, 315, 326
8:4   262
8:5-13   347
8:19   302, 303, 306
8:20   214, 284, 286, 300, 302, 303, 306, 312, 315, 337
8:21,22   201, 214, 286-8, 299-302, 306-8, 315, 317, 319, 325, 330-31, 340-41, 348, 372, 401
9:37   315, 344-5
10:8   273, 315, 372
10:10   315, 344-5, 363, 368, 372-5, 381, 395
10:16   275, 315
10:22   345
10:24,25   309, 315, 322, 327, 330, 332, 333, 334, 342-4
10:26,27   315, 322, 325, 345
10:29   217, 315
10:34   277
10:38,39   247, 267, 346
11:16-19   286, 307, 326, 339-40, 348, 365, 391

11:27	327, 334, 344	**Mark:**	
12:5-6	391-4	1:21-23	279
12:30	333, 335	1:27-28	279
12:33-37	275, 276, 277, 286, 315	2:1-12	330
13:24-30, 36-43	276	2:13-17	289, 327, 330-31, 334
13:53-58	279	2:18-22	390-91
15:11,17	384, 388	2:19	234, 285-65, 289, 314, 325, 327-9, 334, 344, 368, 391-92, 401
15:13	315		
15:14	342-3		
16:2,3	293, 315, 326		
16:25	247	2:21-22	234, 287, 315, 322
17:24-27	394	2:23-28	89, 234, 251, 266, 273, 284-7, 289, 300, 311, 338, 351, 358, 368, 390, 391-4
18:4	260, 262		
18:6-7	264, 314, 337-8		
18:8-9	264		
18:15-20	369		
19:2	368	3:1-6	284, 289, 330, 368, 390, 394-5
19:3-9	377-9		
19:12	311, 313, 344, 372, 373-7, 386, 395, 404	3:24	289, 311
		3:25	311
		4:1-25	234, 252, 253-5, 258, 259, 286, 287, 289, 312, 321, 325, 370, 404
19:30	260, 262		
20:16	260, 262, 263		
20:26-27	260		
21:28-32	312	4:26-33	287
22:1-14	328	5:26	330
22:14	277, 313, 347	6:1-6	279, 280, 332, 365
23:11	260	6:4	148, 278-281, 282, 284, 296, 327, 331-2, 334, 343, 381
23:16	342-3		
23:24	342		
24:26-27	340-41		
24:28	311, 315, 340-41	7:1-23	283, 289, 382, 383, 384, 388, 390, 404
24:35-6	334		
25:1-18	328		
26:24	337	7:15	315, 352, 380, 383-90, 392, 399, 404
26:52	277, 371-72		

7:24-30	278, 326, 347-8, 365, 371, 404		Luke:	
			2:23	331
			2:24	282, 331
8:22	154		3:9	276
8:34	261		4:1-13	288
8:35	247, 267, 284, 313, 319, 345-6		4:16	332
			4:23	234, 281, 321-2, 326, 327, 330, 331, 332, 334, 336
9:33-37	260			
9:35	260-4, 313, 342, 380-81, 400			
			4:24	234, 298, 329, 332
9:40	267, 333		4:16-30	147, 234, 278, 280, 281
9:42-50	264-7, 269, 271, 313, 314, 315, 363-4, 380			
			5:33-39	251, 272, 287, 315
			6:5	287
10:2-12	289, 315, 368, 377-80, 382, 386, 390, 404, 405		6:13	322
			6:27-36	270-2
			6:37-42	255-60, 278, 310, 312, 330, 332, 342-3
10:13-16	260			
10:29-37	404			
10:31	260, 261, 285, 313, 342		6:43-45	275-7, 315, 332
			7:1-10	288
10:35-45	233, 380, 400		7:32	278
10:43-44	260, 261, 262, 263, 284, 286, 313, 338-9, 342, 381, 405		7:31-35	307, 316, 339, 348
			7:36-50	277, 278
			7:47	258, 315
			8:16-18	253, 255, 325
11:15-19	400		9:24	247
12:17	315, 368, 390, 395-8, 400		9:48	260, 262
			9:50	267, 334
12:18-27	289, 300		9:57-62	300-307, 311, 313, 342-4
13:13	286, 314, 346			
13:30	334		9:60	288, 300, 302, 372
13:31	267, 313, 333-5, 345		10:12	293
			10:2-16	275, 293, 297, 344-5, 372
13:32	334			
14:3-9	277		10:22	327
14:21	311, 314, 337		10:29-37	405
			10:38-42	285, 290
			11:23	267, 334

11:33	252
11:34-35	274, 322
12:2	325
12:3	234, 325
12:6	217
12:28	258
12:32	272
12:33-34	272
12:51	277
12:54-56	278, 293, 315, 365
13:6-9	276
13:24	285, 286, 347
13:30	260
14:11	258, 262
14:27	313
14:34-35	266, 313
15:8,9	314
16:8	285, 347
16:10-12	258, 268, 269, 270, 274, 286, 315, 322
16:13	267-70, 274, 322, 370, 404
16:17	267, 286, 288, 313-4, 334
16:18	377
17:1	314, 337
17:23-37	285, 340
17:33	213, 247, 267
18:14	258, 285
21:33	334
22:22	337
22:24-30	381, 400, 405
22:27	74, 88, 260, 263, 332
22:36	277
22:51	277
23:2	
23:31	314, 315

23:35	322
24:56	280

John:

2:1-11	328
3:29	328
4:35	315
4:44	147, 278-281, 282, 332
7:52	332
8:12	335
12:25	247
13:1-20	308, 381, 400, 405
13:2-5	74, 88
13:15-16	263, 309, 330, 332-3
15:1-17	276
15:20	310, 332
18:11	277

Acts:

17:28	271
20:35	372

Romans:

2:1-11	369
13:7	368, 395-8
14:7-21	357, 368, 380, 383, 386-90, 399, 404

1 Corinthians:

5, 6	357
6:13	351, 358, 388
6:16	378, 380
7:1-40	375-7
7:6	368, 377
7:10-11	357, 368, 377-9
7:25	368, 375-7

8:2-3   357
9:1-14   357, 358-9, 363, 368, 372-5
10:23   388
10:24   357
11:23   294
11:23-25   380
11:24-5   357
13:13   357
14:33   357

2 Corinthians:
4:18b   357
7:10   357
9:6-7   357
12:9   357
13:13   357

Galatians:
1:11-24   359
2:6   357

2:21   357, 362
5:9   357
5:25-6:19   232, 357

Philippians:
1:21   357

1 Thessalonians:
4:15-17   380
5:7   357

1 Timothy:
5:18   363, 372-5
6:20   270

Titus:
1:12   298

James:
5:4   363, 372

INDEX OF MODERN AUTHORS

Allison, D.C., 323
Aune, D.E., 219
Barth, K., 60
Beardslee, W.A., 212-5, 219-20, 244, 292, 295-6, 298, 301, 316-20, 324, 346
Berger, K., 174, 177, 227-35, 263, 339, 382, 384, 391, 400
Betz, H.-D., 41-2, 323
Bible and Culture Collective, 64
Bitzer, L., 14
Bjorndalen, A.J., 171
Boismard, M.-E., 253
Boring, M.E., 181
Boswell, J., 210-2
Botha, J.E., 240
Brown, P., 36, 85
Bultmann, R., 76-7, 86-9, 110, 148, 167-8, 197, 198-220, 224, 226, 281, 292, 298, 311, 314, 316
Carlston, C.E., 212, 215-6, 245, 288, 292-3, 295, 297, 305, 323
Cizek, A., 238
Cotter, W., 316

Crépeau, P., 150-3, 156, 163, 172, 177-8, 190, 308-9, 330
Crossan, J.D., 20, 132-3, 142-4, 186, 196, 216-26, 234, 249, 262, 366
Davies, M., 379
Davies, W.D., 402
Dewey, A.J., 313-4
Dibelius, M., 76-8, 202, 404
Dupont, J., 268-9, 322
Edwards, R.A., 293
Eißfeldt, O., 161-7, 169, 178-9, 185, 192, 278
Fischel, H.A., 350, 361
Fontaine, C., 162
Fuchs, E., 336
Geertz,. C., 52
Gerhardsson, B., 192-3, 206
Gerstenberger, E., 169, 171
Goulder, M., 245-6
Greimas, A.J., 149-151
Greßmann, H., 169
Harris, W.V., 21
Hempel, J., 169
Hengel, M., 299-310, 306-7
Hermisson, H.-J., 168-9
Hock, R.F., 103
Jacobson, A.D., 306
Jolles, A., 149, 157, 168, 304

Kelber, W.H., 57, 181-2, 184, 186, 206, 208, 221, 230
Kennedy, G.A., 139-40
Kloppenborg, J.S., 23-4, 48, 178, 180-3, 185-6, 288, 292-3
Küchler, M., 178, 188-9
Kuhn, H.-W., 253
Layton, B., 256
Lindeskog, G., 321
Lowenhaupt Tsing, A., 408-9
Lührmann, D., 298
Mack, B.L., 46-55, 59, 73, 82-3, 97, 100-2, 111-4, 134, 283
Mees, M., 256
Milner, G.B., 150-1
Muilenburg, J., 43-4
Nadeau, R., 137
Neusner, J., 191-5
Noorda, S.J., 321-2, 331
O'Neil, E.N., 103, 134
Philonenko, M., 323
Rabe, H., 134
Richter, W., 169-78, 192
Robinson, J.M., 180, 184
Robbins, V.K., 46-55, 82-3, 87-9, 92, 96, 100, 112-4, 145, 148, 185-6, 208-9, 227, 260-2, 283, 284, 292, 294, 296, 303-5, 407
Sanders, E.P., 90, 299, 379, 385
Sato, M., 293
Schille, G., 392
Schweitzer, A., 196, 292, 298
Scott, B.B., 82

Scroggs, R., 55, 70
Sellew, P., 248-9
Sinclair, P., 97, 124-6
Smith, M., 192
Stamps, D., 38-9, 64
Stuhlmacher, P., 57
Tannehill, R.C., 290
Taylor, A., 149
Taylor, R.O.P., 74
Theißen, G., 47, 207, 326
Vaage, L.E., 301
Vassiliadis, P., 288
Wanke, J., 286
Wettstein, J., 323
Westerholm, S., 383
Wilder, A.N., 43-6, 52, 196-7
Williams, J.G., 163
Winton, A.P., 171, 219-21
Wuellner, W., 242
Zeller, D., 171-7, 180, 183, 185-6, 192, 196, 201
Zimmerli, W., 169-71

BIBLICAL INTERPRETATION SERIES

ISSN 0928-0731

1. VAN DIJK-HEMMES, F. & A. BRENNER. *On Gendering Texts.* Female and Male Voices in the Hebrew Bible. 1993. ISBN 90 04 09642 6
2. VAN TILBORG, S. *Imaginative Love in John.* 1993. ISBN 90 04 09716 3
3. DANOVE, P.L. *The End of Mark's Story.* A Methodological Study. 1993. ISBN 90 04 09717 1
4. WATSON, D.F. & A.J. HAUSER. *Rhetorical Criticism of the Bible.* A Comprehensive Bibliography with Notes on History and Method. 1994. ISBN 90 04 09903 4
5. SEELEY, D. *Deconstructing the New Testament.* 1994. ISBN 90 04 09880 1
6. VAN WOLDE, E. *Words become Worlds.* Semantic Studies of Genesis 1-11. 1994. ISBN 90 04 098879
7. NEUFELD, D. *Reconceiving Texts as Speech Acts.* An Analysis of i John. 1994. ISBN 90 04 09853 4
8. PORTER, S.E., P. JOYCE & D.E. ORTON (eds.). *Crossing the Boundaries.* Essays in Biblical Interpretation in Honour of Michael D. Goulder. 1994. ISBN 90 04 10131 4
9. YEO, K.-K. *Rhetorical Interaction in 1 Corinthians 8 and 10.* A Formal Analysis with Preliminary Suggestions for a Chinese, Cross-Cultural Hermeneutic. 1995. ISBN 90 04 10115 2
10. LETELLIER, R.I. *Day in Mamre, Night in Sodom.* Abraham and Lot in Genesis 18 and 19. 1995. ISBN 90 04 10250 7
12. TOLMIE, D.F. *Jesus' Farewell to the Disciples.* John 13:1-17:26 in Narratological Perspective. 1995. ISBN 90 04 10270 1
13. RYOU, D.H. *Zephaniah's Oracles against the Nations.* A Synchronic and Diachronic Study of Zephaniah 2:1-3:8. 1995. ISBN 90 04 10311 2
14. PORTER, S.E. & J.T. REED. *The Book of Romans.* A Grammatical-rhetorical Commentary. In Preparation. ISBN 90 04 09908 5
15. SELAND, T. *Establishment Violence in Philo and Luke.* A Study of Non-Conformity to the Torah and Jewish Vigilante Reactions. 1995. ISBN 90 04 10252 3
16. NOBLE, P.R *The Canonical Approach.* A Critical Reconstruction of the Hermeneutics of Brevard S. Childs. 1995. ISBN 90 04 10151 9
17. SCHOTTROFF, L.R & M.-T. WACKER (Hrsg.). *Von der Wurzel getragen.* Christlich-feministische Exegese in Auseinandersetzung mit Antijudaismus. 1996. ISBN 90 04 10336 8
18. BECKING, B. & M. DIJKSTRA (eds.). *On Reading Prophetic Texts.* Gender-Specific and Related Studies in Memory of Fokkelien van Dijk-Hemmes. 1996. ISBN 90 04 10274 4
19. BRETT, M.G. (ed.). *Ethnicity and the Bible.* 1996. ISBN 90 04 10317 1
20. HENDERSON, I.A. *Jesus, Rhetoric and Law.* 1996. ISBN 90 04 10377 5